THE
SEVENTH
EARL OF SHAFTESBURY

THE SEVENTH EARL OF SHAFTESBURY
1801–1885

Geoffrey B. A. M. Finlayson

REGENT COLLEGE PUBLISHING
Vancouver, British Columbia

Copyright © 1981 Geoffrey B.A.M. Finlayson
All rights reserved.

First published 1981 by Eyre Methuen Ltd, London, UK

This edition published 2004 by
Regent College Publishing
5800 University Boulevard
Vancouver, BC V6T 2E4 Canada
www.regentpublishing.com

Views expressed in works published by Regent College
Publishing are those of the author and do not
necessarily represent the official position of
Regent College <www.regent-college.edu>.

Library and Archives Canada Cataloguing in Publication Data

Finlayson, Geoffrey B. A. M.
The seventh Earl of Shaftesbury, 1801-1885 /
Geoffrey B.A.M. Finlayson.

ISBN 1-57383-314-2

1. Shaftesbury, Anthony Ashley Cooper, Earl of, 1801-1885.
2. Nobility—Great Britain—Biography. 3. Social reformers—
Great Britain—Biography. I. Title.

HV28.S46F56 2004   941.081'092

C2004-905103-2

Contents

	Abbreviations	6
	Acknowledgments	7
1	Awe, Reserve and Youthful Hope, 1801–1826	11
2	Choosing a Line of Life, 1826–1830	27
3	Zeal and Good Intentions, 1830–1833	57
4	Private Happiness and Public Usefulness, 1830–1835	91
5	Full of Schemes, 1835–1841	109
6	Paths of No Gain and Humility, 1839–1841	137
7	Prophecy and Protestantism, 1841–1846	153
8	Hearts to be won, Souls to be saved, 1841–1843	173
9	Mammon, Moloch, Mens Sana, 1843–1845	207
10	Free Mercy to Past Faith, 1845–1847	239
11	Fresh Toils, Fresh Anxieties, 1848–1851	271
12	Exigencies Spiritual and Personal, 1846–1851	307
13	A New Name, A New Career, 1851–1855	331
14	Near the Fountain Head, 1855–1865	373
15	Unprofitable Labours, 1855–1865	407
16	Righteousness Exalteth a Nation, 1854–1865	439
17	Doubt, Darkness, Discouragement, 1866–1873	467
18	The Juggernaut of Rationalism and Ritualism, 1866–1874	515
19	Notice to Quit, 1873–1878	543
20	The Few Things that Remain, 1879–1885	571
21	Epitaph to a Saint	599
	BIBLIOGRAPHY	611
	INDEX	621

Abbreviations

The following abbreviations have been used in the notes:

B.L.	The British Library, London.
Battiscombe	Battiscombe, G., *Shaftesbury. A Biography of the Seventh Earl, 1801–1885* (1974).
H.R.O.	The Hampshire Record Office, Winchester.
Hammonds	Hammond, J. L. and B., *Lord Shaftesbury* (fourth ed. 1936, reprinted 1969).
Hodder	Hodder, E., *The Life and Work of the Seventh Earl of Shaftesbury, K.G.* (3 vols, 1887).
I.H.R.	The Institute of Historical Research, London.
I.O.R.	India Office Records.
N.RA.	The National Register of Archives, London.
P.R.O.	The Public Record Office, London.
St.G.H.	St Giles's House, Shaftesbury Estates, Dorset.

Place of Publication
Unless otherwise stated, the place of publication is London.

Acknowledgments

In carrying out research for this book, I have been assisted by Travel Grants from the University of Glasgow and I should like to express my appreciation of this help. I also acknowledge with gratitude awards towards publication costs made by the British Academy, the Carnegie Trust for the Universities of Scotland and the University of Glasgow Publications Board.

I am grateful to the following for their kind permission to consult and to use material from papers in their possession: Lady Anne Bentinck, Viscount Cobham, Lord Elphinstone, Sir Charles Graham, Mr George Howard, the Earl of Lonsdale, the National Trust, the Royal Commission on Historical Manuscripts, the Earl of Shaftesbury, the Trustees of the Broadlands Archives Trust, and the Duke of Wellington.

I also wish to record my gratitude to the following institutions and societies: the Bodleian Library, Oxford, the British Library of Political and Economic Science, London, Cumbria County Council Archives Department (Carlisle Record Office), Duke University, Durham, North Carolina (William R. Perkins Library, Manuscripts Department), Harvard University Library, the Huntington Library, San Marino, California, Imperial College of Science and Technology, London, Lambeth Palace Library, London, the Lord's Day Observance Society, London, the New York Public Library, the Shaftesbury Society (Ragged School Union), London, University College, London (the Library), the University of California, Los Angeles (The University Library, Department of Special Collections), the University of Durham (Department of Palaeography and Diplomatic), the University of Glasgow (the University Library and the Photographic Unit), the University of Keele (The Library), the University of Nottingham (The University Library, Manuscripts Department) and the University of Texas at Austin (Humanities Research Centre). Transcripts of Crown Copyright records in the British Library (Additional MSS), in the India Office Records and in the Public Record Office appear by permission of the Controller of Her Majesty's Stationery Office.

I owe a great debt to the many librarians, curators, archivists, and officers of various societies who have gone to considerable trouble to answer my inquiries. In particular, I should like to thank Mrs Felicity Strong (née Ranger) not only for her invaluable professional assistance in the course of my visits to the National Register of Archives but also for her friendship to me and my family and the interest which she has taken in the progress of this book. I should also like to express my appreciation of the assistance which I received from the late Mrs Hilda Stowell, sometime Archivist to the present Earl of Shaftesbury. Her successor, Mrs M. E. Griffiths has also been most helpful. I wish to thank also Dr Richard Bingle of the India Office Library and Records, Mr R. E. Heasman of the Shaftesbury Society and Miss Judith Oppenheimer, Archivist at Castle Howard. I have also received assistance from Mrs Georgina Battiscombe, Mr G. D. Carnall of the University of Edinburgh, Dr J. Jean Hecht, Lady Longford and Professor John Osborne; and permission to quote from their theses has been kindly given by Professor G. M. Ellis, Revd Dr B. E. Hardman, Revd Dr S. C. Orchard and Dr Anne Ruck (née Bentley).

Many colleagues in this and other Universities have been extremely generous with their help. In Glasgow, Professors W. R. Brock, A. L. Brown and A. A. M. Duncan and Dr A. G. R. Smith have taken an interest in the book over many years and have given me much encouragement. Professor K. G. Robbins and Mr D. G. Henry have given me valuable help in the later stages. In the course of his postgraduate research, Mr R. C. Sloan has discovered and drawn my attention to source material which I should otherwise have missed. Historians in other Universities have likewise been most helpful. Mr Michael Brock, Warden of Nuffield College, Oxford, who, in fact, first suggested that I might undertake this book, has kindly put at my disposal his transcripts from the Lonsdale MSS and the Sneyd MSS. Professor G. F. A. Best of the University of Sussex gave me invaluable assistance in the early stages of the book. Professor Norman Gash, late of the University of St Andrews, Mr John Prest of Balliol College, Oxford and Professor John Ward of the University of Strathclyde have given freely of their time and resources in answering my inquiries.

The arduous task of typing the book has been carried out by Miss Patricia Ferguson with her accustomed expertise and meticulousness. Mrs Barbara Beggs has also performed many valuable services. I record my thanks similarly to successive editors at Eyre Methuen and, in particular, to Mr Geoffrey Strachan, Managing Director and Miss Ann Mansbridge, Rights Manager and Senior Editor. They have been courteous and patient in their dealings with me over many years. I am also grateful to Mr Christopher Stafford for his guidance as Copy Editor.

My helpers have, therefore, been legion and to them all I offer my sincere thanks. My greatest helper, deserving of my deepest gratitude, has been my wife, who has contributed in inestimable measure to every stage of the book's preparation and production. She and our two daughters – who have accompanied us on all our research journeys – have been my closest and most constant collaborators in the making of this book. Now that it is finally made, it is dedicated to them.

University of Glasgow   Geoffrey B. A. M. Finlayson
October 1980

For my wife and daughters

I
Awe, Reserve and Youthful Hope, 1801–1826

'There are few characters in English history better worth studying than Anthony Ashley Cooper, first Earl of Shaftesbury. He lived in most momentous times and he played most important parts in them.' Thus opened a review of a nineteenth-century *Life* of the first Earl;[1] and, whether he is seen as Dryden's Achitophel – 'a name to all succeeding ages curst' – or in more moderate terms,[2] such a general assessment of the importance of the Earl's life in the context of late-seventeenth-century England can scarcely be denied. The reviewer, however, also commented on subsequent holders of the title. He recalled that Dryden had extended his satire to the first Earl's son, 'born a shapeless lump, like anarchy'. It was a comment directed less at the second Earl's physical appearance than at his lack of mental powers, or, as the reviewer put it, his 'inferiority of understanding';[3] and it was one which, it appears, was resented by the third Earl, son of the second, more than any other part of Dryden's satire. The third Earl was a man of considerable intellectual stature. He was the author of *Characteristics of Men, Manners, Opinions and Times*, published shortly after his death in 1713, and was described by Voltaire as 'the boldest of English philosophers'.[4] But after his death, the reviewer wrote, there was a 'long interval, during which no lineal descendant rose to celebrity.' Nevertheless, he continued, those who held that genius and character were hereditary should not despair: for Anthony Ashley Cooper, born in 1801 and, from 1851, Seventh Earl measured up to his distinguished ancestors:

> In this instance [the reviewer wrote], we are reminded of the river which, after running many miles underground, emerges clearer, purer and less turbid than at its source. After a noiseless descent of nearly two centuries, the name and honours of the Earls of Shaftesbury have devolved upon

one who inherits all the domestic virtues, with much of the capacity, intellectual vigour, high courage and eager animated eloquence of their founder....[5]

It is, indeed, true that only the first, third and seventh Earls were men of prominence. Yet the reviewer is, perhaps, rather harsh on other holders of the title, and, in particular, on Cropley Ashley Cooper, sixth Earl of Shaftesbury. Born in 1768, Cropley Ashley was the younger son of the fourth Earl and brother of the fifth. After his education at Winchester and Christ Church, he went on the 'Grand Tour' of Europe normal to one of his station; and, in 1790, he entered Parliament. The principal family estates were at Wimborne St Giles in the county of Dorset, and it was for Dorchester, the family borough controlled in the interest of the Earls of Shaftesbury, that Cropley Ashley was returned and for which he sat until 1811. When the Tories assumed office in 1807, Ashley was appointed Clerk of the Ordinance. He held the appointment until 1811, when he succeeded to the title; his elder brother, the fifth Earl, had died without issue. Ashley had, therefore, 'a long apprenticeship to political life',[6] and, once in the Lords, he remained extremely active. In 1811, he temporarily filled the office of Chairman of Committees during the illness of the incumbent, and, in November, 1814, he was appointed permanent Chairman and a Privy Councillor. The office which he filled covered a wide area: he was chairman of the Committee of Appeals, the Committee on Unopposed Private Bills and also that on Standing Orders. In the Commons, such duties were spread among four public officers. He retained his Chairmanship until very shortly before his death in 1851 and thus became a noted figure in the Lords. He was not, it seems, a very impressive figure, being described as 'a man of undignified presence, (and) of indistinct and hurried speech'.[7] But what he lacked in 'presence' he made up for in competence and authority. A man of wide experience as a parliamentary agent was known to say that he remembered only one case in which the House reversed a decision of Shaftesbury, and, on that occasion, it was necessary to persuade the Duke of Wellington to speak to overcome the opinion of the sixth Earl. His reputation was such that it was felt that the House could never have a more efficient chairman. He was, however, known not only for his competence. He was also known and, it would seem, held in some awe, for his 'hasty and brusque manner'. He was impatient with persons who talked at length and to little purpose; he was always anxious to get through the business and, it was said, issued his directions in 'no very gentle terms'. On occasion, he acted as Speaker of the House in the absence of the Lord Chancellor: then, his conduct was dignified and restrained. But once back in his accustomed role, he reverted to his accustomed manner, showing no hesitation, no dubiety, and allowing no one to pause or doubt. 'Give me that clause *now*'; 'That's enough'; 'It will do very well as it is'; 'If you have anything further to propose, move at once'. Such, it was said, were his methods of despatching business.[8]

The wife of the sixth Earl was Lady Anne Spencer, daughter of the fourth Earl of Marlborough,[9] the marriage taking place in 1796. The first three children of the marriage were daughters: Charlotte, Caroline and Harriet. The first son, Anthony, was born on 28 April, 1801, and there followed, between 1803 and 1813, five other sons: William, Henry, John, Francis and Lionel.[10] Anthony's early career was not, indeed, unlike that of his father. He was educated at the Manor House, Chiswick and Harrow, and, after a period of private tuition, went up to Christ Church in 1819. After taking his degree in 1822, he undertook a tour of Europe, and in 1826, entered Parliament as a Tory for Woodstock, a borough where the influence of his mother's family was prevalent.

The fact that Ashley, to some degree, followed in his father's footsteps does not mean, however, that a close affinity existed between him and his parents. Indeed, much of the interest of these early years in his life derives from his distant relationship with them. It was certainly a matter on which he himself often wrote. While at Oxford, he became friendly with George Howard[11] and visited him at his home at Castle Howard, and he developed a warm affection for Howard's mother, Lady Georgiana Morpeth.[12] In the course of correspondence with her, which began after a visit to Castle Howard in 1820, he often mentioned his family. He was anxious that Lady Georgiana should get to know his sisters. He was sure that she would discover many faults in them – as he did: but their merits, he wrote, were great and Lady Georgiana's good opinion, delivered to the world, would be 'a great shield for their reputations'; he knew well that they were traduced by their mother. And he continued:

> Here are the consequences of a Mother's dereliction of her children. How dreadful they are you will neither learn by experience or imagine. Your own feelings are so vivid, so maternal, and so arduous towards your offspring, that you almost doubt my assertion that such *unnatural*, such *deeply horrid examples* are found in a human and a Christian soul.[13]

Later, in 1823, he told Lady Georgiana that his sisters were to visit London, not because of their own inclinations, but because 'imperious and unrelenting words of authority' had forced them to go. They would call on Lady Georgiana. She must, he wrote, be kind to them. 'I assure you they deserve it, and no good natured affections are lost upon them.' Kindness was especially welcome to them, for it was a 'dish which, tho' much relished (was) rarely ever tasted.'[14]

In his own private Diary, which he began to keep in 1825, Ashley also poured out his feelings on his parents. 'What a dreadful woman our mother is!' he wrote in 1825. 'Her whole pleasure is in finding fault.'[15] The following year, he noted that his mother continued in her hardness: 'it is now judicial; away with her Memory! The Idea of such fiend-warmed Hearts is bad for a Christian soul.'[16] Ashley also wrote at length about his father. He felt that he was 'an honest man', who did his duty to the public,[17] but, as a parent, left much to be desired. Ashley had tried to please him but without success. Never a year had passed without an insult, open or implied, and, had Ashley resorted to resistance and complaint, he would have done no more than almost any other son would have done and the world would have taken his part. The Earl's natural tendency was to avoid all his children.

> As to friendship and affection between him and me [Ashley continued], years of Experience had sufficiently proved that outward civility *and only civility* is the utmost that can be looked for. . . . His whole pleasure is in finding fault; he oftener abuses than censures. . . .[18]

He went on to say that his father had for years vented 'malignity and horror' against his eldest sister, Charlotte, and had ceased only because his children began to answer him sternly. Now, he noted, he vented abuse on the servants. Ashley ended his remarks with a prayer that no family might endure from its parents what his family had endured. 'The History of Father and Mother,' he wrote, 'would be incredible to most men and perhaps it would do no good if such facts were recorded.'[19] And very late in life, Ashley, then seventh Earl, returned to such thoughts. He admitted that he had very few recollections of his earliest years, but he recalled that he and his sisters were brought up with 'very great severity, moral and physical, in respect both of mind and body, the opinion of our parents being that, to render a child obedient, it should be in a constant fear of its father and mother.'[20] It was also said that Ashley's father used to knock him down and recommended his tutor at Harrow to do the same.[21]

Ashley always claimed, indeed, that the only real friend of his childhood had been a servant, Maria Millis, who had been a maid to his mother at Blenheim and followed her into service as housekeeper on her marriage. In 1809, on his eighth birthday, Ashley received a poem signed his 'Affectionate friend A.M.M.',[22] and this seems certain to have been Maria Millis. It was religious in tone, wishing for the young Anthony earthly and eternal blessings. When Maria Millis died shortly after this, she left Ashley her watch and seal and he took great pride in wearing the watch to the end of his life, saying that it had been given to him by the best friend he ever had in the world. In 1865, he wrote of 'Anna Maria Millis, the old Housekeeper, to whom, under God, (he owed) the first thoughts of Piety and the first action of Prayer',[23] and, towards the end of his life, he wrote again of her. He remembered that he had passed into her special care at an early age:

> She was an affectionate, pious woman [he wrote]. She taught me many things, directing my thoughts to highest subjects; and I can even now call to my mind many sentences of prayer she made me repeat at her knees. To her, I trace, under God, my first impressions.[24]

Ashley's recollections of his earliest years must, of course, be treated with some care – memories of childhood are notoriously unreliable and subject to exaggeration. Nevertheless, there seems little reason to doubt that his childhood *was* deprived of parental affection and that Maria Millis supplied this need in some measure. Bearing in mind the sixth Earl's strong sense of discipline in his public life, it is not unreasonable to suppose that this also extended to his private dealings with his children. Others, too, commented on the Earl and Countess. Melbourne told Queen Victoria that they disliked their children; and their social activities – Lady Shaftesbury's balls were apparently brilliant occasions – no doubt left little time for attention to family matters, even if there had been the inclination.[25] Henry Fox,[26] whom Ashley knew as a young man at Oxford, described the sixth Earl as 'disgusting, and meaner than any other wretch in the world'.[27] His mother, Lady Holland,[28] wrote that Shaftesbury had never been 'father in the kind sense' to Ashley.[29] While visiting Ashley at St Giles in the early 1820s, George Howard wrote home to his mother, telling her of the household. He wrote on one occasion that, from what he had seen of the Earl himself, he would be inclined to like him, since he appeared to be 'a very good sort of man, with a good deal of a *bluff* sort of good-nature.'[30] Another time he wrote that the Earl was 'very civil'.[31] But he could not help noticing the effect which Shaftesbury had on his family. Thus he wrote of the Earl's impending return after an absence from St Giles. This, Howard wrote, will 'make us all more early at breakfast, more silent at dinner and more attentive at whist.'[32] Another letter referred to Shaftesbury's departure to County Sessions: this, wrote Howard, seemed to be a 'considerable relief' to every member of the family. He noted the 'uncommon awe and reserve' in which the whole family stood of their father. 'It beats the worst moments of Castle Howard hollow, hollow,' he wrote. He thought that the boys felt it more than the girls and he assured his mother 'in plain earnest' that Ashley and William never opened 'either of their well-formed mouths in the presence of their sire.' But – providentially – this was not called for, since, except for three minutes during breakfast and in the evening, the Earl never appeared. In the evening, after the ladies had withdrawn from dinner, the men sat round a small table by the fire and had 'rather a long séance, during which period the same Ashley and William enjoy a deep and unbroken slumber.' On one occasion, after the departure of a guest who had been staying at St Giles, Howard admitted that he had looked forward 'with some dismay to the tête-à-tête' to which he would be reduced with the Earl, but Ashley and William obliged him by keeping awake and other guests were soon expected.[33]

The letters point to the chilling effect which Shaftesbury had on the house and household: but Howard liked the family very much. 'They are really all, I think, uncommonly amiable and warm-hearted people,' he told his mother.[34] The girls were much better educated than he had expected.[35] He had a special liking for Harriet: she was the cleverest.[36] But he also had good words to say about Caroline, except for the fact that she made the tea 'abominably weak' – that was her 'solitary fault'. In all other respects, she was exemplary.[37] The letters also contained interesting observations on the house. On the outside, it was 'nothing remarkable, long and low'. But inside, it was much beyond Howard's expectations, 'both handsome and comfortable'. There were two drawing rooms built by Inigo Jones, full of pictures, and a library – a long room with two fireplaces, in which they had breakfast.[38] And, except for the weak tea, the living was good: there were regular guests, regular games of whist and Caroline played music for an hour every night, 'which she seems to do,' wrote Howard, 'very well and brilliantly.'[39] Thus, especially in the Earl's absence – or when he fell asleep in the evening – the household was not, according to Howard, a gloomy one, and Howard wrote that 'notwithstanding ... the reserve and silence they are all under,' he did not find 'the least gêne in their way of living.'[40] Such comments suggest that, at least at this period of their lives, Ashley and his brothers and sisters suffered little physical deprivation, but they also corroborate Ashley's own comments on the cold and distant relationship between the sixth Earl and his family. They have, however, nothing to say of Lady Shaftesbury.

If Ashley's childhood memories were unhappy, he recalled his school days at Manor House, Chiswick, with equal displeasure. The school was an expensive establishment, much patronised by the sons of the nobility; its Headmaster was the Revd. Dr Thomas Horne, a man of learning and distinction. But Ashley looked back on it with horror. 'Nothing could have surpassed it,' he wrote, 'for filth, bullying, neglect, and hard treatment of every sort,' and he compared it with Dotheboys Hall.[41] In old age, he still shuddered at the thought of the place: it was 'bad, wicked, filthy; and the treatment was starvation and cruelty.'[42] Harrow, by contrast, was more bearable. Life there was, indeed, spartan. Ashley used to recall that his form master was a bad sleeper and held 'first school' at 4 a.m. on a winter morning. The boy for whom Ashley fagged was anxious to excel at recitation and forced Ashley and his fellow fag to listen to his recitations night after night.⁴³ But the worst excesses of behaviour were curbed under the headmastership of Dr George Butler, in whose house Ashley boarded, and Ashley looked back to his days at Harrow with much more pleasure than to those at Manor House. 'Things,' he wrote, 'were there on a very different footing compared with Chiswick.'⁴⁴ But, in retrospect, he blamed himself for not being more diligent at Harrow. He won some prizes, but 'neglected most opportunities of acquiring knowledge.'⁴⁵ One of his most vivid memories, indeed, had nothing to do with his studies. About the age of fourteen, he saw a pauper funeral on Harrow Hill, and the drunkenness and profanity surrounding it deeply shocked him. As late as 1880, he still recalled the event as one which 'brought powerfully before (him) the scorn and neglect manifested towards the poor and helpless.'⁴⁶ Four years later, in 1884, he related the story to the son of Dr Butler, also Headmaster of Harrow, while on a visit to the school, and, after that conversation, a tablet on the wall of the old school was erected to commemorate the spot where Ashley saw the incident. It has been claimed that this marked the beginning of Ashley's social conscience and concern: the tablet states that it 'helped to awaken his life-long devotion to the service of the Poor and oppressed.'⁴⁷ But too much should not be made of this. There is no doubt that the incident etched itself very sharply on Ashley's mind: he was, he recalled in 1880, 'deeply affected'. But he also admitted that, for many years after that, he acted only on 'feeling and sentiment'. It was not until some time later that a sense of duty in such matters began to affect his conduct.⁴⁸

The reason for Ashley's transference from Harrow in 1816 to be tutored by a relative – a clergyman in Derbyshire – is not clear. He later said that it was in order to be 'got out of the way', and he also felt that these years had been completely mis-spent. This may have been too harsh a judgment, for at least he appears to have been relatively happy during the period. He had a horse and enjoyed playing with the dog that belonged to the house. But it does seem that this period of his life contributed little to his academic advancement – the clergyman, he recalled, never professed that he was able to teach him anything, nor did his father require any such services. 'I hardly ever opened a book,' he recalled, 'and seldom heard anything that was worth hearing.'⁴⁹

It was to be different at Oxford, where Ashley went in 1819 – narrowly escaping, it appears, the military career which his father had in mind for him. There, Ashley did work hard and obtained a 'First' in Classics in 1822. The correspondence which he conducted with George Howard's mother, Lady Georgiana, throws considerable light on Ashley's development at this period of his life. In the summer vacation in 1820, Howard and Ashley set out on a tour of Scotland. Ashley wrote to Lady Georgiana giving news of their activities, which included a visit to Sir Walter Scott at Abbotsford. 'He possesses in an eminent degree,' wrote Ashley of Scott, 'the greatest blessing of this life and perhaps the surest guide to another – good temper.'[50] The correspondence continued from Oxford. The original pretence, as Ashley admitted in February, 1821, was to give periodic bulletins on Howard's health,[51] but there is no doubt that he enjoyed their exchange of letters, which extended over the following few years. He wrote in 1821 that he had never experienced such true satisfaction and improvement as he derived and hoped yet to derive from Lady Georgiana's acquaintance and correspondence.[52] It may well be that he found in his relationship with her compensation for the coldness which existed between him and his own mother: Howard told Lady Georgiana that he was 'very tender' about her.[53] As has been seen, he did, on occasion, confide in Lady Georgiana over some of the shortcomings of his parents, although he did not stress such serious topics: on the first occasion on which he told her of the plight of his sisters, he asked her to forgive 'sensations which, tho' not warmer than a brother's should be, are too violent and impetuous at all times to be restrained.'[54] He occasionally mentioned politics, but the Whig allegiance of the Howard family inhibited too much of this – 'let us dismiss politics for in everything else we agree most wonderfully,' he wrote.[55] There was also very little emphasis on religion; indeed, such remarks as he made on the subject were somewhat disparaging. During the tour of Scotland in September, 1820, he wrote of a visit which he and Howard had paid to a Presbyterian Church. There, they found a preacher 'who consigned all absent, present, dead and alive to the inexorable claw of Satan.' But, wrote Ashley, 'he endeavoured but failed to prove me a complete sinner.' If the preacher's argument was strong enough to convince others of its reality, 'he could not,' wrote Ashley, 'prevail on me to repent.' In the evening, on the other hand, they listened to the 'exhortations of one as gentle as the first was ferocious, who solicited so mildly and muttered his curses so softly and ambiguously that none . . . of his brethren could have dived into . . . (his) purport.'[56] Again, writing from Oxford in December, 1820, he said that he would arrange in chronological order the events which had passed; 'not those which are to come,' he wrote, 'as I do not possess the gift of prophecy which was maintained by a pitiable wretch the other day, while examined in Divinity for a degree.'[57] The content of these letters was, for the most part, passing events – and news of Howard – and their tone was light. He wrote in December, 1820, that he was 'dreadfully in love': his 'magnet' was a Mrs Herbert: she was 'exquisitely pretty' and he asked Lady Georgiana to pity the 'real distress of the case . . . the gulf between us – her age – her husband and a variety of obstacles.'[58] He always passed on messages to Lady Georgiana's youngest daughter, Blanche, and she also wrote to him: 'pray mention to Blanche,' he wrote in October, 1820, 'that I am delighted with her epistle. I treasure it in Camphor and sweet odours.'⁵⁹ Again, a year later: 'How is dear Blanche?' he asked. '. . . I should like to be playing at billiards with her now or rolling down the grass slopes (at Castle Howard).'⁶⁰ Ashley also often referred to one of Blanche's older sisters, 'Miss Harriet'; and it may be that it was Harriet rather than Blanche who was the object of his affections.⁶¹

The light and somewhat frivolous nature of these letters may, indeed, have been deliberately cultivated to strike the note of the worldly 'Devonshire' set of Whigs,⁶² but they point to the fact that, despite the parental restraints of his childhood and youth, Ashley was not an excessively shy or solemn young man at Oxford. Indeed, it was Howard who was the quieter of the two. While in Scotland on their visit in 1820, Ashley had been described by a young woman as 'the handsomest young man I ever saw, full of fun and frolic, and his countenance radiant with youthful hope.'⁶³ Other comments also stressed this side of Ashley. In 1823, Lady Holland wrote that 'L(ord) A. is much improved in manner, less stiff.' On one occasion, he had talked a great deal about books, 'which,' she wrote, 'appears always a good sign in a young man.'⁶⁴ On another occasion, however, she was much less approving in her remarks. After Ashley had paid what she regarded as undue attention to her daughter, Mary, Lady Holland wrote that he was 'a male coquet, the cruellest of characters and the most cold-hearted.' But, she added more charitably, 'he is very handsome and captivating; and young ladies are willing to be deceived and from their own vanity often exaggerate affections. . . .'⁶⁵ Thus, in his early twenties, Ashley impressed observers as a handsome and vivacious young man, although their comments also suggest a seriousness and earnestness in his demeanour. These latter aspects were, indeed, to become more pronounced, to the exclusion of his youthful vivacity, but this phase of exuberance should not be telescoped between the rigours of his early years and the sombreness of later life.

Ashley was sorry to leave Oxford. He told Lady Georgiana that he could not but experience regret at his 'departure from Alma Mater'. He had formed friendships he could never forget and acquired pursuits he could never neglect. All around, he added, seemed to be 'in the fairest prospect'; and, he continued, 'if my father behaved with common kindness, I should be at present in perfect tranquillity.'⁶⁶ But, in fact, his father refused him a permanent home, either at his London house at 24 Grosvenor Square, or at St Giles. In 1828, Ashley wrote that his father *'commanded* (him) to leave his house in London and (would) receive (him) nowhere else.' And, he asked, 'Is this right?'⁶⁷ During four years, with the exception of one week spent at Dorset, he had not 'broken bread in his house ten times.' The whole family had, indeed, been refused a settled home. 'I am now sadly vexed,' Ashley wrote. 'I feel that the seat of our Ancestors is closed against us for ever and the family can never more meet in comfort, at least while he lives.'[68] In 1824, Ashley's sister Charlotte, eldest of the three daughters, married Henry Lyster of Rowton Castle, Shropshire. Ashley wrote to Lady Georgiana about the marriage. He thanked her for her congratulations on it: 'Your kindness towards them has been so uniform that I am sure you sincerely rejoice in any happy event which befalls our Family,' he wrote. He did not know Lyster, but such reports as he had heard were favourable, and, he told Lady Georgiana, he had become – or fancied that he had become – 'sufficiently wise to prefer character to Dukedoms and Excellence to Riches.'[69] Certainly Charlotte's marriage opened up a house which Ashley was often to visit. Other members of the family were also scattered. In 1826, Ashley wrote that Henry had a post at Malta and Lionel, the youngest brother, who betrayed a certain weakness of character, was sent to the Navy. 'Dear boy,' Ashley wrote, 'with his many faults (he) promises well. He is with an excellent captain; and had every advantage which can attend one so young and so far removed from his connections.'[70] At this point, Ashley seems to have felt that the younger members of the family were doing well, although, tragically, another brother, Francis, was killed in a fight at Eton in 1825. Again, Ashley had cause to thank Lady Georgiana: 'You have comforted my sisters in their affliction,' he wrote, 'and have not forgotten the Friendship you promised to me and which could not be better shown (than) in kindness towards those that I love.'[71] Ashley was greatly concerned for his unmarried sisters, especially Harriet. He wrote that she was conducting herself with 'all the amiableness that human nature is capable of'[72] and he wished that she were married. Her life was 'heavy and without solace, what will it be hereafter?' It appears that she had opportunities to marry but turned them down. Ashley could not blame her – they were not men of 'quality' to become her 'fit companions': the entire 'range of womankind (would) not furnish a wife so perfect as she . . .'[73] Harriet did marry in 1830, and Ashley's other sister, Caroline, in 1831.[74] Ashley felt that she was 'neither so amiable nor so generous' as Harriet. But she did possess good qualities and, he wrote: 'I do not intend to fall short of their Piety.'[75] Ashley thus showed a considerable solidarity with his sisters; no doubt their upbringing contributed in large measure to this.

Deprived of a parental and family home, Ashley moved from place to place, visiting friends; not, of course, that it was unusual for a young man of his social status to move from one country house to another, but, in Ashley's case, this routine was prompted partly by necessity. He was not well off, being kept on an allowance of £2,000 by his father. The only exception to this appears to have been when he undertook another of the normal activities of one in his position and, in 1823, went on a tour of Europe. He visited France, Switzerland, Italy – where he was visited by

George Howard – and Austria, and was abroad until 1825. On this occasion, it seems, his father made generous financial provision:[76] it may be that the sixth Earl thought well of a project which kept his eldest son out of his way for so long. But, although Ashley did not forget his family while he was away – it was during this period that he wrote to Lady Georgiana about Charlotte and Francis – his mind was taken up with other things. He had not, as has been seen, shown himself indifferent to the company of young women: indeed, Lady Holland told her son Henry that his absence abroad would be a 'blessing' to them.[77] And, while he was away, Ashley was especially susceptible to thoughts of romance. He wrote to Lady Georgiana that Italy was the 'land of deception and charm', although he had no 'personified attachment' there: his heart was free and unaffected 'by any Beauty or talent'.[78] It was to be different in Vienna. There he did form a 'personified attachment': to Antoinette von Leykham.[79] Ashley's feelings for Antoinette – or, as he always called her, 'Liebe' – were extremely strong. Even after his return home in 1825, he poured them into the Diary which he had begun to keep in that year, but most of the pages appear to have been excised in later life. Those that remain give only a fleeting impression of the emotions which affected him and clearly made him think of marriage. On 15 August, 1825, he noted that it was Liebe's birthday; he had sent her a present. In late August or early September, he wrote her two letters.[80] The relationship was still alive at that point, but it was soon to die. On his twenty-fifth birthday, on 28 April, 1826, Ashley looked back on it. He was by then reconciled to having parted with Antoinette, largely, it would seem, because of her 'disreputable' relations. Her father had married an Italian singer and her house was visited by persons regarded as being of dubious character and morality.

> Man never has loved more furiously or more imprudently [he wrote]. The object was, and is, an angel, but she was surrounded by and would have brought with her a halo of hell. I thought the Deity harsh in the obstacles to our Union, obstacles which he raised in my own mind even, but now I confess his Wisdom and tender Providence: 'he doth all for the best.' . . .[81]

Ashley's twenty-fifth birthday was, indeed, a time of stock-taking, not only of this matter, but of many others. Indeed he claimed that his attachment to Antoinette had started a course of self-knowledge for him, and his long Diary entry on 28 April, 1826,[82] was the first of many – often undertaken on a birthday – in which he probed his own character. He felt that, considering his age and station, he had had many sorrows, but he was the better for their discipline: indulgences and prosperity might have exaggerated his weaknesses. He did, indeed, consider that during the last three years he had cured himself of 'several defects . . . almost vices'. He was 'proud in visible Amendment, in the correction of those Errors which began to sprout in younger days, and which, had they not been pursued by an unsparing Hand, might have taken deep Root. . . .' It is not clear what Ashley meant by the 'defects' and 'errors' – it may be that he felt himself guilty of being too light-hearted and frivolous in past years, and his seriousness of character may now have been beginning to predominate. But Ashley went on to mention other aspects of his personality which, as he well knew, had not been 'cured' and which, indeed, were to remain with him throughout his life. One was sensitivity or, as he called it, 'sensibility'. He longed to be rid of it. He wrote that he wished that a 'keen sensibility' to anything like coldness or temporary indifference from his friends were subdued. It led him to 'frequent mistakes by the unreflecting quickness of (his) feelings.' This was, indeed, an important ingredient in Ashley's character. Ashley was always to be over-sensitive to slights, or imagined slights, and, if faced with opposition or criticism, he was apt to take personal offence against the individual who had offered it and pass hasty and uncharitable judgement on him. The other trait of personality of which Ashley gave evidence – and again recognised in himself – was a tendency to varying and fluctuating moods. He had, in fact, already written on this subject. He told Lady Georgiana in 1821 that the 'despondency fits have a tendency to exert their influence;' but, he added, 'stern Philosophy can throw them off.'[83] In 1826, he showed how varying his thoughts about himself could be. He wrote of having 'visions without end . . . all of a noble character.' He fancied himself in wealth and power, exerting his influence for the 'increase of religion and true happiness'; he conceived himself 'the best, the wisest, the most zealous of Ministers.' But he was then overtaken by despondency, for he felt himself incapable of reaching these heights. 'The greater flights are not for such wings as mine,' he wrote. 'I have no talents for that undertaking.' It was enough that he was 'neither gifted, learned, nor profitable'. He was only to be 'numbered with the crowd' and the extent of his ambition should be to carry out his duty 'in this state of insignificance'.[84] This volatility of temperament was, like his sensitivity, to be present throughout his life. He was often to long for fame and recognition and then be overcome by a sense of inadequacy and unworthiness: ambition went hand in hand with self-deprecation. Others recognised this instability in Ashley. Henry Fox initially strongly disliked Ashley, but then came to admire and like him, but he did not understand him. 'Ashley's character,' he wrote in 1820 after a walk with him in Kensington Gardens, 'seems to me quite unintelligible and can only be accounted for by a dash of madness.'[85] In 1822, Fox wrote that a further conversation with Ashley had given him a 'much better opinion of his heart' than he had ever had previously. But, he added, 'his understanding is so warped by the most violent prejudices, that he appears quite ridiculous whenever he finds an opportunity to vent them.'[86]

The Diary entry for Ashley's twenty-fifth birthday did not, however, deal only with matters of character and personality. It also included thoughts on his career. He was greatly dissatisfied with the years which he had spent since leaving Oxford. He had been engaged in 'trifles'. He asked himself what had been performed in these three years: 'not a study had been commenced, not an object pursued; not a good deed done, not a good thought generated.' He had recently 'taken to hard study'; and, indeed, his Diary entries for the previous few months show evidence of his reading in religious and literary works. This, he wrote, amused him and prevented mischief: 'occasionally the question "cui bono" sour(ed) (his) spirit of application;' although – with a reference, it seems, to his attachment to Antoinette – he added: 'I have stilled the passions.' Looking to the future, he confessed that he had no plans, but, he continued, 'Politics seems my career, but they demand talents and wisdom far beyond my feeble reach: at present I am preparing for the Senate, preparing in that unsettled hopeless way which cannot be called a plan. . . .'[87] In his thoughts about his career, as about himself, Ashley thus showed himself in an unsettled and uncertain frame of mind. A 'line of life' had not yet made itself plain to him.

NOTES

1. *A Life of Anthony Ashley, First Earl of Shaftesbury, 1621–1683* (2 vols. 1871), (Reviewed by W. D. Christie in *The Quarterly Review*, cxxx, 287–327).
2. See K. H. D. Haley, *The first Earl of Shaftesbury* (Oxford, 1968), *passim.*
3. *The Quarterly Review*, CXXX, 327. The second Earl lived from 1652–99.
4. P. Townend (ed.), *Burke's Genealogical and Heraldic History of the Peerage, Baronetage and Knightage* (105th ed., 1970), p. 2412. The third Earl lived from 1671–1713.
5. *The Quarterly Review*, CXXX, 327. The fourth Earl lived from 1710–71; the fifth from 1761–1811; the sixth from 1768–1851.
6. *The Times*, 4 June, 1851.
7. ibid.
8. ibid.
9. She died in 1865, in her 91st year.
10. William, 1803–77; Henry, 1807–58; John, 1808–67; Francis, 1810–25; Lionel, 1813–36.
11. George William Frederick Howard (1802–1864), eldest son of George Howard, Sixth Earl of Carlisle, whom he succeeded as Seventh Earl in 1848.
12. Georgiana Dorothy Cavendish, eldest daughter of William, Fifth Duke of Devonshire: married George Howard (see above n. 11) 1801: died 1858, aged 75.
13. Castle Howard Archives, Carlisle MSS, 1st ser., Book 67, 9 Oct., 1821.
14. ibid., 1st ser., Book 67, 27 Jan., 1823.

15. N.R.A., Shaftesbury (Broadlands) MSS, SHA/PD/1, 18–23 Sept., 1825.
16. ibid., SHA/PD/1, 28 Apr., 1826.
17. ibid., SHA/PD/1, 28 Apr., 1826.
18. ibid., SHA/PD/1, 16 Nov., 1828.
19. ibid., SHA/PD/1, 16 Nov., 1828.
20. Hodder, I, 51.
21. G. W. E. Russell, *Collections and Recollections* (1898, new ed. 1903), p. 94.
22. N.R.A., Shaftesbury (Broadlands) MSS, SHA/MIS/62.
23. ibid., SHA/MIS/63.
24. Hodder, I, 50–51.
25. See Battiscombe, p. 4 and also Lady Theresa Lewis (ed.), *Extracts of the Journals and Correspondence of Miss Berry from the year 1783–1852* (3 vols., 1865), II, 352–3 and 418.
26. Henry Edward Fox (1802–1859), fourth Baron Holland from 1840. M.P. 1826–7; thereafter in diplomatic service in Italy.
27. The Earl of Ilchester (ed.), *The Journal of the Hon. Henry Edward Fox, 1818–1830* (1923), p. 131.
28. Elizabeth Vassall Fox (1776–1845), married Lord Holland, 1797: famous Whig hostess at Holland House.
29. The Earl of Ilchester (ed.), *Elizabeth, Lady Holland to her son, 1821–1845* (1946), p. 57.
30. Carlisle MSS, 1st ser., Book 49, letter 35 (not dated).
31. ibid., 1st ser., Book 51, letter 32 (1823, no day or month given).
32. ibid., 1st ser., Book 49, letter 30 (Undated).
33. ibid., 1st ser., Book 49, letter 35 (Undated).
34. ibid., 1st ser., Book 51, letter 32 (1823, no day or month given).
35. ibid., 1st ser., Book 49, letter 35 (Undated).
36. ibid., 1st ser., Book 49, letter 33 (Undated).
37. ibid., 1st ser., Book 49, letter 34 (Undated).
38. ibid., 1st ser., Book 51, letter 32 (1823, no day or month given).
39. ibid., 1st ser., Book 49, letter 30 (Undated).
40. ibid., 1st ser., Book 49, letter 35 (Undated).
41. Hodder, I, 51.
42. ibid., I, 39.
43. G. W. E. Russell, op. cit., p. 29.
44. Hodder, I, 51.
45. ibid.
46. San Marino, Huntington Library MSS, CB 129–361. Shaftesbury to Frances Power Cobbe, 14 Apr., 1880.
47. G. W. E. Russell, op. cit., p. 30.
48. Huntington Library MSS, CB 129–361. Shaftesbury to Frances Power Cobbe, 14 Apr., 1880.
49. Hodder, I, 51.
50. Carlisle MSS, 1st ser., Book 67, 5 Aug., 1820.
51. ibid., 1st ser., Book 67, 8 Feb., 1821.
52. ibid., 1st ser., Book 67, 9 Oct., 1821.
53. ibid., 1st ser., Book 51, letter 32 (1823, no day or month given).
54. ibid., 1st ser., Book 67, 9 Oct., 1821.
55. ibid., 1st ser., Book 67, 13 Sept., 1821.
56. ibid., 1st ser., Book 67, 9 Sept., 1820.
57. ibid., 1st ser., Book 67, 4 Dec., 1820.

58. ibid., 1st ser., Book 67, 4 Dec., 1820.
59. ibid., 1st ser., Book 67, 27 Oct., 1820.
60. ibid., 1st ser., Book 67, 9 Oct., 1821.
61. Battiscombe, p. 14.
62. ibid., p. 15.
63. Quoted in Battiscombe, p. 14.
64. The Earl of Ilchester (ed.), *Elizabeth, Lady Holland to her son*, p. 18.
65. ibid., p. 18 n. 2.
66. Carlisle MSS, 1st ser., Book 67, 13 Jan., 1823.
67. N.R.A., Shaftesbury (Broadlands) MSS, SHA/PD/1, 16 Nov., 1828.
68. ibid., SHA/PD/1, 16 Nov., 1828.
69. Carlisle MSS, 1st ser., Book 67, 11 Dec., 1824.
70. N.R.A., Shaftesbury (Broadlands) MSS, SHA/PD/1, 28 Apr., 1826.
71. Carlisle MSS, 1st ser., Book 67, 27 Mar., 1825. It appears that neither Lord nor Lady Shaftesbury nor any member of the family was present at Francis's funeral. (See A. Tilney Basset (ed.), *Gladstone to His Wife* (1936), pp. 9-10).
72. N.R.A., Shaftesbury (Broadlands) MSS, SHA/PD/1, 28 Apr., 1826.
73. ibid., SHA/PD/1, 20 Nov., 1828.
74. Harriet married Henry Thomas Lowry Corry, M.P. Caroline married Joseph Neeld of Grittleton, Wilts, M.P.
75. N.R.A., Shaftesbury (Broadlands) MSS, SHA/PD/1, 28 Apr., 1826.
76. Battiscombe, p. 20.
77. The Earl of Ilchester (ed.), *Elizabeth, Lady Holland to her son*, p. 18, n. 2.
78. Carlisle MSS, 1st ser., Book 67, 17 Jan., 1824.
79. Daughter of a diplomat, Baron von Leykham. (Battiscombe, p. 21).
80. N.R.A., Shaftesbury (Broadlands) MSS, SHA/PD/1, 31 Aug.-2 Sept., 1825.
81. ibid., SHA/PD/1, 28 Apr., 1826.
82. ibid., SHA/PD/1, 28 Apr., 1826.
83. Carlisle MSS, 1st ser., Book 67, 22 Nov., 1821.
84. N.R.A., Shaftesbury (Broadlands) MSS, SHA/PD/1, 28 Apr., 1826.
85. The Earl of Ilchester (ed.), *The Journal of the Hon. Henry Edward Fox*, pp. 34-5.
86. ibid., p. 116.
87. N.R.A., Shaftesbury (Broadlands) MSS, SHA/PD/1, 28 Apr., 1826.

2

Choosing a Line of Life, 1826–1830

Politics did, indeed, prove to be Ashley's career – it was the normal career for a young man of his social standing. Woodstock was the family borough of his uncle, the Duke of Marlborough, and, at the General Election of 1826, Ashley stood in the borough with his cousin Lord Blandford, eldest son of the Duke. He had mentioned the forthcoming election earlier in the year in a letter to Lady Georgiana, by then Lady Carlisle. If he were, he wrote, fortunate enough to be returned for Woodstock, his brother William would sit for Dorchester. He confessed that he knew nothing which would more impress him with 'an awful Idea of . . . Advance in Age' than to see himself and his brother, their memories 'still alive with the Events of the Nursery' elected members of the 'British Senate': and, he added in his self-critical style: 'it is certainly very disquieting to find myself getting old, without the slightest Symptom of getting wiser.'[1]

Ashley was duly returned for Woodstock, along with his cousin. The Marlborough connection was mentioned in the nomination speeches for both men: Ashley was nominated as a 'proper person to represent the borough in Parliament' and a 'near relation to the noble Duke'.[2] Family influence was, therefore, a powerful weapon to wield among the one hundred and sixty freemen who had the vote, although the election caused some excitement, being contested by two rival candidates, one of whom, J. H. Langton, was a late member for the borough. The two successful candidates thanked the freemen for their confidence: 'We are proud of our success,' they wrote in the local newspaper, 'but still more proud of the hearty zeal and unbiassed friendship with which you have supported our cause. . . .'[3] Before Parliament met, Ashley took a short holiday in France with John Denison.[4] He told Lady Carlisle that they were 'not anxious for society but (went) to improve (their) understanding by a steady course of French plays, fencing and whatever else is improving.'[5] While in Paris, they visited Lady Carlisle's sister and brother-in-law, Lord and Lady Granville, at the British Embassy. Lady Granville wrote to her sister that they were 'behaving beautifully' and went out each morning 'to sit with foreigners of distinction.'[6] Ashley clearly made a good impression on the French ladies whom he met at the Embassy and seemed to be enjoying himself. 'I introduced him to the élégantes, who think him *superbe, magnifique*,' Lady Granville wrote, 'and he is much pleased.'[7] The 'sociable' side of Ashley was thus still in evidence; but so too was the serious. He wrote to Lady Carlisle that Paris was a 'sad place for Idleness'. One could not have regularity, even in amusement, and 'as for seriousness, the mind runs to seed like an old Mustard Plant.' He did not suppose that, if he remained there twenty years, he could do or think a useful thing. ' 'Tis very lucky that Parliament meets on 14th' he continued; 'one's time would otherwise be sadly frittered away, for the Place has attractions, and without powerful Reasons for Resistance, I should undoubtedly yield to them.'[8] On his return, he noted in his Diary that he took the oaths of Parliament 'with great good will', and, he added, with 'a slight prayer for assistance in (his) thoughts and deeds.'[9]

Ashley entered Parliament as a Tory, and his entry coincided with a time of considerable difficulty for the party. The 'liberal Toryism' pursued in the 1820s had always had its critics within the party as being too progressive, but the party had been held together by its leader, Lord Liverpool, partly by his attributes of personality and partly because he avoided any specific commitment to the highly controversial issue of Catholic Emancipation by making it an open question. Liverpool's retirement owing to a stroke in February, 1827, however, removed the stability which he had afforded his Ministry and also brought to the surface many of the latent disagreements over policy. When Canning was finally asked by George IV to form a new Ministry, the Tory party was in a state of disarray. Canning had been associated with a forward and liberal foreign policy which many Tories thought too dangerous, and he was committed to the relief of Catholic disabilities, to which there was strong opposition in the party. Canning, indeed, had great difficulty in forming a Ministry: there were resignations from men who had served under Liverpool and he had to effect a union with the Whigs.

The crisis in the Tory party was to involve Ashley, new as he was to Parliament, for, in April, 1827, he was offered office in Canning's administration. It had been rumoured that his father had resigned as Chairman of Committees, and Mrs Canning wrote to Ashley to discover the truth of this. If it were true, it would prevent her husband from making a direct offer to Ashley for fear of a refusal; but, before final arrangements were made, she had been told to sound Ashley out about a seat at one of the Boards.[10]

Ashley replied that his father had not resigned and, in any event, could not do so before Parliament met. This removed the objection which Mrs Canning had mentioned, and thus a place was offered. Ashley was flattered by Canning's proposal and he was tempted by the prospect of the salary, for he was, he wrote, 'in sad distress'.[11] But he refused it. His reasons were more personal than political. On the major issue of Catholic Emancipation, Ashley had written in his Diary in 1825 that, on occasion, he inclined towards concessions to Catholics, yet 'every second thought hints a Danger.'[12] At his election at Woodstock, his banners had carried the slogan 'No Popery' and, in his speech accepting the nomination, he had professed himself a true friend to the Church and 'decidedly hostile' to any further concessions to the Catholics.[13] But, since then, his views had changed and he came to feel that the dangers to State and Church involved in Emancipation were less great than he had supposed. Indeed, Lady Holland wrote that he 'lament(ed) his promise to his Constituents at Woodstock about the Catholics'; but, she added, 'What will Lord Shaftesbury say of his son if he revolts?' Bearing in mind the sixth Earl's conduct towards Ashley, she wrote: 'It will be one of the few cases I should be for son against father.'[14] And Ashley himself realised that he had to conceal his views about Emancipation lest, as he feared, his father '(went) mad.'[15] But, although he agreed with Canning in 'nine-tenths of his system', he shared with many other Tories a certain personal distrust of him. Canning, he felt, was 'injudicious, hasty, loving show more than substance' and guilty, too, of 'flippancy in foreign matters.'[16] Further, in his view, the fact that Peel and Wellington would not serve in Canning's Ministry removed influences which might have restrained Canning's impetuousness, and it also made him less amenable to the offer. He had a very warm personal regard for the Duke, which sprang partly from a boyhood admiration for his military exploits. When his brother Henry was about to enter the army, he had written to Wellington to ask him about the best military work which he should study, and had received a helpful reply.[17] Ashley was, indeed, a regular visitor to Wellington's estate at Stratfield Saye, and, in May, 1827, wrote to Wellington expressing his high esteem. He might, he admitted, be regarded as going rather far in assuming a kind of intimacy by writing so unreservedly; 'but,' he continued, 'the fact is that I have, as an Englishman, great Gratitude for your public Services and as an Individual, for your frequent kindnesses.'[18] Ashley felt, therefore, that he could not accept Canning's offer and remain loyal to the Duke. With him, the Duke was the 'chief consideration'.[19]

Ashley's loyalty was, however, soon to be rewarded. In August, 1827, Canning died and, after a period of further political confusion, during which Lord Goderich was Prime Minister, Wellington was asked to form a Ministry in January, 1828. He asked Ashley to become a member of the

Administration. Ashley told Mrs Arbuthnot[20] that he and the Duke had had an interview – 'very friendly and short' – in which the Duke told him of his intention to appoint him to a post where he would be the principal spokesman of his department in the House of Commons.[21] The appointment was a Commissionership at the India Board of Control,[22] and it gave Ashley the responsibility of managing the affairs of the Board in the Commons. By the convention of the time, appointment to office necessitated re-election to the Commons, and, on 8 February, 1828, Ashley was duly re-elected at Woodstock without opposition and installed in office, with a salary of £1,500 per annum.[23] The salary was welcome and enabled him to discharge debts which he had contracted.[24] He was grateful for the confidence which the Duke had placed in him, and took his duties at the Board seriously and conscientiously. He had, in fact, been doubtful about the wisdom and propriety of admitting certain Canningites, in particular Lord Dudley, into the Duke's Cabinet; the doubts which he had voiced over this earned him some criticism and he regretted what he had said.[25] In the event, he proved a staunch supporter of Wellington: 'There is nothing I desire more than to serve his Government,' he told Mrs Arbuthnot.[26] He supported Wellington over the major domestic issue of the Ministry, Catholic Emancipation. As has been seen, Ashley already felt that Emancipation should be granted, and he was overjoyed when the Duke finally decided that, in the light of agitation in Ireland, it was necessary that it should be carried. Who but the Duke, Ashley asked, would have 'dared to conceive and execute it – persuade the King and overcome popular abhorrence?'[27] He felt that Peel's decision to support Wellington was praiseworthy and he himself spoke in favour of Emancipation in the Commons.[28] He rejoiced at the prospect of the question being definitely settled. To the argument that the step involved peril, he would answer that this was problematical: the peril of standing still was certain. This would incur the enmity of Ireland, a nation 'which ought to be England's right arm.' And he took the opportunity of expressing his admiration for the Duke. 'Parliament,' he said, 'could have no better security for the safety of the measure ... than the character of his right honourable friend.' But, if Ashley supported the Duke, he went against the wishes of his father. His brother, William, member for Dorchester, proved more amenable to the dictates of the sixth Earl. 'To a certainty the Earl has won him,' Ashley wrote. '... To justify Lord S(haftesbury) is to condemn me. I know that William is always in the hands of that man who last flattered him. ....'[29] Lady Holland wrote that Shaftesbury was 'behaving abominably' and would not allow William, who, she said, had promised support for the measure, to vote for it.[30]

Difficulties with his father apart, Ashley's progress to Parliament and to office had thus seemed relatively painless. But, in his own mind, it was not so. He remained over-sensitive to the opinions of others: 'I am too bilious for public life,' he wrote in 1827.[31] This was a point which did not escape notice. Lord Bathurst, who, with his wife, was on close terms with Ashley, reassured him about his maiden speech in 1828: it had, in fact, been reported as being delivered in too low a tone of voice and almost inaudible,[32] but, Bathurst wrote, it was simply a question of becoming more confident by practice. 'I could not help writing this,' he said, 'as I know you to be mighty sensitive, and may, therefore, take it into your head that there had been a failure, which I can assure you is not the case.'[33] On the other hand, Ashley was gratified by praise. When he heard that Brougham spoke well of him, he wrote that he could not be 'indifferent to the encomiums of a man like Brougham;'[34] and, noting the news that Peel and Wellington also spoke highly of him, he expressed his surprise at the 'wide dissimilarity of persons' with whom he stood 'a great favourite'.[35] He also showed ample evidence of his moods of depression. On 1 April, 1827, he wrote that the curse of God was upon him and blighted all his efforts. He still had 'honourable desires' but he was haunted by a sense of 'predestined failure'.[36] On his twenty-sixth birthday, he reflected that men who had 'obtained a degree of efficiency' in later life had made their mark much earlier than he, and he could not understand why, despite all his efforts, his time was less profitably employed than that of others.[37] He conceded that poor health, from which he had suffered in the past few years, might have contributed to this. In April, 1827, he complained that he had, for some time, suffered from headaches and weakness of the limbs, and he also had a weak stomach. He consulted his doctor, who said that he had never met a person with a more deranged system: 'knew by my symptoms,' Ashley wrote, 'that my brain must be sadly loaded: enough to bring on any excess of bad spirits.'[38] But Ashley felt that this could not be the only explanation: he had to admit to 'painful deficiency'.[39] And such thoughts recurred. On his birthday in 1828 – another occasion for stock-taking – he wrote that he had acquired a 'more enlarged view of things,' but could not 'withstand despondency.'[40] And, in January, 1829, he wrote that he felt a 'peculiar vivacity of . . . heart': there was no special reason for this, and he knew that he would pay for it by a 'corresponding dejection'.[41] Ashley thus well realised this trait in his character: 'how curious and uncertain is my character,' he wrote in 1829: 'sometimes for a while in the wildest and most jovial of spirits; at others and for a longer period in cruel . . . despondency.'[42]

The prospect of office had brought these traits of character into sharp focus. Office greatly excited but also frightened him. In August, 1827, he wrote that he began to tremble as he looked upon himself as 'certain of office and consequently of exposure:'[43] and, in January, 1828, as he contemplated the formation of Wellington's Ministry, he wrote of his sentiments fluttering here and there. He was 'half-anxious for office – half not. Half inclined to expect an Under-Secretaryship and half inclined to think (him)self too despicable.'[44] In February, 1828, once appointed to the India Board and about to stand for re-election at Woodstock, he wrote to Mrs Arbuthnot that he could not 'contain (his) joy at the prospect of (his) future life,' and yet he had nagging doubts about his abilities to discharge the duties of the office in a way that would bring honour to himself or benefit to his party.[45]

It did, indeed, seem at some points that Ashley's doubts about his capacity for public life might drive him into taking refuge in private studies and occupations: 'private life is better for me,' he once wrote.[46] He continued his private studies and his curriculum was wide: Mathematics, Arithmetic, Metaphysics, Welsh – which he studied in the autumn of 1827 after a visit to Aberystwyth – and Hebrew, undertaken in 1829. In 1829, too, he became deeply interested in science, largely through his acquaintanceship with Sir James South, the astronomer,[47] and, in 1830, he approached Wellington and Peel in an attempt to interest them in South's work and to obtain money to assist his researches, thereby preventing South's proposed departure for France. He told Peel that he felt an 'irresistible desire to maintain, as long as God will permit, the Superiority of England in the discovery and perfection of Scientific Truths.'[48] He also took a great interest in the work of Charles Babbage, the mathematician,[49] who had constructed a machine for calculating numerical tables. Babbage had received money from the government to assist with his invention, but certain difficulties occurred over this and Ashley did his best to help and advise him: 'it is for the Cause of Science,' he wrote to Babbage on one occasion.[50] Babbage was grateful for Ashley's assistance – writing that he could not ask any man more capable or willing than Ashley to assist and advise him on the way in which he should approach the government.[51] This interest in Science – and the desire to foster and develop it – was to remain with Ashley throughout his life.

Religion and biblical studies were, however, also a regular part of Ashley's curriculum. His Diary entries contained frequent references to verses in the Old and New Testament which had made an impression on him, sometimes from a literary and sometimes from a spiritual point of view. Often, indeed, his mathematical, scientific or literary studies were allied to his religious ones: the Science of Numbers, he wrote in July, 1826, 'bespeaks the harmonious wisdom of a *God*;'[52] his observation of the heavens through South's telescope induced aspirations towards a higher being and made him wonder at the 'sweet magnificence of the Creator.'[53] Hebrew was undertaken to enable him to read the Septuagint. There was, therefore, an intellectual side to his religion, and also a spiritual and a practical one. In November, 1828, while at Brighton, he walked along the cliffs: 'had an opportunity of what I love,' he wrote, 'a silent prayer in solitude and contemplation.'[54] He felt under an obligation to give money for charity, especially after receipt of a small legacy of £100 and his appointment to office had assisted his financial position. Thus he gave £45 of his legacy to the Revd. Robert Moore, Rector of St Giles, Dorset, for disbursement in charities; he gave £100 to King's College London, a College designed to uphold Anglicanism: this, he wrote, was a large sum for him but was one 'rightly laid out . . .'[55] A sum of £5 was given to a fund which might 'educate a young girl and save her perhaps from misery and prostitution.'[56] A further £8 was given to a church at Barmouth; £2 for a lifeboat. Ashley was also anxious to help his brother William, who was not showing great signs of application. He felt that he must do something to get William settled in life; 'perhaps that will alter his whole Character,' he wrote. 'What is money but a means towards worldly happiness and a Ladder to Eternity?'[57]

But Ashley felt that religion could not only be a matter of personal piety and charitable behaviour. It must inform the whole of public life. During Canning's period as Prime Minister, he expressed the view that no one should hold that office 'unless deeply imbued with religion.' If the Prime Minister did not rely on scripture and 'holy aid' to assist him in the discharge of his office, he must do it 'in that frame of mind and heart which is caused by long and genuine delight in the lessons derived from the truths of wisdom and Christianity.' And the fact that he felt that Canning would do 'none of this' added to his doubts about his fitness for office.[58] He was much distressed, too, when Wellington was elected to the gaming club, Crockford's – 'that hell of all hells', as he described it.[59] He asked Mrs Arbuthnot to remember the country 'wherein, by God's blessing we live; its high moral character, and its curious scrutiny into the actions of those who aspire to rule it.' He felt that the Duke's election, which, he claimed, had been carried without his knowledge, would show him in an unfavourable light and be used as a weapon against him. He urged Mrs Arbuthnot to try by all the means she could to withdraw the Duke's name from the lists.[60] And, amidst all his uncertainty about his own future, he was conscious of an obligation to discharge his responsibilities in a serious and God-fearing manner for the general good. In 1827, he wrote that he must 'choose (his) Line of Life and stand to it manfully.' He could see nothing, he continued, but a political career: 'for everyone must take that in which his various circumstances will give him the best means of doing good.' Where, he asked, could he be so useful as in the public service?[61] In June, 1828, he wrote that he would retire from public life if he did not think that his conscience would 'hereafter smite (him) for having quitted that Station which Providence hath marked out. . . .'[62] In December, 1828, after a few months in office, he asked himself what would be his future career. His despondency prompted him to reflect that he would never be 'fit for a Cabinet'; his seriousness of purpose made him ask: 'and yet if I quit the service of politics, where are my means of utility?'[63]

One of Ashley's very first ventures in Parliament was, indeed, undertaken in this spirit. In 1827, he served on a select committee of the House to investigate the subject of lunacy and, in 1828, seconded the motion of Robert Gordon, a Dorset magistrate, for the introduction of bills to amend the lunacy laws. The main defects of these laws lay in the fact that they imposed very few effective controls over the admission, treatment and release of lunatics. In 1774, an Act — largely a re-enactment of an earlier measure of 1711 — had empowered two or more Justices of the Peace to authorise the arrest of lunatics who were 'furiously mad and dangerous' by the town or parish officials and to order their confinement. Sometimes, this took place in a workhouse or a house of correction, where the lunatic was placed beside the other inmates; on other occasions, when, for example, the case was more severe or chronic, it became common to board the lunatic out in private houses. This Act, for the most part, applied to pauper lunatics, the cost of their detention being borne by the parish of settlement. Lunatics from the wealthier classes were detained — on the authorisation of their relatives — in private madhouses, run on a fee-paying basis. There was, however, no control over the setting up or conduct of such private madhouses and, in the course of the eighteenth century, they acquired a bad reputation for brutality. The principle of licensing and inspecting of private madhouses was first introduced in 1774: this empowered the Royal College of Physicians to appoint annually five of its members to act as Commissioners who would license and inspect, at least once a year, all private houses in which more than one lunatic was confined within the Cities of London and Westminster and within a radius of seven miles. Elsewhere in England and Wales, the task of licensing was to be carried out by magistrates at Quarter Sessions; inspection was to be carried out by two magistrates together with a physician. With regard to the admission of new clients, a medical certificate was necessary, confirming insanity before confinement could take place. The Act remained in force for five years; in 1779 it was extended for another seven years; in 1786 it became permanent.

The Act represented a step towards the regulation of private madhouses, but it was very unsatisfactory in several respects. There was little check on the persons receiving licences and, despite the procedure for inspection, little control on their activities. It is true that the College of Physicians could receive reports of abuses from the five Commissioners or from the persons appointed by Quarter Sessions, but the only grounds on which a licence could be revoked were if the Commissioners or magistrates were denied access to the madhouse and the only punishment for reports of bad conduct was to display a record of offences in the Censor's Room of the College of Physicians. In the country areas, inspection by magistrates was rare, and the apparent safeguard of medical certification against improper admission did not prove to be effective.

Further, the Act of 1774 made no provision for pauper lunatics. It did not apply to public institutions, such as workhouses, and if paupers were in a private madhouse, they were excluded from its terms of reference. In 1807, a select committee was appointed to inquire into the state of criminal and pauper lunatics in England and Wales. This committee observed that the treatment of paupers in private madhouses depended entirely on the good conduct of the keeper, and also that they were kept in very bad conditions. The Report of this committee led in 1808 to the passing of the County Asylums Act: this recommended that asylums should be erected by magistrates of single counties or groups of counties at the expense of the county rates; and these would accommodate pauper lunatics, who would be maintained at the expense of their parish of settlement. The Act was, however, only permissive, and, by 1824, only nine counties had complied with it. Indeed the delay only encouraged the further growth of private madhouses and, despite a further Act of 1815 which provided that counties could borrow money over a period of fourteen years to set up an asylum, private madhouses remained the principal method of housing pauper lunatics. Between 1815 and 1819, there were further efforts to deal with the situation. An Act of 1819 made the first provision for the medical certification of paupers: but most of these efforts met with opposition and came to nothing.

Thus the existing laws on lunacy were severely defective and, in practice, left many persons, especially paupers, outside their scope. It was in this context that another inquiry was set on foot with the appointment of a select committee to investigate the state of pauper lunatics in the County of Middlesex, in particular within the parishes of Marylebone, St George's Hanover Square and St Pancras. Ashley served as a member of this committee; and, after its report was presented, Robert Gordon moved for leave, in February, 1828, to bring in a bill to amend the law for the regulation of lunatic asylums.[64] He surveyed all the defects of existing legislation. There was, he said, too much facility in the granting of certificates to the keepers of lunatic asylums and too few safeguards against improper confinement. The requirement that a certificate had to be produced by a physician, surgeon or apothecary was meaningless: for 'apothecary' could mean merely a seller of drugs and such a person had the right to confine to imprisonment any person whom he deemed insane even if that condition were occasioned only by the delirium of fever or hallucination caused by opium. A certificate might be issued and, as Gordon put it, 'the unfortunate sufferer might for months afterwards remain immured amidst the horrors of a madhouse.' Further, even if there were good cause for confinement, no attempt was made at any corrective treatment and no care taken of bodily health, and there was clear evidence of cruelty and maltreatment having taken place. The procedures for inspection under the Act of 1774 were virtually inoperative. The only check – the placing of a card in the Censor's room – had never even been carried out, at least since 1800. Finally, if the person so confined did ever regain his senses, there was very little chance of his being discharged and returned to society; it was in the interest of the keeper to continue his confinement. Gordon brought a powerful indictment of the system to a close with examples of individual cases of neglect: two patients had been found lying in an outhouse and three others chained down by the arms, wrists and legs, their wrists blistered, their bodies covered only by rags. He was not speaking, he said, of a practice which prevailed in a distant part of the country, but of one to be found within five miles of London. 'No class of sufferers,' he said, 'could have stronger claims on our sympathy and kindness than that which he had brought under the attention of the House.'

Ashley seconded the motion, although, as Hansard reported, 'in so low a tone, that he was nearly inaudible in the gallery.'[65] He alluded to the evidence given before the committee and cited several cases that came within his knowledge, which showed that the present system was defective. The speech was, in fact, his first in Parliament: 'God be praised,' he wrote, 'I did not utterly disgrace myself, tho' the contribution was far from glorious. . . .' He had felt 'unusual sympathy' for those whom the bill was intended to protect and so did not decline Gordon's request to second the motion, more especially since he had learned that his support would render some small service to the cause. 'And so,' he concluded, 'by God's blessing, my first effort has been taken for the advancement of human happiness. May I improve hourly!'[66]

Two Acts followed the efforts of Gordon and Ashley, both passed in 1828. The first, the County Lunatic Asylums Act, was a further attempt to establish institutions for pauper lunatics. It gave Justices of the Peace in Quarter Sessions power to initiate the building of county asylums and levy a rate for the purpose. In fact – as in the past – the Act was little implemented. More important was the Madhouse Act, which modified the legislation of 1774. There were to be more stringent provisions to act as safeguards against improper admission.[67] Further, the Act replaced the five fellows of the College of Physicians by a body of fifteen Commissioners, appointed by the Home Secretary. Five of these were to be physicians, who were to be paid for their service; the others were unpaid. The new Commissioners had wider powers than the old. They could visit with or without notice, even at night, if there had been an allegation of malpractices, and they were obliged to inspect every licensed house in their district at least four times a year. They could revoke a licence or refuse the renewal of a licence after due notice to the Home Secretary, and they could order the release of any person whom they regarded as improperly detained. The Commissioners' powers extended only to the Metropolitan area; elsewhere such functions were carried out by Justices of the Peace in Quarter Sessions, who were obliged to appoint three or more Visitors, with at least one doctor, and they were to visit four times a year and report to the Home Secretary. In addition to such matters of regulation and supervision, the Act also gave consideration to the medical and spiritual care of the patients. There was to be a resident medical officer in institutions which housed one hundred or more patients; if fewer than one hundred, a doctor was to visit twice a week. Divine Service was to be performed every Sunday. There were exclusions from the operation of the Act: all county asylums in existence were excluded, as were institutions such as Guy's Hospital and St Luke's. Nevertheless the Act did answer many of the criticisms which Gordon and Ashley had made of previous legislation. It provided for better safeguards against improper admission, required stricter supervision and control from the newly constituted body, prescribed a degree of medical and spiritual attention and introduced some prospect of release for patients.

The Act of 1828 was thus of considerable importance in the development of lunacy legislation,[68] and its implementation was of great significance in Ashley's career. For he was appointed one of the fifteen Commissioners. He carried out visitations; his name appeared frequently on the lists of visitors and he was also involved in the work of the Board.[69] He took his duties seriously. One Sunday in 1828, he spent from 11 a.m. to 6.30 p.m. 'engaged,' as he put it, 'in the good but wearisome cause of Lunatic Asylums.' He chose a Sunday because that was the day on which 'the keepers of old sought their own amusements and left the unhappy lunatics to pain and filthiness.' He 'did not wish for such an employment, but duty made it imperative.'[70] Again, in November, 1828, he wrote that there was nothing poetical in the duty: 'but every sigh prevented, and every pang subdued, is a song of harmony to the heart.'[71]

Ashley also approached his work at the India Board of Control in the spirit of using the benefits of his station to advance the interests of his fellow men. He was much influenced by the movement of reform in the administration of India which had begun in the late eighteenth century and was, in the early nineteenth, to gain strength and to prevail over the older and more static policies. It derived in part from Evangelical and missionary impulses which sought to spread Christianity; and in part from liberal sentiments which aimed at a more progressive and open administration.[72] These forces combined to produce a generally humanitarian and benevolent policy; and it was such a policy which received cautious implementation from men like Bishop Heber of Calcutta between 1823 and 1826 and Mount Stuart Elphinstone, Commissioner of the Deccan from 1817 to 1819 and Governor of Bombay from 1819 to 1827. The pace of reform quickened in 1828 with the appointment as Governor General of Lord William Bentinck, an Evangelical in religion, who favoured progressive movements.[73] Ashley admired the efforts of all these men. After Heber's death in 1826, he wrote: 'No man ever equalled Bishop Heber. His talents were of the most exquisite character.'[74] He wrote to Elphinstone, saying that he was extremely anxious to make his acquaintance as that of 'a man the most distinguished of many generations for noble sentiments and splendid philanthropy towards the less favoured of our Race.'[75] Ashley wrote to Bentinck that his appointment would begin 'a new century of happiness and progress' in India. 'I go along with you heart and soul in your projected Reform,' he wrote.[76] Ashley's term of office at the India Board thus coincided with the effective beginning of the reform movement and he did his best to promote it. On his twenty-seventh birthday in 1828, he wrote that India with her hundred millions was the 'compass of (his) mind's survey'; it was almost possible that 'some happiness or misery' might depend upon his efforts. Could 'mortal man be raised to a nobler pinnacle here on earth? . . .'[77] he asked. Again, he posed the question: 'India, what can I do for your countless myriads? There are two things – good government and Christianity.'[78] He realised that his capacity to achieve such visionary ambitions was limited, but both occupied his mind. He had a plan to establish scientific corporations for the improvement of horticulture and husbandry throughout the provinces of India. This would remedy the defective state of knowledge among the natives of India and would benefit them economically. It would also lead to more friendly relations between the Europeans and the natives; it might make the natives, he wrote, 'more sensible of our benevolent policy and we more alive to their various capabilities.' What he called the 'rigid characteristics of English demeanour' would be softened by a discovery of 'kind intentions' and a 'community of pursuits'.[79] In his answers to questions in the Commons, Ashley was always at pains to display concern for native Indians and Europeans alike. Thus in answer to a petition presented on behalf of certain native Indians praying for their admission to Grand Juries and to civil offices, Ashley assured the House that this and other matters of importance had not escaped the notice of the Board of Control or the Directors of the East India Company. Much, he said, had been done to increase the power of the native Indians. He defended the record of the Directors, with whom, indeed, he made it his business to enjoy good relations. They had always, he said, shown the strongest disposition to improve the condition of the people and, as proof of this, he pointed to the number of Indians benefiting from the public schools of Madras. The government well realised, he concluded, that

> It was only by the diffusion of education among the natives and by an attention to the improvement of their social and political condition, that they could hope to advance the interests of Europeans or to secure the prosperity of their empire in India.[80]

Ashley did, indeed, pursue the question of the jury further and completed a Minute on it. He wrote to Bentinck saying that he had spent a great deal of time in investigating the 'fitness of the natives in India to participate in the trial of their brothers.' This was not to be in the strict form of a jury, but was to be based on the spirit and principle of that institution. His reading suggested that the system might be 'rationalised' in many parts of the Empire: this could not fail to 'produce a rich harvest of moral improvement.' He had corresponded with John Loch, Deputy Chairman of the East India Company and, as a result, a despatch had been sent to Bombay enjoining the setting up of the system experimentally, the detail being left to the local authority. He hoped that there would be no adherence to a 'magical number such as twelve' – often inconvenient and 'wholly groundless in Reason' – and no necessity for a unanimous verdict being reached. He did not, he told Bentinck, take up the question to indulge a theory: it appeared to him the

> best means for the correction of the various defects which must inevitably be found in the judicial system of men who administer the laws of a Country which, in spite of all our Exertions, is and must yet remain more abstruse than the wildest hieroglyphics.[81]

This interest in the jury question was, therefore, undertaken in a spirit of 'good intention and warm interest towards the natives of India;'[82] and another instance of this was his letter in 1828 to Loch regarding the appointment of an astronomer for Bombay; he resolved to request that one of his assistants be a native.[83] Concern for the advancement of native Indian interests did not, indeed, imply any hostility to European interests. Indeed, Ashley's view was that it was the best way of safeguarding the Europeans. Writing to Bentinck about his plans for civil service reform in Bengal, Ashley commented that 'duty and interest' required Britain 'to confer on the people of India every benefit, moral and political, of which they are capable;' to exclude a man perpetually from one's confidence was not the way to make him ambitious or worthy of attaining it.[84]

But if Ashley was concerned with 'good government', he was also much interested in spreading the principles of Christianity in India. It appears that he thought the practice of 'Sutteeism' – the burning of widows on the death of their husbands – one which was cruel and wrong and that he ran into stiff opposition for expressing such an opinion. But the practice was stopped by Bentinck in 1829: in retrospect, Ashley commented that Bentinck had 'appealed to those great principles of the human heart, which are implanted by the hand of God. . . .'[85] He also gave much thought to the conversion of India; and he felt that the Indian appointed as assistant astronomer would 'by contemplating the purity of Almightiness . . . soon learn to despise Brahma and Vishnu.'[86] Thus, like his fellow-reformers, Ashley sought to sow the 'seeds of freedom, of virtue and of Christianity'[87] in India.

Such efforts did not, indeed, escape criticism and opposition from those who were concerned less with humanitarian principles of trusteeship than with the political and military strength which India afforded Britain. Lord Ellenborough,[88] President of the Board during Ashley's tenure as a Commissioner, was of this latter persuasion. He was dissatisfied with Bentinck's 'goings on' in India and he spoke to Mrs Arbuthnot of Ashley as 'foolish and presumptuous'.[89] Ellenborough, indeed, expressed a strong desire to get rid of Ashley and replace him with Sir James Graham, who could manage the business in the Commons: a task which, Ellenborough felt, Ashley was 'quite unequal to'.[90] Ashley was certainly a disappointment in many Tory circles. Charles Arbuthnot had entertained very high hopes of him but was greatly distressed by his performance at the India office;[91] his wife had also at one time thought well of Ashley, only to be disappointed. In 1826, she wrote that she was 'charmed' with him and commented that he was 'a very clever agreeable young man with excellent principles'. But by 1828, she had revised her opinion, writing that she had never been more deceived in any man than in Ashley, for he had 'proved himself in office to be wholly inefficient.'[92] Ashley's early efforts in the Commons appear to have been marred by inaudibility: but the view that he was incompetent in office was not universally held. After he had given an answer to a point raised in the Commons, his questioner said that 'the noble lord had evinced a knowledge of his subject that did him the greatest honour . . . and an extent of information which might prove highly serviceable to his country.'[93] In criticising Ashley's performance, Ellenborough and the Arbuthnots were no doubt venting their dislike of his principles.[94] Certainly relations between Ashley and Ellenborough were very tense. Ellenborough rejected Ashley's Minute on the jury question. Ashley wrote that he had never expected success: Ellenborough's 'vanity would not like to take from an inferior the hint of so glorious a consummation. His reasoning was short and ridiculous.'[95] In 1829, Ashley wrote to Peel about the appointment to the then vacant Bishopric of Calcutta. He had already, he said, 'in duty bound' mentioned it to Ellenborough, but that was a matter of form. He would rather trust to Peel's 'sober and reflecting mind'.[96] And, in 1830, Ashley had an acrimonious exchange of letters[97] with Ellenborough over a Dr Wallich, the Superintendent of a botanical garden in India, who had spent a period in Britain. Wallich wished to spend further time in Britain to complete his work and Ashley wrote to Ellenborough asking for extra money to finance it. The British government, Ashley wrote, was regarded as 'most indifferent to the spread of scientific knowledge'. Dr Wallich was contributing to such knowledge and was shortly to publish the fruits of twenty years of research. Ellenborough was unsympathetic to the claim. He was disturbed by the fact that Wallich had already been permitted to draw his full Indian allowances for two and a half years as superintendent of a botanical garden in India, and he replied sharply to Ashley that he 'really thought' that Ashley would have understood that he required sufficient ground for an 'unusual grant' of public money. When Ashley sought the opinion of scientists as to the worth of Wallich's work, Ellenborough wrote with growing impatience to the effect that it was 'not their business to report on the continuation of Wallich's Indian allowances,' nor had Ellenborough expected that Ashley would have sought such an opinion. The episode, if a small one, was indicative of the tension between Ellenborough and Ashley: and this was to persist in the future. Ellenborough's policies as Governor-General between 1841 and 1844 were to earn Ashley's unstinted criticism.[98] But Ashley's concern for good government and Christianity in India were also to remain and his short period at the India Board gave him an interest in India which he never lost. Certainly the post itself gave him great pride and pleasure. In 1829, he told Bentinck that it gave him the lead in the House of Commons: 'so you see,' he wrote, 'I am become more of a person than when you left England.'[99]

Public life thus commanded Ashley's serious attention in these years; but not to the exclusion of private life. The question of marriage greatly exercised his mind. His public activity did help to blunt the memory of Antoinette, but at times of solitude he thought of her;[100] and, although he still felt that it had been better for them to part, his emotions and affections could be aroused. In December, 1827, he received news of her marriage to Metternich. He could not, he wrote, but feel some return of love; 'the affection I entertained once was so painfully strong that its impression must endure for a time.' But he rejoiced in her 'bettered condition' and prayed for her happiness, although he could not refrain from wondering if she were worthy of such thoughts: 'I do not like to doubt it and I will not,' he wrote, 'Heaven protect her.'[101] But Antoinette was not to live long: she died in childbirth in 1829. 'This day what did I hear? Liebe, Liebe herself is dead,' he wrote on receipt of the news. It was painful to him: 'how many things will rush upon me by degrees!' he continued: 'The many walks, the many Sentiments, the many Tears we have known together.'[102] Ashley, indeed, went on to fill several pages of his Diary with his recollections of Antoinette. Later, he crossed out most of these entries. It had been a relationship which had deeply touched him – at one time, indeed, he had felt that he should never experience the same intensity of emotion again: 'a man loves fiercely but once; the next time is Reason or Convenience or Fancy or plain matter of fact.'[103]

Nevertheless, even the thought that his feelings for a wife might not match those which he had had for Antoinette did not deter him from doing his utmost to achieve the married state. He felt that marriage would be a stabilising element in his life and would correct his faults. In August, 1827, he wrote that he felt 'great kindness towards a select few'. He was not, it seems, without admirers. He mentioned that he had had a good many compliments. 'Somehow or other I like them and so does everyone,' he commented, and went on to say that he and his brother William were called 'the sublime and beautiful – very flattering!'[104] It was, however, some eighteen months after this was written before Ashley had his first serious romantic encounter since Antoinette, and it may not be without significance that this was after her death. It was in the spring and early summer of 1829 and the young lady in question was Lady Selina Jenkinson, the seventeen-year-old daughter of the third Earl of Liverpool. Ashley first saw her at the opera in March, 1829: she was, he wrote, a 'beautiful girl' who made him dream of things that he had entirely forgotten since the days of Antoinette.[105] Encouraged by his sister Harriet and his brother William, he did his best to present himself to Lady Selina and her relatives as a young man with honourable intentions of matrimony. He spoke of these to Lady Selina's cousin, Lady Cavendish. He pursued the young lady herself to a ball for the purpose of exchanging a few words: 'Oh what a place for nurturing a love such as I wish to feel! ...'[106] he wrote. But it was all to no avail. Lady Cavendish was not encouraging and the third Earl, it seems, was positively discouraging. Ashley, indeed, had always feared that Lady Selina's relatives and her father would want a 'more splendid establishment' than he could give.[107] After his proposal of marriage had finally been refused, he rather ungraciously gave full vent to his disappointment.

> I shall not think (of) you any more Madame Selina [he wrote], no doubt you take after your papa; – this is unjust, probably you do not; ... however as there is no affection as yet existing between us, I shall not

endeavour to wish for one. How odd that I should ever have fancied you! You are (as) stiff as a poker, with no more grace in your movements than a pair of tongs; but see the effect of imagination....'[108]

Ashley did admit that such remarks might be taken as 'sour grapes': but, he continued, 'sweet or sour we shall never eat them together: so I wish you well and myself a little more discernment and patience in my next inquiry after domestic and conjugal happiness.'[109]

The reverse, however, in no way blunted the urgency with which he pursued such inquiries. The difficulty was in knowing exactly where to pursue them.

Where, oh God, tell me where is the woman? [he wrote]. Night and morning I pray for a wife, lovely, beautiful and true: one with whom I may be safe from the snares of temptation; a woman after Thine own heart, the companion of my life and of my mind and with whom I may raise up children to Thine honour and glory, through Jesus Christ our Lord. Can I ask for more? Not in the world – after that cometh Eternity....'[110]

A month later, he returned to the same theme; it was high time, he wrote, that he should marry. He was twenty-eight and it suited neither his 'dignity nor ... Principles to continue the life of a headstrong youngster just emancipated from College.' He had, he continued, 'looked around' and had found many 'amiable girls'. Two or three were especially so, but none seemed entirely satisfactory as a companion. One, however, whom he did not know well, did merit special attention: 'lovely, accomplished, clever, with an almost virgin indifference towards her admirers.'[111] This was the daughter of Lady Emily Cowper,[112] also named Emily and thus called 'Minny' to distinguish her from her mother.

Ashley's attention could scarcely have fallen on anyone who seemed less suitable for him. Minny was descended through her mother from the Lamb family, which had very strong Whig leanings; her uncle was the future Whig Prime Minister, Lord Melbourne. Thus there was a clear political difference between Ashley and Minny's family. But equally great were differences in their manner of life. For in the Lamb family, earnestness and seriousness were not regarded as virtues; indeed, they might almost be regarded as faults. Minny's mother, Lady Cowper, in a sense, epitomised the 'genre'; and Minny seems literally to have personified it. For it is virtually certain that Minny's father was not Lord Cowper but Lord Palmerston. In 1839, after the death of Cowper, Palmerston did, indeed, marry Lady Cowper; and then, of course, Minny became his step-daughter. In 1856, Palmerston wrote to Minny that, when he married Lady Cowper, he considered himself as adopting all her children as his own and had always felt for all of them 'the warm affection which belongs to our reciprocal Relations.'[113] But even before 1839, Palmerston regarded Minny with a special warmth and affection; and, although it can never be proved that he was her father, his feelings for her were akin to those of a father for his daughter. There were various small instances of this. Early in 1829, he sent presents to her which he had brought from Paris and with them he sent his sincerest wishes, as he put it, 'that the return of this season may for many many years bring with it as much Happiness to you, as it now does through you to all those who belong to you.'[114] On another occasion, Palmerston was able to appoint a person whom Minny had suggested to a vacant Clerkship: 'pray, my dear Minny,' he wrote, 'recollect once and for all and for *Life* that you will always be doing me a *real kindness* whenever you can point out to me the means by which I may be able to gratify any wish of yours.'[115] In Shaftesbury's papers is a favour, from Minny's wedding in June, 1830: it is identified in what is almost certainly Palmerston's writing.[116] And it is reported that on his death bed, Palmerston said 'Come in, Minny, come in, you are a sunbeam.'[117]

Lady Cowper's reputation when Ashley first set eyes on her daughter was well known and Ashley himself was aware of it. Rather delicately, he wrote that she had 'laboured under heavy suspicions of faithlessness to her marriage vows;' and he wondered if, on that account, he should 'abstain from enquiring into the Character of a Person whose outward Appearance present(ed) such Qualities.'[118] But then the further thought occurred to him whether he had any right to condemn the child for the sin of the parent. Were there not daughters the very reverse of their mothers – 'domestic, loving, faithful'? Thoughts of his own sisters came to his mind; if he were to judge them by the 'infernal wickedness of the parent that bore us,' would he arrive at a true conclusion? Thus he would inquire further, and he implored Almighty Providence to aid his judgment and direct his choice.[119]

Certainly, Ashley conducted his investigations with great seriousness. He saw Minny constantly in early August, 1829, and later went to Tunbridge Wells where the Cowpers were staying. Every meeting engaged his affections more securely. Minny's beauty was legendary: indeed, Lady Granville told her brother that all the men were 'more or less in love' with her.[120] She was described by Creevey as 'the leading favourite of the town'; and although he – and, it would seem, he alone – did not feel that her looks matched their fame, he wrote that she was 'very natural (&) lovely' and appeared to be a 'good natured young person'.[121] Certainly Ashley was entirely captivated by her beauty and also by her manner. There was, he wrote, 'so much grace and natural and easy indifference in her whole manner; a most lady-like civility.' Her mind, he continued, seemed 'most pure and . . . evidently honest'; and her character gave a 'relish to her Beauty'.[122] He saw 'much, very much in her to charm and satisfy (him),' but he could not be sure of her feelings towards him: 'oh Great God,' he wrote, 'What a Treasure to possess such a Darling!'[123] He was, indeed, making up his mind to ask her to marry him. On 12 August, he wrote that he was sure that he would have proposed had an opportunity offered, but, he continued, 'she fights any Advance tending to a proposal: she seems instantly to change the subject!'[124] He was vexed by this: a rebuff would be terrible'. Yet, she was talking to him 'abundantly and in confidence': what was he to think? He felt that he must propose before long: 'shall I do it by word or by writing?' he wondered. 'I will do it by word.'[125] On 13 August, he saw her again. He said 'everything to elicit a check, if she were inclined to give one:' but he also seized her hand repeatedly and gave 'every possible sign' of his affection. She did not, however, '*correspond*'; nor did she 'discourage' him and did not give the check which he had invited. Thus he approached the 'final question': only to be told by Minny that she had not known him very long. 'I . . . was, I know not what, but certainly *not accepted*,' Ashley wrote dejectedly.[126] He did not take the rebuff well: he became 'very angry and irritated', which appeared to cause Minny some alarm. For her part, she did not treat him unkindly: 'she took my arm,' he wrote, 'was lively but tender;' she was very different from the preceding night and did not leave him once. This threw Ashley into further confusion. 'What am I to understand?' he wrote. 'Good heavens, she *cannot be averse* to my proposal!' He could not decide what to do. He would 'endeavour to pique her by indifference:' he would 'have recourse to prayer:' but, he added, 'Man is so weak that he ceases to repose confidence in the Deity unless his Petition be instantly granted.'[127]

Ashley, indeed, remained in a state of painful uncertainty for the next few months. In September, 1829, he wrote that he felt his love more and more: 'we are made for each other and if *we have feeling and character* we shall be married.'[128] And so his torment continued – unrecorded, however, in his Diary, in which he made no entries for six months after 24 October, and then, after a brief entry, none again for a further six months. Many other comments were, however, made on the relationship. The seeming ill-assortment of the couple attracted a great deal of society gossip. Lord Francis Leveson Gower wrote to Charles Arbuthnot that Ashley had always been 'more or less of an Ishmaelite in the fashionable world.' He had shown 'very distinctly the contempt which most men of study can feel more or less for the idler members of society;' and he could, therefore, have but few friends among the usual entourage of Lady Cowper, who, Leveson Gower imagined, had 'little taste for uncut jewels, but likes those which have taken a high polish from the attrition of society. . . .'[129] Mrs Arbuthnot commented in rather similar vein that Ashley was thinking of marrying into 'one of the most profligate families in the kingdom, he being really as moral and religious a man as exists.'[180] She added later, with, it would seem, some exaggeration, that Lady Cowper was trying to get Ashley out of office and into the ranks of the opposition. She thought she might succeed; 'a man in love is always a fool and I have observed he is becoming a *frondeur*.' And, reverting to her critical attitude to Ashley's public career, she wrote that he would be 'no loss for, in talent and sense, he has disappointed us grievously.'[181] Charles Arbuthnot also clearly thought that Ashley was making a fool of himself by his attachment to Minny: and, for this, he was reproved by Lady Harriet Leveson Gower, who warmly espoused Ashley's cause. She felt that Arbuthnot was allowing his disappointment with Ashley's career at the India Board to colour his judgment and was too ready to find fault with him. 'I dare say he is quite wrong about his India affairs,' she wrote, 'but I cannot agree that he is making so egregious a fool of himself in his love affairs.' She asked what there was 'extraordinary or absurd in a man falling in ... love with the prettiest and most fascinating girl in London.' She admitted that he had, two months previously, thought of marrying Lady Selina Jenkinson: but 'with *that* girl,' she wrote, 'he was no more in love than I am.' With Minny, on the other hand, he was 'desperately in love' and Lady Harriet was glad that he was 'not ... fool enough' to allow politics and political animosities to interfere with his private happiness. It was not right or kind of Arbuthnot to take every opportunity of denigrating Ashley – she liked him 'excessively'. He had 'a thousand excellent and valuable qualities,' she wrote, 'and two or three failings, of which ... falling in love with L(ady) E. Cowper's not one; on the contrary, a proof of great good taste.' She was, however, doubtful if a marriage between them would turn out well, 'his character and that of her family being so different.'[182] She could only hope that it would.

Lady Harriet also wrote in praise of Ashley to Lady Carlisle: indeed, she told her sister that she and Lady Cowper were much more in love with him than Minny. Nevertheless, she thought Minny 'pleased with him' and that she would marry him. He was quite willing, she continued, to 'wait and hope and try everything to gain her affections.' Lady Harriet greatly admired Ashley's 'manner of making up' to Minny. 'So *passioné*, so devoted, yet so manly, *so noble*, nothing of the common place role in it.' It was scarcely possible, she wrote, to judge Minny: 'she has been so perseveringly spoilt, but she is natural, gay, and good humoured.' And, rather changing her view of the likelihood of the success of a marriage to Ashley, she concluded that Minny's 'only chance ... (was) to marry a good sort of man whom she likes very much.'[183]

Other observers, however, were less sympathetic to Ashley: notably

Minny's uncle, Frederick Lamb. 'What,' he asked his sister, Lady Cowper, 'has poor Min done to deserve to be linked to such a fate and in a family generally disliked, reputed mad, and of feelings, opinions, connections directly the reverse of all of ours?' He had an 'odious father and four beggarly brothers.' Ashley's lack of finance was a matter of special concern to Lamb: three thousand pounds a year, a proportion of which derived from his office at the India Board – the latter dependent on political uncertainties – was, he felt, a very meagre allowance for a couple and a family. If Minny 'doated' (*sic*) on him and if he would 'live well' with the Lamb family, then it might be 'endured and softened;' although Lord Cowper thought Ashley 'odd', and Melbourne felt that it was a 'bad look-out and an undesirable connection'. Moreover, Lamb was sure that Minny herself had no affection for Ashley; and as for Ashley's love, he supposed it was 'about as violent as it was for Liverpool's daughter and as it will be for some other six weeks after Minny shall have turned him off.' Lamb could, therefore, see nothing to be said for Ashley and the possibility of a marriage: 'what the devil there is in its favour I am at a loss to perceive,' he wrote. He advised his sister not to be 'balancing about'; she should get rid of Ashley 'at once and forever'. Of all the matches that had been offered, this was, without doubt, the least desirable; 'but,' he added, 'if anything can cloud her happy and brilliant prospects and reduce her ultimately to make an indifferent marriage it will be this way of dallying with undesirable offers. . . .'[134]

Lady Cowper did not, however, follow her brother's advice. Although Ashley himself suspected her of influencing Minny against him, she treated him with considerable kindness. 'You would not look upon me as an enemy if you knew how much I wish for your happiness,' she once wrote;[135] and she also told him that he could not think how anxious she felt about him or how fully she appreciated all his 'great and good qualities'.[136] She could never mention him but 'in the terms of the greatest admiration' and he must be sure that she did him 'full justice'.[137] But at other times, she was less sanguine at the prospect of having Ashley as husband for her daughter. She took advice in various quarters as to what to do: the diarist Greville records that she asked him.[138] Her state of indecision is well illustrated by a letter which she wrote to Mrs Huskisson.[139] If Minny liked Ashley, she wrote, he was a very suitable match for her; if she did not, she would find somebody else she liked better. But Ashley had many 'very agreeable and good qualities' and improved on acquaintance. She found him very 'accommodating and tractable and reasonable', which she had not expected. She had found him 'odd' at first, but had discovered that this was only his manner, and she felt sure that, if Minny chose him, he would make a very good husband, for she never saw 'anybody so in love and so devoted as he is.' Yet she also told Mrs Huskisson that, on the whole, it would be as well for Minny to refuse Ashley, and she thought that this would be the result in the end – but there was 'no knowing'.[140]

What Minny herself thought is less well documented. Her mother told Ashley that Minny had the 'greatest regard' for him, and the 'highest admiration' for his character, but she doubted if her daughter felt that 'love and affection which she ought to have for the person to whom she would dedicate her whole life.'[141] Lady Harriet Leveson Gower told Lady Carlisle that Minny was reported to have said she was not in love, never was and never would be; that she supposed she must marry some day and hoped that when she did, she would 'love her husband, because it is right, but the later the better.'[142] On occasion, Minny appears to have been rude and unkind to Ashley, but this may have been due to irritation at her mother's constant references to the matter. Lady Harriet recounted that Minny had told her mother: 'You tease me so, you talk of nothing else. Let me forget it, and then, perhaps, I shall like him better.'[143] Minny also appears to have been genuinely perplexed and puzzled as to what she should do. Her mother told Lady Harriet that the difficulty of making up her mind caused Minny great anxiety.[144] Throughout all of this, Ashley himself appears to have behaved with considerable restraint, although the lack of entries in his Diary leaves his inmost thoughts unknown. He did threaten at one point to give up his office and go to America.[145] But Lady Cowper told him that Minny would be 'miserable' about this[146] and he did not carry out the threat; how serious it was cannot be known. Later, in February, 1830, Lady Harriet – never, it is true, an unbiassed witness where Ashley was concerned – wrote that he had behaved 'beautifully' at a ball – he had danced all night with other girls and had not followed Minny at all. His spirits appeared good 'without being forced': although Lady Harriet, knowing the true state of his feelings could, she wrote, have 'cried over him.' She wondered how Minny could 'help liking him, seeing his devotion for her, with something so noble, so manly in his whole manner and conduct!'[147]

Finally, however, the matter was resolved. In April, 1830, Lady Cowper, who had been anxious to keep everything shrouded in mystery, was advised by Princess Lieven to make the forthcoming marriage public. 'Your marriage is so well known,' wrote Princess Lieven, 'that everyone takes me for a fool when I deny the rumours.'[148] On 20 April, Lord John Russell, who, it seems, had proposed to Minny in 1829 and had been turned down, wrote to Lady Holland that he had seen Ashley and Minny, who were by then clearly engaged. They were 'much loving, as might have been expected,' he wrote: Ashley 'the most so of the two, but she seems very well pleased with his devotion. I believe him to be an excellent and amiable man and I hope it may all turn out right.'[149] Ashley's persistence had been rewarded: and he and Minny were married on 10 June, 1830, at St George's, Hanover Square.

In the course of these years, Ashley had thus displayed many signs of uncertainty and restlessness in his public and private life. Doubts about his adequacy for public life never left him, and, such was his sensitivity, that he frequently and resentfully imagined that others, too, doubted his capabilities. Nevertheless, these years also witnessed some progress, often painful progress, towards a more settled 'line of life'. In this connection, the question may be posed whether he was, at this time, an Evangelical; and, before this can be answered, some of the characteristics of Evangelicalism must be described, although this cannot amount to a definition of what was always a diffuse phenomenon. What can be said, however, is that the Evangelical revival, as it developed in the late eighteenth century and was to be found, for example, in the Clapham Sect,[150] stressed certain aspects of religion which, in the view of its followers, had been obscured by an undue emphasis on an intellectual approach to the subject. Whereas the Deist tended to regard God as an academic concept explaining the origins and mystery of the Universe, the Evangelical looked upon Him as a Father, who had shown his unspeakable love for mankind by the gift and sacrifice of His son. Man was utterly sinful, but Christ had taken upon Himself the sins of the world and, by His suffering and death, Man was restored to a right relationship with God. Man's first awareness of his sin and his response to the love of God in Christ was the point of his 'conversion'; and, once converted, he became a new creature, justified in the sight of God, not by his own efforts, but by acknowledgment of his unworthiness and of Christ's atoning sacrifice. Evangelicalism, therefore, was concerned less with creation than with redemption, and it saw God's Providence in the role not only of superintending and supervising the whole Universe but also of having a particular relevance to each individual life.[151] The Evangelical was thus acutely aware of the presence of God in his life and the purpose of God for his life: and his belief was nurtured and sustained by prayer and study of the Scriptures, which he regarded as the unerring 'Word of God'. Public worship, too, placed an emphasis on an exposition of the Scriptures rather than on Holy Communion, regarded more as a commemorative occasion than a channel of grace. The Evangelical thus had no need of an intellectual approach to religion, nor of any priestly interposition between him and God; he regarded both, indeed, with acute mistrust. But, although his religious experience was intensely personal, the Evangelical did not wish to keep it to himself. He felt impelled to go out into all the world and save others as he himself was saved. Such missionary enterprise was often seen as a means of making the fields white unto harvest and of cooperating with God to usher in the Second Coming of Christ, for a belief in the Second Coming was essential to the faith of many Evangelicals, if of the more extreme kind. The Evangelical, moreover, was concerned to purge his own life and the world at large of practices which he regarded as inconsistent with the moral precepts of the Bible; and, further, he felt committed to looking on all men as the children of God and to relieving them of temporal obstacles to the fulfilment of their spiritual destinies. In this last context, good works could not purchase man's salvation, since this was the gift of God, but good works should follow his salvation and were, indeed, a mark of it, for faith without works was dead.

There were, therefore, various aspects of Evangelicalism. There was the religious aspect, concerned with the Evangelical's own beliefs and incorporating an emphasis on personal salvation, justification by faith, reliance on the Bible, missionary endeavour and an uncompromising Protestantism. There was also the moral aspect, deriving from the desire to strive for piety and righteousness in private and public conduct. And there was a social aspect, the result of the Evangelical's impulse towards benevolent and philanthropic activity. Such beliefs and practices, it must be said, were not held by all Evangelicals with the same intensity, and, to some, the religious and moral aspects were of considerably more importance than the social. But, whatever their differences, Evangelicals formed a group of 'spiritually aware' Christians within the Churches at the end of the eighteenth and in the early nineteenth century, and the concern of many to reform the manners, morals and social abuses of the country also made them a force to be reckoned with in national life. Finally – and more controversially – it may be argued that there were political overtones to Evangelicalism, especially to that found within the Church of England. Anglican Evangelicals, it may be held, were anxious to promote political stability at a time when the influence of the French Revolution posed a threat to established institutions. Their desire to improve manners and morals may be interpreted as an attempt to thwart infidel and secular ideas; their involvement in 'good works' as an endeavour to stem the dangers of political and social upheaval by schemes of amelioration. Put in such terms, this interpretation is an extreme one and certainly cannot be said to probe the spiritual depths of the movement and to provide an adequate explanation of it. Nevertheless, the political, moral and social conservatism and paternalism of many Evangelicals within the Established Church has often attracted the comment of historians,[152] and it is an aspect of Evangelicalism which cannot be overlooked.

Many of Ashley's thoughts and activities in the late 1820s may, indeed, be seen against this general background. He himself always acknowledged the importance of Maria Millis's influence in his development as an Evangelical: but if this is regarded as too early or too uncertain, his reading of a Commentary of the Bible by an Evangelical clergyman, the Revd Thomas Scott, in 1826 appears to have made a considerable impression on him. Further, much of his reading in the late 1820s was of a religious nature: in 1829, he wrote that he prayed night and morning for God's grace and assistance.[153] Also in 1829, he noted disapprovingly that geology was being used to discredit the Mosaic history of the Deluge: 'at best it savours of presumption,' he wrote, thus showing an early distrust of any form of biblical criticism.[154] Further, in terms of his personal life, he became convinced of his own shortcomings and upbraided himself for wasting time. He was clearly pious in his habits and seen to be such. In April, 1827, he recounted an episode when a man took the opportunity of his presence to teach his child points of religious instruction. 'He sought my applause, I could perceive,' Ashley noted.[155] He also felt an increasing sense of the seriousness of life. In 1829, he spent some time at Windsor as the guest of George IV. He wrote that he had passed 'a most happy time': he had never enjoyed 'such a round of laughing and pleasure'. He had, indeed, been so jovial that he almost forgot himself: and, he continued: 'but now I say with Job "it may be that I have sinned and cursed God in my heart," but I trust not. I was harmless in my mirth.'[156] Twice in 1829, indeed, he was called a 'Saint', the colloquial expression for an Evangelical. On the second occasion, it was Lady Cowper who used the expression. She said that Ashley had a 'high sense of religion' and was 'almost a Saint'.[157] Further, observers of his courtship with Minny were quick to point to his highly moral character, and the courtship itself was conducted partly in terms of an earnest and serious search for a soul mate. Again, if certain of the 'moral' features of Evangelicalism were present in his private life, they were also to be seen in his attitude towards public affairs. There was, for example, his belief that religion should be at the basis of all public life and his disapproval of any association between Wellington and Crockford's. Again, his disbursement of charities, his decision to commit himself to public life as one of service and his activities to improve the treatment of Lunacy and the administration of India were signs of the social and philanthropic side of Evangelicalism. Finally, his attitude towards the Indian question was not without a paternalistic content and the measures which he advocated would, he felt, be conservative of European interests there.

Yet, certain points need to be made in qualification. Ashley's conviction of his own shortcomings was, at this point, more a matter of upbringing and temperament than a consciousness of sin – there was little evidence as yet of an Evangelical doctrine of sin and salvation. His religion rested partly on intellectual processes and not purely on experiential ones. In 1829, he wrote that he prayed 'with all the fervour (he) could command,' but he continued: 'all prayer is infinitely cold to express what is felt, or rather what one wishes to feel.'[158] Such a comment may be suggestive of the language of an Evangelical, but it also lacks the intensity of the Evangelical who has found prayer a vital power in his life. He disapproved of the display of religious sentiment between father and son laid before him in 1827: no doubt the father meant well, he wrote, but the 'pretension' displeased him.[159] Further, Ashley himself disavowed the title of 'Saint'. 'I do not regard it,' he wrote in 1829 after the first occasion on which the title was applied to him.[160] On the second occasion, he again rejected the title. He assured Lady Cowper that he had, indeed, a high sense of religion, but asked if she could see in him 'any moroseness, any fanaticism, any superstitious excess.' 'Oh not at all' was Lady Cowper's comment:[161] one which may have owed something to tact. But even if others saw him as an Evangelical, Ashley did not, as yet, see himself in that light, nor did he wish to do so. Further, his social and philanthropic activities owed something to his seriousness of character and a sense of the duties and obligations of his station in life, and, although a Tory, the paternalistic side of his political beliefs was not yet fully evident. Thus, although the makings of an Evangelical were present and discernible, they required development; a 'line of life' had, indeed, been set out, but some further definition was required before it became firmly established. In this, the events of the early and mid 1830s were to play an important part.

NOTES

1. Carlisle MSS, 1st ser., Book 67, 21 Jan. (1826). (Lady Georgiana became Lady Carlisle in 1825).
2. *Jackson's Oxford Journal*, 10 June, 1826.
3. ibid., 17 June, 1826.
4. John Evelyn Denison (1800–73). Speaker of the House of Commons, 1857–72. Created Visct Ossington, 1872.
5. Carlisle MSS, 1st ser., Book 67, 3 Sept. (1826).
6. The Hon. F. Leveson Gower (ed.), *Letters of Harriet, Countess Granville, 1810–1845* (2 vols, 2nd ed., 1894), I, 400.
7. ibid., p. 397.
8. Carlisle MSS, 1st ser., Book 67, 1 Nov. (1826).
9. N.R.A., Shaftesbury (Broadlands) MSS, SHA/PD/1, 16 Nov., 1826.
10. St G. H., Shaftesbury MSS, C 25016/7th Earl.
11. N.R.A., Shaftesbury (Broadlands) MSS, SHA/PD/1, 18 Apr., 1827.
12. ibid., SHA/PD/1, 31 Aug.–2 Sept., 1825.
13. *Jackson's Oxford Journal*, 10 June, 1826.
14. The Earl of Ilchester (ed.), *Elizabeth, Lady Holland to her son*, p. 57.
15. N.R.A., Shaftesbury (Broadlands) MSS, SHA/PD/1, 18 Apr., 1827.

16. ibid., SHA/PD/1, 18 Apr., 1827.
17. St G.H., Shaftesbury MSS, C 25020.13/7th Earl.
18. Apsley House, Wellington MSS, 3 May, 1827.
19. N.R.A., Shaftesbury (Broadlands) MSS, SHA/PD/1, 18 Apr., 1827.
20. Harriet Arbuthnot (1793–1834), daughter of Hon. Henry Fane of Fulbeck, Lincolnshire and granddaughter of eighth Earl of Westmoreland. Married Charles Arbuthnot, 1814.
21. A. Aspinall (ed.), *The Correspondence of Charles Arbuthnot* (Camden, 3rd ser., LXV, 1941), p. 101.
22. Created by Pitt's India Act of 1784. The Board was appointed by the government of the day and was responsible to Parliament. It had certain supervisory powers over the activities of the East India Company.
23. India Office Library and Records. IOR: F/2/10, Board of Control letter-book 1829–33, p. 305.
24. N.R.A., Shaftesbury (Broadlands) MSS, SHA/PD/1, 27 July, 1828.
25. ibid., SHA/PD/1, 25 Jan., 1828.
26. A. Aspinall (ed.), op. cit., p. 101.
27. N.R.A., Shaftesbury (Broadlands) MSS, SHA/PD/1, 5 Feb., 1829.
28. Hansard, *Parl(iamentary) Debates*, N.S., XX, 97.
29. N.R.A., Shaftesbury (Broadlands) MSS, SHA/PD/1, 9 Jan., 1829.
30. The Earl of Ilchester (ed.), *Elizabeth, Lady Holland to her son*, p. 57.
31. N.R.A., Shaftesbury (Broadlands) MSS, SHA/PD/1, 14 Feb., 1827.
32. Lady Holland wrote in 1829 that Ashley spoke 'so low that I did not hear a word of his speech' (The Earl of Ilchester (ed.), *Elizabeth, Lady Holland to her son*, p. 95. See also p. 36).
33. St G.H., Shaftesbury MSS, C 25020/7th Earl.
34. N.R.A., Shaftesbury (Broadlands) MSS, SHA/PD/1, 1 Apr., 1827.
35. ibid., SHA/PD/1, 13 Nov., 1828.
36. ibid., SHA/PD/1, 1 Apr., 1827.
37. ibid., SHA/PD/1, 28 Apr., 1827.
38. ibid., SHA/PD/1, 17 Apr., 1827.
39. ibid., SHA/PD/1, 28 Apr., 1827.
40. ibid., SHA/PD/1, 28 Apr., 1828.
41. ibid., SHA/PD/1, 18 Jan., 1829.
42. ibid., SHA/PD/1, 3 July, 1829.
43. ibid., SHA/PD/1, 11 Aug., 1827.
44. ibid., SHA/PD/1, 17 Jan., 1828.
45. A. Aspinall (ed.), op. cit., p. 103.
46. N.R.A., Shaftesbury (Broadlands) MSS, SHA/PD/1, 17 Jan., 1828.
47. Sir James South (1785–1867). A founder member of the Astronomical Society, from which he later resigned after various disagreements. Author of several papers on astronomical subjects: e.g. Mars, eclipses, occultations.
48. B.L., Add. MSS, 40, 401, fos 20–22. Ashley's letters to Wellington on the subject are in Apsley House, Wellington MSS, 8 May, 26 Aug., 1830.
49. Charles Babbage (1792–1871) with South (see above n. 47), a critic of the management of scientific societies in England. Largely responsible for the foundation of the Statistical Society of London, 1834.
50. Add. MSS, 35, 185, f. 390.
51. ibid., 37, 184, f. 432.
52. N.R.A., Shaftesbury (Broadlands) MSS, SHA/PD/1, 30 July, 1826.
53. ibid., SHA/PD/1, 22 July, 1829.

54. ibid., SHA/PD/1, 20 Nov., 1828.
55. ibid., SHA/PD/1, 25 July, 1828.
56. ibid., SHA/PD/1, 3 Aug., 1828.
57. ibid., SHA/PD/1, 16 Aug., 1828. Ashley also decided to ask Wellington for a position for William: he wrote that if William did not 'conduct himself with Industry and energetic Principle, (his) heart would be snapped asunder.' (ibid., SHA/PD/1, 16 Aug., 1828).
58. ibid., SHA/PD/1, 17 Apr., 1827.
59. A. Aspinall (ed.), op. cit., pp. 102–3.
60. ibid.
61. N.R.A., Shaftesbury (Broadlands) MSS, SHA/PD/1, 17 Dec., 1827.
62. ibid., SHA/PD/1, 13 Jan., 1828.
63. ibid., SHA/PD/1, 3 Dec., 1828.
64. Hansard, *Parl. Debates,* N.S., XVIII, 575–85.
65. ibid., 583.
66. N.R.A., Shaftesbury (Broadlands) MSS, SHA/PD/1, 20 Feb., 1828.
67. Private patients could not be received into an asylum without a certificate of admission, signed by two doctors who had examined the patient separately within the previous fourteen days. Pauper patients could not be admitted without an order signed by two magistrates or by an overseer and a clergyman of the parish, together with a medical certificate signed by one doctor; but no provision was made for a personal examination. (See W. Ll. Parry-Jones, *The Trade in Lunacy. A Study of Private Madhouses in England in the Eighteenth and Nineteenth Centuries* (1972), p. 17).
68. The Act was replaced by the Care and Treatment of Insane Persons Act in 1832 but its provisions were little altered. (W. Ll. Parry-Jones, op. cit., p. 18).
69. P.R.O., H.O., 44–51.
70. N.R.A., Shaftesbury (Broadlands) MSS, SHA/PD/1, 15 July, 1828.
71. ibid., SHA/PD/1, 13 Nov., 1828.
72. G. D. Bearce, *British Attitudes towards India, 1784–1858* (Oxford, 1961), pp. 65–101.
73. For a study of Bentinck, see J. Rosselli, *Lord William Bentinck. The Making of a Liberal Imperialist, 1774–1839* (1974).
74. N.R.A., Shaftesbury (Broadlands) MSS, SHA/PD/1, 1 June, 1828.
75. IOR: MSS Eur. F. 88, Box 3, no. 19. Ashley to Mount Stuart Elphinstone, 11 May, 1829.
76. University of Nottingham Library, Manuscripts Department, Portland MSS, Ashley to Bentinck, 24 June, 1829.
77. N.R.A., Shaftesbury (Broadlands) MSS, SHA/PD/1, 28 Apr., 1828.
78. ibid., SHA/PD/1, 6 Aug., 1828.
79. Hodder, I, 83. St G.H., Shaftesbury MSS, C 25018. 7/7th Earl.
80. Hansard, *Parl. Debates,* N.S., XXI, 1754.
81. Portland MSS, Ashley to Bentinck, 24 June, 1829.
82. N.R.A., Shaftesbury (Broadlands) MSS, SHA/PD/1, 20 Dec., 1828.
83. ibid., SHA/PD/1, 5 Dec., 1828.
84. Portland MSS, Ashley to Bentinck, 24 June, 1829.
85. Hodder, I, 82.
86. N.R.A., Shaftesbury (Broadlands) MSS, SHA/PD/1, 5 Dec., 1828.
87. ibid., SHA/PD/1, 27 Mar., 1829.
88. Edward Law (1790–1871), Earl of Ellenborough, M.P. 1813–18; succ. father as

CHOOSING A LINE OF LIFE, 1826–1830

second Baron Ellenborough 1818. Lord Privy Seal 1828. Member of Board of Control, 1828–30. Gov. Gen. of India, 1841–4. Created Earl, 1844.
89. F. Bamford and The Duke of Wellington (eds.), *The Journal of Mrs Arbuthnot, 1820–1832* (2 vols, 1950), II, 292–3.
90. ibid., p. 293.
91. A. Aspinall (ed.), op. cit., pp. 119–20.
92. F. Bamford and The Duke of Wellington (eds.), op. cit., p. 48 (comment of 1826); p. 293 (comment of 1828).
93. Hansard, *Parl. Debates*, N.S., XIX, 1416.
94. Mrs Arbuthnot was angered by a story, conveyed to her by Ashley, that she had spoken harshly of George IV. 'Now my dear Mrs Arbuthnot,' Ashley had written, 'you are a marvellous person for prudence nine times out of ten ... but the exception proves the rule, and in a late instance you have proved it indisputably. It is mentioned in London that *your language about our gracious (Sovereign) has been most loud and angry*. Is not that a little ill-judged?' (Quoted in F. Bamford and The Duke of Wellington (eds.), op. cit., p. 110, n. 1). This letter, written in Apr., 1827, may also explain Mrs Arbuthnot's disenchantment with Ashley; she was, she wrote, 'excessively annoyed' at the story (ibid., p. 110).
95. N.R.A., Shaftesbury (Broadlands) MSS, SHA/PD/1, 20 Dec., 1828.
96. Add. MSS, 40, 398, fos 79–80.
97. P.R.O., Ellenborough MSS, 30/12/12, fos. 1744–64.
98. See below pp. 173–4, 207–8.
99. Portland MSS, Ashley to Bentinck, 24 June, 1829.
100. N.R.A., Shaftesbury (Broadlands) MSS, SHA/PD/1, 13 Aug., 1827.
101. ibid., SHA/PD/1, 17 Dec., 1827. See also P. Quennell (ed.), *The Private Letters of Princess Lieven to Prince Metternich, 1820–1826* (1937), p. 369 for Princess Lieven's comments on Metternich's liaison with Antoinette.
102. N.R.A., Shaftesbury (Broadlands) MSS, SHA/PD/1, 29 Jan., 1829.
103. ibid., SHA/PD/1, 13 Aug. 1827.
104. ibid., SHA/PD/1. 13 Aug., 1827.
105. ibid., SHA/PD/1, 22 Mar., 1829.
106. ibid., SHA/PD/1, 6 May, 1829.
107. ibid., SHA/PD/1, 29 Apr., 1829.
108. ibid., SHA/PD/1, 2 July, 1829.
109. ibid., SHA/PD/1, 2 July, 1829.
110. ibid., SHA/PD/1, 2 July, 1829.
111. ibid., SHA/PD/1, 2 Aug., 1829.
112. Emily Mary Cowper (1787–1869), dau. of first Visct Melbourne and sister of William and Frederick Lamb. Married fifth Earl Cowper who died in 1837. Married Lord Palmerston in 1839. A prominent Whig hostess.
113. H.R.O., Shaftesbury (Broadlands) MSS, 27M60, 10 Dec., 1856.
114. ibid., 27M60, 2 Jan., 1829.
115. ibid., 27M60. Undated (1829?).
116. ibid., 27M60. Undated.
117. Mabel, Countess of Airlie, *Lady Palmerston and Her Times* (2 vols, 1922), I, 149.
118. N.R.A., Shaftesbury (Broadlands) MSS, SHA/PD/1, 2 Aug., 1829.
119. ibid., SHA/PD/1, 2 Aug., 1829.
120. The Hon. F. Leveson Gower (ed.), op. cit., II, 42.
121. The Rt Hon. Sir Herbert Maxwell (ed.), *The Creevey Papers. A Selection from the Correspondence and Diaries of the late Thomas Creevey, M.P., 1768–1838* (2 vols, 1904), II, 198.

122. N.R.A., Shaftesbury (Broadlands) MSS, SHA/PD/1, 10 Aug., 1829.
123. ibid., SHA/PD/1, 11 Aug., 1829.
124. ibid., SHA/PD/1, 12 Aug., 1829.
125. ibid., SHA/PD/1, 12 Aug., 1829.
126. ibid., SHA/PD/1, 13 Aug., 1829.
127. ibid., SHA/PD/1, 13 Aug., 1829.
128. ibid., SHA/PD/1, 15 Sept., 1829.
129. A. Aspinall (ed.), op. cit., p. 119.
130. F. Bamford and The Duke of Wellington (eds.), op. cit., II, 306.
131. ibid., 338.
132. A. Aspinall (ed.), op. cit., pp. 119–20.
133. The Hon. F. Leveson Gower (ed.), op cit., II, 42–3.
134. Mabel, Countess of Airlie, op. cit., I, 146–8.
135. H.R.O., Shaftesbury (Broadlands) MSS, 27M60. Undated.
136. ibid., 27M60. Undated.
137. ibid., 27M60. Undated.
138. L. Strachey and R. Fulford (eds.), *The Greville Memoirs 1814–60* (7 vols, 1938), I, 311.
139. T. Lever (ed.), *The Letters of Lady Palmerston* (1957), pp. 183–4.
140. ibid., p. 184.
141. H.R.O., Shaftesbury (Broadlands) MSS, 27M60. Undated.
142. The Hon. F. Leveson Gower (ed.), op. cit., II, 45.
143. ibid.
144. ibid., 43.
145. ibid., 50.
146. H.R.O., Shaftesbury (Broadlands) MSS, 27M60. Undated.
147. The Hon. F. Leveson Gower (ed.), op. cit., II, 59.
148. Lord Sudley (ed.), *The Lieven-Palmerston Correspondence, 1832–1856* (1943), p. 17.
149. Quoted in J. Prest, *Lord John Russell* (1972), p. 71.
150. M. Hennell, *John Venn and the Clapham Sect* (1958), Chapters 3 and 4.
151. I am indebted to Dr G. White, Department of Ecclesiastical History, University of Glasgow, for these points.
152. See, for example, I. Bradley, *The Call to Seriousness, The Evangelical Impact on the Victorians* (1976), pp. 110–15, where the point is discussed.
153. N.R.A., Shaftesbury (Broadlands) MSS, SHA/PD/1, 11 Feb., 1829.
154. ibid., SHA/PD/1, 24 Apr., 1829.
155. ibid., SHA/PD/1, 25 Apr., 1829.
156. ibid., SHA/PD/1, 22 June, 1829.
157. ibid., SHA/PD/1, 24 Aug., 1829.
158. ibid., SHA/PD/1, 2 July, 1829.
159. ibid., SHA/PD/1, 25 Apr., 1829.
160. ibid., SHA/PD/1, 28 Apr., 1829.
161. ibid., SHA/PD/1, 24 Aug., 1829.

3
Zeal and Good Intentions, 1830–1833

The passage of Catholic Emancipation in 1829, establishing the eligibility of Roman Catholics to sit in Parliament, marked the end of the 'Protestant' Constitution, and it did a great deal to hasten the end of the unreformed Parliament.[1] The agitation for Emancipation, organised in O'Connell's Catholic Association in Ireland, encouraged the growth of agencies of reforming sentiment in Britain: and the fact that Wellington's government had felt obliged to concede the measure to prevent the outbreak of large-scale disturbance in Ireland seemed to indicate that success might attend the efforts of extra-parliamentary agitation. Thus the cause of parliamentary reform, already gaining strength in the late 1820s, received a considerable fillip. Moreover, the use to which the Tory government had put the electoral assets of the unreformed system to achieve Catholic Emancipation made many ultra Tories have doubts about a system which could be exploited to achieve a measure of which they strongly disapproved. And the fact that such assets might now be used by Catholics for their own advancement reinforced these doubts. The General Election of July-August, 1830, caused by the death of George IV, took the whole process further. The Election took place at the same time as news of the July Revolution in France reached Britain, although interest in reform was already well developed and did not need the stimulus of foreign example. The Election gave that interest an opportunity to express itself: and the further – if unavailing – manipulation of the system by the government to stave off that sentiment once more raised questionings about the working of unreformed Parliament. But to all those portents of reform, Wellington and his government remained blind. In November, 1830, Wellington expressed his complete confidence in the existing system – an attitude which put him out of touch with the views of the increasing number of members of Parliament, Whig and Tory, who, for varying reasons, felt that a measure of reform was necessary. Wellington suffered defeat in the Civil List debate in November, and, on his resignation, the Whigs assumed office and began to prepare a Reform Bill. It was introduced by Lord John Russell in March, 1831: and this began a period of some sixteen months during which the political world was dominated by the question of parliamentary reform.

Ashley had, indeed, acknowledged the necessity for Catholic Emancipation;[2] and he had also realised the bearing which it had on parliamentary reform. He wrote in 1829 that the 'measure . . . touching relief to the Papists may have, by reflex, as it were, great influence on the question of Reform in Parliament;' and, he added:

> If the Jesuits, who are both rich and enterprising, aided by the Catholic gentry and noblesse, should possess themselves of many close boroughs, and . . . command several votes in the Lower House, there would be an outcry for a more extended interposition of a Protestant people, as an antidote to Papistical ambition. . . .[3]

But, unlike some of his fellow Tories, Ashley did not pursue this line of argument into support for parliamentary reform. At the General Election of 1830, he stood, not for Woodstock, but for Dorchester, the borough with which his family had so long an association. He was returned unopposed. In his speech offering himself for nomination, he did not touch on parliamentary reform as such, but he was at pains to praise the British constitution, to which he was, he said, 'attached both by principle and by education'. The British constitution ensured that power and right were so defined that 'we stood in fear neither of sedition nor of despotism;' and the July Revolution in France was clearly in Ashley's mind when he declared that the Constitution had stood uninjured during the events of the last thirty years and would remain unendangered 'even should the moral and political edifice of a neighbouring nation be again shaken.'[4]

Such sentiments were much in agreement with those expressed by Wellington in his ill-fated speech of November, and Ashley voted with the minority of members who supported the Wellington government in the Civil List division.[5] On the resignation of Wellington on 16 November, Ashley lost his seat at the India Board. He was immediately approached by Palmerston, Foreign Secretary in the new Whig Ministry, as to whether he would accept an under-secretaryship in the Foreign Office. Palmerston wrote[6] that he would not think of making any proposition which, if accepted, Ashley would later regret, and, since he himself was an interested party, he urged Ashley to consult Peel on the offer, but without mentioning that he had given Ashley this advice. He asked Ashley to bear in mind that the offer was a personal and not an official one: it was, in fact, a non-political appointment. Palmerston mentioned that the only person whom he had consulted on the matter was Melbourne, and it seems reasonable to suppose that both men were actuated by a desire to help Minny by offsetting the financial loss which she and Ashley had suffered on Ashley's demission of office at the India Board. Ashley did, indeed, call at Peel's house on 20 November, but was unable to see him because of pressure of business, but he wrote to Palmerston the same day that he did not think that any advice which he might receive from Peel would make him accept the offer.[7] He expressed his gratitude to Palmerston for making it. He said that the post would be suited to his 'taste in public Business and to (his) personal Gratification in the Chief that (he) should officially serve.' This last consideration, indeed, gave him more regret than any other. But he could not see his way to accept Palmerston's proposition. He wrote that the 'peculiarity of circumstances attending Party and the business of Politics' had changed the grounds on which 'public men of different though approximating opinions must regulate their conduct:' acceptance or refusal of office had become a matter of feeling more than of principle, and, he continued: 'feelings, perhaps unfortunately for the Interests of Mankind, maintain their spirit of Exclusiveness long after Principles have ceased to prevent any Distinction.' It was the question of parliamentary reform which, in late 1830, engendered those party feelings and the 'spirit of exclusiveness' which went with them; and, despite his personal regard for Palmerston, Ashley clearly felt too closely identified with the anti-reform cause to serve a Minister in a 'reform' Cabinet, even in a non-party and personal capacity. His decision was applauded by Greville, writing in the Tory interest: Ashley's refusal was, Greville wrote, 'honorable (sic) enough'.[8]

Ashley's early opposition to reform was to be maintained throughout its subsequent stages. The Whig bill introduced by Russell in March, 1831, was more extensive than had been expected and cured even those Tories who had hitherto favoured reform of their earlier inclinations. Ashley voted against the second reading of the bill in March, and when the Whigs, having carried the second reading by only one vote, suffered defeat in Committee and persuaded a reluctant William IV to dissolve Parliament, Ashley stood again for Dorchester. Once more, he promised the electors to 'continue to defend and maintain to the utmost ... our admired and inimitable constitution.'[9] In his nomination speech, he stressed his ancient family connection with the borough: so strongly did he feel on this point, he said, that

> even now when, in this age of innovation, old connections are threatened to be destroyed, and those links which have for ages bound man to man, are about to be torn asunder, I hesitate not to say that I would rather

represent the five hundred voters of Dorchester than the five hundred thousand who, we are told, are to be brought into existence.[10]

No candidate other than Ashley and his fellow member, Robert Williams, presented themselves, despite a rumour that one would be brought forward, and Ashley and Williams were duly declared elected.

The Election as a whole, however, resulted in a large pro-reform majority: and, on 16 June, two days after the meeting of the new Parliament, Ashley was one of a group of Tories who met at Charles Street, St James's Square, and agreed to set up a party headquarters there as a focal point of opposition to reform. Each member of the group paid £5 towards expenses and subscriptions were invited. This was the beginning of the Carlton Club.[11] When the second bill, introduced by Russell in July, 1831, was in Committee, Ashley kept up his efforts to thwart the progress of reform. Thus he tried to save his former seat, Woodstock, from total disfranchisement. He denied that it was under the control of the Duke of Marlborough who, he claimed, could not control ten votes.[12] He also defended the existing two-member representation of Dorchester which the Whigs intended to reduce to one-member status; he asked whether the Whigs proceeded by the principle of population or by that of property. If the former, he admitted that Dorchester by itself would not withstand the test; if the latter, it would do so. He spoke well of his constituents; he had never, he said, been asked for a favour by those who returned him.[13] Althorp replied that Ashley was the last man in the House to whom he would attribute any corrupt or improper election proceeding, a remark which provides a further indication of Ashley's reputation for probity thus early in his career.[14]

The most notable episode in Ashley's opposition to Parliamentary reform was, however, still to come. The second bill passed the Commons in September, 1831, and went to the Lords in October. At the same time, an election was pending in one of the seats for the county of Dorset, owing to the suicide of the incumbent member, John Calcraft. The reformers were immediately active in bringing forward a candidate to succeed Calcraft, who had favoured reform,[15] and a deputation was sent to the Hon. W. F. S. Ponsonby, the brother of Lord Duncannon, one of the Whig 'committee of four' which had drafted the Reform Bill. Ponsonby agreed to stand.[16] There was, however, some difficulty in finding a candidate on the other side. Henry Bankes had been the anti-reform candidate in the General Election earlier in the year, and, on Calcraft's death, it was hoped that he might be persuaded to repeat the struggle. Considerable efforts were, indeed, made to persuade him to do so – Ashley himself taking a letter from Wellington to Bankes on the subject.[17] It was felt by the Tories that the by-election was an excellent opportunity to test public opinion on reform. A Tory victory would, they felt, show that there had been a reaction against reform and would justify opposition to the bill in the Lords. *The Dorset County Chronicle* stated that the 'eyes of all England' were at that moment on Dorset, and the result of the election would have great influence on the ultimate fate of the Reform Bill.[18] The Whigs, on their side, were apprehensive about the election: Lady Holland wrote that if 'old Banks (sic) should stand, he would have a great chance against any other candidate. The getting in an anti-reformer just now would have a bad effect on the House of Lords.'[19] But Bankes – and his son William – refused to stand. Ashley conveyed this news to Wellington on 16 September. The whole county, he wrote, had expected either William or his father to stand, but they would not. There was a good spirit among the gentry, he continued, but the delay in putting forward a candidate was putting the Tories at a disadvantage.[20] The Bankes' refusal certainly caused some consternation and anger in the Tory ranks. William Holmes wrote to Mrs Arbuthnot: 'Old Bankes and his son William have cruelly deceived us as to Dorset,'[21] and Lady Bathurst wrote: 'A nice mess we have been making in Dorsetshire . . . thanks to all the bungling of the Bankes we shall be beat.'[22] It was in these circumstances that an approach was made to Ashley to stand, and, finally, he agreed to do so:[23] on 27 September, he issued his election Address to the 'Gentry, Clergy and Freeholders of the County of Dorset.'[24] As William Holmes wrote to Mrs Arbuthnot on 29 September: 'Ashley's writ has been moved and he stands for the County.'[25]

Ashley had, in fact, been in some doubt whether he should stand. He wrote to Wellington on the subject on 18 September. The reaction in the county, he told Wellington, was 'certain', although not yet sufficient to guarantee a successful contest. Nevertheless, the farmers were 'alive' and, the previous day, had been waiting in crowds to hear whether he would accept the nomination. But Ashley had clearly not given a firm answer on that occasion. He told Wellington that he was very anxious to see him and would call at Apsley House the following day; no doubt the purpose of the visit was to discuss his candidature. He knew that no time must be lost in reaching a final decision, but felt that, even in a few days' time, the contest could still be won; he told the Duke that his name had been well received.[26] What happened at the meeting with Wellington is not altogether clear, but when Ashley did finally decide to stand, he referred in his election Address to the delay in his acceptance of the nomination. On Bankes' refusal to stand, he had, he wrote, been 'urged alike by duty and inclination' to try to persuade him to change his mind. In this he failed, but had still hoped that 'some other Gentleman of similar Principles might be induced to present himself. . . .'[27] Ashley's failure to act more quickly was, indeed, criticised in

Tory circles. Holmes wrote to Mrs Arbuthnot: '*Private*, between ourselves, Ashley *is not* the man I took him for;'[28] and Ellenborough, writing on 26 September, noted that the accounts for Dorset were 'not good'. The gentlemen, he wrote, seemed 'backward'. There had been no requisition to Ashley, and Farquharson, thought to be the most influential man in the county, was 'most cold'. 'They have found out Ashley has no political courage,' Ellenborough continued, 'and they think, and *I think*, he will not stand.'[29]

Such comments were, however, unfair, and that of Ellenborough no doubt owed something to his dislike of Ashley. Ashley's hesitation about accepting the nomination was understandable. County elections were extremely expensive and the sum of between £8,000 and £10,000 was thought necessary to meet the costs of this particular contest.[30] The Tory party did, indeed, make efforts to raise this and felt that if such a sum could be collected and Ashley stood, the election would be won.[31] By 26 September, £10,000 had been collected[32] and, later, the sum reached £11,000,[33] but, at first, the money was rather slow in coming in. On 21 September, only £4,600 had been raised,[34] a fact which may well have made Ashley doubt at that point whether he should commit himself to a contest which might involve him in considerable personal expense. The move to Dorset was, indeed, something of a risk; and his comment in the election Address that, in parting from his 'valued constituents' at Dorchester, he could not 'but experience the liveliest regret'[35] may have been more than a polite civility. It is true that Ashley's family had strong links with the county and he acknowledged these in his Address, adding that 'to represent my native County would be one of the highest Honours I could attain.'[36] But his doubts about standing suggest that he was not, in fact, very covetous of that honour, and he seems finally to have been impelled to stand by a sense of the urgency of the situation. No one else had come forward and the county seemed likely to be denied the opportunity of recording its opinions on reform. The candidature was undertaken, he was to write later to Minny, 'in the hope of maintaining a great Cause and fighting a battle for the institutions of the Country.'[37]

Ashley's election Address certainly gave a much more explicit case against reform than any he had given previously. The bill, he said, was a 'sudden and presumptuous innovation, destructive of the nice balance hitherto maintained between the interests of Land and Manufacturers and subversive of our Civil and Religious Institutions.' The measure was 'violent in its provisions, miscalculated in its effects and eventually injurious to the community; by the aggrandisement of the towns at the expense of the Agriculturalists.' He thought that after the 'destruction of Equipoise and the consequent ... collision of interests', the Corn Laws would be ultimately overthrown, perpetual change would take the place of stability, laws and institutions would be as 'variable as the weather': and the final settlement of one day would be revised by the final settlement of the next. In all this, the British farmer would be the first to suffer, but the distress of the landed interest would rapidly spread to the whole body of the nation.[38] Here, indeed, Ashley put various 'Tory' arguments against reform very forcibly.

The election opened on 30 September and continued until 17 October. It was thus open for fifteen days, a period not unusual for county elections at the time. Each day's figures indicated fluctuating fortunes.[39] Ponsonby finished the first day twenty-eight votes ahead, but by the end of the second, Ashley had gone ahead with a 'gross' – as against a daily – majority of one hundred and twenty six. On 6 October, *The Dorset County Chronicle* reported that Ashley's voters 'poured into every booth ... whilst the visits of the Reform voters were "like those of angels, brief and far between".' But Ponsonby pulled back. By the end of the sixth day, he had a gross majority of one vote and he remained narrowly in the lead for the seventh and eighth days. Thereafter, however, Ashley made up ground and by the close of the poll was thirty six votes ahead of Ponsonby and had won the seat.[40]

The progress of the election was closely followed in political circles, coinciding, as it did, with the debate in the Lords on the bill and its eventual defeat on the second reading on 8 October. The Tories were delighted that the election was so close-run and felt that this clearly showed that reforming opinion had spent itself. Even former critics of Ashley were forced to admit that he had made a brave showing. Ellenborough commented during the election that Ashley was making a good fight.[41] He thought that the news of Ashley's early lead might make Grey resign; Brougham might form a government, offering Peel an appointment.[42] Later, on 11 October, Ellenborough noted that Ashley had, at that point, polled nearly seven hundred more votes than Bankes at the previous election: 'and yet,' he added sardonically, 'there is no *reaction*.'[43] Mrs Arbuthnot wrote that Dorsetshire was 'an immense triumph and proves how extraordinarily the public mind is changed.'[44] Ashley himself was certain that there had been a reaction. He wrote to Wellington telling him of the support and attention which he had received: 'the fact is that popular excitement is *down* and cannot be resuscitated ... no one except those whose *hearts* are revolutionary, now think of the bill except to ridicule it. ... ' The prevailing cry, he added, was 'Ashley and old England'; and this was 'a good symptom of returning sense and attachment to ... ancient Institutions.'[45] He repeated these views in the Commons on taking his seat. Many of the electors, he said, had told him at the hustings that they had voted for the reform candidate at the previous election, but were now satisfied that the bill was 'a great humbug'.[46] The

Dorset election thus made many Tories hopeful that the pro-reform mood had spent itself, and they were further cheered by the news that on 21 October, a radical reformer had been defeated at Liverpool. Another fillip was the victory of the anti-reform candidate at Pembrokeshire.

Such hopes, however, received a setback with the victory of the reform candidate in an election at Cambridgeshire, declared on 1 November, 1831. The Tories had been very hopeful that this by-election would give further proof of a reaction in public opinion, but R. G. Townley, a reformer, was returned. In any event, Tory reliance on the evidence of the Dorset by-election – and on those at Liverpool and Pembrokeshire – was unduly optimistic. Greville had sounded a more cautious note than many of his fellow Tories. He had, in fact, felt that the by-election victories were unfortunate, since they encouraged the Tories to persevere in opposition 'under the false notion that this supposed reaction will every day gain ground.' He himself wished that it were so, but he knew that it was not. There might, he wrote, be fewer friends of the bill, especially among the agriculturalists, but reform was 'not a whit less popular with the mass of the people in the manufacturing districts, throughout the (Political) Unions, and generally amongst all classes in all parts of the country.'[47] He was correct. Moreover, the rejection of the bill by the Lords on 8 October strengthened the popular feeling in favour of reform. This provided the Whigs with an overwhelming argument for proceeding with the bill without substantial alteration; any compromise with the Lords might provoke a still more explosive popular reaction. Thus the Whigs moved ahead to introduce a further bill in December, 1831.

If the Dorset by-election did not, in the event, have great public or political repercussions, it was to bring Ashley himself very considerable private trouble and embarrassment. The election had, in fact, proved to be extremely expensive: much more expensive than had been predicted and than the funds which had been raised could bear. Some £11,000 had been raised by subscription, yet Ashley's expenses amounted to some £28,000.[48] It appears that Ashley himself had to borrow to meet some of the balance – indeed, in 1851, when he succeeded his father as seventh Earl, he had to re-pay a principal of £1,500; 'a debt', as he then put it, 'contracted to pay election expenses (which others had undertaken to bear) for the County in 1831; and which had borne interest for 20 years!'[49] But worse was to come, for, when the election was finally over, a movement was started to present a petition against his return. Ashley was later to recall that he returned to London on 19 October; and on 20th – or 21st at the latest – the whole town was placarded with appeals to the County to drive him from his seat. Four days after his return, he recalled, a committee met in

Cockspur Street and issued placards, calling on all who advocated reform principles to subscribe to a fund which would be used to contest his victory.[50] The prospect of having to defend his election in a disputed election case filled Ashley with alarm. He wrote to Wellington in late November on the subject, and thus began a somewhat strained correspondence with the Duke. In his letter, Ashley wrote that he felt it his duty to inform Wellington, 'not only as the head of the party' to which he belonged but also as 'having taken so great an interest in the struggle for Dorsetshire', that if Ponsonby presented the petition, he did not intend to resist it. This was not because he thought Ponsonby's case was a good one – it was, indeed, in his view, 'uncommonly bad'. But he could not undertake the further expense which would be incurred in defending his return. His election expenses, he wrote, were still unpaid: indeed, even the amount nominally subscribed had not been placed in the Banker's hands. He had, therefore, the prospect of 'debts and incumbrances' which he himself could never discharge, and, in these circumstances, it would be 'dishonourable to incur any further expenses.' He asked Wellington not to divulge his intentions, since this might resolve any doubts in Ponsonby's mind about presenting a petition.[51] The Duke's reply was somewhat terse. When Ashley addressed him as a person greatly interested in his honour and success and as one who felt an anxious interest in Ashley's success in Dorset, he was willing to reply: but he disclaimed the title of 'the head of a party' which Ashley had used. 'I protest,' Wellington wrote, 'against being supposed to be the head of any party, or responsible for anybody's acts excepting my own.' He expressed sympathy for Ashley's plight, but little more. 'I am very sorry,' he wrote, 'you should find yourself under the necessity of retiring in case Mr Ponsonby should petition. I did everything in my power to support you. I did more even than I promised.' And he promised to pay Ashley what he owed him when they next met.[52]

This prompted a pained reply from Ashley. He had embarked on the contest 'for no motives of private ambition whatever' but was induced to it by 'political feelings and the persuasion of those who felt strongly on the Reform Question.' He had had reason to hope and was encouraged to think that he would not be expected to bear any burden, and, although he well realised the difference between a 'positive promise' and a 'reasonable expectation', he assured Wellington that he had letters in his possession which warranted that conclusion. None of these was from the Duke himself, but he had hoped that the Duke and others in the party would have taken an interest in trying to extricate him from his difficulties. It was simply to draw the Duke's attention to this matter that his 'much misconstrued' letter had been sent, not to 'extort any compliance' on his part. And, he ended:

Excuse me my Lord if I say that in terming you the head of a great party I was only asserting to you that position which your eminent services, talents and high station have ensured you in the eyes of all the country as well as in those of your obedient and devoted servant.[53]

Again, in a further letter, Ashley returned to his description of Wellington as 'head of a party'. He had, he wrote, no intention of fixing responsibility on Wellington, but he felt obliged to inform Wellington of his intention to retire so that the Duke might calculate the strength of the opposition in the Commons.[54] The letters, however, provoked no more favourable a response from Wellington. The Duke pointed out that Ashley had asked him to keep his intentions a secret; thus he could not approach others on the subject. And he added: 'the truth is that I cannot interfere in these matters any more.'[55] Ashley replied that it would have been possible for Wellington to act without mentioning any names, and, had the Duke raised the matter, he would have had no objection to anyone else being admitted to the secret if that had been thought expedient.[56] But there the matter rested: Ashley clearly sensed the Duke's evident desire to end the correspondence.

On 7 December, the petition was duly presented against Ashley's return. It argued that Ashley obtained 'a colourable majority and was returned to serve in Parliament in open violation of the law and freedom of Election.'[57] The grounds on which it made this case were various. It was argued that the Sheriff and his Assessors had shown partiality towards Ashley: thus, many legally qualified voters, who declared their intention of voting for Ponsonby, were not allowed to vote and many persons not qualified to vote were permitted to cast their vote for Ashley. Moreover, the Sheriff and his Assessors, it was said, had turned down repeated requests made on Ponsonby's behalf to appoint an additional assessor to hear objections which had been made to voters, and, it was claimed, had these cases been properly heard, the validity of their votes would have been established and, since most had been in Ponsonby's interest, Ashley's slender majority would have been overturned. Charges were also made against Ashley himself and his agents. By gifts and by treating, he and his supporters had been guilty, so the petition ran, of 'extensive bribery and corrupt practices'; and, by threats and promises, they had employed undue influences and improper means. The petition was due to be considered on 26 December, 1831; but on 17 December it was deferred until 24 January.

Ashley was quick to disclaim any responsibility for the expenditure which resistance to the petition would incur. On 20 December, he wrote to two of his agents to tell them of his refusal to authorise any expenses in that connection. He did not know what might be done to defend the seat by his friends, but, he told T. G. Read, one of his agents: 'I have written this note simply to declare myself wholly irresponsible for any debts whatsoever that may be incurred by such a measure.'[58] The same day, he issued a public statement, expressing his 'present but final determination'. If the party thought the seat worth defending, he wrote, they were quite at liberty to undertake the defence. But he himself could do nothing in that respect. His 'whole endeavours' would be directed towards the discharge of his election debts: that was the only course by which he could 'stand justified before the world, the creditors and (his) own conscience.' He would not spend a farthing in resisting Ponsonby's petition, and, whatever the party might do in their own name, he could not permit even the smallest charge in his.[59] Read felt that Ashley's attitude was somewhat unwise. He told Ashley that the agents of Ponsonby had been active in every part of the county in investigating the votes. It was necessary for Ashley's agents to do the same and such efforts as had been made had revealed great numbers of bad votes registered for Ponsonby. If he now had to write to the agents to say that Ashley would not be responsible for any further expenses, without at the same time stating in what manner they would be discharged, everything would be dropped.

> I feel very much for your Lordship's situation [Read continued] and I am aware that the Expense must be a most serious consideration, but I trust some arrangement will be made for raising the funds, as it is a great pity so good a cause should be abandoned....[60]

But Ashley adhered to his previous view. He was determined, he told Read, to 'get out of it as soon as possible.' As a man of sense and a man of honour, he could not consent to become responsible for more debts while the first remained unpaid.[61] On 17 January, 1832, in the House of Commons, he publicly announced his intention to retire from the representation of Dorset. He was not afraid, he said, of the result of an examination before an election committee, but he had decided to retire, lest such an examination might render him liable to 'pecuniary inconveniences'. It was necessity and nothing else that drove him from the field.[62]

Ashley felt a keen sense of grievance at the way in which he had been treated by the party. He was, it was reported in January, 'very sulky and cross'.[63] He told Read that the party, having put him forward, was unwilling – so it seemed – to meet the expenses: 'in short,' he wrote, 'they have deserted me, but the debt remains.'[64] And, in a letter to the Duke of Cumberland thanking him for the 'kind feeling' which the Duke had expressed on his behalf, Ashley referred to the 'general desertion of (his) friends'.[65] The Duke, in reply, expressed the view that, since the Tory party had persuaded Ashley to stand in the election rather against his own wishes, it was bound now to do its utmost to help him – the question was one in which 'the honour and character of us Tories is most entirely concerned.'[66] And such views were shared by others. Greville wrote in January, 1832, that Ashley was

> very low and unhappy about his election concerns, having been pushed into the contest by the Tories, who now abandon him to the bills which it has entailed – they have subscribed 12,000£ and (the) accounts amount to 30,000 – the enthusiasm has evaporated, and though he explained in the outset that he could not spend a guinea, and they were profuse in promises to bear him harmless, nobody seems disposed to come forward with a guinea.[67]

Ashley was not, therefore, without sympathy in his plight, but what was felt even more acutely by the Tory party was the fact that, if the petition were not contested, it would amount to an admission that the charges of bribery and partiality were accurate. This point was forcibly expressed in a letter from William Bankes to Mrs Arbuthnot in December, 1831. Bankes wrote that he had not been a party to the original decision to embark on the election, but defending it was a different matter. 'We owe it to Ashley,' he wrote, 'and we owe it still more (I mean the whole party) to our character.' He envisaged the reception which would be given to a failure to defend the seat. There could be no question that a party which included the Dukes of Northumberland and Buccleuch could not afford to contest the petition, and any failure to do so could only be ascribed to a knowledge that the election could not be defended because it had been won by bribery. This was, moreover, the election which supposedly witnessed a 'spontaneous reaction and exhibition of strong and altered feeling'. Money had been found for that and could, Bankes felt, also be found as readily now, but it was 'pleasanter to pay for a triumph than a disgrace and to retreat quietly than to brave an expulsion.' Bankes thus felt that not only honour but also political necessity demanded that the petition be contested. He himself had been active in raising subscriptions to pay for it and he urged Mrs Arbuthnot to do the same: it was, he wrote, 'worth almost any exertion' to avoid embarrassment to the party.[68]

Thus Ponsonby's petition *was* contested. A committee was formed in London to collect funds subscribed by Tories who had no connection with Dorset but who felt it either a matter of duty or interest to contest the petition. There was also very considerable local effort in Dorset. *The Dorset County Chronicle* reported that the freeholders of Dorset had come forward 'with zeal and alacrity' to defend Ashley. The subscriptions amounted to some £6,000 and were daily increasing.[69] Further reports gave news of other subscriptions: the lists of subscribers comprised 'a multitude of names of the first respectability, for property, for rank and for learning' and there was a greater number of clergymen of the Church of England than of any other category.[70] A committee was formed in the county to correspond and cooperate with the committee in London.[71] It was reported that more 'handsome subscriptions' had been added to the lists and that many had promised 'double if required'.[72] It appears, indeed, that more money was subscribed than was actually required. Read wrote in April that, since there was a surplus, the various agents could 'with great propriety be paid for their services in getting up their cases which they agreed to do gratuitously if . . . there might not be money sufficient.'[73] The actual procedure for contesting the petition was set in motion on 8 February in the form of another petition: this went in the name of eight men,[74] who prayed that, since Ashley did not intend to defend his election and return, they might be admitted as 'Parties in the room of the said Lord Ashley to defend the said Election and Return.'[75] The petition was accepted and on 1 March the House appointed a select committee to try and determine the merits of Ponsonby's petition.

The committee did not, in fact, have to pronounce upon the question of the conduct of the Sheriff and the Assessor, nor upon the alleged bribery and undue influence employed by Ashley and his supporters. These complaints, made in Ponsonby's petition, were abandoned early in the committee's deliberations by Ponsonby's solicitor. Instead, the committee's time was taken up by a consideration of disputed votes. The poll book was examined and disputed votes on both sides settled in each division. In the end, Ponsonby's solicitor retired from the hearings and virtually conceded victory to Ashley, and the decision of the committee, reported to the Commons on 19 March, 1832, was that Ashley was 'duly elected a Knight of the shire to serve in the present Parliament for the County of Dorset.'[76] Ashley was thus able to take his seat, and, on 22 March, 1832, he issued a statement to the Gentry, Clergy and Freeholders of the County of Dorset, stating that the honour which he had received at their hands at the election had been increased and confirmed by the result of the investigation; not a single name had been struck from the list of the majority. He acknowledged 'with heartfelt gratitude' their 'activity and kindness', displayed in the resistance to the petition against him no less than in the Election itself.[77]

Nevertheless, the whole episode had been a painful and somewhat disillusioning one for Ashley. The election had, to some extent, been forced upon him; the victory had been marred by the petition against his return and by the financial difficulties in which he had been placed. Further, although the county and the party did finally come to his rescue, he had had sharp exchanges with his former patron, Wellington. He had also been involved in acrimonious dealings with his fellow member in Dorset, E.

Berkeley Portman, whom, indeed, he had known at Christ Church and who sat for Dorset as a Whig. Portman had not been in favour of Ashley's candidature in Dorset; he had written to Ashley on 28 September of the 'impolicy of the contest'.[78] If Ashley succeeded in the election, he would expose the County to the reproach of being 'a weathercock County': indeed, Portman said that if Ashley were returned, he himself would retire and give the freeholders the opportunity of choosing another Tory candidate. Ashley replied that nothing was more usual in counties than for two colleagues to differ on subjects of great moment: there was no need for either to retire. He promised to cooperate in promoting the prosperity of Dorset.[79] Portman's letter was, however, made public, and, after Ashley's election had been confirmed, Portman was asked in the Commons if he intended to retire.[80] He replied that when the committee decided in favour of Ashley, he had felt obliged to keep his pledge and had tendered his resignation, but a requisition from the county had begged him not to hazard its peace by another election. He wished to say that he had personally no objection to acting with Ashley as a colleague, but he objected to his letter threatening resignation being made public.[81] Ashley, however, claimed that, since Portman had saddled him with the responsibility of exposing the county to another election, he saw no reason to consider the letter as a private communication.

Thus, despite the favourable outcome of the election and the petition, Ashley had been involved in a good deal of unpleasantness. Further, he chafed at the fact that he had to remain in London during the inquiry of the select committee and was thus apart from his young wife, who was out of town. 'It makes me wretched to say that I cannot come to you,' he wrote to Minny in March, 'but really my affairs look so ill that I am unwilling to leave London in such a state of uncertainty.'[82] He felt that Ponsonby's great object was to make a series of frivolous objections and exhaust the money which might otherwise be the means of his relief. 'This cannot be helped,' he wrote, 'and we must submit to the evils which await an insolvent debtor.' And, he continued, 'God be praised, I have done nothing to disgrace my character, tho' much to diminish our happiness.'[83]

Although he had been personally vindicated, the costly stand which he had taken in defence of the unreformed Parliament finally proved to be in vain. The Whigs did, indeed, encounter further difficulties with their bill introduced in December, 1831. In May, 1832, they resigned when a hostile amendment was carried in the Lords, and attempts were made to form a Tory Ministry. This, however, failed, and the Whigs returned, having finally extracted from William IV the assurance that he would create sufficient peers to overcome any continuing resistance. The Lords thus dropped their opposition and the bill passed in June, 1832. Ashley played no part in these final proceedings, and the part which he had played earlier, with all its accompanying unpleasantness and distress, had no effect on them.

The final passing of the bill was followed in December, 1832, by the first elections under the reformed system. Ashley was depressed by the future prospects of the country. It seemed to him likely that reform of Parliament would be followed by encroachments on another great institution which, it could be argued, was also in need of reform: the Church. 'Infidels by the score, many more lukewarm, and a few deeply impressed with the duties of religion! Such will be the House of Commons,' he wrote to Minny. And he felt that it might fall to him to stand up for the 'remnant of God's Church and name'.[84] Certainly, the Tory party was virtually annihilated in the General Election. 'Where are the Conservatives to be found?' he asked Minny. 'What places, excepting a few, have sent them to Parliament?'[85] The only possible consolation was that the very weakness of the Conservatives might stave off further reforming efforts by the Whigs; 'having nothing more to fear from a ruined party,' he wrote to Minny, 'the Administration may be less eager to destroy the Institutions which that party upheld....'[86]

Ashley himself stood once again for Dorset. At his speech accepting the nomination, he referred to his election the previous autumn. He was surprised, he said, to be received with such unanimity and found it gratifying that this was so; it was 'convincing proof that he had given no offence.'[87] But he was most anxious to avoid a contest on this occasion, for, as he put it to Minny, 'it . . . would be impossible to withstand one.'[88] There were various rumours that a candidate would be put up against him: one was that Russell, if defeated in Devonshire, might stand against him,[89] and, when that rumour proved false, others were started. 'London and Manchester,' Ashley told Minny, 'have been ransacked for a Candidate; the cheapest, tho' they don't know it, would be enough for me.'[90] He wrote that he would go to the hustings with two advertisements in his pocket: 'one to thank the electors for their kindness; another to decline paying any expense in a contest.' But, despite all such rumours, Ashley was confident that the 'thanking one' would be the more likely to be used.[91] And so it proved: Ashley was returned without a contest. Under the terms of the Reform Act, the representation of Dorset was increased from two members to three. Ashley's fellow members were Ponsonby, his opponent of October, and Bankes, who now stood and was returned.

Yet, in personal terms, as in national ones, the political future looked bleak to Ashley. In the new House, he would, he thought, feel 'like a pelican . . . in the wilderness, amongst so many Jacobins, Atheists, radical Dissenters and Whig place hunters.' And, he continued, it had only been curiosity which had urged him to desire a seat in Parliament: 'pleasure, interests, ambitions, hope of doing good, chance of averting evil are so many dead and corrupt imaginations.'[92] Certainly the immediate post Reform Act period, with the Whigs firmly entrenched in office, must have opened up an unpromising and barren prospect for a young Tory politician. Yet these years were to prove of crucial importance to Ashley. For, within a few months of his writing that there was nothing for him to do in politics, Ashley was to become involved in an issue which was to remain an urgent concern in his life for many years to come and was to have a great bearing on his political fortunes: factory reform.

Ashley embarked on the question of factory reform after the initiative had been taken by others. Popular agitation for a shorter working day had first been organised in Lancashire in the years after 1815, but in the later 1820s and early 1830s was centred mainly on Yorkshire.[93] The formation of short-time committees was further stimulated by disappointment at an Act passed in 1831 – Hobhouse's Act[94] – for the regulation of hours in cotton factories, and efforts were made to obtain the support of a member of Parliament who would sponsor a bill which would be an improvement on Hobhouse's Act. Popular leadership of the Ten Hours Movement, as it became known, was provided notably by Richard Oastler, a steward on an estate near Huddersfield, who became converted to the cause in 1830 after visiting a neighbouring factory.[95] Parliamentary leadership was given by Michael Sadler, Tory member for Newark, who agreed to the Movement's request that a further measure should be introduced. Sadler's bill,[96] first proposed in December, 1831, provided a focal point for the energies of the Movement; but it was given a second reading in March, 1832, only on the condition that it be referred to a select committee. This met under Sadler's chairmanship. The publication of the factory workers' evidence to the select committee in January, 1833, provoked further agitation by the Ten Hours Movement. On the other hand, it also prompted resistance from the opponents of the Movement on the grounds that it presented an unfair case. It was, therefore, necessary for the Movement to mount a campaign to ensure that Sadler's initiative was not lost, but Sadler himself was defeated at the General Election of December, 1832.[97] The Movement had by now regained support in its original home, Lancashire, and a joint committee of Lancashire and Yorkshire Short-Time Committees was held at Bradford in January, 1833.[98] One of the tasks which was clearly necessary was to obtain the support of another member of Parliament to take Sadler's place. An active member of the Movement, the Revd. G. S. Bull,[99] was sent to London to achieve this, and it was Bull who finally approached Ashley with the request that he take up Sadler's bill.

Ashley's involvement with the Factory Movement was, therefore, dictated by circumstances over which he himself had no control; but involved he became. On 5 February, 1833, he gave notice in the Commons that he would re-introduce Sadler's bill a month later. The following day, Bull wrote to the Short-Time Committee to inform them of his success in securing a parliamentary spokesman. He was full of praise for Ashley, whom he described as 'noble, benevolent, and resolute in mind, as he is manly in person.' He had been favoured with several interviews with Ashley, 'all of the most satisfactory kind.' On one occasion, Ashley had said that he had only 'zeal and good intentions' to bring to the work; he could have no merit in it, since that belonged to Sadler. 'It seems no one else will undertake it,' Bull reported Ashley to say, 'so I will; and without cant or hypocrisy, which I hate, I assure you I dare not refuse the request you have so earnestly pressed. . . .'[100]

In describing Ashley as 'resolute in mind', Bull almost certainly exaggerated the extent of Ashley's commitment to the question – or knowledge of it – when he was first approached. Looking back on the episode in 1838, Ashley recalled[101] that it was only in the autumn and winter of 1832 that he had happened to read in *The Times* some extracts of evidence taken before Sadler's committee. He had heard nothing of the question previously and was not aware that an inquiry had been instituted by the Commons. He had, however, been 'astonished and disgusted' by his reading of the evidence: and knowing that Sadler was out of Parliament, he had written to him to offer his services in presenting petitions 'or doing any other small work that the cause might require.' He had, however, received no answer and had forgotten the matter. He recalled his 'astonishment . . . doubt and terror' when Bull approached him in early February, 1833, with the proposition that he should take the lead in Parliament. He had asked for time to consider it, but Bull had replied that an immediate decision was necessary, since Morpeth – Ashley's old friend – would otherwise give notice of a bill which would introduce an eleven-hour day and thus defraud the operatives of a ten-hour day. Ashley recollected that he had obtained a respite from Bull until the following morning and set himself 'to reflection and inquiry'. He had consulted two members,[102] who urged him to adopt the question, and he had gone home, armed with their opinions, to decide for himself 'after meditation and prayer and "divination" (as it were) by the Word of God.'

Such comments – written five years after the event – must, of course, be treated with some caution, but they are corroborated by Ashley's correspondence at the time. Ashley wrote to Bull on 5 February telling him how ill-equipped he was to undertake the cause: he could bring nothing to it except 'hearty zeal'. He only agreed to Bull's request because others whom Sadler had approached to take his place had refused to do so, but he had felt under the strongest temptation to follow their example.[103] Further, Morpeth wrote to Ashley on 6 February to express the hope that Ashley would not think it discourteous or unfair of him to have given notice on the factory question, despite Ashley's initiative; Morpeth had already told his constituents that, if Sadler were not elected, he would take up the matter 'in such a shape as would best suit the interest of all classes among them.'[104] Ashley replied that he did not feel Morpeth's motion to be 'quite conformable to the usages of the House': but he would say nothing more about it since Morpeth seemed to be 'greatly embarrassed' by the interests of his constituents. He went on to tell Morpeth that it would be difficult to describe the reluctance with which he had undertaken to bring forward Sadler's bill. He had, he said, pointed out to Bull how unfit he was to be the head of such a cause, although this had been met by the observation that, as the representative of a southern and agricultural county, he could not be justly suspected of furthering his own political interests. Nevertheless, he had withheld his consent until almost all Sadler's friends had been approached and had refused, and, having consented, he did not conceal from Morpeth that his heart sank within him. If Morpeth's bill met the demands of the Ten Hours Movement – the total abolition of night work, a ten-hour day between the ages of nine and eighteen and eight hours on a Saturday – he would be delighted to retire from his commitment to Sadler's measure and give Morpeth every support.[105] And Ashley also wrote to Oastler on 16 February. He acknowledged the part which Sadler had played: if he succeeded, he would simply be terminating 'in the twelfth hour (Sadler's) labour of the eleven.' But he 'greatly fear(ed)' his ability to carry on this measure: he wished 'most ardently ... that some other had been found to undertake the cause.'[106] Further, Oastler himself well realised another aspect of the situation which seemed to militate against a close association between Ashley and the Ten Hours Movement: the fact that, as an aristocrat, Ashley was likely to have little in common with the Movement's leadership and rank and file. 'I would not on any occasion forget,' Oastler once wrote to Ashley, 'that I am a poor servant and that your Lordship is a Noble and an Aristocrat.'[107]

Nevertheless, despite the doubts and the discrepancies, the question of factory reform was one which accorded with certain aspects of Ashley's development which were already evident. The sense of duty which he had shown in the 1820s had been strengthened by a friendship which had developed with the poet, Robert Southey, an exponent of the Tory paternalist school of thought.[108] Ashley greatly admired Southey, and, in 1828, he had made an appeal for financial support on Southey's behalf. In this, he described Southey as 'the most distinguished man of his day for learning and acquirements'; one whose writings would be 'esteemed true *national*

Treasures, so long as there shall be wisdom, Morality and Religion among the inhabitants of our Country.'[109] He felt that Southey's merits had not been adequately rewarded. In September, 1830, he had taken a further step to assist his new-found friend. He wrote to him, expressing his admiration for Southey's work and asking if, as a measure of his gratitude, he could use his good offices with the Directors of the East India Company to secure an appointment with the company for a son or nephew.[110] Southey was glad to accept the offer on behalf of his nephew, and, thereafter, the two men corresponded regularly.

Their correspondence ranged over the political issues of the time. Initially, Southey took a rather more optimistic view than Ashley of the political situation at the time of the Reform Bill: he wrote in February, 1831, that the Whigs would become Conservatives now that they were in power, and that the Conservatives themselves would come back to power 'at no very distant day'.[111] He took a keen interest in the Dorset election and greatly sympathised with Ashley's plight over the petition;[112] but he thought that Ashley's return in the election was a manifestation of a change in public opinion towards reform. Time, he felt, might 'set this question asleep.' But he also added — with more pessimism than his earlier comments had shown — that the men in power would not allow this;[113] and, as time went on, he became reconciled to the fact that reform would come. The Conservatives, he wrote in January, 1832, would have to 'submit patiently to the evils which they (could) no longer hope to avert.'[114] And, throughout the Reform Bill episode, he always felt that attention to political and institutional reform was severely misguided. In April, 1831, he wrote to Ashley that, whatever government was in office, it must endeavour to better the condition of the people: 'this must be amended or we perish,' he wrote.[115] In January, 1832, he told Ashley that he wished that the Conservative party would occupy one ground while the 'peer mongering factions are busy in schemes of revolutionary reform;' and this was to call attention to 'those real reforms which would benefit all classes and which alone, with God's help, can save us.' The state of the poor, he continued, could not be discussed too much, for until it was 'improved physically and morally and religiously we shall be in more danger from them than the West Indian planters are from their slaves.'[116] He could, however, see very little prospect of such improvement coming from the Parliament elected under the reformed system. The ten pounders, he wrote to Ashley in January, 1833, had sent 'just such members as might be expected to *Parledemonium* from the great manufacturing towns.' But he was more sorry to see what good men had been excluded from Parliament than 'what scamps and miscreants' had got in. And he was particularly sorry to see the loss of Sadler; Sadler might not have been popular in the House or in London society, but his speeches did good in the country and he was a 'singularly able, right-minded, religious man'. And, Southey continued, who was there 'to take up the question of our white-slave trade with equal feeling?' He went on to condemn the factory system: those who grew cotton, he wrote, were merciful task masters compared with those who manufactured it. Negroes in a plantation might be made happy by kind treatment, but, wrote Southey, 'I know not how a cotton mill can be otherwise than an abomination to God and man.'[117] And, later, he wrote to Ashley that Sadler's Report had deeply shocked him: 'for one or two nights,' he wrote, 'it disturbed my sleep, in a way that no book ever did before.'[118]

Ashley's correspondence with Southey thus exposed him to the central points of Tory paternalistic thought: its distrust of changes in the political structure; its ideal of a stable and hierarchic society bound together by mutual obligations between rich and poor; its belief that only by showing care and concern for the poor could the rich hope to survive. Factory reform was, indeed, a clear and obvious issue for the Tory paternalist to espouse. Further, overlapping with this, it was also much in accordance with the social and, to some degree too, the political aspects of Evangelicalism. Ashley's association with Evangelicalism had become closer in the early 1830s: he was a member of a select committee appointed in 1832 to investigate Sunday observance, a matter of great concern to Evangelicals.[119] Indeed, it was said that it was in this committee that the young Ashley first began to be noticed as an Evangelical,[120] and it was his membership of the committee which led to the approach by Bull. Bull first approached Sir Andrew Agnew, a noted Evangelical, who was chairman of the committee, but Agnew himself was heavily occupied with the Sunday question. He introduced Bull to Ashley, and, it is said, 'laid squarely before (Ashley) that he was the man for the job.'[121]

Thus there were strong pressures on Ashley to make him overcome his reluctance to undertake such a prominent role over factory reform. The influence of Southey is discernible in a letter which Ashley wrote to Brougham in February, 1833, in which he referred to a petition forwarded to Brougham from Bradford and signed by some 10,000 persons. 'You will not, I am sure, be backward to support this righteous cause,' Ashley wrote, '. . . because West Indian slavery, which you combated for so many years is a state of Paradise compared with this accursed system.'[122] Certainly, Southey approved of Ashley's decision to take the bill in hand. 'Thousands of thousands will bless you for taking up the cause of these poor children,' he wrote. 'I do not believe that anything more inhuman than the system has ever disgraced human nature, in any age or country.'[123] The more specifically Evangelical influence on Ashley came through his comment to Oastler that he entertained such strong opinions on the matter that he did not '*dare*, as a Christian, to let... diffidence or love of ease, prevail over the demands of morality and religion.'[124] And that the political, in addition to the religious and moral, aspect did not escape him is shown in remarks which he made in a speech to the London Society for the Improvement of the Condition of the Factory Children. The matter was, indeed, a great moral and religious question; it was moral because 'it would decide whether the rising generation should learn to distinguish between good and evil'; it was religious since it 'involved the means to thousands and tens of thousands of being brought up in the faith and fear of the God that created them.' But Ashley also mentioned the political dimension: it was a political question 'because it would decide whether thousands should be left in discontent, aye, and just discontent.'[125]

In accordance with the notice which he had already given on 5 March, Ashley moved for leave to bring in a bill to regulate the labour of children in factories.[126] This proposed the same regulations as Sadler's bill had done: no child should be employed under the age of nine; no person between the ages of nine and eighteen was to be employed for more than ten hours a day and eight hours on a Saturday; and there was to be no night work – defined as 7 p.m. to 6 a.m. – for anyone under the age of twenty-one. Despite opposition from Althorp, the leader of the House, who would have preferred to finish some uncompleted business, Ashley was given leave to bring in the bill. Its supporters in the country, however, clearly anticipated opposition. On 14 March, Ashley presented petitions in favour of the bill, and one of these, from Little Bolton and neighbouring places in Lancashire, prayed that the House would not grant a Commission of Inquiry on the bill, since this would only tend to delay it.[127] There was, indeed, the distinct possibility that such a Commission would be demanded on the grounds that the Sadler committee had not taken evidence from the manufacturers and had thus been biassed in its findings. This point was made by Wilson Patten, Conservative member for North Lancashire, on 14 March – he felt that it was necessary to ensure that the matter was better understood and also to clear the characters of the employers 'from these imputations, which seemed to be cast on them by the friends of this measure, but which further evidence would prove to be utterly unjustifiable.'[128] Ashley replied that the House ought not to be stopped for legislating on the subject 'merely because ten or twelve gentlemen fancied themselves aggrieved by the tendency of the matter already known to the public.' He knew that they had had an opportunity of considering the provisions of the bill, since he had sent one hundred copies of it to the country to those most interested in the matter. The only effect of a Commission would be to delay the bill so that it would be lost this session as it had been lost in the last.[129]

The opposition of which Patten had given notice was not, however, to be overcome easily. On 25 March, 1833, a petition was presented from the master cotton spinners of the town and neighbourhood of Lancaster praying that the House would grant a Commission to take evidence on the subject of labour in cotton factories before it proceeded with Ashley's bill.[130] Ashley assured the House that there was great agitation in the manufacturing districts on the subject. It was impossible, he said, that the present system could be allowed to go on and he would resist a motion for a Commission 'to the utmost'.[131] Patten, however, stated his determination to bring in such a motion whenever he had the opportunity, and on 3 April, he was as good as his word.[132] Ashley once more strenuously opposed Patten's request that a Commission should be set up to collect more information. Such a step was, he felt, quite unnecessary. He did not, he said, rest his case on the inquiries of any committee. He was 'struck with the whole system.' It was time it should be checked and he would 'push the bill as long as he breathed.' In any event, he said, the whole matter had been under discussion for forty years and an abundance of evidence, especially medical evidence, obtained by earlier inquiries had clearly shown that a measure such as he had introduced was necessary. He quoted this medical evidence at some length. It had been given, he said, by persons who had 'no motive beyond the influence of their feelings as humane and Christian men, who felt for the unjust sufferings of their fellow creatures.' And he concluded his speech by expressing the view that every member who considered the subject for a moment must be of the opinion that ten hours a day was a sufficient period during which children should labour in a factory; further, those most interested in the matter would, he said, be obliged to assent to it 'as a relief to their own wounded consciences.'[133]

After the delivery of various speeches in support of Patten and Ashley, Spring Rice, Secretary to the Treasury, said that, in his view, the weight of the arguments was in favour of a Commission being appointed. The interests of the manufacturers were too vast and important to be lightly dealt with and they were entitled to the attention which they claimed.[134] Russell felt that legislation was necessary, but on full evidence. Althorp, who was absent from the House owing to illness, had told him that the government would not object to a Commission if the feeling of the House were in favour of it, but a better course of action might be to appoint a select committee.[135] But Patten's motion prevailed by one vote in a small House: 74 votes for and 73 against. Ashley had thus suffered a setback, and he asked the government to appoint the Commission immediately and to place on it medical men of the highest skill and eminence. He wondered if it could report in time for the present session, as Patten's motion had said it should, and he was afraid that its evidence might be 'too particular'. He disclaimed all desire of obtaining popularity by bringing forward the measure, and expressed the belief that his bill would be of as much advantage to the Ministers as to himself.[136]

The appointment of the Royal Commission on 19 April, 1833, was greeted with strong disapproval by the Ten Hours Movement, which regarded it as simply an attempt on the part of the government to give the manufacturers an opportunity to present their case. Oastler denounced it as 'a trick of the government' intended to save 'their dear friends the capitalists'.[137] Such was his fury that an elaborate protest campaign was organised by many of the Short Time Committees and directed against the itinerant Factory Commissioners. Ashley himself also refused to assist the work of the Commission. The Board of Commissioners, it appears, wrote to him offering an opportunity for interested parties to appear before it. He replied that he had 'no communication' to make to it.[138] In the House, Ashley criticised the conduct of the inquiry. He objected to the fact that the evidence of witnesses was being taken in private and not recorded by a short-hand writer. He had a right, he said, to expect that the whole testimonies should be laid on the table of the House, and, if this were not done, he would protest against all the evidence of every individual which was calculated to affect the evidence already before Sadler's committee.[139] This was a point which he also mentioned to S. L. Giffard, proprietor of *The Standard*. 'Now it appears that these unfortunate Operatives are to be judged in secret,' he wrote, 'and nothing of their testimony will be reported except the "substance"!' This, he felt, clearly opened up the possibility that the evidence might be 'transformed in passing through the minds of selfish and partial and perhaps interested political Economists!'[140] In making such appeals for increased publicity of evidence, Ashley was, as he freely told the House, responding to requests made to him by operatives in Lancashire, the West Riding and in Scotland. Indeed, this led to a protest from one member against 'the noble Lord styling himself the Representative of the Operatives.'[141] In reply, Ashley justified his action. He referred to the fact that four delegates, elected on the basis of universal suffrage by the operatives of the West Riding and Lancashire, were in London; they had entrusted their case to him and thus he was, he claimed, 'entitled to say that he was as much the Representative of the operatives as any Member of that House was the Representative of his constituency.'[142] Moreover, despite the appointment of the Royal Commission, Ashley did not abandon his bill. On 17 June, he moved its second reading, and he also repeated his request that the evidence of the Commissioners should be laid on the Table and printed and circulated as publicly as possible.[143] In all of this, therefore, Ashley identified himself closely with the opposition and objections of the Movement to the Royal Commission.

The appointment and progress of the Commission had, however, considerably altered the situation. For one thing, it had taken the initiative away from the Ten Hours Movement. The Commission set an extremely fast pace in its proceedings and completed its task remarkably quickly: the first draft of its Report was in the hands of the government within forty-five days and it was presented in June, 1833. The Commissioners were not, indeed, uncritical of factory conditions and their Report[144] did not amount to a whitewashing of the manufacturers, as the Ten Hours Movement had feared. But they did not wholly share Ashley's concern for religious and moral considerations. Their approach was more a utilitarian one, which, indeed, reflected the Benthamite views of some of the most influential members of the Commission, such as Edwin Chadwick. The Report claimed that conditions had, in many cases, improved, but, where criticism and condemnation were in place, these were on grounds that bad conditions led to an unavoidable wastage of human resources rather than to moral or spiritual degradation. The Commissioners were 'disinterested men, cool, analytical and unsentimental';[145] and their Report was couched in unsentimental terms. Moreover, whereas the Ten Hours Movement and Ashley wanted a ten-hour day up to the age of eighteen – and hoped that this might indirectly lead to a ten-hour day for adults – the Commission felt that limitation of hours should apply only to children and should not extend beyond the age of thirteen. Until they reached that age, children were not free agents but were let out to hire, and, in fact, they required more protection than Ashley's bill had given them. The Commissioners thus favoured an eight-hour day between the ages of nine and thirteen; after the age of thirteen, all protection should cease and contracts should be freely negotiated. The Report was, therefore, critical of Ashley's bill on the grounds that it gave insufficient protection up to the age of thirteen and undue protection thereafter. It also criticised the bill because it did not provide for the occupation of any part of the day in educational purposes either before or after the hours of labour, and it was especially critical of the bill's failure to ensure that the legislation should be enforced. There was, the Report argued, little point in leaving enforcement in the hands of parents and employers who had an interest in evading the requirements – rather, enforcement should be put in the hands of disinterested parties. The Report therefore recommended the appointment of inspectors to see that the legislation was implemented.

The Commissioners thus approached the question from a somewhat different standpoint from that of Ashley, and they gave the government a different set of proposals. When Ashley proposed the second reading of the bill on 17 June, the final version of the Report was not, however, in the hands of the government but was due the following week. Althorp did not, in fact, oppose Ashley's bill going to a second reading, but he hinted that once in Committee on the bill, the House might consider the Report when it became available.[146] Ashley was delighted that his bill had passed its second reading. 'We have triumphed gloriously,' he wrote to Giffard. 'The Government who, five months ago, would have driven out the bill with contempt, permitted the second Reading and *acknowledged the principle of it without a discussion.*' He felt 'assured that Providence is working with us' and told Giffard that Sadler was 'in raptures', adding that 'whatever be the honour, the merit, the success or the blessing that follows upon this measure, *all is his!*'[147]

Nevertheless, he recognised that there might well be difficulties ahead, and, on 24 June, he wrote to Althorp with a view, it would seem, to overcoming such difficulties by warning Althorp of the dangers of disappointing the Ten Hours Movement. He stated his view – which, he said, was that of every man 'who supported this question from his heart' – that if the labour of adults were not indirectly limited, half of the benefits expected from the measure would not come about, and he assured Althorp that any scheme for imposing more than ten hours on young persons between the ages of fourteen and eighteen would be 'stoutly *and even fiercely opposed.*' He recalled the hostile reception which the Commissioners had been given in Bradford and enclosed newspaper accounts of it for Althorp to read; he told Althorp of a remark which he had heard that should more than ten hours be imposed between the ages of fourteen and eighteen 'perhaps scarcely one Factory will escape the fire.' He himself was convinced of this but would not state it openly in the House 'because arguments drawn from intimidation are both unfit for the ears of a legislature and to the parties whose Cause is urged.' Nevertheless, he wished Althorp to know that the people were '*desperate*', and knowing this, he felt it his duty to pass on this private information.[148]

His letter, however, had little effect. When the Committee stage began on 5 July, Althorp was forced to admit that, although the Report had been laid on the table of the House, it had not been placed in the hands of members. It would not, he felt, be correct to proceed on that basis, and thus he proposed that Ashley's bill be referred to a select committee of the House which would, in effect, amend it in accordance with the Report's proposals. He was critical of Ashley's measure: it would, he argued, be disastrous in the manufacturing districts and would play into the hands of foreign competitors. So far from being a measure of humanity, it would become 'one of the greatest acts of cruelty that could be inflicted.' Ashley's bill should thus be amended so that protection be given only to those who could not protect themselves. The measure of protection should be increased for children under thirteen; but the labour of adults, 'who were in a state to decide for themselves,' should be unrestricted. Further, provision should also be made for education and enforcement.[149]

In reply,[150] Ashley stated that he had no objection to restricting the labour of children under fourteen to eight hours, and he was willing to accept the point about education and inspection. He felt that the 'great moral defect' in society sprang from the lack of education for the 'lower orders'; and he would like to see further educational opportunities given to children, whether employed in factories or not. He also entirely agreed with the proposals for inspectors; had he not, indeed, been afraid of giving additional offence to the opponents of his measure, provision for inspection would have formed part of his bill. In these respects, therefore, he was not opposed to Althorp's suggestions. But in others, he remained committed to his original proposals. One related to accidents. Althorp had rejected Ashley's proposal that an accident which caused death should carry the penalty of manslaughter for the master; this, Althorp had argued, would place the masters in an intolerable position. But Ashley would not accept any alteration of his proposal. He would also hold to his own proposition about protection extending beyond the age of fourteen, and he drew particular attention to the position of females at this age. Medical evidence had been cited to show that more than ten hours had a very bad effect on females in their mid-teens; there was, he said, 'no period of a female life in which she required more care, attention and protection, than at the very age at which the noble Lord required that care, attention and protection should cease.' More generally, he confessed himself at a loss to understand why Althorp had not made his propositions at the second reading. Why his bill should have been allowed to come to the Committee and 'then be scouted out of the House like a mad dog, to be carried by a Committee upstairs,' he could not see. If the principle of his bill were adhered to, he would not object to Althorp's suggestion for a committee, but he would much prefer the matter to be dealt with publicly rather than to be referred to a private tribunal – there had, he felt, been 'quite enough of secrecy in the progress of the bill already.' When put to the vote, Ashley's views prevailed: Althorp's proposal for a select committee was defeated by a majority of twenty-three.[151]

Ashley's victory, however, had been a Pyrrhic one. For when on 18 July, 1833, the House once more resolved itself into a Committee on his bill, its second clause, limiting the labour of persons under eighteen, met with strong opposition. Althorp reiterated his earlier points about the dangers which it presented to the manufacturing interests of the country. He proposed that the age of thirteen should be substituted for that of eighteen, and he would, he said, afterwards propose an amendment limiting the hours of children under thirteen to eight hours.¹⁵² Ashley rejected Althorp's arguments;¹⁵³ foreign competition was problematical and, in any event, he would prefer that danger to the moral degradation of the people. There would be no large-scale unemployment, despite the fact that his bill would have the indirect effect of limiting the hours of adults, and such a limitation would have the thoroughly desirable effect of promoting 'a return of the working classes . . . to domestic habits and comforts' and thereby counteracting the 'complete disruption which now took place of all domestic ties in our manufacturing districts.' Although he had previously agreed to eight hours for children under thirteen, he did not feel that such a limitation was necessary, and he raised the objection that an eight-hour day between the ages of eight and thirteen would lead to the employment of two sets of children. This would, in fact, increase the working day for adults and it would also expose the children to the danger of being employed in two different factories in the same day. He thus took his stand on his original proposal of a ten-hour day for all between the ages of nine and eighteen. But all his arguments were unavailing. The motion that protection of ten hours should extend to the age of eighteen was lost by a majority of one hundred and forty-five. At that point, Ashley admitted defeat. He found, he said, that Althorp had 'completely defeated him.' He would, therefore, surrender the bill into Althorp's hands, but, having taken it up with a view to do good to the classes which were interested in it, he would only say 'into whatever hands it might pass, God prosper it.'¹⁵⁴ The following day, he wrote to Oastler. He told him that he had never – not even on the Reform Bill – witnessed 'such unity, zeal and determination' as had been manifested by his opponents. He refused to bear the responsibility of an altered bill, believing that the government would 'produce tenfold misery and tenfold crime.'¹⁵⁵

Thus on Ashley's surrender, a bill was prepared by Edwin Chadwick. It bore a close resemblance to the Royal Commission Report and it was introduced for the government by Althorp on 9 August.¹⁵⁶ It had a rapid passage through Parliament and on 29 August, 1833, received the royal assent. Ashley took no part at all in these proceedings. The Act applied to all textile factories, with the major exception of the silk and lace trades. There was to be no employment under the age of nine. Children between nine and thirteen were to work for not more than forty-eight hours a week or nine hours a day. A further provision, which owed its origin not to the Commissioners but to Althorp, extended a measure of protection beyond the age of thirteen: thus young persons between thirteen and eighteen were to work for not more than sixty-nine hours a week or twelve hours in any one day. There was to be no night work – defined as lasting between 8.30 p.m. and

5.30 a.m. – under the age of eighteen. The Act also required children between nine and thirteen to attend a school. The question of enforcement was given attention. No child between nine and thirteen could be employed in any factory without a certificate to the effect that he was 'of the ordinary strength and appearance' of a child of or exceeding the age of nine – this was to be given by a doctor of the neighbourhood, who had to examine the child, and the certificate had to be countersigned by a magistrate within three months. Four inspectors were appointed to attend to the enforcement of the Act.

The Factory Act thus fell short of what the Ten Hours Movement and Ashley had campaigned for and demanded. At the parliamentary level, Ashley had, indeed, been outmanoeuvred. His position had always been somewhat vulnerable. In part, this derived from his lack of direct knowledge of the issues on which he spoke. He was, indeed, advised by Southey not to be totally preoccupied with the factory question in case he would be overwhelmed by it – Southey reminded him that Clarkson's 'gigantic strength' had almost broken down under the exertions for the abolition of the slave trade.[157] He also advised Ashley not to go to the manufacturing districts on the grounds that what he would see there would be too distressing and might injure his health.[158] Ashley certainly tried to become familiar with all the available evidence on the subject, medical and otherwise, and he was in touch with the delegates of the Short-Time Committees in London throughout the struggles over the bill. But the fact that he did not actually *know* the factory districts at first hand meant that he was open to question and contradiction from the interests ranged against the measure. Sir George Phillips remarked in the debates that he himself had been engaged in the manufacturing business; he had lived all his life in a manufacturing district; and he frankly confessed that he could not speak on the subject with Ashley's confidence. It was generally known, Phillips tartly remarked, that confidence was in proportion to want of knowledge.[159] Allied to this charge was the criticism that Ashley's righteous commitment to the cause of factory reform blinded him to the existence of masters who took a benevolent interest in their employees, and, in time, this was to be developed into the point that the condition of agricultural workers on the Shaftesbury estates might well be considerably worse than that of manufacturing workers. Further, it seems that, at first, Ashley substantially underestimated the extent of the opposition with which he would be faced: it will be recalled that he once referred to the supposed objections of 'ten or twelve gentlemen' who disliked the way in which the Sadler committee had done its work and desired a Royal Commission. When he took up the matter, it is unlikely that Ashley realised the long struggle which lay ahead.

Nor did he realise the effect which it would have on his own political future; to argue that he willingly sacrificed that future in 1833 is to imply a much greater degree of foreknowledge of future events than was possible at the time.

Nevertheless, Ashley had inherited a situation which had its difficulties. The criticism of the Sadler committee opened the way for the Royal Commission and, although Ashley may have underestimated the strength of the opposition, he cannot bear any responsibility for the situation which gave rise to it. Moreover, the cause itself – apart from its sponsor – did run counter to much contemporary economic wisdom, which held that regulation of the labour market was wrong in principle and harmful in its effects, and, although Ashley may have failed to give such opinions due weight, he did have to contend in the reformed Parliament with the representatives of the newly enfranchised manufacturing towns – Althorp clearly paid considerable attention to what he called the 'strong good sense' of their speeches.[160] Further, the fact that a Factory Act was passed at all was certainly due in part to Ashley's prompting: after Ashley had surrendered the matter, Southey wrote consolingly that whatever good was done and whatever mitigation of evil effected, it would be through Ashley's efforts. 'The manufacturers and the Ministers would have done nothing unless you had forced them to it,' he wrote.[161] This obviously contains an element of exaggeration, but also a good deal of truth. And, although he shared the disappointment of the Ten Hours Movement at the final measure, Ashley was not dismayed. He wrote to the Chairman of the Manchester Short Time Committee that, by surrendering the matter, its opponents had been denied the means of 'cloaking their *hostility* to a remedial measure under the pretence of resistance to an "offensive and violent" interference (as they termed it) with the disposal of capital.'[162] He felt, moreover, that the measure contained 'some humane and highly useful provisions'.[163]

In the course of the first three years of the decade, Ashley thus showed his Toryism in his resistance to parliamentary reform, and also his increasing commitment to paternalism and evangelicalism in his efforts over factory reform. His Toryism had, indeed, at first exposed him to suspicion in certain sections of the Ten Hours Movement. John Doherty, a factory reformer who was also active in trade unionism and political radicalism, wrote that he had initially been prejudiced against Ashley on political grounds, but after frequent dealings, he was glad to concede that in no walk of life had he found 'so honourable, so straightforward, kind and condescending and at the same time, talented and fearless a person as that young man.'[164] Moreover, Ashley's association with the Movement and with the cause of factory reform was, in time, to have a great bearing on his political career. In Ashley's public life, these were, then, eventful years in addition to being extremely active ones: and in his private life, they were the first three years of his marriage.

NOTES

1. M. Brock, *The Great Reform Act* (1973), pp. 55–8.
2. See above p. 29.
3. N.R.A., Shaftesbury (Broadlands) MSS, SHA/PD/1, 25 Feb., 1829.
4. *The Dorset County Chronicle and Somersetshire Gazette*, 5 Aug., 1830.
5. Hansard, *Parl. Debates*, 3rd ser., I, 551.
6. N.R.A., Shaftesbury (Broadlands) MSS, SHA/PC/62/1.
7. ibid., Palmerston (Broadlands) MSS, GC/SH/2.
8. L. Strachey and R. Fulford (eds.), op. cit., II, 106.
9. *The Dorset County Chronicle and Somersetshire Gazette*, 28 Apr., 1831.
10. ibid., 5 May, 1831.
11. A. Aspinall, *Politics and the Press, 1780–1850* (1949), p. 336.
12. Hansard, *Parl. Debates*, 3rd ser., V, 378.
13. ibid., 492.
14. ibid., 493.
15. Calcraft had taken office under Wellington in 1828, but later changed his views to supporting parliamentary reform. He voted for the second reading of the Reform Bill in Mar. 1831 and stood successfully in Dorset at the General Election of Apr. 1831 as a pro-reformer. *The Dorset County Chronicle and Somersetshire Gazette* (15 Sept., 1831) suggested that he had been worried by the cool reception which he had received in the House of Commons and that this prompted him to commit suicide. Other accounts (e.g. The Earl of Ilchester (Ed.), *Elizabeth, Lady Holland to her son*, p. 116) suggest that Calcraft had long been in a despondent frame of mind and this is attributed to the death of Huskisson in 1828.
16. *The Dorset County Chronicle and Somersetshire Gazette*, 15 Sept., 1831. Ponsonby, it appears, did not wish to stand, but felt that the Whigs would not have brought the bill into the Lords had he not done so. (A. Aspinall, (ed.), *Three Early Nineteenth Century Diaries* (1952), p. 136).
17. A. Aspinall (ed.), *The Correspondence of Charles Arbuthnot*, p. 144.
18. *The Dorset County Chronicle and Somersetshire Gazette*, 22 Sept., 1831.
19. The Earl of Ilchester (Ed.), *Elizabeth, Lady Holland to her son*, p. 116.
20. Apsley House, Wellington MSS, 16 Sept., 1831.
21. A. Aspinall (ed.), *The Correspondence of Charles Arbuthnot*, p. 145.
22. University of Keele, Sneyd MSS, Countess Bathurst (Georgiana) to Ralph Sneyd (undated, but end of Sept., 1831. I owe this reference to Mr M. G. Brock, of Nuffield College, Oxford).
23. F. Bamford and The Duke of Wellington (eds.), op. cit., II, p. 433.
24. N.R.A., Shaftesbury (Broadlands) MSS, SHA/MIS/22.
25. A. Aspinall (ed.), *The Correspondence of Charles Arbuthnot*, p. 146.
26. Apsley House, Wellington MSS, 18 Sept., 1831.
27. N.R.A., Shaftesbury (Broadlands) MSS, SHA/MIS/22.
28. A. Aspinall (ed.), *The Correspondence of Charles Arbuthnot*, p. 146.

29. A. Aspinall (ed.), *Three Early Nineteenth Century Diaries*, p. 134. Countess Bathurst thought that had Ashley consented to stand immediately, Ponsonby would not have stood. (Sneyd MSS, undated but end of Sept., 1831. I owe this reference to Mr Brock).
30. A. Aspinall (ed.), *Three Early Nineteenth Century Diaries*, p. 130.
31. ibid. Also Record Office, Carlisle, Lonsdale MSS, Visc. Lowther to Earl of Lonsdale (undated, but late Sept., 1831). Lowther wrote that Ashley would be 'a much more popular candidate than Bankes'. £4,000 had been promised; 'if we can but double it', Lowther wrote, 'we shall gain the election.' (I owe this reference to Mr. Brock).
32. A. Aspinall (ed.), *Three Early Nineteenth Century Diaries*, p. 134.
33. ibid., p. 148.
34. ibid., p. 130.
35. N.R.A., Shaftesbury (Broadlands) MSS, SHA/MIS/22. Ashley resigned the seat by accepting the stewardship of the Chiltern Hundreds (J. Holladay Philbin, *Parliamentary Representation, 1832. England and Wales* (New Haven, 1965), p. 61). Ashley's brother Henry took his place at Dorchester: he was elected unopposed in a by-election in October 1831.
36. N.R.A., Shaftesbury (Broadlands) MSS, SHA/MIS/22.
37. ibid., SHA/PC/128/2.
38. ibid., SHA/MIS/22.
39. I.H.R., Dorset Poll Book, 1831.
40. Ashley polled 1847 votes and Ponsonby 1811. (ibid.)
41. A. Aspinall (ed.), *Three Early Nineteenth Century Diaries*, p. 142.
42. ibid., p. 140.
43. ibid., p. 149.
44. F. Bamford and The Duke of Wellington, op. cit., II, 432.
45. Apsley House, Wellington MSS, Oct., 1831 (no day given).
46. Hansard, *Parl. Debates*, 3rd ser., VIII, 932.
47. L. Strachey and R. Fulford (eds.), op. cit., II, 210.
48. St G.H., Shaftesbury MSS, 25153.32/7th Earl. Hodder, I, 120, puts the expenses at £15,600. This is too low a figure.
49. N.R.A., Shaftesbury (Broadlands) MSS, SHA/EST/7.
50. Hansard, *Parl. Debates*, 3rd ser., XXXIX, 774–5.
51. Apsley House, Wellington MSS, 30 Nov., 1831.
52. St G.H., Shaftesbury MSS, C 25020.10/7th Earl.
53. ibid., C 25020.22/7th Earl (not dated, but end of 1831, copy).
54. Apsley House, Wellington MSS, 2 Dec., 1831.
55. St G.H., Shaftesbury MSS, C 25020.4/7th Earl.
56. Apsley House, Wellington MSS, 7 Dec., 1831.
57. *Commons Journals*, LXXXVII, 8–9.
58. St G.H., Shaftesbury MSS, C 25018.26/7th Earl.
59. ibid., C 25020.8/7th Earl.
60. ibid., C 25017/7th Earl.
61. ibid. (Copy).
62. Hansard, *Parl. Debates*, 3rd ser., IX, 560–61.
63. A. Aspinall (ed.), *The Correspondence of Charles Arbuthnot*, p. 154.
64. St G.H., Shaftesbury MSS, C 25017/7th Earl. (Copy).
65. Hodder, I, 123–4.
66. ibid., 124.

67. Sneyd MSS, Charles Greville to Ralph Sneyd, 4 Jan., 1832. (I owe this reference to Mr. Brock).
68. A. Aspinall (ed.), *The Correspondence of Charles Arbuthnot*, pp. 151-2.
69. *The Dorset County Chronicle and Somersetshire Gazette*, 12 Jan., 1832.
70. ibid., 2 Feb., 1832.
71. ibid., 9 Feb., 1832.
72. ibid., 1 Mar., 1832.
73. St G.H., Shaftesbury MSS, C 25153.27/7th Earl.
74. *The Dorset County Chronicle and Somersetshire Gazette*, 9 Feb., 1832. They were described as 2 country gentlemen, 2 clergymen, 2 agriculturalists and 2 merchants: all men of 'great respectability'.
75. *Commons Journals*, LXXXVII, 82-3.
76. ibid., 202. *The Dorset County Chronicle and Somersetshire Gazette*, 1, 8, 15, 22 Mar., carried reports of the committee's deliberations.
77. *The Dorset County Chronicle and Somersetshire Gazette*, 29 Mar., 1832.
78. St G.H., Shaftesbury MSS, C 25153.5/7th Earl.
79. ibid., C 25153.6/7th Earl.
80. Hansard, *Parl. Debates*, 3rd ser., XII, 1038.
81. ibid., 1038-40.
82. N.R.A., Shaftesbury (Broadlands) MSS, SHA/PC/128/2.
83. ibid., SHA/PC/128/2.
84. ibid., SHA/PC/131.
85. ibid., SHA/PC/131.
86. ibid., SHA/PC/132.
87. *The Dorset County Chronicle and Somersetshire Gazette*, 20 Dec., 1832.
88. N.R.A., Shaftesbury (Broadlands) MSS, SHA/PC/132.
89. ibid., SHA/PC/130.
90. ibid., SHA/PC/133.
91. ibid., SHA/PC/133.
92. ibid., SHA/PC/133.
93. R. G. Kirby and A. E. Musson, *The Voice of the People. John Doherty, 1798-1854 Trade Unionist, radical and factory reformer* (Manchester, 1975), p. 346 ff.
94. Hobhouse originally proposed that all employment should be prohibited under 9 and all night employment prohibited between 9 and 18; and that between 9 and 18, the working day should be limited to $11\frac{1}{2}$ hours. As a result of opposition and amendment, however, the proposals regulating night work were weakened and the working day for children and young persons between 9 and 18 extended to 12 hours. The Act applied only to cotton factories. (See M. W. Thomas, *The Early Factory Legislation* (Leigh-on-Sea, 1948), pp. 29-31).
95. For his biography, see C. Driver, *Tory Radical. The Life of Richard Oastler* (New York, 1946).
96. Sadler's bill prohibited work under 9; prescribed a 10 hour day for children and young persons between 9 and 18; and prohibited night work (to be counted between 7 p.m. and 6 a.m.) for all under 21.
97. He stood at Leeds on the issue of ten hours but was beaten into third place by T. B. Macaulay.
98. R. G. Kirby and A. E. Musson, op. cit., p. 379.
99. For his biography, see J. C. Gill, *The Ten Hours Parson* (1959) and *Parson Bull of Byerley* (1963).
100. Hodder, I, 147-8.
101. ibid., 148-9.

102. W. N. Peach, M.P. for Truro, who had taken an active part in the Dorset by-election in 1831 and Sir James Scarlett, first Baron Abinger, Attorney General in the Wellington Ministry and subsequently M.P. for Cockermouth.
103. St G.H., Shaftesbury MSS, C 25001/7th Earl. (Copy).
104. ibid., C 25018.30/7th Earl. (Copy).
105. Carlisle MSS, 2nd ser., Book 15, 6 Feb., 1833.
106. Hodder, I, 152–3.
107. St G.H., Shaftesbury MSS, C 25035/7th Earl. 17 Apr., 1835.
108. See G. Carnall, *Robert Southey and His Age. The Development of a Conservative Mind* (Oxford, 1960), esp. Chapter III. Also D. Roberts, *Paternalism in Early Victorian England* (1979), pp. 68–9, 222–3.
109. Humanities Research Center, The University of Texas at Austin. Anthony Ashley Cooper/Shaftesbury Collection. A portion of this appeal is missing and there is no date. But the paper is water marked 1828.
110. The New York Public Library, Astor, Lenox and Tilden Foundations, Henry W. and Albert A. Berg Collection, 12 Sept., 1830.
111. ibid., 12 Feb., 1831.
112. ibid., 16 Jan., 1832.
113. ibid., 24 Oct., 1831.
114. ibid., 16 Jan., 1832.
115. ibid., 10 Apr., 1831.
116. ibid., Jan., 1832 (no day given).
117. ibid., 13 Jan., 1832. Oastler also stressed the theme of West Indian slavery in connection with factory labour in the series of letters which he sent to the *Leeds Mercury* in the early 1830s on 'Yorkshire Slavery'. (J. T. Ward, *The Factory System* (Newton Abbot, 2 vols, 1970), II, 73–9).
118. Quoted in G. Carnall, op. cit., p. 190.
119. See below Chapter 4.
120. *The Record*, 11 Feb., 1833.
121. J. Bridges, *Memoir of Sir Andrew Agnew of Lochnow*, Bart (Edinburgh, 1849), p. 15.
122. The Library, University College London, Brougham MSS, 44, 489.
123. Quoted in Hodder, I, 157.
124. Quoted ibid., 153.
125. Quoted ibid., 154–5.
126. Hansard, *Parl. Debates*, 3rd ser., XVI, 199.
127. ibid., 640.
128. ibid., 640–41.
129. ibid., 641.
130. ibid., 1001.
131. ibid.
132. ibid., XVII, 79–84.
133. ibid., 85–90.
134. ibid., 105–7.
135. ibid., 111–12.
136. ibid., 114–15.
137. Quoted in J. T. Ward, *The Factory Movement, 1830–55* (1962), p. 97.
138. The Library, University College London, Chadwick MSS, 23 Apr. (1833).
139. Hansard, *Parl. Debates*, 3rd ser., XVIII, 305–6.
140. Add. MSS, 56, 368, fos 37–8. For comments on Giffard, see D. Roberts, op. cit., p. 193.
141. Hansard, *Parl. Debates*, 3rd ser., XVIII, 307.

142. ibid., 308.
143. ibid., 914–15.
144. P.P. 1833, XX.
145. J. T. Ward, *The Factory Movement*, p. 94.
146. Hansard, *Parl. Debates*, 3rd ser., XVIII, 914–15.
147. Add. MSS, 56, 368, fos 23–4.
148. St G.H., Shaftesbury MSS, C 25033/7th Earl (Copy).
149. Hansard, *Parl. Debates*, 3rd ser., XIX, 221–3.
150. ibid., 224–7.
151. ibid., 254.
152. ibid., 885–8.
153. ibid., 888–91.
154. ibid., 913.
155. Quoted in J. G. Gill, *The Ten Hours Parson*, p. 115.
156. Hansard, *Parl. Debates*, 3rd ser., XX, 449.
157. Henry W. and Albert A. Berg Collection, 6 Feb., 1833.
158. ibid., 11 May, 1833.
159. Hansard, *Parl. Debates*, 3rd ser., XIX, 891.
160. ibid., 912–13.
161. Quoted in Hodder, I, 169.
162. St G.H., Shaftesbury MSS, C 25034/7th Earl.
163. *Speeches of the Earl of Shaftesbury, K.G. Upon Subjects Having Relation chiefly to the Claims and Interests of the Labouring Class.* (1868, reprinted by Irish University Press, Shannon, Ireland, 1971), V.
164. J. G. Gill, *The Ten Hours Parson*, p. 112.

4
Private Happiness and Public Usefulness, 1830–1835

Throughout the public events to which he had been exposed since 1830, Ashley's marriage proved to be a source of strength and comfort. Despite their points of dissimilarity, Ashley's relationship with his mother-in-law was, on the whole, a happy one and was certainly better than that with his own parents. His father refused to attend his wedding in 1830. A few days later, however, he tried to make amends and invited the Cowper family to meet him. Lady Cowper was reluctant to accept the invitation and did not do so until she had consulted Ashley's sister, Caroline. She regretted that she had decided to go when she discovered that Ashley himself had not been in favour of it, but she wrote to Ashley, explaining that her sole object had been to try to improve relations between the Earl and his son and daughter-in-law. She had felt that this might be achieved by accepting the invitation rather than rejecting it. She told Ashley that his father had told everybody that he was prevented by business from attending the wedding: 'We know this is not true,' she wrote, 'but still as he makes the excuse, one may accept it.' She went on to give her opinion that it was wise 'to accept his overtures than to have the satisfaction of giving him a slap in the face by refusing them. Odious as he is, we cannot prevent his being your Father, or his having the power of annoying you in various ways.' Thus she thought it preferable for him to be conciliated rather than kept at arm's length, and she hoped that Ashley would find his father more anxious to be well disposed towards him for being 'on decent terms' with the Cowper family.[1] Her efforts appear to have had some success, for, within a few weeks, the Earl showed himself happy to accept Minny as his daughter-in-law.[2]

Ashley's candidature at the Dorset election of 1831, however, incurred the wrath of his father; according to Lady Cowper, he was 'furious at the idea of (Ashley's) standing for the County.'[3] She did not explain the reasons for his displeasure, but she herself once more proved to be a good friend. Although a Whig, she did not favour parliamentary reform, but it was more Ashley's financial predicament over the petition presented against his return that concerned her. She advised him to contest it and not to resign the seat. She did not wish to incur any more expense, but felt that he was more likely to have money advanced if he retained his seat; and, she added: 'I am putting all irons in the fire to see if anything can be done . . . I am so grieved to think you are so worried.'[4] She was certainly active: 'Mama is indefatigable,' Minny wrote to Ashley, 'and goes on writing the most *violent language* right and left.'[5] One of Lady Cowper's letters was to Wellington. She was in great anxiety, she wrote, about Ashley's affairs and appealed to Wellington to use his influence to help him. Were she a Tory, she said, she would feel it a deep disgrace to the party if it were to allow expenses to fall on Ashley, especially in the light of his unwillingness to stand and the sacrifice which he had made to do so. He had stood on the understanding that he would receive financial assistance, but this was now insufficient and, she wrote, he 'finds himself left to get out of the scrape as he can and this without any *means* of extricating himself from his difficulties.' Surely the 'great Tories who are rolling in riches' would not let Ashley be the victim of his devotion to their cause. And, she continued:

> I was born, and brought up a Whig, and although I have nearly ceased being so, from disgust at their proceedings for the last year and a half yet this I will say in their favour that I never knew them to leave a friend in the lurch or refuse to contribute with their money to support the principles they professed.[6]

Thus in Lady Cowper, Ashley found a loyal mother-in-law. And in Minny, he found a devoted wife. In the summer of 1830, when they were parted for two days, Minny wrote to Ashley, 'My dearest Love, I really am *quite* miserable without you. I would not have believed that I should have minded your being away for two days.' She begged him to come back the following day, if he could: 'It would make me very happy,' she wrote. 'There certainly never was such a darling as you are dearest Ashley and I really think I love you more and more every day.'[7] Whenever the couple were apart, Minny wrote in similar vein. In the autumn of 1831, when Ashley was in London and Minny at her parents' home at Panshanger, she wrote urging him to take care of himself, especially at a time when there was an outbreak of cholera: 'don't think me very foolish but when you are away from me I keep thinking of all the things that can by any possibility happen to you – it is really *almost* a misfortune to doat (*sic*) upon anybody as much as I do upon you.'[8] And another letter ran: 'I think of nothing but you. The fact is, I love you almost *too* dearly. . . .'[9] Ashley's feelings were equally warm. 'Believe me my sweet soul,' he wrote in 1832, 'I love you more than ... I thought I ever *could* love. It is a great happiness to have one whom I so completely adore.'[10] In June, 1831, their first child was born, Anthony, nicknamed 'Sir Babkins'. Letters between Minny and Ashley contained frequent references to him. Minny wrote, with due motherly pride, in August, 1831, that he grew 'more beautiful every day';[11] later, while in Brighton, she wrote that 'Babkins is the admiration of the town, but he grows so wilful, there is hardly any managing him, *so violent*. It is *astonishing how like his father he is!!*'[12] Ashley's comments, if more suitably flattering, were on the same theme: 'And so Babkins grows in beauty ... he must if he grows like you,' he wrote in 1832;[13] and while in Dorset for the Election of December, 1832, he finished a letter to Minny, 'Well, darling, give a thousand kisses from me to Sir Babkins – and tell him not to forget me.'[14]

Personal endearments were not, however, the only matters contained in these early letters. Minny showed a natural concern about the Dorset election and petition. She wrote to Ashley at the end of 1831 complaining of the 'shabby' behaviour of the Tories and saying how sorry she was to think of him in London in the middle of all his troubles: 'it is really too vexatious the state of your affairs,' she wrote. '... Upon my word the conduct of all these people is outrageous. ...'[15] She was not in favour of his defending the petition, if he could not get any of his election expenses paid, and, she added: 'I hope you love me and are not angry with me for thinking that I could be very happy if you were out of Parliament for a little while.'[16] However, she was soon to write again to say that she was delighted that things looked better 'tho' ever so little', and she passed on news that her mother had received a letter to the effect that more money would be subscribed.[17] On his side, Ashley gave Minny news of his political and public affairs: as has been seen,[18] he wrote of his frustrations over the petition and of his feelings about the new Parliament. Moreover, he discussed with her what was to be for them both the most important event of the new Parliament: the invitation of the Ten Hours Movement to take up Sadler's bill. 'It is your duty,' she said, 'and the consequences we must leave. Go forward, and to Victory!'[19]

Despite their seeming ill-assortment, Ashley and Minny thus proved to be a close and devoted couple. Lady Lyttelton, Lady-in-Waiting to Queen Victoria and later Governess to the royal children, commented in 1838 that the Ashleys were 'a very interesting ménage to watch'. She felt that Ashley – 'a very sensible and most highly principled man, full of useful good qualities' – had done his 'beautiful wife' a great deal of good: he had taught her 'all the good she could not learn from her mother, so that, from being a flirting, unpromising girl she is grown a nice happy wife and mother.'[20] In the mid forties, Lady Lyttelton once again commented on the Ashleys, remarking also on Ashley's eccentricities of behaviour. After a dinner at Windsor, she recounted her surprise at Ashley's choice of the character of St Paul as a subject for conversation before the first course had been served: and, after the Queen had gone to bed, Ashley had come up to Lady Lyttelton, taken her by both hands and said 'Heaven bless you ten thousand times!' She was, she wrote, 'rather astonished, but pleased too. It felt warm and comfortable from a person so sincere, mad though he be. ....' Such were Ashley's interests and idiosyncracies that she wondered 'how in the world he gets on with his whole kin-in-law ... Indeed, his wife and he are as wide asunder as this world and the next.' But, she added: 'he is very fond of her and she of him, and it is always so pretty to see his awfully handsome face soften whenever his eye meets hers.'[21]

In a real sense, therefore, Ashley and Minny were good for each other. Ashley's seriousness might, on occasion, be somewhat oppressive for Minny and the zeal with which he was to follow some of his projects excessive, but he was extremely fond and protective of his young wife. His influence acted as a ballast to the light-hearted and somewhat frivolous elements in her nature, but did not crush them, and in fact, she willingly absorbed his religious faith, if never quite to the extent that he was absorbed by it. Similarly, Minny's gaiety of spirit and sunny disposition were an invaluable corrective to the solemn, dark and brooding side of Ashley's nature; and he always – and very often on his wedding anniversaries – offered thanks to God for the gift of his wife.

After the activities of the 1833 session, Ashley and Minny set out on holiday. Southey had urged on Ashley the need for rest after his preoccupation with the factory question[22] and hoped that Ashley would visit him in Keswick, where he would find new scenes and quietness. But – probably in deference to Minny, who always liked to travel abroad – it was to Italy that they set out. A second son, Francis, had been born in March; he was left at home and Ashley and Minny were accompanied on their journey by Anthony and by Minny's parents. The party did not return until April, 1834, and in the six months a great number of places were visited. Milan was reached by November, 1833, and there, Ashley and Minny left Anthony with his grandparents and travelled for six weeks on their own. All the major towns and 'sights' were visited: Venice, Bologna, San Marino, Rome, where they spent Christmas, Siena, Florence, Pisa, San Remo. By early February, the party was re-united in Nice. They travelled through France, paying a visit to Paris *en route*, and in April, they were home: 'Thus ends our tour,' Ashley wrote. 'It has been very entertaining and I hope instructive.'[23]

These months saw Ashley as a purely private man, away from his public concerns and causes. He continued to rejoice in the company of his wife, and he took much pleasure in his changed status since his last visit to Italy some ten years earlier. He followed almost exactly the same route as he had done on the previous occasion, but he found himself a much happier man.

> I believed myself fitted for domestic life, and God willing, I entered into that state [he wrote]. Little did I think, when pacing these streets, that I should next visit them as paterfamilias; but often have I occasion to bless that Providence that put into my soul to desire a wife, and then guided my choice to rest upon one, who must, if I be capable of any goodness, insure to me a perpetuity of earthly happiness.[24]

The Journal which Ashley kept throughout the tour[25] contained many admiring references to Minny. After a Ball which they attended in Rome, Ashley wrote, 'Minny looked heavenly ... Is it wrong to be so entirely proud and happy in one's wife's beauty? But surely there is nothing so pretty and fascinating as my Min.' The places which they visited together were faithfully catalogued and commented on, and many of Ashley's remarks were those which almost any traveller, anxious to see as much as possible in the time at his disposal, might make. Venice was a 'glory of human skill': Bologna 'alone would occupy a month and we can spare it a day:' the Catacombs prompted the remark 'Now what a compass your thoughts must embrace if you stand in the narrow chapel of the catacombs and reflect on St Peter's, or in St Peter's and reflect on the catacombs.' There had been an abundance of sights to see, but after it all, Ashley was clearly glad to be re-united with his son. On their arrival in Nice in February, he wrote: 'Arrived at four; thanks be to God, found them all well, and especially our darling child, who knew us again, and showed evident joy at our return....'

The Journal, however, was not just a record of passing events; it also contained references to Ashley's reading and reflections. Gibbon and Massillon were his main sources of study, and many of his thoughts were on historical and religious themes. There were, indeed, many inducements to such thoughts in his surroundings. The Colliseum brought to mind 'the sufferings of the early Christians and the heroism of those faithful ones, whose blood under Providence, has been the "seed of the Church"'; and he was moved to 'utter a prayer of thanksgiving to God for all who had departed this life in His faith and fear.' The Catacombs, 'low, wretched and dismal', were yet 'the nursery of the Christian faith'. It is true that not all that Ashley saw pleased him. Since there was no Protestant place of worship in Milan, he and Minny went to High Mass in the Cathedral. But what he saw and heard gave him little spiritual nourishment. The ceremonies at St Peter's on Christmas Day were 'grand indeed': but he could find in them little 'worship ... love ... humility and gratitude'. Nevertheless, Ashley's mind was by no means closed to good points which he detected in the Roman

Catholic Church. In Milan Cathedral, he was impressed by the varied social composition of the congregation. He also reacted favourably to the Roman practice of leaving churches open for casual worshippers, and he recorded with approval Minny's observation that 'one great and honourable characteristic of this religion is . . . that no one is ashamed to exhibit devotion.' Further, while his seriousness and earnestness were amply evident during the visit, there was time for relaxation and gaiety: he and Minny went to Balls, they visited galleries and the opera; and in Rome, a large part of their time was spent in 'card leaving'.

Ashley left Italy having formed a considerable affection for her people. He saw them as the victims of centuries of misgovernment and suffering and yet having within them the potential of greatness. They were, after all, the 'instructors of Europe' in art, science, trade, literature, politics; and surely 'virtue and genius' could again take root. Ashley, indeed, looked to the establishment of a Kingdom of Italy as 'the millenium of European policy', although he well realised the problems and difficulties in the path of its achievement. But, as he left, he offered his blessing: 'Peace be within thy walls and plenteousness within thy palaces. I wish thee good luck.' The prospect of the return to political life did not, however, fill Ashley with enthusiasm. The tour had marked a 'happy freedom from politics'; he had carefully avoided newspapers and conversation on 'that odious subject'. But now, the respite was over: he had to renew his 'intercourse with vice and misery'. The visit to Paris on the way home – to please Minny and her mother it would seem – did not lighten his spirits but rather depressed them still more. There, 'everything amused, dissipated and corrupted the mind, without either giving cause, or leaving time, for the slightest reflection.' He was glad to 'quit the place, earnestly hoping that no child of (his) might ever pass many days in that pavilion of Belial.'

The political world to which Ashley returned presented no more attractions to him in reality than it had done in prospect. He wrote in May that he hated the House of Commons because he always felt his inferiority there – he could never hear anyone speaking without being conscious of his own limitations. He felt that he must consider whether he had the power of discharging public duties with any degree of skill or service, and, in June, came the plaintive comment: 'I wish I knew what I am, or what I was fitted for!'[26] Before the end of the year, however, political events took a turn which arrested his attention. In November, 1834, William IV dismissed the Whigs and called upon the Tories to form a Ministry. Throughout the struggles over the Reform Bill in 1831–2, William had accepted the Whigs' proposals to secure the passage of the Bill with increasing reluctance, and after 1832, he grew more and more apprehensive that the Whigs, with their large majority, would move forward to carry further reforms, especially in the Church. He was anxious to establish a coalition ministry in the anti-reform interest. This, however, proved to be impossible, and William thus turned to the more extreme step of dismissing the Whigs. Melbourne's proposal that Russell should succeed Althorp as leader of the House of Commons on Althorp's elevation to the Lords gave William his opportunity. Russell had been closely associated with reform proposals for the Irish Church, having committed himself in May to the policy of appropriating the surplus revenues of the Irish Church to secular purposes, and his elevation was altogether too much for William. Making a pretext of the possibility that, without Althorp, the Whigs would have difficulty in controlling the House of Commons, William dismissed Melbourne in November, 1834. Peel, called home suddenly from Italy, was required to form a Ministry.[27]

Ashley followed these events with keen interest. Amid 'all the chops and changes', he wondered what would be his fate. He wrote that he regarded the prospect of office 'with dismay'; it would mean long absences from home and the total disruption of his domestic life. Further, he felt himself unfit for it.[28] But Peel sent for him and duly asked him to serve in his administration. The actual office was not specified, but, according to Ashley, it was clear that Peel did not have in mind the India Board where Ashley had previously served, but some 'more confined Department', such as the Admiralty. Ashley protested his unfitness and reluctance: he had nothing to offer Peel, he said, except 'sound principles and by God's blessing, a good character'. Peel explained that he required the 'union of ability and integrity' and that it was on these grounds that he invited Ashley into the King's service. Ashley finally agreed to accept whatever office was to be offered: 'I yielded,' he wrote, 'because I had nothing to oppose to his wishes but my own feelings and disinclination.'[29]

Having declared his willingness to join Peel, Ashley proceeded to agonise over his decision. He had, he felt, made too many sacrifices: he would have no time for the education of his children, for the company of his wife, for the 'superintendence of the Poor', and for the study of religion. And there was little to compensate for this loss of 'everything of taste, utility and enjoyment': he was greatly disappointed to have had such a meagre offer put before him. An office such as Peel had proposed afforded very little scope for independent opinion or judgment: all that it called for was 'neither to do nor to think any more than may be done or thought by any quill-driver in the Establishment.' Thus he felt himself required to do 'what (his) valet could probably do better.'[30] The offer was confirmed some days after the interview in a letter from Peel: it was the post of Civil Lord of the Admiralty in the House of Commons.[31] Ashley replied, once more expressing his reluctance to accept an office which would afford so few opportunities of useful service. He admitted that it was as much as he was worth, but he pointed out that all his contemporaries had been promoted, whereas he was to occupy a less important post than that which he had previously held, and, since he could make no advance, he felt that he must give way to other men. If he accepted, it would give rise to the suspicion that he was so anxious for place that he would accept any offer. His letter was, therefore, a refusal of the post which Peel had offered to him, but it ended with an expression of his willingness to act not only as an 'honest, and wise, and able Minister but also . . . as (a) personal friend:' he would always, he said, be at Peel's 'command to undergo any Labour or any odium' to support the 'sacred principles' for which Peel stood.[32]

The letter was received by Lord Granville Somerset, who sent it on to Peel. Somerset expressed his surprise at Ashley's final statement of willingness to serve Peel, coming, as it did, immediately after his refusal of the office offered to him: 'the latter part of the accompanying letter,' Somerset commented, 'astonishes me exceedingly, following the first part.'[33] Somerset answered on Peel's behalf that the Admiralty Commission was all but completed when Ashley's letter was received, and Peel was anxious to know if Ashley's intention was now definitely to refuse it. He explained that Ashley's role would be to act as the Civil representative of the Board of Admiralty in the Commons, whose business it was to move the estimates and be the 'leading person' on all topics connected with the civil side of the Admiralty. He mentioned this, he said, in reply to Ashley's observation that his political position had been diminished. Peel had selected Ashley 'out of *numerous* Applicants' and his motives were of 'the kindest nature'.[34] In his reply, Ashley was at pains to dispel the impression which he felt he had given that he aspired to or deserved a higher office. He had declined the post because he felt that he would not be of service in it. Nevertheless, he continued:

> My business and duty . . . are to serve him, in his way, not my own; and since he is willing to bear the responsibility of having appointed me to an active situation and is kind enough to say that I can really contribute somewhat in his aid, I am perfectly ready, however conscious of my own weakness, to undertake the charge he has been pleased to assign me.[35]

Ashley thus finally accepted the offer, if in a highly tortuous way. Not for the first time nor for the last, he had shown the various aspects of his personality: his feelings of uncertainty about his own capacities and yet his sense of grievance when these capacities were not recognised by others; his desire to be 'of service' and yet his disappointment that a better offer had not been made. 'What a humiliation for an ambitious man!' he wrote of it.[36] Somerset – and, it would seem, Peel himself – realised that Ashley would have to be persuaded that the post was not, in fact, a humble one, but was well sought after. The contents of Somerset's letter to Ashley suggest this, and Somerset added a note to Peel: 'Perhaps I ought to add my condolence and apologies for having (as you feared) convinced Ashley for *his* benefit.'[37]

The formation of Peel's Ministry was followed by a General Election, held in January, 1835. Ashley once again offered himself for Dorset, Lady Cowper, it appears, undertaking to meet the expenses. 'Pray tell your mother,' Ashley wrote to Minny on 9 January, 'that no time must be allowed before she calls for the election Bills. The sooner she has them in, the smaller they will be.'[38] On 12 January, two days before the hustings, he wrote to Minny that all promised to be 'extremely quiet'; everything would probably be over in half an hour.[39] Yet, once more, he was afflicted by uncertainty and lack of confidence. He told Minny that he was 'inclined to despair'; he felt that he had 'sadly mistaken (his) calling': he had 'dashed into public life, almost as a matter of course' and had winced ever since under a sense of his inadequacy.[40] He trembled at the prospect of 'a public exhibition'; his eloquence on the Factory Bill was the very utmost of his powers. He had embarked on public life and could not now 'go ashore'; he had been forced, against his better judgment, to engage in office, 'feeling that every self-sufficient Whipper-snapper (was) more than a match for (him) in the field of oratory.' He also felt discontented at being separated from Minny. 'My child,' he wrote 'we never intended that we should live apart even for a day; yet I think you bear it better than I do. To be sure you have the children who must console you.' There was, however, the fact that he and Minny had a new home in London, at Upper Brook Street, having moved there on their return from the Continent. It appears to have been more suitable as a family home than their previous house at Norfolk Street and possibly meant that Minny would not have to spend so much time with her parents at Panshanger. Whatever the reason, Ashley felt 'less repugnance to office' when he recollected that the separation from Minny would not be so long and constant as when they lived in Norfolk Street, and this was, he wrote, 'a very great alleviation of the immense burden of a public career.'[41]

The election itself in Dorset proved to be as uneventful as Ashley had prophesied. He was nominated on 1 January and in his speech promised to maintain the Church, for, he believed, 'Providence never bestowed a greater blessing on any country.' He also referred to his recent association with factory reform; he had proposed one thing and the government another, but he had been and would continue to be 'engaged for the public benefit'. When challenged that he now had a place, he assured the electors that this would never induce him to neglect their interests. 'It shall be my unceasing aim,' he said, 'to promote your real interests and to maintain the institutions of this country in Church and State.'[42] Such sentiments proved acceptable, and Ashley, returned unopposed, was confirmed in his office at the Admiralty.

The fortunes of the Tory party as a whole at the Election showed a considerable recovery from the bleak and disastrous days of December, 1832. The assurance of moderate and measured reforms, which was the theme of Peel's Tamworth Manifesto, proved attractive to men of property and conservative instincts. But the growing support for Conservatism was not yet sufficient to provide Peel with a majority in the Commons, and, on the assembly of Parliament in February, 1835, the Conservative Ministry found itself in a minority and confronted with the opposition of Whigs, radicals and Irish. At once, the Speakership was contested. Manners Sutton, who had been Speaker in the unreformed House and had continued in that office in the reformed, was considered by the Whigs to have departed from strict neutrality and to have been a party to their dismissal in November, 1834. It was decided to oppose his re-election in the new House by the candidature of Abercromby, a Whig. On 19 February, Manners Sutton was defeated by 316 votes to 306. Peel, however, remained in office after the vote, and thus the Whigs, the radicals and the Irish agreed to move an amendment to the Address. This insisted on the continuance of reform and deplored the late dissolution of Parliament, and was carried by 309 votes to 302. Once again, Peel did not resign, and there was, indeed, a feeling among certain moderate Whigs that Peel, as the King's Minister, should be given a fair chance. But his position was always weak, and, even if his Ministry did not suffer a frontal attack, it was open to 'sniper's bullets'. One method used in this type of warfare was the obstruction of supply.[43]

At the Admiralty, Ashley was to find himself especially vulnerable to such attacks, and, added to this, he had to face the criticism of the archopponent of expenditure, Joseph Hume. It seems clear that the naval estimates were already virtually prepared by the outgoing government and that the new Board could only make very minor revisions in the time available to it. The estimates showed a reduction in proposed expenditure over the previous year, and Ashley announced this on 13 March, when moving them.[44] Even so, he was constantly under attack from Hume on various items and, although some of Hume's amendments were defeated, the government was seriously embarrassed by the difficulty which it encountered in getting all its naval estimates passed. Ashley pointed this out to the House on 25 March,[45] and, in particular, he mentioned the fact that the government would not be in a position to give notice that pensions would become payable the following month unless it was provided with the funds necessary to meet them. Since certain votes had passed, there was the question whether it would be constitutionally correct to appropriate public money to a purpose other than that to which it had been specifically assigned. Peel himself intervened in the debate, stating that the most prudent course for the House would be to sanction the vote asked for and not leave any payments necessary for the public service to be made from money intended for other purposes.[46] This was accepted and the particular difficulty resolved. But on 6 April, there were further problems over the vote for the expenses of the Marine Establishment at home.[47] On this occasion, the Chancellor of the Exchequer was at pains to point out that the votes for which the government had asked over the Naval Estimates were 'indispensably necessary': one of these, not yet passed, related to the payment of the wages of the artificers in the docks and victualling yards, due on 10 April. Hume asked whether any Navy Bills had been refused payment owing to the Estimates not having been passed. He also denied that the opposition was to blame for not allowing the estimates to be passed – the fault lay with Peel's dissolution of Parliament. Another speaker, Labouchere, regretted that Ashley had not explained the emergency to the House more clearly: he felt that votes would have been passed had this been done. The government countered all such points. Ashley himself explained that the Admiralty had not gone to the extent of dishonouring any Bill, but since no money was in hand to meet certain accounts and no money had been voted, the Admiralty had thought it right to delay payment of these accounts. The Chancellor denied that any blame attached to the government. The main cause was that the government had been obstructed. After this wrangle, the particular vote relating to the Marine Establishment was accepted, but no sooner was this done than a further vote, requesting money to defray the expense of naval stores and materials for the building and repairs of ships and docks, ran into difficulties and economies were requested. Ashley stressed that it was most important that there be no delay, and he pointed out that there were at present fewer ships-in-ordinary than ever before.[48] Finally the vote was passed.

The difficulties of getting the naval estimates passed were symptomatic of the problems of the Peel Ministry. On 25 March, Peel had issued a cabinet paper, drawing the attention of his colleagues to the position of his government in the Commons. He reviewed the situation since he had formed his administration, noting the defeats on the Speakership and the amendment to the Address, and he mentioned that no progress had been made with the public business. In the face of such constant obstruction, government was impossible. In his paper, Peel also referred to the fact that the issue of Irish appropriation was once again to be raised by Russell. This was a point of principle to which the government could not accede, and, in his view, the only course would be for it to resign if appropriation were upheld.⁴⁹ The matter was debated between 30 March and 7 April. In the course of these debates, the government suffered a number of defeats, culminating in a defeat on 7 April on the issue of appropriation. Peel resigned on 8 April. Ashley noted in his Diary: 'We are out. Peel has resigned. It is evident that the Commons would not accept *any* measures at his hands and they prefer anarchy under themselves to order under him.'⁵⁰

Thus ended Ashley's brief but troubled spell at the Admiralty. The episode was, in fact, to be revived at the end of the decade. When the naval estimates were being discussed in 1839, there was a feeling that the international situation called for a larger naval establishment, and charges were made in the Commons that the Conservative government of 1834–5 had made reductions in the estimates at the risk of impairing the navy for the sake of winning popularity. Ashley strenuously rebutted these charges. He pointed out that the estimates were already almost complete when he came to the Board and that economies had been envisaged by the previous government. The Conservative government had, indeed, slightly increased the estimates over those made by the outgoing Whigs and had left a rather larger supply of stores than it had inherited. Peel also spoke in defence of his government in 1834–5, and he recalled that it had been faced not by calls for increased expenditure but by demands for further economies and by constant obstruction. In 1839, opinion had set in against economy, but his government could not be blamed for this.⁵¹ Thus even after four years, the controversies of 1835 had not been wholly laid to rest.

Political life was, therefore, a pressing concern for Ashley in 1834–5, but not to the exclusion of everything else. Religion had occupied much of his thought in Italy, and after he returned in April, 1834, it did so to an increasing extent. While visiting Oxford in June, 1834, to attend the installation of the Duke of Wellington as Chancellor of the University, he took the opportunity to look back on the eleven and a half years since he had completed his undergraduate days, and he asked himself whether his mind was now 'more powerful and better instructed'. 'Certainly,' he wrote, 'but not in the proportion of time, experience and other men. But I have, by God's grace, a deeper sense (and yet how shallow!) of His religion; ... that being obtained, all other things will be added thereunto!'⁵² The following month, he upbraided himself for his lack of systematic study of any one subject, but he confessed his preference for theology above all others. Finance, corn laws, foreign policy or poor laws would give him 'more public usefulness' but they would not give more 'private happiness'. And he continued: 'I shall be content henceforward to float down the stream of time, and put ashore at any point whither the Almighty in His wisdom may command me!'[53]

Much of this was in accordance with his previously held and expressed views on religion, but it is also true that, at this time, Ashley displayed more distinctively Evangelical characteristics than he had done before, especially in matters of belief. There still appears to have been no dramatic conversion experience, but he became more convinced of human depravity and the necessity of the Atonement. In August, 1834, he wrote that he believed the human heart to be 'so corrupt that, if we could, in every instance, see our motives as God sees them, we should be equally surprised and disgusted.' And, he continued, 'nothing but a disbelief of, or a disinclination to, this truth could possibly affect our eager acceptance of the great, necessary and most comfortable doctrine of the Atonement.'[54] About this time, too, he began to keep volumes of his religious reflections, and in these there were many thoughts about human depravity. One long passage on the betrayal of Christ by Judas Iscariot contained the comment that the human heart was 'deceitful above all things and desperately wicked';[55] on Christmas Eve, 1834, he wrote that the great doctrine of Man's corruption and infirmity, 'coupled with the prodigy of the Atonement' was 'far more comfortable than any reliance on Man's perfection. By God's grace, I hold such a doctrine in terror and abhorrence.'[56] Religion thus became for Ashley less intellectual and more personal: not only a way of explaining the mysteries and beauties of Creation, but a vital means of releasing man from his incorrigible sinfulness. Man had no chance of releasing himself from sin and could never rely on his own merit. Ashley's reading of the memoirs of Hannah More in the autumn of 1834 prompted the thought that those who relied on works for justification should 'cease to hope until they shall at least have equalled her, and then they will begin to despair; for, finding no consolation in self-meritoriousness . . . they will look around for something else to assuage their souls.'[57] Man could only find justification by acknowledging God's redeeming love.

Another aspect of Ashley's beliefs which showed prominence at this time was in the area of eschatological issues, which was also a common tendency among certain Evangelicals.[58] His diaries of religious reflections ranged over such matters as eternal life and the Day of Judgment, 'the period of final adjudication,' he wrote, 'when the Son of Man shall sit upon the Throne of His Glory.'[59] Another Evangelical belief, closely associated with this, was that of the Second Coming of Christ. This was not only a spiritual coming into the life of the believer; it was a literal coming of Christ Himself and the foundation of God's Kingdom on earth. There was room for disagreement as to the sequence of events between this and the Day of Judgment. Some Evangelicals believed that Christ would come and usher in a thousand years of blessedness and peace – the Millennium – during which He reigned in glory with the Saints: and at the end of this would come the Final Judgment. This was the pre-Millenarian school. Others again thought that the Second Coming would coincide with the Millennium; and yet others – the post-Millenarians – that Christ would come at the end of the Millennium and Judgment would take place then. Ashley became increasingly preoccupied with such matters in the second half of the thirties, and of great importance in this respect was his meeting with Edward Bickersteth in 1835. A former secretary of the Church Missionary Society, Bickersteth had become ordained and was a leading Evangelical; he firmly belonged to the pre-Millenarian school. His book, a *Practical Guide to the Prophecies*, first published in 1823 and re-issued as an enlarged fourth edition in 1835, set out his ideas on the Second Coming,[60] in addition to various other prophetical matters. Ashley became very friendly with Bickersteth, whose teaching had a great influence on him, and he, too, became a convinced pre-Millenarian.

Ashley's beliefs thus took on an increasingly Evangelical tinge, and this was also true of his conduct. He showed a greater tendency than before to feel deeply about his religion and to make a display of it. He expressed his dislike of formal religion consisting only of respectable Church-going.[61] He wrote that after reading the Bible aloud to Minny, he 'all but burst into tears at the mere dignity of the subject and the language.'[62] He spoke at a meeting of the Society for the Promotion of Christian Knowledge in Hertford in September, 1834: he was depressed by his performance, but he rejoiced to have expressed his belief.[63] He was also increasingly concerned for the salvation of those near to him. When, in November, 1834, Lady Cowper showed an interest in a Bible lying on Minny's table, Ashley felt that he must make the attempt to 'reach her soul' and trusted to God 'to send her Grace and Aid and Illumination on the passages of Holy Writ.' He was somewhat doubtful if his mother-in-law would make a very willing convert, but the first step had been made and, he wrote, 'we will hope for better things.'[64] For Minny and his family, he continued to be deeply thankful. He told Minny in January, 1835, that when he thought of her, he was 'lost in wonder in the reflection that all (his) prayers (had) been so truly and beautifully accomplished.' And, he continued: 'God knows that, so far as human Nature in its corruption, can be grateful, I feel and confess a most humble thankfulness. I cannot, I fear, do more and God grant that I may never do less than train you all towards Eternity in His faith and fear.'[65] And, if he sought to instil his religious concern into his family circle, he deplored the lack of that concern in public men. In July, 1834, when it was rumoured that Peel might be asked to form a Ministry, Ashley complained that he neither saw nor heard 'any symptom of awakened religion among those who aspire to be our rulers;' and, he added, 'what security does any other principle afford?'[66] When Peel did form his Ministry in December and asked Ashley to join it, one of Ashley's objections was, as has been seen, that it would interfere with his study of Religion, which, he wrote, was 'the most delightful (as well as the *only important*) study of a human Being. . . .'[67] And his feelings about the Cabinet were lukewarm. Few, he thought, could be regarded as men of piety: 'I had hoped at any rate,' he wrote, 'for honest, right-minded and feeling Colleagues.'[68] The episode with Peel also showed Ashley's Evangelical Sabbatarianism. When Peel asked Ashley to go to see him as quickly as possible, Ashley travelled on a Sunday to do so. 'I thought it a matter of necessity in an urgent case such as this to obey his summons,'[69] he wrote: he found it necessary to justify to himself the breaking of the Sabbath.

Thus if Ashley had been at pains to rebut the description of 'Saint' in 1829, by 1834–5 he was coming to think of himself in these terms. Since no conversion experience is recorded, it is impossible to be precise about the date on which Ashley became a fully committed Evangelical. A further difficulty is that few of the entries in his volume of religious reflections are dated. There was, clearly, some continuity between his earlier position and his 'new' one, but these years were of distinct importance in Ashley's religious development. He became more concerned with Man's bondage to sin, to be broken only through justification by faith; more interested in 'eschatological issues'; more self-consciously pious; more concerned that others, too, should be pious. The 'religious' aspect of Evangelicalism, concerned with matters of belief, became more firmly established; the 'moral' aspect of private and public conduct more fully developed. His involvement in Peel's Ministry and the concerns at the Admiralty may have briefly interrupted such interests, and the deepening tone of his religious life did not leave him immune from thoughts about the political world and his own advancement in it. But in April, 1835, the Conservatives were once more in opposition and, with a brief interlude in 1839, when it seemed that they might have office, were to remain so until the Whigs finally went out of power in 1841. Thus for Ashley, political events in the second half of the decade became less pressing and he was able to turn his attention to the concerns now so near to his heart and soul.

NOTES

1. H.R.O., Shaftesbury (Broadlands) MSS, 27M60. 1830 (no day or month given).
2. Battiscombe, p. 66.
3. Apsley House, Wellington MSS, Lady Cowper to Wellington, 1831 (no day or

month given). Ashley was distressed by the fact that he received little interest or support from his family during his canvass in Dorset in Dec. 1832. He told Minny that the 'St Giles' People' had not been kind to him. Neither Henry nor Lionel had paid him a visit and his sister had only seen him once. 'The fact is,' he wrote, 'they have not sufficient affection to overcome their fear of Lord S(haftesbury)'s disapprobation.' (N.R.A., Shaftesbury (Broadlands) MSS, SHA/PC/133).
4. H.R.O., Shaftesbury (Broadlands) MSS, 27M60. (Undated).
5. ibid., 27M60, 17 Dec. (1831).
6. Apsley House, Wellington MSS, 1831 (no day or month given).
7. H.R.O., Shaftesbury (Broadlands) MSS, 27M60. (Postmarked 26 July, 1830: otherwise undated).
8. ibid., 27M60. (Postmarked 18 Aug., 1831: otherwise undated).
9. ibid., 27M60. (Undated).
10. N.R.A., Shaftesbury (Broadlands) MSS, SHA/PC/129.
11. H.R.O., Shaftesbury (Broadlands) MSS, 27M60. (Postmarked 18 Aug., 1830: otherwise undated).
12. ibid., 27M60. (Undated).
13. N.R.A., Shaftesbury (Broadlands) MSS, SHA/PC/132.
14. ibid., SHA/PC/133.
15. H.R.O., Shaftesbury (Broadlands) MSS, 27M60. 14 Dec., 1831.
16. ibid., 27M60. 17 Dec., 1831.
17. ibid., 27M60. (Undated).
18. See above pp. 70, 71.
19. Hodder, I, 151.
20. The Hon. Mrs Hugh Wyndham (ed.), *Correspondence of Sarah Spencer, Lady Lyttelton, 1787–1870* (1912), p. 283.
21. ibid., p. 351. In 1837, Melbourne told the Queen that Ashley adored Lady Ashley. (Viscount Esher (ed.), *The Girlhood of Queen Victoria. A Selection of Her Majesty's Diaries between the years 1832 and 1840* (2 vols, 1912), I, 242–3).
22. Henry W. and Albert A. Berg Collection, 24 July, 14 Oct., 1833.
23. Hodder, I, 193.
24. ibid., 175–6.
25. ibid., 170–93, contain extracts from this Journal and all references quoted in the text on pp. 95–96 are taken from these extracts.
26. N.R.A., Shaftesbury (Broadlands) MSS, SHA/PD/1, 27 June, 1834.
27. N. Gash, *Sir Robert Peel. The Life of Sir Robert Peel after 1830* (1972), p. 82 ff.
28. N.R.A., Shaftesbury (Broadlands) MSS, SHA/PD/1, 26 Nov., 1834.
29. ibid., SHA/PD/1, 15 Dec., 1834. This extract covers the interview with Peel, as reconstructed by Ashley.
30. ibid., SHA/PD/1, 15 Dec., 1834.
31. Hodder, I, 203–4.
32. Add. MSS, 40, 407, fos 7–11.
33. ibid., fos 95–6.
34. St G.H., Shaftesbury MSS, C 25022.1/7th Earl.
35. Add. MSS, 40, 407, fos 97–8.
36. N.R.A., Shaftesbury (Broadlands) MSS, SHA/PD/1, 22 Dec., 1834.
37. Add. MSS, 40, 407, fos 95–6.
38. N.R.A., Shaftesbury (Broadlands) MSS, SHA/PC/146.
39. ibid., SHA/PC/148.
40. ibid., SHA/PC/145.
41. ibid., SHA/PC/148.

42. *The Dorset County Chronicle and Somersetshire Gazette*, 15 Jan., 1835.
43. G. Kitson Clark, *Peel and the Conservative Party* (2nd ed., 1964), pp. 241–2.
44. Hansard, *Parl. Debates*, 3rd ser., XXVI, 990–94.
45. ibid., XXVII, 225.
46. ibid., 231. Greville recorded Ashley's annoyance at Peel's interference in such matters. Ashley, he wrote, was 'furious' when Peel would not allow him to give an answer to Hume which Ashley had taken pains to prepare himself. (L. Strachey and R. Fulford (eds.), op. cit., III, 176).
47. Hansard, *Parl. Debates*, 3rd ser., XXVII, 864–71.
48. ibid., 872.
49. N. Gash, op. cit., p. 114.
50. N.R.A., Shaftesbury (Broadlands) MSS, SHA/PD/1, 8 Apr., 1835.
51. Hansard, *Parl. Debates*, 3rd ser., XLV, 1368–71; XLVI, 243–73.
52. N.R.A., Shaftesbury (Broadlands) MSS, SHA/PD/1, 9 June, 1834.
53. ibid., SHA/PD/1, 3 July, 1834.
54. ibid., SHA/PD/1, 7 Aug., 1834.
55. ibid., SHA/MIS/1. (Undated).
56. ibid., SHA/PD/1, 24 Dec., 1834.
57. ibid., SHA/PD/1, 7 Sept., 1834.
58. See S. C. Orchard, 'English Evangelical Eschatology 1790–1850' (Ph.D., Cambridge, 1968), *passim*.
59. N.R.A., Shaftesbury (Broadlands) MSS, SHA/MIS/1. (Undated).
60. E. Bickersteth, *A Practical Guide to the Prophecies* (4th ed., 1835), pp. 100–14. See also G. F. A. Best, *Shaftesbury* (1964), pp. 67–8 and J. F. C. Harrison, *The Second Coming, Popular Millenarianism, 1780–1850* (1979), p. 4.
61. N.R.A., Shaftesbury (Broadlands) MSS, SHA/PD/1, 10 Dec., 1834.
62. ibid., SHA/PD/1, 14 June, 1834.
63. ibid., SHA/PD/1, 7 Sept., 1834.
64. ibid., SHA/PD/1, 20 Nov., 1834.
65. ibid., SHA/PC/137.
66. ibid., SHA/PD/1, 14 July, 1834.
67. ibid., SHA/PD/1, 15 Dec., 1834.
68. ibid., SHA/PD/1, 16 Dec., 1834.
69. ibid., SHA/PD/1, 15 Dec., 1834.

5
Full of Schemes, 1835–1841

The Evangelical faith to which Ashley became firmly committed in the mid 1830s was, of course, more than a number of doctrines and attitudes held by individual Evangelicals. In terms of the Church of England, it was to be found among certain of the clergy and laity and, although they were not a united or homogeneous body and did not form a majority party in the Church, they were a forceful element within it. Evangelicalism in a corporate sense was also to be found in the Nonconformist Churches, and, in addition, in a host of societies concerned with religious endeavour, public morality and philanthropic effort. Some of these societies were limited to members of the Church of England; others straddled different denominations and involved the cooperation of persons of Evangelical views in the Established Church and the Nonconformist Churches. Exeter Hall in the Strand was the 'headquarters' of many of these societies, and to it, every May, their faithful members were wont to travel to hear the speeches of their Presidents and officials at the annual meetings. The influence of such societies on Victorian England is hard to measure with any accuracy, but their conspicuousness as a feature of Victorian England is an undoubted fact. And with this world of Evangelical zeal and effort, Ashley was now to become ever more closely associated, both in a private capacity and also as a member of Parliament.

One notable area of Evangelical activity was that of Sunday observance.[1] This was founded on a strict interpretation of the fourth commandment, the binding nature of which on the Evangelical was not affected by the fact that the Christian religion spoke in terms of Sunday being the first day of the week rather than the seventh. Whether first or seventh did not matter; what did matter was God's will, which the Evangelical found clearly expressed in the Bible, that the Sabbath be properly observed. Such sentiments resulted in the formation of the Lord's Day Observance Society in January,

1831. The General Committee of the Society was limited to members of the Church of England, but it also tried to enlist support outside the Establishment. The Society was greatly concerned with the subject of Sunday legislation. By law, activity on a Sunday was curtailed by an Act of 1677, still on the statute book, according to which no one, unless engaged in food service, was to pursue any occupation on a Sunday – all trading and travelling were forbidden. The Act, however, was ineffective and widely ignored. The Lord's Day Observance Society saw as one of its primary objects the enlistment of parliamentary support to promote legislation to remedy this situation, and, throughout the 1830s, various efforts were made by members sympathetic to its point of view. The leading spokesman was Sir Andrew Agnew, an Evangelical member of Parliament, who, in July, 1832, moved for a select committee to investigate the question of Sunday observance, and Agnew remained active in the cause until he lost his seat in Parliament in 1837. Agnew's interests have, indeed, already been mentioned.

Parliamentary efforts on the subject in the 1830s fell broadly into two categories. One was the introduction of widely ranging bills which sought to revive and make more stringent the legislation of 1677; and bills which came into this category were introduced in 1833, 1834, 1836 and 1837. The other category was more limited in scope and kept to the one issue of Sunday trading; and bills to limit trading were introduced in 1833, 1834, 1835 and 1838. Both categories of bill, however, failed. They ran into opposition or, more often, indifference – their fate was often to meet defeat in a poorly-attended House. The end of the decade saw much Evangelical activity in this area concentrated on the question of Sunday labour in the post office. There was no delivery of post in London on a Sunday: the only work done was by a few clerks in the central office, handling government letters. But in the provincial offices, there was a Sunday delivery after the Church services. In 1838, various changes were proposed by a parliamentary select committee and these included the Sunday opening of the London General Post Office and every branch office in London for a number of hours for the receipt and delivery of letters. These recommendations roused the Lord's Day Observance Society into activity. Deputations were appointed to wait on the government and discover its intentions, and one such deputation saw Melbourne. He assured it that the government had no thought of carrying out the recommendations of the select committee, and the matter was dropped. Here, Evangelical activity did enjoy some success, although the question was later to be revived.[2]

In all this flurry of Evangelical activity, Ashley took his part. As has been noted,[3] he was a member of Agnew's select committee of 1832, and he supported many of the parliamentary efforts which were made in the decade. In 1835, he voted for the second reading of the Sunday Observance

Bill, which was concerned with Sunday trading[4] and he supported a further bill on trading in 1838.[5] He also voted for a wider measure proposed in 1837.[6] He was approached in 1836 by a sub-committee of the Lord's Day Observance Society on the question of Sunday railways, being described by Lord Sandon – who was also approached, but felt he could not comply with the Society's request to press for the prohibition of Sunday travel – as a 'most proper individual' to attend to the matter.[7] It has been seen that Ashley had travelled on a Sunday to see Peel in 1834 only on the grounds of 'necessity',[8] and in 1837 he supported a clause in the Glasgow Railway Bill which prevented travelling on a Sunday.[9] And, at the end of the decade, Ashley gave his support to the campaign to stop Sunday labour in the Post Office; he took part in the deputation which called on Melbourne.[10] In 1839, Ashley noted that the longer he lived, the more he reverenced and adored 'the benevolent wisdom of God, which has set apart one day in seven for His service and man's refreshment....'[11] His activities in the late thirties contributed to the Evangelical attempt to translate the 'wisdom of God' into the practice for man.

The thrust towards missionary enterprise, also essential to Evangelicalism, was much in evidence in the latter half of the decade. It was, indeed, the duty, as well as the delight of the Evangelical to share his faith with others, and this was not unconnected with the Second Coming. It would not bring in the Millennium, but it would prepare for it and ensure that, at the Second Coming, the earth was 'filled with the glory of the Lord'.[12] Many missionary societies were devoted to work in 'heathen lands'; but this was supplemented by activity devoted to the domestic situation. In the early nineteenth century, the spiritual welfare of the urban working classes presented an enormous challenge to all Christians and all Churches. To Evangelicals, the need for action was inescapable and, on occasion, they drew together from different denominations to work for the spreading of the Gospel. Thus the London City Mission, founded in May, 1835, was inter-denominational; its object was to take the Gospel to the poor of London without regard for distinctive forms of Church government. It performed its work by means of lay agents carrying out home visitations, conducting prayer meetings and distributing tracts, but this was not in the interests of any one Church.[13] Other societies, if similar in purpose, were limited to one denomination. Such was the Church Pastoral Aid Society, founded in February, 1836, which was restricted to members of the Church of England. The purpose of the Society was to provide funds to go towards the appointment of clergy who would undertake duties in parishes where their efforts were required and to provide lay assistance for the clergy in matters which were not ministerial – for example, in carrying out visitations. This, then, was an attempt to increase the effectiveness of the parochial ministry of the Church in highly populated urban parishes.

It is not clear whether Ashley took any part in the activities of the London City Mission in the 1830s, although in the 1840s he was to become closely associated with many of its efforts. But he was involved in the establishment of the Church Pastoral Aid Society. He took the chair at its foundation meeting in February, 1836, and, in May, he stated that the founders had 'perceived that the population of the country had outgrown the means of instruction which the established Church was able to provide.'[14] He remained President of the Society for the rest of his life and his speech at the annual May meeting was always a major event in the Evangelical calendar. In 1838, he wrote that the Society had made great progress in its work of assisting clergymen and had opened up new channels for the Gospel. 'I never was called by God's mercy,' he continued, 'to so happy and blessed a work as to labour on behalf of this Society and preside at its head. . . .'[15] And these were to remain his sentiments: amidst all the societies with which he was to become involved, Ashley always regarded the Church Pastoral Aid Society with special warmth. He was fully committed to its missionary purposes, and he fully approved of the lay agency which it employed. For Ashley, laity who could speak directly and simply of their faith from their own experience had a vital role to play in the task of mission.

A further area of Evangelical activity which occupied much of Ashley's time in the late thirties arose from concern over the fortunes of the Jews. Although all Evangelical missionary enterprise had an eschatological content, in that it was directed towards preparing a final state of readiness for the working out of God's ultimate purposes, missionary enterprise to the Jews was of a rather special nature. Many Evangelicals were led by Biblical prophecies to believe that the restoration of the Jews to the Holy Land and their conversion to Christianity was a sign of the 'last days', a necessary prelude to the Second Coming; or, as was also believed in some Evangelical circles, an accompaniment to it; or again, according to another theory, a postscript to it.[16] Whatever the precise timing, however, there was, to many Evangelicals, no doubt that the fate of the Jews and the Second Coming were closely linked. Ashley displayed great interest in the repatriation of the Jews to Palestine in the late 1830s. He was especially pleased with the appointment in 1838 of a British Consul at Jerusalem, William Young: indeed, it was he who made representations to Palmerston, the Foreign Secretary, for Young's appointment, which, he felt, might act as an encouragement to the Jews to return by offering them special consular protection.[17] He was also anxious to take advantage of the opportunities presented by the Near East Crisis of 1839–41, which was precipitated by the desire of the Sultan to recover the provinces, which included Palestine, held since 1833 by his rebellious subject, Mehemet Ali, pasha of Egypt. Ashley followed the war between Egypt and Turkey, the participation of the powers and their efforts to settle it, with keen interest. He felt that if the powers could be 'induced to guarantee security of life and possessions to the Hebrew race they would flock back in rapidly augmenting numbers.'[18] He resolved to prepare a document on the subject for Palmerston,[19] and, in September, 1840, he presented it to the Foreign Secretary.[20]

Ashley also showed great interest in the conversion of the Jews and wrote on the subject in a review article in *The Quarterly Review* in 1839. That the Jews were at present 'degraded and despised' was, he admitted, 'part of their chastisement and the fulfilment of prophecy'. But the dawn of a better day was at hand: 'a day of regeneration and deliverance' which would 'set them at large in the glorious liberty of the Gospel.'[21] He mentioned various societies in Europe which existed to promote Christianity among the Jews, one of which was the London Society, founded in 1809, and, in particular, he wrote of a plan favoured by the Society for the establishment of a Protestant Church at Jerusalem. A considerable sum of money had been collected for the purpose and all that was required was the purchase of ground on which the Church could be built. An appointment had been made to the charge, a Dane, Nicolayson, who had, since 1826, been a missionary employed by the London Society in Jerusalem. Ashley made the point in his article that for centuries, Greek, Romanist, Armenian and Turk had their places of worship at Jerusalem; 'the pure doctrines of the Reformation, as embodied and professed in the Church of England,' he continued, 'have alone been unrepresented amidst all those corruptions.' It was of vital importance to the cause of Christianity that

> we should exhibit it in its pure and apostolical form to the children of Israel . . . they are returning in crowds to their ancient land; we must provide for the converts an orthodox spiritual service, and set before the rest whether residents or pilgrims, a worship as enjoined by our Saviour himself, 'a worship in spirit and in truth.'[22]

Some progress was, indeed, made towards securing increased protection for the Jews in the Ottoman Empire. Young's powers as Consul were quickly extended to offer protection to Jews generally living in the Holy Land.[23] Ashley was delighted at this; he approved of Young as one sympathetic to his ideas and felt that his extended powers would reap great fruit. 'He is . . . accredited, as it were, to the former Kingdom of David and the Twelve Tribes . . .' Ashley wrote. The Jews might thus be encouraged to return 'in yet greater numbers and become once more the husbandmen of Judea and Galilee.'[24] Ashley also found Palmerston ready to listen to his plans for offering the Jews greater safeguards in the peace arrangements at the close of the Turco-Egyptian war. 'Palmerston has already been chosen by God to be an instrument of good to His ancient people,' was Ashley's comment.[25] Thus, when the provinces occupied by Mehemet Ali were once more restored to the Sultan in 1841, Palmerston was hopeful that the Sultan would make laws favourable to the Jews, so that they would enjoy special rights and privileges as his subjects and thus be induced to make their home in Palestine.[26] But his representations to the Sultan on this point failed, and Ashley's larger hopes were disappointed.

The other project, for the establishment of a Protestant presence at Jerusalem, was to enjoy greater success. Young, an eager advocate of the conversion of the Jews, had pressed for the founding of a Protestant Church while the territories were still under the control of Mehemet Ali. This ran into difficulties, not from the Egyptians, but from the Sultan, whose official permission was sought, but not granted.[27] But such difficulties were ignored. Advantage was taken of the fact that the occupying Egyptian authorities were not unfavourably disposed to the idea, and premises were rented for holding services. The purchase of land was more difficult; but Nicolayson, who, in cooperation with the London Society, took much of the initiative in the matter, succeeded in obtaining plots of land through an intermediary, and despite opposition from the local Muslim population, Nicolayson was authorised by the London Society to start building operations. In February, 1840, the foundation stone of the church was laid.[28] Once the provinces were returned to the Sultan in 1841, there were to be further difficulties in the building of the church. Nevertheless, the restoration of the Sultan's control provoked the powers to reaffirm or to establish their claims to missionary enterprise and protection of Christian communities. And the plans for a Protestant presence in the Near East gained a powerful ally in Frederick William IV of Prussia, who had visionary ideas for the unity of the Protestant Church world-wide and felt that cooperative action between Britain and Prussia in the project at Jerusalem would be a start towards the fulfilment of his ambitions. With this in view he sent Chevalier – later Baron – Bunsen to negotiate with Britain in the summer of 1841, and arrangements were quickly made for what was to be a Bishopric at Jerusalem, funded in part by Britain and in part by Prussia, with each power nominating alternate bishops.

The idea of a Bishopric, rather than simply a church, had, indeed, been in the plans of the London Society: it had long supported the creation of a Bishopric in the East and, by 1840, had felt that this should be at Jerusalem. Similarly, this had been in Ashley's mind. 'Could we not erect a Protestant Bishopric at Jerusalem . . . ?' he had written as early as 1838.[29] He was thus extremely enthusiastic towards the Prussian initiative: Bunsen's mission was, he wrote, 'a wonder'.[30] He already knew Bunsen, having met him during his holiday in Italy in 1834 and the two men were on close terms. Ashley's cooperation with Bunsen in the summer of 1841 did a great deal to pave the way for the establishment of the Bishopric later in the year. The mission coincided with the last months of the Whig and the first months of the Conservative government. Ashley acted as an intermediary with the Archbishop of Canterbury, with Palmerston and with Peel, the new Prime Minister. There were, it is true, difficulties ahead when Peel actually assumed office,[31] but, by that time, much of the work had been done towards the creation of the Bishopric.

Ashley's work on behalf of the Jews and in the cause of their conversion was thus a major concern in the late thirties and early forties. He was, of course, not alone in the efforts which he made, and religious considerations did not always dictate what was attempted and achieved. There were strong political and economic interests at stake for Britain in the Ottoman Empire, and the appointment of the Consul at Jerusalem and Palmerston's willingness to press the claims of the Jews certainly owed a great deal to such considerations. The return of the Jews to Palestine would, Palmerston felt, strengthen the Ottoman Empire politically and also bring economic benefit. The plans for the church and later Bishopric at Jerusalem were also advanced for secular in addition to religious reasons. Religious communities and the rights which they afforded their protectors were useful diplomatic weapons and such advantages of the Jerusalem Bishopric were well realised in Prussian and British official circles. But Ashley also grasped these points. He stressed the political and economic effects of the return of the Jews in his representations to Palmerston over Young's appointment to Jerusalem in 1838 and also in his memorandum of 1840; these, he felt, would weigh with Palmerston more than purely religious considerations.[32] Similarly, with the Jerusalem Bishopric, Ashley wrote of it as a matter 'political and religious . . . a combination of Protestant thrones, bound by temporal interests and eternal principles, to plant under the banner of the Cross, God's people on the mountains of Jerusalem. . . .'[33] Ashley thus combined political with apocalyptic considerations, and, although his influence on either project must not be exaggerated, it was important. He was a consistent spokesman and zealous worker for the restoration and conversion of the Jews. His concern for the latter meant that his efforts for the former went unapplauded by the Jews themselves, but both formed essential ingredients of his Evangelicalism. He did wonder, on occasion, if his efforts amounted to an improper hastening of the 'times and seasons'; and these questionings illustrate the difficulties sometimes felt by Evangelicals about the propriety of carrying out God's work for Him in ushering in the Second Coming. In Ashley's case, his scruples were overcome by Bickersteth, who assured him that his conduct over the Jews did not amount to undue interference with the Divine plan, but was, rather, cooperation with it, and Ashley's continuing efforts in this field were a mark of his close association with Bickersteth.[34]

A further characteristic of Ashley's Evangelicalism evident in the late thirties was a staunch advocacy of Protestantism. Certain Catholic practices had attracted him in Italy in 1833–4;[35] few were to do so thereafter. Ashley, indeed, became increasingly convinced that Roman Catholicism presented a considerable threat to Protestantism and had to be resisted. He appears to have 'inspired'[36] an article in *The Quarterly Review* in 1839 on the subject of an alleged encroachment by the Archbishop of Cologne on the rights of the King of Prussia; the vigilance of the Prussian ambassador at Rome and the firmness of the Prussian government on the matter had, so the article ran, 'forced the (papal) conspiracy into the light of day and thus conferred an overwhelming obligation on all Protestant Europe. A secret plan for the universal overthrow of Protestant thrones,' it continued, 'has been for some time in operation.'[37] These were very much Ashley's sentiments, and he took every opportunity to express them. He was anxious to mark the Tercentenary of the Reformation in October, 1835, by calling on 'all who entertain(ed) the slightest regard for the Protestant Faith' to contribute to the wants of the Protestant clergy in Ireland. He wrote to S. L. Giffard in these terms, commenting also that these 'meritorious servants of God' had been placed 'in the forefront of the Battle that evangelical Religion is now sustaining against Popery; the religion of Christ against the religion of human nature.'[38] There were also battles to be fought nearer home. In 1839, in his address to the Church Pastoral Aid Society, Ashley referred to rumours that there was to be a Roman Catholic Cathedral in London, 'rivalling', as he put it, 'the temple of Solomon in splendour, though not in purity;' and he asked his audience if it was nothing to see that Papists gave or bequested enormous sums for the advancement of their religion, while the members of the Protestant Established Church did not contribute one tenth of what they ought to contribute. 'Let us then, as Protestants,' he urged, 'stand by that which alone was the pillar and ground of the truth – the Bible, the whole Bible and nothing but the Bible.'[39]

The Church of England, then, must be shown to be a truly Protestant church, based on the Bible. Ashley was anxious that Giffard should make it known through *The Standard* that the King had made a special request for the Bishop of Winchester to preach before him on the Sunday nearest the Tercentenary of the Reformation on the subject of the Reformation. Ashley told Giffard that a 'most beautiful and vigorous sermon' was preached by the Bishop, who 'enlarged with much truth and unction on the blessed event ... Thus the King ... was led in his private capacity to acknowledge the wisdom and goodness of Providence.'[40] Later in October, 1835, he noted that the Tercentenary had been 'observed with much reverence and sincerity. It was far more general than I had ventured to hope.'[41] Ashley's desire to stress the Protestant legacy of the Church of England was the more urgent in the context of the development in the 1830s of the Oxford Movement, with its emphasis on High Churchmanship. This, to Ashley, was more sinister than overt Catholicism since it was, in his view, crypto-Catholicism masquerading as Anglicanism. The beliefs of the Oxford Movement in a Church Universal but not papal were, he felt, nonsensical; they were also dangerous because they were ill-defined. The Romanists, he wrote, 'when they assert their one Universal Church show us something visible and definite,' which could, he felt, be disproved or rejected 'by every force of History and Scripture'. But the High Church party would commit themselves to nothing 'comprehensible and definite'.[42] Again, the emphasis of the Oxford Movement on the Apostolic Succession of Bishops and on the absolute necessity of a priesthood ordained by such bishops smacked of sacerdotalism to Ashley, and it conflicted with his views on the rôle of the laity. In one of his entries to his book of religious reflections in the mid thirties, he observed that throughout the Book of Acts – 'the first and the inspired ecclesiastical History' – the word 'church' was never used to denote the clergy only – it included the whole congregation and recognised 'no distinctive position and powers for the "ordained" Ministry'.[43] Disputes on this point marked the early meetings of the Church Pastoral Aid Society. High Churchmen who joined the Society took exception to the work to be performed by the laity and they withdrew to found their own Society, the Additional Curates Society, in 1837.[44] These controversies were the occasion of Ashley's first struggles with the High Church party – struggles which were to become more bitter in later years. But his views on the men involved in the Oxford Movement – the Tractarians or Puseyites,[45] as they were commonly called – were sufficiently well developed to prompt a letter from the young Benjamin Jowett[46] expressing the opinion that Ashley's fears about Oxford Popery were groundless. He pointed out that many strong sentiments against Popery were to be found in the works of the Oxford scholars, and that 'the charge of a leaning towards Romanism is a difficulty which those who hold high church views . . . have always had to struggle with.'[47] But Ashley was far from convinced, regarding the Puseyites as undermining the Protestant heritage of the Church of England. One of his chief delights about the foundation of the Jerusalem Bishopric, involving the cooperation of Britain and Prussia, was its truly Protestant parentage.[48]

Further, if Ashley was concerned to protect the Church of England as the embodiment of Protestantism, he was also anxious to maintain it as the upholder of orthodoxy. He was alarmed by any evidence of liberal theology and was especially shocked if it appeared that such opinion was in any way countenanced in official circles in Church and State. When two Bishops put their names as subscribers to a volume of sermons published by a clergyman of liberal views, Ashley wrote that things had reached 'a high pass ... as old ladies say, what next?'[49] He was outraged when, in 1838, Dr Lant Carpenter, a Unitarian clergyman in Bristol, published an Apostolic Harmony and obtained permission to present it to the Queen. Ashley wrote to Melbourne to protest, but Melbourne replied to say that he could see no harm in it, provided the work itself was not of a Unitarian character.[50] Ashley found little reassurance in this; the episode suggested to him, as he wrote, that 'heresy is in high feather. Were Arius alive now, he would be promoted to Canterbury.'[51]

Ashley's Evangelical views did not, it is true, exclude cooperation on certain issues with Anglicans of a different shade. Thus, in 1839, Ashley shared in the general opposition of the Church of England to the Whig plans for education. These departed from the practice established in 1833, whereby £20,000 had been granted to the two major voluntary religious educational societies, the National Society, limited to members of the Church of England, and the British and Foreign Bible Schools Society, open to Anglicans and Dissenters. The grant made in 1839 – increased to £30,000 – was not limited to schools run by these two societies; it was, moreover to be administered by a secular agency, a committee of the Privy Council, and schools in receipt of money from it were to be inspected. There was also a proposal to set up a training college for teachers, in which religious teaching was to be 'general', supplemented only by denominational teaching by visiting clergymen for members of their particular church. Members of the Church of England had foreseen such a development before 1839 and had made strenuous efforts to extend the work of the National Society in an attempt to counter the Whig claim that insufficient education was being provided by the two major societies. Ashley wrote to Wellington in August, 1838, telling him of such efforts; they were, he said, sanctioned by the Archbishop of Canterbury and most of the Bishops 'who are extremely anxious to devise some means of resisting the infidel and jacobinical schemes of "national" Education which will assuredly be propounded ... in the next session of Parliament.'[52] When it *was* propounded in 1839, Ashley was also active: he wrote to Peel in May, 1839, telling him that he had been engaged in 'going from one Bishop to another, writing to Archdeacons, issuing Circulars, in short (as the phrase is) "getting up the steam".'[53] He was also in touch once more with Wellington to tell him of a meeting to be held on 28 May, the purpose of which was to explain what the Church had done to discharge its educational responsibilities,[54] and, in the House, he spoke at length in criticism of the Whig plans. The scheme, he said, involved 'the control over and possession of the youthful mind of the country and consequently the temporal and eternal destinies of countless millions.'[55] To give this to a secular authority, on which no Church representative was present, would deprive the Church of England of its influence. The plans for 'general' religion in the training college were equally unacceptable. He supposed that this meant 'moral principles' as opposed to the 'special doctrines and peculiar truths of the Gospel'. The effect of this proposal would be 'universal scepticism or an universal belief that there was nothing necessary, nothing certain.'[56] The provision for special denominational teaching would also mean that Roman Catholics and Socinians were to be trained at the expense of the state to enter schools licensed and supported by the state to teach their respective doctrines, and Ashley declared his vehement opposition to any such departure from the 'true and simple faith of the Gospel' and to the establishment of a system of education which inculcated 'the worship of Saints or ... the denial of the Trinity'.[57] In the face of opposition such as this, the Whigs dropped their plans for the training college. Their other plans, however, went forward, although the Church did gain a right of veto on the appointment of the inspectors of the schools run by the National Society.

On this issue, Ashley did not, indeed, adopt a stance peculiar to the Evangelicals, although his opposition to the religion to be taught in the training college reflected his Evangelical principles. But if he shared in the general opposition of the Church of England to the Whig proposals, it was from the Evangelical wing of the Church that he did so. His religious activities in the later thirties had confirmed him in that position, and from it he was, in the future, to continue to fight many of the battles begun in these years: battles for Sabbatarianism, for missionary enterprise at home and abroad; battles against Roman Catholicism, Puseyism, liberal theology and secular influences.

Although many of Ashley's efforts in the later 1830s were of a religious nature, social concerns were by no means absent. The concentrated activity over factory reform which had marked the earlier part of the decade was not, it is true, sustained in the middle years of the decade, and in 1835 it seemed as if Ashley's position as parliamentary spokesman for the Ten Hours Movement was to be supplanted. The Lancashire operatives in 1835 secured the agreement of Charles Hindley, a millowner and member for Ashton-under-Lyme, to introduce a new ten hours bill, with a clause restricting machine hours. Hindley's business and northern connections may have made him appear a more suitable choice than Ashley,[58] and Ashley had, indeed, remained aloof from attempts to revive the factory question in 1834 and 1835 on the grounds that it was premature to re-open it before the Act of 1833 had come fully into force. For this, he had suffered criticism from those involved in the Lancashire Ten Hours Movement, such as John Doherty.[59] Oastler also had some complaints. Writing to Ashley in April, 1835, he conceded that Ashley could not take the lead in the factory question while he held office, but he might have been more active in countering expressions of opposition to the Act in the House and he might also have kept more regularly in touch with Oastler himself and with Bull.[60] Hindley's initiative was not, in fact, a very convincing one: he was more concerned to restrict hours during which machinery was in action than hours of work, and, although he pledged himself to divide the House on the question of ten hours, this was only to allow both sides to state their case and he was not committed to securing all that the operatives desired.[61] Despite their earlier criticism of Ashley's 'neglect', Oastler and Bull remained loyal to him and distrusted Hindley. Nevertheless, Hindley's move did re-open the matter and in the early months of 1836 the Ten Hours Movement revived as support was organised.

Events, however, were quickly to restore Ashley to his former position as primary parliamentary spokesman for the Movement. For while Hindley was preparing his bill, the government in March, 1836, introduced a bill cutting short the protection of the 1833 Act to children under twelve – thus the regulation of an eight-hour day was not to extend to children between twelve and thirteen, as it should have begun to do, in terms of the Act, in March, 1836. Twelve-year-olds would now count as young persons and work a twelve-hour day. The government had been under pressure from both inspectors and masters to make this move. The inspectors argued that to limit the hours of children between twelve and thirteen to eight hours a day would interfere with adult labour, and the masters were quick to point out that such interference would be ruinous to their interests. But the government's decision spurred the Ten Hours Movement to strenuous efforts: great meetings were held in the country to denounce it, and in London, parliamentary opposition was planned to block the government. It was agreed that Ashley should move the rejection of the bill.[62]

The role prescribed for Ashley implied that he, rather than Hindley, was to play the dominant part. And so it proved, when on 9 May, 1836, the second reading of the government's bill was moved. Ashley spoke at some length.[63] He admitted that he had said nothing about the factory question during the past two sessions – he had been anxious, he said, to give the Act of 1833 a fair chance. But its proposed curtailment aroused his strenuous opposition. It seemed as if it might be the thin end of the wedge towards the total repeal of the clauses protecting children. The second reading was, in fact, carried by only two votes. On 10 June, Ashley asked if it was the intention of the government to take any further steps. The reply was that the division had been too narrow and the matter was to be dropped.⁶⁴

Opposition had, therefore, been successful. The Ten Hours Movement was highly encouraged, and Ashley was restored to his former role as parliamentary spokesman. It is true that, in response to continuing demands for a ten hours bill, Hindley moved in June, 1836, for leave to bring in a bill to amend the Act of 1833. Ashley was opposed to this. He felt that, with the session nearing its end, the time was not favourable for such a proposal and he tried to dissuade Hindley from making it. He expressed such views to the House, but added that should Hindley succeed, he would offer his cordial support.⁶⁵ But Hindley did not succeed. His motion met with a cold reception from the House and the government, and he withdrew it. The episode did nothing to enhance his reputation in the eyes of the operatives – indeed, it reinforced that of Ashley.

In rejecting Hindley's motion, Russell had pledged the government to ensure that the Act of 1833 was enforced. That such a pledge was necessary was an indication of the extent to which the Act had been evaded. The inspectors – only four in number – were too few to cover the whole country; and although they were assisted by superintendents, the powers of superintendents were not clearly defined in such matters as the right to enter all parts of the factory. Again, the arrangement laid down by the Act governing the entry of the child to the factory for work did not work well. The certificate which doctors had to sign and magistrates to countersign to the effect that a child entering a factory was of the 'ordinary strength and appearance of a child of nine years' proved an inadequate safeguard. There were those who posed as doctors and issued fraudulent certificates and magistrates were not required by the Act to see the children for whom they counter-signed certificates. Certificates were lost and sold and children were smuggled into factories without certificates. Further, if action were taken against a factory owner who was alleged to have broken the law, it was often difficult to obtain an impartial hearing, since factory owners might well be among the magistrates who heard the case.

Such evasions always aroused bitterness in the Ten Hours Movement. On occasion, extreme action was advocated, as in September, 1836, when Oastler urged a meeting of operatives at Bradford to counter failure to enforce the law by sabotaging machinery. This went too far for many of Oastler's associates: Bull was distressed by it and Ashley was 'exceedingly grieved' and broke off his correspondence with Oastler.⁶⁶ He himself, however, was not inactive in bringing cases of infringement of the law to the government's attention and, in July, 1836, asked in the House if it were intended to increase the number of inspectors, the present number, he claimed, being inadequate.⁶⁷ In December, 1836, he wrote an article in *The*

Quarterly Review, in which he described the Act of 1833 as 'impracticable' and asserted that it was known to be so by the government and the mill-owners; they had 'obtained a law which they had previously determined should remain a dead letter.'[68]

By the end of 1836, Ashley had also come to the view that the protection given by the Act of 1833 should be extended. In his *Quarterly Review* article, he called for a ten hours bill. 'One thing is certain,' he wrote, 'the people of the manufacturing districts . . . are determined that they will never be quiet till Parliament grant them a ten hours bill. How long is their cry to be trifled with?'[69] In January, 1837, indeed, factory delegates at Manchester formulated a bill according to which no child would enter a factory until the age of ten and no employee would work for more than ten hours a day. In February, 1837, Ashley gave notice in the Commons of his intention to re-commit his bill of 1833 to limit factory workers under eighteen to fifty-eight hours a week. The operatives planned to press for amendments to Ashley's bill to bring it into conformity with their own ideas. But the campaign aroused little support, and Ashley felt that his own efforts would command insufficient acceptance. There was also the consideration that a ten hours bill would involve an increase in the number of hours worked by children, and the government would then have a plausible reason for resisting it. Thus, in April, Ashley decided to drop his proposal.[70]

For the rest of the decade, however, he took every opportunity to ensure that the 1833 Act was implemented, and also to widen its scope. In 1838 and 1839, he spoke at length on the subject of enforcement.[71] If the 1833 Act were good, he said in 1838, let the government enforce it; if bad, let them amend it; and if unnecessary or dangerous, let them repeal it. In 1839, Ashley introduced an amendment to a government bill, which did attend to various matters of enforcement; the amendment proposed a ten-hour day for young persons between thirteen and eighteen. He could not, he said, find it in his heart to let the opportunity go past without asserting the principles which he had so long entertained. He also proposed a further amendment extending the protection of the 1833 Act to silk and lace factories.[72] But all his efforts failed. His attempts to raise the question of implementation in 1838 met with resistance, and so too did the amendments to extend the scope of protection in 1839.[73] Among his critics was Peel, who, in 1838, said that he thought some final settlement of the question was desirable to remove uncertainty among the capitalists; but he was 'no advocate of the plan of Lord Ashley'; he had never taken 'the popular view of the subject'. He felt that the country was threatened with competition and argued that 'the interests of humanity in the large view of the question are to be less consulted by the short-sighted restriction of labour than they are by its perfect freedom. . . .'[74] The division between Ashley and Peel on the issue was a portent for the future.

The decade thus ended on a note of disappointment. In 1839, Ashley was dispirited. He wrote to Giffard that he despaired of any solid and lasting benefit to the operatives. But, he continued, it is 'our duty to labour and faint not – there are few who think with me and still fewer who act with me.'[75] In 1840, indeed, Ashley undertook various important initiatives. The Act of 1833 had made no provision for the fencing of dangerous machinery. The inspectors had no power in such matters and did not have to report accidents. Thus individuals had to seek redress privately through the courts for any injuries which they sustained in the course of their work. In 1840, Ashley, employing H. S. Law as his solicitor, brought actions at his own risk and cost against the proprietors of certain mills in Lancashire on behalf of employees who had suffered injuries.[76] This was successful. Thus compensation of £50 was paid – in a settlement out of court – to Mary Howarth who had been injured and whose family's economic position had been adversely affected by her injury.[77] In another case, which did come to court, the employer admitted liability and paid his employee – Elizabeth Cotterell – £100.[78] Apart from the benefit which these efforts brought to the particular individuals and their families, public interest and comment was aroused. *The Times* carried a leading article in October in which it commented that Ashley was performing for the slave children of Britain what Wilberforce had done for the black slaves.[79] Further, in his parliamentary capacity, Ashley, in March 1840, moved for the appointment of a select committee to inquire into the operation of the Act of 1833.[80] This was accepted by the government and the committee of fourteen members, under the chairmanship of Ashley himself, sat between 11 March and 14 July. It published its Report and recommendations in February, 1841. 'To God above be all the glory!' Ashley wrote, 'Great and signal has been the support that I have received under great difficulties; may He continue it in the final difficulties of its passage through Parliament.'[81] This time it seemed as if his prayers might be fulfilled. On 26 March, the government introduced a measure drafted by the inspectors, which followed the main recommendations of Ashley's committee. More stringent control was to be exercised over the doctors who issued the certificates enabling the children to work and also over the magistrates who countersigned them; children between nine and thirteen were to have their hours of work restricted to seven hours a day, which had to be worked either in the morning or in the afternoon; this would prevent the practice of spreading the hours over the whole day and would make schooling arrangements easier; the protection of a twelve-hour day was extended to the age of twenty-one; a more extensive enforcement agency was to be set up; and millowners were to be banned from acting as magistrates in all cases. Further, on 30 March, another bill was introduced to regulate the position in the silk mills. These proposals represented a considerable step forward in matters of enforcement, and although they did not introduce a ten-hour day, they involved a widening of protection. But none of this was to reach the statute book. The Whig government's tenure of office was slipping away, and Ashley heard that the bills were to be suspended. 'Suspended forsooth!' wrote Ashley, 'and thus another year is added to the period over which wrong and violence are to reign without control!'[82]

Ashley was not, of course, alone in the efforts which were made in the late thirties over factory reform. In addition to the activities of the popular movement, an important impetus towards improvement came from the reports of the inspectors appointed under the Act of 1833. But he remained the foremost parliamentary spokesman on the factory question and kept his contacts – except those with Oastler – with the leaders of the movement in the country. Frances Trollope, mother of Anthony, went to the North of England in 1839, and Ashley sent letters with her to provide introductions to individuals such as Doherty.[83] At the end of the decade, moreover, he extended his efforts in other directions. In 1840, he showed a keen interest in proposals to protect children employed as chimney sweeps. Earlier legislation on the subject had proved ineffective, and the most recent Act – that of 1834 – was due to expire in 1840.[84] The Whigs introduced a further measure in that year, restricting the age of apprenticeship to sixteen and of employment to twenty-one years of age, and Ashley gave it his wholehearted support. The House, he said, had been kind and benevolent towards children employed in factories, and the condition of these children was tenfold better than that of chimney sweepers; he trusted that the system of sweeping chimneys by children would shortly pass away, for it led to more misery and degradation than prevailed in any other Christian country.[85] The Whig bill passed the Commons, but the Lords threatened strong opposition. 'Anxious, very anxious about my sweeps,' Ashley wrote in July. 'The Conservative . . . Peers threaten a fierce opposition . . . I shall have no ease of pleasure in the recess, should these poor children be despised by the Lords, and tossed to the mercy of their savage purchasers. . . .'[86] The Lords did, indeed, put up a strong resistance, but the bill finally passed and received the royal assent, coming into effect in 1842. But even so, it proved to be ineffective in some places and disregarded in others.

Interest in factory children and chimney sweeps did not, however, exhaust Ashley's efforts. He felt that he must concern himself with children not protected by any legislation. In the course of a speech in the Commons on 4 August, 1840,[87] he said that he had 'long been taunted with narrow and exclusive attention to the children in factories alone.' His reply to this was that he had long contemplated action on a broader front and that as soon as he could see the factory children 'as it were safe in harbour, (he) would undertake a new task.' He felt that the time had now come to attempt such a task, and the House responded to his initiative and passed his motion. A Commission was, therefore, set up to inquire into the employment of children in mines and in various branches of trade and manufactures not affected by legislation. Considering the extent of his activities, it was with some justice that Ashley wrote in 1840: 'My hands are too full, Jews, chimney Sweeps, Factory children, all children. . . .'[88]

The impulses behind Ashley's social efforts in the late thirties were, of course, similar to those already evident in the twenties and early thirties, but they were considerably stronger. There was, he felt, a greater need than ever for the governing classes to show an interest in and concern for the working classes. For, by the end of the decade, working-class discontent had reached considerable proportions. In 1837, much of the energy of the Ten Hours Movement had been channelled into resistance to the implementation of the Poor Law Amendment Act of 1834. There were various ways in which the two questions overlapped. It could be argued that the abolition of outdoor relief and the workhouse test of less eligibility – whereby relief could only be obtained inside a workhouse where conditions would be less preferable than those of the lowest paid worker in independent employment – would have the effect of depressing wages and compelling workers to accept long hours in factories;[89] and further, the plans of the Poor Law Commissioners to encourage migration from rural areas with a low demand for labour, to factory districts, with a high demand, was seen as an attempt to flood the labour market in the north with cheap labour.[90] The fact that the implementation of the new Poor Law in the north coincided with a trade depression and unemployment exacerbated feelings of bitterness and discontent; and to many active in the Ten Hours Movement, the Poor Law was simply another manifestation of the hostility which, they felt, the reformed Parliament had shown to the working classes throughout the thirties. Yet the newly established Anti-Poor Law Movement was itself soon to be superseded. In 1838, many popular radicals began to stress the need for further electoral reform, arguing that energy should not be dispersed into campaigns for factory reform or poor law repeal: only a basic change in the distribution of political power, brought about by adult manhood suffrage, could bring about real improvement. Such an avowedly radical political programme – to be enshrined in the People's Charter – did not, it is true, commend itself to all those involved in the earlier movements. Oastler and Bull had willingly turned their attention from factory reform to Poor Law repeal, but neither favoured the Chartist demands, and both retired from active political involvement in the late thirties. Bull began to do so in the summer of 1837; Oastler, always more extreme, remained active for longer. But he too became depressed and disillusioned as he saw Chartism supersede the Anti-Poor Law Movement.[91] Thus Chartism did not swallow up the earlier movements without leaving behind some of the advocates of these movements, but by 1838–9, it had become the dominant working-class movement.

These developments were of great importance to Ashley. He had, after all, taken up the distinct question of factory reform in 1833. When the Poor Law Amendment bill had passed Parliament in 1834, he had been abroad, although he does not appear to have been opposed to it, and he was not involved in the Anti-Poor Law Movement.[92] And, as a Tory, he could have no sympathy for the radical political demands of the Charter. But he did have great sympathy for the circumstances which, he felt, led to the development of discontent. In his speeches in 1838 on the evasions of the Factory Act, he asked the House if it was surprising that there should be grievances among the operatives in the manufacturing districts when they saw a law passed for the protection of young children daily violated 'not only with impunity, but also with the most unblushing effrontery.' The House gave the impression that it was inclined to legislate for the richer rather than the poorer classes; it was thus to be expected that the law would be held in contempt.[93] In an article in *The Quarterly Review* in December 1840, on the subject of 'Infant Labour', Ashley wrote of the 'two great demons in morals and politics, Socialism and Chartism . . . stalking through the land'; and he went on to argue that this was not to be wondered at when so little thought and attention was given to social problems.

> Our system [he wrote] begets the vast and inflammable mass that lies waiting, day by day, for the spark to explode it into mischief . . . all these vast multitudes, ignorant and excitable in themselves, and rendered still more so by oppression and neglect, are surrendered, almost without a struggle, to the experimental philosophy of infidels and democrats.[94]

Thus to Ashley, social effort was vital. He regarded his endeavours in 1840 over the court cases in the light of defending the poor: 'to see that the poor and miserable had their rights.' He had stood to lose several hundreds of pounds but, he wrote, 'had not lost a farthing'. He had done individual justice, anticipated further injuries and soothed, he hoped, 'many angry, discontented Chartist spirits by showing them that men of rank and property can, and do, care for the rights and feelings of all their brethren.'[95]

Paternalism was, therefore, urgently necessary; the governing classes must, in their own interest, meet their responsibilities to the less fortunate. But there were, too, higher considerations at stake. Ashley's new-found Evangelical zeal reinforced his existing tendency to see social questions in religious terms. Individuals could not be expected to lead a spiritual life amidst circumstances of social deprivation. This attitude was evident in his article in *The Quarterly Review* of 1836. What wonder, he wrote, that the factory worker limited 'the operations of an immortal soul to unceasing labour and disgusting sensuality' and never looked higher.[96] The public was under an obligation to see that he had 'both time and opportunity for the cultivation and exercise of his immortal part.'[97] He justified his motion for the appointment of the Children's Employment Commission in 1840 partly on grounds of the effects of work on health and morals: it was right that the country should know at what cost its preeminence was purchased. But more than this was involved; the objects of the investigation were 'beings created, as ourselves, by the same Maker, redeemed by the same Saviour and destined to the same immortality.'[98] They must, therefore, be relieved of the evils which so grievously afflicted them. Thus relieved, they would be enabled to look to their immortal destiny and prepare for the Second Coming. As a firm believer in Providence, Ashley trusted that everything was in God's hands: but he also believed that he should spend his time attempting to do the Lord's work 'till he comes'. In 1841, he reported a remark made by Russell that, in legislative deliberations, no cognisance must be taken of the prophetic scriptures. God, said Russell, had no need of our cooperation to carry out His wise purposes. 'Most true,' Ashley commented, 'but has not the Almighty been pleased to command that we shall do nothing to thwart them?'[99] Social endeavour, like missionary work, was not a way of forcing God's hand: it was a way of harmonising with God's will. For Ashley, then, social endeavour was not only a means of preventing men from becoming Chartists: much more it was a means of enabling them to become Christians and to face their Maker. He wrote in 1840 that laws should assume the proper function of protecting the helpless, but it was more important to spend money on the building of churches and to send forth ministers of religion. 'All hopes are groundless, all legislation weak, all conservatism nonsense,' he wrote, 'without this alpha and omega of policy. . . .'[100]

Ashley was, therefore, as he put it in 1840, 'full of schemes'. He was devising undertakings, 'worthy of all the statesmen thrown into a mass, that ever existed;' and, he added, 'with Parliamentary and oratorical abilities diametrically opposite.'[101] In 1838, however, an anonymous word portrait had commented on the 'faultless' nature of his addresses as pieces of composition. Every sentence was perfect in form; his delivery was 'fluent but not rapid, his voice fine and rich in tone, but not sufficiently exerted to be generally audible; and his manner, though evidently he is quite in earnest, is animated but somewhat cold. . . .' The writer also mentioned as the most striking feature of Ashley's public deportment his 'apparently rigid self-possession'.[102] It would seem then, that Ashley still suffered from an inability to make himself heard, but the portrait is considerably more favourable than Ashley's estimate of himself. Nevertheless, as is clear from his remark of 1840, he still suffered from the nervousness and sense of inferiority which had long been apparent. He chided himself for his defective memory and scanty knowledge and his inability to speak without careful preparation. In 1841, he wrote that he never heard a speech without feeling that, despite its faults, it was better than he could make. He remained 'overwhelmed by (his) own deficiency'.[103] And yet, although he could indulge in such self-criticism, he admitted that he would be 'mightily distressed' if he believed that anyone else thought in similar terms. 'I am,' as he put it succinctly, 'peculiarly constituted.'[104]

Amidst his political duties, there were times for rest and relaxation. There were still visits to the Cowpers' home at Panshanger, although the death of Lord Cowper in 1837 did somewhat change the situation there – he now felt himself more a guest than a member of the family.[105] He took pleasure in the home of his sister and brother-in-law at Rowton. In 1839, Ashley undertook an extensive tour in the North of England and in Scotland.[106] It was, in some measure, a grand tour of aristocratic houses. Thus in Scotland, Ashley stayed at Newbattle Abbey, seat of the Marquis of Lothian, and also at Rossie Priory, the home of Lord Kinnaird; and in England, at Chillingworth Castle, Alnwick Castle, Ravensworth, Newby, Castle Howard and Chatsworth. There were, too, many visits to Cathedrals and Churches: Carlisle Cathedral, Durham Cathedral, Ripon Minster, York Minster – 'the most lovely of all perishable buildings', as he described it. He attended the services in the Cathedrals and also in smaller churches, and, while in Scotland, attended the Church of Scotland. This, however, was more a matter of necessity than of choice, and the service was not to his liking. It was too much dominated by the Minister: 'No responses, No Amens; all is silent, save the minister, who discharges the whole ceremony and labours under the weight of his own tautologies. . . .'

The visit to the Church of Scotland apart, the tour showed Ashley's liking for the traditional and established elements of national life. He had, indeed, contacts with the world of the Ten Hours Movement, but he also moved easily in the world of the country house and enjoyed doing so. Visits such as these, he wrote, revived friendships, made new ones, enlarged the mind and softened the spirit. Ashley had, and always retained, a strong sense of the due place of the aristocracy. Similarly he took great pleasure in the buildings and services of the Church of England: when he heard that hundreds had come by train from Leeds to hear an anthem at York Minster, he wrote that 'taste and due reverence will thus again be diffused and our

Cathedrals will thus again become the boast and glory of our land.' But his own distinctive views and interests also found full expression. Aristocracy was, indeed, desirable, but aristocracy tempered by a sense of responsibility. Thus Chatsworth struck him as too grand: 'everything is magnificent and half of it unnecessary, even to the just display of the dignity suited to the rank and influence of the proprietor – everything in the wildest abundance that constitutes wealth.' On the religious side, too, his evangelicalism was apparent. He found the sermon at Netherby 'good and pious'; and although the Church of Scotland did not please him, the Episcopal Church which he attended in Glasgow did. There, he heard a sermon by Robert Montgomery 'directed against the intellectual scepticism of the day' and inspired, it appears, by the presence of a committee of Socialists. Ashley did not approve of all of it, but he thanked God 'for raising up such a man at such a time for such an audience.' Also in Glasgow, Ashley was heartened by a visit to a Blind School. He was President of the Indigent Blind Visiting Society in England, the purpose of which was to provide scriptural instruction for blind persons, and, on his visit to the blind in Glasgow, he could hardly refrain from tears when he saw 'their easy and happy acquaintanceship with the art of reading the Scriptures.' Social matters, too, did not escape his notice. His holiday reading consisted of the poet Crabbe: 'however represented in poetry or in prose,' Ashley commented, 'I enter fully into all the images and distresses of the poor; it is not, alas, everyone that does so, and Crabbe directs his great powers to the elevation of their cause.' In more practical terms, he visited a calico printing works and an iron works in Glasgow; he walked through the 'dreadful' parts of 'this amoral city' and realised full well the ways in which the 'small alleys, like gutters, crowded with houses, dunghills and human beings' gave rise to disease and crime. Health, in such circumstances, was impossible, and, he asked 'is moral propriety and moral cleanliness ... more probable? Quite the reverse. Discontent, malignity, filthy and vicious habits, beastly thoughts and beastly actions must be, and are, the results of such associations.' Ashley thus showed an interest in matters of public health; an interest later to become more prominent. One great disappointment of the tour was that Ashley failed to see Southey who had, indeed, frequently asked him to take a holiday at the Lakes. Ashley had long wanted to do this, and one of the motives behind the tour was to call on his mentor. But when he visited his house, he found him absent, much to his regret, and he did not, in fact, see Southey again before his death in 1840. Nevertheless, it was a full and varied tour and one which well reflected Ashley's interests: it appears, moreover, to have marked the first occasion on which Ashley actually visited factories and gained some first-hand knowledge of them. He returned to London in November, 1839, 'strengthened in body and mind'.

Throughout the holiday, he had been accompanied by Minny. They were now the parents of five sons and a daughter: the births of Anthony and Francis have already been noted, and the mid and later thirties saw the births of three more sons, Maurice in 1835, Evelyn in 1836 and Lionel in 1838; and of a daughter Victoria in 1837. The company of his wife on the holiday inspired Ashley's gratitude to God that He had granted his prayers for a wife for his 'comfort, improvement and safety; He has granted me to the full all that I desired,' Ashley wrote, 'and far *more* than I deserved.' On their return from holiday, two events took place which were of importance in their lives. One was that Ashley became reconciled to his father. He had not visited St Giles since 1829. His public career had done nothing to overcome the estrangement with his father but had only made it worse. In November, 1839, however, he visited St Giles once again. He wrote that he could hardly believe his senses; 'here I am in St Giles,' he continued, 'reconciled to my father, and actually receiving from him, ardent and sincere marks of kindness and affection! Who would have thought, not I at least, when I quitted this house *ten* years (!) ago, that I should never return to it, until I came a married man, with six children!'[107] But he rejoiced that the reconciliation had taken place and derived great satisfaction from his period of residence at St Giles over the Christmas season. 'It cannot be disguised, I do enjoy being here,' he wrote; and he thanked God for His mercy in softening his father's heart.[108] Sad to relate, it was not to be a permanent reconciliation: in the 1840s, Ashley's activities were once more to provoke his father's wrath. The other event to take place in 1839 was the marriage of Lady Cowper to Palmerston. Ashley looked on his mother-in-law with mixed feelings. On the one hand, he had received great kindness, hospitality and generosity from her and these he could not forget. On the other hand, he could not approve of her style of life. Palmerston was also seen in a double light. It is clear that Ashley had warm regard for Palmerston at the beginning of the decade and had refused Palmerston's offer of office with some regret.[109] But he did not share Palmerston's support for the Reform Bill, and, again, he certainly could not assent to Palmerston's personal conduct. The open liaison between Lady Cowper and Palmerston was an affront to Ashley's Evangelical conscience. He and Minny had not actively encouraged or discouraged their marriage, but it finally came to the point where, as Ashley put it, 'one of two courses was inevitable, at least if public decency was of any value. Either she should marry him or should decline the frequency and familiarity of his visits.' Lady Cowper would not do the second; thus Ashley counselled the first. Lady Cowper, it appears, 'agreed and retracted and agreed again, accepted Palmerston's offer, then postponed it;' but on 16 December, 1839, the marriage finally took place.[110]

Although he had favoured the marriage as the only decent thing which could be done, Ashley felt that the whole episode betrayed a woeful worldliness and vanity. Instead of beginning the 'vanities of life anew and making her account with Politics and fashion,' Lady Cowper should be 'making her account with God.' When he and Minny paid their first visit to Lord and Lady Palmerston at Broadlands just before Christmas in 1839, Ashley wrote that he had found all as he had expected: his mother-in-law

> installed in all the delights and occupations of juvenile life, happy as a bride and thoughtless as an animal. The world and all its fascinations floating before her eyes, balls, dinners, parties, foreign Ministers and foreign ladies, drawing rooms and royalty all thrown together in her exotic imagination to make a very Macedoine of future pleasure.

In the light of his mother-in-law's past kindness to him and his family, Ashley wished her well and desired 'much her happiness on earth'. But he desired 'much more her happiness in heaven' and he prayed that even now it might be 'in the rule of Providence to wean her from the world by giving her a surfeit of it.' Lady Palmerston did not always take kindly to the views of her son-in-law and, after a visit in 1840, it seems that she vented her feelings to Minny: Ashley wrote that Minny 'poor darling, had a sad conflict to sustain after my departure; . . . her mother was seized by her fits of blasphemy . . . and selected me as her object of displeasure. . . . She spoke scornfully of everyone and everything which bordered in the least on serious views and seemed unusually animated in her feelings of abhorrence. . . .'[111] Ashley could clearly be a trial to his mother-in-law, and in 1841, his zeal for the Jerusalem Bishopric, it seems, aroused even Minny's displeasure: 'You din this perpetually in my ears,' she appears to have said 'and it sets my back up against it. . . .'[112] But such expressions of impatience were very short-lived; harmony with Minny was soon restored and relations with her mother were, on the whole, to remain cordial. Ashley was to have further cause for gratitude for her hospitality and generosity and this was also to be true of his dealings with Palmerston.

The later 1830s were, then, important in Ashley's private and family life. And they were significant in the development of his public life. The impulses – religious, moral, social and political – of his Evangelicalism assumed greater strength and increasingly dictated his activities, and his 'schemes' became more varied in their range. His career in party political terms was, for the moment, in abeyance, and yet that, too, was to come into prominence. For, as the decade closed and a new one opened, political events once more focused attention on the Conservative party and on Ashley's role within it.

NOTES

1. See G. M. Ellis, 'The Evangelicals and the Sunday Question, 1830–1860. Organised Sabbatarianism as an Aspect of the Evangelical Movement' (Ph.D., Harvard, 1952), pp. 71–126, for a full analysis of this subject in the 1830s.
2. See below pp. 313–6.
3. See above p. 76.
4. Hansard, *Parl. Debates,* 3rd ser., XXVII, 244.
5. ibid., XL, 1116.
6. ibid., XXXVIII, 545.
7. London, L(ord's) D(ay) O(bservance) S(ociety). Minute Books. Book 2, pp. 80–89.
8. See above p. 105.
9. Hansard, *Parl. Debates,* 3rd ser., XXXVIII, 858, 905.
10. G. M. Ellis, op. cit., p. 118.
11. Hodder, I, 263.
12. S. C. Orchard, op. cit., p. 33.
13. G. M. Ellis, op. cit., p. 50.
14. *The Record,* 16 May, 1836.
15. N.R.A., Shaftesbury (Broadlands) MSS, SHA/PD/2, 4 Oct., 1838.
16. G. F. A. Best, op. cit., p. 68. See also E. Bickersteth, op. cit., pp. 45–59.
17. N.R.A., Palmerston (Broadlands) MSS, GC/SH/4.
18. ibid., Shaftesbury (Broadlands) MSS, SHA/PD/2, 31 July, 1840. His comments on the progress of the war and the conduct of the powers are also to be found in SHA/PD/2 under the entries of 7, 9, 12, 16 Nov., 8 Dec., 1840. Ashley was critical of the sympathy shown by the French to Mehemet Ali and wrote to Palmerston about the war and the French role in it. (ibid., Palmerston (Broadlands) MSS, GC/SH/7–9, 11–15).
19. ibid., Shaftesbury (Broadlands) MSS, SHA/PD/2, 31 July, 1840.
20. ibid., SHA/PD/2, 25 Sept., 1840. A copy of this memorandum is in St G.H., Shaftesbury MSS, C 25019/7th Earl.
21. *The Quarterly Review* (1839), LXIII, 182.
22. ibid., 187.
23. A. L. Tibawi, *British Interests in Palestine, 1800–1901. A Study of Religious and Educational Enterprise* (Oxford, 1961), p. 33.
24. N.R.A., Shaftesbury (Broadlands) MSS, SHA/PD/2, 29 Sept., 1839.
25. ibid., SHA/PD/2, 1 Aug., 1840.
26. Sir C. Webster, *The Foreign Policy of Palmerston, 1830–1841. Britain, The Liberal Movement and the Eastern Question* (2 vols., 1951), II, 762.
27. A. L. Tibawi, op. cit., pp. 38–9.
28. ibid., pp. 40–41.
29. N.R.A., Shaftesbury (Broadlands) MSS, SHA/PD/2, 8 Oct., 1838.
30. ibid., SHA/PD/2, 24 June, 1841. See also R. W. Greaves, 'The Jerusalem Bishopric, 1841' (*English Historical Review,* LXIV, 330–52). The first rough plan for the Bishopric was worked out between Ashley and Bunsen in Dec., 1838 (R. W. Greaves, op. cit., p. 341. See also F. Bunsen, *Memoir of Baron Bunsen* (2 vols, 1886), I, 608).
31. See below pp. 155–6.
32. N.R.A., Shaftesbury (Broadlands) MSS, SHA/PD/2, 1 Aug., 1840.
33. ibid., SHA/PD/2, 12 July, 1841.
34. ibid., SHA/PD/2, 31 July, 1840. See also S. C. Orchard, op. cit., p. 217.
35. See above pp. 95–6.

36. N.R.A., Shaftesbury (Broadlands) MSS, SHA/PD/2, 2 Feb., 1839. Ashley wrote to Peel about the article. He told him that Peel might rely on every statement in it. It was 'as important as any State Paper'. (Add. MSS, 40, 425, fos 403–4).
37. The *Quarterly Review* (1839), LXIII, 104.
38. Add. MSS, 56, 368, f. 31.
39. *The Record*, 16 May, 1839.
40. Add. MSS, 56, 368, fos 2–3.
41. N.R.A., Shaftesbury (Broadlands) MSS, SHA/PD/1, 14 Oct., 1835.
42. ibid., SHA/MIS/1.
43. ibid., SHA/MIS/1.
44. G. M. Ellis, op. cit., pp. 50–53. Hodder, I, 210–12.
45. E. B. Pusey (1800–82), an almost exact contemporary of Ashley, was his cousin. See below pp. 162, 163, 164, 167, 365, 395, 396, 400, 506, 524, 528, 579, 607 for Ashley's dealings with Pusey.
46. Benjamin Jowett (1817–93), son of a collaborator of Ashley in the Ten Hours Movement. See below pp. 516, 527 for Ashley's comments on Jowett's academic and theological career.
47. N.R.A., Shaftesbury (Broadlands) MSS, SHA/PC/45/1.
48. See below pp. 161–2.
49. N.R.A., Shaftesbury (Broadlands) MSS, SHA/PD/2, 19 Oct., 1838.
50. St G.H., Shaftesbury MSS, C 25026.2/7th Earl.
51. N.R.A., Shaftesbury (Broadlands) MSS, SHA/PD/2, 19 Oct., 1838. See also O. Chadwick *The Victorian Church* (2 vols, 1966), I, 395.
52. N.R.A., Wellington MSS, 21 Aug., 1838.
53. Add. MSS, 40, 427, fos 25–6.
54. N.R.A., Wellington MSS, 22, 24, 27 May, 1839. Wellington also strongly objected to the Whig plans and told Ashley that he would refuse to contribute towards the establishment of the system unless compelled by law to do so. (ibid., Wellington MSS, 20 May, 1839). He also wrote a memorandum on the subject (Hodder, I, 250–52). He would not, however, attend the meeting of which Ashley told him since he did not know what policy was to be followed by the Tories in the Commons; and he would not allow Ashley or the Archbishop to quote his opinions. 'If my opinion is to be stated ... in my absence,' he wrote, 'I should have done better to attend and state for myself.' (N.R.A., Wellington MSS, 28 May, 1839. Copy).
55. Hansard, *Parl. Debates*, 3rd ser., XLVIII, 270.
56. ibid., 277–9.
57. ibid., 284.
58. C. Driver, op. cit., p. 311.
59. R. G. Kirby and A. E. Musson, op. cit., p. 385.
60. St G.H., Shaftesbury MSS, C 25035/7th Earl.
61. J. T. Ward, *The Factory Movement*, p. 146.
62. R. G. Kirby and A. E. Musson, op. cit., p. 388. J. T. Ward, *The Factory Movement*, p. 154.
63. Hansard, *Parl. Debates*, 3rd ser., XXXIII, 740–48.
64. ibid., XXXIV, 306–7.
65. ibid., 839–40.
66. C. Driver, op. cit., p. 328. Oastler's letter of Apr. 1835 had urged—in frenzied terms—the need to denounce the Act of 1833 as, among other things, impracticable. (St G. H., Shaftesbury MSS, C 25035/7th Earl).
67. Hansard, *Parl. Debates*, 3rd ser., XXXV, 268. In 1837, Ashley took up certain

recommendations made by one of the Inspectors, Leonard Horner, to help clarify the age at which children were admitted to factories. This involved the deduction of age from height. The Manchester Short Time Committee claimed that this was not in conformity with the Act and was illegal; and Ashley gave notice of a motion on the Committee's behalf, questioning the recommendation. This prompted a letter from Russell, telling Ashley that he himself had received a memorial from the Committee and had consulted the Law Officers of the Crown. As Russell told Ashley in the letter (N.R.A., Shaftesbury (Broadlands) MSS, SHA/PC/87) and in the House (Hansard, *Parl. Debates*, 3rd ser., XXXVII, 665-6), the Law Officers ruled that Horner's recommendation did not conform with the Act, which related only to the strength and appearance of the child and not to his age; thus the recommendations made by Horner were altered. Had they been acted upon, they might have resulted in a more effective implementation of the Act.

68. *The Quarterly Review* (1836), LVII, 416-17.
69. ibid., 442.
70. R. G. Kirby and A. E. Musson, op. cit., pp. 393-4. J. T. Ward, *The Factory Movement*, pp. 168-72.
71. Hansard, *Parl. Debates*, 3rd ser., XLIII, 968-70; XLIV, 187-8, 383-98; 418; XLV, 886-7.
72. ibid., XLVIII, 1073-4, 1078.
73. The ten-hour amendment was defeated by 94 votes to 62. (ibid., XLVIII, 1081). The amendment extending protection to silk and lace factories was carried by 55 votes to 49 (ibid., 1077); but this provoked resistance from the manufacturers and Ashley refused to come to a compromise over it. Thus Russell withdrew the whole bill. (M. W. Thomas, op. cit., p. 156).
74. Hansard, *Parl. Debates*, 3rd ser., XLIII, 975.
75. Add. MSS, 56, 368, f. 9.
76. St G.H., Shaftesbury MSS, C 25155 to C 25158.6/7th Earl.
77. ibid., C 25155.5/7th Earl. £20 of this was used for her apprenticeship in millinery; £20 was paid to her father for clothing; and £10 placed in a savings bank for the girl to start in business. (ibid., C 25155.8/7th Earl).
78. ibid., C 25155.6/7th Earl.
79. *The Times*, 6 Oct., 1840.
80. See M. W. Thomas, op. cit., pp. 175-91.
81. N.R.A., Shaftesbury (Broadlands) MSS, SHA/PD/2, 18 Feb., 1841.
82. ibid., SHA/PD/2, 4 May, 1841.
83. R. G. Kirby and A. E. Musson, op. cit., p. 397.
84. Hodder, I, 295-302. See also Hammonds, pp. 218-20.
85. Hansard, *Parl. Debates*, 3rd ser., LIII, 1092.
86. N.R.A., Shaftesbury (Broadlands) MSS, SHA/PD/2, 4 July, 1840.
87. Hansard, *Parl. Debates*, 3rd ser., LV, 1260-74.
88. N.R.A., Shaftesbury (Broadlands) MSS, SHA/PD/2, 1 July, 1840.
89. N. C. Edsall, *The Anti-Poor Law Movement, 1834-1844* (Manchester), p. 57.
90. ibid., p. 52.
91. C. Driver, op. cit., pp. 393-401.
92. He did, however, ask Oastler how the poor law was received in the north, and received a vehemently worded reply that it would be resisted 'to the *Death*'. Oastler added the comment: 'Oh my Lord, you once had the opportunity of being the Saviour of your Country—but you slumbered and slept and now the Giant is awakening.' (St G.H., Shaftesbury MSS, C 25001/7th Earl). This may be

a reference to Ashley's lack of involvement in the anti-poor law movement.
93. Hansard, *Parl. Debates,* 3rd ser., XLIV, 393.
94. *The Quarterly Review* (1840), LXVII, 181.
95. N.R.A., Shaftesbury (Broadlands) MSS, SHA/PD/2, 24 Aug., 1840.
96. *The Quarterly Review* (1836), LVII, 398.
97. ibid., 422.
98. Hansard, *Parl. Debates,* 3rd ser., LV, 1273.
99. N.R.A., Shaftesbury (Broadlands) MSS, SHA/PD/2, 12 Mar., 1841.
100. *The Quarterly Review* (1840), LXVII, 181.
101. N.R.A., Shaftesbury (Broadlands), MSS, SHA/PD/2, 6 Mar., 1840.
102. Quoted in Hodder, I, 228–9.
103. N.R.A., Shaftesbury (Broadlands) MSS, SHA/PD/2, 13, 20 May, 1841.
104. ibid., SHA/PD/2, 12 June, 1840.
105. ibid., SHA/PD/2, 8 Oct., 1838.
106. This is covered in Hodder, I, 256–81. All quotations on pp. 128–9 are from these references in Hodder.
107. N.R.A., Shaftesbury (Broadlands) MSS, SHA/PD/2, 23 Nov., 1839.
108. ibid., SHA/PD/2, 3 Dec., 1839.
109. See above pp. 58–9.
110. N.R.A., Shaftesbury (Broadlands) MSS, 16 Dec. and 25 Dec., 1839 contain all Ashley's references to this subject.
111. ibid., SHA/PD/2, 5 Sept., 1840.
112. ibid., SHA/PD/2, 22 Aug., 1841.

6
Paths of No Gain and Humility, 1839-1841

The politics of the second half of the eighteen thirties were characterised by the growing weakness of the Whigs and the increasing strength of the Conservatives. The beginnings of this process have already been seen in the General Election of 1835, and the Election of 1837, caused by the death of William IV in that year, provided further evidence of it. The parliamentary position of Melbourne's government remained tenable, but it was precarious, and, in May, 1839, Melbourne felt that his majority was so small and unreliable that he decided to resign.[1] Peel then attempted to form a Conservative Ministry, but this came to nothing owing to difficulties between him and the Queen over certain Household appointments. The Whigs returned and held office until 1841, when they felt obliged to advise a dissolution of Parliament. After the subsequent General Election, Peel had a clear majority of seats in the new House and formed an administration. Thus by the end of the decade, the fortunes of the Conservatives, at so low an ebb in 1832, had been transformed, and this raised the question of Ashley's political future. He was returned for Dorset in 1837 and thereafter, as before, remained actively committed to his 'schemes'. It was to be seen in 1839 and again in 1841 what bearing these would have on his prospects as a Conservative politician.

Since her accession in 1837, Victoria had been on very close terms with her Whig ministers and, in particular, with Melbourne. She looked upon Melbourne as a trusted counsellor, who advised her on the constitutional niceties of her role, but Melbourne was more father than counsellor to the young Queen and she regarded him with warmth and affection.[2] It is not, therefore, surprising that when Melbourne felt obliged to offer his resignation in 1839, Victoria was distraught. Peel realised the delicacy of his position, and, as a token of the Queen's confidence in her new Ministers, asked permission to submit names for the principal offices in the Royal Household.

Agreement was reached over a number of these, but difficulties arose over appointments in the Household held by ladies related to the outgoing Whig Ministers: Peel felt that it was only right for them to join the Ministers in retiring. But the Queen would not part with any of the ladies and, without the demonstration of support which accession to his request would have implied, Peel felt unable to serve. Thus after the Bedchamber Incident, as it was called, the Whigs returned to office, to remain there for two further years. The episode had been very largely dictated by personal considerations. The Queen was young and inexperienced and her attitude to the ladies was caused by her distress at losing Melbourne. She kept in touch with him throughout her dealings with Peel and, indeed, exaggerated the extent of Peel's request. Melbourne continued to give advice, although this was based on the Queen's unreliable version of what was happening and influenced by the views of colleagues more anxious than he to come to the Queen's rescue.[3] No doubt, too, Peel's somewhat cold and reserved manner only made the Queen more than ever determined to keep Melbourne. That she was able to do so, however, was due more to political circumstances than to personal preference: despite his difficulties, Melbourne was able to keep his parliamentary majority intact until 1841 and thus remain as the 'Queen's Minister'. Thereafter, his majority was gone, and, as Melbourne told the Queen, Peel then had the power to extort what he pleased.

The major participants in the episode were clearly the Queen, Melbourne and Peel. But it also had a bearing on Ashley. He was well known to all three. In 1838, he wrote that ever since her accession, Victoria had treated him with kindness. He and his family had spent a few days at Windsor as the Queen's guests in October, 1838: 'unquestionably a great honour,' he commented, 'which demands all gratitude and loyalty from us.'[4] The Queen liked Minny and found her natural and charming, but Ashley's views and personality were less congenial. It may be that the Queen was influenced here, as in most other things, by Melbourne, who was, of course, Minny's uncle, but there was little in common between him and Ashley. Both were prepared to concede the other's good points: Melbourne that Ashley was worthy and Ashley that Melbourne was 'engaging'. But Ashley was too narrow and sober for Melbourne, and Melbourne altogether too frivolous and worldly for Ashley.[5] Ashley was worried about the Whig leader's influence on the young Queen. It was natural, he felt, that Victoria should have turned to Melbourne at her accession and he was prepared to admit that Melbourne did have the Queen's interests at heart. But Ashley also realised, with some perception, that such a close relationship between Queen and Minister was undesirable; her next Prime Minister could never fill the same role and this could only cause pain and distress. And meantime,

Melbourne's influence was unlikely to be for the Queen's good. As a public minister, Melbourne would 'tarnish her reputation and destroy her kingdom.' As her private counsellor, he would, indeed, seek her comfort and welfare, but, Ashley added, 'according to the best of his judgment'.[6] That judgment was, in Ashley's eyes, sadly defective in its appreciation of the Queen's true welfare.

Ashley thus had his own thoughts about the Queen and Melbourne, and the Bedchamber Incident was to bring him into closer dealings with Peel than he had had since 1835. On 9 May, he received a letter from Peel, asking him to an interview. Ashley found Peel in the midst of his difficulties over the Household. Peel was concerned to ensure that the personal attendants of the young Queen would contribute to her moral well-being and he wanted to ask Ashley's advice over this: but, more than that, he wanted Ashley to take a place himself in the Household. Ashley's influence, he felt, would be for the Queen's good – he would bring a serious moral purpose to bear. Ashley appears to have been completely unprepared for the offer and he was, as he put it, 'thunderstruck' by it. He was appalled at the prospect of Court life, which would be trivial, time-wasting and would involve the surrender of his occupations and ambition: 'instead of being a Minister,' he wrote, 'to become a mere puppet.' According to Ashley's account,[7] Peel admitted that the place was unworthy of him, but Ashley feared that the offer would give the impression that Household office was all that Peel considered him fit for, and this wounded his pride. It appears, too, that Ashley mentioned the factory question as a bar to his acceptance of office, but this was 'pooh-poohed' by Peel.[8] Nevertheless, despite his misgivings, Ashley accepted the office on grounds of public duty. He wrote the following day to confirm his acceptance, telling Peel that he was as ready after mature reflection as he had been before to make any sacrifice which Peel might think necessary for his purpose.[9] He had also discussed other Household appointments with Peel and felt that he could suggest many that would be acceptable to the Queen and the public.[10] His own appointment did prove to be to the Queen's liking,[11] but he was, of course, never to occupy it. On 12 May, he wrote to Peel telling him that the Whigs had finally decided to support the Queen in her stance over the ladies of the Household and would thus resume the government,[12] and when he next saw Peel, it was to hear of the difficulties which Peel had experienced and his refusal to serve in the face of them. 'I told him at the end he was a fine fellow,' Ashley wrote in his Diary, 'and that I rejoiced both in his conduct and the step he had taken.'[13]

Although it came to nothing, the episode was not without significance. Peel's request for Ashley to serve in the Household indicated the reputation which Ashley had established by the late thirties. Under the Whigs, the

Court had become known for moral laxity, and Peel clearly felt that Ashley's presence would help to rectify this. 'Your character is such in the country,' he told Ashley, 'you are so connected with the religious societies and the religion of the country; you are so well known and enjoy so high a reputation, that you can do more than any man. . . .'[14] That Ashley enjoyed such a standing might be expected to be a matter of gratification to him, but he was clearly displeased with the offer to which it led. His reaction to Peel's offer of 1839 was, indeed, similar to his attitude in 1834.[15] He protested that he did not want office and that it would interfere with his pursuits. Yet he was hurt that a more substantial offer was not made. This aspect of the matter once more showed the ambition and thirst for recognition which always lurked in Ashley, although it is also true that his acceptance of the offer reflects his sense of duty. 'No man should live for himself alone,' he wrote, 'but should do his duty in that state of life to which it should please God to call him.'[16] And if it was not the first occasion on which such characteristics were evident, it was not to be the last.

Once the crisis was over, Ashley was able to observe events at Court again as a spectator. He dined at the Palace on 21 May and thought the Queen in low spirits. 'Uneasy lies the head that wears a crown,' he reflected, and added: 'Oh, that she knew what alone makes a yoke easy and a burden light!'[17] But he came increasingly to doubt if any such knowledge was to be had from Melbourne, now back in office. He did, indeed, write to Peel, saying that he had heard that Melbourne, alarmed at the progress of radicalism and the 'Jacobinical hodge podge in the House of Commons', was trying to persuade the Queen to revert to the Tories as the real defenders of the Throne, and he also thought that, if Melbourne honestly advised her about the dangers that threatened her Empire, she would get over her long-standing dislike of the Tories.[18] But, in private, he was considerably less sanguine. Melbourne, he wrote in his Diary, might have a 'sincere and even ardent affection for the Queen'; but he had neither knowledge nor courage to advise her according to her best interests. He would be, if not checked, her political and moral destroyer – his society and conversation were 'pernicious to a young mind'. And for all his sympathy for Victoria, he thought that she had revealed herself over the Bedchamber Incident as 'wilful, unthinking, untaught', and he was not confident for the future, for she was 'obstinate to madness'.[19]

Such comments – over-harsh in their verdict on Melbourne and the Queen – remained private, but Ashley was soon to incur the Queen's displeasure over her marriage to Albert in February, 1840. He had written to Peel the previous autumn on the subject of the forthcoming marriage. He had heard that Albert had been selected as a 'young Gentleman' who would not concern himself with politics or affairs of state, but 'would pursue hunting, shooting, dancing and other amiable distractions'. But he warned Peel that, according to the Duchess of Cambridge, this was untrue; the prince was, indeed, the reverse of what was said and entertained 'very stirring and ambitious views'.[20] Such views did not, initially, seem promising to Ashley. The fact that they had been acquired in Germany and might, therefore, smack of theological liberalism, was not a recommendation, and the literary and scientific tastes which the prince was reputed to cultivate might lead him into 'very pernicious society'.[21] Ashley also disapproved of the proposed annuity of £50,000 for Albert. He told Bonham that the existing establishment of Windsor was ample for the Crown, married or single: 'we must not allow the public money to be given to these Adventurers,' he wrote. He was also afraid that large funds might be the source of political patronage and thus recommend that Albert should have 'a sufficiency of pocket money, and a fitting suite of Equerries, but no more.'[22] The annuity was, in fact, reduced in the Commons from £50,000 to £30,000 and the idea, much favoured by the Queen, that Albert should be given precedence next to her had to be abandoned in the face of Tory resistance. The Queen was angry with this, and especially angry, it seems, with Ashley, who had abstained from voting on the annuity as a way of registering his disapproval of the original figure. He had been invited to dine with the Queen, but received a message that he was not to come, as the Queen 'could not receive those who opposed Her Ministers. . . .'[23] Despite this, Ashley and Minny were present at the wedding ceremony, the family relationship with Melbourne apparently having secured the invitation. Ashley was not altogether pleased with the occasion. The overwhelming preponderance of Whig guests demonstrated, he felt, an unacceptable degree of partisanship on the Queen's part, and the ceremony itself was too 'showy' for his taste, lacking in 'enthusiasm and impressiveness'.[24] In future years, it is true, Ashley was very largely to overcome his initial suspicion of Albert, and, more immediately, he felt that Albert's influence on the Queen was for her good. In 1841, he noted that she was less dependent on Melbourne's 'Whiggery' for her social contacts than she had been before her marriage. Nevertheless, she was, he wrote, still 'very zealous to retain them' and he feared that her 'total ignorance of the country and the constitution, her natural violence and false courage, her extreme and ungovernable wilfulness' would lead her to act in a way that would be harmful to herself and the Crown.[25] Thus, although in public a strong supporter of Victoria's monarchy, in private, Ashley was critical of her personality and doubtful if she had the qualities which he considered necessary for her role.

If the Whigs had just enough parliamentary strength to enable the Queen's wishes to be effective in 1839, their position remained weak, and, almost from Melbourne's return, there were rumours that his Ministry could not last very long. In the spring and early summer of 1841, it seemed that the end could not be long delayed. Ashley followed events with interest. On 13 May, he wrote of a 'labyrinth of speculation . . . World busy in assigning offices to men and men to offices.'[26] Finally, on 4 June, Peel carried a motion of no confidence in the government by one vote and the Whigs acted on their decision to advise the Queen to dissolve Parliament and hold a General Election: a decision which Melbourne regarded with some misgivings. He was well justified, for the reaction in favour of the Conservatives, steadily building up in the latter half of the thirties, had reached a high point and was skilfully exploited by party organisation. When the new Parliament met, the Conservatives had a large majority of seats; Melbourne had no choice but to resign and it was for Peel to compose his new administration. The Whigs' tenure of office, which had lasted for some ten years, was at an end. At an end, too, was the period of wilderness for the Tories. Ashley put it this way: '. . . Shortly will begin a new Administration, and God grant it may open new hopes and new principles.'[27]

Ashley himself had been returned, for the fourth time, at Dorset – he was, in fact, returned unopposed 'without trouble and without expense'.[28] His speech at the declaration of the result was indicative of his major concerns in politics. He urged his hearers to stand by the Church, and he also stressed social questions, particularly in relation to the Corn Laws, lately brought into prominence by the activities of the Anti-Corn Law League. He expressed his support for protection, which ensured the 'due maintenance and proper remuneration of the honest industry of this realm'; and he discounted free trade propaganda that Corn Law repeal would be in the interests of the working classes by reducing the price of bread. This, he said, was only one half of the truth; the other half lay in low wages. And he would never consent to any arrangement that would 'abate by one farthing the wages of labour either in the county of Dorset or in the Town of Manchester;' nor would he agree to any scheme which would drive the labourers from the country to the towns. This would simply swell the already over-supplied labour market and lead to work in unpleasant factories for low wages. Ashley thus made clear his support for some form of protection, and this was to be important later, when he had to consider the implications of changing his mind. It is, however, worth noting that he saw the matter in a broader social context than simply the interests of the agricultural and landed classes.[29]

It remained to be seen how far the administration shortly to be formed would satisfy Ashley on grounds of religious, social and economic policy. In personal terms he found Peel difficult to guage. 'Sat next to Peel at dinner last Saturday,' he wrote on 12 July. 'What possesses that man? It was the neighbourhood of an iceberg with a slight thaw on the surface.'[30] He felt that Peel was an honest and upright man, but doubted if there was the true spark of religion in him: a man, he wrote, who would never do a dishonourable thing but would be ashamed of doing a religious one.[31] Further, there was the question whether Peel would appoint 'Puseyite bishops' and elevate liberal theologians. Ashley, indeed, wrote at length to Peel immediately on his accession to office urging on him the perils to which the whole Church would be exposed if men of Puseyite views were elevated to high office in the Church: the Church would be shaken by 'violent commotions'. The Low Church would believe and preach that Popery was encouraged and promoted and Ashley himself would share this view. He did not disguise from Peel his belief that many among the Puseyites were 'Romanists in creed' and would declare themselves to be so 'whenever conscience gets the better of Jesuitry.' Ashley ended his letter by reminding Peel of his awesome responsibilities: tens of thousands had daily earnestly prayed that Peel 'might become an instrument, in the hands of Almighty God, for the advancement and glory of His Church, the welfare of this people, and of all mankind. . . .'[32]

The letter had been mainly concerned with the future of the Church. It had said nothing specific about social matters. But on these grounds, too, Ashley wondered if the new Ministry would be sympathetic towards him. He had certainly disliked the Whigs on political and religious grounds; he had, too, criticised them for their lack of energy on the factory question and, towards the end of the decade, had despaired of any progress being made. But in February, 1841, when there had been rumours that Parliament would be dissolved, Ashley expressed misgivings about a change of government. His major concern, he wrote in his Diary, was to carry factory reform, but, he continued, 'sure I am ("tell it not in Gath") that I have got more and may get more from the Whigs than I shall ever get from my own friends.'[33] At the Election of 1841, Ashley was, in fact, invited by Conservatives at Leeds to stand as their candidate on the factory question. He was gratified at the offer, but declined it. But Lord Jocelyn, who had married Ashley's sister-in-law, Fanny,[34] stood in the election. Ashley did his best to promote Jocelyn's return by means of his name and influence in the north and he was pleased at the reception which, at his request, Jocelyn was given. But despite this, Jocelyn was defeated: 'thus fall my hopes and efforts,' Ashley wrote. 'The Ten Hours Bill, if not retarded, has lost a grand means of advance. . . .'[35] But factory matters still occupied a great deal of his time and attention. In July, he visited Oastler,[36] with whom he had not had any dealings since 1836, when he had been antagonised by Oastler's violent language. Again, in August, 1841, Ashley went on a tour of the factory districts, his first visit to the north devoted solely to this purpose. He visited

Manchester, Bolton, Ashton, Huddersfield and Leeds. He made a speech at each place.[37] Thus at Leeds, he said that he had come to find out what the operatives wanted and to give details of his plans. He told his audience that he had no political object: factory reform was a 'great national question' on which all could unite on neutral ground. His own political views were, he said, 'Blue', but his Conservatism taught him to look on station and property as given to him not for himself alone but as a trust for the benefit of his fellow men. He looked forward to the passing of a ten hours bill as bringing an incalculable blessing to the working classes in the manufacturing districts and as a prelude to other 'healing and beneficial measures'.[38] He was well received, being presented with various addresses of thanks for his past efforts, and he wrote in his Diary of the 'sterling merit and value' of those who had greeted him with 'such respect and affection'. He was reminded and felt the truth of Oastler's observation that the working classes were neither infidels nor Jacobins but loved the Monarchy and religion. But, he added, 'they have been denied the blessings of the one and excluded from the benefits of the other.'[39]

The change in the political situation did, however, raise Ashley's own future: he might be offered office. This was, indeed, a point which had not escaped the notice of the West Riding operatives. Earlier in the summer, their secretary, Mark Crabtree, had approached Ashley, expressing the fear that, should Ashley accept office under Peel, his freedom of action on factory matters would be restricted.[40] Some months earlier, Ashley had already turned the matter over in his own mind. He wrote that he did not 'greatly fancy' office – he would be equally useful and far more happy in a 'private station', since he could not submit to be controlled in all his 'peculiar views and independent action'.[41] Crabtree's letter brought the subject up again, and this time, Ashley was obliged to state his position to others. He replied on 1 June, 1841, giving Crabtree and his friends reassurance. He would never, he said, place himself in any situation where he would not be 'as free as the air' to do everything that he might believe to be 'conducive to the happiness, comfort and welfare of that portion of the working classes who had so long and so confidently entrusted to (him) the care of their hopes and interests.'[42] Towards the end of August, 1841, a further development took place, occasioned by a meeting of master spinners in Manchester, which appears to have been a counter-demonstration to the meetings of operatives which had greeted Ashley. At the meeting, the spinners declared themselves against any bill which Ashley might introduce. Ashley noted in his Diary that this determined much of his course. He was convinced that Peel would 'succumb to the capitalists' and reject a ten hours bill. No human power, therefore, would induce him to accept office. 'I am bound by every obligation, human and Divine,' he wrote, 'not to allow myself to be placed in any situation where I may not be equally, if not better, circumstanced to advance these great interests. . . .'⁴³

The matter did, indeed, reach the point of decision in late August and early September, 1841. On 30 August, Peel sent for Ashley, and, as in 1839, asked him to serve in the Queen's Household. There was to be a further interview on the subject on 2 September. According to Ashley's reconstruction of these interviews,⁴⁴ Peel went over much the same ground as he had done two years earlier. He mentioned the desirability of surrounding the Queen with sound moral influences and praised Ashley's 'unblemished reputation'. Ashley was also seen by Goulburn and was urged to accept Peel's offer; Goulburn's own tenure of office, Ashley reported him to say, would be very much more pleasant if he had Ashley as a colleague. For his part, Ashley displayed no more willingness to accept the offer than he had done in 1839. He told Peel that the situation at Court was different: the Queen was two years older and had a husband. He also mentioned the pledge which he had given to the Factory Movement; he could not, he said, withdraw or modify his principles on this issue without losing the moral character to which Peel attached so much importance. He also rejected various middle courses offered to him: that he might, for example, take office, reserving the right to enter some other arrangement with the Factory Movement. He might then, it was suggested, be able to resume his interest in the subject, although he would not be able to indulge in open agitation. But this, Ashley felt, would restrict his freedom to deal with the matter as he saw best. It would also be damaging to himself and to the government if he were to join Peel's Ministry and then resign from it in a few months in the event of difficulties over the factory question. It would be better for him to decline office on the grounds that the Ministry's mind was not fully decided on the subject. Ashley thus put up strong resistance to Peel's offer, but he agreed to comply with Peel's request that he should discuss it with others: '*although I was resolved*,' he wrote, 'it seemed delicate and polite so to do.'

But the discussions which followed confirmed Ashley in his opinions. The advice of Seeley,⁴⁵ whom Ashley regarded to be a man of good judgment and wide experience, was important. This was firmly against acceptance of office. Seeley wrote to Ashley saying that he could not desire office for him at the expense of character, and, for Ashley to accept office, keeping the factory question in abeyance for a few months and then to resign, would be 'worse than nothing': it would injure Ashley's reputation and be even more damaging to the government. Fortified by this advice, Ashley wrote to Peel, reporting his discussions and enclosing Seeley's letter.⁴⁶ He told Peel that he would 'cheerfully make any *personal* sacrifice' if, by so doing, he would contribute, however slightly, to the welfare of Peel's government.

But he was not willing to sacrifice his principles. On receipt of the letter, Peel again sent for Ashley and told him that the Queen wished to know if he were to be at Court. But Ashley repeated his objections, telling Peel, as he noted in his Diary, that 'a solemn principle and deep feeling of conscience' stood between him and acceptance of office.[47] On 4 September, Ashley wrote to Crabtree to say that he had, indeed, been offered office by Peel, but, having discovered that Peel's views on the factory question were not fully formed, he had declined the acceptance of any place under circumstances which would restrict his 'full and free action' to advance a measure which he considered essential to the 'welfare of the working classes and the real interests of the country'.[48]

This seemed to close the matter, but there was one final episode. On 7 and 9 September, Ashley noted that he had had further interviews with Peel.[49] These were to urge him to accept office in Albert's Household. Peel was, indeed, in correspondence with Anson, the prince's Private Secretary, on the subject.[50] Anson wrote that the same objections need not apply to Ashley's acceptance of an offer from the prince as had applied when the offer came from Peel. A place in the prince's Household would not be a public office; it would not even involve Ashley in vacating his seat and would not prevent his being transferred to another office when the factory question was disposed of. Anson also said that Albert had wished to have a peer for the office of Lord-in-Waiting and would only have made an exception to secure such a man as Ashley. But when Peel put these points to Ashley, he still met with a refusal. Although conscious of the 'kind expressions', Ashley felt that the offer raised the same principle as the previous one, a point which Peel appears to have accepted. Thus Peel had finally to write to Anson on 9 September that he had discussed the proposal with Ashley a second time; but, he wrote, 'I fear his scruples are invincible.'

Thus ended the matter. But it is one worth analysing rather more fully, since it is revealing of Ashley's temperament and personality and it had an important bearing on his political future. It does, indeed, seem clear that Ashley had decided by the end of August – before Peel's offer – to refuse to serve in the new administration. The acceptance of any office would have imposed certain restrictions on his conduct over factory reform, and this is what he ruled out in his letter to Crabtree, with his comments – which he later described as 'calculated words'[51] – that he must be as 'free as the air' to pursue his interest in a factory bill. It was a self-denying ordinance: just as a sense of public duty impelled him to accept Peel's offer in 1839, the same sense, if in a somewhat different context, impelled him to reject the offer of 1841. Ashley, indeed, used very similar words to justify his decision in 1841 as he had in 1839: 'a man is not his own,' he wrote, 'he must do his duty and give himself to whatever it may please God to assign him....'[52]

And both decisions were made after seeking Divine guidance. His action was well received in the north as being consistent with his previous undertaking to Crabtree. The Huddersfield Short-Time Committee passed a resolution on 13 September, thanking Ashley for the 'prompt and independent manner' in which he had declined the acceptance of a place in Peel's government: 'all seem quite delighted with the stand you took,' wrote the Secretary of the Committee. And the Bradford Short Time Committee likewise thanked Ashley for 'resisting the alluring considerations of Government Station.'[53]

Ashley himself, however, was appalled at the 'Station' offered to him and was greatly disappointed that it was not more 'alluring'. He felt that he had given good service to the Conservative cause since his entry to Parliament; his efforts over factory reform had, he considered, 'conciliated thousands of hearts to our blessed constitution' and his influence had been of some importance during the recent General Election, especially in the West Riding. Ashley also wrote bitterly that his pen 'would blush' if he were to detail the praise which he had received from members of Parliament and of the Tory Carlton Club for his services to the state. And after all this, he reflected, he was given the opportunity of employment in the Household '. . . ordering dinners and carrying a white wand.' Ashley would almost certainly have turned down a much better offer, but he was deeply hurt that he was not given the chance. Having been prepared to reject an important office, he was called upon to reject a small one.

Furthermore, Ashley castigated Peel in his Diary, ascribing to him the worst of motives in making the offer. Sometimes, his feeling was that Peel, who, in his view, 'always avoided any principles at all,' only wanted his 'name' to give the government a cloak of morality: otherwise, he would never have pressed on him a department in which, as Ashley put it, he could 'exhibit nothing good but (his) legs in white shorts' and would be taken further and further away from political occupation. At other times, Ashley was less sure of this. The appointment as Lord-in-Waiting of Lord Powerscourt, 'one of the most profligate men of the day', Ashley noted, seemed to destroy the argument that Peel was interested only in Ashley's moral stature. There must be something else. He heard rumours that he had been discussed for a variety of offices, including the Secretaryship for Ireland: but Peel thought him 'impracticable', which, Ashley wrote, meant that he had an opinion and principles of his own. Thus he was relegated to a very minor office, where his principles could do no harm. Ashley at times also resented the way in which Peel made the offer of Household employment: he was hurt that Peel did not say that it was unworthy of him, as he had done in 1839, and he complained that Peel was 'cold and careless'.[54]

Peel's side of the question is, inevitably, less fully documented than

Ashley's. His dealings with Ashley were only a part, and a small part, of the task of forming his Ministry, and he could not be expected to write about them at such length as Ashley, to whom the matter was all-absorbing. It is certainly true that Peel knew Ashley to be a man of firmly-held views, and the somewhat portentous letter which Ashley had sent him on his accession to office can only have confirmed him in this knowledge. Further, Peel did not approve of the ten hours limitation, which he regarded as too severe, and he did not like the agitation surrounding the matter. There were clearly differences between the two men: differences of personality and of view. Yet it can be argued that, far from emphasising these differences, Peel did his best to overcome them. His reply to Ashley's early letter was very polite: Ashley, he wrote, need never make the 'slightest apology' in communicating to him, frankly and without reserve, his own views on public matters or those of others.[55] Again, throughout the interviews over the appointment to his government, it is clear, even from parts of Ashley's own account, that Peel was trying to be as accommodating as possible. He made the point that Household office left Ashley freer than a political appointment would have done, and he appears even to have gone as far as offering Ashley a civil post if he preferred it.[56] And, although he did rule out Ashley's ability to indulge in open agitation while in office, he did not reject the possibility of some arrangement on the question of the factory bill. After certain remarks which Peel made, Ashley was, indeed, under the impression that Peel 'meant to investigate the question with a strong bias to concede it.'[57] Thus Ashley's interpretation that Peel passed him over for high office because he thought him too difficult on a number of issues is scarcely tenable; and also unfair was the further view expressed by Ashley that Peel only offered him civil office once he was sure that this would be rejected. If anything, Peel was trying to find ways and means of getting round difficulties for the sake of securing Ashley. And his desire to secure Ashley owed a great deal to the wishes of the Queen and, perhaps, more particularly, of Albert. Although, on this occasion, Peel was in a much more powerful position than he had been in 1839, he allowed the royal wishes very wide rein. The fact, indeed, that he *was* in a powerful position meant that he could afford to do so, and to give the Queen her wishes over Household matters might well secure her support. The Queen later admitted to Ashley that Peel had behaved generously to her.[58] Thus Ashley was unjust to Peel in his accusation that Peel simply wanted his 'name' as a cloak of morality for his government, and, indeed, his subsequent doubts about this on the grounds of other Household appointments were also unfounded. Ashley himself noted that Peel thanked him for drawing to his notice the failings of Powerscourt; before Peel received Ashley's letter on the subject, he appears to have thought Powerscourt 'among the most moral of mankind' and, when he learned otherwise, he cancelled the appointment.[59] Peel *did* want to make 'moral' appointments to the Household, and that Ashley was among them owed as much to the royal wishes as his own. Finally, if Ashley, on occasion, complained of Peel's demeanour, at others, he acknowledged that Peel was 'very kind in manner' and, indeed, reported Peel as saying that he had never in the whole of his public life 'experienced half so much pain' as he did on Ashley's refusal of office.[60]

Ashley's comments on his dealings with Peel have, therefore, to be treated with some care. It was certainly unfortunate that he was offered a post over which he had shown such reluctance two years earlier – his feelings of distress and disappointment were understandable and no doubt contributed to the frame of mind in which he accused Peel of sinister and unworthy motives. But he had accepted a Household office in 1839, and, especially in view of the Queen's and Albert's feelings, it was not unnatural that he was offered it again in 1841. Peel cannot be said to have wanted to make use of Ashley's morality; nor did he seek to make Ashley's independent views a pretext for relegating him to an unimportant office. Rather, he misjudged the extent of Ashley's morality and independence in the light of the undertaking which Ashley had given to Crabtree. The episode showed even more clearly than those of 1834 and 1839 what Ashley was made of. His rejection of Peel's offer showed his sense of duty and principle; his reaction to it revealed the more human traits of wounded self-esteem and hasty and irrational judgment.

In the course of a few days, it is true, milder counsels prevailed. At Broadlands on 11 September, Ashley reflected on the fact that Peel had completed his Ministry, and, as he put it, revised his own course of action. He felt more and more assured that he had been led to a right judgment and was conscious of a 'real solid peace and internal satisfaction'. And looking to the future he wrote:

> I want not office. I will run, by God's help, the course I have begun, steering clear between right-hand defections and left-hand fallings off. My finances are low, very low, but I and mine have yet, blessed be His name, the barrel of meal and the cruse of oil.[61]

Further, relations with Peel were soon to be on a more cordial note. On 18 September Peel wrote to Ashley, asking for permission to submit Ashley's name to the Queen for appointment to a vacancy in the Ecclesiastical Commission. Such an appointment would, Peel wrote, 'secure to the Church the valuable services of a most able and zealous friend to the best interests of the Establishment.'[62] Ashley replied, saying that it gave him great pleasure to learn that Peel entertained 'so favourable an opinion of (his) zeal and capacity to serve the true interests of our Established Church.'[63] Thus he accepted the offer, noting in his Diary that it brought 'no salary and no official restraint'.[64] It did not, therefore, restrict his activities over factory reform, but the exchange of letters with Peel bore little trace of the earlier bitterness of Ashley's feelings.

Nevertheless, the events of 1841 did have considerable significance for the future. Although he had, for several years, been involved in extra-parliamentary pursuits, it seems that it was only in 1841 that Ashley fully realised the bearing which they were to have on his political career. He had, indeed, protested in 1834 that office would interfere with his various activities; he did the same in 1839. But on both occasions, he accepted office. In 1841, he rejected it. He claimed that he had 'foreseen and forechosen' the issue and that he had known that his commitment to the operatives before the dissolution had shut the 'door of power against (his) own entrance'. But the matter was put to the test by Peel's offer and, in rejecting it, Ashley realised that he had taken a decisive step and was not simply contemplating it. 'I have taken that course,' he wrote, 'which will exclude me, perhaps for ever, from a share in the official government of this kingdom.' There were 'paths of profit and honour' : there were 'paths of "no gain" and humility'.[65] The realisation that he had finally decided to follow the latter was a painful one: he wrote that it took from him all the pleasure and much of the hope which he had in public life.[66] All this, no doubt, served to heighten the emotion which Ashley displayed at the time and may also explain some of the venom which he heaped on Peel as the man who brought him face to face with the consequences of his actions. And, although in the immediate aftermath, Ashley showed signs of being resigned to his political lot and reconciled to his party leader, it remained to be seen how far these would last as the new Ministry set out on its business.

NOTES

1. The government's majority was reduced to 5 on its decision to suspend the legislative assembly of Jamaica.
2. See P. Ziegler, *Melbourne* (1976), p. 256 ff.
3. ibid., pp. 290–98.
4. N.R.A., Shaftesbury (Broadlands) MSS, 11 Oct., 1838.
5. See Battiscombe, p. 112.
6. N.R.A., Shaftesbury (Broadlands) MSS, SHA/PD/2, 13 Oct., 1838.
7. ibid., SHA/PD/2, 11 May, 1839. This entry covers the whole interview.
8. ibid., SHA/PD/2, 31 Aug., 1841. This was written more than two years after the event.
9. Add. MSS, 40, 426, f. 337.
10. N.R.A., Shaftesbury (Broadlands) MSS, SHA/PD/2, 11 May, 1839. Also Add. MSS, 40, 426, f. 264.

PATHS OF NO GAIN AND HUMILITY, 1839–1841   151

11. A. C. Benson and Viscount Esher (eds.), *The Letters of Queen Victoria, 1837–1861* (3 vols 1907) I, 207.
12. Add. MSS, 40, 426, f. 380.
13. N.R.A., Shaftesbury (Broadlands) MSS, SHA/PD/2, 14 May, 1839.
14. ibid., SHA/PD/2, 11 May, 1839.
15. See above pp. 97–9.
16. N.R.A., Shaftesbury (Broadlands) MSS, SHA/PD/2, 11 May, 1839.
17. ibid., SHA/PD/2, 21 May, 1839.
18. Add. MSS, 40, 427, fos 15–16.
19. N.R.A., Shaftesbury (Broadlands) MSS, SHA/PD/2, 21 May, 1839.
20. Add. MSS, 40, 427, fos 199–200.
21. N.R.A., Shaftesbury (Broadlands) MSS, SHA/PD/2, 6 Feb., 1840.
22. Add. MSS, 40, 427, fos 269–70.
23. The Seventh Duke of Wellington (ed.), *Wellington and his Friends: Letters of the First Duke* (1965), p. 131.
24. N.R.A., Shaftesbury (Broadlands) MSS, SHA/PD/2, 10 May, 1840.
25. ibid., SHA/PD/2, 29 June, 1841.
26. ibid., SHA/PD/2, 13 May, 1841.
27. ibid., SHA/PD/2, 24 July, 1841.
28. ibid., SHA/PD/2, 6 July, 1841.
29. ibid., SHA/MIS/9.
30. ibid., SHA/PD/2, 12 July, 1841.
31. ibid., SHA/PD/2, 24 July, 1841.
32. Add. MSS, 40, 483, fos 12–15.
33. N.R.A., Shaftesbury (Broadlands) MSS, SHA/PD/2, 13 Feb., 1841.
34. See Battiscombe, p. 131.
35. N.R.A., Shaftesbury (Broadlands) MSS, SHA/PD/2, 3 July, 1841.
36. Oastler had been imprisoned for debt owed to his employer, Thomas Thornhill in Dec. 1840. (C. Driver, op. cit., p. 413).
37. N.R.A., Shaftesbury (Broadlands) MSS, SHA/PD/2, 2, 6 Aug., 1841.
38. *The Leeds Intelligencer*, 7 Aug., 1841.
39. N.R.A., Shaftesbury (Broadlands) MSS, SHA/PD/2, 6 Aug., 1841.
40. Hodder, I, 339–40.
41. N.R.A., Shaftesbury (Broadlands) MSS, SHA/PD/2, 18 Feb., 1841.
42. St G.H., Shaftesbury MSS, C 25039/7th Earl. 1 June, 1841 (Copy).
43. N.R.A., Shaftesbury (Broadlands) MSS, SHA/PD/2, 27 Aug., 1841.
44. ibid., SHA/PD/2, 30 Aug., 3 Sept., 1841.
45. R. B. Seeley (1798–1886). A publisher, book-seller and author, who had been a founder-member of the Church Pastoral Aid Society and was active in many evangelical pursuits.
46. Add. MSS, 40, 483, fos 16–17 (Ashley to Peel) and fos 18–19 (Seeley to Ashley).
47. N.R.A., Shaftesbury (Broadlands) MSS, SHA/PD/2, 3 Sept., 1841.
48. Quoted by Hodder, I, 359. Ashley wrote in similar terms to James Turner, the chairman of the Lancashire Central Committee. (J. T. Ward, *The Factory Movement*, p. 228).
49. N.R.A., Shaftesbury (Broadlands) MSS, SHA/PD/2, 7, 9 Sept., 1841.
50. Add. MSS, 40, 432, fos 67–8, 100, 102, 104.
51. N.R.A., Shaftesbury (Broadlands) MSS, SHA/PD/2, 3 Sept., 1841.
52. ibid., SHA/PD/2, 3 Sept., 1841.
53. St G.H., Shaftesbury MSS, C 25018.25/7th Earl (Huddersfield): C 25018.31/7th Earl (Bradford).

54. Ashley's expressions of disappointment and disapproval of Peel are in N.R.A., Shaftesbury (Broadlands) MSS, SHA/PD/2, 1, 2, 3 Sept., 1841.
55. Quoted by Hodder, I, 347–8.
56. Ashley makes a brief reference to this in N.R.A., Shaftesbury (Broadlands) MSS, SHA/PD/2, 3 Sept., 1841.
57. ibid., SHA/PD/2, 3 Sept., 1841.
58. N. Gash, op. cit., p. 275.
59. N.R.A., Shaftesbury (Broadlands) MSS, SHA/PD/2, 7 Sept., 1841. See also N. Gash, op. cit., p. 274.
60. N.R.A., Shaftesbury (Broadlands) MSS, SHA/PD/2, 3 Sept., 1841.
61. Ibid., SHA/PD/2, 11 Sept., 1841.
62. St G.H., Shaftesbury MSS, C 25022.11/7th Earl.
63. Add. MSS, 40, 483, fos 24–5.
64. N.R.A., Shaftesbury (Broadlands) MSS, SHA/PD/2, 17 Sept., 1841. (This would seem to be mis-dated, since Peel's letter is dated 18 Sept.).
65. ibid., SHA/PD/2, 3 Sept., 1841.
66. Add. MSS, 40, 483, f. 17.

7
Prophecy and Protestantism, 1841–1846

In October, 1841, Ashley took his seat on the Ecclesiastical Commission to which Peel had appointed him the previous month. The efforts of the Commission to strengthen the Established Church by making its organisation more efficient and effective[1] had much in common with what Ashley desired for the Church, but his first experience of it did not greatly impress him. 'I see clearly I shall not like it,' he wrote.[2] It may be that the Commission was too closely bound up with the authority of the Bishops for Ashley's liking; whatever the reason, he was not to be a frequent attender at its meetings,[3] although this was often true of the lay members. His membership of the Commission certainly did not diminish his commitment to the Evangelical wing of the Church of England nor did it detract from his participation in the Evangelical societies which he had begun fully to support in the 1830s. The Church Pastoral Aid Society retained his firm adherence and he was present regularly at its annual meetings in May, reviewing the previous year's efforts and urging its members to greater endeavours to 'promote the diffusion of Evangelical truth.'[4] Ashley also retained his chairmanship of other Evangelical bodies, such as the Indigent Blind Visiting Society, with its missionary role to blind persons; he was a member of the committee of the Scripture Readers' Society, founded in 1844[5] with the object of providing laymen as Scripture readers who would act with the approval of the Bishop of the diocese and under the direction of the incumbent of the parish; and he was chairman of a committee set up in 1844 to arrange for the distribution of funds for Church Extension. This scheme was one of several which were mooted and put forward for this purpose in the 1840s. Peel himself in 1843 introduced a bill which increased the funds at the disposal of the Ecclesiastical Commissioners so that new churches might be built and new parishes created,[6] and Ashley consulted Peel over the scheme in which he was privately involved.[7] This entailed the distribution of funds which were voluntarily donated; the committee which made arrangements for the spending of these funds through trustees was entirely lay; and in every case in which a church was built wholly or partly, from the fund, particular care had to be taken that 'good and ample accommodation for the poor of the parish' was provided.[8] Ashley was thus concerned to spread the gospel by such 'unofficial' means, and he saw an urgent need to do so. In 1845, he told the annual meeting of the Church Pastoral Aid Society that foreign missions were very necessary: but it was wise to begin with those who might be considered as 'of the household of our faith, who are at the moment just as much in need of evangelicization as many of the most benighted Heathens to which Missions can be directed.'[9] Not, indeed, that Ashley neglected foreign missions. He became Vice-President of the Church Missionary Society in 1845 and, in an address to its annual meeting that year, commended its efforts to employ missionaries indigenous to the country concerned: 'rely on it,' he said, 'that this is the surest way to evangelise a country. . . .'[10] And, in 1845, he deputised for the chairman of the Irish Society of London, the purpose of which was to use the Irish language for missionary endeavour in Ireland. This, Ashley said, was the 'only way in which we can carry the light of the Gospel to the remotest parts of Ireland.'[11] In 1846, Ashley's efforts in these directions were well illustrated by his chairmanship of the Church of England's Young Men's Society for Aiding Missions at Home and Abroad. This had been founded in 1845 and aimed to spread 'a missionary spirit' among young men by disseminating missionary knowledge and promoting a 'heartfelt interest' in four agencies of the Church of England which embraced the mission field: the Church Pastoral Aid Society, the Colonial Church Society, the Society for the Conversion of Jews and the Church Missionary Society. Ashley was, he said, delighted to contemplate a society of this kind.[12]

Ashley's missionary zeal was thus in full prominence in the first half of the forties, but the mission to the Jews, in particular, occupied a great deal of his time and attention, especially at the beginning of Peel's Ministry. Negotiations for the Jerusalem Bishopric were well advanced when the change of Ministry took place and, by early October, 1841, a bill giving the Crown power to authorise the consecration of a Bishop had passed Parliament and was on the statute book.[13] Britain was to nominate the first Bishop. The appointment was offered first to Alexander McCaul, a Hebrew scholar of Trinity College, Dublin, and a leading member of the London Society for the Conversion of the Jews, but he declined it on the grounds that it would be better filled by a Jewish convert. This suggestion was adopted and the Bishopric was, therefore, offered to and accepted by Michael Solomon Alexander, who had been born in Poland as a Russian subject and had come to Britain in 1820. He had been a rabbi in Plymouth until his conversion to Christianity in 1825. He became a missionary of the Jews Society, and, in the years immediately before his appointment to the Bishopric, had taught Hebrew at King's College, London.[14]

Ashley took a very active part in all of this. In August, he had written to Frederick William IV thanking him for 'the noble and unparalleled part that, as a Christian and Protestant Monarch (he had) begun, under the blessing of Almighty God, to sustain in the history of His Church and people.'[15] The letter evoked a warm response, which was delivered by Bunsen to Ashley: the King wrote that he had been much encouraged by the zeal which Ashley had devoted to the cause.[16] Ashley cooperated[17] very closely with Bunsen in the negotiations over the creation of the Bishopric; he was present with Bunsen at a meeting held in early September at Addington Lodge, near Croydon, the official property of the Archbishop of Canterbury, at which the basis of the arrangement was set out.[18] He was also active in further meetings which tidied up the details: on 8 September, he noted in his Diary that he and Bunsen had spent two hours with the Archbishop, Howley, talking about the Jews.[19] When the bill creating the Bishopric passed Parliament, Ashley recorded his delight. His prayer was that 'the blessing of the God of Abraham, of Isaac, and of Jacob, the Father of our Lord Jesus Christ, be with it now and for ever.'[20] And, according to Bunsen, it was Ashley who suggested the name of Alexander as the first Bishop, after McCaul had turned it down.[21]

Nevertheless, there were certain difficulties before Alexander was finally consecrated and set sail. The new government was not as sympathetic to the whole matter as the previous one had been. This was not primarily on religious grounds: Peel said that, as a religious enterprise, they were prepared to give aid to its success.[22] The government was, however, less enthusiastic than the Whigs on diplomatic grounds. Peel and, more especially, Aberdeen, the Foreign Secretary, were more anxious than Palmerston had been for good relations with France and less hostile in their attitude to Russia. The supporters of the project had, indeed, been aware that difficulties might occur on the change of government and this was one reason for the speed with which the negotiations were conducted. Bunsen certainly found Aberdeen much less well disposed than Palmerston. He had an interview with Aberdeen which, it appears, was difficult and unpleasant. This aroused Ashley's anger: 'a wary, comfortless creature' was his description of Aberdeen: 'he has no more *religion* than Palmerston and far less will, experience, generosity and British feeling.'[23] To counteract Aberdeen's influence, Ashley wrote to Peel on 29 September, sending him an extract from a letter which he had received from Bickersteth telling of large meetings in Derby and Liverpool on behalf of the Jews Society – twenty-four sermons had been preached on a single Sunday for the Society. Ashley wrote that he was anxious to bring this to Peel's attention as a sample of the feeling which prevailed on the subject, since he had heard that there might be 'difficulties raised against the progress of these great measures.' He hoped that nothing would come of these. 'The *unparalleled* aid which the late government afforded to us in these respects,' he added, 'would form a painful and *pernicious* contrast with any obstruction or doubts that might be suggested on the part of (the) Conservatives.'[24] Ashley appears to have been re-assured by Peel's reply, for he wrote to Peel again on 30 September, saying that the difficulty had been with Aberdeen: but if Peel raised no objection, none could be raised 'at least so as to be effective.'[25] On 12 October, Ashley was hopeful that all difficulties had been set at rest, and commented that had Bunsen arrived a month later the whole matter would have been much delayed.[26] But Ashley's optimism was even yet somewhat premature. Archbishop Howley had been enthusiastic for the project but then appeared to have second thoughts. He felt that he needed to take time to consider the propriety of consecrating a former Jew: this might not be acceptable to Greek Christians. Howley asked Ashley to see him on three occasions and said that he himself was not averse to the project, and Ashley felt that the doubts had been sown in the Archbishop's mind by Aberdeen.[27] Further, there were misgivings about the project among certain of the High Church party in the Church of England who disliked the strongly Protestant overtones of an ecclesiastical alliance with the United Evangelical Church of Prussia, which incorporated Lutherans and Calvinists. Howley thus felt it necessary to tread warily, and the consecration of Alexander was postponed on more than one occasion. Moreover, Ashley still had difficulties with Peel. He met Peel on 22 October; he recorded later the same day that he never wished to have another interview. 'He was an exaggeration and caricature,' Ashley wrote, 'of his habitual coldness.' Ashley pressed on Peel the desirability of a steamboat being provided by the government to take the Bishop to Jaffa. The land journey, he said, would take much too long. The Bishop had a large family and his wife was pregnant, and there was a 'large suite of persons connected with the mission.' But Ashley noted: 'nothing of this touched him.' Peel talked of provoking the Ottoman Porte and the need to do things quietly. According to his report, Ashley did not neglect the opportunity of saying that the Conservative government had done nothing towards the project; the Prussian King had contributed half of the endowment of the Bishopric and the British public the other half; there was deep and intense interest in the country in the subject. As Ashley recorded the interview, he concluded: '*all* we ask of *our own* Government is the loan of a steamboat to carry out the Bishop.' Peel said that he would speak to Aberdeen: 'thus ended a short interview,' Ashley noted, 'equally unpleasant and odious, I should think, to both parties.'[28]

Nevertheless, the difficulties were soon to be resolved. On 24 October, Ashley received a short letter from Peel,[29] stating that orders would be given for an Admiralty steamboat to carry the Bishop and his immediate suite to the coast of Syria. Ashley wrote in his Diary that had he not been almost accustomed, 'so to speak,' to God's mercies, he would have disbelieved it.[30] He replied to Peel's letter, thanking him,[31] although privately, he felt that Peel's concession had been one of 'calculation' not sympathy; he recalled that he had enumerated the services of the late government and had indicated the contrast between this and the conduct of Peel's Ministry.[32] This, however, was a step forward, and on 26 October, Ashley recorded his pleasure at hearing that many of the High Church were in favour of the Bishopric – the more moderate among the High Churchmen, indeed, felt that the project offered an opportunity to introduce a fully episcopal system to Prussia. Finally, on 7 November, Alexander's consecration by the Archbishop, assisted by the Bishops of London and Rochester, took place in the chapel of Lambeth Palace. Ashley was present at the ceremony. He felt that Howley had risen 'infinitely above himself' in his conduct of the consecration, and he was elated by the occasion:

> The whole thing [he wrote] was wonderful, and to those who have long laboured and prayed in the Jewish cause, nearly overwhelming to see a native Hebrew appointed, under God, to revive the Episcopate of St James, and carry back to the Holy City the truths and blessings we Gentiles had received from it....[33]

A further delight to Ashley was the first service conducted by Alexander as Bishop the night after the consecration. The sermon was, Ashley wrote, 'deep and feeling' and well suited to the occasion,[34] and the benediction was the 'first episcopal benediction that had fallen from Hebrew lips for seventeen hundred years.'[35] There was some delay over the vessel on which Alexander was to sail to take up his charge. He refused to sail on the first ship supplied by the Admiralty: H.M.S. *Infernal*. A second ship bore the name H.M.S. *Devastation*. This proved acceptable to the new Bishop, and, on 29 November, he set sail.[36] Ashley noted that this was the day after the first Sunday in Advent: the departure of the 'one who telleth good tidings to Zion' struck him as a remarkable coincidence.[37] It certainly marked the completion of a project on which he had long set his heart. His absorption in the project had caused some temporary domestic friction with Minny,[38] but he recorded with pride in November that his four 'blessed boys', Anthony, Francis, Maurice and Evelyn, had brought him some money for the Bishopric; he had spoken to the elder boys and they had 'cheerfully acquiesced'; and the 'little ones, hearing from them, burned to do likewise.'[39]

To mark the successful achievement of their joint effort, Ashley sent his portrait to Bunsen together with a book of prayers from the writings of the English Fathers. It was suitably inscribed as a memorial

> of our solemn, anxious and by God's goodness, successful labours, which, under His grace, we have sustained for the consolidation of Protestant truth, the welfare of Israel and the extension of the Kingdom of our blessed Lord.[40]

And he was overjoyed when, on 24 November, he received news from Bunsen that the Queen wished the King of Prussia to be Godfather to her newly born son – this had been announced by Prince Albert at an interview between Bunsen and the Prince, which, indeed, Ashley had obtained. 'Where are we? What will happen next? There is no end to God's goodness,' Ashley wrote. Such an event would have been satisfactory at any time; now it was 'clearly providential', coming as it did after the union of the Anglican and German Churches.[41] Ashley wrote to Bunsen that the King must accept the invitation and come,[42] and this, indeed, happened in January, 1842. Ashley noted on 28 January that he was to meet the King the following day at Bunsen's house and had asked leave to take Anthony and Francis, for they would 'long remember the sight of a "good King".'[43] At the lunch held at Bunsen's house, he proposed the King's health. Ashley also went to Windsor in connection with the visit, but he did not approve of the arrangements for the departure of the guests: 'turned out on *Sunday morning!* That was a great indecency,' he wrote.[44] It appears to have arisen from a miscalculation of dates by the Queen: 'nevertheless she would not correct it,' wrote Ashley. Nor would Ashley travel: he went for the remainder of Sunday to Salt Hill, nearby. Frederick William, however, travelled to London. This, Ashley felt, was a 'sad error' and would offend many religious people. Another error of which he thought the King guilty was a visit to the theatre – this was 'almost incompatible with the great and holy mission' on which he had come. Ashley was 'sadly grieved' by anything which tended to 'abate the effect of his presence,' and wrote to Bunsen – in vain – about the theatre expedition.[45] Nevertheless, these incidents apart, Ashley derived great pleasure and satisfaction from the visit and, early in February, presented an address to the King on behalf of the London Society for the Conversion of the Jews, welcoming Frederick William to Britain and expressing gratitude for the part which he had played in the setting up of the Jerusalem Bishopric.[46] It was warmly received by the King.[47]

The fortunes of the Bishopric[48] were not, in fact, to be very happy. There were difficulties over the endowment fund. It was not raised in time to yield an income for the first year and, on Ashley's prompting, the London Jews

Society had to grant £600 from its funds to make up the Bishop's revenues for the first year.[49] Again, the role of the Bishop was circumscribed by assurances given to the Turkish envoy by Aberdeen, anxious to minimise the possible diplomatic repercussions of the Bishopric: these were to the effect that no special protection or privileges were requested for the Bishop and that his mission was not to extend to Mohammedans or Christian subjects of the Sultan. His mission was only to be to the Jews, and even this presented difficulties since, although most Jews in Palestine were Turkish subjects, there were many who came from Russia and elsewhere in Europe and who were under the protection of the Russian Consul. Thus Alexander could only extend his missionary efforts to Jews who were subjects of the Ottoman Empire and the British Consul was under orders to abstain from assisting his endeavours even in this task.[50] Alexander himself was a sincere and well-intentioned man. It may be that he lacked the qualities of diplomacy necessary for his work, but there is no doubt that the work was very difficult.[51] The Jews, moreover, proved intractable and unamenable to such efforts as were made to convert them, and very few converts were made. With the exception of the Armenian Church in Palestine, Alexander's relations with the Eastern Orthodox Churches were never very close, and relations with the Presbyterian mission were somewhat tense. There were, too, great difficulties with the Sultan. The unauthorised start to the building of the church was not allowed to proceed. In 1845, Ashley presented a memorial to Aberdeen signed by the Archbishop of Canterbury, the Bishop of London and numerous clergy and laity of the Church of England,[52] and representations were made to the Sultan on the subject. But he still refused to grant full permission for the building plans, and, when Alexander died in 1845, the church was still not built. The difficulties distressed Ashley and he was much dismayed by Alexander's death: 'it buries at once half my hopes for the speedy welfare of our Church, our nation and the Children of Israel! What an overthrow to our plans,' he wrote.[53] Nevertheless, he did not lose faith in the work of the London Jews Society. In May 1845, he told it that he rejoiced that it was 'called to advance by their instrumentality the practical and spiritual welfare of the Hebrew people,'[54] and, at the 1846 meeting, although expressing regret at the death of Alexander, 'cut off in the midst of his labours,' he also expressed confidence in his successor, Samuel Gobat, who was appointed to the see by Prussia. Gobat, a French-speaking Swiss, had come to Britain in 1825 and had worked as a missionary for the Church Missionary Society in Abyssinia. Ashley referred to him as a 'distinguished missionary' and rejoiced that 'a man of (his) temper, character and principles ... should have been appointed to that high post.'[55]

Far from being discouraged by the difficulties of the Jerusalem Bishopric, Ashley became deeply involved in another project of a similar nature. In

1842, the Church Missionary Society had had to wind up its missionary station at Malta owing to financial problems. The gap was filled by the establishment in 1845 of a Protestant College at Malta for the training of missionaries. Ashley was chairman of a provisional committee set up to plan the College. In 1844, he wrote that half his time was taken up in signing circulars begging money for the College.[56] As with the Jerusalem Bishopric, it was hoped to unite the orthodox Protestants of Germany and the rest of Continental Europe with British Christians in the venture; Bunsen was a member of the committee and Gobat was Vice Principal of the College for a short time before he became Bishop of Jerusalem. The appeal for subscriptions for the College, published in the press, stated that the work envisaged was 'of the most urgent importance'. Its object was to spread the 'pure light of revealed religion, with the blessings of moral and intellectual cultivation among nations now sunk in the lowest state of degradation.'[57] Ashley himself wrote of the project as a 'great effort for the diffusion of saving truth through every region of the East.'[58]

In his involvement in all of this missionary enterprise, Ashley and his friends never lost sight of its close relationship with the working out of prophecy. The sermon at Alexander's consecration in 1841 was preached by McCaul, who stressed that the event signified that the Second Advent was near. 'Signs such as these,' he said, 'proclaim that, if the set time to favour Zion has not yet fully arrived, it can hardly be far distant.'[59] In 1845, Ashley told the London Jews Society that the purpose which it pursued and the principles it professed could only be maintained 'by the perpetual study of the word of God and especially the prophetical parts.'[60] In 1845, Ashley wrote that he had 'ardently but fondly believed' that the Jerusalem Bishopric and Alexander's appointment had been 'an accomplishment of the prophecy of Isaiah'. Alexander's death awakened his old doubts whether the scheme had been a presumptuous attempt to define the 'times and seasons which the Father has put in His own power;' it now seemed that 'the thing was amiss and not according to God's wisdom and pleasure.'[61] But his faith was soon restored. After attending Gobat's consecration as Bishop in succession to Alexander, Ashley expressed his hope that this might 'tend to hasten the Second and glorious Advent.'[62]

But if missionary endeavour was essential to the fulfilment of prophecy, it was also necessary for the upholding of Protestantism and combating the activities of the Oxford Movement, or, as Ashley always preferred to call it, 'Puseyism'. In 1842, he told the Church Pastoral Aid Society that he blessed God for raising up such a body 'to protest against all (the) heresy and schisms, whether they be presented under the gorgeous mantle of Romanism or under the more insinuating garb of Anglo-Catholicity.'[63] In 1846, he rejoiced that the Society proceeded on 'those great and glorious principles that were restored at the blessed Reformation.'[64] He told the Church Missionary Society in 1845 that it was necessary to support its efforts because 'it asserts for Protestants and Protestantism a claim to missionary character and missionary spirit as fervent ... as ever animated the Roman Catholic Church.'[65] But it was over the Jerusalem Bishopric that his missionary endeavour brought Ashley into most heated conflict with the Oxford Movement. The cooperation with Prussia in the establishment of the Bishopric had, as Ashley put it in his memorial to Bunsen in 1841, meant the 'consolidation of Protestant truth'. The subsequent visit of Frederick William to act as Godfather to the Prince of Wales also involved, he wrote, 'the most intimate friendship of the two great Protestant Powers; the open avowal of the Royal attachment to the principles of the Reformation.'[66] Ashley had been much gratified by the public response to the King: it was worthy of 'a great, glowing open-hearted Protestant nation'.[67] But, if such events were welcome in many Evangelical circles, they furthered the divisions within the Church of England of which the Oxford Movement had been both symptom and cause. Newman's Tract XC, published in February 1841 and giving an interpretation of the Thirty-Nine Articles which seemed to many to come close to Roman Catholic doctrine, had been condemned by the heads of the Oxford Colleges and disapproved of by the Bishops. The establishment of the Jerusalem Bishopric, coming immediately after this, was a further setback to Newman and a major influence in undermining his confidence in the Anglican Church.[68] He regarded the foundation of the Bishopric as inspired solely by the political considerations of increasing British influence in the Ottoman Empire, and he was bitterly opposed to the cooperation of the Church of England with a Church attached to Lutheranism and Calvinism, doctrines which he regarded as heretical. He wrote of 'this atrocious Jerusalem Bishopric affair', adding that the Archbishop was doing all he could 'to unchurch us,'[69] and, in November, he sent a formal protest to the Bishop of Oxford.[70]

On his side, Ashley was incensed by High Church opposition to the Bishopric. He wrote of the 'monstrosities of Puseyism', and noted that the Bishop of London was 'beset, and half-brow beaten by the clamorous and uncatholic race.' The Bishop had shown Bunsen a letter from Pusey which began with the comment that it was now 'for the first time that the Church of England holds communication with those that are *without the Church!*' Ashley was scandalised by this comment: 'This,' he wrote, 'is the holy, Christian, Catholic way in which he speaks of all the congregations of Protestant Germany.'[71] Pusey did not, indeed, approve of the alliance with Prussian Protestants, but he was at one point less opposed to the Bishopric than Newman[72], and, as has been seen, certain High Churchmen favoured the project, as Ashley was glad to acknowledge. He was especially pleased that Gladstone, as he put it, 'stripped himself of a part of his Puseyite garments' and spoke in support of the Bishop and Bishopric at a dinner held in October 1841 at Bunsen's house to celebrate Frederick William's birthday. This, wrote Ashley, was 'delightful; for he is a good man, and a clever man, and an industrious man. I praise God that he is now nearer to us.'[73] But Pusey became more hostile to the scheme and approved of Newman's protest,[74] and McCaul's strongly Evangelical sermon at Alexander's consecration offended some High Churchmen, including Gladstone. Ashley noted that Gladstone's 'Puseyism had returned up on him in full flood' and, reversing his earlier opinion, added: 'strange and useless will he be throughout life.'[75]

Nevertheless, although High Church opposition to the Bishopric angered Ashley, in a sense he welcomed it as bringing to a head the conflict within the Church of England. He felt that the stance of 'Newman and his crew' over the Bishopric had made them appear in their true colours and also hastened their departure from the Church of England. 'Thus because we manifest a love of God's ancient people,' he wrote, 'we are to be delivered (for secession must follow) from the plague spot of Puseyism! This is indeed a mercy. . . .'[76] He was also glad of the effects of the visit of Frederick William: 'we must build a new and large ward for the Puseyites in Bedlam!' he wrote.[77] In 1843, he told the London Jews Society that it must adhere to its task: 'it is our duty and our interest to show that our blessed Church . . . has other men and other theology than those of Oxford.'[78] In 1846, Ashley was once more involved in a dispute with certain of the High Church party over the Bishopric, for the death of Alexander and the appointment of Gobat again precipitated opposition. Gobat was attacked as a man of heretical opinions and also on grounds of personal conduct. Ashley was at pains to defend him. He told the London Jews Society in 1846 that it pleased 'certain fantastic persons . . . to endeavour to throw some odium . . . on the character and conduct of that Evangelical person.' But he was assured that 'these miserable efforts, many of which are wicked and all of which are foolish will only tend, under God's good providence, to show how utterly unassailable he is by darts such as these. . . .'[79]

The Jerusalem Bishopric was thus a major issue of contention between Puseyite and Evangelical in the 1840s: but it was not the only one. In 1841-2, Ashley became deeply embroiled in the controversy surrounding the election of a successor to Keble as Professor of Poetry at Oxford. The Fellows of Trinity College put forward one of their number as a candidate, the Revd. Isaac Williams, and a rival candidate, James Garbett, was nominated by Brasenose College. Neither was an outstanding candidate in terms of poetic achievement, although Williams had written poetry, whereas

Garbett was a translator of classical verse and a literary critic. But the issue was not to be contested on these grounds. Although not a prominent Tractarian nor a controversial figure, Williams had written three of the Tracts and thus had associations with the Tractarian party. Pusey, fearing that these associations would harm Williams's prospects, issued a circular to all members of Convocation in which he described Williams's qualities as a poet and suggested that Garbett's supporters were activated solely by a desire to prevent the election of Williams.[80] Ashley became the chairman of Garbett's election committee and was involved in the strenuous exchanges which the issue evoked. He reacted very strongly to Pusey's circular, writing that he never had 'much predilection for the peculiar doctrines of the party to which Mr Williams belongs:' but their recent opposition to the Jerusalem Bishopric had made him 'abhor their opinions as much in practice, as (he) before feared them in speculation.'[81] Pusey replied, asking if Ashley was quite sure whether he knew what the opinions which he said he abhorred were, and he suggested that there was less difference between Ashley and his opponents than Ashley thought to be the case. And, he added, 'try and think more mildly of us; love us more; perhaps you will understand us better; pray for us as I do daily for you.'[82] Ashley responded to the personal note in Pusey's letter, writing that he 'must ever entertain real kindness and esteem' for Pusey himself. He added that it was sad that they differed, but hoped that the differences might not 'amount to enmity'. However, he was in no doubt as to the existence of differences with Pusey on religious grounds and he spelled these out very clearly. He took special exception to Pusey's reference to the Jerusalem Bishopric as 'countenancing heresy'. This, Ashley wrote, was the 'necessary language, the inevitable issue' of Pusey's principles.[83] Ashley also had a spirited exchange of letters with Roundell Palmer, a leading Tractarian layman who, on behalf of Williams's committee, asked for Ashley's support. Ashley replied, firmly refusing it. Williams might, indeed, have 'amiable qualities and high attainments' as a private person, but he was seeking a public post and was to be invested with public authority. Further, Williams aspired to be a moral teacher – the Professor of Poetry was bound to impart his views and principles to his writings and lectures. Ashley was willing to acknowledge the 'latitude of speculation that must be permitted to all the members of a common Church,' but there were limits which must not be overlooked and Williams's participation in the writing of some of the Tracts put him well beyond these. Ashley thus refused his support for 'exotic and esoteric doctrines in the Church of England' which obscured 'the perspicuity of the Gospel by the philosophy of Paganism'.[84] This prompted a strong reply from Palmer, implying that Ashley had not read Williams's works, or, at least, that he had completely misrepresented them.[85]

Ashley's views, however, commanded considerable support and he received several letters, congratulating him on the stance which he had taken. Bickersteth was the author of one of these, and another writer commended him for taking a 'noble dash ... at the Puseyites'.[86] There were also letters on the other side, and the positions of the two became so entrenched that an attempt initiated by certain clerical and lay members of Convocation to persuade Williams and Garbett to withdraw and to run a compromise candidate failed.[87] In the end, however, Williams withdrew: his committee tested pledged votes and found that Garbett had a majority of these.[88] Ashley was delighted and saw God's blessing in the victory over the Puseyite party brought about by Williams's retirement.[89]

Despite the victory, however, Ashley felt that he must be vigilant about future events in Oxford. He wrote to Goulburn in April, 1842, about the new Professorship of Pastoral Theology. All Oxford, he said, was alive on the subject: the Puseyites were very anxious to get him.[90] To Peel, he suggested various persons of the anti-Tractarian school, and, for the Professorship of Ecclesiastical History, advised Peel to beware of Mr Brewer of King's College, London, whose views were 'Puseyitish'.[91] Peel replied that he had already consulted the Archbishop of Canterbury.[92] Ashley acknowledged that Peel had, indeed, to do this, but he warned Peel against taking the Archbishop's advice in this matter. He cited the case of the chaplain to the Bishop of Jerusalem, claiming that the Archbishop had forced through the appointment of a young man who had been tainted with Puseyism. The Archbishop had denied this, but Ashley told Peel that he had heard that the Archbishop had gone to Oxford and '*absolutely was closetted with the Heads of the Sect and received from them instructions how he should act!*' The Archbishop, he added, is 'very timid and easily influenced by those about him!'[93] Ashley also took a keen interest in the other events in Oxford in the mid forties. In 1843, Pusey was suspended from preaching for two years for a sermon on the Real Presence. It was, Ashley felt, a sermon 'strongly savouring of Popery' and he approved of Pusey's suspension.[94] In July, he took the chair at a meeting at Freemason's Tavern to consider the best way of uniting the laity in 'one general movement against Puseyism'. A memorial was signed, addressed to the 'Powers of the University'.[95] In December, it was presented. 'I suppose I shall be roasted!' Ashley wrote.[96] Later he went to Oxford to take part in the condemnation of W. G. Ward for the publication of his book *The Ideal of a Christian Church, Considered in Comparison with Existing Practice*. This was condemned by Convocation as inconsistent with the articles of Religion of the Church of England: Ward was censured and deprived of his degree. Ashley heartily approved of this: it was, he felt, 'most necessary, becoming and just.'[97] The treatment of Ward was, indeed, a final blow against the

Oxford Movement, and the reception of Ward, Newman and several other of its members into the Roman Catholic Church in 1845 witnessed the Movement's culmination – and also its nadir.

Throughout the Peel ministry, Ashley was, therefore, ever vigilant to further the fulfilment of 'prophecy' and uphold the Protestant Establishment against Puseyite influences. Peel was, indeed, sympathetic to the idea of extending the influence of the Church and, as has been seen, increased the money at the disposal of the Ecclesiastical Commissioners for the building of new churches. For mission allied to prophecy, he was, however, less enthusiastic. He did not share the Evangelicals' concern for interpreting the Biblical prophecies and working for their fulfilment. But if Peel lacked the Evangelical zeal which Ashley always looked for in political leaders, he did share Ashley's dislike of Puseyism and scarcely required Ashley's promptings and warnings to make him steer clear of appointments which were of a Puseyite character. In 1841, Ashley sent Peel a strongly worded letter from William Palmer, President of Magdalen and an extreme Tractarian, to Golightly, an extreme anti-Tractarian. He did this, he said, so that Peel might 'see and hear what things are said and done in the church.'[98] Peel replied that he had already seen the letter: he was thankful to God, he wrote, that the 'power to revive the functions of the Inquisition does not correspond with the inclination if this pamphlet be a fair specimen of the theology of Magdalen College.'[99] Peel disliked religious extremism at both ends of the theological and ecclesiastical spectrum, and the majority of his appointments were 'safe, solid and dull.'[100] Two exceptions to this were the appointment of Samuel Wilberforce to the Deanery of Westminster and subsequently to the See of Oxford, and of Professor Buckland of Oxford, a noted geologist, to the Deanery of Westminster on Wilberforce's elevation.[101] Ashley strongly disapproved of the appointment of Buckland. He wrote of him in his Diary as a 'joking geologist who has hardly ever preached and whose language oftentimes borders on the profane.'[102] And he wrote to Bonham of his utter astonishment that Peel should have done such a thing. He reflected on what could have been effected by a 'pious, active Dean in stimulating the indolence of the Cathedral Dignitaries and aiding to supply the deplorable, the perilous deficiency of provision for "things religious" in the City of Westminster. . . .'[103] Ashley did feel that Peel could have appointed men more fitted to the 'emergencies of the times',[104] and, on occasion, he wondered if Peel's dislike of Tractarianism was entirely thoroughgoing: 'he disliked the forms but not the tenets,' he wrote in 1846.[105] But on the whole, he found Peel reassuring on this issue: he noted in 1843 that he had dined with Peel and had been asked many questions about Puseyism. 'He now seems to hold it in horror,' he wrote, 'and well he may!'[106]

Peel's handling of certain religious matters, however, aroused Ashley's strong criticism. One example of this was in connection with the Dissenters' Chapels Act in 1844, which was designed to safeguard endowments enjoyed by Unitarian congregations. These endowments had often been inherited from periods when Unitarians had not been allowed to practise their religion. Once Unitarians were granted toleration, it was still doubtfully legal for them to take over endowments previously held by other denominations, in particular, the Presbyterians. The Act of 1844 declared that where no trust deed defining doctrine existed, usage of a specified period would be sufficient to prove the right of any congregation to possess a chapel or school, burial grounds or endowments. Ashley was strongly critical of this: he told Bonham that 'a blow had been struck from which we shall never recover . . . say what you will, they have passed a law against the will of this country to give to Socinians the funds assigned to the spiritual teaching of the Believers in the Holy Trinity. . . .'[107] The following year, Ashley was involved in a more spectacular disagreement with Peel. In 1845, Peel, as part of his policy to conciliate Ireland, announced his government's intention to increase the grant given to the College for the education of Roman Catholic priests and laity at Maynooth.[108] This caused a great outcry in Protestant circles, both within the Church of England and among Dissenters, and, in this, Ashley played his part. He spoke on the subject in the Commons at the second reading on 16 April[109] and stressed the dangers inherent in granting public money to a Roman Catholic institution – this amounted to a recognition of the Roman Catholic Church as one of the 'standing institutions of the Empire', which the state would be bound to uphold. It would have a highly damaging effect on the Protestant Establishment since there would be, in effect, two co-existent established churches in the same country and there would be constant conflict. Ashley voted against the second reading, but his efforts were to no avail and the grant was carried. Ashley felt that Peel's determination to keep to the bill in the face of the enormous opposition to it in the country showed 'a strange ignorance, or haughty contempt of the deep, solemn Protestant feeling in the hearts of the British people.'[110]

The efforts of Ashley throughout these years to uphold the 'deep solemn Protestant feeling' may be regarded as betraying a narrowly partisan Evangelicalism. It is certainly true that he took an oversimplified view of the complexities of the Oxford Movement by his constant insistence that all Puseyites were Papists in disguise. 'The Puseyite object is this "to effect a reconciliation with Rome",' he wrote in 1841, 'ours, with Protestantism.'[111] Some of the Puseyites did, indeed, finally become reconciled to the Roman Catholic Church: but not all did so, notably Pusey himself.

But Ashley's mind was too firmly committed to an Evangelical position to take account of such distinctions, and, equally, he could discern little or nothing of the scholarly and spiritual qualities of the Oxford apostles. It is also true that he did see partisan issues in several matters – missionary endeavour, especially over the Jerusalem Bishopric, and elections at Oxford; and, in the Williams case, he was accused by Roundell Palmer of introducing theological considerations into an academic election.[112] Ashley *did* contribute to the tension and bitterness which characterised relations within the Church of England at this time. But, of course, the same could be said of many of the activities of the Puseyite party. Again, to take the Williams election as an example, Pusey saw the question in very extreme terms and did as much as Ashley to introduce religion into the contest.[113] Ashley, indeed, told Bonham that he had no doubt that the 'theological ground was taken first by the Puseyites.'[114] He wrote in his Diary that he did not seek the controversy; 'but the occasion seemed to call for an avowal of sentiment: and, not hesitating to believe, I did not fear to speak.'[115] Thus, as Ashley saw it, it was the Puseyites who were dividing the Church: and to Pusey's claims that there was less difference between them than Ashley supposed, he retorted that this might have been true before the publication of the Tracts. But, he added: 'you have ebbed since that time and ... left me stranded.'[116] And, of course, the views and activities of the Puseyites left more persons than Ashley 'stranded' – they were too extreme for most Anglicans, whether Evangelical or not. And even within the Evangelical party, Ashley was not the most extreme. The sequel to Williams election also raised a controversial matter: for, immediately after Williams's withdrawal, Gilbert of Brasenose, who had been Garbett's chief supporter, was nominated by Peel to be the new Bishop of Chichester. It might have been thought that Ashley would have rejoiced in the appointment. Peel, indeed, wrote that he thought that Ashley would have approved of his choice.[117] But Ashley did not. He wrote that he regarded it as too much of a 'political coup'; and he did not approve of the enthusiasm shown by *The Record* newspaper, an organ of Anglican Evangelicalism, towards Gilbert's appointment. 'It is a sad pity,' Ashley wrote, 'that this journal is so ungovernably violent in spirit and language.' He applauded its opposition to Popery but shrank 'constantly from its motives and expressions.' He disapproved of its language in calling Williams 'a heretical person'. This, he felt, was 'the false and unChristian spirit we charge upon the Puseyites! So extremes meet.'[118] Ashley, therefore, was not the most violent and outspoken critic of Puseyism; and, equally on the Maynooth question, his attitude was not an extreme one. He spoke of his repugnance at 'incurring the appearance of casting reflections on the principles and practices of these Gentlemen who conscientiously believe the religion they profess.'[119] In his opposition to the proposals, he was not, he said, activated by illiberal motives nor by any hostility towards the people of Ireland. And in his comments on his speech, he wrote that he did all that he could to avoid 'harsh or personal expressions against Roman Catholics . . . and yet to assert (his) Protestant principles.'[120] His speech was well received in many circles: he reported Disraeli as having described it as *'great conciliation with steady and full assertion of Protestantism.'*[121] Greville wrote that Ashley had 'put himself at the head of the Low Church party' and would 'make a great clatter.'[122] But there were Evangelicals who would have preferred a greater clatter: Ashley himself noted that his language was distasteful to the people of Exeter Hall – 'not half fiery enough' he wrote.[123]

Ashley, then, was not the most bitter or fanatical of the Evangelicals. But his pursuits in the first half of the 1840s had witnessed a further development of his Evangelicalism in its religious facet. Mission, prophecy, defence of Protestantism against its assailants, Socinian, Puseyite or Roman: all these were in full evidence. But religious and ecclesiastical issues were far from being Ashley's only, or even major, concern in these years, for the events of the early and mid forties provided full scope for the expression of his Evangelicalism in its moral, social and political aspects.

NOTES

1. See G. F. A. Best, *Temporal Pillars: Queen Anne's Bounty, the Ecclesiastical Commissioners and the Church of England* (Cambridge, 1964), p. 296 ff.
2. N.R.A., Shaftesbury (Broadlands) MSS, SHA/PD/2, 5 Oct., 1841.
3. The Commission held 189 general meetings between 1840–41 and 1846–7: Ashley attended 27 of these. There were also 317 committee meetings held in these years, of which Ashley attended 12. (P.P., 1847, IX, App. H, pp. 232–3).
4. *The Record*, 15 May, 1841.
5. ibid., 2 June, 1845.
6. G. F. A. Best, *Temporal Pillars*, pp. 356–8.
7. Add. MSS, 40, 483, fos 160, 162, 165, 166.
8. *The Record*, 8 May, 1845.
9. ibid., 14 May, 1845.
10. ibid., 8 May, 1845.
11. ibid., 17 May, 1845.
12. ibid., 13 May, 1846.
13. There was no precedent in England for the consecration of a British subject as Bishop to minister in foreign territories and to foreigners. Thus authority for such a proceeding had to be sought from the Crown in Parliament. The bill was introduced on 30 Aug., 1841, and received the royal assent on 5 Oct., 1841.
14. A. L. Tibawi, op. cit., p. 50.
15. Quoted in Hodder, I, 372.
16. ibid., 374–5.
17. See above pp. 114–15.

18. R. W. Greaves, op. cit., p. 342.
19. N.R.A., Shaftesbury (Broadlands) MSS, SHA/PD/2, 8 Sept., 1841.
20. ibid., SHA/PD/2, 23 Sept., 1841.
21. Hodder, I, 371-2.
22. Hansard, *Parl. Debates*, 3rd ser., LXVIII, 853. R. W. Greaves, op. cit., p. 349.
23. N.R.A., Shaftesbury (Broadlands) MSS, SHA/PD/2, 23 Sept., 1841.
24. Add. MSS, 40, 483, fos 27-8.
25. ibid., f. 26.
26. N.R.A., Shaftesbury (Broadlands) MSS, SHA/PD/2, 12 Oct., 1841.
27. ibid., SHA/PD/2, 5 Oct., 1841.
28. ibid., SHA/PD/2, 22 Oct., 1841.
29. Add. MSS, 40, 483, f. 27.
30. N.R.A., Shaftesbury (Broadlands) MSS, SHA/PD/2, 25 Oct., 1841.
31. Add. MSS, 40, 483, f. 29.
32. N.R.A., Shaftesbury (Broadlands) MSS, SHA/PD/2, 25 Oct., 1841.
33. ibid., SHA/PD/2, 12 Nov., 1841.
34. The text was Acts XX, 22-4.
    (ibid., SHA/PD/2, 8 Nov., 1841).
35. ibid., SHA/PD/2, 8 Nov., 1841.
36. A. L. Tibawi, op. cit., pp. 50-51.
37. N.R.A., Shaftesbury (Broadlands) MSS, SHA/PD/2, 29 Nov., 1841.
38. See above p. 131.
39. N.R.A., Shaftesbury (Broadlands) MSS, SHA/PD/2, 20 Nov., 1841.
40. Hodder, I, 380.
41. N.R.A., Shaftesbury (Broadlands) MSS, SHA/PD/2, 26 Nov., 1841.
42. Battiscombe, p. 139.
43. N.R.A., Shaftesbury (Broadlands) MSS, SHA/PD/2, 28 Jan., 1842.
44. ibid., SHA/PD/2, 31 Jan., 1842.
45. ibid., SHA/PD/2, 31 Jan., 1842.
46. Hodder, I, 402.
47. N.R.A., Shaftesbury (Broadlands) MSS, SHA/PD/2, 3 Feb., 1841.
48. The title of the Bishopric was not 'Bishop of Jerusalem' but 'Bishop of the United Church of England and Ireland in Jerusalem'. (O. Chadwick, op. cit., I, 239).
49. S. C. Orchard, op. cit., p. 239.
50. A. L. Tibawi, op. cit., pp. 55-6.
51. ibid., p. 58 ff.
52. ibid., p. 73.
53. N.R.A., Shaftesbury (Broadlands) MSS, SHA/PD/4, 15 Dec., 1845. Ashley gave £25 as a donation to a fund set up as a testimonial of respect to the memory of Bishop Alexander. The money was to be spent in helping the Bishop's family: he left a widow and eight young children. A committee was set up to gather contributions to the fund: Ashley was the chairman of this. (*The Record*, 12 Feb., 26 Mar., 21 May, 1846).
54. *The Record*, 14 May, 1845.
55. ibid., 11 May, 1846.
56. N.R.A., Shaftesbury (Broadlands) MSS, SHA/PD/3, 26 Nov., 1844.
57. *The Record*, 2 Apr., 1846.
58. N.R.A., Shaftesbury (Broadlands) MSS, SHA/PD/3, 6 Mar., 1845.
59. S. C. Orchard, op. cit., p. 236.
60. *The Record*, 11 May, 1846.

61. N.R.A., Shaftesbury (Broadlands) MSS, SHA/PD/4, 15 Dec., 1845.
62. ibid., SHA/PD/4, 5 July, 1846.
63. *The Record*, 14 May, 1842.
64. ibid., 14 May, 1846.
65. ibid., 8 May, 1845.
66. N.R.A., Shaftesbury (Broadlands) MSS, SHA/PD/2, 26 Nov., 1841.
67. ibid., SHA/PD/2, 25 Jan., 1842.
68. J. H. Newman, *Apologia Pro Vita Sua* (1864), p. 248.
69. A. Mozley (ed.), *Letters and Correspondence of John Henry Newman* (2 vols, 1891), II, 352. Greville writing in 1842 commented that he had heard that the 'history of our consenting to that ridiculous appointment was that it was given to Ashley as the price of his negotiating with *The Times* their support of, or cessation of opposition to, the Syrian War.' (L. Strachey and R. Fulford (eds.), op. cit., V, 64).
70. A. Mozley (ed.), op. cit., II, 362–3.
71. N.R.A., Shaftesbury (Broadlands) MSS, SHA/PD/2, 12 Oct., 1841.
72. H. P. Liddon, *The Life of Edward Bouverie Pusey* (4 vols, 1894), II, 249–52.
73. N.R.A., Shaftesbury (Broadlands) MSS, SHA/PD/2, 16 Oct., 1841.
74. H. P. Liddon, op. cit., II, pp. 256–7. Pusey, however, felt that some good might come of the scheme; unlike Newman, who thought that none could. (ibid., II, pp. 259–60).
75. N.R.A., Shaftesbury (Broadlands) MSS, SHA/PD/2, 12 Nov., 1841.
76. ibid., SHA/PD/2, 18 Nov., 1841. Newman also attached great importance to the episode. It was, he wrote, 'one of the greatest of mercies. It brought me on to the beginning of the end.' (J. H. Newman, op. cit., p. 253).
77. N.R.A., Shaftesbury (Broadlands) MSS, SHA/PD/2, 26 Nov., 1841.
78. *The Record*, 10 May, 1843.
79. ibid., 11 May, 1846. See also A. L. Tibawi, op. cit., p. 88 and Hodder, II, 171–2.
80. H. P. Liddon, op. cit., II, 261–3.
81. Quoted in H. P. Liddon, op. cit., II, p. 264.
82. Quoted in Hodder, I, 394–5.
83. ibid., 395–7.
84. Written on 11 Dec., 1841. Printed in *The Record*, 16 Dec., 1841.
85. Lambeth Palace Library, Selborne MSS, 1861, f. 61.
86. Hodder, I, 392–3.
87. H. P. Liddon, op. cit., II, 266–7.
88. Hodder, I, 398.
89. N.R.A., Shaftesbury (Broadlands) MSS, SHA/PD/2, 24 Jan., 1842.
90. Add. MSS, 40, 443, fos 175–6.
91. ibid., 40, 483, fos 55–6.
92. ibid., 40, 483, f. 57.
93. ibid., fos 58–9.
94. N.R.A., Shaftesbury (Broadlands) MSS, SHA/PD/3, 30 May, 3 June, 1843.
95. ibid., SHA/PD/3, 18 July, 1843.
96. ibid., SHA/PD/3, 19 Dec., 1843.
97. ibid., SHA/PD/3, 13 Feb., 1845.
98. Add. MSS, 40, 483, f. 38.
99. ibid., 40, 483, fos 40–41.
100. O. Chadwick, op. cit., I, 228.
101. Ibid., I, 229.
102. N.R.A., Shaftesbury (Broadlands) MSS, SHA/PD/4, 17 Nov., 1845.
103. Add. MSS, 40, 617, fos 206–7.

104. N.R.A., Shaftesbury (Broadlands) MSS, SHA/PD/3, 1 Nov., 1843.
105. ibid., SHA/PD/4, 17 Jan., 1846.
106. ibid., SHA/PD/2, 23 Feb., 1843.
107. Add. MSS, 40, 617, f. 159. See also Hodder, II, 57–8.
108. N. Gash, op. cit., p. 414 ff.
109. Hansard, *Parl. Debates*, 3rd ser., LXXIX, 774–81.
110. N.R.A., Shaftesbury (Broadlands) MSS, SHA/PD/3, 7 Apr., 1845.
111. ibid., SHA/PD/2, 14 Oct., 1841.
112. Selborne MSS, 1861, f. 61.
113. O. Chadwick, op. cit., I, 204.
114. Add. MSS, 40, 617, f. 111. H. P. Liddon, op. cit., I, 262–3 disputes this point, but he does admit that Pusey's circular, ascribing partisan motives to Garbett's committee, was 'not justified'.
115. N.R.A., Shaftesbury (Broadlands) MSS, SHA/PD/2, 21 Dec., 1841.
116. Quoted in Hodder, I, 396.
117. Add. MSS, 40, 483, f. 46.
118. N.R.A., Shaftesbury (Broadlands) MSS, SHA/PD/2, 24 Jan., 1842.
119. Hansard, *Parl. Debates*, 3rd ser., LXXIX, 774.
120. N.R.A., Shaftesbury (Broadlands) MSS, SHA/PD/3, 18 Apr., 1845.
121. ibid., SHA/PD/3, 18 Apr., 1845.
122. L. Strachey and R. Fulford (eds.), op. cit., V, 205.
123. N.R.A., Shaftesbury (Broadlands) MSS, SHA/PD/3, 2 May, 1845.

8
Hearts to be won, Souls to be saved, 1841–1843

One of the first problems facing the new Peel Ministry in 1841 was in the area of foreign affairs. An expedition had been sent in 1839–40 to pacify the confused internal condition of Afghanistan so that Russian influences in the North West frontier of India could be counter-balanced. After some initial success, the expedition ran into difficulties and, by 1841, the British forces were retreating from Kabul. In general, a policy of withdrawal from Afghanistan was favoured by Peel's government and by Ellenborough, who arrived in India as Governor-General in 1842, but it was also felt that an effort should be made to restore British prestige and rescue prisoners. This was done in the course of the withdrawal and met with some success, and Ellenborough gave orders that the gates of the Temple of Somnauth, an alleged Hindu religious relic, removed from India by pillaging Mohammedans in 1024, should be restored. When the armies returned to India with the gates – or, more accurately, copies of the originals, a fact unknown to Ellenborough – the Governor-General issued a proclamation to the Princes and Chiefs of the Peoples of India in which he declared that the insult of eight hundred years was at last erased. He intended to place the relic in the Temple of Somnauth and set over it the Imperial Crown, as a public demonstration of the achievements of British power and authority.

Ashley followed these events with keen interest. He had not favoured the original invasion of Afghanistan in the late thirties, and stories of atrocities carried out in the course of the withdrawal aroused his criticism. The activities of Ellenborough, moreover, moved him to voice strong opposition. This was not, perhaps, surprising in view of his earlier dealings with Ellenborough, but the proclamation issued by the Governor-General was, in Ashley's opinion, bombastic and offensive. He took exception to the fact that Britain, instead of being concerned with extending Christianity, was assisting towards the restoration of a Hindu religious shrine. 'Is Ellenborough mad?' he wrote in January, 1843. 'Has any person, private or royal, ever uttered such a speech, or sent such a circular since the days of Herod? . . . But this folly is serious; it vitally affects the honour and service of Christianity; the British Government is to conciliate the Hindoos (sic) by the repair of their temples and by the adoration of their idols!'[1] Ashley wrote to Peel in February on the subject of a possible vote of thanks to Ellenborough. Such a suggestion, he wrote, had made many laugh, but a few weep. All who believed that God had given Britain an Empire in India for the advancement of His name 'tremble to see the power prostituted to the service of Heathen temples.' Ashley was prepared to believe that Ellenborough did not intend this, but such 'unheard of liberality' would be ascribed by the Hindus to a 'most godless indifference'.[2] Ashley was also critical of Peel's conduct in Parliament when Ellenborough's proclamation was debated in early February. Peel simply mentioned the military victories in Afghanistan – he admitted that Ellenborough might have been indiscreet, but asked if the Governor-General were to suffer disgrace on that account alone. Ashley felt that Peel would have acted more honourably, if less astutely, by simply acknowledging that an error had been made. On 9 March, a motion of censure was proposed on Ellenborough's proclamation. Ashley argued that the Whigs were inspired by partisan motives in bringing it forward; but, if he disapproved of this, he disapproved even more of the government's defence of Ellenborough:

> never did I feel less regard for public men [he wrote], or less pleasure in public life. The character of the Proclamation, its effects on the native race, on Christians in India, on Christians in England, were quite forgotten: everything sacrificed to the defence of the Governor General. God be praised, I voted against Sir Robert Peel![3]

Another area of foreign policy in which government policy was to arouse Ashley's displeasure concerned the Opium question. He disapproved of the war between Britain and China, precipitated in 1839 by various trading disputes, including the smuggling of opium by British merchants, and he took little pleasure in the British victory, consolidated by the Treaty of Nanking in 1842. He felt that Britain had triumphed 'in one of the most lawless, unnecessary, and unfair struggles in the records of History.'[4] He sent Peel extracts from *The Times* and *The Standard* giving accounts of horrors: it was not a war, he told Peel, but a horrific massacre of several thousand men who made no resistance.[5] Yet the peace, too, brought with it disadvantages: it would stimulate trade with China and result in cotton factories being worked to capacity.[6] Further, he strongly disapproved of the fact that, despite the treaty, the Opium Trade continued. In February, 1843, he was asked to lay the state of the trade before Parliament 'as a grand question of national morality and religion.'⁷ He agreed to do so, with some trepidation: but he felt that it was 'the cause of Christianity and of God'.⁸ Thus on 4 April, 1843, he presented numerous petitions against the trade on behalf of various religious bodies and moved that steps be taken to abolish it. He supported this in a long speech,⁹ in which he condemned the trade on various grounds: that it caused ill-feeling between China and Britain; that it had a bad effect on legitimate trade with China; but, most of all, that it did immense harm and damage to the moral welfare of nations and individuals. British encouragement of the 'infamous traffic' checked the progress of Christianity and impeded the civilisation of mankind. But here was an opportunity to set this right: let Britain direct all her energies and vows to 'that one great end of human existence: "Glory to God in the highest; on earth peace, good will towards men".'

The speech made a considerable impression in Parliament and out of it. But Peel asked Ashley to withdraw his motion on the grounds that a vote would prejudice negotiations pending in China. Ashley felt obliged to accede to the request, but was not without dark thoughts about Peel's conduct. He had expected Peel to express disapproval of the trade; but, instead of that, Ashley wrote, Peel '*sneered* at our care for the health and morals of the Chinese.' He

> assumed the tone of a low, mercantile, financial soul, incapable of conceiving or urging a principle, which finally disgusted me, and placed him in my mind much below the Christian level, and not any higher than the heathen. It passed again and again through my heart, 'I will never serve under such a fellow as *you!*'¹⁰

In his views and activities in these two areas of foreign policy, Ashley clearly showed the moral dimension of Evangelicalism. In his view, Britain must always act honourably in its dealings with foreign powers and must uphold moral standards. He was outraged when she did not do so. Thus in his speech on the Opium question, he said that although Britain wore 'a certain appearance of power and majesty,' in too many instances she was trampling underfoot every moral and religious obligation.¹¹ He was not, indeed, opposed to Britain asserting herself in the world and using her power for good: but if Britain used her superiority in arts, arms, science and knowledge to the injury and not to the advantage of mankind, then he would prefer her to descend to the level of a third-rate power.¹² International conduct, no less than personal conduct, must accord with the moral precepts of Christianity. In failing – as Ashley saw it – to uphold these standards, Peel was falling far short of what might be expected from a British Minister. There was in Peel, he thought, no force of moral power or, as he once put it, 'nothing of faith, and a vast deal of policy.'¹³ The accuracy of such an assessment is, of course, open to question. Peel did not, in fact, favour the Afghan war nor did he approve of Ellenborough's conduct. But he inherited the war and found Ellenborough difficult to restrain.[14] And over the Opium question, the government did have responsibilities in undertaking negotiations; Ashley was free of these and thus found it easier to see the matter in clear-cut terms. Thus while Ashley's views bring out the moral nature of his concern, his comments on the lack of that concern in others must be approached with caution.

If foreign affairs provided Ashley with an area for comment in the early 1840s, the same was true of the domestic situation in its social and economic aspects. The economic recession of the late 1830s became worse: 1842 was a particularly bad year, marked by factory closures, unemployment and unrest, both industrial and political. There was, therefore, Ashley felt, greater need than ever for the ruling classes to undertake measures of social improvement. If they did not, they were leaving the field open for the Anti-Corn Law League and the Chartists, and, on a higher plane, they were neglecting the opportunities for developing the spiritual capacities of the working classes. All this was much on Ashley's mind and conscience as Peel came into office, and, of course, the social issues of which he was so acutely aware were also the problems of the incoming Ministry. In social matters, indeed, more than in religious or foreign, Ashley was to have constant dealings with the Peel Ministry.

The issue of factory reform was raised soon after the formation of Peel's Ministry. Deputations from the factory districts called on Peel and other Conservative leaders in October, 1841, and felt heartened at their reception, at least by Peel. They felt that he was aware of their difficulties and was sympathetic to them, but they were less certain of Graham, who seemed to them too much influenced by economic liberalism to have any understanding of their position.[15] Ashley wrote to Peel in November, 1841, passing on such impressions, which he himself shared.[16] Ashley's distrust of Graham was taken a stage further by an exchange of letters in December.[17] Graham wrote to Ashley on 27 December, telling him that he had read the reports of the factory inspectors and had also examined the bill which the Whigs had introduced in the last months of their administration.[18] He wrote that he was aware that Ashley advocated the prohibition of machinery being worked for more than ten hours of each twenty-four and added that he was not prepared to say that this was his view; but he was anxious to know if Ashley regarded the Whig bill as an improvement on the existing law. Ashley replied on 28 December that he approved of almost every provision of the Whig bill, except that governing the hours of labour. But he corrected Graham on his remarks about the limitation on the hours during which machinery was run. This was not his concern; he was anxious only to secure a ten-hour day for operatives under eighteen. And he asked Graham if his refusal to commit himself to ten hours was the final answer to the factory question which, he claimed, Peel had promised him in September on behalf of the government. Graham replied that the point about restricting the operation of machinery to ten hours had been made to him by the deputation from Yorkshire, and it was to this that he had refused his assent. But he was at pains to point out that he had written to Ashley without having consulted any of his colleagues and was not aware of any promise given to Ashley by Peel. A factory bill had not yet been discussed by the Cabinet and his letter had been a private one, with no bearing on any decision on the part of the government.

This exchange of letters, somewhat at cross-purposes, was an unfortunate beginning to Ashley's dealings with the government over the factory question, and it was the more unfortunate in that, despite Graham's final remarks, it gave Ashley the impression that the government had finally decided against ten hours. For, in January, 1842, Ashley wrote to Bonham,[19] that he had reason to believe that Peel intended not to concede the 'great factory principle' for which he had so long and so ardently fought. This, Ashley felt, was deplorable, if only on the grounds that the new Ministry might have had the working classes with them; these classes, despairing of any other redress, would now be driven to ally with the League. But Ashley's purpose in writing to Bonham was not primarily to comment on the broader consequences of what he took to be the government's attitude. He was concerned with his own position. He told Bonham that he intended to 'push the question irrespective of all party;' he had an account to render and he must discharge it. Thus, assuming that the government was fully opposed to his demand, he would begin by moving an Address to the Crown and would pursue the matter on supply days and lodge other motions or petitions. He was anxious to know Bonham's views on how such a course of determined opposition would leave him as a member of the Carlton Club, of which he had been a founder member in 1831, and he suggested that the correct action would be for him to resign, once the government had formally stated its opposition.

On receipt of the letter, Bonham asked Ashley's permission to show it to others, and, on 20 January, Ashley wrote consenting to this and emphasising that he was most anxious to avoid 'anything like a Manifestation'; all he desired was, as he put it, 'simply the opinion of a good-hearted, honourable man. . . .'[20] It is not clear what Bonham wrote in reply, but it would seem that his advice was that Ashley should keep his membership of the Carlton, since Ashley did not carry out his threat to resign. But Bonham also showed Ashley's letter to Graham, who replied on 21 January to the effect that he hoped that some kind of compromise might be reached with Ashley and that relations might be more cordial than had been implied by Ashley's letter.[21]

But any possibility of an agreement between Ashley and the Conservative leadership was ruled out by an exchange of letters between Ashley and Peel,[22] the first of which was written by Ashley on 21 January, the very day on which Graham was writing to Bonham expressing hopes of an accommodation. In this letter, Ashley asked Peel to inform him whether a decision had been reached on the question of a further limitation of hours for persons between the years of thirteen and twenty-one, the latter being the upper age proposed by the Whig bill of 1841 for the protection of a twelve-hour day. Since Parliament was due to open, Peel would, perhaps, 'feel no objection to remove the suspense in which so many thousands (were) at present detained.' The letter drew a somewhat sharp reply from Peel to the effect that he was not prepared to pledge himself or the government to the support of a ten hours bill for such persons, and he asked Ashley to call on Graham, who had a measure affecting labour in factories under consideration. Ashley replied to this on 24 January, asking for a more explicit statement; it was, he said, extremely desirable that he 'should be able to give a distinct and complete answer to the Short-Time Committees. . . .' He understood that the government had decided not to support a bill for the limitation of hours of labour between the ages of thirteen and eighteen or twenty-one, but Peel had said nothing about the government's determination to oppose one, if brought in from another quarter. Peel replied on 26 January in even sharper terms than previously: he considered that he had already given Ashley 'information sufficiently explicit' and had done so in time to enable Ashley to introduce a measure of his own to Parliament, if he wished to do so. He never had any wish to impose a restraint on Ashley's conduct. Ashley closed the correspondence on 31 January: once again, he stated that he might have expected an explicit answer, but he would not persist in asking for one. And he finished with the observation:

> I fear that I must conclude with the deepest regret that Her Majesty's Government, avoiding all open questions, are determined to oppose any measure which shall propose to carry out a limitation of labour to ten hours in the day.

Having closed an acrimonious correspondence, Ashley then wrote to the Short-Time Committees of Cheshire, Lancashire and Yorkshire on 2 February. He was, he wrote, obliged to announce that Peel had signified his opposition to the ten hours bill, and concluded that Peel's reply must be taken as the reply of the whole government. Ashley, however, pledged his own continued efforts, and he exhorted the Committees to do likewise in a legitimate and peaceful way. They must 'infringe no law and offend no properties: all must work together as responsible men, who will one day give account of their motives and actions. . . .' If this course were approved, nothing would detach him from the cause – if not, they must elect another advocate. Ashley ended the statement by saying that he knew that in taking this step, he excluded himself from office, but he rejoiced in the sacrifice and was happy to devote the rest of his days to an effort to improve the operatives' moral and social condition.[23] The letter was sent not only to the Short-Time Committees; it was also sent to *The Times*.

The line between Ashley and the Conservative Ministry on the issue had thus been clearly drawn, and a further development came on 4 February, when a short leader appeared in a Conservative newspaper, *The Morning Post*. This argued that Ashley should have stated the terms on which Peel had signified his opposition to the ten hours bill; if the public were to see the communication, 'it might lead to a rather different impression from that which the noble lord's peevish letter, in allusion to it, is calculated to create.' It also launched an attack on Ashley's reference to his exclusion from office: he would have acted more gracefully if he had left to others 'the task of exhibiting his self-denial to the public.' And it wished that Ashley would abandon using 'sanctimonious phraseology, resembling that of the Conventicle in his communications with the public.'[24] Ashley was dismayed when he read the article. It was, he said, the 'most violent and venomous article' which he had ever read against any public man. Moreover, he felt that it must have been made on the authority of some one other than the writer: it could be that Peel was the writer or promoter; or it could be a Puseyite attack.[25] Ashley felt that it called for a reply. Thus on 5 February, 1842, he wrote to Bonham, no doubt in the hope that the substance of the letter would be passed on to the Conservative leaders. He told Bonham that he had 'urged and implored in the most emphatic manner, an answer that *could not possibly be misunderstood;*' he could not believe that the matter could be left an 'open question'. On the second point, relating to his language about office, he explained that he had to deal with large masses who 'from long suffering and frequent deception, are extremely suspicious;' in order to retain influence over them, he had to make it clear that he was asserting an irrevocable line of conduct, was true to their welfare and was forming no compromise with their opponents. Thus he had to state publicly his disavowal of office. The third charge about his method of address, Ashley shrugged off: it required 'only forgiveness for its enormous uncharitableness' and that Ashley freely gave. In writing to Bonham, Ashley made it clear that he was convinced that some one other than the editor of *The Morning Post* had written or inspired the article: 'I should not have troubled you with this letter,' he wrote, 'had I not felt convinced that the Editor must have written from another man's notes.'[26]

Here, then, was another unhappy episode in Ashley's dealings with his party. It can, indeed, be argued that Ashley himself must bear some of the responsibility for it. He jumped to the conclusion, from Graham's letter of 27 December, that the government had decided against the ten hours principle; as has been seen, this conclusion was not really warranted by what Graham said. And Ashley did ignore the suggestion made by both Graham and Peel that he should discuss the measure which Graham had inherited from the Whigs and had under consideration. Further, it is understandable that Peel found Ashley's letters demanding explicit statements irritating – it did look as if he was deliberately trying to provoke a refusal in order to safeguard his own position in relation to the Ten Hours Movement and appear in a favourable light. Thus Peel wrote to Graham, when forwarding the correspondence between Ashley and himself: 'there are limits to coaxing a Gentleman who is angry with everybody because he had embarrassed himself.'[27] Again, Ashley's statement to the Short-Time Committees that Peel had declared his opposition to the ten hours bill was not strictly accurate. What Peel had said was that neither he nor his government could undertake to bring in such a measure – he did not positively say that he would oppose one. Finally, as far as the leader in *The Morning Post* is concerned, Ashley's view that it was inspired by the government appears to have been mistaken. He himself noted on 6 February that he had heard that Peel and Graham condemned the article, but he still felt that the first charge originated from Peel, even if the composer of the 'Diatribe' used it without Peel's knowledge.[28] This was unduly suspicious on Ashley's part. Thus it can be argued that Ashley acted over-hastily, unreasonably and out of an exaggerated sense of victimisation.

Looking at the matter from Ashley's side, however, it is true that he had discussed the matter fully with Peel in September, 1841 and, in his letter to Crabtree on 4 September, had stated that Peel required further time for deliberation on the subject.[29] By January, Ashley thought that Peel had had sufficient time. He also felt that the situation in the country meant that time was, indeed, running out for Peel. On 1 January, 1842, he wrote to Peel warning of the consequences of inaction: 'if the working classes be with you, you may defy all the Leagues and Leaguers of every sort and description; but ... we shall be in a very bad plight without them.'[30] Again, his desire to clarify his own position in relation to the Ten Hours Movement by asking for an explicit statement was not based on purely selfish considerations. He was always conscious of his unique role as an aristocrat dealing with the people. In 1841, he had commented that he was 'no doubt unworthily, the representative of the whole aristocracy in respect of the operatives – should (he) deceive them, they will never henceforward believe that there exists a single man of station or fortune who is worthy to be trusted.'[31] Thus in 1842, he was anxious – as his final letter to Bonham showed – not to put himself in a position in which he could be accused of deceit. Further, although it must be admitted that Ashley did not coooperate with Graham over the inherited Whig bill, it is doubtful if there was room for cooperation. When asked about the government's policy in the House on 7 February, Graham replied that he would re-introduce the measure brought forward at the end of the Whig administration with some alterations, but it was not his intention to bring in a ten-hour day for those between thirteen and eighteen.[32] All this cannot completely exculpate Ashley: he could have approached the question with less haste and more patience. But to him, it appeared that the government was adopting a dangerously prevaricating attitude and was asking him to cooperate on a measure in which he saw no room for cooperation, and he thus felt driven to establish his own position for fear that his actions might be misunderstood.

The episode left Ashley low and depressed in spirits. It was not that he regretted sending the letter to the Short-Time Committees: on 11 February he wrote of it as 'the famous and fatal letter', but, he added: 'I approve it heartily after mature reflection.'[33] But he also admitted later in the month that he had been 'much depressed and harassed . . . very distrustful of (himself) and fearing that all looked gloomy on (his) endeavours.'[34] There were times when the depression lifted, and Ashley betrayed that fitfulness of temperament which so afflicted him. On 9 March, he recorded that he 'awoke in high spirits' and was hopeful that all would go well;[35] yet the next entry of 11 March records that he was 'quite down again; easily raised, easily depressed. . . .'[36] It was not, indeed, that he was inactive, with time to brood on past sores. He was busy with the hearing of disputed elections: 'fresh labour added to old sinews', he wrote. 'I am like a factory spinner – more toil and less wages.'[37] He also retained all his work in connection with lunacy and, on 17 March, 1842, spoke on a bill concerned with the subject.[38] But his performance depressed him, and he wondered how he could succeed in the 'great measures' which he proposed, if he were so weak in the smaller.[39] And, as for the 'great measures', he could see very little hope. He contrasted his position with that of Wilberforce and his efforts over slavery. Wilberforce was active in a question 'which interested people but remotely;' he, on the other hand, had a body of opponents on the spot.[40] Towards the end of March, 1842, there was, it is true, a reconciliation with Peel – they 'shook hands and avoided all explanations,' and Ashley records that Peel was 'very cordial and clearly much pleased.'[41] But the meeting did not make Ashley any more hopeful for the success of his 'schemes'. At the end of April, he wrote that he saw 'the setting of the wind' :

> People are already beginning to say [he wrote] 'you will get nothing this year with your Factory Bill; the Government will have no time' etc. etc. . . . Thus it is that I am tossed about from one session to another, and have not strength enough even to obtain a hearing of my Cause. Meanwhile, wrong, oppression, mutilation, death, with all the grim roll of physical and moral evils, are in full liberty. My labour seems in vain, ever wearisome, ever new. . . .[42]

Yet the future was not quite as dark as Ashley painted it. The first Report of the Commission inquiring into Child Employment, appointed in 1840, was published in May – it was concerned with employment in mines. It has been described as the 'most famous Blue Book of the century',[43] and the revelations which it made of conditions in mines, accompanied by sketches, did, indeed, make an immediate and very considerable impression. Ashley described the Report as a 'noble document . . . Perhaps even "Civilisation" itself never exhibited such a mass of sin and cruelty. The disgust felt is very great, thank God;' but he wondered if it would be reduced to action when he called for a remedy.[44] He was clearly intent on introducing a measure, and such was the feeling in the country and in the press, that he was confident of success. There were certain delays ahead and Ashley grew irritated and impatient and unjustly accused the government of putting obstacles in his way.[45] The bill was finally arranged for 31 May but was again delayed owing to an adjournment of the House on an attempted assassination of the Queen. This time, Ashley allowed Peel to have precedence over him since the government had lost a day's business and Peel replied with a 'grateful acceptance'. In more charitable mood, Ashley wrote that he was glad that he had given way to Peel. Nevertheless, he foresaw a 'covert and spiteful opposition'. Some of the Northern coal owners had produced a document defending themselves: 'a vain, insolent and feeble paper', Ashley wrote, 'quite in the style of the old apologies of the factory masters.'[46]

The delays had preyed on Ashley's nerves, but, once he was given the opportunity to speak on 7 June, 1842, he did so at great length – for over two hours – and with considerable effect.[47] Once again, he sounded a note of urgency : it was not enough to say that vice had occurred before and would do so again :

> I maintain [he said] that our danger is absolute and not comparative – our forefathers had to deal with thousands, we with millions. We must

address ourselves to the evil boldly and faithfully, or it will soon acquire so enormous a magnitude as to be insuperable by any effort . . . of genius or principle.

Moving on to the condition of the working classes in the mines, Ashley drew heavily on the details of the Report. He had found the task of reading and summarising the Report a difficult one: 'great labour, great difficulty, first to read, and then to select and arrange the matter,' he had written.[48] But he showed an impressive mastery of its details. He cited numerous examples of young children being employed in heavy work – dragging coal loads by chains attached to the waist – in conditions which lacked ventilation. He dwelt on the physical effects of coal mining: stunted growth, crippled gait, irritation of the head, back and feet, early exhaustion, early death. He was particularly concerned about the moral effects on girls and women of working naked, the cruelty and ferocity of colliers towards children and the ignorance of domestic duties among women induced by working in mines. It is arguable that all this presented the situation at its worst, but Ashley did not indulge in 'blanket condemnation'. He admitted that there was considerable local variation and, despite the threatened opposition, he even went so far as to say that, if it had only been the great coal owners of the North with whom he had to deal, the necessity for a bill might never have existed – they had 'exhibited in many respects care and kindness towards their people.' Ashley also spoke well of the Irish coal owners. And he acknowledged that, where a remedy was needed, it was sought by 'many well-intentioned and honest proprietors'. But the evils that did exist were, in his mind, 'both disgusting and intolerable – disgusting they would be in a heathen country and perfectly intolerable they are in one that professes to call itself Christian;' thus the 'vigorous and immediate interposition of the legislature' was essential to remove or to mitigate them.

Ashley's main proposals were, in the first place, the total exclusion of all females from the mines and collieries, and he quoted instances where this had already been done without any effects on the price of coal. The second proposal was the exclusion of boys under thirteen – he would have preferred the age of fourteen, but since thirteen was the age limit used in the Factory Acts for purposes of maximum protection, he would not deviate from it. Thirdly, no person should be employed to be in charge of an engine or engine house under the age of twenty-one. These were the mechanisms used to draw up and let down the work people and accidents were common. And finally, the system of assigning boys as apprentices should be stopped: these had often been pauper children, who had been badly treated. In some general remarks at the conclusion of his speech, Ashley pointed out the limited scope of his efforts. He had never attempted, he said, to legislate for adults nor to interfere between master and man in the matter of wages. But what he had done was to attempt to bring children and young persons within the reach of moral and religious education, knowing full well that they were the seeds of future generations.

> For twenty millions of money [he concluded] you purchased the liberation of the negro; and it was a blessed deed. You may, this night, by a cheap and harmless vote, invigorate the hearts of thousands of your country people, enable them to walk erect in newness of life, to enter on the enjoyment of their inherited freedom, and avail themselves (if they will accept them) of the opportunities of virtue, of morality and religion.

The words well illustrated the sources of Ashley's social concern.

Ashley's long speech met with an assurance of support from Graham on the part of the government, although he reserved its position on the proposed exclusion of boys at the age of thirteen. Other speakers expressed support and admiration for Ashley's endeavours. All his depression was banished: 'The success,' he wrote, 'has been *wonderful* . . . for two hours the House listened so attentively that you might have heard a pin drop, broken only by loud and repeated marks of approbation. . . .'[49] He saw in his success evidence that God had bestowed on his speech 'acceptance and favour'.[50] And he wrote to Graham that the reception given by the House had 'already done good to the cause of steady and constitutional Government. The people are not a little pleased by the sympathy of those in higher station.'[51] The bill passed its first and second readings without difficulty, but, by 20 June, Ashley was beginning to feel more anxious. He wrote of a combination of the coalowners to reduce the age at which boys might work to ten, and there were, he continued, 'interviews without end'.[52] In the event, Ashley decided to concede this reduction in age at a meeting with a deputation representing the Northern owners, which included Lord Wharncliffe, Lord Lambton and John Buddle, principal agent of the Colliery owners of the North East. He appears to have hoped that the concession would bring opposition to the measure to an end and ensure some degree of regulation. He wrote well of the deputation; they had promised full support and had assured Graham of this.[53] Thus at the Committee stage, Ashley himself proposed the new age limit of ten rather than thirteen. He would have preferred the latter figure as the proper limit under which no boy should be employed, but he recognised that these differences of opinion 'arose from the best motives;' and he again acknowledged the kindness and courtesy of those who had formed the deputation.[54] The new proposal – which included the provision that between the ages of ten and thirteen, boys should work on only three days a week, every alternate day and for not more than twelve hours a day[55] – was accepted and the remaining clauses were agreed to with little trouble. Opposition from mining members, in particular Ainsworth, gave Ashley cause for disquiet, but he was cheered by a letter from the Prince Consort, to whom he had sent a copy of his speech: this – and an interview with the Prince – made him revise his earlier unfavourable opinion of Albert. 'Found him hearty, kind, sensible and zealous,' Ashley wrote. 'He is an admirable man.'[56] And on 24 June, despite continuing resistance from Ainsworth, Ashley got the bill through the Report stage. 'Thank God!' he wrote, 'but the day is not yet won.'[57]

There was, indeed, further delay and resistance before the bill finally passed the Commons. Thus on 4 July, when Ashley moved the third reading, two motions were proposed by Ainsworth for an adjournment.[58] Both, however, were substantially defeated and the bill was read a third time with certain additional clauses held over for discussion. When these were taken on 5 July, Ainsworth once again spoke in opposition, but said that he would not persist in it, although he added ominously that he was glad that the whole matter was to be considered in another House.[59] Thus the bill finally passed the Commons.

The delays over the latter stages of the bill had reduced Ashley's confidence and he was not optimistic as he viewed the prospect of the bill in the Lords. On 28 June, he wrote of a deputation from South Staffordshire: 'very positive, very unreasonable ... The whole struggle is reserved for the Upper House. God be with us!'[60] Ashley, moreover, found considerable difficulty in persuading anyone to take charge of the bill in the Lords. He approached the Duke of Buccleuch, Lord Privy Seal; after some hesitation, Buccleuch undertook at the end of June to take charge of it, only to tell Ashley within a few days that his colleagues objected and refused him permission to proceed.[61] This prompted bitter remarks from Ashley on the conduct of the government: he felt that after Graham's promises of support and the general unanimity of the Commons in favour of the bill, it should have been made a government measure. The fact that it had not been given this status made Ashley believe that the ministers were ill-disposed. On 5 July, he wrote of his difficulties in finding a patron for the bill in the Lords: he had approached Buccleuch, Richmond and Sutherland, but 'to no purpose'.[62] On 8 July, he was still writing of his troubles. He had been so often refused that he felt 'quite humbled ... All had some excuse or other; praised it, but avoided it. ... All seek their own, not the things that are Jesus Christ's.'[63]

At last, however, on the evening of 8 July, Ashley found Lord Devon to sponsor his bill. At once, it ran into trouble. Lord Hatherton gave notice of referring the bill to a select committee, a proposal supported by Wellington.[64] A select committee was indeed appointed on 8 July to consider whether the bill was fit to be read a second time. But when Devon offered to make certain concessions on 14 July,[65] it was agreed to give it a second reading, although Lord Londonderry, who had already spoken strongly against the bill, wanted to postpone the second reading for six months, during which a select committee could examine it. He did not press the point to a division on this occasion, but he did do so after the Committee stage on 25th.[66] This, however, was defeated and the bill received its third reading.[67] Throughout all these threats to the bill, Ashley was on edge. He was bitter at the attitude taken by Wellington. He had, indeed, been in correspondence with Wellington on the matter for some weeks; on 25 June, he had been gratified that the Duke had been willing to accept a copy of his speech in the Commons, and wrote to express his 'heartfelt delight' that Wellington approved of the measure.[68] On 4 July, he appealed to the Duke to see that he had 'fair play' in the Lords since there was no party in the House to back it up.[69] Wellington replied that he must take 'the course ... of the Minister of the Crown in the House of Commons;' and he hoped that no individuals would take any course on it that would be 'otherwise than fair'.[70] Ashley was angered at Wellington's support for a select committee on 8 July; he felt that this was going back on his pledge to support the line taken by the government in the Commons.[71] Ashley was also angry at the conduct of Wharncliffe, Lord President of the Council. In reply to a question put by Londonderry on 12 July as to the government's attitude to the bill, Wharncliffe said that the government had taken no part in it whatever and intended to remain perfectly passive.[72] So much, Ashley thought, for the government's promises of assistance: 'it is impossible to keep terms with this Ministry,' he wrote, 'their promises are worth nothing.'[73] And, if Ashley felt betrayed by the government, he also felt betrayed by those in the coalmining business who had, he claimed, dishonoured their agreement of the previous month by their vigorous opposition in the Lords. He had told Wellington on 25 June that all the great coal owners of the North 'entirely concur(red) with (him) in *every* provision.'[74] Londonderry, however, refuted this in the Lords on 12 and 14 July. His agent, Buddle, did, indeed, meet Ashley during his visit to London in June, but, Londonderry claimed, the coalowners had not authorised Buddle to enter into any compromise, and he had not done so.[75] Londonderry quoted a letter from Ashley to Buddle in which Ashley had expressed astonishment at the owners' intention to depart from the 'engagement' which had been reached, but Buddle had replied in terms which suggested that there had been no such engagement. Thus, said Londonderry on 14 July, the intention of not opposing the bill had never been intimated and the Lords felt under no constraint in vigorously attacking it.[76]

Ashley's criticisms of the government certainly had some force. The government's conduct was, to say the least, ambivalent. After Wharncliffe's comment in the Lords that the government intended to remain 'perfectly passive', Palmerston in the Commons asked who spoke for the government, Graham or Wharncliffe.[77] Graham was taken off guard by the question and said that he had had no opportunity of consulting Wharncliffe. But he repeated his earlier undertaking to support the bill both as an individual and as a member of the government, although reserving the right of considering the details; he could only believe that Wharncliffe had done the same.[78] It was an explanation which was less than wholly convincing. With regard to the other 'betrayal', it is hard to establish exactly what did happen at the meeting of 20 June and whether this was understood by the coalowners as a binding engagement, although Ashley's view of the episode as a binding agreement appears to have been shared by another person present at the meeting, Hedworth Lambton.[79] But whatever the rights and wrongs of the two 'betrayals', there is no doubt that the bill's original proposals underwent considerable revision, either by concessions on the part of Devon or by amendments. Women and children were to be allowed to enter coal mines, although not to work underground; the arrangement whereby boys were to work on alternate days was dropped; the minimum age for looking after an engine or engine house was lowered from twenty-one to fifteen; the apprenticing of pauper children was virtually re-introduced, although not under the age of ten and not beyond the age of eighteen. Further, inspectors appointed under the Act were not authorised to report on the condition and state of the mines, as had been originally proposed, but only on the condition of persons employed in the mines and on the operation of the Act.[80] Ashley felt that the Lords had 'left (the bill) far worse than they found it.'[81] He wrote to Peel on 2 August, once the bill had returned to the Commons, that the amendments would reduce the protection at first contemplated. He had had, he said, 'but little reason to anticipate' the alterations – this presumably was a reference to the 'engagement' of 20 June. But he was prepared to acquiesce in them.[82] One amendment which caused Ashley particular concern, however, related to the admission of women and children to the mines. He felt that if this were left in the bill, it would neutralise it, for, once women were admitted to the mines, it was almost certain that they would be employed underground. He asked Peel to resist the amendment.[83] Peel was sympathetic, but felt that he could not do so. To exclude women from the mines for any purpose whatever, as the original bill had done, would mean, for example, that a man who met with a serious accident could not be visited by his wife or daughter, or that a girl could not carry her father's dinner to him in pits which were easily accessible for such purposes.[84] Ashley still felt that this left an undesirable loophole, but, on 6 August, he invited the House to accede to the bill. He regretted the amendments, but the measure 'went to establish a great and valuable principle.'[85] Thus the bill was passed, and, despite his disappointments, Ashley still felt thankful to God for the

> undeserved measure of success with which He hath blessed my effort for the glory of His name and the welfare of His creatures. Oh that it may be the beginning of good to all mankind! ... Whatever has been done, is but the millionth part of what there is to do ... The more I labour, the more I see of labour to be performed ... Our prayer must be for the Second Advent, our toil 'that we be found watching.'[86]

There was, indeed, no resting for Ashley. A visit to St Giles in August, finding it 'in beauty and in peace' perhaps pointed the contrast to the situation in the country 'distracted by lawless mobs and sudden insurrections throughout the trading districts.'[87] The appeal of Chartism at such a time of economic grievance and social distress was considerable. Ashley wrote that all smaller concerns, such as the poor law and the factory bill, were 'subordinate to the grand and final remedy of the Charter!'[88] It seemed to him not unlikely that the existing distribution of property would soon come under critical scrutiny. There was, then, urgent need to spread reconciling and healing influences and to work for the physical and moral education of the working classes. Ashley wrote of the 'frightful consequences of (their) prolonged neglect' and of the 'danger of disregarding and opposing these mighty and increasing multitudes.'[89] And these feelings were brought home the more sharply to Ashley when he and Minny, after a short holiday in Wales, toured the manufacturing districts of the North in September, 1842. In the course of his journey, he spent three days with Kay Shuttleworth,[90] Secretary to the Committee on Education and, as such, an adversary of Ashley. But as a Manchester doctor, Kay Shuttleworth was also much concerned with matters of public health and thus shared many of Ashley's interests: the two men had long conversations on issues affecting the condition of the poor. Ashley also walked round Manchester on a Saturday night and, as he reported this in his Diary, 'passed through cellars, garrets, gin palaces, beer-houses, brothels, gaming-houses and every resort of vice and violence. ...' He also went down a coal mine: 'thought it a duty; easier to talk after you have seen.'[91]

The most interesting and significant part of Ashley's travels, however, was the meeting which he had in Manchester with the Central Short-Time Committee. Throughout his struggles over mines reform, Ashley had not lost sight of factory reform. He had corresponded with Peel on the subject in July.[92] He recalled Graham's statement of February promising a bill amending the Act of 1833; this, and remarks made by others, gave him grounds for believing that the government would do 'at least as much as the late Government'. But nothing had been done and he himself was now suspected of negligence by those whose interests he represented. Peel replied that Graham had, indeed, contemplated a measure early in the session, but that he could not have foreseen the extent to which the government would be occupied with other matters. Ashley was not wholly satisfied with this. He thought that Graham ought to have done more, but he told Peel that he would not press the point at that stage. Now, as Ashley toured the Northern districts and met the Central Short-Time Committee, the matter was – inevitably – raised. If Ashley had entertained fears that the delays over the factory bill might cause him unpopularity, these were set at rest by the presentation of a loyal address by the Committee approving of his past efforts. Ashley replied[93] that he was 'honoured and satisfied' by the Committee's approval and he drew attention to the recent passing of the Mines bill, backed as it had been, by considerable unanimity of public feeling: this might encourage the Committee to persevere in its 'just and necessary demands for a reasonable Time Bill': and he assured the Committee that his own resolution to persevere had undergone 'no abatement'. Ashley also took the opportunity to discuss the evils of society as he saw them. Individuals were being debased and demoralised by the effects of 'the manufacture of wealth'. The country faced the prospect of men with 'feeble bodies and untaught minds, the perilous materials of present and future pauperism, of violence and infidelity;' of women untrained in domestic accomplishments and virtues by hours of employment in factories[94]; of children brought up in ignorance and sin by neglect of their immortal souls. The family unit would be eliminated and society destroyed at its core.

Throughout 1843, Ashley was to be constantly preoccupied in Parliament with the themes stated in his speech. At the very beginning of the year, however, he was pessimistic about the future. The Mines Act did not seem to be working as well as he had hoped; the ten hours bill still found no favour; and efforts which he felt he must make in education were, as he put it, 'below the horizon'.[95] He noted on 10 January that Gladstone had made a 'grand oration' at Liverpool in favour of education for the middle classes. The speech had met with great praise. 'Well be it so,' wrote Ashley; 'there is no lack of effort and declamation in behalf of fine edifices and the wealthier classes; but where is the zeal for ragged pin-makers, brats in calico works and dirty colliers?'[96] But, in fact, the fortunes of such sections of society were to be exposed by the publication on 30 January, 1843, of the second Report of the Children's Employment Commission, dealing with the conditions of children and young persons employed in various branches of industry not covered by the Factory Act. This included a wide variety of trades, ranging from metal work to needle work, lace work, hosiery and calico printing. The Report stated that regular employment often started in such works at seven or eight years old; that, with the exception of certain processes in the manufacture of metalware, earthenware and glass, the work itself was not oppressive but it was often carried out over long hours, resulting in considerable damage to health. The Report also mentioned the moral condition of the children and young workers. This was usually very low; parents took no interest in the children apart from the wages which they brought in; and means of secular and religious education were totally lacking.[97]

The Report did not make the impression on the public which that on Mines had done, and Ashley made no immediate move to act upon it. Nevertheless, its publication reinforced his desire to take up the question of education, and, on 28 February, 1843, he moved an Address in the Commons praying Her Majesty 'to take into her instant and serious consideration the best means of diffusing the benefits and blessings of a moral and religious education amongst the working classes of her people.' He supported this in a long speech[98] which ranged over various issues in addition to education: 'our duty,' he said, 'is to examine the moral state of the country.' He drew heavily on the Report of the Children's Employment Commissioners, and he called on Parliament to discharge its responsibilities to the poor and to 'seek their temporal through their eternal welfare'. There were, he said, 'many hearts to be won, many minds to be instructed, and many souls to be saved.' He called for laws and regulations not to curtail freedom but to enlarge it – not to 'limit rights but to multiply opportunities for enjoying them.'

The speech met with considerable approval and Ashley's spirits were buoyed up. Graham willingly accepted the substance of Ashley's Address.[99] He agreed that there had been a neglect of moral training and religious education, and also that recent events in the manufacturing districts were 'pregnant with solemn warning'. He told the House that he had given thought to a system of education and well knew its difficulties, especially in relation to denominational rivalries. But he hoped to persuade the House to set aside party feeling and religious differences and to try to find 'neutral ground' on which a system of national education could be established, with due regard for the interests of the established Church on the one hand and the 'honest scruples' of the Dissenters on the other. He then stated that he had a measure in preparation for factory children which would involve educational provisions: this was, in fact, the bill on which he had been working ever since the Tories took office. Thus Ashley's Address was accepted, and, on 1 March, Ashley wrote in glowing terms to Graham, saying that the events of the previous night would 'under God's good Providence' make his 'administration of affairs very happy . . . and a period of new and lasting blessings to the country.'[100] Graham replied that Ashley's note had 'gratified him sincerely.' And, he continued:

> I am willing to hope that the new Factory Bill will in the most important particulars satisfy your wishes; and since the foundation of this Administration, no circumstance has been more deeply regretted by me than the obstacles which this question has presented to your acceptance of office. It would delight me, if the reasonable settlement proposed should in any degree remove your honourable scruples, and smooth the way to future arrangements, which I consider so desirable to the public service.[101]

On 7 March, 1843, Graham introduced the promised measure.[102] It was, indeed, similar to that introduced by the Whigs in the last days of their administration. It established the minimum age for employment at eight years rather than nine, but it reduced the maximum working day for children between eight and thirteen to six-and-a-half hours. Young persons between the ages of thirteen and eighteen were to continue to work a twelve-hour day: women were to be limited to the twelve-hour day until they reached the age of twenty-one. It was, however, the educational provisions of the bill which constituted its main novelty. Children were to attend school for at least three hours a day on five days a week. The bill made an effort to placate various religious persuasions in the arrangements which it provided for the administration of the schools and the teaching to be carried out within them. It was, as Graham put it, an attempt at 'national education... a scheme of comprehension and concord.' But as such it failed completely.[103] There were numerous objections to the bill, both from the Anglican and, more especially, from the Dissenting side. Certain Anglicans objected to the proposals for the governing body of the schools, for these included the appointment of four trustees by the secular authority of the magistrates. On the other hand, the Dissenters strongly objected to the fact that the chairman of the board, with a casting vote, was to be a clergyman of the Church of England and that two other members of the board were to be church wardens. Again, on matters of religious teaching, some Anglicans objected to the fact that there was to be no doctrinal interpretation attached to the daily reading of the Bible; and, on the Dissenting side, there was criticism of the provision whereby the clerical trustees on the board might, on certain occasions, require the schoolmaster to teach the Catechism and use the Book of Common Prayer, and they were not satisfied by the saving clause that a parent could have his child withdrawn from such instruction. The bill was subjected to strenuous criticism in the House, but it passed its second reading on 24 March. Opposition in the country, however, was overwhelming. Petitions, especially from the Dissenters, poured in on the government objecting to the bill. Various attempts were made to meet these. The Committee stage was delayed to allow time for reconsideration of various points. On 1 May, Graham offered what he called an 'olive branch' by announcing several important concessions. Thus the four trustees originally to be appointed by the magistrates were to be elected by the ratepayers, and, although the clerical trustee was to remain chairman, there was to be only one church warden and not two. The proposals about religious teaching were also modified. The religious services and teaching were to be on a 'contracting in' rather than 'contracting out' basis, and provision was made for the Dissenting clergyman of the district to give religious instruction to children from his congregation. The concessions on the side of the Church of England were considerable, but there was still widespread and vocal opposition from the Dissenters, in particular from the Wesleyan Methodists. A last effort at compromise between representatives of the United Wesleyan Committee and Peel and Graham failed; and on 15 June, Graham announced that the government intended to drop the educational clauses of the bill.[104]

Throughout the episode, Ashley gave the matter his full attention. When the bill was introduced, he expressed approval of it, although he regretted that it did not further reduce the hours of labour. He did not fully approve of the educational provisions – he did not like the lack of doctrinal explanation of the Bible. Nevertheless, he was willing to accept the bill[105]; he felt that it was the best that could have been devised and a considerable improvement on the educational provisions of the Act of 1833. In Parliament[106] and outside it, he did his best to defend it. To the Church Pastoral Aid Society on 9 May, he argued that the system of education, despite its defects, was worthy of acceptance: it was aimed to bring 'within the pale of Christianity ... thousands, nay, many more than that, hundreds of thousands, and almost millions of children and young persons who now live in a state of more than practical heathenism....'[107]

Nevertheless, Ashley always appreciated the strength of the opposition ranged against the scheme. Writing to Sir John Easthope on 18 March, he commented that hopes of national education were to be 'blasted by the Dissenters on the one hand and the Puseyites on the other. It may be that by God's blessing on so good a work, the measure may slide in between the two extremes.'[108] But, as this became increasingly unlikely, Ashley resigned himself to a long struggle. On 28 March, he wrote to Graham, asking whether he had decided to postpone the bill. He urged Graham to do so, for another debate on education would be likely to yield little progress.[109] He ascribed the vigorous opposition, particularly from the Wesleyan Methodists – who had supported the Anglicans against the Whig educational plans in 1839 – to fears of Popery in the Church of England. He told Graham on 26 April that no falsehood had been spared to excite and terrify the people, and, such, he wrote, was the 'sad state of our Church' that such stories were believed. The people would 'believe anything just now and more especially anything that asserts the perilous effects of Puseyism on religious liberty.'[110] There was, indeed, some substance in this statement for there was widespread distrust among Dissenters of events in Tractarian circles in 1843, such as Pusey's sermon in Oxford.[111] Ashley was not, however, opposed to the concessions which Graham made to the Dissenters. He was asked by Graham to a meeting to hear the amendments which Graham proposed on 1 May and gave his opinion that they would serve the purpose. But 'not a hair's breadth more must be yielded.'[112] And, when the amendments did not conciliate the Dissenters, Ashley felt that the government took the correct course in withdrawing the educational clauses. They could not have been carried in the House except by 'forced and small majorities', and the scheme could not have been put into effect in the country without 'fierce and everlasting collisions'.[113] He ascribed the failure of the proposed system not only to the strength of the Dissenting opposition, but also to the fact that Anglicans, clerical and lay, had not given it enough support: 'foes active,' as he put it, 'friends supine.'[114] And he concluded that 'Combined Education' must never again be attempted: it had proved impossible to achieve and had also resulted in agitation and the establishment of claims to equality on the part of the Dissenters to which the Church of England could not assent. '. . . Let us have our own schools, our Catechism, our Liturgy, our Articles, our Homilies, our faith, our own *teaching* of God's word,' he wrote.[115]

Although Ashley felt that the government had been correct in abandoning the educational clauses of the bill, he was most insistent that the other parts of it should be retained. He had written to Graham on 28 March expressing his determination to persevere in his efforts to reduce the hours of work. He was, he said, bound to the parties at whose 'earnest solicitations he had taken the matter up, and he told Graham that he strongly shared in their desires: 'I entertain so deep a feeling,' he wrote, 'on the horrid *individual* and *national* Sin of this accursed system that I do not dare to treat the question as I would a turnpike bill or any secondary matter.'[116] On 14 June, he wrote to Peel, releasing the government from any implied engagement to him on the educational clauses of their factory bill; Peel could 'advance or recede here.' But, as to the regulation parts of the bill, the 'case (stood) differently.'[117] He followed this with another letter to Peel the very next day, complaining of a statement made by Graham in the House that the factory bill might have to be deferred owing to the difficulties over the education clauses: these clauses were, he wrote, engrafted onto a bill which the Tories had inherited from the Whigs; this bill was a 'complete measure,' even if shorn of the educational clauses and should not be withdrawn. 'Such a step,' wrote Ashley, 'would be a departure from what is due to the House, to the operatives, and I may say, to myself.' He recalled that he had hoped for progress in 1841 but had been disappointed; a measure had been anticipated in 1842, but 'excuses were assigned;' thus he lived on the promise for 1843.[118]

Peel had replied to Ashley's first letter of 14 June, expressing gratitude that Ashley had released the government from the 'great embarrassment' which it would have felt in abandoning the educational clauses if Ashley had been in favour of perseverance. Dissent had achieved 'a sorry and lamentable triumph'.[119] A further letter from Peel on 17 June answered Ashley's second letter on the subject of possible abandonment of the bill as a whole. He wrote that 'from the extreme pressure of public business', Graham had not had the opportunity of conferring with his colleagues as to what should be done about the remaining clauses. But, after consideration, the government had decided not to abandon nor to postpone the remaining portions of the bill.[120] Thus on 19 June, the bill was re-committed and went into Committee.[121] However, it was too late in the session to go further and Graham announced at the end of June that a further measure would be introduced when the time was more opportune.[122] The matter was, therefore, deferred. 'Factory bill to be postponed again,' wrote Ashley on 30 June. And, he added, 'Is it not evident that Sir James is meditating a trick?'[123] Ashley was, therefore, suspicious of the government's intentions. He did, indeed, admit to Peel in mid-July that the pressure of business and the advanced stage of the session made it difficult for the government to proceed with the factory question; it was better to have it stand over till next session. But he asked Peel explicitly to express regret that he could not go further this session and to announce that he would take the matter up again next session.[124] When he did not get immediate satisfaction on these points, he became mistrustful again and wrote to Peel on 21 July urging recollection of the various public and private engagements on the matter, the reports of the inspectors, the 'necessity of the case': Peel would surely be the first to recognise that the matter must be set at rest.[125] Finally, on 21 July, Peel confirmed that the bill would be re-introduced early in the following session.[126]

Thus on social issues, Ashley's dealings with the government had been varied in nature. There were occasions when he cooperated with the government and was ready to express his appreciation for its help. But, more frequently, he felt that his efforts found little favour in official Tory circles, and beside the politeness of some of the letters must be set the suspicions and dislikes which he poured into his Diary. Graham earned his especially severe private criticism: 'The most dishonest of all public officers', he wrote of him in June, 1843.[127] And Ashley thought that the government's conduct in failing to accept his proposals over factory reform was alienating working-class sympathies and providing material for the League and the Chartists. Peel's 'refusals create an appetite for O'Connor's offers,' he wrote.[128] Ashley was quite out of sympathy with the economic liberalism favoured by Peel. To him, this was dull, soulless and materialistic. 'Imports and exports,' he wrote in 1842, 'here is Peel's philosophy! There it begins and there it ends!'[129] Such methods could, he felt, make no appeal to people in distress. 'All Peel's affinities,' he once wrote, 'are towards wealth and capital . . . *What* has he ever done or proposed for the working classes? . . . Cotton is everything, man nothing.'[130] Thus Ashley expressed his dissatisfaction with the record of the Peel Ministry: 'men looked for high sentiments and heard small opinions; for principles and were put off with expediency.'[131]

But, as in the case of Ashley's strictures on the conduct of the government in the area of foreign policy, certain qualifications must be made. There was, in fact, much in common between the ultimate aims of Ashley and those of Peel. Both wanted to provide a cure for social distress; both wanted to preserve the existing political and social order; both wanted to outflank radical criticism of it, whether represented in the League or in Chartism. The difference was one of method. Ashley favoured paternalistic measures for social improvement: Peel put his faith in creating the conditions for economic prosperity which would bring greater satisfaction and contentment. It may, indeed, be argued that Peel's opposition to Ashley's factory proposals as adversely affecting the prospect of economic recovery was exaggerated and ill-founded; but, equally, Ashley was unfair in accusing Peel of complete indifference to social matters and in dismissing his policies as being concerned only with 'imports and exports' and not having any wider social purpose. Further, although there was a difference in method between Ashley and Peel, the government was not as antagonistic towards Ashley's efforts as he made out. Graham told Bonham in 1842 that anything which he could do to satisfy Ashley consistently with his sense of duty would be done.[132] Graham on one occasion wrote to Ashley that the 'rigours and hard duties' of his office might have given to his conduct 'an appearance of cold severity'. This, he wrote, was not in his nature: 'the wish of my heart,' he continued, 'is to cooperate cordially in your good works to the utmost extent that my sense of public duty will allow.'[133] Peel, too, expressed his admiration for Ashley's qualities 'of heart and head',[134] and he told Ashley that he was always obliged by the frank communication of his opinions even if these were critical of the government.[135] Peel and Graham were, therefore, consistently courteous to Ashley in their dealings with him. Further, they were under a very considerable pressure of business and responsibility. Graham wrote to Ashley that he worked fourteen hours a day; that he could do no more; and, that, with every effort, he was scarcely able to transact the business in a manner satisfactory even to himself.[136] Ashley was not under these pressures; he was free to pursue his own line of policy. All this must be set against Ashley's comments on the government to obtain a more balanced view. Ashley undoubtedly performed an invaluable role as a spokesman for much of the moral and social comment and criticism of the time: his contribution in this respect was similar to that of the 'Young England' group of Tories[137], if much more practical and realistic than it. He claimed in May 1843 that he might rejoice that he had 'given a direction to men's thoughts and turned them into deep and flowing channels which carries (*sic*) to the great sea of duty to the Poor and the whole aggregate of moral and religious obligations.'[138] It was a role which, as many were prepared to admit, was a noble one, but it was the role of the moralist and the independent, and it may be too much to expect any government always to follow the course preached by those who do not shoulder its day-to-day responsibilities. It may be, too, that Ashley did not always credit the government as generously as he might have done for the efforts which it did make in this field, even if different in method from his own.

Amidst Ashley's public efforts during these years, he displayed his habitual volatility: elation, depression, mistrust of himself, suspicion of others were – as has been seen – much in evidence. His feelings of isolation also increased. He was worried at having, as he thought, so many enemies: millowners, coalowners, government and Puseyites. He was, he wrote in 1842, like a 'pelican in the wilderness'.[139] He also felt that he did not receive sufficient support from his co-religionists in matters of social improvement. Already in 1840, he had written that he could not rely on 'evangelical religionists' in causes for 'what is called "Humanity".'[140] And in 1842, the same thoughts returned to him: 'will the religious public . . . do anything for me?' he asked.[141] Some of these comments, of course, reflected his tendency to see every hand against him, and, as in the past, he admitted this fault. 'I am by nature,' he wrote in 1843, 'foolishly sensitive.'[142] And, if he did not have the pressures of office, he was certainly conscious of the heavy burden of public life. He wrote that if the day were five times as long, it would be filled up: he never had time to read a book.[143] He was 'hurried beyond all precedent'; he never had a moment to himself; amidst all the interruptions, he had lost all power of 'consecutive meditation'.[144] There were, moreover, worries over Minny's health in the summer of 1843. In July 1842, she gave birth to a second daughter, Mary, although not without the threat of a miscarriage earlier in the year. In July 1843, however, she did suffer a miscarriage and, although she recovered quite quickly, the doctor recommended a holiday at Carlsbad. Thus from late July until October, Ashley was abroad with Minny, taking with them Anthony and Francis and their tutor, but leaving behind the younger children. They reached Carlsbad on 12 August.[145] There, Ashley, as well as Minny, took the waters; the local doctor suggested that he might well do so since he was there and recommended that he should drink seven goblets every day. 'It is the life of a whale,' Ashley wrote, but he noted that the waters seemed to do him 'neither good nor evil; a hogshead of the Thames would be quite as effective.' Nevertheless, the rest and change, if not the waters, clearly did Ashley good. He now had time for reading, one of his books being Seeley's abridgement of Wilberforce's *Life*. 'How many things have we felt alike,' Ashley wrote. 'What similar disappointments, misgivings and disgusts!' After five weeks, the party left Carlsbad. Their further journeyings took them to Prague, where Ashley visited a hospital and a lunatic asylum, and to Vienna. There, he tried to re-visit his 'old haunts', wandering about alone. 'After an interval of eighteen years I find myself once more at Vienna, a married man with seven children! What a change since the time I first arrived here....' The visit included a talk with Metternich and an inspection of cotton mills, where he thought that the conditions left much to be desired, although he had seen 'far worse in England'. In early October, the party began their homeward journey and reached London on 20 October. Ashley felt that it had been a good and worthwhile holiday, filled with amusement and instruction, and he and Minny returned in better health. But he had been glad to turn homeward to his 'own precious land, the abode of all (he held) most dear and the field of all (his) duties.' And, once home, he prayed that all might be turned to 'greater, more zealous, more faithful service in the cause of our Lord and Redeemer.'

On his return, Ashley found a backlog of letters and papers to attend to: 'old story of postmen, knockers, bells, visitors, business, questions, answers, hopes, fears, doubts, difficulties....'[146] Family business occupied his attention. He went to St Giles in October, 1843, 'with the whole cavalcade of brats and nurses...'[147] and he was much concerned with the entry of Anthony to a boarding school on the Isle of Wight at the end of October. Ashley had taken a keen interest in the boy's education and, in particular, his spiritual instruction. Every morning for many years, he had spent time with him hearing and reading the Bible. He had also watched his son's 'every moment, weighed every expression, considered every thought and seized every opportunity to drop a word in season.' To part with him and entrust him to others was, for Ashley, a great wrench, but he was convinced that the step was for the boy's good: '... *he* must be gradually introduced to the world,' Ashley wrote, 'and *we* gradually severed from him.'[148] Thoughts, too, about his public efforts, past and future, crowded into

Ashley's mind as he walked in the country near St Giles. Seed had been sown, but no harvest yet reaped. But he prayed that he might trust in God's 'blessed Providence' and be content that he was called 'even to the proposal of good things'.[149] As it happened, Ashley was, once more, soon to propose 'good things', and he was to do so amidst the countryside in which he stood as he pondered his career.

That so strong a critic of the abuses of the factory system as Ashley was himself of a landed family having large Estates did not escape notice. His criticisms of the factories and mills in the north of England invited comparison between conditions there and on the family Estates. Already in 1843, the matter had been touched upon when the system of truck, whereby wages were made up in kind, was mentioned in the House and Ashley was asked if he would take action on abuses held to be prevalent in Dorset.[150] The matter was, moreover, given added point with the publication in 1843 of a Report on the Employment of Women and Children in Agriculture.[151] Dorset had been visited by Alfred Austin in the course of the investigation on which the Report was based, and adverse comments were made on the cottage accommodation in the county for agricultural labourers. Further, if the Report drew attention to Dorset, the activities of the Anti-Corn Law League did likewise: the League took delight in drawing attention to conditions in Dorset as part of their propaganda.

Ashley's position was, therefore, vulnerable. He showed himself willing to investigate the abuses over truck and told Giffard that the system was the most oppressive and ruinous among the grievances of which the working classes complained.[152] But the date at which he realised that conditions on his father's Estates left room for criticism is hard to determine. As early as December, 1832, during the Dorset election of that month, he wrote to his wife: 'My Minny, if we lived here, how much good we might do. . . . But we never shall; let us hope therefore that "what was in our hearts may be accounted to us for righteousness".'[153] Why Ashley ruled out the prospect of one day living in Dorset is uncertain; it may be that, at the time of reform, he felt that the future succession of landed property was uncertain and unlikely to survive. Nor is it clear whether his remarks were meant to be an implied criticism of conditions in the county. Certainly, after his reconciliation with his father in 1839, his remarks, while staying at St Giles, show his pleasure in his ancestral surroundings, and there was little hint of criticism. But in January, 1840, Ashley had his first experience as a magistrate in Dorset in Quarter Sessions and it may be that his experience in this capacity were to engender doubts about the conditions in the county. In January, 1842, he wrote of the dangers of coming into collision with his father if he were to take a more active role,[154] and, in January, 1843, when again in

Quarter Sessions, he noted 'the same vice, the same misery'. The population was increasing and so too was crime, but there was no attempt at remedy.[155]

Certainly by late 1843, Ashley was well aware of the need to counteract criticisms of social conditions in agricultural areas. He had been displeased by the appointment of the Commission to inquire into the employment of women and children in agriculture, seeing this as a ruse by Graham to thwart his efforts at factory reform. Graham, he felt, would allow him to do nothing until the Report had been made and then 'qualify (his) doings by arguing that agriculturalists are no better off.' This, Ashley thought, was quite untrue; factory work, he argued, involved a far larger proportion of women, far harder work, longer hours of work and longer absences from home.[156] Nevertheless, the findings of the Commission would draw the whole question to parliamentary and public notice, and Ashley felt that the time had come for a statement on the other side. A further consideration was that a speech criticising the condition of the agricultural labourer in Dorset had been made by R. B. Sheridan[157] at a meeting of the West Dorset Agricultural Society in October. The speech caused a great deal of unfavourable comment in the local press. Ashley did not feel that Sheridan had spoken from spite or malice, but from a sense of duty, but this, coming so soon after the official report on Dorset, made him feel that it was necessary to speak on the matter.[158]

This, then, was the background to a speech which Ashley made at the annual cattle show and dinner of the Sturminster Agricultural Society at Sturminster Newton in Dorset in November, 1843. It was common practice for the local members of Parliament to attend such dinners, and they were the occasion for comment on any topical points affecting agriculture. Ashley took the chair at the dinner and had his health proposed by Lord Grosvenor, who said that Ashley was entitled to the highest respect, possessing, as he did, 'talents of a rare order'.[159] Ashley took the opportunity of his reply[160] to answer the various points which had been made in recent weeks and months about the county. He said he could speak with freedom because 'no one present was chargeable with any share in the mischiefs so much deplored.' Further, the charges had been exaggerated and much that was good had been ignored. Nevertheless, the statements were 'weighty' and had been made 'by no nameless or spiteful reporter, but by an officer of the Government and a landed proprietor of (the) county.' They had, therefore, to be taken seriously, and he himself had to guard against inconsistency in his own principles. 'I ought not to be lynx-eyed to the misconduct of manufacturers and blind to the faults of landowners.' Ashley thus urged his hearers 'to mitigate the severity of the poor law . . . begin a more frequent and friendly intercourse with the labouring man . . . respect his feelings; respect his rights; pay him in solid money . . . pay him in due time.' Above all, he counselled them never to close their fields in time of harvest: 'give to the gleaner his ancient, his Scriptural right; throw open your gates, throw them wide open, to the poor, the fatherless and the widow.' At the close of his speech, Ashley developed his view of 'stewardship'. All wealth, talent, rank and power were given by God for His Own service, not for man's luxury: 'for the benefit of others, not for the pride of ourselves.' An account would have to be given of 'privileges misused, of means perverted, of opportunities thrown away;' but if these were used aright, they would 'sanctify the possession of property, bless its use and grace its enjoyment;' and would also accomplish 'still higher and better ends by leading the Poor, who experience their value, to thoughts of Piety and peace and . . . to bless Almighty God that men like these . . . are invested with station and leisure and power.'

Ashley was told that he had made a deep impression and he hoped that what he had said might turn 'to the honour of our blessed Lord and the welfare of the People!'[161] *The Dorset County Chronicle* reported that 'the eloquent and impressive speech of the Noble Lord was followed by great applause.'[162] But, at the end of December, the newspaper reported another agricultural dinner which had taken place on 10 December at Blandford. At this, Ashley spoke again, and, once more, he urged the need for good understanding between landlord and tenant which would wipe out the stain cast unjustly on the county by exaggerated reports. His speech was cheered, but it appears that his fellow member, Bankes, was more warmly received. He was 'greeted with prolonged cheers.' He attacked Austin for spending such a short time in Dorset and for the partiality of his report. He also mentioned the Revd. Sydney Godolphin Osborne, whose parish was at Darveston in Dorset. Osborne was chairman of the Board of Poor Law Guardians and showed considerable sympathy for the plight of the poor. Ashley approved of Osborne, whose efforts, he felt, were actuated by high and pure motives. But Bankes was critical of Osborne and claimed that he had contributed to Austin's report. Osborne defended himself against Bankes's attack, but although he was given a hearing, he was interrupted and it was clear that the sympathy of the audience was with Bankes.[163] Thus local opinion showed some signs of being offended at Ashley's comments and unsympathetic to the paternalistic policy which he advocated.

The most marked effect of Ashley's speech, however, was on relations with his father. Ashley was disturbed by a letter which he received on 10 December saying that the writer, a Mr Crofts, and others, all of whom admired Ashley, were often 'perplexed to defend (his) consistency . . . and then to quote the state of the schoolhouse at Woodlands and certain other cottages.' Ashley commented that this was only too true, but he did not know how he could prevent it. How could he dare to attempt any interference with his father's affairs? Would he succeed if he did? And he soon received confirmation of what he already suspected. His father took great exception to his speech at Sturminster and told him that he was inducing the people to make extortionate demands. They got on very well with their present wages and they could not be raised: as for the dwellings, the evils could easily be pointed out, but he could not afford any remedy. Throughout his father's tirade, Ashley kept silence: 'defence,' he wrote, 'exasperates him.' But he thought to himself that £900 had been spent in the previous year for a hothouse, £600 for game and £800 for a farmhouse, which was 'wholly unnecessary, at least just now.' However, he could only have his thoughts; he felt powerless to act. He could not attend the Quarter Sessions for fear of collision or the board of guardians for fear of misrepresentation. He was, as he put it, 'posted between two forces': the League and his father. If he suppressed the faults of the landed proprietors, he was accused by the League; if he rebuked them, he stirred the resentment of his father.[164] He did not regret the speech at Sturminster, but the damage which it did to relations with his father must have caused him pain, both mental and, indeed, physical. In early November, he had already complained of noises in his ears, a complaint which may well have been connected with the moods of depression to which he was subject, and in December, after the quarrel with his father, he wrote of 'long and violent billious attacks' and of pains and was forced to consult a doctor. Again, the complaints may have been associated with nervous tension; he himself wrote that his billious attacks were 'the *accompaniments* and *consequences* of a stirring question hotly opposed.'[165] The Sturminster speech thus exacted its toll on Ashley's own health, and the damage which it did to relations with his father was never to be repaired. Ashley had prayed that God might open his father's eyes and touch his heart; certainly these were things which Ashley himself could never again achieve when, after Sturminster, father and son became finally estranged.

NOTES

1. N.R.A., Shaftesbury (Broadlands) MSS, SHA/PD/2, 12 Jan., 1843.
2. Add. MSS, 40, 483, fos 92-3.
3. N.R.A., Shaftesbury (Broadlands) MSS, SHA/PD/3, 10 Mar., 1843.
4. ibid., SHA/PD/2, 22 Nov., 1842.
5. Add. MSS, 40, 483, fos 84-5, 86-7.
6. N.R.A., Shaftesbury (Broadlands) MSS, SHA/PD/3, 25 Nov., 1843.
7. ibid., SHA/PD/2, 13 Feb., 1843.
8. ibid., SHA/PD/3, 15 Mar., 1843.
9. Hansard, *Parl. Debates*, 3rd ser., LXVIII, 362-405.

10. N.R.A., Shaftesbury (Broadlands) MSS, SHA/PD/3, 5 Apr., 1843.
11. Hansard, *Parl. Debates*, 3rd ser., LXVIII, 405.
12. ibid.
13. N.R.A., Shaftesbury (Broadlands) MSS, SHA/PD/3, 8 July, 1843.
14. N. Gash, op. cit., p. 482 ff.
15. J. T. Ward, *The Factory Movement*, p. 233.
16. Add. MSS, 40, 483, f. 37.
17. St G.H., Shaftesbury MSS, C 25044–C 25046/7th Earl.
18. For proposals of this bill, see above p. 123.
19. Add. MSS, 40, 617, fos 112–13. See also N. Gash, 'Ashley and the Conservative Party in 1842' (*E.H.R.*, LIII, 679–81).
20. Add. MSS, 40, 617, f. 114.
21. ibid., 40, 616, f. 237.
22. ibid., 40, 483, fos 44–52.
23. ibid., fos 53–4.
24. *The Morning Post*, 4 Feb., 1842.
25. N.R.A., Shaftesbury (Broadlands) MSS, SHA/PD/2, 4 Feb., 1842.
26. Add. MSS, 40, 617, fos 115–17.
27. Bodleian Library, Graham MSS (on microfilm). Film 113, 26 Jan., 1842.
28. N.R.A., Shaftesbury (Broadlands) MSS, SHA/PD/2, 6 Feb., 1842. Ashley wrote that he was 'increasingly entertained' by the general concurrence that the author of the article was Roundall Palmer (ibid.).
29. See above, p. 46.
30. Add. MSS, 40, 483, f. 42.
31. N.R.A., Shaftesbury (Broadlands) MSS, SHA/PD/2, 3 Sept., 1841.
32. Hansard, *Parl. Debates*, 3rd ser., LX, 101.
33. N.R.A., Shaftesbury (Broadlands) MSS, SHA/PD/2, 11 Feb., 1842.
34. ibid., SHA/PD/2, 28 Feb., 1842.
35. ibid., SHA/PD/2, 9 Mar., 1842.
36. ibid., SHA/PD/2, 11 Mar., 1842.
37. ibid., SHA/PD/2, 5 Mar., 1842.
38. See below p. 229.
39. N.R.A., Shaftesbury (Broadlands) MSS, SHA/PD/2, 18 Mar., 1842.
40. ibid., SHA/PD/2, 11 Mar., 1842.
41. ibid., SHA/PD/2, 29 Mar., 1842.
42. ibid., SHA/PD/2, 26 Apr., 1842.
43. N. Gash, *Peel*, p. 334.
44. N.R.A., Shaftesbury (Broadlands) MSS, SHA/PD/2, 7 May, 1842.
45. ibid., SHA/PD/2, 21, 24 May, 1842.
46. ibid., SHA/PD/2, 31 May, 1 June, 1842.
47. Hansard, *Parl. Debates*, 3rd ser., LXIII, 1320–52.
48. N.R.A., Shaftesbury (Broadlands) MSS, SHA/PD/2, 9 Apr., 1842.
49. ibid., SHA/PD/2, 9 June, 1842.
50. ibid., SHA/PD/2, 11 June, 1842.
51. Graham MSS (on microfilm). Film 113, 15 June, 1842.
52. N.R.A., Shaftesbury (Broadlands) MSS, SHA/PD/2, 20 June, 1842.
53. ibid., SHA/PD/2, 23 June, 1842.
54. Hansard, *Parl. Debates*, 3rd ser., LXIV, 426.
55. ibid.
56. N.R.A., Shaftesbury (Broadlands) MSS, SHA/PD/2, 25 June, 1842.
57. ibid., SHA/PD/2, 25 June, 1842.

58. Hansard, *Parl. Debates*, 3rd ser., LXIV, 937.
59. ibid., 1001-2.
60. N.R.A., Shaftesbury (Broadlands) MSS, SHA/PD/2, 28 June, 1842.
61. Buccleuch wrote to Peel about Ashley's approach to him. He felt that the bill in the Lords should be under the charge of 'someone not directly concerned with the Government', for if he were to take charge of it, it would be 'tantamount to the adoption of the bill by the Government, who would thus become responsible not only for the principle but also the details of the measure.' (Add. MSS 40, 511, f 174. I owe this reference to Mr R. C. Sloan).
62. N.R.A., Shaftesbury (Broadlands) MSS, SHA/PD/2, 5 July, 1842.
63. ibid., SHA/PD/2, 8 July, 1842.
64. Hansard, *Parl. Debates*, 3rd ser., LXIV, 1166-8.
65. ibid., LXV, 105-10.
66. ibid., 583.
67. ibid., 588.
68. N.R.A., Wellington MSS, 25 June, 1842.
69. N.R.A., ibid., 4 July, 1842.
70. N.R.A., ibid., 5 July, 1842.
71. N.R.A., Shaftesbury (Broadlands) MSS, SHA/PD/2, 8 July, 1842.
72. Hansard, *Parl. Debates*, 3rd ser., LXV, 7.
73. N.R.A., Shaftesbury (Broadlands) MSS, SHA/PD/2, 13 July, 1842.
74. N.R.A., Wellington MSS, 25 June, 1842.
75. Hansard, *Parl. Debates*, 3rd ser., LXV, 2-4.
76. ibid., 101-3.
77. ibid., 84.
78. ibid., 86. There were, in fact, divided counsels in the Tory party. Londonderry wrote to Peel in July, 1842, declaring his intention to oppose the bill in the Lords. (Add. MSS 40, 512, f 35). Peel regretted this step: he told Londonderry that the part taken by the majority of members of the House of Commons connected with the coal trade district of Northumberland and Durham led him to infer that the bill did not meet with much opposition in these districts (ibid., f 71). Londonderry wrote again in October 1842, reiterating his opposition and enclosing a copy of a letter which he had written to Ashley on the subject. He realised that in expressing his opinions so freely, he would probably incur displeasure (Add. MSS 40, 517, f 22). Peel replied, rather icily, that he had not had the leisure to read the letter to Ashley but would do so as soon as possible (ibid., f 24). (I owe these references to Mr R. C. Sloan).
79. Hansard *Parl. Debates*, 3rd ser., LXV, 104.
80. O. O. G. M. MacDonagh, 'Coal Mines Regulation: The First Decade, 1842-1852' (in R. Robson (ed.), *Ideas and Institutions of Victorian Britain* (1967), p. 63).
81. N.R.A., Shaftesbury (Broadlands) MSS, SHA/PD/2, 26 July, 1842.
82. Add. MSS, 40, 483, fos 7, 8.
83. ibid.
84. ibid., fos 80-81. See also N. Gash, *Peel*, 334-5.
85. Hansard, *Parl. Debates*, LXV, 1097.
86. N.R.A., Shaftesbury (Broadlands) MSS, SHA/PD/2, 8 Aug., 1842.
87. ibid., SHA/PD/2, 18 Aug., 1842.
88. ibid., SHA/PD/2, 18 Aug., 1842.
89. Bodleian Library, Oxford, MSS Eng. Lett., c 250, f. 161. (Ashley to Lt-Col Napier), 28 Sept., 1842.

90. Dr James Phillips Kay (1804–77). Assumed the name 'Kay-Shuttleworth'; Sir James Kay-Shuttleworth, 1st Bt from 1849.
91. N.R.A., Shaftesbury (Broadlands) MSS, SHA/PD/2, 29 Sept., 1842.
92. Add. MSS, 40, 483, fos 72–7.
93. Quoted in Hodder, I, 435–7.
94. For a critical assessment of Ashley's comments on the effects of factory labour on the domestic lives of women, see M. Hewitt, *Wives and Mothers in Victorian Industry* (1958), pp. 100–101, 182–4.
95. N.R.A., Shaftesbury (Broadlands) MSS, SHA/PD/2, 10 Jan., 1843.
96. ibid., SHA/PD/2, 10 Jan., 1843.
97. M. W. Thomas, op. cit., 269–70.
98. Hansard, *Parl. Debates*, 3rd ser., LXVII, 47–75.
99. ibid., 75–91.
100. Graham MSS (on microfilm). Film 115, 1 Mar., 1843.
101. ibid., 4 Mar., 1843.
102. Hansard, *Parl. Debates*, 3rd ser., LXVII, 422 ff.
103. J. T. Ward, 'A Lost Opportunity in Education: 1843' (*Researches and Studies*, No 20, Oct., 1959). See also J. T. Ward and J. H. Treble, 'Religion and Education in 1843. Reaction to the "Factory Education Bill".' (*Journal of Ecclesiastical History*, XX, 79–110).
104. Hansard, *Parl. Debates*, 3rd ser., LXIX, 1567–9.
105. N.R.A., Shaftesbury (Broadlands) MSS, SHA/PD/2, 11 May, 1843.
106. Hansard, *Parl. Debates*, 3rd ser., LXVII, 1465–9.
107. Quoted in Hodder, I, 458.
108. Duke University, Durham, North Carolina, William R. Perkins Libr., Manuscript Dept., John Easthope MSS, Ashley to Easthope, 18 Mar., 1843.
109. Graham MSS (on microfilm). Film 115, 28 Mar., 1843.
110. ibid., 26 Apr., 1843.
111. J. T. Ward, 'A Lost Opportunity in Education: 1843', pp. 44–5.
112. N.R.A., Shaftesbury (Broadlands) MSS, SHA/PD/3, 1 May, 1843.
113. ibid., SHA/PD/3, 16 June, 1843.
114. ibid., SHA/PD/3, 11 May, 1843.
115. ibid., SHA/PD/3, 16 June, 1843. Ashley also expressed this view in a letter to Peel on 17 June, 1843 (Add. MSS, 40, 483, fos 114–15): 'The Dissenters and the Church,' he wrote, 'have each laid down their limits which they will not pass; and there is no power which can either force, persuade or delude them.'
116. Graham MSS (on microfilm). Film 115, 28 Mar., 1843.
117. Add. MSS, 40, 483, fos 106–7.
118. ibid., fos 108–9.
119. ibid., fos 110–11.
120. ibid., fos 112–13.
121. Hansard, *Parl. Debates*, 3rd ser., LXX, 94.
122. ibid., 483.
123. N.R.A., Shaftesbury (Broadlands) MSS, SHA/PD/3, 30 June, 1843.
124. Add. MSS, 40, 483, fos 122–3.
125. ibid., fos 124–5.
126. Hansard, *Parl. Debates*, 3rd ser., LXX, 1299–1300.
127. N.R.A., Shaftesbury (Broadlands) MSS, SHA/PD/3, 30 June, 1843.
128. ibid., SHA/PD/2, 18 Aug., 1842.
129. ibid., SHA/PD/2, 6 Sept., 1842.
130. ibid., SHA/PD/2, 24 Feb., 1842.

131. ibid., SHA/PD/2, 8 July, 1842.
132. Add. MSS, 40, 416, f. 237.
133. Graham MSS (on microfilm). Film 113, 15 June, 1842.
134. Add. MSS, 40, 483, fos 70–71.
135. ibid., fos 74–5.
136. Graham MSS (on microfilm). Film 115, 1 Apr., 1843.
137. For a consideration of this group's activities and criticisms of Peel in the 1840s, see R. Blake, *The Conservative Party from Peel to Churchill* (1970), pp. 55–7. Ashley strongly disliked the High Churchmanship associated with the group.
138. N.R.A., Shaftesbury (Broadlands) MSS, SHA/PD/3, 25 May, 1843.
139. ibid., SHA/PD/2, 3 Feb., 1842. The phrase was a favourite one with Ashley. See above p. 71.
140. ibid., SHA/PD/2, 4 July, 1840.
141. ibid., SHA/PD/2, 16 May, 1842.
142. ibid., SHA/PD/3, 25 May, 1843.
143. ibid., SHA/PD/3, 15 May, 1843.
144. ibid., SHA/PD/3, 15 July, 1843.
145. The Diary kept by Ashley on this holiday is quoted by Hodder, I, 497–514. Quotations on p. 197 are taken from Hodder's extracts.
146 N.R.A., Shaftesbury (Broadlands) MSS, SHA/PD/3, 21 Oct., 1843.
147. ibid., SHA/PD/3, 26 Oct., 1843.
148. ibid., SHA/PD/3, 30 Oct., 1843.
149. ibid., SHA/PD/3, 27 Oct., 1843.
150. Hansard, *Parl. Debates*, 3rd ser., LXVI, 1158.
151. P.P., 1843, XII.
152. Add. MSS, 56, 368, fos 10–11.
153. N.R.A., Shaftesbury (Broadlands) MSS, SHA/PC/133.
154. ibid., SHA/PD/2, 3 Jan., 1842.
155. ibid., SHA/PD/2, 1 Jan., 1843.
156. ibid., SHA/PD/2, 16 Dec., 1842.
157. Son of R. B. Sheridan (1751–1816) the dramatist. Member of Parliament from 1845 to 1868.
158. *The Dorset County Chronicle and Somersetshire Gazette*, 7 Dec., 1843.
159. ibid.
160. *Speeches of the Earl of Shaftesbury*, pp. 87–90.
161. N.R.A., Shaftesbury (Broadlands) MSS, SHA/PD/3, 1 Dec., 1843.
162. *The Dorset County Chronicle and Somersetshire Gazette*, 7 Dec., 1843.
163. ibid., 28 Dec., 1843.
164. N.R.A., Shaftesbury (Broadlands) MSS, SHA/PD/3, 11 Dec., 1843.
165. ibid., SHA/PD/3, 14 Dec., 1843.

9
Mammon, Moloch, Mens Sana, 1843–1845

As Ashley spent Christmas Day 1843 at St Giles – the last he was to spend there during his father's lifetime – he rose before six o'clock to pray and meditate. His thoughts wandered to those who, even on Christmas Day, had risen at four 'to toil and suffering'; and this led him to reflect on the 'mockery of an enactment which we cannot enforce, and which, year after year, we vainly endeavour to strengthen.'[1] In the months ahead, Ashley was, indeed, to be much occupied with the factory question, but the first major parliamentary issue of the year which concerned him related to foreign and not domestic affairs. It was over the annexation of Scinde, which had been carried out in the spring of 1843. Scinde lay on the North-West frontier of the Indian Empire and was ruled by a family of princes known as the Ameers. Relations with the Ameers had, on the whole, been friendly, but they had been disturbed by the Afghan war, since the invasion of Afghanistan had involved the passage of troops through territory belonging to the Ameers and the imposition on them of a new treaty in 1839. At the end of the Afghan war, a further treaty was imposed by Ellenborough, involving the surrender of territory. This resulted in the outbreak of violence, including the expulsion of the British resident from Hyderabad. Retaliatory measures quickly followed; a native army was defeated, the Ameers thrown into prison and Scinde annexed to the British Empire.

This, then, was a further episode in the aggressive imperial policy followed under Ellenborough, and, predictably, Ashley expressed severe disapproval of it. In June, 1843, he wrote to Peel to say that the late events in Scinde distressed many persons who wished Peel's government and the British Empire well, and, he continued, he himself could 'not do less than join in any vote of condemnation of the Policy pursued by the Governor General.' He had been 'pained and shocked' by reading various letters and papers which had illustrated his part in the matter.[2] He followed this with another letter to Peel in July, 1843, imploring the Prime Minister to do justice to the Ameers and redress a 'tyrannical and dishonest' act.[3] Before the 1843 session closed, Ashley gave notice of a motion on the subject; he waited until then, hoping that appeals might come from the imprisoned Ameers. By the end of the session, however, these had not come and Ashley intended to abandon his motion lest he might harm their interests. But he was impelled to take action early in 1844 by a letter of 8 January from Sir Henry Pottinger, an Anglo-Indian official, to *The Morning Chronicle* which castigated the treatment accorded to the Ameers as 'the most unprincipled and disgraceful that had ever stamped the annals of our Empire in India.'[4]

Two days later, Ashley wrote to Easthope. He had, he wrote, never read 'such a tremendous document' as Pottinger's letter, and, since he had given notice during the previous session to bring forward the case of the Ameers, he was anxious to obtain authentication of the letter.[5] Easthope's reply has not survived, but it appears that Ashley was satisfied of the authenticity of Pottinger's letter, for, on 8 February, 1844, he introduced a motion for an Address to the Crown, asking for the Ameers to be restored to liberty and the enjoyment of their estates. It was a long speech,[6] in which Ashley surveyed relations over many years between Britain and the Ameers and criticised the recent conduct of the British government. He ended his speech by developing the theme of the 'generosity of absolute power' and the effectiveness of 'true principle'. It remained to be seen whether Britain would accomplish the dominion of the East by these means: 'we have not, I fear, made an auspicious beginning,' he said, 'but if we are to gain no more by virtue, let us not lose what we have by injustice.' Ashley was satisfied by the speech and the reception given to it; but he was depressed by the result of the debate, for his motion was heavily defeated. He attributed his defeat to 'the pernicious effect of party on the moral sense; most were satisfied and yet voted because Peel did, point-blank against me!' And Peel himself was 'narrow, selfish and in a tone of morality lower, by far, than the ordinary run of Ministers.'[7]

Hard on the heels of the Scinde episode came that of Tahiti. For many years, British and French influences had jockeyed for position in Tahiti. British missionaries had long been present on the island and Queen Pomare had, in 1826 and 1838, asked for formal British protection. This, however, had been refused. The French, on the other hand, were more ready to take action, although not of an official nature. This came to a head in 1843, when a French admiral, Dupetit-Thouars, annexed the island without authorisation. The Queen was deposed and the British consul, Pritchard, was arrested, imprisoned and deported. Ashley followed these events with great concern. 'A peaceable and helpless people,' he wrote, '. . . are subjugated by savages and powerful Europeans, and inundated with bloodshed, devastation, profligacy and crime. . . .'[8] The French action, moreover, was not only reprehensible on moral grounds; it was highly objectionable in religious terms. For it meant the overthrow of a Protestant régime: 'a Christian State,' Ashley wrote of it, 'founded on the truths of the Gospel, and governed by the simplicity of God's word.' Popery would now 'reign without control, with all its train of spiritual, moral, and physical evils.'[9] Pritchard, who was a former missionary, attended a great meeting at Exeter Hall in August and Evangelical consciences were roused.[10] The matter was resolved in September, with the payment of compensation to Pritchard and the restoration of Queen Pomare, but French influences remained predominant. Ashley felt that the British government had acted feebly. Aberdeen had, he wrote, 'surrendered all that can be interesting to Protestantism.'[11] And, he continued on another occasion: 'what a disgusting and cowardly attitude for England, thus to stand by and raise not a hand in defence of this merciful gift of Providence!'[12]

Thus over Scinde and Tahiti, Ashley had once more stood out as an upholder of morality in international affairs and, over Tahiti, as a defender of Protestantism. Once more, Peel's government had incurred his severe condemnation, and, once more, it did not deserve it. Peel himself was far from satisfied with the Scinde episode and expressed strong criticism of it privately to Lord Ripon, President of the India Board of Control. It was only with reluctance that the Cabinet decided to accept the annexation of Scinde,[13] and, although Peel often felt obliged to defend Ellenborough's conduct in public and dissociated his government from the Governor-General's dismissal by the Board in April, 1844, he did not share Ellenborough's grandiose ideas.[14] There was, in fact, to be greater harmony between Ashley and Peel under Ellenborough's successor as Governor-General, Lord Hardinge. After a victory over the Sikhs in February, 1846, Hardinge behaved with restraint towards them and offered public prayers and thanksgiving to God for the success of the army. Ashley felt that Hardinge had done a great service to 'the character of his country'; he had been an instrument of 'Divine retribution' towards the warlike Sikhs and had duly acknowledged the aid of the Almighty.[15] Peel shared Ashley's views; Ashley noted that he had heard from Peel telling him that a thanksgiving was to be appointed in Britain, and Peel had added that this would be a departure from 'a bad principle' which had previously prevailed of 'not returning thanks to God for Indian successes.' Ashley approved of Peel's attitude on this occasion.[16] Further, on the Tahiti episode, Peel was not by any means submissive towards France and expressed his views forcibly on the matter and on the necessity for compensation. Aberdeen, it is true, was less abrasive and more willing to be conciliatory[17]; but it was Peel's views over the need for immediate compensation which prevailed.

The major issue concerning Ashley's relations with the Ministry was, however, to be the factory question. Already in November, 1843, the Cabinet had decided to re-introduce the previous session's factory bill, without the educational clauses. A further change was that the age at which work was to start was raised from eight to nine. Thus the bill introduced by Graham on 6 February, 1844,[18] proposed that children between the ages of nine and thirteen should work for six-and-a-half hours a day either in the morning or the afternoon, and they were to receive daily education, although not on the lines suggested in the 1843 bill. Young persons between thirteen and eighteen were to work a maximum of twelve hours, as before; but the bill also proposed that adult women should be limited to these hours, whereas the 1843 bill had proposed that the twelve-hour day should only be for women under the age of twenty-one. Silk mills were to come under the same regulations as other textile factories, and there were also clauses to strengthen the powers of the inspectors and to fence dangerous machinery for the safety of the workers.

The bill did not, of course, concede the ten-hour day. The Ten Hours Movement had been given a new lease of life by Graham's proposals the previous year and had remained active throughout 1843. A great deal of effort was devoted in the latter months of 1843 to a campaign to secure the release of Oastler, who had been imprisoned in 1840 for debt; but every meeting held with this in view also called for 'Ten Hours' and the abolition of the Poor Law.[19] Finally, in February, 1844, Oastler was released, and, coming just at the time when Graham's new proposals were being announced, this injected further life into the Movement. Great meetings were held in the north, many addressed by Oastler himself, and twelve delegates were sent to Westminster to canvass and lobby members of Parliament.

On his return from holiday in October, 1843, Ashley had seen Crabtree to discuss policy and, as has been seen, the factory question was never far from his thoughts. When Graham asked leave on 6 February, 1844, to introduce his bill, Ashley expressed his gratitude to the government.[20] But when delays and postponements occurred after the second reading on 15 February, Ashley began to wonder if he would ever see it succeed and he was disturbed by rumours that John Bright was waiting for an opportunity to make an attack on him.[21] He was also worried by a revival of an issue which had preoccupied him at the end of 1843. Godolphin Osborne wrote to Ashley through the column of *The Times* on the condition of the agricultural labourer and lamented the fact that few persons who had taken an active part in Parliament on this matter had been acquainted with the habits of this particular class of worker. He also said that the agricultural labourers in Dorset had been prevented from making any attempt to set forth their grievances, and suggested that between one seventh and one eighth of the labouring population of Dorset were in a state of pauperism. *The Times* used this as an opportunity to attack the Poor Law and asked 'which of the most philanthropic orators of Exeter Hall has ever come forward manfully to denounce it?' It also asked which supporter of the ten hours bill had 'stirred one foot to raise the wages, increase the comforts and alleviate the hardships of the agricultural labourer in his own district until compelled to do so by very shame?'[22] Such comments distressed Ashley. The question of agricultural grievances, he wrote, was 'not uppermost and . . . barely thought of' when he took up the factory question in 1833, and he reflected that he had 'lost office and every hope of political aggrandisement by (his) adoption of this career;' he had had 'years of trouble, anxiety and expense'; and further, 'eight years of exclusion from the paternal house, and three of *utter impossibility* to interfere while there.'[23] Some days later he sat through a speech by Cobden in the House on conditions in Dorset. It was, he conceded, 'often true'; but Cobden had made no disguise that he wished to 'pay (Ashley) off' for exposing conditions in factories. All this made Ashley feel 'humbled, dejected, and incompetent'.[24]

Nevertheless, when the factory bill went into Committee on 15 March, Ashley moved an amendment to a clause dealing with the hours during which work was prohibited at night, and the effect of this amendment would have been to introduce a ten-hour day for workers between the ages of thirteen and eighteen.[25] The previous day, Ashley had written to Easthope mentioning this amendment;[26] it was not, he said, 'altogether the most intelligible course' but he had adopted it to 'suit . . . Graham's convenience.' He was, however, anxious lest his speech on the subject might not receive very much publicity – reporters, he told Easthope, were inclined to treat speeches made in Committee as 'secondary affairs'. Thus he asked Easthope to make it known to *The Morning Chronicle* that the subject and the debate were of great importance and to ensure that a full report was given. Ashley's speech[27] lasted for two hours and a quarter. Many of the points in it had been made in earlier speeches: individuals were being harmed in body, mind and spirit; homes were being disrupted; the peace of society threatened; the laws of God flouted. The state, he said, had the duty to concern itself in the physical and moral well-being of persons under age; the principle of interference, after all, had been conceded and it was only a question of degree. But Ashley also referred to the points which had recently been made over 'land' and 'industry'. He denied that he was animated by any 'peculiar hostility' towards factory masters and that he had selected them as exclusive objects for attack; avarice and cruelty were not the inherent qualities of any one class or occupation. He freely acknowledged that the prosperity of the manufacturing interest was essential to the welfare and even to the existence of the British Empire.

> No [he concluded], we fear not the increase of your political power, nor envy your stupendous riches: 'Peace be within your walls, and plenteousness within your palaces.' We ask but a slight relaxation of toil, a time to live and a time to die, a time for those comforts that sweeten life, and a time for those duties that adorn it. . . .

The amendment, however, ran into strong opposition from Graham.[28] He was prepared to commend Ashley for his benevolent intentions, but he defended his original proposal. Any reduction of time worked by women and young persons below twelve hours would affect the hours of adults and reduce their wages, and this would not be popular since adult workers preferred establishments where most work was done and the highest wages paid. This point was also made by Milner Gibson, Member for Manchester: a ten-hour day for women and children would, in effect, mean a ten-hour day for adults and this would interfere with the only property which most operatives had to dispose of: their labour.[29] Others spoke in support of Ashley on this point, but the most notable feature of the debate was a vigorous attack on Ashley by Bright.[30] Bright challenged many of the statements which Ashley had made in the course of his speech, claiming that Ashley had exaggerated the evils of the manufacturing districts and neglected those of the countryside; and also that much of his information had come from Dodd, a factory worker crippled in the course of his employment. Dodd's evidence, said Bright, was worthless. 'I am free to tell the noble lord,' Bright said, 'that unless he employs agents more respectable, his statements and his professions of benevolence will ever be viewed with suspicion by the manufacturers of the north. . . .' And Bright also added the accusation that Ashley had been guilty of deserting Dodd once Dodd had ceased to be useful to him.

Ashley recorded that he 'never had a greater weight on his spirits' than when he made his speech, but he felt that the speech had gone well and that he had obtained 'outstanding personal success'. He was, however, bitterly critical of Graham: 'mean, false and hard hearted beyond himself', he wrote.[31] And he had been greatly hurt by Bright's accusations over Dodd. These accusations had stung him to defend himself in the debate.[32] He admitted that he had known Dodd; he had received a letter from Dodd saying that he had been injured in a factory and Dodd had called on him. Ashley had, he said, never seen such a wretched figure; he had given him a meal with the servants and after Dodd had returned to the manufacturing districts, had received letters from him about conditions there. Ashley claimed, however, that he had only once quoted from these letters. As for the accusation that he had cast Dodd off, this had arisen from the fact that Dodd had written to Ashley asking for money for the services which he had rendered the Ten Hours Movement. Ashley had refused this, and Dodd had then written to Messrs. Ashworth of Bolton, claiming that he had been misused by the Movement and offering his services in countering the accusations which it had made against the factory owners. Ashley felt that Dodd had behaved very badly and had been unworthy of the kindness which he had shown him. It must be said that Ashley's comments on this occasion were somewhat selective. Dodd had been paid to send Ashley information about the factory districts and Ashley thought well of his efforts. He wrote of Dodd as a 'jewell' and praised his talent and skill in providing 'invaluable evidence'.[33] And, although he strongly disapproved of Dodd's later conduct, he still thought that Bright and his friends must have bribed him to 'trump up a case' against his former patrons.[34] It was an accusation almost certainly without foundation, and, in making it – as in forming his association with Dodd – Ashley showed that waywardness of judgment of which he could be guilty.[35]

The debate had been adjourned on 15 March, and Ashley wondered what would be the issue. He was told that, had there been a division at the end of the debate, the government would have been beaten, but the interval, he thought, would assist the government: 'official whips', he wrote, 'will produce official votes.'[36] The government certainly took the possibility of defeat on the amendment seriously. Peel knew that many country gentry might be disposed to vote for Ashley from resentment against the Anti-Corn Law League, and the government also felt that such a vote could only intensify the anti-aristocratic sentiment of the League.[37] Indeed, Graham was of the view the Corn Laws would not last twelve months if Ashley's amendment were adopted. The Cabinet discussed its tactics on 16 March. The possibility of a collective resignation or the resignation of Graham individually was not fully explored, but Graham was clear that he would not accept the ten-hour clause even if it were passed. He had Peel's support in this, although others in the Cabinet were less decided. Feelers were put out to Ashley to discover if a way out of the situation could be found. According to Ashley's account of this episode,[38] Stanley approached Ashley's brother-in-law, Jocelyn, and told him of the government's predicament: if Ashley's amendment were carried, as seemed likely, the government would have to abandon the bill, since Graham was committed to carrying it as it was – or surrendering it into Ashley's hands. Stanley dwelt on the likely effect of the amendment, if carried, on the repeal of the Corn Laws. Ashley's comment on this interview was that Jocelyn 'without delivering a direct message, was to inform me of the Ministerial mind. He did so.' Ashley's reply was that if his perseverance 'involved ten thousand Corn Laws and the desertion of as many governments (he) would go on with all the vigour (he) could command;' and that, even if he were disposed to concede, he could not do so without incurring the charge of being a hypocrite. Jocelyn passed this on to Stanley and subsequently reported to Ashley the substance of Stanley's reply. This was to the effect that Stanley never thought that Ashley could abandon the question; on the other hand, the government would appear in an unfavourable light if it resisted a measure which had a majority in the House. Thus Stanley suggested that Tory sympathisers with Ashley should not make vigorous attempts to gain votes and Ashley himself might 'save his character by maintaining his point and *yet allowing himself to be beaten.*' Ashley also dismissed this suggestion: 'the only difference,' he told Jocelyn, 'was whether I should be an open or a secret scoundrel.' He added that he would 'exhaust all legitimate means to obtain (his) end and that, if defeated . . . would never cease to work on the sympathies of the country.'

The adjourned debate was resumed on 28 March, and the strength of feeling in favour of Ashley was indicated by speeches from a wide cross-section of members, Tory and Whig. Peel, however, spoke at length against Ashley's amendment.[39] He stressed the view that loss of working time would lead to reduced production; this would result in loss of markets; and the net effect would be reduced wages. Ashley's proposal would, Peel felt, cut across his plans for economic expansion as the means to increased prosperity and greater social harmony. He also asked whether it was right to deal with only this one branch of industry and leave others – in which conditions were worse – untouched; but extensive intervention would be a task 'above all human strength and pregnant with great injustice to individuals.' The arguments in Peel's speech were not new, but Peel gave them added weight and authority; yet the House refused to follow his lead. At the division, the original clause was lost and Ashley's amendment carried. Graham commented dryly that the decision was 'a virtual adoption of a Ten Hours Bill without modification'; and he added that 'this, with all respect for the Committee, he had a decided objection to.'[40] He suggested that the question might be reconsidered in the debate on a further clause which was concerned with the hours of work of young persons.[41]

Ashley could hardly believe the result of the division. 'Oh gracious God,' he wrote on 19 March, 'keep me from unseemly exultation, that I may creep alow by the ground to Thine honour and to the recovery of the people from Egyptian bondage!'[42] He was pleased that his supporters had been faithful to him, even without any 'whipper-in', but he felt that the government would use the interval until the next division to erode his support by influence and coercion. He wondered what he could do to counteract this.

But, for the moment, he was elated by his success and confident of the final outcome.

On 22 March, the Committee resumed. The previous day, Ashley had written of the efforts made by the ministers to try to reverse the earlier vote: 'Ministers quite mad, using every exertion, no reasoning, no mis-statement, no falsehood almost spared!'[43] But the government itself was defeated. Despite all the efforts and Graham's further plea that a ten-hour day for women and young persons would lead to a diminution of wages, the proposal of the government on clause eight – that the period of work for young males between thirteen and eighteen should be twelve – was rejected by 186 to 183. On the other hand, Ashley's amendment for a ten-hour day was also defeated: on this the voting was 181 to 180. The reason for this was that five members voted against the government's twelve-hour proposal and also against Ashley's ten-hour proposal. This was not entirely due to confusion on their part, for an eleven-hour compromise was favoured in some quarters.[44] But if the members were not themselves confused, the situation to which they contributed certainly was, and Graham could only announce a postponement of the matter until 25 March.[45] Ashley announced that he would persevere, and expressed confidence in his final victory – he wrote next day that, despite the confusion, the cause was 'mightily advanced'. Peel, true to form, had cast away his 'patrimony ... the especial protection of the working classes'; and Ashley was disappointed at 'some sad and grievous fallings off'. Nevertheless, party feeling on all sides had, he felt, been resigned 'to the assertion of a great act of humanity'; and he was delighted by the measure of support which his cause had commanded.[46]

The interval until 25 March was filled with speculation. It was widely expected that the government would compromise with an eleven hours bill. But at a Cabinet meeting on the morning of the 25th, a compromise of this kind was rejected. Peel was strongly opposed to it on the grounds that it would only be a temporary measure and would not settle the matter.[47] Thus, later in the day in the House, Graham once again rejected ten hours and attacked the idea that legislative interference with the free market of labour should be made a general rule: this would be the commencement of a 'Jack Cade' system of legislation. He asked leave to withdraw the bill and replace it with a measure which amended the present law and introduced such improvements and modifications as had already received the sanction of the House.[48] This he did on 29 March. The bill limited children between the ages of eight and eleven in silk mills and eight and thirteen in other mills to six-and-a-half hours: young persons were still to work twelve hours.

The government's continuing hostility provoked resentment in the Ten Hours Movement: the Lancashire Committee petitioned the Queen for Graham's dismissal[49] and protested against his 'ill advised perseverance in a course of cruelty and injustice'.[50] Twenty-two Short-Time Committees signed the protest. Ashley himself would have been willing to accept an eleven hours bill; this, he felt, would have settled the question for two years. He objected to Graham's reference to 'Jack Cade' legislation: 'indecent, foolish and stupid', he wrote.[51] Nevertheless, he was disposed to allow the government to withdraw the bill. He felt that when Graham brought in a new bill, he could precipitate a division on the simple question of ten hours. His decision did not escape criticism; Ashley noted that *The Times* had accused him of preferring 'the existence of government to the affirmation of (his) principle.'[52] But he felt that to have insisted on another debate and division would have been proceeding on technicalities and points of order and this was something which he had never done.[53] He also felt that he would have had a large majority against him, and there was the further point that the bill was at present a 'nonsense – it contained nothing but contradictions.'[54] Thus Ashley felt justified in his course of action, but he thought it necessary to write a letter to the operatives to appear in *The Times* explaining his decision: 'statement in debate,' he wrote, 'has no effect – they will read and will believe a letter signed by my name.'[55]

Before the matter could be resumed, the House rose for the Easter recess. Ashley had complained at the end of March of feeling 'no fire, great difficulty in speaking, not so much through fear as apparent defects of energy and intellectual power.'[56] Over Easter, Ashley went to Dover for a few days' rest. He enjoyed walks and fresh air. But the factory question was never far from his mind. He reflected on the work and effort which had been undertaken in the cause of reform, and yet, he felt, no effect had been produced. After a walk along the cliffs, he returned home feeling tired: 'I often think when fatigued,' he wrote, 'how much less my weariness must be than that of the wretched factory women. It has, at any rate, this good result – that I feel and make additional resolutions to persevere in their behalf.'[57] On Good Friday, he felt 'haunted . . . by debates, divisions, spectres of attacks, defences, failure, success;' and he reflected on his 'very nervous and excitable temperament'.[58] On Easter Sunday, he wrote that this was a 'Christian country'; and yet there were thousands and tens of thousands who did not know the difference between this Sunday and any other. 'Toil, excessive toil,' he wrote, 'is the lot of multitudes. . . . The pauses from labour are the triumphs of exhaustion, not the periods of refreshment to soul or body. . . .'[59]

Ashley was especially concerned at a memorial produced by the mill-owners who had contradicted his speech in Parliament and his remarks on the distances walked by the piecers in the course of their work. This was a task performed by children and involved walking between the machines on various errands, such as picking up pieces of thread and broken ends. With the help of a mathematician, Ashley had estimated this distance at over twenty miles a day, and this was attacked by the masters as a great exaggeration. He wrote that he held to his statements; if he were refuted, he would never again make a speech in the House or elsewhere.[60] Yet, in the face of this opposition, he was heartened by great meetings in the North, organised over Easter by the Ten Hours Movement, and delegates to a meeting in Manchester were told to bring information on the issue of the distances. They reported that the piecers walked at least a third further than the spinners and challenged those who doubted this to hold an investigation.[61] Ashley did, indeed, write to two masters, Ashworth and Greg, challenging them to meet Fielden and Kenworthy, two other masters, and, in the presence of delegates of the operatives, superintend the re-measurement of the distances by the same mathematician who made the original calculation. A long correspondence followed on this matter.[62] Ashworth and Greg were willing to provide further information on the subject and did so, and, if this appeared open to doubt, they were willing to meet Ashley or any other member of Parliament or any master manufacturer and have the measurements made. But they were unwilling to have the same mathematician carry out the task, nor were they disposed to have the delegates of the operatives present. Ashley, on his side, was unwilling to depart from the methods of re-measurement which he had laid down, and, later, he told the House that it was impossible to accept Ashworth's and Greg's suggestions; that he had confirmed his own previous findings and that these had, indeed, been exceeded by the findings of the delegates of the operative spinners from Lancashire.[63] Moreover, Ashley felt not only that he was in the right, but that he had the better of the argument. He had not thought it likely that Greg and Ashworth would accept the invitation. However, if they did, he was confident that he would be proved correct; if they did not, he would prove their dishonesty.[64] This was a somewhat oversimplified view of a complicated and technical subject, but it gave Ashley grounds for encouragement.

Despite this, however, Ashley felt gloomy at the political prospects. He felt that many members of Parliament – even religious men – would be prepared to reverse their votes on the factory question because they believed that perseverance would endanger the government. 'Alas,' he wrote, 'is Peel everything? Is God nothing?'[65] Further, Ashley heard from Bonham that Peel had decided to offer him the Lord Lieutenancy of Ireland, vacant on the resignation of Lord de Grey. According to Ashley's account of his conversation with Bonham,[66] Bonham told him that Peel and Graham were convinced that no one could bring about such good in Ireland as Ashley; he could 'grapple with the landlords and the prelates and maintain, against influence, the rights of the working clergy.' Ashley recorded his reaction to Bonham's news as one of astonishment and gratification. Even to be considered for office came to him as a surprise, if also a pleasant one. But there was also the point that the offer could be interpreted as a way of overcoming Ashley's opposition to the government on the factory question. Despite his gratification, Ashley was not unaware of this aspect: 'pray how could I work the factory question as Lord Lieutenant of Ireland? Answer me that,' he wrote. He also wrote of his determination to do and to accept nothing which would limit his free action over the ten hours bill. These suspicions were, in fact, unwarranted. Ashley *was* considered as a possibility for the appointment among several others, and Graham felt that he would do 'well for this particular appointment.'[67] But both he and Peel realised that there were difficulties in the way, and it appears that Peel told Bonham that no mention whatever would be made of the matter until after the factory bill was disposed of. Bonham, indeed, admitted to Ashley that he had 'done wrong' in mentioning it at that point, and it was unfortunate, since it tended only to increase Ashley's suspicions of the government.

Nonetheless, Ashley was not deterred. On 17 April – the same day on which he recorded the conversation with Bonham – he wrote to Graham, telling him the course which he intended to take over the factory bill which Graham had introduced on 29 March.[68] No difficulty would be offered to the second reading on 22 April, but before going into Committee, Ashley proposed to move an instruction, directing the Committee to insert clauses for the limitation of the hours of young persons to ten a day. 'This,' he wrote, 'will be at once the speediest and most intelligible course.' Graham replied later on the same day,[69] saying that his 'private wishes and feelings' would lead him to agree to this arrangement, but he had to adhere strictly to the rules of the House. It would be open to Ashley to propose an amendment in Committee to the clause which limited the hours of young persons to twelve, but the rule of the House was, Graham said, 'that a Committee of the whole House could not be instructed to do what it was already competent to do without instruction.' Graham advised Ashley to communicate with the Speaker before committing himself in public to a precise course of action; if the Speaker did not agree with Graham's view, Graham would accept Ashley's suggestion, but, if the Speaker confirmed his opinion, then he would be willing to consult with Ashley to find some way of raising the point in Committee. Ashley replied to Graham the following day:[70] he had, in fact, consulted the Speaker before writing to Graham, but could not, he admitted, have explained the situation with sufficient clarity. He had now asked the Speaker again and had received confirmation of Graham's view. Ashley had then asked the Speaker's opinion on the next course that he had in mind: that of moving the clauses on the third reading. The Speaker accepted this, preferring it to the Report stage. Ashley thus told Graham that he would take the liberty of giving such a notice. He thought that the bill would pass easily through the Committee in one night, and when it came to the third reading 'one discussion and one division would settle the matter. . . .'

Thus when Graham introduced the bill on 18 April, 1844,[71] Ashley gave notice that he would, at the third reading, move the addition of clauses which would limit the hours of young persons after 1 October, 1844, to eleven hours a day and after 1 October, 1847, to ten. On 22 April, the bill was given a second reading. Ashley's decision not to say anything at this point was commented on: Duncombe said that Ashley was only to take a flying shot at the bill as it was about to pass and warned that the operatives would think that their interests were being trifled with.[72] Ashley, however, quoted from a letter of the Central Short-Time Committee approving of his conduct on the matter.[73] The House went into Committee on the bill on 26 April and various points were made about it,[74] but the question of ten hours for young persons between thirteen and eighteen was not raised. This was reserved for the future, and the bill passed the Committee on 6 May.

On 1 May, as great meetings were held in the country, Ashley wrote of the 'serious task' ahead of him. He felt apprehensive at the prospect of a threat of resignation from the government if his motion were carried; he looked, too, for resistance from a body of capitalists 'the wealthiest, the most united, the most selfish that have ever resisted a just proposition.' On his side, he had 'a few masters, very moderate funds, no decided party, very little to threaten and nothing to promise. . . .'[75] On 3 May, Ashley was greatly depressed by a debate prompted by a motion put forward by Roebuck that there should be no interference with the power of adult labourers to make contracts over their hours. In the course of the debate, Ashley was singled out for attack.[76] Roebuck referred slightingly to the 'gratuitous humanity of the noble lord'. Ashley had been 'misled by his sympathies'; the factory worker was better fed, better paid, better clothed than any other kind of worker in the kingdom. Roebuck revived the argument which had haunted Ashley in the past: 'however disagreeable it may be to the agricultural nobles and to the ignorant country gentlemen,' he said, 'it was the manufacturer who applied his mind to business and who carried with him the manliness to do so – while our aristocracy were spending their lives in the fox chase. . . .' Ashley was greatly distressed. He wrote that he had been the 'direct and indirect target. They fired at me without mercy, and left me, like a portrait of St Sebastian, shot through and through by their arrows.'[77] He had replied to the criticisms and once again denied that he was 'anti-millowner';[78] but his reply left him dissatisfied and dispirited – the House had not been willing to listen to him. And, as he contemplated the struggle ahead, he felt 'languid, weary, diffident'; on other issues – in Mines, Education and Opium – he had an inner conviction of support but on this occasion, he never experienced a cheering thought, an invigorating grace. Was he right in his purpose: was it according to God's will?[79] Thus, as the third reading approached, Ashley's spirits were at a low ebb. But he still summoned enough energy to castigate Peel's speech in the debate: 'worse than usual in sentiment,' he wrote:

> (Peel) sneered at moral legislation, at attempts to make people moral by Act of Parliament; maintained that Government had nothing to do with the morality of the people; it should provide them walks and spaces and means of amusement! What a Minister! What a Conservative! What a Christian![80]

The test came on 10 and 13 May at the third reading. On 10th, Ashley moved the clauses of which he had given notice: these would have brought about a ten-hour day by October, 1847. His speech[81] in support of the clauses was severely technical; he attempted to answer the economic objections to ten hours in their own terms. Thus he took the main points commonly made against ten hours: its unfavourable effect on production, on the value of fixed capital, on wages and on British competitiveness in foreign markets. He drew on figures and statistics to refute all these arguments, using, on occasion, the views of certain manufacturers to support his conclusions. And he made the point that the House had already voted on this issue and it was now called upon to cancel it 'not because new facts or new conditions have appeared, but to save a Government. . . .' And Ashley widened this into a constitutional argument: the whole question of representative government was at stake: members were being required to give up their liberty and independence. Yet the speech was not all technical and constitutional. The old theme of paternalistic concern came through, when, in his concluding remarks, Ashley dared to hope for 'restored affections, for renewed understanding between master and man, for combined general efforts, for large and mutual concessions of all classes of the wealthy for the benefit of the common welfare and especially of the labouring people.'

The speech was enthusiastically greeted, but the government's reaction was soon evident.[82] Graham answered some of the economic points; a daily reduction of two hours meant an annual loss of six weeks. He also countered the constitutional point, refuting Ashley's argument that the government was exercising a tyranny: the real tyranny was for the House to demand that a Minister take a course of action which he believed to be fatal to the best interests of the country. And he made it quite evident that, if the House supported Ashley, he would 'seek a private station.' The debate was finally adjourned. On 12 May – a Sunday – Ashley was glad of 'at least a day of repose!' He had been in 'a whirl by night and by day: sleepless, or if sleeping, like a drunken man, all night; (his) head quite giddy, and (his) heart absolutely fainting; too much to do, in quantity, in variety and importance.' Nevertheless, he was relieved that the speech of 10th was over: 'Oh what trouble, time and perplexity removed!' he wrote.[83]

But perplexity was again ahead. When the debate was resumed on 13 May, there were, once more, speeches on both sides: Bright in particular voiced his vehement opposition to Ashley.[84] But the major speech was by Peel. As Graham had done, Peel dwelt to some degree on the economic aspects and re-affirmed his views that ten hours would have disastrous results; but the crucial part of his speech was the unmistakeable threat of resignation if the government were defeated.[85] Under such a threat, the vote on Ashley's clause was decisive: for 159, against 297. Thus the bill passed the Commons in a form acceptable to the government, without the ten-hours clause.

Ashley wrote on 14 May, he had been 'utterly, singularly, prodigiously defeated by a majority of 138!' This, he wrote, was a higher majority than the thirty or forty that had been expected – 'such is the power and such the exercise of Ministerial influence.'[86] Nevertheless, he was not unduly discouraged. On 15 May, he dined at the Lord Mayor's feast and noted that he found 'much sympathy' there, as everywhere. The size of the majority was, he felt, a positive advantage – it was better than one of, say, twenty-five, since it proved that there was 'no division *against the principle*, but one to save the Ministry.' And looking back over the period since Graham had withdrawn his bill, Ashley felt justified in his conduct. He was 'amply satisfied' that he had permitted the withdrawal of the bill; had he persevered in it at that time, he would have suffered an equally large defeat and there the matter would have rested for the session. Instead of that, it had been kept alive and before the public, and in the interval, there had been meetings held throughout the country on the subject; and now he had obtained a debate and division on the true issue of ten hours, not a mere technicality. Further, the bill, 'with all its valuable clauses' had been saved and had gone to the Lords; had he behaved differently, the government might not have gone as far as they had. Thus Ashley was 'cast down but not destroyed.' He felt 'no abatement of faith, no sinking of hopes, no relaxation of perseverance.'[87]

The bill encountered some opposition in the Lords, but it finally passed on 6 June, 1844. The Act reduced the minimum age for employment from nine to eight years, but between the ages of eight and thirteen no child was to be employed for more than six-and-a-half hours in any one day, and these hours were to fall either before 1 p.m. or after it; there was to be a half-day for education and recreation. The hours of young persons were to remain the same as under the 1833 Act: twelve hours a day or sixty-nine a week, but all women were to be restricted to these hours and were to be excluded from night work. Provision was made for the fencing of dangerous machinery; and machinery in motion was not to be cleaned by any child, young person or woman. The question of enforcement was also further regulated. A certificate had to be produced before a child could enter a factory; but in addition to fitness, this had also to testify to age. This was now much more possible than it had been in 1833 owing to the introduction of registration of births in 1836. Such certificates could only be granted on personal inspection where the child was to be employed. Again, the inspectors were given the power of appointing certifying doctors, of issuing regulations for their guidance and of laying down the factories or districts in which they might act. This gave the inspectors power which they had long requested. Further, inspectors were authorised, as were superintendents, or sub-inspectors as they were now called, to summon offenders and witnesses to appear before the courts, and inspectors and sub-inspectors were to have the right to enter every part of the factories at any time by day or night when any person was employed in it. Complaints about the breaking of the law were to be heard before two or more magistrates and not one as previously, but these could not be the occupier of the factory where the alleged offence had taken place, nor could they be the father, son or brother of the occupier. The Act did, therefore, represent a considerable step forward in matters of enforcement. It was welcomed by the inspectors as a measure which reduced many of the opportunities for evasion which had so vitiated the 1833 Act. And even although it was still not perfect in these respects and, of course, did not introduce a ten-hour day, Ashley had some reason to be glad that the bill had been saved. It was, he felt, a further useful instalment. 'Although you may not pass the stream of Jordan,' he had written, 'it is something that God has permitted you to wash your feet in the waters of the promised land.'[88]

Nevertheless, Ashley's dealings with the government over the matter had left another legacy of bitterness. The episode had once again illustrated the division between Ashley and Peel over the methods which each favoured to solve social problems. But there had also, on this occasion, been the constitutional issue. Ashley had felt that ministerial influence had been quite improperly used: Peel, on the other hand, resented the fact that many in the party had deserted him to support Ashley and deplored the way in which this left his government at the mercy of the House – in such circumstances, firm government was impossible.[89] And this was a matter very soon to be raised again, for, on 14 June, a motion on the Sugar Duties Bill was carried against the government. Peel contemplated resignation, and this, along with certain small concessions made by the government, was enough to give the government a majority when the matter was discussed on 17

June.⁹⁰ Although technically not quite a reversal of the earlier vote, substantially it amounted to this: once more, the government had brought its will to bear on its recalcitrant supporters. Ashley did not let the matter pass without comment. He wrote to Peel on the subject having, after some hesitation, decided to do so 'because it is right to undeceive a leader who believes, or may believe, that one is an unqualified adviser and supporter; and because if all would tell Peel the truth, which he never hears, he might be wiser and better.'⁹¹ The correspondence extended over some days.⁹² Ashley told Peel that the government's conduct was 'unconstitutional and tending to dictatorship, under the forms of free government.' He also wrote that he felt it was his duty to tell Peel that it was now no longer possible for him to continue 'to entertain the hopes and feelings of former days.' Peel interpreted this to mean that Ashley proposed to withdraw his support altogether from the government; in his reply, he expressed sincere regret at this. Ashley, however, replied further, saying that Peel had misunderstood him – he would still support most of Peel's measures and was not about to seek a political leader among Peel's opponents. What he had meant was that his support might be given 'with less confidence and hope'. Peel in a letter of 21 July expressed his 'great satisfaction' at Ashley's clarification of his previous remarks, but, even had Ashley intended to withdraw all support, this would not have altered his 'feelings of personal respect and esteem'. This, Ashley acknowledged, was a 'kind reply'; and he felt that the exchange of letters had been good. 'His tone is altered; he has spoken in a conciliatory manner, and, in fact, cried "peccavi". I cannot doubt that my letter has materially contributed to it. . . .'⁹³ This almost certainly exaggerated the effects of his original letter to Peel, but the letter had expressed a sentiment which many in the party shared. At a time when patronage had declined and party was not all-embracing, members of the Commons did enjoy a measure of independence and freedom and cherished it, and Peel's tendency to override the views of the Commons in the interests of executive government caused deep resentment within his own party. The episode of 1844 contributed further to this feeling and, although Peel won the day, it was at the cost of building up frustration and bitterness for the future.⁹⁴ 'But alas! The mischief is done,' Ashley wrote, 'it can never be repaired.'⁹⁵

The passing of the 1844 Act, even with the benefits which it brought, did not satisfy the Ten Hours Movement, and activity in the country continued. After a short holiday in August on the Isle of Wight, Ashley set out in September on a tour of the manufacturing districts. His tour coincided with an improvement in trade and an increase in wages, and Ashley noted his impressions.⁹⁶ The manufacturing world was 'breathless with anxiety and haste ... mills, new machinery, new speculation.' It made him reflect that 'had we for God a tenth part of their zeal for Mammon, we might hope to see the truly *Golden Age*;' and he was privately critical of much of the activity. He repeatedly asked why this improvement had taken place, but found no satisfactory answer. He also wondered if it would last. The operatives, he found, were distrustful of it. Nevertheless, there were some 'indications of hope'. One was that he found the manufacturers willing to talk of an eleven hours bill, although not yet a ten hours one; further, he was greatly impressed by some of the mills which he visited. Ashley was, indeed, now at pains to emphasise that he was not the enemy of the factory masters. He told the Lancashire Short-Time Committee that he would be ashamed to harbour hostility against a class which included men who were generous and benevolent. Nor was he hostile to the factory system – it would be absurd to be the enemy to a system which gave employment to tens of thousands. He was the enemy only to the abuses of the factory system, and he asked his hearers to seek remedies of such abuses 'with forbearance'.[97] Thus during the tour, Ashley recommended 'conciliatory sentiments towards employers', as he put it in his Diary;[98] but he was also anxious to affirm that the principle of ten hours had not been lost sight of. He explained to the Lancashire Short-Time Committee the difficulties which he had encountered in Parliament over the 1844 measure; he felt that the measure, as passed, offered many advantages, but he reassured his audience that he still believed in a shorter working day. It could give time for self-improvement and domestic life; if reformed in this way, the factory system might become the channel of comforts and even blessings. He urged them to pray for all of this: and, once their objects were achieved, they were to be used for 'high purposes' – not for mere amusement, but as a preparation for eternity.[99] A ten-hour bill was thus in the forefront of Ashley's mind for the following session. He intended to write to the Secretary of the Short-Time Committee announcing the re-opening of the question, and in mid November promised the Lancashire reformers that he would introduce a bill as soon as possible.[100]

Even after his strenuous efforts over factory reform, both in Parliament and the country, there was very little relaxation or rest. Public activities continued to claim his attention: 'All sorts of things . . .' he wrote. 'Good deal of work . . . no repose.'[101] Amidst it all – a visit to an asylum, an interview with the Secretary for the Protection of Needlewomen, the chair of a meeting on behalf of seamstresses – Ashley felt in good health: but he looked to the Second Advent as the '*only* hope for the temporal world'.[102] Certain matters at the close of 1844 were, however, of a family and personal nature. In November, he went to Rugby to see if the school would be suitable for Anthony. He feared Eton, dreading the 'proximity of Windsor, with all its ... allurements'; and he disapproved of the 'tone and atmosphere of the school'. It gave a man only social graces, he felt; the need was for

> nobler, deeper and sterner stuff ... more of the inward, not so much of the outward gentleman; a rigid sense of duty, not a 'delicate sense of honour'; a just estimate of rank and property, not as matters of personal enjoyment and display, but as gifts from God, bringing with them serious responsibilities and involving a fearful account.[103]

Another family preoccupation was with his father. Ashley was distressed by a visit to St Giles in mid-December. It was, indeed, a painful experience.[104] He found his father aged, head sunk between his shoulders, voice thicker. But, Ashley wrote, there was still 'the same wilfulness, the same determination to defy the Doctors, treating all the symptoms and the advice with affected contempt and exceeding in wine (in *Port* wine!) beyond his ordinary excess.' The sight was to Ashley 'melancholy, heart breaking, frightful ... it is beyond endurance and beyond remedy. ...' There was also the pain inflicted by his father's open hostility towards his public life. The Sturminster speech, Ashley noted, was 'not forgotten' and was one of the ingredients of his father's hatred. Ashley heard, too, that his father spoke angrily of certain motions which he had proposed and of his connections with religious societies. The Earl was very anxious for Ashley to leave St Giles and told him to do so; 'cannot, by word or deed, do good,' Ashley wrote. 'My presence even is hateful.' He reflected wryly on the attacks which he was still suffering from the Anti-Corn Law League. 'Curious occurrence,' he wrote, 'the League are reviling me for doing *nothing*, at the moment I am turned out of my father's house for doing *too much*.'

Christmas and New Year were spent at Broadlands. During a visit earlier in December, Ashley had written of the 'kind dear people' there, but, he added, 'what wasters of time ... killers of precious moments ... ravagers of systematic habits.' He was not able while at Broadlands to adhere to his normal custom of rising at 6 a.m. and having two hours of solitude and 'several more of *occupied* exercise'.[105] And, as Ashley settled in at Broadlands for Christmas, he could not refrain from commenting again on his hosts. Their kindness was unbounded, but their activities on a Sunday grieved his soul. In preparation for a reception the following day, there was 'the business of trumpery and decoration ... upholsterers laying down carpets and beautifying rooms ... What a predominance of worldly spirit! What a selfish demand made upon a workman's necessities.' Ashley could only think such things to himself; he could not speak or hint. But, he wrote, 'woe is me. that I am constrained to dwell in the tens of Kedar.'[106] He felt less well than he had done: 'weak in body and mind,' he wrote. 'The truth is that this place disagrees with me.'[107]

His thoughts while at Broadlands also turned to the future. He wondered what he would do in the coming year, or, rather, what he would be permitted to do. The factory question was still much on his mind, and yet he was unsure whether he would be able to pursue it. It was not unlikely, he felt, that the coming session would be his last in the House of Commons, for he thought that his father could not live much longer. If he were removed to the House of Lords, he would be 'taken to an assembly where it would be vain to propose such measures.' He could think of no one who would be prepared to undertake the cause in the Commons. And he brooded over the sacrifices which he had made by 'endeavouring to alleviate the wrongs of working people:' he had made many enemies and shaken the confidence of many friends. He had borrowed and spent 'enormous sums of money' in proportion to his income; he had been excluded from 'every path of emolument and every path of honourable ambition'. His own near kinsfolk disliked his opinions and some persecuted him.

> No one but myself can estimate the amount of toil by day and by night, of fears and disappointments, of prayers and tears, of repugnances contended against and overcome, of long journeys and unceasing letters; and will all this have no greater result than the simple . . . issue of the Colliery Bill? 'I will stand on my watch tower and will see.' He alone is good and merciful and *wise*.[108]

Ashley thus contemplated the New Year in sombre mood.

In late January, there were again rumours that Ashley was being considered for an Irish appointment: on this occasion, Chief Secretary.[109] Once more, his informant was Bonham, who told him that both Peel and Graham wanted Ashley to take the post. The factory question, they said, was settled, and there was also the point that Ashley was likely soon to be in the Lords and could not take a real part in any further activity on the matter. He would, therefore, be free to join the government. Ashley expressed his willingness to discuss the matter with Peel, although he also mentioned serious doubts and reservations. His career, he wrote, lay among the 'questions and labours of social interests', and he told Bonham that his unwillingness to accept office sprang not only from the resistance of the government to the ten-hour day but from its 'language and conduct on all social questions.' In fact, nothing came of the rumours nor of the proposal, which, it appears, commended itself to Graham on the grounds that Ashley's philanthropic endeavours would have an opportunity for full expression in Ireland.

On 4 February, 1845, Parliament was opened by the Queen. Clearly,

Ashley intended to give a great deal of his attention to the factory question, but, more immediately, he was occupied with two other issues: children in cotton printworks and the subject of lunacy. In the course of his tour of the factory districts in 1844, he had visited printwork factories and found that children employed in them worked long hours, and he had made up his mind to give this 'abomination' his early attention.[110] He kept to his resolution. On 5 February, he gained precedence by ballot for a motion on the subject, and on the 18th, moved for leave to introduce a bill. He based much of his speech[111] on the report of the Children's Employment Commission published in 1843.[112] He dwelt on the long hours worked in exhausting conditions: there were, he said, some twenty-five-thousand children, many between eight and nine years of age, working sometimes for sixteen, seventeen or eighteen hours a day. He proposed that all females and all boys under thirteen should be excluded from night work, and children under thirteen should be limited to eight hours a day for six days of the week, or twelve hours on three alternate days. These regulations should apply to printworks and also to factories engaged in the allied processes of dyeing, bleaching and calendering. Ashley had expected a 'dreadful onslaught', as he put it, from Cobden since he was invading his 'peculiar manor'.[113] He tried to anticipate this in his speech. Thus he said that he might be accused of 'a narrow and one-sided humanity' and of leaving 'untouched much worse things.' He thought it likely that such critics would divert his attention to the Corn Laws, but, he argued, repeal of the Corn Laws 'would leave these infants as it found them, neither worse nor better. . . .' Britain might, indeed, 'obtain a surplus and reduce taxes, increase (her) fleets and extend (her) armies;' all those things were 'excellent in their way'. But they were all 'unavailing if they rest not on the moral and physical prosperity of the great mass of (her) people.'[114] Cobden did, indeed, prove sensitive to the charges made about calico printers by Ashley in the course of his speech; it would lead the public to think, he said, that there was something 'peculiarly demoralised about the printers of calico.'[115] Graham was somewhat lukewarm. He was unable, he said, to prevent the introduction of the bill but pointed to the difficulties of legislating effectively on the particular case. He also expressed apprehension at the way in which Ashley was extending his efforts to afford protection and at the further efforts to this end to which he had pledged his energies in the course of his speech; this, Graham argued, would have a fatal effect on trade and manufacture.[116] Ashley was only moderately pleased with the debate: 'a painful affair,' he wrote, 'and dubious success,' and he felt that there was little public interest in the affair.[117]

The bill was given a first reading on 12 March, and, between then and the second reading, Graham consulted the factory inspectors to obtain further information on the subject; and on 2 April, at the second reading, reported on these inquiries and on deputations which he had received from employers.[118] From all this, he concluded that some regulation was necessary, but this should apply only to cotton printworkers and not to factories engaged in dyeing, bleaching and calendering. He accepted the proposal that children under eight should be prohibited from employment in printworks; he also agreed that time should be allowed for education, although he argued the need for flexibility in this respect to take account of busy and slack times. Ashley was willing to accept terms which fell short of his original proposals – in particular, this would involve sacrificing the eight-hour day – or twelve on alternate days – for children under thirteen. This sacrifice was made with regret: but he saw himself as almost alone, confronted by the government and the great mass of the master printers. The struggle was thus hopeless and he would be delaying the measure by further persistence.[119] The bill was, therefore, read a second time; it passed through its Report stages and, on 30 April, received a third reading. It also passed the Lords and received royal assent on 30 June. Thus after 1 January, 1846, no child under eight was to be employed in a printworks, and no child between the ages of eight and thirteen and no woman was to work at night. The Act was to be enforced by the factory inspectors. There was no stipulation for hours worked during the day and no regulation beyond the age of thirteen. There were also difficulties over the educational provisions and further legislation was necessary in 1847. Nevertheless, this was a first attempt to legislate for cotton printworks: and Ashley was moderately pleased. As he put it, he had not got 'the whole' but had got 'a great deal'.[120]

The question of lunacy had been one which had absorbed Ashley ever since he had first become interested and involved in the subject in 1828. His work on the Metropolitan Commission in Lunacy, of which he had become Chairman in 1833, had been unspectacular, but onerous and time-consuming: and his Diary contained frequent references to time spent transacting 'business in Lunacy'. On the whole, he felt satisfied with what the Commission had achieved. In 1841, in a debate on the subject, he stated that the Commissioners had done all that could reasonably be expected of them.[121] Their powers were those of control, but a great deal had been done by advice and suggestion and not by authority. Thus one power was to refuse licences, but this had been used very sparingly.[122] He felt that within the Metropolitan area and for several miles around, the Commissioners had brought the asylums into 'a most complete state of order'. At the same time, Ashley felt that there was ample room for further reform. He regretted the fact that the Commissioners' powers were restricted to the London area and felt that there was an urgent need to put the management of lunacy throughout the country on to a more uniform and general footing. He knew the difficulties of this: in 1842, he told the House that complete uniformity in many matters – for example in those of treatment – would be extremely difficult to attain.[123] But he was much in favour of stricter visitation of provincial asylums, and he supported the principle of a bill introduced in 1842 by Lord George Somerset, a lay member of the Metropolitan Commission, which proposed that more effective inspection of asylums licensed by magistrates in Quarter Sessions should be carried out by the members of the London Commission.[124] Somerset's initiative resulted in an Act of 1842, which was to last for three years. This widened the Commission to include four lawyers and six or seven physicians. At least two of them, one a lawyer and one a doctor, were to visit all provincial licensed asylums twice a year and all county asylums once a year and were to send in a full report on their condition. This, then, meant that the London Commission extended its investigations. England and Wales were divided for the purpose into four districts and each was subdivided into two parts. The investigations were completed by 1844. As chairman of the Board, Ashley was involved in it. He did not take part in the tour, but went through the material which was received and wrote most of the Report.[125] On 2 July, 1844, he wrote: 'Finished at last Report of Commission in Lunacy. Good thing over. Sat for many days in review. God prosper it! It contains much for the alleviation of physical and moral suffering.'[126]

The presentation of the Report gave Ashley an opportunity to raise the matter in Parliament, and, on 23 July, 1844, he brought forward a motion for an Address to the Crown, praying Her Majesty to take the Report of the Metropolitan Commission into consideration, since the following session the statute under which they operated would expire.[127] He developed his ideas on various aspects of regulation on the one hand and treatment and care on the other. Thus he was critical of the immunity from inspection of houses for single patients. The only control which existed over single houses was that the owner of the house must communicate the names of the patients to the Clerk of the Commission if they resided more than twelve months. But this rule was either disregarded or evaded by removing the patients every eleven months. He also disliked and disapproved of the profit motive in the running of many private asylums – this was especially true of pauper patients who were admitted – and Ashley expressed his belief in the need for the provision of more county asylums. Again, Ashley argued the case for the treatment of lunacy in its early stages, and urged that separate arrangements should be made for incurable patients from those for patients who could be restored to health. He praised the efforts of those who had 'laboured to make the rational and humane treatment to be the rule and principle of the government of lunacy.' By this, Ashley meant the principle of non-restraint which the Metropolitan Commissioners had been concerned to introduce in asylums under their jurisdiction in place of mechanical restraint. Thus better regulation could prevent the occurrence of 'frightful cruelties': better treatment would 'soothe the days of the incurable and restore many sufferers to health and usefulness.'

Graham assured the House that the matter would receive attention the following session, and Ashley withdrew his motion. He noted that his speech had 'done its work so far as to obtain a recognition from the Secretary of State that legislation was necessary and should be taken up in my sense of it.'[128] On this occasion, indeed, there was to be considerable cooperation between Ashley and the government. In March, 1844, Ashley noted that Graham had asked him to undertake the lunacy bill: he had agreed to do so 'on full condition of *full government support* in every respect.' It was 'prodigious work', but he could not 'refuse to lighten the burden on a Minister's shoulders.'[129] In March, 1845, he wrote to Graham, asking him to come to no final decisions on the bills before he had heard all that Ashley urged on the matter. 'These bills,' he wrote, 'have been constructed with great care and after serious deliberation; we have proposed no more than we think and we believe we can prove to be absolutely necessary.' He continued that he had a 'deep and anxious interest in the propriety and effectiveness of the Commission.'

> I have acted now for many years as its Chairman [he continued]; and numberless are the hours and days that I have given to the service. I am convinced that we can render it an honour to the nation and a benefit even to mankind.[130]

On 6 June, Ashley brought in two bills on the subject.[131] The first replaced the Metropolitan Lunacy Commission by the Lunacy Commission, a permanent body responsible to the Lord Chancellor, consisting of five unpaid Commissioners and six whole-time professional Commissioners, three doctors and three barristers, each paid a salary of £1,500. There was also to be a secretary, to be paid £800, and two clerks. The second bill made it obligatory on Justices of the Peace of a county or a borough to make provision for asylums if they had not already done so. In his speech introducing the measures, Ashley reverted to the themes which he had mentioned in his speech the previous year. Thus, in relation to the first bill, the new Commission would involve increased control and regulation. Its scope was extended to include institutions not previously within its control. Certain hospitals and workhouses which admitted lunatics were to be brought under its supervision and solitary patients were to be looked after by a small private committee of the Commission. The Commission would also exercise control by its powers of licensing, visitation[132] and inspection. Ashley also mentioned the stricter regulations to be adopted for the admission and certification of patients, especially pauper patients, into licensed houses.[133] All this, then, amounted to a consolidation and extension of the authority and control of the central body, and the regulations which it laid down would prevent abuse. Ashley also looked for better treatment through the county asylums which would be built under the second bill. These would be erected from public funds and this would reduce the profit motive, which Ashley was so anxious to eliminate, especially for pauper patients. Further, the construction of new asylums – plans for which had to be submitted to the Commissioners – would, Ashley hoped, provide the opportunity to plan the buildings in such a way as to separate the incurable patients from those who were curable, and this would give methods of non-restraint a better chance of success in restoring patients to health.

In introducing his bills, Ashley felt it unnecessary to urge on the House – 'as an assembly of educated, humane and Christian men' – the duty of coming to the aid and protection' of this utterly helpless class who, under the marked visitation of a wise though unscrutable Providence, demand an unusual measure of our sympathy.'[134] Graham did, indeed, second Ashley's motion; Ashley recorded that he made 'a very kind and fervid speech and announced the full support of the Government.'[135] He acknowledged his gratitude in a letter to Graham of 7 June in which he wrote that this day 'must not close before I express to you my sincere thanks for the patience and zeal you exhibited yesterday on the introduction of the bills for the protection and treatment of the unhappy lunatics.'[136] There were, however, difficulties ahead, and, on 30 June, Ashley noted that he had never suffered more anxiety than on the lunacy bills.[137] In particular, he was much concerned by the opposition of Duncombe, who was a severe critic of the Commission.[138] Duncombe objected to the salaries to be paid to the Commissioners and, indeed, referred to it as a body 'hateful and foreign to the Constitution'. He tried to postpone the measure until the following session, but failed and the bill went into Committee. Nevertheless, he kept up his opposition and initiated several divisions; and when these failed, he was active at the third reading on 22 July. Ashley noted that he had 'toiled through obstruction, insult, delay, desertion. . . .'[139] However, the bill finally passed on 23 July. But there was still the Lords to contend with: 'we pass from Scylla to Charybdis,' wrote Ashley. 'My father as usual, taking the lead in hatred and resistance to anything of mine. God turn his heart and give prosperity to the bill.'[140] However, by the end of the month, both bills had passed the Lords and were safe: on 4 August, they received the royal assent. Ashley thanked God for his success, and, on this occasion, he was quite prepared to give the government credit. He wrote that Graham's 'conduct in this affair had been bold, feeling and faithful.'[141]

These two Acts marked an extremely important stage in the history of lunacy legislation, and Ashley was to play as important a part in their implementation as he had done in their initiation. At the first meeting of the new Commission, on 24 August, 1845, he was elected permanent Chairman of the Commission.[142] The Commission met on a weekly, monthly and quarterly basis. The weekly meetings were for ordinary business and had to be attended by at least one medical and one legal commissioner: the other meetings were envisaged as occasions for the conduct of more important business, at which all medical and legal commissioners were present unless they were urgently required elsewhere.[143] The fullest attendance was at the Quarterly meetings. The duties of the Commission included the receipt and consideration of reports from the visiting Commissioners, and it scrutinised the certificates required on the admission, discharge, death, removal and escape of every lunatic to ensure that they were in order. The Commission received and considered letters about alleged mismanagement, neglect of patients or undue detention; these were often referred to the visiting Commissioners for further investigation and report before a decision was reached in individual cases. Plans for the construction of new institutions were discussed and considered. The Commission thus had a great deal of material referred to it for examination, consideration and decision, and, in addition, it issued circulars to the proprietor of institutions on various topics[144] and engaged in correspondence with individual proprietors about any irregularities in their conduct. It also exercised the important duty of licensing: renewal of licences was usually considered at the well-attended Quarterly meetings but might be considered at other meetings. Ashley regularly presided over the various meetings. The Minutes of these meetings[145] do not, of course, reveal the part which he played as an individual, but it is clear that he was responsible for the conduct of meetings at which a great deal of detailed and technical work was done. He also took part in the visitations in the early years of the Commission. England and Wales were divided into several districts; and on every visit at least one medical and one legal Commissioner had to be present. Their duties were to inspect the premises, examine the registers, see all the patients and report to the Commission.[146]

Thus by the autumn of 1845, Ashley had seen the completion of measures on two of the subjects which he had contemplated at the beginning of the session: cotton printers and lunacy.

> Such a thing almost before unknown [he wrote], that a man, without a party, unsupported by anything private or public, but God and His Truth, should have overcome Mammon and Moloch, and have carried, in one

Session, three such measures as the Print-works Regulation and the two Bills for the erection and government of Lunatic Asylums! Non Nobis, Domine. . . .[147]

But there was still the factory question. There was, indeed, some resentment in the factory districts that no bill had been introduced. Ashley grew somewhat exasperated at this: 'it is not their intention,' Ashley had written in June, 'but they are monstrously unjust. No man, living or dead, has sacrificed the tenth part that I have done; and what motive can I have, but their interest, to be silent even for an hour?'[148] A joint Conference of Yorkshire and Lancashire operatives was summoned so that the difficulties of introducing a bill during the present session could be explained. They accepted the position,[149] but there were still dangers that the Movement would become impatient, and thus, in October, Ashley undertook a tour to spread reassurance. At meetings which he addressed in Manchester and Bradford,[150] he explained that, during 1845, there had been no opportunity for him to bring the ten hours question forward. The House had been too preoccupied with railway business and various other matters to allow a calm consideration of the subject. He also mentioned the advantages which the 1844 Act had brought, and he thought, too, that there was an 'improved tone and temper of all classes of station and property towards working people.' He applauded the operatives on the manner in which they had conducted the question: no violence of language or action, no threats, no expressions of vengeance, no bitter accusations, no unhealable wounds. 'This,' he told the Bradford meeting, was 'a bright example to the whole world of the mode in which a people should demand and will obtain, their inalienable rights.'[151] Ashley also stressed his own efforts in the cause – his involvement in it had sacrificed many political friends and had closed against himself the pleasures and benefits of many honours. And he pledged his continued efforts; he announced his intention to introduce a ten hours bill on the re-assembly of Parliament. He counselled patience and perseverance. These efforts met with considerable success. In Manchester, a vote of confidence was passed in Ashley's favour and at Bradford, three cheers rang out for 'Ten Hours and Lord Ashley'.[152]

Ashley thus reassured the Movement that the time had almost come for the achievement of its aims, or, as he put it in his Diary, the cause had 'long been in the ground; now surely, it is time for it to bear fruit upward.'[153] Thus, after all the disappointments and setbacks of the 1840s, in 1845 he felt some confidence. And he was correct: the time had almost come. But before it did, the political world was shaken by the issue of Corn Law repeal, a matter which was to bear closely on Ashley's own political future.

NOTES

1. N.R.A., Shaftesbury (Broadlands) MSS, SHA/PD/3, 25 Dec., 1843.
2. Add. MSS, 40, 483, fos 103-4.
3. ibid., f. 121.
4. Quoted in Hodder, II, 5.
5. John Easthope MSS, Ashley to Easthope, 10 Jan., 1844.
6. Hansard, *Parl. Debates*, 3rd ser., LXXII, 342-64.
7. N.R.A., Shaftesbury (Broadlands) MSS, SHA/PD/3, 9 Feb., 1844.
8. ibid., SHA/PD/3, 4 Oct., 1844.
9. ibid., SHA/PD/3, 21 Feb., 1844.
10. N. Gash, *Peel*, p. 508.
11. N.R.A., Shaftesbury (Broadlands) MSS, SHA/PD/3, 12 Sept., 1844.
12. ibid., SHA/PD/3, 4 Oct., 1844.
13. N. Gash, *Peel*, p. 489.
14. ibid., p. 494.
15. N.R.A., Shaftesbury (Broadlands) MSS, SHA/PD/4, 1, 2, 3 Apr., 1846.
16. ibid., SHA/PD/4, 5 Apr., 1846.
17. N. Gash, *Peel*, pp. 508-17.
18. Hansard, *Parl. Debates*, 3rd ser., LXXII, 277-81.
19. J. T. Ward, *The Factory Movement*, pp. 269, 276.
20. Hansard, *Parl. Debates*, 3rd ser., LXXII, 285.
21. N.R.A., Shaftesbury (Broadlands) MSS, SHA/PD/3, 27 Feb., 1844.
22. *The Times*, 8 Mar., 1844.
23. N.R.A., Shaftesbury (Broadlands) MSS, SHA/PD/3, 8, 9 Mar., 1844.
24. ibid., SHA/PD/3, 12 Mar., 1844.
25. Hansard, *Parl. Debates*, 3rd ser., LXXIII, 1073. The amendment was that the word 'night' should be taken to mean 6 p.m. to 6 a.m., instead of 8 p.m. to 6 a.m. as the clause proposed. If work were prohibited during this period, this left a 12-hour day; but, with a break for 2 hours for meals, the working day would be reduced to 10.
26. John Easthope MSS, Ashley to Easthope, 14 Mar., 1844.
27. Hansard, *Parl. Debates*, 3rd ser., LXXIII, 1073-1101.
28. ibid., 1101-10.
29. ibid., 1110-17.
30. ibid., 1132-51. See also Keith Robbins, *John Bright* (1979), pp. 50-51.
31. N.R.A., Shaftesbury (Broadlands) MSS, SHA/PD/3, 16 Mar., 1844.
32. Hansard, *Parl. Debates*, LXXIII, 1151, 1152, 1154, 1155.
33. N.R.A., Shaftesbury (Broadlands) MSS, SHA/PD/2, 3 Dec., 1841. One of Dodd's books, *The factory system illustrated: in a series of Letters to the Right Hon. Lord Ashley* (1842) was based on Dodd's investigations in factory districts and contains accounts of accidents and descriptions of cripples (See R. Boyson, *The Ashworth Cotton Enterprise. The Rise and Fall of a Family Firm, 1818-1880* (Oxford, 1970), pp. 180-81). The book of Dodd referred to has been reissued in a new edition (1968), with an introduction by W. H. Chaloner.
34. N.R.A., Shaftesbury (Broadlands) MSS, SHA/PD/3, 16 Mar., 1844.
35. R. Boyson, op. cit., p. 181. When Ashley visited Ashworth in Sept., 1844, the subject of Dodd was raised. Ashley denied that he had advised Dodd to go to Lancashire to obtain information about the factory owners but had simply encouraged him to visit his sister there. Earlier, however, Ashley had written: 'I sent down Dodd, or rather Dodd went down, to the manufacturing districts. We

paid his expenses—he gave me abundant information.' (N.R.A., Shaftesbury (Broadlands) MSS, SHA/PD/3, 9 Apr., 1844. See also R. Boyson, op. cit., p. 183). W. H. Chaloner in his introduction to Dodd's book quotes evidence that Ashley paid Dodd 45s a week and coach hire while he was visiting the manufacturing districts and 20s a week while he was in London. (William Dodd, *The factory system illustrated* new ed. (1968), p. xiii).

36. N.R.A., Shaftesbury (Broadlands) MSS, SHA/PD/3, 16 Mar., 1844.
37. N. Gash, *Peel*, p. 439 ff.
38. N.R.A., Shaftesbury (Broadlands) MSS, SHA/PD/3, 18 Mar., 1844.
39. Hansard, *Parl. Debates*, 3rd ser., LXXIII, 1241–55. Before the debate, he had been at pains to confirm his view that the ten-hour restriction would mean a considerable reduction in wages and profits. On 17 Mar., 1844, he wrote to Graham asking for a meeting with one of the Inspectors, Horner, and with any other informed person, to find out whether employers who at present voluntarily worked their factories for only ten hours paid smaller wages than others, and, if they did, whether a forced reduction would lead to a diminution of wages to the extent of 25%. The meeting took place on the morning of 18 Mar., 1844, with Horner and another Inspector, Saunders. (Graham MSS (on microfilm). Film 117, 17 Mar., 1844. See also N. Gash, *Peel*, p. 440. On 19 Mar., 1844, Peel wrote to Lord Sandon that the government's bill carried the principle of restriction 'quite as far' as it could, in his opinion, be carried with safety. (Add. MSS 40, 541, f. 292. I owe this reference to Mr R. C. Sloan).
40. Hansard, *Parl. Debates*, 3rd ser., LXXIII, 1266.
41. ibid., 1267.
42. N.R.A., Shaftesbury (Broadlands) MSS, SHA/PD/3, 19 Mar., 1844.
43. N.R.A., Shaftesbury (Broadlands) MSS, SHA/PD/3, 21 Mar., 1844.
44. J. T. Ward, *The Factory Movement*, p. 290.
45. Hansard, *Parl. Debates*, 3rd ser., LXXIII, 1463.
46. N.R.A., Shaftesbury (Broadlands) MSS, SHA/PD/3, 23 Mar., 1844.
47. N. Gash, *Peel*, pp. 442–3.
48. Hansard, *Parl. Debates*, 3rd ser., LXXIII, 1490–91.
49. J. T. Ward, *The Factory Movement*, p. 292.
50. Hodder, II, 37.
51. N.R.A., Shaftesbury (Broadlands) MSS, SHA/PD/3, 25 Mar., 1844.
52. ibid., SHA/PD/3, 28 Mar., 1844.
53. He justified his conduct in the House of Commons on 29 Mar., 1844. (Hansard, *Parl. Debates*, LXXIII, 624–5). Greville commented that some 'abused Ashley for not going on and fighting again,' but that Ashley 'knew well enough it would be of no use.' The government, Greville said, would carry their bill and Ashley would be able to do nothing. Nevertheless, he would 'go on agitating session after session: and a Philanthropic agitator is more dangerous than a repealer, either of the Union or the Corn Laws.' Greville concluded with distaste: 'We are just now overrun with philanthropy, and God knows where it will stop, or whither it will lead us.' (L. Strachey and R. Fulford, op. cit., V, 169).
54. N.R.A., Shaftesbury (Broadlands) MSS, SHA/PD/3, 28 Mar., 1844.
55. ibid., SHA/PD/3, 30 Mar., 1844.
56. ibid., SHA/PD/3, 30 Mar., 1844.
57. ibid., SHA/PD/3, 3 Apr., 1844.
58. ibid., SHA/PD/3, 5 Apr., 1844.
59. ibid., SHA/PD/3, 7 Apr., 1844.
60. ibid., SHA/PD/3, 6 Apr., 1844.

61. J. T. Ward, *The Factory Movement*, p. 295.
62. St G.H., Shaftesbury MSS, C 25018.10/7th Earl; C 25018.17/7th Earl; C 25018.24/7th Earl; C 25018.28/7th Earl; C 25018.33/7th Earl; C 25018.38/7th Earl; C 25050/7th Earl; C 25052/7th Earl; C 25057/7th Earl; C 25057.1/7th Earl; C 25058/7th Earl.
63. Hansard, *Parl. Debates*, 3rd ser., LXXIV, 671-2.
64. N.R.A., Shaftesbury (Broadlands) MSS, SHA/PD/3, 15 Apr., 1844.
65. ibid., SHA/PD/3, 12 Apr., 1844.
66. ibid., SHA/PD/3, 17 Apr., 1844.
67. Add. MSS, 40, 450, fos 54-5.
68. Graham MSS (on microfilm). Film 117, 17 Apr., 1844.
69. ibid., Film 118, 18 Apr., 1844.
70. ibid., 18 Apr., 1844.
71. Hansard, *Parl. Debates*, 3rd ser., LXXIV, 89.
72. ibid., 131.
73. ibid., 132.
74. ibid., 335 ff.
75. N.R.A., Shaftesbury (Broadlands) MSS, SHA/PD/3, 1 May, 1844.
76. Hansard, *Parl. Debates*, 3rd ser., LXXIV, 613 ff.
77. N.R.A., Shaftesbury (Broadlands) MSS, SHA/PD/3, 4 May, 1844.
78. Hansard, *Parl. Debates*, 3rd ser., LXXIV, 669-80.
79. N.R.A., Shaftesbury (Broadlands) MSS, SHA/PD/3, 4 May, 1844.
80. ibid., SHA/PD/3, 4 May, 1844.
81. Hansard, *Parl. Debates*, 3rd ser., LXXIV, 889 ff.
82. ibid., 915 ff.
83. N.R.A., Shaftesbury (Broadlands) MSS, SHA/PD/3, 12 May, 1844.
84. Hansard, *Parl. Debates*, 3rd ser., LXXIV, 1063-70.
85. ibid., 1094. See also N. Gash, *Peel*, p. 443-4.
86. N.R.A., Shaftesbury (Broadlands) MSS, SHA/PD/3, 14 May, 1844.
87. ibid., SHA/PD/3, 16 May, 1844.
88. ibid., SHA/PD/3, 16 May, 1844.
89. N. Gash, *Peel*, pp. 443-4.
90. ibid., pp. 445-51.
91. N.R.A., Shaftesbury (Broadlands) MSS, SHA/PD/3, 20 June, 1844.
92. Add. MSS, 40, 483, fos 134-41.
93. N.R.A., Shaftesbury (Broadlands) MSS, SHA/PD/3, 22 June, 1844.
94. N. Gash, *Peel*, p. 453.
95. N.R.A., Shaftesbury (Broadlands) MSS, SHA/PD/3, 22 June, 1844.
96. ibid., SHA/PD/3, 7, 1, 17 Oct., 1844.
97. *The Manchester Courier and Lancashire General Advertiser*, 26 Oct., 1844.
98. N.R.A., Shaftesbury (Broadlands) MSS, SHA/PD/3, 19 Oct., 1844.
99. *The Manchester Courier and Lancashire General Advertiser*, 26 Oct., 1844.
100. J. T. Ward, *The Factory Movement*, pp. 304-5.
101. N.R.A., Shaftesbury (Broadlands) MSS, SHA/PD/3, 15 Nov., 1844.
102. ibid., SHA/PD/3, 9 Dec., 1844.
103. ibid., SHA/PD/3, 21 Nov., 1844.
104. ibid., SHA/PD/3, 13, 16 Dec., 1844. These entries contain the references to Ashley's visit.
105. ibid., SHA/PD/3, 11 Dec., 1844.
106. ibid., SHA/PD/3, 22 Dec., 1844.
107. ibid., SHA/PD/3, 2 Jan., 1845.

108. ibid., SHA/PD/3, 11 Jan., 1845.
109. ibid., SHA/PD/3, 24 Jan., 1, 5, 7 Feb., 1845. (I am grateful to Mr R. C. Sloan for providing me with information on this subject).
110. ibid., SHA/PD/3, 19 Oct., 1844.
111. Hansard, *Parl. Debates,* 3rd ser., LXXVII, 638–56.
112. P.P., 1843, XIII.
113. N.R.A., Shaftesbury (Broadlands) MSS, SHA/PD/3, 14 Feb., 1845.
114. Hansard, *Parl. Debates,* 3rd ser., LXXVII, 655.
115. ibid., 622.
116. ibid., 659.
117. N.R.A., Shaftesbury (Broadlands) MSS, SHA/PD/3, 15 Feb., 1844.
118. Hansard, *Parl. Debates,* 3rd ser., LXXVIII, 1369 ff.
119. ibid., 1376.
120. ibid., 1376.
121. ibid., LIX, 697–9.
122. Ashley was, however, aware of the importance of the legal Commissioners. He wrote to Brougham on 18 July, 1845, that Brougham had been the first to determine that barristers should sit on the Commission. 'I do not hesitate to assert,' Ashley wrote, 'that without the aid of legal persons the Doctor would have been nearly powerless and the whole Commission would have stagnated.' (Brougham MSS, 33, 670, 18 July, 1845).
123. Hansard, *Parl. Debates,* 3rd ser., LXI, 806.
124. ibid., 797–803.
125. K. Jones, *Mental Health and Social Policy, 1845–1959* (1960), p. 175.
126. N.R.A., Shaftesbury (Broadlands) MSS, SHA/PD/3, 2 July, 1844.
127. Hansard, *Parl. Debates,* 3rd ser., LXXVI, 1257–71.
128. N.R.A., Shaftesbury (Broadlands) MSS, SHA/PD/3, 24 July, 1844.
129. ibid., SHA/PD/3, 21 Nov., 1844.
130. Graham MSS (on microfilm). Film 120, 24 Mar., 1845.
131. Hansard, *Parl. Debates,* 3rd ser., LXXXI, 180 ff.
132. Metropolitan licensed houses were to be visited four times a year; provincial licensed houses twice a year (also four times by visiting Justices appointed in Quarter Sessions); county and borough asylums once a year; single patients once a year (by a small private committee of the Commission); workhouses once a year.
133. Admission and certification procedures had been raised in various pamphlets written by persons who claimed that they had suffered improper seizure and detention (W. Ll. Parry-Jones, op. cit., pp. 227–30). Thus, after 1845, the documents submitted to the proprietor of a licensed house on admission of a private patient had to contain more detailed information than previously, and the same amount of detail was required for the admission documents of a pauper patient. Further, in the case of a private patient, the medical certificates had to contain a statement by the doctor of the facts on which he based his opinion. The proprietor had to send copies of all documents to the Commissioners within seven days and further copies, outside London, to the Clerk of the Visitors. (W. Ll. Parry-Jones, op. cit., p. 301, K. Jones, op. cit., pp. 192–3).
134. Hansard, *Parl. Debates,* 3rd ser., LXXXI, 194.
135. N.R.A., Shaftesbury (Broadlands) MSS, SHA/PD/3, 7 June, 1845.
136. Graham MSS (on microfilm). Film 120, 7 June, 1845.
137. N.R.A., Shaftesbury (Broadlands) MSS, SHA/PD/4, 30 June, 1845.
138. Hansard, *Parl. Debates,* 3rd ser., LXXXI, 1414–15; LXXXII, 395, 530, 615, 891.
139. N.R.A., Shaftesbury (Broadlands) MSS, SHA/PD/4, 22 July, 1845.

140. ibid., SHA/PD/4, 23 July, 1845.
141. ibid., SHA/PD/4, 30 July, 1845.
142. P.R.O., M.H./50/1.
143. P.P., 1847, XXXIII, 5-6.
144. P.R.O., M.H./51/236.
145. ibid., M.H./50/1-24 covering the period 1845-85.
146. P.P., 1847, XXXIII, 2-4.
147. N.R.A., Shaftesbury (Broadlands) MSS, SHA/PD/4, 30 July, 1845.
148. ibid., SHA/PD/3, 7 June, 1845.
149. J. T. Ward, *The Factory Movement*, p. 312.
150. *The Leeds Intelligencer*, 18 Oct., 1845.
151. N.R.A., Shaftesbury (Broadlands) MSS, SHA/PD/4, 17 Oct., 1845.
152. *The Leeds Intelligencer*, 18 Oct., 1845.
153. N.R.A., Shaftesbury (Broadlands) MSS, SHA/PD/4, 14 Oct., 1845.

10

Free Mercy to Past Faith, 1845-1847

Before the question of repeal came into full prominence, Ashley's political standing in Dorset was already weakening. In December, 1844, he had written in his Diary of 'private hints', which, allied to his own suspicions, had led him to believe that his 'favour' had for some time been on the decline in the county. The only occasion on which he had been outspoken had been at Sturminster in November, 1843, but, he felt, he was disliked not only for what he had said but for what he had omitted to say. He wrote that he could not – as his fellow member Bankes could – attend agricultural meetings and farmers' clubs and, as he put it:

> roar about protection, the superhuman excellence of landlords, the positively divine character of tenants, tickle the ears with fulsome flattery and rise in popularity as you rise in declamation.

He still felt that the labourers were seriously ill-treated. The gentry and the farmers knew his views, 'hence their aversion'. He was confirmed in his opinion by what had happened at an agricultural meeting at Blandford at the end of 1844; his name had been mentioned only once and had attracted 'but a cold "Hear, hear".' But, he continued, 'let them do as they like: I know ... that I am right; and I will not abate one breath of my lips to save the seat for the county.'[1]

Thus there was already unease between Ashley and his constituents before Corn Law repeal brought it to a head. Ashley had, indeed, been a supporter of Protection, and his speech at the General Election of 1841 had given the clear understanding that he would seek to maintain it.[2] But, by 1845, he had changed his mind. For one thing he had come to regard the Corn Laws as an obstacle to his cherished desire of a ten-hours bill. The protection which the Laws afforded the landed interest could be used as a justification by the manufacturing interest for refusing to reduce the safeguards which it enjoyed and thus for resisting a ten-hour day. Part of the argument against the Corn Laws was that they restricted the free flow of trade and put British manufacturers at a disadvantage in foreign markets. Thus, if the Laws were repealed, manufacturers might feel sufficiently confident of their markets to be able to concede a ten-hour day, or, at least, their resistance to ten hours might be less strong. In February, 1846, Ashley wrote to Easthope that he had in the past always regarded the Corn Laws as 'things to be taken for granted', but he had found that 'they met (him) as fact or argument at every step and thwarted almost every undertaking.'[3] Further, by 1845, Ashley had come to regard repeal as inevitable. He believed that unconditional resistance to repeal would be unavailing; commercial difficulty or the prevailing mood of the government of the day would ultimately require the agricultural interest to reverse its continuing opposition to repeal. And given this situation, the landed interest, he thought, ought to accept repeal. If it did so, it would get better terms than if it were compelled to concede at some future point.

All these issues were present in a letter which Ashley addressed to the 'Gentry, Clergy and Freeholders of the County of Dorset', written while he was in the north of England in October, 1845.[4] The letter was prompted by news which Ashley had received that a requisition had been signed and circulated throughout the country to ask some other person whose views were more in accordance with those of the signatories to stand at the next General Election. He did not complain of this development, which was constitutionally perfectly correct, but it made it essential for him to make an open statement of his position and he chose to do this by letter, since he was unable to attend any of the forthcoming agricultural dinners. He regretted that, for the first time in the fourteen years during which he had been a member for the constituency, he found himself at variance with those who had previously supported him. But he emphasised his view that repeal was just a matter of time; the opinions of the prominent politicians were hardening against the Laws. It was, therefore, 'needless to argue the policy or impolicy of such a change; it would rather be wise to consider in what way you can break the force of an inevitable blow.'

Ashley had – as he put it in his Diary – spoken his mind honestly and had given what he regarded as the best advice which the present position would allow.[5] The letter, however, earned him severe rebuke in many quarters. *The Dorset County Chronicle*, hitherto favourable to Ashley, asked why there was a difference between his conduct over factory children and his treatment of his agricultural constituency. 'Has his Lordship's mind,' it asked, 'been of late so much accustomed to the misuses of a small fraction of the population that he has become insensible to the requirements of a most numerous and important class of the community?'[6] *The Morning*

Post described the letter as a 'miserable display of peevishness' and criticised Ashley for not declaring his views openly at an agricultural meeting. This was an example of what it described as Ashley's fondness for meddling in important matters and yet lack of 'manly spirit and resolute good sense which are necessary for bringing any important affair to a desirable issue.' The writer of the leading article bore Ashley 'no ill will' but heartily wished him to be in 'the situation for which he is best fitted . . . out of parliament and well settled as secretary and manager of some Ladies' Bible Society.'[7] But, if the letter exposed Ashley to bitter attack from the Protectionist side, it did not appease the Free Traders, for he had not proposed the League's aim of total and immediate repeal, but the moderate policy of gradual decline towards a small fixed duty. *The League*, the newspaper of the Anti-Corn Law League, wrote that it had seldom read any document from a public man which evinced 'a more complete and cowardly disregard of public duty'. Ashley had not faced up to the question whether Protection was right or wrong, good or bad: he had simply said that its destiny was fixed. To submit to destiny was 'a convenient cloak for cowardice or treachery'; and from this 'senatorial epistle' farmers might see what they had to expect from those in whom they had put their trust.[8]

Ashley attributed the attack of *The Morning Post* to Tractarian dislike; it was, he wrote, 'the explosion of that heavenly substance, the Tractarian mind.'[9] He felt that the bitterness of *The League* was due to the fact that the millowners would never forgive him nor cease to seek his injury. He was comforted by the consideration that, in taking a middle course on the issue, he was bound to exasperate the extremists on either side, and their opposition suggested to him that he had 'hit the mean'.[10] Nevertheless, he was deeply offended and hurt at the violence of the attacks on him – the episode, he felt, simply furnished proof of what he had long suspected: that he had many enemies and few friends. In November, he developed this theme further and catalogued all the 'constant, minute and pointed hatred' which he had provoked not only on this issue but on many others. The Anti-Corn Law League hated him as an aristocrat; the landowners as a radical; the wealthy of all opinions as a 'mover of inconvenient principles'. The Tractarians loathed him as an ultra-Protestant; the Dissenters as a Churchman; the High Church thought him 'abominably low'; the Low Church some degrees too high. He had no political party. The Whigs regarded him as leaning to the Conservatives; the Conservatives declared that he had greatly injured Peel's government. He had, therefore, the approval and support of neither; and the 'floating men' disliking what they called a 'saint', joined in the hatred and rejoiced in it. Every class was thus against him.[11] Earlier, Ashley had written that all who had regard for him were in the 'poorer or inferior walks of life';[12] now he feared that they too could catch the infection and turn against him: thus, he wrote, ' "farewell King": farewell any hopes of further usefulness.'[13]

Such an outburst was, of course, grossly exaggerated and revealed once more Ashley's tendency to indulge in excessive self-pity, although it was true that the issue had been the occasion for a great deal of criticism, some of it – such as that of *The Morning Post* – of a very unfair and vituperative nature. But despite it, Ashley stood his ground and felt justified in his course. There were times, he wrote, when it was wise to be silent, but '*here* (he) could not with propriety refrain from speaking out.' He could not deceive his constituents by advising them to carry out a protracted resistance to repeal and by promising results which he was sure would never come about. This would not be in their interests and would be contrary to his own judgment. But he could now only await the 'personal consequences'.[14]

There was not, in fact, very long to wait. The Irish Famine of 1845 brought repeal into full prominence and made it the dominant political issue in 1846. Peel – like Ashley – was already disposed against the Corn Laws; indeed, as early as 1843, he had decided that the Laws could not long remain an exception to the policy of free trade enshrined in his Budgets. Repeal would not, in Peel's view, harm the landed interest – it would, in fact, save it from the radical assaults of the Anti-Corn Law League. But Peel's hand was forced by the failure of the Irish potato crop in the autumn of 1845. Parliament, in his view, could scarcely be expected to vote public funds for relief and yet maintain restrictions on the import of corn, and, if the Laws were suspended to help promote the supply of food during the crisis, they could not, Peel felt, be re-imposed without serious discontent in Britain.[15] Thus, in November, 1845, Peel put proposals before the Cabinet for a review of the Corn Laws with repeal as the ultimate outcome of that review, and thus began the process which led to the repeal of the Laws in May 1846. But it also brought into the open the splits and divisions within the Conservative party which had lain below the surface for a number of years. In the face of opposition within the Cabinet, Peel resigned on 6 December. Russell, who on 22 November had publicly declared himself in favour of repeal in the *Edinburgh Letter,* tried to form a Whig administration but without success, and on 20 December, Peel returned to office. Stanley still refused to be a party to repeal, but Russell's failure to deal with the question strengthened Peel's position with the rest of the Cabinet and the way was open for repeal proposals to be introduced on 27 January. But having secured the support of the Cabinet, Peel still did not have the support of the bulk of the party. After four months of activity, during which Peel made five major speeches, the Corn Laws were repealed in May in the face of 222 Conservative Protectionist votes and with the support of only 106 Peelite votes. Whig-Peelites votes carried the day in the Commons and the Lords. But Peel's Ministry was not long to survive the Laws; in June, 1846, he was defeated over an Irish Coercion Bill and resigned. He was succeeded by a Whig government under Russell.

Ashley was keenly interested in these events. Russell's statement in favour of Free Trade simply confirmed his view that the political leaders were turning against Protection. Events were happening as he had foretold them; perhaps, he thought, the landed interest would now listen to him or at least be less inclined to revile him.[16] Ashley admitted that he was out of touch with politicians and had no certain information as to what was happening in Peel's Cabinet; but, when Peel returned to office after Russell's failure to form a government, he realised that members of Parliament 'of a certain complexion' – and these included himself – would shortly be called upon to decide whether they would vote for the removal of protective duties from British agriculture, which Peel would shortly propose. If those members decided that circumstances had made this inevitable, and, provided it were carefully done, not injurious, they would have to vote for abolition – but had they a right to do so? Ashley scrutinised his own case. He had been elected by an agricultural body which expected that Protection would be maintained, although no distinct pledge on his part had been given. Now the question of abolition had arisen: and it seemed to Ashley that if he were to vote for it, he would be acting 'in a sense diametrically opposite' to the views of his constituents when they elected him; indeed, had they foreseen such a vote, he would almost certainly not have been elected at all.[17] A few days later, he put the matter succinctly: 'if Peel's plan be for total abolition and I be disposed to support it, must I not previously resign my seat?'[18]

As the time came for Parliament to re-assemble, these thoughts grew stronger in Ashley's mind. Thus, on 20 January, he wrote of the time being at hand for 'fixing (his) political destiny'.[19] That destiny approached nearer when Peel announced his proposals on 27 January: for Ashley approved of the arrangements for a gradual relaxation of the protective duties on imported corn, leading to expiry in February, 1849. He thought this entirely satisfactory; the landed interest ought to be content with the proposed adjustment. He wrote that he rejoiced that repeal would compel the landed gentry to improve their estates and the condition of those who worked on them – if they did this, they would be richer and more powerful than ever. If he remained a member of Parliament, he would vote for every part of Peel's proposals. But could he remain so? And here, Ashley once again rehearsed the difficulties of his position, and he considered, too, the point that his reputation was that of a man of principle and character. If he acted in a way contrary to this, it would give rise to the criticism that, when it came to the test, 'religious men' were no better than anyone else. Thus

Ashley felt that he must resign his seat. By so doing he would surrender all his 'beloved projects'; but he would keep his integrity.[20]

It appears that, when Peel announced his proposals, Ashley wrote to J. J. Farquharson, a leading member of the Conservatives in Dorset, asking him to sound out opinion in the county as to whether he would be acting in opposition to his previously expressed opinions if he voted for repeal. It also seems that Farquharson took it upon himself to say that he would be so acting and that this would be the view of the yeomanry.[21] This finally determined Ashley's conduct. On 31 January, he applied for the Chiltern Hundreds, and the same day he sent an Address to the electors of Dorset explaining his position. He wrote of his reasons for supporting Peel's proposals and also of the 'honourable understanding' between himself and his electors, dating from 1841, which he would break if he were to retain his seat and vote for the measure. He expressed his regret that he had found such a step necessary, but he announced his intention to appear on the hustings on the day of nomination and call for a show of hands to discover, beyond any doubt, the feelings of the county.

Before this happened, however, there were some further developments. Dorset was deprived of two of its members by the issue, for one of Ashley's fellow members, Sturt, also resigned. Thus on 6 February, a special general meeting of the Dorchester Agricultural Protection Society was convened to meet deputations from several other district associations to take steps to fill the vacancies caused by the retirement of Ashley and Sturt; these would be 'staunch Protectionists'. Two persons were, indeed, proposed, Seymer and Floyer; a requisition asking them to stand and pledging support was signed; and a central committee was set up to canvass votes.[22] But other efforts were being made to assist the return of Ashley. On 6 February, Ashley noted in his Diary that Bonham had been anxious to see him the previous day. This was to say that some persons had contributed £2,000 towards the expense of Ashley being re-elected. Ashley found, as he put it, 'that Peel and Graham (is there an end of wonders?) were among them!' According to Ashley, they had told Bonham to say that they considered 'a great public principle' to be at stake in Ashley's re-election and that their assurances did not imply any obligation; thus Ashley's freedom of action over the introduction of a ten-hours bill would be unimpaired.[23] But Ashley felt that he could not accept the offer. He wrote to Bonham that he fully appreciated 'the generosity as well as the *delicacy* of the proposition', but he would feel himself embarrassed if he were to accept it.[24] By this he meant – as he wrote in his Diary – that he would lose his independence of thought and action, even if this had not been intended by those who made the offer; he should feel 'fettered' were he to accept it.[25] It seems that a further offer of help was made by Easthope, for, on 10 February, Ashley wrote to Palmerston saying that there was 'not a more kind hearted man alive' than Easthope, but he feared that Easthope's liberality would be 'of little avail'. He would need to feel sure of 'a very large sum indeed, several thousand pounds', before he could enter on such a contest. And he added that the county were fully aware of the uselessness of resistance to repeal, but were resolved to punish him personally.[26] Ashley thus addressed another letter to the electors of Dorset, dated 12 February. He informed them that it would not be possible for him to bear the cost of a contest, and, so that his opponents would not require to incur any financial responsibilities, announced that, although he would be present at the nomination, he would not demand a poll.[27]

At the nomination meeting, Ashley spoke for an hour and a half. He urged his hearers to accept a compromise over Protection and dismissed the arguments that farmers would be ruined or that the country would be made dependent on foreign supplies. The measure before Parliament would give a great stimulus to agriculture and would confer considerable benefits on the working classes. More capital would be expended on the land; a larger yield would be obtained and food would be cheapened. There would also be a larger demand for labour and thus wages would be maintained, or even raised. He stressed his knowledge of all classes, derived from his tours of the manufacturing districts; in such districts, he said, those who condemned him would find 'a new world to contemplate, a new state of things to legislate for.' He was also firmly of the view that the manufacturing and commercial classes were not the enemy of agriculture, nor were they disaffected to the monarchy and the constitution. The millowners of the North, he said, were men of vast capital 'who by their wealth, their numbers and their intelligence, now constituted a distinct order in the state and they must be attended to.' He thus urged his hearers 'so to act that this great country might present the spectacle of a united kingdom – strong for external action and strong in harmony for internal improvement.' He also pointed out that if repeal had adverse consequences for the landed interest, he stood to lose a great deal: he had many children to maintain and all his expectations derived from the land. Ashley ended by mentioning his public position: he had laid himself open to being rejected by his former constituents, 'sentenced to a private situation and deprived of all hope of carrying those measures of social improvement to which (he) had devoted the better part of (his) life.' At the end of the speech, his name was, indeed, put forward in addition to that of Seymer and of Floyer, but he declined the nomination and Seymer and Floyer were returned.[28]

It was an eloquent and memorable leave-taking. Ashley himself noted in his Diary that he had never spoken so forcibly in his life.[29] He was, in fact, well pleased with the occasion. He wrote to Peel on 19 February and said that he never saw 'such a display' in his life: 'several thousand people were assembled and their whole heart was in my favour . . . (The) people listened with the utmost attention, but they would not hear another soul.' He had no doubt that, had he possessed £5,000 on the evening he accepted the Chiltern Hundreds, he would have carried the county.[30] Peel replied that he rejoiced to hear, not so much for Ashley's sake as for 'that of the credit and honour of the County of Dorset,' that the electors on taking leave of Ashley had 'redeemed in some degree their conduct in permitting (his) retirement.'[31] Ashley thus relinquished his seat, and he felt that he had done right. He wrote in his Diary that he had not brought his principles and past professions into dishonour – he would not recall one single word nor retrieve one single step.[32] He had, however, been disappointed at the attitude of some of his Evangelical friends. Earlier in the month, he had, indeed, received 'kind, Christianlike and most acceptable letters' from McCaul and Bickersteth, but Seeley had been 'bitter, fanatical and evidently rejoicing in (his) dismissal' and Jowett had expressed no regrets.

> Is this evangelical religion? [Ashley wrote]. I have been true to every principle in Politics and Religion. I have resisted Tractarians, maintained Protestantism, upheld every good work and every religious society, have laboured and suffered in person and purse for the poor and helpless; and yet because I entertain a different opinion on the Corn Laws, I am to be set aside for someone perhaps who will either do nothing or the reverse of all this![33]

Repeal thus severed Ashley's relationship with his former electors and strained that with some of his former Evangelical friends. Despite all their past differences, it was, indeed, with Peel that Ashley was in closest agreement in the issue. His remarks about the good which repeal would bring to all sections of the community might almost have been made by Peel himself. And yet Ashley was critical of Peel's handling of the matter. He felt that Peel exaggerated the Irish Famine, which, in his view, could have been met by a temporary opening of the ports. He also felt – and this was a recurrent theme in his comments – that Peel should not have tried to make his party desert its past professions; it was the duty of Peel to consider the honour of his party, of public men and of himself. He thus thought that Peel had made a great mistake in putting a repeal proposal to his Cabinet – he should never have tried to persuade his colleagues 'to violate every honourable understanding.' Once convinced of the necessity of repeal, Peel should have resigned and left it to the Whigs to take up the matter; had Russell then failed, Peel might have returned 'on the ground of public exigencies, with a clear conscience and a clear character.' But he made no effort to try out the Whigs' capacity to undertake office until he had attempted to handle the question himself.[34] Further, Ashley was not only critical of Peel for attempting to make his supporters turn back on a previously held policy; he was resentful that Peel should have expected them to do so. He commented bitterly on what he regarded as Peel's arrogance and 'despotic Dominion', demanding absolute allegiance from his followers whether he himself was 'steady and consistent or chopping and changing'.[35] The changes were, Ashley felt, more conspicuous than the consistency; Peel had 'begun by opposing and ended by carrying (not simply supporting) almost every great question of the day.' And, in such changes, he had 'seduced some of his followers and browbeat the others.'[36] Corn Law repeal was yet another example of this. Peel had turned round

> externally at least with the rapidity of a Dervish and thought that his dictation alone was sufficient to command a similar revolution on the part of his followers. One half of the opposition he has encountered has arisen from personal feelings and personal indignation against his conduct.[37]

In his view that Peel exaggerated the Famine, Ashley was voicing a criticism made of Peel both at the time of repeal and since. It is a view which is clearly open to argument. What may be said is that a serious, and even over-serious, assessment of the situation in Ireland was understandable in the light of the evidence presented, and there seems no doubt that Peel himself was genuinely convinced of the severity of the crisis – as, indeed, Ashley was prepared to admit. The criticism that Peel should have suspended the laws is also debatable, but there is considerable weight in Professor Gash's view[38] that since the Famine was likely to last longer than one year, suspension would have to be prolonged and might have to last until 1850. Before that, a General Election would have to take place, which would have given the opportunity for agitation in favour of complete repeal, and this would not have served the interests of the established order, which both Peel and Ashley wanted to preserve. The further point made by Ashley – that Peel should have resigned and let the Whigs try to deal with the situation before he put forward any repeal proposals – does not take account of the urgency of the situation, as Peel saw it, nor of Peel's feeling that this would be an evasion of his duty; and there is also the consideration that it was not until 20 November that Russell declared openly in favour of repeal. As Professor Gash has written, the Irish question 'made (Peel) do hastily and without warning what he intended to do later and after due notice.'[39] But it is true that, at this point, Peel put what he felt to be his duty to his country ahead of duty to his party; and, even if the Irish Famine had not taken place and due notice had been served of Peel's intentions to repeal the Laws, there would still have been great difficulties for Conservative members who felt pledged to Protection. Although his sense of duty dictated it, Peel did find it easier to 'turn round', as Ashley put it, and change course than many, and he tended to expect others to do the same and follow his lead. Setting aside the merits of the issue which made him 'turn round', it is understandable that such conduct alienated opinion in the party, and Ashley's comments on this aspect of the question certainly echoed those of many others.

One of Ashley's major regrets at his retirement from Parliament was that he would not be in a position to complete the measures of social improvement to which he had devoted so much time. The most important of these was, of course, factory reform. On 29 January, two days before his resignation, Ashley had re-introduced a ten-hours bill for women and young persons. Before he did so, he had corresponded with Graham on the matter. Graham had written that in the 'peculiar circumstances of the time', he did not think he would 'consult the public good by resisting the introduction of the Ten Hours Bill,' but he assumed that Ashley would be willing to postpone its second reading until after the Corn Law question had been settled.[40] Ashley agreed to this and promised to say as little as he could in the debate; he only sought to justify his conduct in resuming the matter.[41] In his speech,[42] he said that the main issue was whether ten hours would lead to injury to the manufacturers and a reduction of wages. He thus took up the issues which Peel had raised in 1844. Ashley refuted these possibilities. The 1833 Act had not produced the ruination of the textile industry prophesied at the time; in addition, manufacturers who had tried the experiment of an eleven-hour day had found no harmful effects. On the contrary, production had been kept up, the quality of goods was better, the workers were healthier and their earnings had not been depressed. There was, therefore, no reason why the further limitation of hours should not now be imposed, and there was every reason to protect female workers in their early teens. Ashley was, however, severely attacked by Bright, who claimed that he did not know enough on the subject and looked too much on one side of it.[43] Various other speakers were also critical and, although Graham did not offer resistance to the introduction of the bill, he made it clear that, in his view, further government interference would be a dangerous experiment. Ashley recorded that Graham was 'very hostile, clearly there must have been some personal feeling ... The House ... very cold and comfortless, scarcely one approving voice;' and he also mentioned that he had been 'most awfully reviled' by Bright and others. 'The truth is,' he wrote, 'that I am much fallen in public estimation.'[44] The bill was read a first time, but this was almost immediately followed by Ashley's resignation. The resignation caused alarm in the Ten Hours Movement and a meeting of the Central Short-Time Committee of Lancashire was quickly summoned. A letter from Ashley was read, expressing his reasons for resigning and his regrets, but urging the Committees not to despair. John Fielden, Radical member for Oldham and – despite being a cotton master at Todmorden – a supporter of a ten hours limitation, would bring the bill to a second reading, and Ashley would still do all he could. Ashley received a reply expressing regret at his loss, gratitude for his past services and relief that the matter would not be dropped. Despite the relief, however, the Committee agreed to send an address to the electors of Dorset, asking them to re-elect Ashley.[45] Their requests were, of course, unavailing.

Once finally out of Parliament, Ashley undertook an extensive tour of the factory districts in March, 1846. He found it 'monstrous difficult to find a fresh speech every night,'[46] which is not surprising since the tour included visits to at least nine different places.[47] He sought to guide and steer the campaign which had started in support of Fielden. He wanted to 'propitiate the masters and yet encourage the work people.' This he found a difficult task for 'soft sawder to the millowners (unless... skilfully applied) is a damper to the men; and a stirrer to the men is a damper to the millowners.'[48] It was, also, he wrote, a 'novel form of agitation to abstain from excitement and appeal; and to adopt rebuke, exhortation and counsel to the people whom you address.'[49] But he thought that to adopt such a moderate line was the best way forward. And he also considered it his duty to exhort his hearers to 'use aright' the blessings of a shorter working day and to turn it to the honour of God and the moral improvement of themselves and their children.[50] He had, he wrote, always been concerned to raise the moral character and feelings of the working classes, and this could only be done by 'instructing them of their real dignity as immortal beings and treating them as such.'[51] Ashley was also concerned to explain his own position. Thus he told his audience at Manchester that he had no means of serving them except with his personal character; if he had remained in Parliament, he would have lost his reputation. And he felt that he had succeeded in so persuading them. 'Operatives in general,' he wrote, 'feel that I have advanced the question by the mode and subject of my retirement.'[52]

Absence from Parliament, however, did not mean relaxation of effort. Although he was not now responsible for the question of factory reform in Parliament, Ashley was heavily involved in various extra-parliamentary pursuits concerned with social matters. There was, for example, the question of housing for the working classes. This was, indeed, a matter in which Ashley had been interested since the late 1830s. He visited areas of bad housing in Glasgow in 1839;[53] in September, 1841, he recorded in his Diary a walk which he had taken in Whitechapel and Bethnal Green in London and wrote of the 'scenes of filth, discomfort, disease' and of the 'suffering and degradation which unwholesome residences inflict on the poorer classes'.[54] Such interests inevitably brought Ashley into contact with those involved in the public health movement. He had been disappointed that the Tory government after 1841 failed to follow up bills introduced in the last years of the Whigs for ventilation and drainage, and he was even more outraged when Graham did not take action on these bills after the publication in 1842 of the Report of the Sanitary Condition of the Labouring Classes. The appointment by the government in 1843 of a Health of Towns Commission was, Ashley thought, a delaying tactic: and he was very active in the Health of Towns Association founded in 1844, to give publicity to sanitary reform and keep the subject before the public. In these efforts, Ashley acted in association with Edwin Chadwick, who was largely responsible for the Report of 1842. There were, indeed, many differences between the two men.[55] Ashley's approach was inspired primarily by Evangelical and paternalistic concern, whereas Chadwick argued the case for public health in terms of national self-interest and efficiency rather than of charity. But if Ashley saw the matter in religious and moral terms and Chadwick in terms of public administration and social science, both were agreed that action was essential; and, in the mid-forties, they began the active cooperation which was later to be a marked feature of the public health movement. One area where Ashley acted in cooperation with enthusiasts for public health was in the foundation of the Society for Improving the Condition of the Labouring Classes in May, 1844. This Society had a forerunner in the Labourers' Friend Society, which was founded in the early 1830s and had been concerned with providing allotments for rural labourers. The Society founded in 1844 retained this as one of its objects – the allotments were to be used for leisure pursuits. But it was felt that considerably more than this was now required and thus the Society also aimed to improve the houses of the poor in the town and the country, and to form friendly loan societies. It was an experiment 'undertaken on Christian principles for the attainment of Christian ends.'[56] As a pilot scheme, it resolved to build a certain number of houses as models of the different kinds of house which it thought fit for the working classes in heavily populated towns. It took heed of the recommendations of the Health of Towns Commission, and in the arrangement of the buildings, care was taken 'to combine every point essential to the health, comfort and moral habits of the industrious classes and their families ... particularly with respect to ventilation, drainage and an ample supply of water.'[57] Ashley was chairman of the Committee appointed to manage the affairs of the Society, and he gave a donation of £50 to its activities.[58] The Society offered 4% as a return on capital subscribed to assist its operations. It found that its early efforts in building model housing at Pentonville were expensive, and, in December, 1844, as a part of an appeal for more funds, Ashley wrote to Peel, asking for his interest and support.[59] 'The state of our labouring people,' he wrote, 'demands the most extensive and immediate exertions.' It is not clear what Peel's response was, but the Society did attract interest in high places: its patrons were the Queen and Queen Dowager, who subscribed £20 and £10 respectively, and Prince Albert was its President. And it did achieve some success. In the area of the Old Pancras Road and Mile End New Town, where it built two blocks of model lodging houses, the mortality rate dropped to 13.6 per 1,000.[60] But it did not succeed in setting speculative builders an example to invest in working-class housing. The return of 4% offered by the Society on capital subscribed was regarded by Chadwick as too low, and even Prince Albert thought that it would be necessary to offer 7% to 8% to induce builders to invest capital in such houses.[61]

A further subject in which Ashley took an active personal interest in the mid 1840s was the establishment of Ragged Schools for destitute children. Ragged Schools were founded in London in the first few years of the decade by Sunday School teachers associated with the London City Mission; their purpose was to instruct children who 'from their poverty or ragged condition (were) prevented attending any other place of religious instruction.'[62] In 1844, a number of Ragged School teachers in London met together to found the Ragged School Union, which was intended to give encouragement and permanency to existing Ragged Schools in the metropolis and help promote the establishment of new ones; and the organisation developed separately from the London City Mission, which felt unable to add to its burden by undertaking further work of this kind. The Schools did provide a certain elementary education in reading, writing and counting and they also offered various social and recreational facilities. In addition, they were regarded as valuable in inculcating useful and industrious habits among destitute children and in restraining them from a life of mischief and crime. But their primary purpose was to impart religious instruction; all other objects were 'subordinated to the chief end of bringing neglected and ignorant children within the reach of the doctrine of Christ.'[63]

Ashley's attention to the schools appears to have been first attracted by an advertisement in *The Times* in February, 1843, inserted by the teachers of the Field Lane Sabbath School in Saffron Hill, appealing for assistance in the running of the School, which was situated in a 'most wretched and demoralised locality', and which, since 1841, had been open on Sunday and Thursday evenings.[64] Ashley at once became interested in the work of such Schools and in November, 1844, responded to a request to become President of the Ragged School Union.[65] As President, he took the chair at its annual meetings and he attended numerous meetings of individual Ragged Schools to give encouragement and advice. Although he had expressed opposition to the idea of 'combined education' with Dissenters in 1844, the attendance of Dissenters at Ragged Schools did not worry him. In November, 1845, he recorded a visit to Broadwall Infant Ragged School: 'Many Dissenters,' he wrote, 'but it is high time to be thinking where we agree, not where we differ. Tens of thousands of untaught heathens in the heart of a Christian metropolis cry aloud to God for vengeance.'[66] And in the following month, after a visit to a tea meeting at Jurston Street Sunday School for the 'ragged, half-starved, neglected children of the locality,' he wrote that he regarded himself as acting in the spirit of the Bible and of the Church of England. He was violating none of the Church's 'laws, precepts, principles or prayers'; but, if his conduct were judged to be at variance with the doctrines of the Established Church, he would 'prefer to renounce communion with the Church to abandoning those wretched infants of oppression, infidelity and crime.'[67] In fact, this did not prove to be necessary, but the comment illustrated the force of his views on the importance of the work done by the Schools.

Ashley's release from parliamentary duties in January, 1846, gave him more freedom to devote to these interests and, for the rest of the year, he was extremely busy with them. He set himself to use the time now at his disposal to increase his knowledge of the worst parts of London by making personal visits accompanied by a doctor and a missionary from the London City Mission. At a meeting of the Society for Improving the Condition of the Labouring Classes in May, 1846, Ashley explained how his changed circumstances had given him the opportunity to explore the worst areas of the Metropolis. He did not now, he said, speak merely from what he had read in books or accounts – he spoke from what he had seen. Ashley told the Society of his explorations and announced that it was proposed, if funds permitted, to build a model lodging house in the parish of St Giles with accommodation at a reasonable rent.[68] He also kept up his activities in the Health of Towns Association and retained his links with Chadwick. In November, 1846, Chadwick sent him a review of progress made in public health since 1837: 'a singularly important' paper, wrote Ashley in reply.[69] Also in November, Ashley acted as chairman of a deputation to the Home Office on behalf of a bill for ventilation and drainage.[70] Public health pursuits thus engaged his attention, and, throughout the year, he was constantly occupied in visiting and helping to found Ragged Schools, often in places where his perambulations had taken him. His Diary for the year is, indeed, full of such engagements – the entry for 6 June: 'busied about erection of "Ragged Schools" '[71] would serve as an illustration of many. In December, he wrote an article on the subject of the schools in *The*

Quarterly Review;[72] he hoped that the payment for it would meet the cost — which he himself had undertaken — of running an evening class to teach tailoring, shoemaking and needlework at the ragged school at Broadwall.[73] Not only did he describe graphically the conditions which he had seen, but he also praised the efforts of those active in the work of Ragged Schools. 'Ladies and gentlemen who walk in purple and fine linen and fare sumptuously every day' could have no idea of the 'pain and toil which the founders and conductors of these schools have joyfully sustained in their simple and fervent piety. . . .' They sought to 'reclaim a wild and lawless race, unaccustomed from their earlier years to the slightest moral influence, or even restraint, and bring them back to notions of civilization and domestic life.' And he answered the question as to what would be done with the children in the Schools when they had been educated with another question: what would be done with them if their education were neglected? They were the seeds of future generations. Thus, he continued:

> The wheat or tares will predominate, as Christian principle or ignorant selfishness shall, hereafter, govern our conduct. We must cease, if we would be safe, to trust in measures of coercion and chastisement for our juvenile vagrants; they are not too many to be educated as infants; they are far too many to be punished as adults. We must entertain higher thoughts for them and for England, and, with a just appreciation of their rights and our own duties, not only help them, by God's blessing, from those depths of degradation, but raise them to a level on which they may run the course that is set before them, as citizens of the British Empire, and heirs of a glorious immortality.

In addition to such activities, Ashley retained, throughout 1846, other extra-parliamentary pursuits. The regular meetings of the Commission in Lunacy were burdensome: 'six hours this day' ran a Diary entry in October referring to a meeting of the Commission.[74] The same month, he recorded a visit of some hours to a 'large madhouse', after which he returned home half-exhausted, but thankful that much had been done to improve the condition of the insane.[75] Such long-standing interests, along with the more recent ones, kept Ashley at full stretch. Already in March, 1846, he complained that he had more business out of Parliament than in it,[76] and, in November, he wrote that the Society for Improving the Condition of the Labouring Classes, the Ragged Schools and the Lunacy Commission kept him 'in unceasing occupation'; he had hardly a moment to himself.[77]

There were, of course, also in this period family and personal concerns. Some were happy; a third daughter, Constance, had been born in November, 1845. Others were less so. Ashley was anxious about Anthony, for reports from Rugby were disturbing. 'Is Anthony a bad boy,' he wrote in July, 1846, 'is he a heartless contumacious boy? Alas, I see in him many signs of a wilful, selfish spirit. I cannot see in him many signs of duty and affection to his parents – and yet God knows how we have watched over him. . . .' The particular incident which gave rise to this entry ended with Anthony expressing remorse and shedding tears; 'all is well,' wrote Ashley.[78] But not for long. In September, Anthony wrote to demand more money: 'Alas,' wrote Ashley, 'he *never* writes but when he wants some addition to his luxury. The boy seems utterly damaged.'[79] In November, Ashley wrote that it was evident that Anthony was 'set for the trial, if not the grief of his parents:' the boy had taken to smoking.[80] Later in the month, there was more bad news from Rugby about Anthony's 'indolence and carelessness': he had contracted large debts. 'What can I do,' wrote Ashley. 'I am at my wits end.'[81] Again, there was solace to come: a letter was received from Anthony expressing regret. These entries in 1846 were, however, the first of many in the future: anxiety at Anthony's conduct, followed by comfort at the boy's expression of regret, was a pattern to be repeated on innumerable occasions. There were, too, other worries over the health of Maurice, and largely for his sake, Ashley, Minny and the four eldest boys set out in July for a spa in Germany and a period in Switzerland. Although tired and weary, Ashley was reluctant to take himself away from the many duties demanding his attention. While in Switzerland, he was heartened by the amount of Evangelical activity in Basle, but considerably distressed at the reports of free thinking and intellectual scepticism in Germany. The holiday was not, in fact, a great success in restoring either Ashley or Maurice to health. There were days in the Alps when Ashley felt refreshed, or, as he put it, 'elastic', but they were few. And in early August, Maurice took ill and it was decided to return home as soon as possible – the party returned that month.[82] The expense of the holiday must have added to Ashley's personal problems. Indeed, the very last day of the year found him complaining about lack of money. 'Croesus would be pauperised if he were to meet half the demands that are made upon me every month,' he wrote. He had to refuse most of the demands and give sparingly to the rest, and he knew that this would lead to misrepresentation and misunderstandings.

> Many people choose to believe that I am rich [he continued] and ask accordingly; and yet more than half of my income is borrowed, to be repaid at some future day, with heavy accumulations of interest; eight children, the two eldest costing me more than £200 a year each; a ninth coming,[83] and an allowance from my father of only £100 annually more than I had as a Bachelor at Oxford! Are these sources of wealth? . . .[84]

The year 1846 had, therefore, begun for Ashley on a note of anxiety about his political and parliamentary career; the subsequent months had been filled with effort in various extra-parliamentary causes; causes which were demanding on his purse in addition to his time and energy and which contributed to the worries which Ashley harboured as the year closed. It has, indeed, been argued that Ashley's retirement from Parliament in January, 1846, was a turning-point in his career. Thus the Hammonds have written that Ashley's retirement:

> altered profoundly his whole life. That event marks a decisive turning-point in his career. It was while he was out of the House of Commons that he became absorbed in philanthropic work and this new interest gradually dominated his life, turning him from a politician striving to serve his Christian conscience into a monk or missionary who remained in politics with less than half of his mind.[85]

Mrs Battiscombe writes that Ashley's 'departure from the House of Commons marks a watershed in his life.' She argues that until then, he believed that 'his chief vocation was to act as Parliamentary spokesman for the poor, the oppressed and the outcast, who had no votes and could not speak for themselves.' The period during which he was out of Parliament, however, showed Ashley that he could do 'as much good work outside Parliament as ever he could achieve inside it.'[86] Thus it may be held that, from this period, the bias of Ashley's life tended to be towards philanthropic rather than parliamentary efforts. Such points of view do, indeed, have much validity. There is no doubt that Ashley did strive to develop his extra-parliamentary pursuits while out of Parliament, and, the more he saw, the more he was convinced there was to do. In December, 1846, he wrote of his Ragged School work: 'expulsion from Parliament has led me to this pursuit which I could not undertake had I remained in the House of Commons; thank heaven I thus changed my front but did not retreat from duty and it will not be, God helping me, altogether useless.'[87] As Mrs Battiscombe writes, this remark might be 'applied equally to his philanthropic work as a whole.'[88] And for the first few months of 1847, these interests continued to dominate his time and energy. There was the work of the Association of Health of Towns – Ashley recorded that he took the chair of a meeting in February.[89] There were also the efforts of The Society for the Improvement of the Condition of the Labouring Classes to set up lodging houses to assist strangers who arrived in London with no accommodation and eventually found themselves squalid and overcrowded rooms – Ashley wrote an article in *The Quarterly Review* on this subject.[90] And there was constant activity over Ragged Schools. On 19 February, he wrote at 10.30 p.m. that he had just returned from the chair of a Ragged School meeting. 'I go from chair to chair and make one appeal after another,'[91] he wrote. There were the customary 'May' meetings of societies devoted to Evangelical and philanthropic work: on 8 May, 1847, he wrote that he was 'not roasted whole, but hashed and minced by engagements, Chairs, speeches, Committees etc.'[92]

But, as Mrs Battiscombe rightly says,[93] too much should not be made of the 'break' in Ashley's life in 1846-7. For one thing, the causes which he espoused in these years – matters concerned with public health and Ragged Schools – were not, in fact, new; Ashley was already interested in them. Further, Ashley's earlier major concern for factory reform remained a major preoccupation, even if he was no longer in Parliament to promote it. He was acutely anxious for the success of the bill which he himself had introduced in January, 1846. His efforts in the campaign of March of that year in support of Fielden have already been noted. In April, he was distressed by rumours that the operatives had yielded to the intrigues of Hindley and would ask for an eleven-hours bill. As long as he himself had been in charge of the measure, he wrote, Hindley's efforts had been unsuccessful: 'but now that the cat is away, the mice will play.' He did not favour eleven hours; it had the bad effects of twelve hours and none of the good effects of ten, and he felt that the departure from the 'just and righteous principle of Ten Hours' would be regarded as a sign of weakness.[94] He looked forward to the second reading of his bill, although he knew that he must not interfere with Fielden's efforts. When Fielden did move the second reading on 29 April, 1846, Ashley waited in the lobby: 'had not the spirit to attend the gallery', he wrote. And, he added sadly: 'Many things will be started in debate which no one can refute but myself. Alas! Alas!'[95] Once more, the bill ran into government opposition. Ashley noted this on 30 April: 'heartless and dishonest men!' he wrote. 'The whole debate proceeded, and will proceed, on a lie: on the lie that the bill is directed to the control of the labour of grown men!'[96] Fears such as this did, indeed, contribute to the bill's defeat, although it was a narrow one – when the vote was taken on 22 May, the majority against it was only ten. Ashley was heartened by the result. He told the Lancashire Committee that 'although not a victory, it is the next best thing to one' and he advised the workers to 'redouble their efforts.'[97]

The fall of Peel's government in June, 1846, encouraged the reformers to keep up their pressure, for Russell, the new Prime Minister, had supported the bill lost the previous month. The Ten Hours Movement intensified its efforts. Ashley refused to take part in a newly organised body, a Society for Bettering the Condition of Female Factory Operatives, since its programme did not include shorter hours: but he did exhort the Movement to undertake further efforts and to set up as many committees as it could.[98] The campaign kept up its momentum throughout late 1846 and early 1847 in anticipation of the new parliamentary session, in which Fielden would resume his efforts in the cause. In January, 1847, Ashley made a tour of Lancashire, with many speaking engagements. He took Anthony with him hoping 'to provoke him to emulation and give him a taste for usefulness and kindle the dormant spark of zeal for God's service.' At least, it would keep the boy from the temptations of London.[99] On 26 January, he spoke at a meeting at Bolton: 'great, glorious, enthusiastic,' and, he added: 'my duty is clear – I must labour and urge and compel, as tho' I were in Parliament and the measure would be called by my name. . . .'[100] He wrote to Bonham the following day from Manchester, telling him that the feeling in the district was 'enthusiastic', and that the affection which they showed towards himself was 'very striking'.[101] At Manchester, he urged his audience to keep to the cause in lawful ways, arguing that the old obstacle of foreign competition had been removed now that manufacturers were not hindered by the Corn Laws from competing on equal terms with their counterparts abroad. He also dismissed the case that ten hours would mean a reduction of wages, and rejected the argument about complete non-interference between employer and employed. The principle of interference had long been attained, and 'all the arguments against it ought to be buried and go to the tomb of all the Capitalists.'[102]

Finally, on 26 January, 1847, Fielden was given leave to bring in a ten-hours bill. The second reading came on 10 February. Once again, Ashley could not quite bring himself to go into the House: 'I lingered in the lobby,' he wrote on 10th: 'had not spirit to enter the House: should have been nervously excited to reply, and grieved by inability to do so.'[103] He was distressed by the fact that opposition was still offered, but felt that resistance was now on the decline, and, indeed, Sir George Grey, the Home Secretary, expressed general support for the measure, although he would have preferred eleven hours.[104] On 17 February, when the debate was resumed, an eleven hours amendment was, indeed, proposed, but it was defeated. Again Ashley was tantalised by his position on the wings. 'I could have wished,' he wrote, 'to have taken my part in these things and to have tasted a portion of the fruits of my watching; but my sentence is the sentence of the Jews, "others shall reap the harvest" . . .'[105] The bill passed its second reading on 19 February but, even although this was a step forward, Ashley's interest and concern did not cease. There was a real possibility that an eleven hours amendment would be proposed later in Committee. On 1 March, Ashley wrote of his 'intense anxiety' about the bill and recorded that he dreamt of it by day and night and worked as though he had charge of it.[106] On 2 March, he wrote to Russell, asking him to present a petition from the Short-Time Committees. He described the excitement on the subject as greater than at any former period in the manufacturing districts and trusted that the people would not again be disappointed, especially at a time of distress and unemployment. 'Hitherto,' he wrote, 'the great defeats have occurred in periods of prosperity: a repulse would now happen at a moment when they could and would, I fear, brood over their sufferings.'[107]

On 3 March, the House rejected a motion that the Committee be postponed for six months.[108] This was a step forward, but Ashley was still anxious: on 12 March he wrote that the 'sky lowers – damps and fog hang over the Committee. . . .'[109] On 16 March, he was occupied in providing Russell with notes for a speech: but he still feared delays.[110] But on 17 March, at 11 p.m., he finally expressed relief. The House had at last gone into Committee and a clause giving a ten-hour day after 1 May, 1848, was carried.[111] Ashley could scarcely believe that there was 'no mischief . . . no plan, no strategem' in this; but even if this were so, the question had 'gained a mighty stride' and he wondered if the government would dare 'disappoint the people.'[112] Russell would have preferred an eleven-hours measure, but he accepted the vote of the Committee and urged that there should be no further delay.[113] There was, it is true, a last-ditch effort to delay the bill, but two hostile amendments were defeated and on 21 April, the bill passed through Committee.[114] Ashley joined in a deputation to Russell, and Russell agreed to allow the third reading to take place on 3 May. 'God bless him for it,' Ashley wrote.[115] The third reading was duly carried; 'blessed be His holy and gracious name,' wrote Ashley.[116]

Ashley had not been inactive about the prospects of the bill in the Lords. While the bill was still in the Commons, he had visited Lord Ellesmere to request him to take charge of the bill in the Lords. On 19 March, he recorded rumours that the Lords would turn the bill into an eleven-hours measure. 'I foresee another journey into Lancashire to keep up their spirits,' he wrote. 'The labour of this cause is terrible.'[117] Again, on 22 March, Ashley was anxious at reports that the Lords would move for a committee of inquiry to delay the matter. In an effort to recruit support for the bill, Ashley wrote to Wilberforce, Bishop of Oxford, in the hope of 'stirring (his) sympathies on behalf of half a million of operatives' and of persuading him to use 'that eloquence which God had given (him) for the temporal and spiritual welfare of His creatures.'[118] Wilberforce agreed to do so, and Ashley wrote to thank him. Ashley mentioned to Wilberforce that objections to the measure had changed their character over the past fourteen years. At first it had been argued that there was no need at all for interference: all was 'Elysium in these districts'. But now, the existence of physical and moral evils was admitted and twelve hours of labour for women and young persons – involving fifteen hours away from home – were seen as too many. The resistance now was on financial grounds: that it would reduce wages, cut profits and drive capital out of the country. Ashley sent Wilberforce an extract from *Hansard* giving a review which he had made in January, 1846, of the benefits of factory legislation, and he wrote of his anxiety that Wilberforce should speak, not only that he might support the bill and 'grace the question', but, he continued, 'because it is very desirable that these mighty masses should be attached to the Constitution in Church and State, by finding their advocates and protectors in the Bishops and the laws.'[119]

The bill was duly introduced by Ellesmere on 4 May, 1847. By 8 May, Ashley felt that the prospects were better: 'but I can take no rest,' he wrote, 'nor shall I.'[120] There was, indeed, no rest: he was hard at work preparing notes for Ellesmere. The Lords debated the matter at some length at the second reading on 17 May. Wilberforce kept his promise and spoke in favour of the bill,[121] as did the Bishop of St Davids.[122] When the bill passed its second reading, Ashley was delighted: 'How can we praise Thee or thank Thee, O Lord? One step more and all will be safe.' He felt that the Bishops had 'behaved gallantly'; their conduct would 'do very much to win the hearts of the manufacturing people to Bishops and Lords. . . .'[123] On 31 May, the bill went into Committee in the Lords: Ashley was confident that God would be with it and thus relieve its supporters from 'this long terrible anxiety and toil'.[124] Finally, on 1 June, he received the news that the factory bill had passed its third reading. He was deeply thankful: 'what reward shall we give unto the Lord for all the benefits He hath conferred upon us?' he wrote.[125]

It is, of course, true that the final achievement of the measure was partly due to the circumstances of the time. In 1847, short-time working was, in fact, almost in operation without the Act: it was a period of economic recession and trade was slack. By 1847, there was not the same opposition from the employers as there had been earlier – many larger firms offered no resistance to it, and smaller employers were also well disposed, fearing that, on the resumption of trade, they would be swallowed up by the larger firms. Yet Ashley well recognised that circumstances were favourable in 1847 and was anxious to exploit the position and keep up the pressure. He told Russell in March, 1847, of the support for the measure among the manufacturers, large and small,[126] but he was anxious to secure legislation on the subject and not rely on local agreements. He told the factory operatives in Manchester in January, 1847, that he could not believe that those who advised them to rely on private arrangements were serious – the law was the only safeguard and the law was their right.[127]

Thus the leadership of the cause of factory reform which Ashley had provided since 1833 was still exercised even when his parliamentary position was lost. *The Ten Hours Advocate* – published for the first time in

September, 1846, and described by Ashley as the 'operatives' own paper'[128] – still named him as 'our great leader';[129] and when the bill passed through Committee in the Commons, the Bolton reformers made a presentation to Ashley.[130] Once the bill had finally passed both Commons and Lords, Ashley enjoyed as much acclaim as Fielden. Further, some days after the bill had passed the Lords, Ashley sent a letter to the Short-Time Committees and thus, in a sense, re-affirmed himself in his old role.[131] He did, indeed, pay tribute to Fielden as one who, ever since 1833, had been the Movement's 'able, energetic and unshrinking advocate'. But Ashley could not 'after so many years of labour, take leave of it altogether without a few words . . . of advice and congratulation.' The letter urged the factory workers to put the hours gained by the new legislation to good effect in pursuits which would lead to 'moral improvement', especially among the female workers. There would now be 'far better opportunities both of learning and practising those duties which must be known and discharged if we would have a comfortable, decent and happy population.' Assistance towards this would be received from clergymen and medical men in the district. And Ashley further exhorted the Committees to 'an oblivion of past conflicts and to hearty endeavour for future harmony.' There should be no language of triumph, as though an enemy had been defeated; now that the struggle was over, interests and feelings of employer and employed could be combined 'in a mutual understanding for the comfort and benefit of each other, and for the welfare of the whole community.' Ashley thus saw 1847 as a culmination of the appeals made over the years to Parliament on behalf of the operatives' rights 'as immortal beings, as citizens and Christians'.

Absence from Parliament did not, therefore, mark a major change in Ashley's interests. Further, Ashley was not wholly reconciled to his role outside Parliament. It is, indeed, true that he sometimes felt that his parliamentary career was at an end. It appears that, when he resigned his seat, his thoughts ran along these lines. Thus he wrote to Brougham in February, 1847, looking back on his introduction of the ten-hours bill in January, 1846: 'knowing that I was about to resign my seat,' he wrote, 'I wished before I closed my career in Parliament to state what had been effected by law and public opinion towards the amelioration of that large class of human beings.'[132] And, thereafter, he had doubts whether he would return. He was not without offers. In August, 1846, he received letters from Bath and also from the City of Oxford, asking him to become a candidate in each of these constituencies.[133] Little more came of the Oxford offer, but in October, he received another message from Bath, asking him to stand at the next election. He replied that he wanted assurances and a guarantee about support and expenses:[134] and, in December, he noted the 'lamentable truth' that he must either be returned for some place 'scot free or not at all'.[135] Later in December, he received a further letter from Bath, urging him to stand and promising to bear all the expenses. But he was not anxious to accept the offer. 'I have indeed,' he wrote, 'ceased to be anxious, at least I fancy so, to enter Parliament again.' He would, in any event, have preferred an 'honourable return' to his own County, but his enemies were bitter and his friends slow.[136] Thus at certain times, Ashley felt that his parliamentary career *was* at an end, and, when addressing the Annual Meeting of the Ragged School Union in 1847, he said that, having lost the letters 'M.P.' after his name, he should feel satisfied with supplying the letters 'C.R.S.U.' or Chairman of the Ragged School Union.[137] But, at other times, Ashley hankered after a return to Parliament. In April, 1846, he wrote that he had no 'idle time', and yet he felt 'like a man at sea without a rudder'. He was 'collecting facts, and examining books and instituting inquiries', but he felt dissatisfied that he could turn none of this to account. 'Literature,' he commented, 'may be pursued for its own sake, but there is no attraction or compensation in the study of human misery and degradation, except the prospect of abating them.'[138] His exclusion from Parliament, 'the great scene of the nation', as he put it, made him feel '*much enfeebled* . . . in general influence.'[139] and he considered that any influence which he did possess depended on the prospect of a return to Parliament.[140] Here again, therefore, there was no real break with the past. Ashley did not turn his back irrevocably on Parliament to enter a sphere of activity outside it, and he felt that he had to be in Parliament to give effective expression to his pursuits.

The period of indecision was, indeed, shortlived. In early January, he met a further deputation from Bath. He was given evidence of a general desire that he should become the representative of the constituency, assurance of probable success and a guarantee of payment of all expenses. Ashley refused to give conditional acceptance of the requisition – which had been signed by more than one thousand electors : he felt this was 'too much of a negotiation'. Nevertheless, he was greatly impressed by the approach; and also by the fact that no pledge was required, that strong hopes of success were held out and that the trades people undertook to conduct the canvassing and bear the costs themselves. Thus he thought the deputation 'on the whole, very satisfactory'.[141] In May, 1847, there was a faint possibility that he might stand as a candidate for Oxford University : this would be to aid the Protestant cause against the candidatures of Gladstone and Cardwell. Ashley certainly distrusted both men : Gladstone, in his view, was a 'mystified, slippery, uncertain, politico-Churchman, a non-Romanist Jesuit'; and Cardwell a 'clever time serving, simple lawyer, the mere creature of Peel and pledged to all his policy.'[142] But Ashley did not wish to be a candidate. He heard objections to himself : that he was the son of a peer, advanced in life, the President of the Church Pastoral Aid Society, a low churchman. All this convinced him that he was regarded as totally unfit, and he was led to dark and sombre thoughts about the real extent of the 'influence' which was attributed to him. In any event, he was, as he wrote, 'three parts engaged to Bath'.[143] And a few days later, on 25 May, he signified his full engagement in a speech to the electors. In this, he mentioned the temptations which he had felt to retire from public life. But there was still the need to defend the principles of the Constitution in Church and State, even if too bigoted an adherence to details was not practicable and institutions had to be adapted to the necessities of the times. And there were also the social questions to which he felt committed: 'private duty' might do much, but legislation would do more by giving direction and purpose to that duty when it tended to grow weary.[144] Thus Ashley threw his hat into the ring for the General Election of the summer of 1847. Even while suggesting that he might be content with the letters 'C.R.S.U.' after his name, he was actively trying to restore those of 'M.P.'

As the Election approached, Ashley was a prey to his usual conflict of emotions. He was gratified that Lancashire sent a deputation of three in early July to address the workpeople of Bath, but, a week later, he was asking himself if he would succeed, and, even more urgently, what he would do if he failed. Then his 'means of usefulness' would be greatly curtailed and all his efforts, even on behalf of Ragged Schools, would die away.[145] He noted that government influence was working against him. This, indeed, was a point on which he had written a month earlier to Russell,[146] prompted by a statement made to him by Russell that the government would use all its weight at Bath in favour of Ashley's opponent, Roebuck, who was one of the sitting members. Ashley had commented that he did not expect the government to work against Roebuck, but he recalled that Roebuck had bitterly attacked him for the part which he had played in securing the assent of the Wesleyans to educational proposals put forward by the Whigs.[147] This had been in cooperation with Russell, who had thanked Ashley for his services.[148] The government's open hostility to his candidature at Bath thus struck Ashley as somewhat ungrateful, and its support for Roebuck surprising. It is true that the influence which the government could bring to bear at Bath was small, and Ashley knew this, but the fact that it was being used against him may have contributed to his pessimistic mood: and he arrived in Bath in low spirits. But, characteristically, his mood was soon to change. He had, it is true, been mobbed and had a blow aimed at him, and violence, he noted, was expected at the hustings. But, having attended several committees – 'very crowded and very hot' – he wrote that all looked 'pretty well'.[149]

The nomination was held on 28 July. Lord Duncan, Roebuck and Ashley were proposed. Roebuck admitted that Ashley was a humane man, but accused him of changing his opinions: with Wellington over Catholic Emancipation and with Peel over the Corn Laws. Ashley rebutted these charges, and he mentioned his work over factory reform and the sacrifices which he had made on its behalf. Looking to the forthcoming session of Parliament, he felt that the questions likely to be discussed would be of a social character, affecting the condition of the working classes, and he said that, if elected, he would devote time and energy to their consideration.[150] Ashley felt that the nomination had passed quietly – he had expected much more bitter criticism from Roebuck. Towards the end of his speech, he felt he detected a growing measure of support,[151] but the show of hands at the close went in favour of Duncan and Roebuck and a poll was demanded for Ashley.[152]

Polling began on 29 July and the official declaration of the result was made by the mayor as returning officer on 30th. It showed Ashley and Duncan elected, with Roebuck third. At the declaration, there was some violence, and several stones were thrown at Ashley, one hitting him on the hand and one on the chest. The latter, according to the local press, he picked up 'exhibited ... for a moment and with a smile and polite bow dropped ... into the breast pocket of his coat.' He declined to speak, but left the hustings surrounded by a body of his supporters and escorted by the police. At his hotel, he did speak, saying that the disturbance had been caused by twenty-five or thirty people who had come to the hustings with the deliberate intention of causing it, and he referred to a criticism made by Roebuck before the election that, while he tried to 'elevate men in the social scale, he did not endeavour to confer on them political rights.' Ashley declared his conviction that when men were prepared to exercise their right responsibly for the welfare of the state and had religious principles instilled into their hearts, he would be as ready as any man to confer on them an extension of the franchise.[153] He thus neatly used the disorderly episode to counter Roebuck's criticism.

Ashley was highly delighted and gratified at his success. He had written to Bonham on 29 July at the close of the poll, giving the figures at that point: 'Thank God,' he wrote, 'the whole thing has been admirably conducted.'[154] It appears that Roebuck had been well supported from various quarters: it was said that the Jews had submitted £2,000 on his behalf.[155] Ashley's campaign, on the other hand, had been strictly controlled and no money had been spent beyond what was necessary. He had, moreover, forbidden everything that tended to excite the people: music, processions, beer. And he felt that all this was of great importance – the conduct of his election had been a 'model for elections'. He had been excluded from Parliament for two sessions; the time had not, indeed, been entirely lost, but he was well pleased that he had been returned to Parliament and to public usefulness in such a pleasant and honourable way.

After the summer's exertions, Ashley went on holiday to Scotland. It was a happy time. In October, he wrote that he had been in good spirits since his arrival in Scotland; he had laughed a great deal 'and perhaps too much'.[156] He was, no doubt, elated by his success at Bath, and he always liked Scotland. The scenery, especially in the Highlands, had a restorative effect on him and while at Achnacarry, he wrote that the fascination of the Highlands could not be described: 'The hills must be seen and the air must be breathed; one's old limbs become elastic.'[157] In Glasgow in late September, he visited a model lodging house and a Ragged School: 'a good specimen of rags and dirt,' he wrote of the latter, and he rejoiced in the effort to evangelise 'this wretched tribe'.[158] While staying at Rossie Priory, he visited a Lunatic Asylum in Dundee and spoke on Ragged Schools.[159] But, even in the midst of his enjoyment and relaxation, he was anxious to return. He wanted to take up all the 'sleeping duties' which he had left and to have time and opportunity to make preparations for the next session of Parliament.[160] On his way south, an incident took place which recalled past efforts and gave him great pleasure. Minny was presented by the Short-Time Committees for the West Riding with a full-length portrait of Ashley: 'an excellent likeness and . . . a memorial of gratitude for my services,' Ashley wrote: 'nothing could have been more acceptable in every sense.'[161]

On his return to London, Ashley found himself busy with extra-parliamentary duties. He attended a meeting of the Lambeth Ragged School which he had helped to found in July, 1846, and found there three hundred and seventy children, 'orderly decent, happy'.[162] There were also private engagements: dinner with Russell, at which the two men resumed their earlier friendly relations before the Bath episode, although at first, Ashley had some thoughts of avoiding such civilities.[163] There was also a visit to Windsor Castle. Ashley found the Queen very 'kind and hospitable' but wrote disapprovingly of the bad example which the Queen and Albert set in their rare attendance at morning prayers – if they considered them as 'subordinate duties', the domestics would also do so.[164] But political and parliamentary matters now once more actively occupied his attention. Parliament was opened by the Queen on 23 November. Despite his keen anticipation of his return to Parliament, Ashley's nerve seemed to fail him. He wrote that the House made him 'quite timid'; he felt as if he had never sat in it; and he was conscious once more of his isolation.[165] The issue of Jewish disabilities, moreover, caused him some anxiety. This was brought to the forefront of parliamentary attention by the return of Baron Rothschild for the City of London. Under existing legislation, he was debarred from taking his seat. Russell and the Whigs favoured the admission of the Jews to Parliament, and Russell proposed on 16 December that the House should consider the removal of the civil and political disabilities which affected the Jews in Britain.[166] Ashley felt that he must speak on the subject and this would be his first major speech since his return to Parliament. The prospect made him nervous: his spirit, he wrote, was 'far from elastic' and, he added, 'I am always easily depressed, I am more so now.'[167]

Ashley did, indeed, speak in the debate.[168] and did so with some effect. He was at pains to emphasise his admiration for the Jews, the 'most talented of all races', and he was not ashamed to confess that he looked upon the 'poorest Israelite with feelings akin to reverence, as one of the descendants of the most remarkable race that has ever appeared on the face of the earth and one of the forefathers of those who were yet to play the noblest part in the history of mankind.' Ashley thus made due reference to his belief in the role which the Jews were to play in the Second Coming. Despite all this, however, he had to oppose the bill admitting the Jews to Parliament. The reason was that the proposals involved the alteration of the parliamentary oath so that it might be taken by non-Christians, and this meant the deletion of the words 'on the true faith of a Christian'. This Ashley could not tolerate: religion and politics must be conjoined and, although the present oath ran the risk of involving some hypocrisy, it did at least preserve the principle. Russell's proposal was accepted in the Commons, but it was later to be overturned in the Lords. Ashley's speech was well received, and his spirits once more became 'elastic'. He recalled his earlier doubts and hesitations, so severe that he had almost decided not to speak: 'Who ever trusted in God and was disappointed,' he wrote.[169]

The year thus ended for Ashley on a note of success and satisfaction. In personal terms, he had in September mused over his family and felt more confident about the future. Francis, who had now started school at Harrow, was always 'a safe boy' and his good qualities were developing; Anthony, too, seemed 'vastly improved' and Ashley thought that this marked the 'formulation of better things'.[170] On Christmas Day, 1847, Ashley was in the company of his wife and all their children and spent the day 'in peace and safety. Is this not a mighty blessing?' he wrote.[171] And there was also the satisfaction of his return to Parliament and the praise which his speech in December had received. Ashley, indeed, saw his political position in the context of what had happened since 1845. He had resigned his seat and all his public hopes and career so that he might not 'give occasion to the enemies of God to blaspheme' and he had surrendered everything to God's keeping.

Mark the issue [he continued]; My Ten Hours Bill is carried in my absence. I am returned to Parliament in a singularly and unusually honourable way, and within three weeks I begin to occupy a higher position than at any antecedent period: surely it is a completion of the promise 'Them that honour me, I will honour.'

God had thus shown 'free mercy to past faith'.[172]

NOTES

1. N.R.A., Shaftesbury (Broadlands) MSS, SHA/PD/3, 28 Dec., 1844.
2. See above p. 142.
3. John Easthope MSS, 23 Feb., 1846.
4. *The Dorset County Chronicle and Somersetshire Gazette*, 16 Oct., 1845.
5. N.R.A., Shaftesbury (Broadlands) MSS, SHA/PD/4, 13 Oct., 1845.
6. *The Dorset County Chronicle and Somersetshire Gazette*, 23 Oct., 1845.
7. *The Morning Post*, 22 Oct., 1845.
8. *The League*, 25 Oct., 1845.
9. N.R.A., Shaftesbury (Broadlands) MSS, SHA/PD/4, 23 Oct., 1845.
10. ibid., SHA/PD/4, 27 Oct., 1845.
11. ibid., SHA/PD/4, 24 Nov., 1845.
12. ibid., SHA/PD/4, 30 Oct., 1845.
13. ibid., SHA/PD/4, 24 Nov., 1845.
14. ibid., SHA/PD/4, 27 Oct., 1845.
15. N. Gash, *Peel*, p. 537 ff.
16. N.R.A., Shaftesbury (Broadlands) MSS, SHA/PD/4, 27 Nov., 1845.
17. ibid., SHA/PD/4, 23 Dec., 1845.
18. ibid., SHA/PD/4, 31 Dec., 1845.
19. ibid., SHA/PD/4, 20 Jan., 1846.
20. ibid., SHA/PD/4, 27 Jan., 1846.
21. *The Dorset County Chronicle and Somersetshire Gazette*, 12 Feb., 1846 (supplement).
22. ibid., 5 and 12 Feb., 1846.
23. N.R.A., Shaftesbury (Broadlands) MSS, SHA/PD/4, 6 Feb., 1844.
24. Add. MSS, 40, 617, f. 218.
25. N.R.A., Shaftesbury (Broadlands) MSS, SHA/PD/4, 6 Feb., 1844.
26. ibid., Palmerston (Broadlands) MSS, GC/SH/19. Ashley also wrote in his Diary that if he had a responsible Committee and £1,000 in the Banker's hands, he might sustain a successful fight, but he could not begin with less security. (ibid., Shaftesbury (Broadlands) MSS, SHA/PD/4, 9 Feb., 1846).
27. *The Dorset County Chronicle and Somersetshire Gazette*, 19 Feb., 1846.
28. ibid., 26 Feb., 1846.
29. N.R.A., Shaftesbury (Broadlands) MSS, SHA/PD/4, 19 Feb., 1846.
30. Add. MSS, 40, 483, fos 171-2. *The Record* (23 Feb., 1846) reported some 'occasional interruption', but noted that Ashley was heard with respect and thst he was cheered on retiring.
31. Add. MSS, 40, 483, f. 173. Previous correspondence between Ashley and Peel on the subject is in ibid., fos 365, 367, 368. In this Ashley had notified Peel of his intention to resign his seat (f. 365): Peel had doubted if the electors of Dorset

would seek to replace Ashley (f. 367): and Ashley expressed *his* doubts if the electors shared Peel's opinions respecting his fitness to represent them (f. 368).
32. N.R.A., Shaftesbury (Broadlands) MSS, SHA/PD/4, 21 Feb., 1846.
33. ibid., SHA/PD/4, 4 Feb., 1846. Within a few days, however, Ashley received a letter from Seeley 'in milder and better terms' than his previous one. 'Then let all be forgotten,' he wrote. (ibid., SHA/PD/4, 11 Feb., 1846).
34. ibid., SHA/PD/4, 30 Mar., 1846.
35. ibid., SHA/PD/4, 23 Jan., 1846.
36. ibid., SHA/PD/4, 18 May, 1846.
37. ibid., SHA/PD/4, 1 July, 1846.
38. N. Gash, *Peel*, p. 611.
39. ibid., p. 612.
40. Graham MSS (on microfilm). Film 121, 29 Jan., 1846.
41. ibid.
42. Hansard, *Parl. Debates*, 3rd ser., LXXXIII, 378 ff.
43. ibid., 408–9.
44. N.R.A., Shaftesbury (Broadlands) MSS, SHA/PD/4, 30 Jan., 1846.
45. *The Record*, 2 Feb., 1846. *The Times*, 6 Feb., 1846.
46. N.R.A., Shaftesbury (Broadlands) MSS, SHA/PD/4, 4 Mar., 1846.
47. Manchester, Preston, Ashton, Bolton, Oldham, Bradford, Halifax, Huddersfield, Leeds.
48. N.R.A., Shaftesbury (Broadlands) MSS, SHA/PD/4, 4 Mar., 1846.
49. ibid., SHA/PD/4, 17 Mar., 1846.
50. ibid., SHA/PD/4, 6 Mar., 1846.
51. ibid., SHA/PD/4, 17 Mar., 1846.
52. ibid., SHA/PD/4, 2 Mar., 1846.
53. See above p. 129.
54. N.R.A., Shaftesbury (Broadlands) MSS, SHA/PD/2, 27 Sept., 1841.
55. R. A. Lewis, *Edwin Chadwick and the Public Health Movement, 1832–1854* (1952), p. 183.
56. *The Record*, 15 May, 1844.
57. Add. MSS, 40, 483, f. 145.
58. *The Record*, 23 May, 1844.
59. Add. MSS, 40, 483, fos 142–5.
60. R. A. Lewis, op. cit., p. 343.
61. E. Gauldie, *Cruel Habitations. A History of Working-Class Housing, 1780–1918* (1974), p. 226, pp. 233–4.
62. Quoted in Hodder, I, 481.
63. *Ragged School Union Magazine* (1856), p. 232.
64. Hodder, I, 481–2.
65. Ibid., II, 147–8.
66. N.R.A., Shaftesbury (Broadlands) MSS, SHA/PD/4, 27 Nov., 1845.
67. ibid., SHA/PD/4, 11 Dec., 1845.
68. Hodder, II, 160.
69. Quoted in R. A. Lewis, op. cit., p. 113.
70. N.R.A., Shaftesbury (Broadlands) MSS, SHA/PD/4, 21 Nov., 1846.
71. ibid., SHA/PD/4, 6 June, 1846.
72. *The Quarterly Review*, LXXIX, 127–41.
73. N.R.A., Shaftesbury (Broadlands) MSS, SHA/PD/4, 14 Nov., 1846.
74. ibid., SHA/PD/4, 1 Oct., 1846.
75. ibid., SHA/PD/4, 13 Oct., 1846.

76. ibid., SHA/PD/4, 24 Mar., 1846.
77. ibid., SHA/PD/4, 24 Nov., 1846.
78. ibid., SHA/PD/4, 6 July, 1846.
79. ibid., SHA/PD/4, 26 Sept., 1846.
80. ibid., SHA/PD/4, 4 Nov., 1846.
81. ibid., SHA/PD/4, 27 Nov., 1846.
82. See Hodder, II, 173–81 for details of the holiday.
83. A ninth child and fourth daughter, Hilda, was born in Apr., 1847.
84. N.R.A., Shaftesbury (Broadlands) MSS, SHA/PD/4, 31 Dec., 1846. In 1856, Ashley wrote that he had only £900 of income 'to sustain, educate the whole family and meet the many and various charges of (his) career and situation during twenty years.' He and his wife had lived 'closely' during the whole of that time; they had only a small house, kept one man-servant and a boy but no carriage or horses of any kind. They had indulged in no expensive tastes; the only luxury had consisted of going abroad and, in the summer, of taking a house at the sea. 'No doubt too much was given away' he added: 'and besides, the cost of fighting all my measures in Parliament, travelling, subsidising etc etc was excessive.' (ibid., SHA/EST/7, Jan., 1856).
85. Hammonds, p. 124.
86. Battiscombe, p. 191.
87. N.R.A., Shaftesbury (Broadlands) MSS, SHA/PD/4, 8 Dec., 1846.
88. Battiscombe, p. 192.
89. N.R.A., Shaftesbury (Broadlands) MSS, SHA/PD/4, 25 Feb., 1847.
90. *The Quarterly Review*, LXXXII, 142–52.
91. N.R.A., Shaftesbury (Broadlands) MSS, SHA/PD/4, 19 Feb., 1847.
92. ibid., SHA/PD/4, 8 May, 1847.
93. Battiscombe, p. 191. J. Wesley Bready, *Lord Shaftesbury and Social-Industrial Progress* (1926), p. 400, also argues against regarding 1846 as a turning-point in Ashley's career.
94. N.R.A., Shaftesbury (Broadlands) MSS, SHA/PD/4, 27 Apr., 1846.
95. ibid., SHA/PD/4, 29 Apr., 1846.
96. ibid., SHA/PD/4, 30 Apr., 1846.
97. J. T. Ward, *The Factory Movement*, p. 325.
98. ibid., pp. 327–8.
99. N.R.A., Shaftesbury (Broadlands) MSS, SHA/PD/4, 21 Jan., 1847.
100. ibid., SHA/PD/4, 26 Jan., 1847.
101. Add. MSS, 40, 617, fos 226–7.
102. *The Manchester Courier and Lancashire General Advertiser*, 23 Jan., 1847.
103. N.R.A., Shaftesbury (Broadlands) MSS, SHA/PD/4, 10 Feb., 1847.
104. Hansard, *Parl. Debates*, 3rd ser., LXXXIX, 107 ff.
105. N.R.A., Shaftesbury (Broadlands) MSS, SHA/PD/4, 17 Feb., 1847.
106. ibid., SHA/PD/4, 1 Mar., 1847.
107. P.R.O., Russell MSS, 30/22/6B, fos 182–3.
108. Hansard, *Parl. Debates*, 3rd ser., XC, 819.
109. N.R.A., Shaftesbury (Broadlands) MSS, SHA/PD/4, 12 Mar., 1847.
110. ibid., SHA/PD/4, 17 Mar., 1847.
111. Hansard, *Parl. Debates*, 3rd ser., XCI, 146.
112. N.R.A., Shaftesbury (Broadlands) MSS, SHA/PD/4, 17 Mar., 1847.
113. Hansard, *Parl. Debates*, 3rd ser., XCI, 1127–9.
114. ibid., 1130, 1141, 1142.
115. N.R.A., Shaftesbury (Broadlands) MSS, SHA/PD/4, 25 Apr., 1847.

116. ibid., SHA/PD/4, 4 May, 1847.
117. ibid., SHA/PD/4, 19 Mar., 1847.
118. Bodleian Libr., Wilberforce MSS, C 8, fos 176–7.
119. ibid., fos. 178–9.
120. N.R.A., Shaftesbury (Broadlands) MSS, SHA/PD/4, 8 May, 1847.
121. Hansard, *Parl. Debates*, 3rd ser., XCII, 936–43.
122. ibid., 944–5.
123. N.R.A., Shaftesbury (Broadlands) MSS, SHA/PD/4, 18 May, 1847.
124. ibid., SHA/PD/4, 31 May, 1847.
125. ibid., SHA/PD/4, 1 June, 1847. From May, 1848, women and young persons were to be restricted to a ten-hour day (fifty-eight in the week).
126. Russell MSS, 30/22/6B, fos 182, 3.
127. *The Manchester Courier and Lancashire General Advertiser*, 23 Jan., 1847.
128. Add. MSS, 40, 617, f. 226.
129. *The Ten Hours Advocate*, 23 Jan., 1847.
130. J. T. Ward, *The Factory Movement*, p. 341.
131. Letter quoted in Hodder, II, 195–6.
132. Brougham MSS, 24, 710, 26 Feb., 1847.
133. N.R.A., Shaftesbury (Broadlands) MSS, SHA/PD/4, 28 Aug., 1846.
134. ibid., SHA/PD/4, 3 Oct., 1846.
135. ibid., SHA/PD/4, 8 Dec., 1846.
136. ibid., SHA/PD/4, 26 Dec., 1846.
137. *Ragged School Union Magazine* (1847), p. 6.
138. N.R.A., Shaftesbury (Broadlands) MSS, SHA/PD/4, 15 Apr., 1846.
139. ibid., SHA/PD/4, 26 Sept., 1846.
140. ibid., SHA/PD/4, 14 July, 1846.
141. ibid., SHA/PD/4, 9 Jan., 1847.
142. ibid., SHA/PD/4, 17 May, 1847.
143. ibid., SHA/PD/4, 17 May, 1847.
144. *The Times*, 26 May, 1847.
145. N.R.A., Shaftesbury (Broadlands) MSS, SHA/PD/4, 14 July, 1847.
146. Russell MSS, 30/22/6D, fos 73–4.
147. See Hodder, II, 214.
148. Russell MSS, 30/22/6C, fos 35–6.
149. N.R.A., Shaftesbury (Broadlands) MSS, SHA/PD/4, 26 July, 1847.
150. *The Bath and Cheltenham Gazette*, 28 July, 1847.
151. N.R.A., Shaftesbury (Broadlands) MSS, SHA/PD/4, 28 July, 1847.
152. *The Bath and Cheltenham Gazette*, 28 July, 1847.
153. ibid., 4 Aug., 1847.
154. Add. MSS, 40, 617, f. 252.
155. *The Record*. 9 Aug., 1847.
156. N.R.A., Shaftesbury (Broadlands) MSS, SHA/PD/4, 9 Oct., 1847.
157. ibid., SHA/PD/4, 2 Oct., 1847.
158. ibid., SHA/PD/4, 27 Sept., 1847.
159. ibid., SHA/PD/4, 9 Oct., 1847.
160. ibid., SHA/PD/4, 30 Sept., 1847.
161. ibid., SHA/PD/4, 20 Oct., 1847.
162. ibid., SHA/PD/4, 25 Nov., 1847.
163. ibid., SHA/PD/4, 15 Nov., 1847.
164. ibid., SHA/PD/4, 19 Nov., 1847.
165. ibid., SHA/PD/4, 30 Nov., 1847.

166. Hansard, *Parl. Debates*, 3rd ser., XCV, 1249.
167. N.R.A., Shaftesbury (Broadlands) MSS, SHA/PD/4, 15 Dec., 1847.
168. Hansard, *Parl. Debates*, 3rd ser., XCII, 1272 ff.
169. N.R.A., Shaftesbury (Broadlands) MSS, SHA/PD/4, 17 Dec., 1847.
170. ibid., SHA/PD/4, 8 Sept., 1847.
171. ibid., SHA/PD/4, 26 Dec., 1847.
172. ibid., SHA/PD/4, 20 Dec., 1847.

11

Fresh Toils, Fresh Anxieties, 1848–1851

Ashley's return to Parliament preceded by a few months the revolutionary disturbances which were to sweep Europe in 1848. These events gave him an opportunity to exercise his considerable interest in foreign affairs. He was surprised by the suddenness of Louis Philippe's fall in February, 1848, and, as he viewed the insurrections at Berlin and Vienna and the deposition of Metternich in March, he remarked how astounding it was to see the fall of these great monarchies. 'They seem as though they had no roots, nor ever had any,' he wrote.[1] As the disturbances spread to Italy, he commented that revolutions went off 'like pop-guns'.[2] He felt that the makings of the disturbances had long been present. Thus Louis Philippe had, in his view, spent the past seventeen years resisting the principles which had placed him on the throne. The very limited electoral system of his monarchy could not hope to satisfy the country; he had been guilty of errors and miscalculations and had neglected the social welfare of his people.[3] The foundations of the Hapsburg Empire, he thought, had for years been rotten. Yet, if the revolutions had been long in the making, the forces which they unleashed were, in Ashley's view, highly dangerous, and he was much concerned about the fate of his fellow-countrymen in France as the revolution there developed. Ashley was, indeed, quick to devise ways and means for their relief. He presided over a committee which was set up to collect money to assist British workers in France deprived of their employment and their savings; and the initiative which he took was followed up by government action, as a result of which more than six thousand refugees were brought back to Britain and given assistance on their arrival.[4]

If events abroad gave grounds for anxiety, there was also the possibility of disturbance at home. A recession in industry in 1847–8 brought precariousness of employment and this contributed to a further upsurge of Chartist activity – the third Chartist petition was presented in 1848. At times, Ashley confessed that he was anxious for the future: in February, 1848, he wrote that he had never known such a time of distrust, perplexity and apprehension[5] and later had visions of himself and his family 'fleeing in terror and distress like the scattered and innocent victims of the Orleanist family.'[6] But, on the whole, Ashley's sentiments were ones of relief that serious trouble did not break out in Britain, and he was especially thankful that the ten hours question had been resolved the previous year. He wondered if Lancashire and Yorkshire would have remained quiet in 1848 if resistance had still been offered to the ten-hours bill. But the year passed without severe disturbance: 'such, under God,' wrote Ashley, 'is the fruit of many years of sympathy and generous legislation.'[7] The prospect of the Chartist demonstration in April caused Ashley some alarm, although he thought it would end peaceably. The fact that it did was a further cause of thanksgiving to God 'who stilleth the raging of the sea, and the madness of the people.'[8]

Yet, although reassured at the peaceful turn of events, Ashley did not feel complacent. He saw around him signs of restlessness and change and doubted if aristocratic institutions would survive his lifetime.[9] There was, therefore, ample room for further paternalistic effort. Restored to Parliament, he was once again at the centre of political life, but his aloofness from party ties continued. He was at odds with the Whigs on political grounds and regarded Russell as too willing to consider further parliamentary reform. Equally, he was out of sympathy with both sections of the old Conservative party, Peelite and Protectionist. He paid very few visits to the Carlton Club. He was, it is true, included among possible office-holders in a Protectionist ministry projected in 1849: the office placed opposite his name was the Colonial Office. Derby later suggested that this should be changed to the India Board on the grounds that Ashley was 'impracticable'.[10] But nothing came of these suggestions, since no Protectionist Ministry was formed in 1849, and it is unlikely that Ashley knew anything about them. Nor, moreover, is it by any means certain that he would have accepted office had the occasion arisen. Although he continued to complain about his political isolation, it was, in fact, in accordance with his inclinations: it allowed him opportunity to continue his efforts in the cause of social and moral improvement and yet to use his regained parliamentary position to give them greater prominence and effectiveness.

In April and May, 1848, Ashley spent a great deal of time and effort in enlisting the support of Prince Albert for his schemes for social betterment. In April, he was summoned by the Queen, who was at Osborne, to discuss the condition of the working classes; he wrote that he found the Queen 'very amiable and very considerate for the poor.'[11] In a subsequent conversation with Albert, Ashley urged the Prince to attend the annual meeting of the Society for Improving the Condition of the Labouring Classes, due to be held on 18 May, 1848. This, Ashley felt, would show that Royalty took an interest in the happiness of the Kingdom. Albert was happy to agree to the suggestion and the arrangements were made. Russell, however, made certain difficulties – he was afraid of a disturbance breaking out at the meeting from Chartist or other sources – and, at one point, it seemed that the plan would come to nothing. But Albert himself was anxious for the meeting to take place: he felt that it would be an excellent opportunity to refute anti-monarchial sentiment and criticism.[12] Thus, in the end, Ashley had his way. Albert went on a tour of inspection of the St Giles area in London along with Ashley and later took the chair at the public meeting. Ashley was gratified and felt that the occasion did much to assist the anti-revolutionary cause.

> Aye, truly [he wrote] this is the way to stifle Chartism ... Rank, leisure, station are gifts of God, for which man must give an account. Here is a full proof, a glowing instance! The aristocracy, after a long separation, are re-approaching the people; and the people the aristocracy. Oh Cobden, Bright and all that dismal crew, you will be crushed in the friendly collision![13]

This, then, was a spectacular occasion which Ashley had worked hard to achieve. And during the summer of 1848, his interest in what he called the 'pariah' race remained unabated. It extended to the opening of a reading room for 'dirty, forgotten workpeople of Duck Lane and Pye Street';[14] and, at the end of July, he recorded a meeting among thieves, organised by a missionary, Thomas Jackson. Ashley prayed with them, read them the Bible and gave an Address, and he discussed ways of putting an end to their criminal habits.[15]

In Parliament, Ashley was also anxious to promote his favourite schemes. His very first task on his return to Parliament had been to sit on a committee to investigate the recent election at Lyme; he was frustrated at the time which this involved and wondered if he would be able to put forward any of the ideas which he had in mind. He was also distressed that the members were not more attentive to their duties. The adjournment of the House on 25 May so that members might attend racing at Epsom was, Ashley felt, 'grievous for private morals, grievous for public character ... Balls, races, festivals ... as tho' nothing had happened in adjacent countries and that we had (an) assurance of perpetual enjoyment. ... Oh that we might apply our hearts unto wisdom. ...'[16] He was much concerned with Ragged Schools: they were, he wrote, 'the conservative principle, the salt for our destitute population,' but he was depressed by the fact that they enjoyed little support from the 'rich and dignified'.[17] One scheme much in his mind in the early months of 1848 concerned the provision of assistance to enable ragged scholars to emigrate, and a committee to investigate the matter was formed. As it happened, emigration regulations had been stiffened by Acts of 1847 and 1848: and, in April, 1848, Ashley wrote to Earl Grey, Secretary for War and Colonies, complaining that the Emigration Board was being over-strict in the conditions which it had made for the clothing of the emigrants: this involved increased expenditure on each child.[18] Grey denied this; strictness, he said, was necessary and, in any event, the Board had relaxed its regulations in Ashley's favour.[19] Thus Ashley felt sufficiently confident of the scheme to raise it in Parliament in June, 1848.[20] He proposed that funds should be provided annually to assist young persons educated in Ragged Schools to emigrate on a voluntary basis to a colony. The colony which he had in mind was Southern Australia, since the demand for labour was greatest there, and he felt that about five hundred boys and five hundred girls might emigrate in this way each year. The Emigration Commissioners saw no difficulties – the scheme was practicable and required only determination to put it into effect. Ashley's speech on the matter was, indeed, reminiscent of those of earlier days, ranging over facts and figures and providing vivid impressions of his subject. He analysed the results of a survey of fifteen Ragged Schools: the number of children attending them; the number without shoes or stockings; without caps or hats; the number who never slept in beds. And he argued that the scheme could be justified on grounds of policy and of religion. Colonisation would no longer be regarded as a way of getting rid of criminals. It would be held up as 'an object of ambition, the recompense of moral exertion'. And the State would prevent the commission of crime by aiding those who might, if left in their present circumstances, become criminals. On a higher plane, the scheme would lead to the spiritual growth of those who were helped by it, for, among the ragged children, there were many thousands who, if they had the opportunity of a new life, would 'walk in all the dignity of honest men and Christian citizens'.

The speech met with some support, and Ashley did not press his motion, fearing that this might provoke opposition.[21] A grant of £1,500 was, indeed, made available by the government for a trial period to see how the scheme worked. Ashley had hoped for a grant of £2,000 to cover the total costs[22] and had to resort to raising money from other sources – and there were delays. Ashley wrote to Grey on 10 July[23] asking if he might have authority to proceed: five weeks had elapsed since the debate in the Commons and no official communication from the Colonial Office had been received. Ashley grew impatient at the delays, and he also encountered some opposition from the parents of the potential emigrants. But the scheme did start in late July, 1848. Ashley took a keen personal interest in the departures of the ragged children. He visited them as they embarked and urged them to use their new opportunities in such a way as to bring credit to themselves and to their country and thereby enhance the chances of others following them. He urged them, too, never to forget prayer.[24] On 27 July, he recounted a tea party given to take leave of the ragged emigrants to Australia: 'ragged no longer, thank God,' he wrote. They were financed from private funds, including money from Ashley's sister Charlotte. It was a 'deeply religious meeting', pervaded by a 'feeling of piety and gratitude'. And he commended them to God's care: 'make them Thy servants in this life and Thy saints in the next, in the mediation and everlasting love of Christ, our only Saviour and Redeemer!' he wrote.[25] Such meetings between Ragged School teachers and their emigrant children were, indeed, commonly held on the eve of departure. A teacher for each vessel was appointed by the Emigration Commissioners and arrangements were made to ensure 'diligence and industry' during the passage. Between October, 1848, and June, 1849, some thirty Schools participated in the scheme and one hundred and fifty scholars were sent.[26]

In July, 1849, Ashley resumed his efforts in Parliament to continue the scheme, moving that a further grant be made available by the government.[27] Once again, he deployed all his arguments: that it was in the interest of the House to prevent crime, lawlessness and disorder by encouraging emigration; that it was the duty of the House to 'consider the case of these desperate sufferers'. Ashley read out letters from boys who had emigrated under the scheme during the past year; these expressed gratitude for what had been done for them and an appreciation of their new life. The scheme had thus benefited them and would act as an inducement to good behaviour in those who hoped still to go. There were certain standards which had to be achieved before a child could qualify for an assisted passage: regular attendance at a Ragged School for at least six months and an industrial class for at least four; ability to write a sentence from dictation, do simple arithmetic, read the Lord's Prayer and Ten Commandments. The emigration scheme would thus encourage the attainment of these standards. But, on this occasion, Ashley's pleas were unavailing. Various points were made in criticism of the scheme: that there had been complaints from cities outside London – for example, from Glasgow – that they had not participated in the project; that it was not the duty of the government to provide for any portion of the population; that such support as had been given by financing the scheme tended to reward the undeserving and the criminal and encourage parents to neglect their children. Any continuation of the scheme, it was argued, would require to be on a voluntary basis. In the face of this opposition, Ashley withdrew his motion. The emigration scheme was thus to be privately financed, and the fact that pupils able to do so now worked their passage helped to reduce the cost.[28]

Thus, as he had foreseen, Ashley made use of his return to Parliament to promote his schemes and develop his interests. And, if this was true of Ragged Schools, it was also true of measures concerned with health. One of his first speeches on his return was in March, 1848, on the subject of providing better medical relief under the Poor Law: he was especially concerned to assist the conditions of the woman who applied to the Poor Law Union for medical assistance with the delivery of her child. His proposals, however, met with opposition and were withdrawn.[29] But if success was not achieved in this area of health provision, progress was soon to be made in the field of public health. And here, too, Ashley was extremely active. He kept up his earlier peregrinations into the neglected areas of London. In April, 1848, he wrote of a walk to inspect the courts and alleys in many parts of the city. The conditions which he saw – 'utterly unchristian and anti-christian' – aroused his sympathy and anger: 'by turns was sad, by turns was wild. I felt and I now feel, indignant to fury . . .'[30] he wrote. Sanitary reform was urgently necessary: like emigration, it would assist in reducing discontent; together, they would be a 'panacea for the difficulties of England'.[31] And measures for sanitary improvement would also provide decent living conditions in which morality and religion could flourish. It would be a recognition of the right of the 'unhappy people' who lived in wretched conditions to be 'placed on a level with sentient and immortal beings.'[32] And, in fact, the investigations and preparations of the mid-forties were soon to bear fruit. There had, it is true, been various false starts and delays. In 1845, a Public Health bill had been introduced by Lord Lincoln, Commissioner of Woods and Forests. It had been withdrawn and re-introduced in 1846. But the Corn Laws dominated events in that year and the matter was again deferred. In March, 1847, Lord Morpeth, Ashley's long-standing friend, who was Commissioner of Woods and Forests in the Whig government, introduced a further measure, but it ran into difficulties and was dropped in July. In February, 1848, however, a revised form of this bill was brought in again by Morpeth and this finally passed in August, 1848. The Act set up a Central Commission, appointed for five years and composed of three members, with the First Commissioner of Woods and Forests as President. The Commission could initiate public health measures in places where the death rate from all causes reached the figure of twenty three per thousand – elsewhere, it had to await a petition signed by one tenth of the ratepayers. Once the Act was applied, the Commission had powers to introduce the machinery of local administration: in incorporated towns, this was to be the town council, but, in towns where no council existed, local boards of health were to be elected on a propertied franchise and a plural voting scale. Such local units were empowered to levy rates and appoint certain officials and were to be responsible for attending to such matters as water supply, drainage and paving, under the supervision of the Central Commission. This supervision was to be exercised by circulars and a superintending Inspectorate.

All the measures introduced since 1845 had been controversial. The elements of centralisation involved in them were criticised as an undesirable and unwarranted interference with local initiative. Equally, the measures incurred certain criticisms from public health reformers themselves, notably Chadwick. All, in their view, had certain defects in their machinery of administration. There was also much in the 1848 Act of which Chadwick disapproved, and he was dissatisfied that it did not apply to London. Nevertheless, the Act did appear to represent a considerable step forward for the Movement. Ashley spoke in favour of the measure when first introduced by Morpeth in 1847.[33] He admitted that local interests and local feelings presented difficulties, but these could not be allowed to obstruct legislation which was so urgently required for the physical and moral improvement of the people. Further, Ashley was to be very actively involved in the implementation of the Act, for, in September, he was asked by the government to accept the unpaid office of third Commissioner. The other two members were Southwood Smith and Edwin Chadwick. When asked by the government to accept the post, Ashley felt that he could not refuse. He had, he wrote, always attached 'immense and unparalleled value ... to the sanitary question, as second only to the religious, and in some respects, inseparable from it.'[34] Moreover, having pressed the government to take action, he could not now reject its request for assistance, and he recalled the services which the Whig government had given over the ten-hours bill. Thus he accepted the post, although he realised that it would involve 'trouble, anxiety, reproach, abuse, unpopularity'.[35] It may, indeed, be that it was to offset some of this 'abuse (and) unpopularity' that Ashley was appointed; the task of the Commission was likely to involve disputes with various interested parties and, if Chadwick himself was quite equal to dealing with them, his arrogant and overbearing manner was not likely to make them any the less intractable.[36] Chadwick was surprised by Ashley's appointment – there had been a delay in making it and this, Chadwick felt, was having a bad effect on public opinion.[37] But he greatly approved of the appointment once made. Ashley wrote to Chadwick on 25 September saying that Morpeth had conveyed to him Chadwick's approval of his appointment. 'I am grateful that you think me a worthy co-adjutor,' he wrote, 'God grant that we may effect all the good that we have so often imagined.'[38] Chadwick replied that, for more reasons than he could express in a short letter, it gave him 'extreme pleasure' to hear of Ashley's appointment: 'it afforded to the country a guarantee of earnestness, sympathy for suffering, singleness of purpose in labouring for its relief.'[39] Chadwick clearly grasped the value of Ashley's reputation in assisting the work of the Commission. And Ashley himself was glad to have the prospect of working with Morpeth. Writing to Morpeth in September, he mentioned past differences between them over social and political issues,[40] and he also told him of his misgivings about accepting the appointment. He shrank from it, 'trembling at the responsibility of the office, the hardness of the way and the consumption of time and strength already over taxed by many undertakings.' But, after some days' thought, he felt required by a sense of public duty to accept the office; and, he added:

> it will be no small gratification to me . . . to be at last associated with the friend of my youth in a labour for the happiness of the nation; and I shall humbly and heartily pray to Almighty God that it may please Him, for the sake of our blessed Redeemer, to prosper this work to the glory of His own name, and the permanent welfare (of) our beloved Country.[41]

Ashley's primary role was to act as parliamentary spokesman for the Commission. It seems clear that, at first, Chadwick did not envisage that Ashley would play a very active part in the day-to-day administration of the Commission. This would be Chadwick's own responsibility, aided by the small number of officials who were to be appointed. He thus asked Ashley to let him know of the extent to which Ashley would want to be kept informed of the Commission's proceedings, and he promised to have the facts on which decisions had to be reached made fully available so that Ashley could help with his 'independent judgment'. The Minutes would also be kept to enable Ashley, during any temporary absences, to 'resume the thread of the proceedings.'[42] But, in fact, Ashley was to play a very active part in the administration of the Commission – he was constantly in attendance at the Headquarters at Gwydyr House. Thus Ashley's cooperation with the more 'professional' public health campaigners became even closer than it had been in the past, and there developed a considerable bond of harmony and respect between him and Chadwick.

One reason for this close involvement of Ashley in the day-to-day administration of the Commission lay in the circumstances of its first year of existence. In September, 1848, an outbreak of cholera occurred and was soon to spread. It reached a high point in January, 1849, and then receded, but, in the summer of 1849, it returned with even greater devastation. The fatalities were enormous: seven hundred deaths in Manchester, two thousand in Leeds, three thousand in Liverpool. And London, not greatly affected by the first outbreak, was worst of all: in one week in August, 1849, one thousand two hundred and seven persons died of cholera in

London alone. Only in September, 1849, a year after its first visitation, did the disease show signs of abating. Thus the Commission could hardly have come into existence at a more difficult time, and the problems which it encountered forced all its members into intense activity. Regulations were issued which aimed at preventing the spread of the disease and remedying it once it had taken hold. Many of these, it is true, were based on a false understanding of the causes of cholera and of the circumstances under which it spread,[43] although, in this respect, the Board simply shared the general ignorance of the subject at the time. Nevertheless, certain of the practices which it did enjoin by regulation – such as house-to-house visitations to administer drugs to those thought to be in the early stages of the disease and to remove those who were still healthy to refuges – did have some effect, if not always for the reasons which the Board advanced for them. In fact, they would have had more effect had they been fully acted upon, but the Board encountered serious difficulties. In issuing its regulations, it was acting under the Nuisances Removal Act of 1848, supplemented by an Order in Council which empowered the Board to use powers vested in it by the Act in the circumstances of an epidemic. The regulations had to be issued to the Poor Law Guardians, who were to put them into effect, but the Board had no power to force the Guardians to act. And, in fact, for the most part, the Guardians refused to enforce the regulations; only when a medical inspector from the Board arrived in person was any measure of success achieved in inducing the Guardians to comply with the regulations. And the extent to which such success could be achieved was severely circumscribed by the fact that, initially, the Board had only two inspectors for the whole country and there was strong resistance to further appointments on grounds of economy. Thus the period of the cholera outbreak was not only an extremely active one for the newly created Board, stretching its resources to the full – it was also a very frustrating one.

Ashley shared fully in both the activity and the frustrations. He and his colleagues, he wrote, had 'toiled unceasingly, and not as mere officials, but with earnestness and feeling.'[44] He remained in London throughout August and into September, 1849, when the disease was at its worst, and only when it began to decline did he take a holiday, going to Tunbridge Wells for some weeks. Even then, he remained in close touch with Chadwick and the Board, and, on one occasion, in late September, members of the Board travelled to Tunbridge Wells and a Board meeting was held there.[45] His work while in London in August and early September was incessant. He attended numerous meetings of the Board, and, at one point in September, 1849, he alone was able to deal with its business for two days since Southwood Smith and Chadwick – and the officials – were themselves ill. He wrote to Chadwick telling him that he could act 'singly as a Board' and counselled him to 'stay away'.[46] Ashley was deeply grateful that he himself was spared the disease. On 9 September, he wrote that London was empty. 'Cholera worse than ever . . . Have been mercifully preserved through this pestilence. Have not, I thank God, shrunk from one hour of duty in the midst of this City of the Plague, and yet it has not approached either me or my dwelling.'[47] He was full of praise for the work of his colleagues. Chadwick and Southwood Smith were men who might 'feel, but who *know* not fatigue or satiety in business, when necessity urges, or duty calls.'[48] As for the officials of the Board, Ashley was unable to speak highly enough of them: they had worked until no longer able to do so, and, when they had become ill, had hastened back to work 'not for emolument . . . but for conscience sake.'[49] Equally, Ashley received high praise for *his* efforts. Russell wrote to him in September, 1849, urging him to take a holiday: he owed it to himself and to his family. Russell added that, had he foreseen that Ashley's duties would be so severe, he might well not have suggested that he take the office. But, he wrote: 'though unpaid, you will, I am sure, feel the satisfaction of having worked for the health and life of your fellow-creatures, in a way that hardly any other person would have done.'[50] Further, Chadwick paid Ashley a glowing tribute. 'But for the gallantry of Lord Ashley,' Chadwick wrote in 1850, 'we must have been brought to a standstill.'[51]

But, like his colleagues, Ashley was constantly aggrieved at and aggravated by the difficulties encountered by the Board in its work. As early as October, 1848, he noted with dismay that there was much public indifference on the subject. The poor, he wrote, paid little attention to the spread of cholera and the rich thought that it was confined to the poor.[52] And, in the face of the resistance and obstructiveness offered by the Boards of Guardians, Ashley's dismay turned to anger. He also chafed at the Board's lack of power in London. In the Commons on 12 July, 1849, in reply to a question on the sanitary state of London, Ashley asserted that the Board was 'utterly powerless' in these matters. It had no jurisdiction in the Metropolis, except where cholera had broken out – there, it could give certain directions for visitations and cleansings: these had some effect, but it had no power to try to remove the permanent sources of the disease.[53] Later in the month, he was responsible for the passage of amendments to the Nuisances Removal Act.[54] These gave powers to the Board to start prosecutions for the infraction or neglect of the Board's regulations,[55] and they also empowered the Board of Health to inspect and inquire into metropolitan burial grounds which were a source of infection. Medical inspectors were sent out by the Board and special orders were issued to close the worst graveyards to any further burial. But this ran into intense opposition: the church guardians or wardens strongly resented the interference of the central Board and asked what alternative there was to continued burials. Ashley grew exasperated with these objections which, he felt, sprang from failure to spend money on providing adequate burial grounds. He noted on 11 September, 1849: 'Boards, Boards, and fights with Guardians! Obstinate and parsimonious wretches!'[56] On the 12th, he wrote of the continuing 'sad resistance' by the guardians and remarked that he had to write three letters to Chadwick that day.[57] One of these urged resolution on the part of the central Board in the face of resistance; the Board must, he said, refuse to receive any deputations or Committees or countenance any form of resistance to its provisional orders.[58] In another letter of the 12th, Ashley wrote that he had just seen a report in *The Daily News* that the church wardens of St Saviour's, Southwark, had decided to resist the Board, and resistance was also offered by various other parishes. Ashley felt that the Board must immediately take legal action against St Saviour's '*at all hazards*'.[59] Despite his resolution, Ashley was not very hopeful of the outcome: he felt that the magistrates were hostile to the Board and that all its proceedings would be reversed. 'Then what a career for the cholera!' he commented.[60] He wrote to Chadwick that the affairs of the Board were coming to a crisis and that the Board must meet and debate what to do in the event of adverse decisions. 'It will be necessary,' he wrote, 'to report to the Government that the Board has no powers equal to the terrible exigency of the times.'[61] Ashley's fears were well founded, for the magistrates found in favour of the churchwardens of St Saviour's. But Ashley felt that the stand which the Board had made was worthwhile:

> ... we have acted rightly, boldly, wisely. I never thought that our interpretation of the Law would stand before a Magistrate. But public opinion and feeling demanded such an act of Heroism on our part. Our counsel must urge very strongly the public overruling necessity of our course.[62]

In the light of such resistance, the Board had recourse to regulations prescribing that quicklime be used at every burial, for purposes of disinfecting the ground. This was an unpopular practice, since it was thought that the quicklime would poison the water supplies[63] and Ashley was at pains to ensure that the orders made it clear that the Board was forced to adopt this course only because the magistrates refused to uphold its prohibition of interments. 'Public opinion would then support us,' he wrote to Chadwick on 16 September, 'but without some such necessity we should encounter a very heavy force of popular Prejudice.'[64] When the Board lost another legal case against the managers of Whitefield Chapel on the issue of closing the burial ground, Ashley felt that the time had come to move ahead. He wrote to Chadwick on 28 September, saying that not a moment should be lost; the quicklime order should be issued immediately and reminded him that the order must make it clear that it was to be used in each grave at each interment and not simply spread on the surface.[65] Ashley was to write to Chadwick again on the subject on 2 October, complaining that the Board was not, in fact, adhering to this practice of individual applications of quicklime: general sprinkling could prevent surface exhalations, but it would not prevent the evil effects of water percolating through the burial grounds into the wells for the supply of water and the adjoining tombs.[66] Ashley, commenting on this in his absence from London, wrote: 'a good long correspondence with B(oard) of H(ealth) – things in my absence hardly to my liking.'[67]

Another aspect of Ashley's activities lay in his attempts to overcome the Treasury's reluctance to finance the appointment of more officials for the Board. A notable instance of this was in the summer and autumn of 1849. In August, 1849, when the disease was at its height, the Treasury, after much prompting, finally agreed to appoint – for two weeks only – one medical inspector and four assistants in London.[68] They immediately set to work in the worst affected areas and it appeared that their efforts in prodding the vestries or Unions into appointing medical visitors were enjoying some success. But, by early September, the situation was once again becoming desperate, and the first week of September was the worst of all for fatalities. The Board, therefore, asked the parliamentary secretary of the Treasury, Hayter, for funds to appoint an additional four medical inspectors in London. But Hayter refused to give any answer until he had consulted the Chancellor of the Exchequer. This moved Ashley to action. 'Mr Hayter's conduct is very bad,' he wrote to Chadwick,[69] and, as the only member of the Board still well, he went to the Treasury himself to ask for the immediate appointment of the officials. The Treasury, however, was deserted; thus Ashley returned to Gwydyr House and recorded that, since the appointments were essential, and any delay would result in serious injury and loss of life, they should be made at once. He notified the Treasury of his action, but the Treasury ratified the appointments only after further considerable delay and at the same time took the Board to task for what it had done.[70] A further annoyance in the midst of all the difficulties was the Treasury's demand that the Board should send in its accounts, with the threat that, till they were made up, the quarterly payment of their parliamentary grant would be suspended. At this point, indeed, Chadwick and Southwood Smith had to put their salaries together to pay office expenses.[71] Ashley was angered at all of this: in October, 1849, while on holiday, he wrote to Chadwick that the Treasury was and doubtless would continue to be 'very vexatious'. He would, however, on his return take his share of 'fighting for the rights of the Board'. And, he continued, 'we have rendered the Government good service; and we are not now to be treated as swindlers and vagabonds.'[72]

Ashley's frustrations and difficulties at the Board of Health during the cholera epidemic were, indeed, representative of the obstacles which prevailing attitudes placed in the way of those who advocated activity by the central government in the cause of social improvement in the mid-nineteenth century. Dislike of interference from the centre; defence of property rights; suspicion of prescribed remedies as sinister and expensive – these were common reactions to schemes such as the Board proposed in 1848–9. As has been seen, Ashley met these with energy and resolution: he was willing to meet local resistance from churchwardens or guardians; to discount popular dislike of quicklime; to set aside property rights where these interfered with public advantage; to battle for more staff to meet the needs of the situation. In these respects, his activities were little different from those of his colleagues on the Board, but his peculiarly religious outlook was also evident. He told Russell that the Board of Health was carrying into effect 'all the wise, beautiful and sanitary regulations of the Levitical Code'.[73] He wrote to the Duchess of Beaufort in November, 1849, that he thought that God had brought good out of evil in the Epidemic: religion had made 'a visible progress among the poorer sort and many of the wealthy are turning their minds to the improvement of society. We shall have a day of thanksgiving as much because the cholera ever came, as because it was driven away.'[74] Ashley was very anxious that there should be special public prayer, or even a fast day, which he would have preferred, for deliverance from the disease, and he made great efforts to obtain this. He wrote on several occasions to the Archbishop of Canterbury, the Bishop of London, Russell and Sir George Grey, the Home Secretary. At first, his efforts to secure, as he put it, 'some open recognition of the Hand from which the scourge has come, and which alone can avert the terrible results'[75] met with resistance. Russell, having received a request for a special prayer from the Archbishop of Canterbury, asked the Queen for an expression of her wishes and was told that, in the Queen's view, the prayer in the Prayer Book on the subject of a common plague or sickness should be used.[76] Grey was of a similar mind: he argued that the existing prayer could be used where appropriate, but need not be used where the cholera had not spread and circumstances did not justify it. But Ashley was not content with this. A special prayer might be framed for use in places untouched by cholera and might be effective in averting its arrival; the ordinary prayer could be used where the plague was present. Finally, in September, as the disease spread rapidly, the government agreed that a special prayer should be prepared on account of the cholera, and, on Sunday, 16 September, it was read in the churches. Ashley regarded it as a 'poor substitute for a day of repentance and humiliation; but thank God, better than nothing.'[77] He was especially critical of the role of the clergy: the Bishops, he felt, had done little or nothing to direct their flocks to prayer and repentance in the crisis.[78] Here, indeed, Ashley showed himself in distinctive colours.

After the abatement of the disease, Ashley felt that sanitary improvement must continue, but realised that this might be difficult: 'we must, if we can, keep up the spirit of physical reform,' he wrote to Chadwick on 29 October, 1849.[79] 'The cholera, thank God, has passed – is not the wholesome fear passing also?' There were, indeed, many battles still to fight. Two, in particular, were to occupy the Board's attention in 1850 and 1851: a further attempt to close the London burial grounds and a plan for re-organising and re-locating London's water supply. By December, 1849, the burial plans were complete. The speed with which the Board acted was largely due to the fact that Chadwick's report on Interments had been available since 1843 and the Board thus simply gathered further information in support of the earlier recommendations.[80] Ten resolutions were put before the Cabinet, the effect of which would have been to place the whole practice of burial on the basis of a public service rather than that of a private, or business, undertaking. The proposals involved the prohibition of all private arrangements for burial within the metropolitan area, whether in parish churchyards, private burial grounds or grounds administered by the eight joint-stock companies in existence at that time. All such burial places would be closed, compensation being paid to clergymen deprived of burial fees and to the cemetery companies. In future, all burials would take place in national cemeteries, laid out beyond the metropolitan area, in which there would be a consecrated portion with an Anglican Church and an unconsecrated part with a chapel for the use of Dissenters. All the arrangements for the laying out of these cemeteries and for their use would be supervised by a Burial Commission, appointed by the Home Secretary. Charges for the use of the cemeteries would be regulated on a scale and, although the Commission was empowered to levy rates, it was envisaged that receipts would be sufficient to discharge a loan to be taken out to defray the initial expenses of compensation and construction and to meet the administrative costs.[81]

The question of London's water supply was another matter which had long occupied the attention of sanitary reformers. The activities of the eight joint-stock companies which provided the water supply of London from the Thames had often been condemned as wholly inefficient and unreliable – and, indeed, they were. Many parts of London, particularly the poorer areas, had no water at all, and, of London's two hundred and seventy thousand houses, seventy thousand drew water from communal pipes from which water was available only on certain restricted occasions.[82] Half the population of the city drew supplies from the tideway of the Thames, which was also used by two hundred sewers for the discharge of sewage. There had, indeed, been previous attempts to remedy the situation and Chadwick had been at work on the subject for much of the 1840s. But, after the cholera epidemic, the time was ripe for another effort, and, in May, 1850, Chadwick produced his *Report on the Supply of Water to the Metropolis*. It made proposals which were rather similar to those relating to burials. Thus the private water companies would be bought out and their functions consolidated; the Thames would be abandoned as a source of supply and new areas of supply would be opened up, providing a much softer water, which, filtered and purified, would be continually available; and an executive Board would be set up to administer the provision of the new water supplies and would combine with this the provision of drainage facilities.

The aftermath of cholera thus provided the Board with an opportunity to present its schemes affecting burials and water supply, and, with both, Ashley was deeply concerned. He had written to Chadwick on 27 October, 1849, on the interment question that he would 'positively refuse to undertake or support any half-measure. The thing shall be complete or not at all.'[83] He warmly approved of the proposals of the Board, telling Carlisle – as Morpeth had become on his father's death – that if he and the government had 'ordinary "pluck", we shall have the noblest interment bill that ever was propounded.'[84] In December, he was present with Carlisle at the Home Office and took part in conversations with Grey, who appears to have suggested that certain of Chadwick's proposals should be modified.[85] There seems no doubt that he fully expected that he himself would introduce an interment bill, based on the Board's proposals and modified in accordance with conversations with the government. But in this he was mistaken. He heard from Carlisle in January, 1850, that the government itself was to introduce the measure. It was a bitter disappointment, and his outpourings in his Diary on the subject once again displayed the measure of his ambition and also his sensitivity to slights and setbacks. He freely admitted his hope that, after all his labours, he would have the satisfaction of seeing his name inseparably linked with a great reforming measure of this kind. And yet he was to be denied it. He bitterly reflected that he was to be reduced to 'the station of a senior clerk in the Home Office', and, meantime, all his other projects languished because he had no time to attend to them. The government expected him to

> devote (his) time, thoughts, almost life to the business of the Board of Health; to prepare the plans and Bills, but then to have no voice or discretion in the proposal or conduct of them, nor any little honour that may accrue from the scheme and the industry bestowed upon it. . . .

The government burdened him with the 'small tedious harassing details of the Provisional Orders', but reserved for itself 'the measures of credit'. And, reverting to a familiar theme, he wrote: 'this has been my fate in many, many things and doubtless humiliation is good for me.'[86]

Nevertheless, his response was not dictated entirely by disappointed ambition; he felt that the government's decision was not in the best interests of the measure, since, in his view, Grey neither understood nor liked it. Further, despite the setback, Ashley expressed his intention to work for the bill 'in and out of the House to pass it into a law', and, once this was done, he would retire from the Board and 'resume social questions that have fallen into comparative neglect.'[87] He felt, however, that the government was making very slow progress: in mid-January, he wrote that he was labouring hard on the 'hopeless interment plan'. He felt that it was one of 'the best ever devised and likely to be productive of real moral effects on the poorer population,' but it would not be carried and probably never proposed. Grey, he wrote, was 'evidently under another and a hostile influence.'[88] By this, Ashley presumably meant the influence of the Treasury, which, indeed, never looked upon the activities of Chadwick or the Board of Health with any measure of favour. Thus in the early months of 1850, Ashley was restless and impatient, and further setbacks were ahead. In March, Carlisle was appointed Chancellor of the Duchy of Lancaster and resigned his position at Woods and Forests and thus his Presidency of the Board of Health. Since his succession to the title in 1848, Carlisle had wanted to have more time to devote to personal and family affairs. He was not sorry to be quit of Woods and Forests, and he hoped he did 'not wrong' in thereby severing his connection with the Board of Health. He realised that there was 'great good to be done' by the Board, but he felt that the intermediate position between Chadwick and the Treasury had become 'intolerable' and he found it difficult to 'bully either'. He still thought that Chadwick had 'greater powers of doing good than any one else'; but, he continued, 'the yoke-fellow's is an uneasy place.'[89] Chadwick was distressed at Carlisle's retirement. He wrote to Carlisle expressing regret and also concern about the succession, especially if this went to a person with whom Ashley might not cooperate – 'and,' he added, 'he is not likely to cooperate with anyone who has not hitherto manifested zeal for our common public objects.' Chadwick felt that any change in the Board would be especially hazardous when the interment question was being discussed; it was important that the confidence of both the Church of England and the Dissenters should be maintained in the Board, and he thought that the present Board, and especially Ashley, did enjoy that confidence. 'I cannot but perceive,' Chadwick concluded, 'that he is discomposed and anxious on the subject of a change.'[90] Ashley was, indeed, depressed and somewhat restless. Carlisle's removal to the Lords made him uncertain of his own position. He had pointed out in 1848 that, in the light of this removal, he was the sole representative of the Board in the Commons, and, although he was willing to try to fill the void left by Carlisle's absence, this might not be altogether to the liking of the government. He quite understood that it might be necessary to replace him with a Whig, and he was ready to retain the position or to surrender it as the government might decide.[91] Ashley did, indeed, keep his place; but he was still unsettled. He wrote to Carlisle on 25 February, 1850, acknowledging the existence of a tie that had bound the members of the Board together 'in perfect harmony'. He felt that it would not be easy, if at all possible, to replace Carlisle; not only ability, but zeal in the cause was necessary and also 'many of the qualities that adorn and endear the private gentleman.' And, as for his own position, much would depend on the appointment of Carlisle's successor as to whether he could remain a member of the Board.[92]

A month later, on 25 March, Ashley wrote again to Carlisle to inform him that he had tendered his resignation from the Board to Russell. He had clearly become impatient to breaking-point with the delay over the interment bill. Grey had refused to fix a day for its introduction and had told Ashley that he must wait until Carlisle's successor had given his opinion of the bill. This, Ashley felt, indicated that Grey had no confidence in the Board's existing membership. He also felt aggrieved at the way in which the Board had been treated – and was still being treated – by the Treasury. He had been happy to serve under Carlisle; but, he continued:

> I do not know what sort of officer may succeed you, and I should be unwilling to assign any personal grounds for retirement; but sure I am that there will be no consideration for my feelings.
> All that I ask [he continued] is a testimony that, to the extent of my ability, I have done my duty; God knows that I have spared neither expense, toil nor health. I have never worked so harmoniously with any men as with our Board; and could I be of any use (it is now impossible) I would not withdraw.[93]

Carlisle's successor as First Commissioner of Woods and Forests and President of the Board of Health was Lord Seymour, heir of the Duke of Somerset. It is sometimes suggested that Ashley resigned from the Board out of wounded pride at Seymour's appointment, since he himself had hoped for the post. But it is clear that, ever since Morpeth's elevation to the Lords, Ashley had been uncertain about his own future as a member of the Board, and his final decision to resign was due to impatience at the interment bill, dissatisfaction with the Treasury's attitude and continuing doubts about the future after Carlisle's resignation. Not that Seymour's appointment in any way reassured him or made him feel that he might not, after all, resign. Carlisle, writing in his Diary of his 'great concern' at Ashley's resignation, mentioned Ashley's impatience at the delay over the interment bill and long-standing dissatisfaction at the 'stiffness of the Treasury', but he also mentioned a meeting with Ashley after the announcement of Seymour's appointment: 'this,' he wrote, '. . . had rather wounded him, as he did not like the notion of Seymour being put over him.' Possibly bearing in mind Ashley's letter to him in 1848, Carlisle did not think that Ashley ought to object to this, since he did not belong to the Whig party nor did he act with the Whigs, but, he added, 'it may be natural.'[94] No doubt some injured pride at Seymour's appointment was involved – such a reaction was certainly natural and was scarcely, in this instance, a case of over-sensitivity on Ashley's part. Seymour was considerably younger than Ashley and had shown no interest in public health matters. His appointment was distinctly unpromising for any further endeavour at the Board. The episode, therefore, did not prompt Ashley's actual decision to resign; but it did nothing to resolve – and can only have exacerbated – the depressed and unsettled state of mind which led him to the point of offering his resignation.

Chadwick was appalled at Ashley's resignation. Coming so soon after Carlisle's resignation, it would, he wrote, be 'a disaster, which should by all means be averted.'[95] And it is, indeed, a mark of Ashley's commitment to the cause that he was persuaded by Grey and Russell to change his mind and remain at the Board, at least until the interment bill had been carried and the water bill put in hand. The interment bill was finally introduced by Grey on 15 April, 1850.[96] The bill, based to a considerable extent on the Board's proposals, finally received the royal assent in August. But this had not been without difficulty. Its far-reaching proposals encountered criticism from advocates of private property, local government and from Dissenters. Ashley was extremely active in defence of the bill. He defended the cost of the Metropolitan Burial Board against attack;[97] he spoke in support of the transfer of the duties of the existing companies to the new Board, which, he felt, would discharge them more responsibly;[98] and he denied the accusation that the fees to be charged would bear harshly on the poorer classes.[99] Ashley thus gave the bill detailed and careful attention. On 7 June, he noted that only three clauses had been passed in about five hours: 'much attacked and reviled . . . These are the sweets of unremunerated public life!'[100] Ashley was thus a more active protagonist of the bill than Seymour; he was to write later that he had been compelled to take an active role in Parliament on public health matters since Seymour knew nothing about them.[101]

Relations with Seymour did, indeed, prove to be difficult. Ashley wrote to Carlisle in August, 1850, reminding him of the harmony which had prevailed at the Board during Carlisle's Presidency – if anything went wrong, the fault would lie with Seymour and his tendency to 'rub the hair the wrong way'. And in January, 1851, he wrote again to Carlisle saying that he had never to deal with a man 'more thoroughly and, it seems, intentionally offensive than Lord Seymour.' He also found Grey 'not very pleasant'. But he said he was willing to bear with all this to carry the water question, and he was anxious to serve the government.[102] Certainly, he was very active on the water supply question. In May, 1850, he successfully resisted a bill which embodied an attempt by a private water company to supply water to London; Ashley said that this would be done much more effectively by a government board.[103] His efforts also extended to taking a walking tour over the heaths of Surrey, around Farnham, looking for springs and sources for a new supply for the metropolis. This was in July, 1850, in the company of the other members of the Board; 'started at ten,' he wrote, 'and returned at ten.'[104] He was satisfied with what they had found: 'rivers to break out in the desert.' God was bountiful, but, he reflected, would man be so? It was 'overwhelming, heart-breaking, awful to reflect, how many thousands are deprived, in this *Christian* city, of the prime requisite for health, comfort, decency, of an essential prop and handmaid to morality! . . .'[105] During a holiday in Scotland in the autumn of 1850, Ashley wrote to Chadwick to say that he had devoted a day to an inspection of the Greenock gathering grounds. He was, he wrote, delighted to have seen them and had come to the conclusion that the Board could easily do the same, very cheaply, for London. He added that he would be in London in November, for the campaign at the Board: 'we must pipe all hands, God helping us, for the water supply.'[106] In October, he wrote again to Chadwick, saying that a start should be made on the water supply question in the first week of November and he hoped that Grey would send the Board instructions to act:[107] later in the month, he made up his mind to write to Grey and ask him for authority to prepare a bill.[108]

But there were to be considerable difficulties ahead. On his return to London in November, Ashley began to wonder if any progress would be made. He wrote on 7 November that he feared not. He distrusted the government and more than distrusted Seymour: 'They worship sanitary measures with their lips, but their hearts are far from it.'[109] Seymour, indeed, scarcely even paid lip service: his attendances at the Board since his appointment had been very sparse.[110] He was also under pressure from the Treasury to keep a watchful eye on the Board's activities and financial expenditure.[111] Certainly, Seymour had made it clear that he held the Board in very low regard and was openly hostile to its efforts and activities.[112] All these restraints and discouragements dampened Ashley's spirits. On 12 December, he wrote that the water supply question would be set aside or emasculated by the government, and yet he had made the measure a condition of his remaining at the Board. His situation, he wrote, was 'painful'; it had become that of a clerk and he was made to feel it hourly by Seymour and Grey. The Board had no free action, no power to give effect to any of its decisions. The Treasury and the Home Office refused or thwarted every proposition 'at the secret dictation of Lord Seymour. . . .'[113] Ashley had had a long interview with Grey on the water question on 20 November, but he had been kept waiting for several weeks for an answer whether the government would proceed with the matter or not. Nevertheless, he was still willing to bear 'almost anything', so deep was his 'conviction of the benefit of the Poor' should he finally prevail.[114] But by 23 December, he was even more despondent: all that he could expect from Grey and Seymour were 'disappointment and affront' – he had been 'without fee or reward' but had found 'nothing but failure and contempt'.[115]

In January, 1851, Ashley became involved in a sharp dispute and exchange of letters with Seymour.[116] The occasion was the publication of a report on the Farnham gathering grounds by the Hon. William Napier who, at Chadwick's request in 1850, had made an examination of the grounds and had written his report in very favourable, if also somewhat highly coloured, terms. On its publication, the Report came to Seymour's notice; he at once came to the conclusion that Napier had been acting without his authority and approval, and he wrote to the Secretary of the Board raising the matter. Ashley took it upon himself to reply and thus began an acrimonious correspondence which lasted for some ten days. On one day alone – 10 January – four letters were exchanged. Seymour was strongly critical of Napier's appointment and his Report, which he regarded as wholly unscientific. Another issue was the method which Seymour had adopted in approaching the Board – Ashley objected to the written approach which Seymour had made to the Secretary, arguing that it would have been much preferable if Seymour had called a meeting of the Board to hear his colleagues' personal explanation of the matter. But the main point of contention arose from a statement made by Seymour in one of his letters to Ashley that the Treasury had sent 'explicit directions' to the Board that any proposals involving expenditure should be submitted to him. Ashley was anxious to discover the precise nature of these directions, since he himself had never heard of them, and he pressed Seymour to give exact information about them. He claimed that such directions would have been illegal – they would have meant that three Commissioners were forced to submit their actions to the fourth, who was never present at the meetings; and moreover, such an act of authority would 'deprive the Board of independent action.'

Ashley had much the better of the exchange. He countered Seymour's complaint that he had not been informed of Napier's appointment by sending him the letter which notified Seymour of the appointment and

Seymour's reply that he had no objections. 'Such,' he wrote, 'is the want of consideration with which you attack your colleagues.' And he forced Seymour to admit that he had 'simply understood' that the 'explicit directions' from the Treasury to which he had referred had been given either by the Treasury or by the Chancellor. Ashley was thus able to reply that a statement based on 'understanding' was weakly based. Ashley also proposed a resolution to the Board, which was carried, to the effect that the Board would send copies of its Minutes to Seymour, but this did not involve any recognition of the right of one Board member to control the proceedings of the others. And, further, if the President wanted to question the conduct of the other members of the Board, he must do so by attending the Board in person. To this, Seymour agreed and asked to be told in advance of occasions on which the Board was about to take important decisions.

The dispute was certainly conducted with energy on both sides. Clearly an element of personal animosity was involved. Ashley wrote in his Diary that Seymour's 'insolence' was intolerable,[117] and, a few days later, that he was 'harassed by this fellow Seymour'. Seymour refused to give direct answers to his questions: 'never was man treated with such contempt!'[118] When it became clear that Ashley had won his points, Seymour did not acknowledge it. 'What a man!' Ashley wrote. 'Beaten at every point and shifting his ground he will not say that he has made a mistake, or regret that he has given pain . . .'[119] On 18 January, however, Ashley told Chadwick that he had received a 'becoming letter' from Seymour and added that he hoped for peace;[120] this suggests that Seymour had apologised for certain of the statements he had made. In any event, there was more to the argument than a clash of personalities. Ashley certainly feared that Seymour's influence would retard progress. Thus Ashley complained of Seymour's refusal to say a 'civil word', but, he continued, 'this I care not for; but I do care lest he should have influence over Sir G. Grey and the two stop the water question.'[121] There was also the important matter of the status of the Board.[122] Throughout the debate, Ashley was anxious, as he put it, to 'maintain the independence of the Commission.'[123] In fact, the Board's position and that of the President were not altogether certain. The President was one of the four Commissioners and, in a sense, was simply chairman of the Board. On the other hand, he was also a member of the government, and he was President of the Board by virtue of being First Commissioner of Woods and Forests, traditionally a subordinate branch of the Treasury. The distinction had never manifested itself under Carlisle's Presidency, but it did emerge under that of Seymour. Ashley and Chadwick took the view that the Board was independent and that the Treasury could only take decisions on its advice: the Treasury – and, under its influence, Seymour – took the view that it controlled Woods and Forests and thus the Board of

Health. It was entirely natural that Ashley should have fought to maintain the independence of the Board, but the other view, held by the Treasury, was also a tenable one, and it was this which was the basic issue in the dispute.

Ashley, indeed, won the dispute, but scarcely the issue. The months after January were to show that the Treasury's influence was still important, even if it was now exercised openly by instruction to the whole Board. And Ashley well realised this. He wrote at the end of January that the Treasury had 'conceived a dislike' of Chadwick and were determined to thwart the Board, 'which they do most effectively.' Seymour adopted the same attitude and had 'over and above that, a dislike of sanitary progress and a reluctance, as he himself admitted, "to do more than he is forced to do".'[124] Ashley, therefore, thought that the implementation of the interment act and the introduction of a water supply bill would be considerably delayed. There was, in fact, to be rather more progress on both issues than Ashley had predicted. In March, 1851, after further skirmishes with the Treasury, the Board was authorised to buy out the interment companies and, the following month, a water bill was introduced. But such progress was to prove insufficient to dispel the mood of frustration and discontent which both Chadwick and Ashley felt over sanitary matters in the first few months of 1851. Both felt that their efforts were being countered by sinister forces: official hostility, vested private interests, localism or 'vestryism'. The battle had, indeed, existed since 1848. By early and mid-1851 it was going against the public health movement. Thereafter, it was to move more decisively against it.[125]

Public health was, therefore, extremely burdensome to Ashley in the years after his return to Parliament. In a sense, it might be argued that Ashley's frenzied activity with public health after 1848 replaced his earlier activity over factory reform. Yet, despite the achievement of the Ten Hours Act in 1847, the factory question was to cause him further worries in the closing years of the decade. The Ten Hours Act was designed to come into operation gradually: from 1 July, 1847, young persons and women were restricted to eleven hours' work a day or sixty-three hours a week; from 1 May, 1848, the limitation was to be ten hours a day or fifty-eight hours a week. The first effects of the Act were, in certain cases, not very noticeable, since they took place in circumstances of depression; and short-time working was being practised irrespective of any statutory limitations. But, even then, there were manufacturers who protested that the reduction to eleven hours was having a ruinous effect on their fortunes, and, at the end of the year and in early 1848, Ashley was beginning to feel alarm that the manufacturers were about to launch an attack aimed at repealing the Act. He wrote more than once to Fielden, expressing these fears; he also said that he had received reports that some employers were trying to win the assistance of their employees, no doubt short of money after the slump, to support petitions for its repeal.[126] He was anxious to strengthen the resistance of the operatives to such efforts. He was in favour of public demonstrations in support of the 1847 Act and supported a plan put forward by Hindley that there should be a Ten Hours Tea Party in the Free Trade Hall in Manchester and that medals commemorating the Act should be struck. Despite some resistance from Fielden, who was less worried at this point than Ashley about future prospects, the rally went ahead in June, 1848, the anniversary of the parliamentary victory: a gold medal was struck for the Queen and twenty silver medals were struck for the leaders of the Movement. Ashley was well pleased with the rally – it was, he wrote, a 'glorious gathering and eminently successful' and he was confident that the resolution of those present was such that no one would 'venture to touch the blessed measure.'[127] But, despite this, Ashley still had anxieties about the Act. In August, he wondered what was ahead. He noted that Horner, one of the Inspectors, had denounced the Act as 'injudicious, oppressive, ruinous to master and man'. This, Ashley felt, was 'arrogant and wicked' on Horner's part; the Act had only come into force on 1 May and Horner had written on 2 June. And he was depressed by what Horner had added: that the workpeople hated it 'as the cause of much privation to them'. In that case, Ashley wrote, he was 'singularly humbled': this was the question, he reflected, for which he had foregone office, ease, political connections, personal friendships; he had also incurred expense and endured anxiety and toil. And it was all for nothing: 'I made myself hated,' he wrote. 'I shall end by being contemptible.'[128]

The achievement of the ten-hour day did not, therefore, mean that Ashley was able to close his mind to the question. But, although he feared the repeal of the Act, the principal threat to it lay more in its evasion by means of a relay system, whereby staggered sets of young persons and women were employed. Their working day did not, in total, exceed the legal limit, but it was divided into separate relays, which involved their remaining on the factory premises for considerably longer than the working hours prescribed by the 1847 Act – they might, indeed, have to remain for the full fifteen hours during which the factory was open. The inspectors had tried to counter this by informing the masters that, under the 1844 Act, the system was illegal. But in 1848, as trade revived and the masters were anxious to run their factories to maximum capacity, the system was extended. The inspectors instituted prosecutions, but many magistrates refused to convict. Ashley wrote to Fielden in February, 1849, of the desire of the inspectors to enforce their interpretations of the law, but he feared that the government was timid and might even legalise relays. In that event, all the 'social and domestic benefits' of the Act of 1847 would be lost.[129] In March, he noted in his Diary that a powerful minority of masters had discovered a means of evasion; the government felt that it could not prevent it and would, therefore, legalise it. 'Here is fresh toil, fresh anxiety. Would to God it were settled forever.'[130] He told Grant, a member of the Lancashire Short-Time Committee, that, although he did not believe that the introduction of legislation was imminent, no time should be lost in collecting all the evidence that could be had on the good working of the 1847 Act.[131] He also took part in meetings with the Home Secretary: on 24 May he called on Grey, with others, to present a memorial and various petitions. A further meeting followed in early June. After it, Ashley commented sadly that Grey and Russell 'quail before capital and power and would force unjust concessions with the operatives.'[132]

At this point, however, Ashley committed himself to a proposal which was to cause him considerable unpopularity in certain sections of the Ten Hours Movement. There had already been negotiations in February between a delegation of the Millowners Association and the government on the subject of a possible compromise over the relay system. This was that, if the Ten Hours Act were replaced by an Eleven Hours Act, the system of relays would be abandoned for females and young persons under the age of eighteen. Nothing came of the plan at that point, but, in June, it was revived. *The Manchester Guardian* carried a report of a meeting between a delegation of Lancashire masters and the government at the Home Office, at which, the report alleged, Grey promised to legalise relays, and it also stated that Ashley had received two of the deputation in a friendly spirit and, in the interests of reaching a settlement, had expressed his willingness to support a compromise of ten-and-a-half or eleven hours if the operatives agreed. This was denounced by *The Manchester Guardian* as 'ministerial treachery to the ten hours bill,'[133] and, indeed, a counter-deputation of masters and men, including Samuel Fielden, son of John Fielden, who had died a few days earlier, went to London to tell Grey and Ashley that there would be no compromise. Ashley, in a letter to *The Manchester Guardian*, denied its earlier report, but he did admit that he had seen two members of the delegation, who had informed him of the plan proposed by the masters. He told them that the law was 'now the property and right of the factory workers;' that he could not assent to or reject the proposition of the masters, since this was a matter for the operatives. But he had added that, as far as he was concerned, he would be ready to consider the proposal of ten-and-a-half hours of labour and probably accede to it, provided that this was taken between the hours of 6 a.m. and 6 p.m. and provided that the operatives agreed to it. He had, however, spoken of an Eleven Hours Bill as an 'arrangement utterly inadmissable'.[134]

The episode, in fact, proved deeply devisive within the popular movement. The Manchester Central Committee, under its secretary, Mawdsley, came to accept the idea of compromise, considering that the extra half-hour was a reasonable price to pay for the abolition of the relays.[135] But another section, gathered round Oastler, Stephens and the Fielden family, opposed all compromise, denounced Ashley and called for an entirely new organisation. A Fielden Society was, indeed, formed in September, 1849, with the object of protecting and enforcing the 1847 Act. Ashley was resentful of these developments. He noted on 4 October that Oastler and Stephens had seized the opportunity to revile him and place themselves at the head of the operatives, 'but,' he added, 'I rejoice to say that the operatives will neither believe them nor accept them.'[136] But the Fielden section gathered strength and again Ashley was provoked to express his annoyance. In November, he wrote that Oastler and 'a crew of others (I can use no milder terms) . . . are denouncing and reviling me in every society, by day and by night, in speech and on paper, as a traitor, and a thousand other things, to the Ten Hours Bill. God knows my sincerity, my labours, vexations, losses, injuries to health, fortune, comfort, position in that cause.'[137] It seemed that the two sections might unite and a meeting was planned for January. But this came to grief over Ashley's position. The Central Committee had, on 11 January, accepted Ashley as their parliamentary leader and this was sufficient to make the opposing section boycott the conference. Fielden stated that the operatives 'must decide whether they would follow the man who attempted to betray them,' held a separate conference, and, on 27 January, 1850, rejected Ashley.[138]

The following month, a further stage in the question of relays was reached when a judgment was given on a test case, Ryder v. Mills, heard on appeal in the Exchequer court. The ruling was to the effect that relays were legal. On 15 February, Ashley noted the judgment: 'great remedial measure, the Ten Hours Act, nullified. The work to be done all over again; and I seventeen years older than when I began!'[139] There was, however, the question of whether Ashley would be asked to do the work. Mawdsley's Central Committee took the initiative by calling a conference in Manchester for 17 February and invited Ashley to be present at it. Ashley did not, in fact, attend, but wrote to the Committee urging the operatives to send petitions, memorials and deputations to Parliament to state their claims to a ten-hour day, worked continuously from the hour at which it was begun and not interrupted by shifts and relays.[140] But, once again, divisions appeared within the Movement. The group around Stephens and Fielden distrusted the Central Committee; it hoped that 'some honest and far more capable man' would succeed Ashley, whom it condemned as 'incompetent, vacillating, time-serving (and) treacherous'.[141] The two groups met on 16 February to try to reach a common policy and a conference took place on 17 February, attended by both. A resolution calling for a simple ten-hour day was passed, and finally Ashley *was* nominated as parliamentary spokesman, along with two others, Lord John Manners and Bankes. Four operatives were also chosen to go as delegates to London. This, indeed, seemed to end the schism between the two groups, and the meeting passed a resolution calling for a re-organisation of the Central Committee with the purpose of widening its base and making it more representative of various opinions. The Committee agreed to undertake this task. But, a week later, Mawdsley held a second conference, attended by thirty delegates who were invited to be present by private ticket. The object of this meeting was to 'wipe away the stain cast on Lord Ashley.' It was argued that the first meeting had been packed; its resolutions were rescinded; nothing was done about re-organisation; and it was agreed to appoint Ashley as sole leader.[142] This move naturally ended the brief period of harmony. It was bitterly criticised by Fielden's supporters, who held a further meeting on 3 March. At this, Fielden attacked the Central Committee and denounced it, and the meeting confirmed the resolutions which had been passed at the conference of 17 February. Further, a solicitor, Cobbett, was asked to prepare a bill on behalf of a new provisional Central Committee which was to be set up. The Movement was once again at loggerheads.

Ashley was anxious to avoid all contact with the Fielden group. Thus, when a draft of the bill prepared by Cobbett was sent to him – and to the two others chosen to take up the matter – he did not acknowledge it. Instead, he decided to go ahead with a bill of his own and introduced this on 14 March.[143] In his speech, Ashley drew attention to the evils of relays, but his bill did not explicitly forbid them. It proposed that the hours of labour, including intervals allowed for meals, should be reckoned continuously from the moment any young person, woman or child first began work in the morning. He stressed that he was concerned only with this point of the continuity of labour, and, in so doing, he felt that he would have the support of the House. The bill was given a second reading on 19 March. But it was not stringent enough for Cobbett, who told Ashley that it was questionable if the bill would have the desired effect, and he suggested a meeting of counsel to strengthen it.[144] But Ashley did not take this up, merely replying that the clause would be amended on 22 March. At the Report stage, certain amendments were introduced to tighten up the bill. But these were still not stringent enough for the Fielden group, and, on 29 March, the new provisional Central Committee condemned the bill and Ashley. Cobbett once again asked for a meeting and Ashley was still unwilling to agree. But his position was weakened when, on 14 April, the old Central Committee came out against his bill. Then, on 16 April, Cobbett, with help from Manners and Bankes, finally persuaded Ashley to attend a meeting, at which a new bill was agreed to, to be drafted by Ashley's solicitor. But Ashley still had doubts and expressed these in a letter to Mawdsley on 27 April. The new provisions agreed on at the meeting with Cobbett contained a great deal of new material for regulating meal times, and it raised three difficulties. In the first place, it was contrary to his statement to the House that he would not raise any issue other than that of continuity of labour; secondly, it would give rise to much debate and opposition; and finally it would lose him support. Ashley thus told Mawdsley that the choice was between accepting the present proposal — which, it was argued, would be violated — and adopting the proposals put forward at the conference — and this latter course would involve an explanation on his part and the likely postponement of the measure to another session. He asked Mawdsley to say which of these 'hazards' he preferred.[145]

Ashley was thus caught in a state of indecision. Meantime, however, the initiative was taken elsewhere. This was in the form of a letter signed by a 'manufacturer' in *The Times* on 25 April which proposed that the working day should stretch from 6 a.m. to 6 p.m. with one-and-a-half hours for meals. Work would thus be done for ten-and-a-half hours. On a Saturday, the hours should be between 6 a.m. and 2 p.m. and work would be performed for seven-and-a-half hours. This, it was argued in the letter, would effect the object more 'simply and certainly than Ashley's plan.'[146] The letter met with considerable opposition, and a meeting of operatives held at Manchester on 28 April, 1850, declared unswerving support for a ten-hour day. Ashley took this as the advice which he had sought from the operatives, and, on 30 April, gave notice of his intention to move a clause, forbidding relays; this was a 'new matter'[147] and thus he gave warning, so that the House would not be taken by surprise.

When the debate resumed on 3 May, Ashley asked for a statement from the government on rumours which were current about its intentions, for it was thought likely that the government intended to propose a scheme of its own. The matter, he said, required clarification. And it did, indeed, become clear that the government favoured the compromise proposal which had been put forward in *The Times*. It was pointed out on the government's behalf that the difficulty of defining a true ten-hour day was primarily due to the fact that the factory was open for fifteen hours per day (5.30 a.m. to 8.30 p.m.); it was this which made it possible to run relays. But this would be resolved if the factory were open for twelve hours on a weekday (6 a.m. to 6 p.m.) and eight hours on a Saturday (6 a.m. to 2 p.m.) with one-and-a-half hours for meals. This would, admittedly, increase the working day to ten-and-a-half hours, which meant an addition of two-and-a-half hours per week, but the working day on a Saturday would be reduced by half-an-hour: thus the net addition to the working week would be two hours. There would, however, be advantages – the factory day would start half-an-hour later in the morning, operatives would finish work earlier in the evening and work would cease at 2 p.m. on a Saturday.[148]

Ashley was clearly attracted to this suggestion. He wrote on 7 May that he was harassed day after day by the factory bill. It was impossible, he wrote, to get a clause stringent enough to prohibit relays. Thus he had resolved 'as (the) only hope of getting anything good and secure for the operatives, to accept (the) Government's amendments.' He was sure that they were the best terms that would be offered, and this would probably be the last time that they would be offered.[149] His decision to accept the compromise was publicly announced in a letter in *The Times*, addressed to the Short-Time Committees of Lancashire and Yorkshire. In this, he stressed the difficulties of finding a clause to prohibit relays and the postponement which such a search would mean. He mentioned the advantages which the proposals offered, with factories open for twelve hours instead of fifteen: there could be no possibility of shifts, relays or other evasions. The plan also provided a later starting time in the morning, the whole of every evening after 6 p.m. for 'recreation and domestic duty' and additional leisure-time on a Saturday. Ashley also felt that the arrangement would secure 'the cooperation of the employers – a matter of no slight importance in the good working of any measure and essential to the harmony and good feeling we all desire to see in the vast districts of our manufactures.'[150] Next day in his Diary, he mentioned this letter: 'expect from (the) manufacturing districts a storm of violence and hatred,' he wrote.[151]

His expectation was well founded. Abuse did, indeed, pour in on him. Oastler said that Ashley had 'betrayed the poor'; Stephens that he had 'at length removed the mask of affected sympathy' and had deserted his former colleagues 'with the most unparalleled baseness'.[152] In Manchester, the new Central Committee for the Protection of the Ten Hours Act passed a resolution deploring the 'infatuation which led to the cause of the factory workers being entrusted to Lord Ashley.' It denounced the government measure, as recommended by Ashley, to extend the working day of young persons and children as 'unjust and evil', and it gratefully accepted an offer which Lord John Manners made to secure a ten-hours bill. Thanks were expressed to Lord John for the generous manner in which he had come forward when the 'base and deliberate treachery of our pretended friends seem to have assured our defeat.' A meeting of the old Central Committee was, as usual, more restrained in its tones. There, the feeling was that, if Manners persisted in his amendment, the bill would simply be abandoned for the session. A resolution was, therefore, passed with only one dissentient – that an opening time of 6 a.m. to 6 p.m. was very desirable; that an effort should be made to engraft a fifty-eight hour week on to it; but, failing this, no effort should be made to endanger the government's plan, reserving the right to re-open the matter another session.[153]

The matter was, indeed, resolved in the summer of 1850. On 13 May, Ashley moved that the clause which he had prepared be withdrawn and the amendment of the government substituted: that the working day of young persons and women be calculated within the hours of 6 a.m. to 6 p.m.[154] One further difficulty concerned the working day of children. Ashley had stated in his letter to the Short-Time Committees that it would be necessary to include children in a working day of 6 a.m. to 6 p.m.; their day was limited by the Act of 1844 to six-and-a-half hours, but this was calculated between the hours of 5.30 a.m. to 8.30 p.m. On 6 June, Ashley moved an amendment that children be included in the set day of 6 a.m. to 6 p.m. – this, he said, would make the law uniform with regard to children, young persons and women.[155] But the government resisted his amendment; Grey stated that children were not affected by the bill and they must continue to work under the protection of the 1844 Act, which, he said, had been beneficial to them.[156] Ashley's amendment was defeated by 102 votes to 72. Ashley was furious at this and said that he felt relieved of the obligation which he had entered into over the bill.[157] He returned to the matter on 14 April and again proposed an amendment that no child should be employed except between 6 a.m. and 6 p.m.[158] He refuted Grey's suggestion that the position of children was not affected by the bill: parents would be leaving the factory at 6 p.m. but the children would have to stay until 8.30 p.m. They would have no one to take them home, and would be kept out of bed until 10 or 10.30 p.m. But Grey again refused to agree. He referred to the two sets of children which were employed under the 1844 Act: some for seven hours, others for six-and-a-half hours – together these came to more than the twelve hours during which Ashley proposed hours should be calculated. Ashley's amendment would, therefore, be a serious restraint on the motive power and productive capacity of the factories.[159] Other speakers made similar points: at present adult labour might be thirteen or fourteen hours and children were employed in two sets to help them. If children were restricted in the way that Ashley proposed, the motive power of the factory would be effectively restricted to ten hours in the day. Ashley's amendment was lost – but only by one vote. Ashley was downcast and depressed: the House, he wrote, would not listen to him – 'they never will listen to me now,' he wrote, 'and who can blame them?'[160] An amendment proposed by Manners that the working day should not extend beyond 5.30 p.m. was also lost,[161] and, on 20 June, the bill was read a third time and sent to the Lords. Ashley made efforts to gain support among the peers for the inclusion of children, and Harrowby did propose an amendment along these lines, but it was defeated.[162] On 5 August, the measure reached the statute book.

Ashley's role in the episode was a controversial one. In his own private reflections on the matter, he felt that his decision to accept the compromise of a ten-and-a-half hour day was justified. He argued that the majority in favour of the bill of 1847 was governed not by devotion to the cause of ten hours, but by anger towards Peel and the Anti-Corn Law League: 'had not these passions interposed,' he wrote, 'there would have been no unusual humanity.' This was not the position in 1850. Further, he did not think that the extra two hours in the week added anything of value to the amount of production for the employers, nor did they take anything of importance from the operatives. Little, therefore, was to be gained or lost; it was simply a struggle for victory – 'no side chooses to be beaten,' he wrote. He admitted that this might be natural, but he could not consent to be the 'tool' of such an attitude. It would, he added, doubtless be a blow to his reputation, because his position and conduct would be misunderstood, and he could not resist the temptation to think of the way in which all his efforts and sacrifices were to end in abuse and hatred. 'Thus it is to serve Man!' he concluded. 'Praise to God; my trust and comfort are in Him!'[163]

The attitude of contemporaries has already been examined, and the attitude of some historians has also been very critical. Thus C. H. Driver in his biography of Oastler writes that in his letter urging the operatives to accept the government compromise, Ashley 'sold the pass' and was guilty of an 'astonishing *volte face*'. Driver discounts Ashley's justification of his acceptance of the compromise, and criticises Ashley for abandoning the responsibilities towards the operatives which he had carried for seventeen years. Driver is also critical of the suddenness of Ashley's change of attitude, for, having told the workers to hold fast to their rights, he suddenly changed his position and persuaded them to give them up.[164]

The validity of such a view is open to argument. There was much to be said for the compromise: Ashley was almost certainly correct in his belief that it was the best that could be achieved, and it should be remembered that he did retain the support of a section of the Ten Hours Movement. That children were not included in the new arrangement was, indeed, unfortunate, but this was not Ashley's fault. He tried to include them but was opposed by the government. But there is some truth in the criticism that Ashley did not handle the matter as well as he might have done. He had always said that, irrespective of his own views, it was for the operatives to decide: he asked for their advice on 25 and 27 April and on 30 April he seemed to be following it by moving a clause to abolish relays. A week later, without further consultation, he informed the Committees that he had decided otherwise, and he did so, not directly, but through the press. The reason for his conduct may possibly lie in his dislike of the criticism which he had suffered at the hands of the Fieldenites and, despite his stated willingness to follow advice, a certain distaste at being dictated to. He told the Committees in his letter of 7 February that he was bound to act not as their delegate, but as their friend, and this was a phrase which he repeated in the House of Commons on 6 June: 'never have I considered myself as their champion,' he said, 'but I did consider myself as their best friend.'[165] Thus an element of 'paternalism' may explain Ashley's conduct. Further, it would seem that by the late 1840s Ashley had little inclination to fight old battles afresh. When he suffered criticism for his willingness to consider a ten-and-a-half hour day, he was somewhat impatient: 'Here is my offence,' he wrote in November, 1849, 'and I am too busy and also too tired to begin a controversial defence. Like Hezekiah, I "spread it before the Lord".'[166] In February, 1850, he wrote that the ten-hours bill was again on his hands and would occupy all the time, health and energy he might have given to other things: 'and now I am nearly fifty years old!' he added, 'oh, what a prospect.'[167] When asked to attend a meeting on 17 February, 1850, to discuss what action should be taken after the adverse ruling of the Exchequer Court, he did not attend, but only sent a letter; indeed he attended no meetings in the north at this time. Finally, although clearly hurt and offended by the criticism and abuse heaped upon him after he accepted the compromise, he did not – as has been perceptively pointed out[168] – fill his Diary with ranting against Oastler – the matter seems to have left him relatively unscathed. Disputes and controversies over what he regarded as an insignificant concession had no attractions for him and, moreover, his energies at the time were fully deployed elsewhere; not only in the cause of public health but also in religious pursuits and in personal and family concerns.

NOTES

1. N.R.A., Shaftesbury (Broadlands) MSS, SHA/PD/5, 21 Mar., 1848.
2. ibid., SHA/PD/5, 25 Mar., 1848.
3. ibid., SHA/PD/5, 24, 25 Feb., 1848.
4. Hodder, II, 239–40.
5. N.R.A., Shaftesbury (Broadlands) MSS, SHA/PD/5, 21 Feb., 1848.
6. ibid., SHA/PD/5, 29 Feb., 1848.
7. ibid., SHA/PD/5, 21 Mar., 1848.
8. ibid., SHA/PD/5, 12 Apr., 1848.
9. ibid., SHA/PD/5, 13 Apr., 1848.

10. For the infrequency of Ashley's visits to the Carlton Club, see Add. MSS 40, 617, fos 272–3. For the projected offers of office, see J. R. Vincent (ed.), *Disraeli, Derby and the Conservative Party. The Political Journals of Lord Stanley 1849–1869* (1978), pp. 2, 6.
11. N.R.A., Shaftesbury (Broadlands) MSS, SHA/PD/5, 19 Apr., 1848.
12. Hodder, II, 246–8.
13. N.R.A., Shaftesbury (Broadlands) MSS, SHA/PD/5, 20 May, 1848.
14. ibid., SHA/PD/5, 8 July, 1848.
15. ibid., SHA/PD/5, 27 July, 1848. (See also Hodder, II, 264–8).
16. ibid., SHA/PD/5, 25 May, 1848.
17. ibid., SHA/PD/5, 23 Mar., 1848.
18. University of Durham, Department of Palaeography and Diplomatic, 3rd Earl Grey MSS, 22 Apr., 1848.
19. ibid., 24 Apr., 1848.
20. Hansard, *Parl. Debates*, XCIC, 429–55.
21. ibid., 470.
22. 3rd Earl Grey MSS, 23 June, 1848.
23. ibid., 10 July, 1848.
24. Hodder, II, 259–60.
25. N.R.A., Shaftesbury (Broadlands) MSS, SHA/PD/5, 27 July, 1848.
26. *Ragged School Union Magazine* (1849), pp. 5–7.
27. Hansard, *Parl. Debates*, 3rd ser., CVII, 897 ff.
28. H.R.O., Shaftesbury (Broadlands) MSS, 27M60, 2 May, 1850.
29. Under the existing system, this assistance could only be given if the Poor Law Guardians or the relieving officer authorised it, and if the Medical officer of the Union attended the woman without an order from the Guardians or officer, he would not be remunerated. Equally, no remuneration would be paid if the Guardians did not feel that the woman required assistance. The Guardians also insisted on the attendance of the husband, and it was unlikely that he could comply with this without the loss of a day's pay. With these restrictions, women were apt to call on unskilled midwives to assist with the delivery, and this could lead to medical complications and even death in childbirth. Ashley thus proposed that every woman claiming medical assistance for childbirth under the Poor Law should be entitled to the aid of the medical officer with the birth of her first child and also with subsequent children, provided the medical officer who had attended her previous confinement testified by certificate that this was medically desirable. There would be no need to obtain the authorisation of the Guardians or the relieving officer, and relief would, therefore, be given promptly. Ashly also proposed that, if an abortion had to be carried out, a second doctor should be called in, and he should be paid for his services. A final proposal was that a medical inspector should be added to the Central Poor Law Commission, with the task of inspecting and reporting on the condition of those treated under the Poor Law. In resistance to these proposals, it was argued that the Guardians were not inhumane and were easily accessible, and that, in any case, this was a matter for the Poor Law Commissioners and not for Parliament. Ashley, therefore, withdrew his proposals. (Hansard, *Parl. Debates*, 3rd ser., XCVII, 632 ff).
30. N.R.A., Shaftesbury (Broadlands) MSS, SHA/PD/5, 9 Apr., 1848.
31. ibid., SHA/PD/5, 14 July, 1848.
32. Hansard, *Parl. Debates*, 3rd ser., XCVIII, 779.
33. ibid., 779–87.
34. N.R.A., Shaftesbury (Broadlands) MSS., SHA/PD/5, 26 Sept., 1848.

35. ibid., SHA/PD/5, 26 Sept., 1848.
36. Battiscombe, p. 221.
37. S. E. Finer, *The Life and Times of Sir Edwin Chadwick* (1952), p. 338.
38. The Library, University College London, Chadwick MSS, 25 Sept., 1848.
39. ibid., 28 Sept., 1848.
40. Ashley wrote in 1846 that Morpeth's behaviour over Ten Hours since 1833 had 'never exhibited either sincerity, honour or feeling.' (N.R.A., Shaftesbury (Broadlands) MSS, SHA/PD/4, 6 May, 1846).
41. Carlisle MSS, 2nd ser., Book 67, 9 Sept., 1848.
42. Chadwick MSS, 28 Sept., 1848.
43. See R. A. Lewis, op. cit., pp. 41–3, 190–91, 346. See also ibid., p. 357, n. 1 for mention of Dr John Snow's pamphlet of 1849 which stated the—correct—theory of the transmission of the disease by water.
44. N.R.A., Shaftesbury (Broadlands) MSS, SHA/PD/5, 17 Sept., 1849. Ashley told Morpeth in 1848 that he would be willing to give 'a good portion of the day and night'. (Carlisle MSS, 2nd ser., Book 67, 9 Sept., 1848). He can scarcely have foreseen how far this would be necessary.
45. N.R.A., Shaftesbury (Broadlands) MSS, SHA/PD/5, 27 Sept., 1848.
46. Chadwick MSS, 3 Sept., 1849.
47. N.R.A., Shaftesbury (Broadlands) MSS, SHA/PD/5, 9 Sept., 1849.
48. ibid., SHA/PD/5, 17 Sept., 1849.
49. ibid., SHA/PD/5, 17 Sept., 1849.
50. St G.H., Shaftesbury MSS, 25026.7/7th Earl.
51. S. Finer, op. cit., p. 352. Ashley wrote to Carlisle in 1851, thanking him for his 'friendly recognition of those services which God in His goodness, has enabled me to perform.' He also rejoiced that their friendship had been strengthened. (Carlisle MSS, 2nd ser., Book 67, 19 Mar., 1851).
52. N.R.A., Shaftesbury (Broadlands) MSS, SHA/PD/5, 24 Oct., 1848.
53. Hansard, *Parl. Debates*, 3rd ser., CVII, 250.
54. ibid., 950–51.
55. R. A. Lewis, op. cit., pp. 207–8.
56. N.R.A., Shaftesbury (Broadlands) MSS, SHA/PD/5, 11 Sept., 1849.
57. ibid., SHA/PD/5, 12 Sept., 1849. Bishop Blomfield of London also expressed 'very strong objections' to the Board's orders over the closure of burial grounds. No opportunity was given to the Bishop of the diocese for discussing the orders and the expense would be considerable. (Lambeth Palace Libr., Blomfield Letter Books, Vol. 397, pp. 370–2. Blomfield to Ashley. Not dated, but mid-1849).
58. Chadwick MSS, 12 Sept., 1849.
59. ibid.
60. N.R.A., Shaftesbury (Broadlands) MSS, SHA/PD/5, 13 Sept., 1848.
61. Chadwick MSS, 13 Sept., 1849.
62. ibid., 13 Sept., 1849.
63. R. A. Lewis, op. cit., p. 209.
64. Chadwick MSS, 16 Sept., 1849.
65. ibid., 28 Sept., 1849.
66. ibid., 2 Oct., 1849.
67. N.R.A., Shaftesbury (Broadlands) MSS, SHA/PD/5, 2 Oct., 1849.
68. R. A. Lewis, op. cit., p. 212.
69. Chadwick MSS, 13 Sept., 1849.
70. S. Finer, op. cit., p. 350. R. A. Lewis, op. cit., p. 212. The Minute of the Board concerning the appointments is in P.R.O., M.H. 5/2, 7 Sept., 1849.

71. R. A. Lewis, op. cit., p. 211.
72. Chadwick MSS, 25 Oct., 1849.
73. Russell MSS, 30/22/8B, 7 Nov., 1849.
74. N.R.A., Shaftesbury (Broadlands) MSS, SHA/PC/18/1.
75. Hodder, II, 297.
76. ibid., 297-8.
77. N.R.A., Shaftesbury (Broadlands) MSS, SHA/PD/5, 17 Sept., 1849.
78. ibid., SHA/PD/5, 17, 20 Sept., 1849.
79. Chadwick MSS, 29 Oct., 1849.
80. There had also been a select committee on Interments in 1842, of which Ashley had been a member.
81. R. A. Lewis, op. cit., p. 238.
82. S. Finer, op. cit., p. 392.
83. Chadwick MSS, 27 Oct., 1849.
84. Carlisle MSS, 2nd ser., Book 59, 19 Nov., 1849.
85. R. A. Lewis, op. cit., p. 240.
86. N.R.A., Shaftesbury (Broadlands) MSS, SHA/PD/5, 1 Jan., 1850.
87. Hodder, II, 318-19 and R. A. Lewis, op. cit., p. 243 say that Ashley resigned over this, but this would seem to be in error.
88. N.R.A., Shaftesbury (Broadlands) MSS, SHA/PD/5, 14 Jan., 1850.
89. Carlisle MSS, Diary of 7th Earl of Carlisle, 27 Mar., 1850.
90. ibid., 2nd ser., Book 60, 6 Mar., 1850.
91. ibid., 2nd ser., Book 58, 6 Dec., 1848.
92. ibid., 2nd ser., Book 60, 25 Feb., 1850.
93. ibid., 2nd ser., Book 60, 25 Mar., 1850.
94. ibid., Diary of the 7th Earl of Carlisle, 25 Mar., 1850.
95. ibid., 2nd ser., Book 60, 27 Mar., 1850.
96. Hansard, *Parl. Debates*, 3rd ser., CX, 354.
97. ibid., CXI, 698-700.
98. ibid., 708.
99. ibid., 857.
100. N.R.A., Shaftesbury (Broadlands) MSS, SHA/PD/5, 7 June, 1850.
101. ibid., SHA/PD/6, 12 Dec., 1850.
102. Letters and in Carlisle MSS, 2nd ser., Book 60, 14 Aug., 1850, and Book 61, 16 Jan., 1851.
103. Hansard, *Parl. Debates*, 3rd ser., CXI, 15-16. The bill was the Metropolitan Water Works (Henley on Thames and London Viaduct) Bill.
104. N.R.A., Shaftesbury (Broadlands) MSS, SHA/PD/5, 18 July, 1850.
105. ibid., SHA/PD/5, 18 July, 1850.
106. Chadwick MSS, 18 Sept., 1850.
107. ibid., 12 Oct., 1850.
108. ibid., 25 Oct., 1850.
109. N.R.A., Shaftesbury (Broadlands) MSS, SHA/PD/6, 7 Nov., 1850.
110. He attended only three meetings during the two years of his Presidency. (R.A. Lewis, op. cit., p. 245).
111. N.R.A., Shaftesbury (Broadlands) MSS, SHA/PD/6, 12 Dec., 1850.
112. R. A. Lewis, op. cit., 244-5.
113. N.R.A., Shaftesbury (Broadlands) MSS, SHA/PD/6, 12 Dec., 1850.
114. ibid., SHA/PD/6, 12 Dec., 1850.
115. ibid., SHA/PD/6, 23 Dec., 1850.

116. R. A. Lewis, op. cit., pp. 264–6. Letters are quoted on pp. 265–6. The Minutes of the Board relating to the dispute are in P.R.O., M.H. 5/4, 15, 16, 21 Jan., 1851.
117. N.R.A., Shaftesbury (Broadlands) MSS, SHA/PD/6, 8 Jan., 1851.
118. ibid., SHA/PD/6, 11 Jan., 1851.
119. ibid., SHA/PD/6, 15 Jan., 1851.
120. Chadwick MSS, 18 Jan., 1851.
121. N.R.A., Shaftesbury (Broadlands) MSS, SHA/PD/6, 9 Jan., 1851.
122. R. A. Lewis, op. cit., pp. 267–8.
123. N.R.A., Shaftesbury (Broadlands) MSS, SHA/PD/6, 15 Jan., 1851.
124. ibid., SHA/PD/6, 31 Jan., 1851.
125. See below p. 352–361.
126. J. T. Ward, *The Factory Movement*, pp. 348–52.
127. N.R.A., Shaftesbury (Broadlands) MSS, SHA/PD/5, 9 June, 1848.
128. ibid., SHA/PD/5, 1 Aug., 1848.
129. J. T. Ward, *The Factory Movement*, p. 358.
130. N.R.A., Shaftesbury (Broadlands) MSS, SHA/PD/5, 5 Mar., 1849.
131. J. T. Ward, *The Factory Movement*, p. 360.
132. N.R.A., Shaftesbury (Broadlands) MSS, SHA/PD/5, 9 June, 1849.
133. *The Manchester Guardian*, 13 June, 1849.
134. ibid., 20 June, 1849.
135. J. T. Ward, *The Factory Movement*, p. 370.
136. N.R.A., Shaftesbury (Broadlands) MSS, SHA/PD/5, 4 Oct., 1849.
137. ibid., SHA/PD/5, 1 Nov., 1849.
138. J. T. Ward, *The Factory Movement*, p. 370.
139. N.R.A., Shaftesbury (Broadlands) MSS, SHA/PD/5, 15 Feb., 1850.
140. Hammonds, p. 136.
141. J. T. Ward, *The Factory Movement*, p. 373.
142. *The Manchester Guardian*, 27 Feb., 1850. It was also hoped that Ashley would be given assistance from Lord John Manners and George Bankes.
143. Hansard, *Parl. Debates*, 3rd ser., CIX, 883 ff.
144. J. T. Ward, *The Factory Movement*, p. 379.
145. *The Times*, 27 Apr., 1850. See also J. T. Ward, *The Factory Movement*, pp 381–2.
146. *The Times*, 25 Apr., 1850.
147. Hansard, *Parl. Debates*, 3rd ser., CX, 1058.
148. ibid., 1133–4.
149. N.R.A., Shaftesbury (Broadlands) MSS, SHA/PD/5, 7 May, 1850.
150. *The Times*, 9 May, 1850.
151. N.R.A., Shaftesbury (Broadlands) MSS, SHA/PD/5, 8 May, 1850.
152. Hammonds, p. 144.
153. Both meetings are reported in *The Manchester Examiner and Times*, 15 May, 1850.
154. Hansard, *Parl. Debates*, 3rd ser., CX, 1431.
155. ibid., CXI, 846.
156. ibid., 852–3.
157. ibid., 855.
158. ibid., 1234–5.
159. ibid., 1235–6.
160. N.R.A., Shaftesbury (Broadlands) MSS, SHA/PD/5, 15 June, 1850.
161. Hansard, *Parl. Debates*, 3rd ser., CXI, 1283.
162. ibid., CXII, 1354.
163. N.R.A., Shaftesbury (Broadlands) MSS, SHA/PD/5, 9 May, 1850.

164. C. Driver, op. cit., pp. 502-3.
165. Hansard, *Parl. Debates,* 3rd ser., CXI, 832-5.
166. N.R.A., Shaftesbury (Broadlands) MSS, SHA/PD/5, 1 Nov., 1849.
167. ibid., SHA/PD/5, 22 Feb., 1850.
168. Battiscombe, p. 216.

12
Exigencies Spiritual and Personal, 1846–1851

Ashley's activities in the Evangelical world in the later 1840s and at the beginning of the 1850s were channelled in directions similar to those evident in the first half of the decade. He retained his interest in the numerous Evangelical societies devoted to mission at home and abroad in which he had already become a leading figure. Indeed, he succeeded to the Presidency of two important societies on the deaths of the previous Presidents: the London Jews Society in 1848 and the British and Foreign Bible Society in 1851. In the late 1840s, the Jerusalem Bishopric, in which the former society had such a close interest, was undergoing changes in policy.[1] The new Bishop, Gobat, was less concerned than Alexander had been to carry out a mission exclusively to the Jews. Gobat, indeed, was more interested in winning over to Protestantism the native Arab members of the Greek Orthodox Church and, with this in view, he set about establishing primary schools for the children of Greek Orthodox parents in the hope that they would provide a basis for his missionary work. Such an extension of the scope of the Bishopric from exclusive attention to Jews to increasing concern for Arabs aroused a great deal of criticism, both secular and ecclesiastical. The British Consul in Jerusalem felt that Gobat was considerably exceeding his authority, defined at the time of the creation of the Bishopric. The Greek Patriarchate was resentful of the Bishop's encroachments, and the Tractarian party in the Church of England – still active despite the demise of the Oxford Movement – was similarly opposed to his interference with the authority of the Greek Orthodox Church. The London Jews Society itself was by no means satisfied with the change of emphasis from Jew to Arab. Nevertheless, Gobat did achieve a measure of success. Various schools were established for Arab children; the church at Jerusalem – still unbuilt on Alexander's death – was completed and consecrated in January, 1849; the Foreign Secretary and the Archbishop of Canterbury both refused to forbid Gobat's activities in granting instruction and guidance to Christians of a different Church who sought it from him – an attitude which to all intents and purposes sanctioned his proselytising endeavours; and the Ottoman authorities acknowledged and declared legal the conversion of Christian Ottoman subjects to Protestantism. Even the London Jews Society came to acquiesce in Gobat's activities.

Ashley's attitude to the issue was more balanced than that of many others. In his speech to the London Jews Society in 1848, he mentioned that the Ottoman authorities had given recognition to Protestants as a distinct and separate element in the Ottoman Empire – they now stood, he said, on the same footing as the Greek, Armenian and Latin Churches. This, he argued, was one of the first fruits of the appointment of a Protestant Bishop, since the Ottoman authorities would recognise no sect or body not represented by some responsible head. He also pointed out that American Protestant missionaries had also benefited from the recognition. It would thus appear that Ashley did not object to the widening of the scope of the Bishopric and felt that it had certain advantages. But he still kept in sight the ultimate aim of the conversion of the Jews. He argued that the recognition given by the Ottoman Empire opened up the field for further effort in that direction; a vigorous but 'holy rivalry' could be entered into with the American missionaries to see who could do more good in the 'great cause' which had been undertaken; and, 'by communicating the Gospel to the Jews, be the means through them of finally propagating the Gospel over all the nations of the world.'[2] Ashley, therefore, did not regard Gobat's activities as incompatible with the original objects of the Jerusalem Bishopric. And he still regarded the Jewish question as a means to the Second Advent. At the end of 1848, he looked to the 'regathering and restoration of the Jewish people' as an event to be followed by 'scriptural results'.[3]

As in the case of the London Jews Society, Ashley's Presidency of the British and Foreign Bible Society marked the recognition of a long-standing interest in and support for its objectives. As a Vice-President, he had spoken in praise of the Society's 'great and leading principle': that the Scriptures should be distributed in a language which would be understood by the people.[4] These, he said, had always been his own principles. He wondered if he should accept the invitation to become President of the Society on the grounds that he was already President of several important societies – he might appear 'a monopolist of place and power' and not be able to give as much time to it as he would wish. But he did finally accept the invitation and was happy to become head of what he called 'the greatest and noblest of the Societies'.[5] One of his first efforts on its behalf was to secure a place at the Great Exhibition of 1851 for its translations of the Bible. He felt that it was especially necessary to display the translations as 'proofs of all that we had done to the praise of God and all that we are capable of doing'; these should be set beside all other objects on display, many of them being implements of war. This, however, met with some resistance, and it appears that Ashley had an interview with Prince Albert on the subject. Ashley had to urge the case in intellectual terms: the numerous translations were surely a 'wonderful proof of intellectual power'. This seems finally to have convinced Albert, who promised to help the Society to secure a place at the Exhibition. He succeeded, although Ashley was not very happy with the place that was given, nor was he altogether impressed with the general tone of the Exhibition. It put too much stress on intellectual, scientific and material advancement as signs of moral progress, whereas, Ashley wrote, all such advancement 'may consist with the hardest and vilest hearts.' Only the one hundred and forty eight translations of the Bible – 'thrust . . . into a remote corner' – distinguished a moral from a material existence, a Christian from a heathen generation. 'And yet we are told that this "great fair" is to show the world's progress.'[6]

In these years, however, Ashley not only confirmed his place in two societies in which he had long shown close interest. Other more recently acquired activities were also a matter of concern to him. The Malta College proved a source of anxiety. The first Master of the College, the Revd. J. Hickman, had to be dismissed: he was, Ashley wrote, a 'proud, wilful and rebellious spirit' – the committee had thought him 'at least a Christian', but his letters seemed to prove that he was a pantheist.[7] In 1849, however, Ashley was pleased with the College's progress, feeling that it promised to be a centre of religious life and civilisation to the people of the East.[8] Events nearer home also occupied him. In the aftermath of the Irish Famine of 1845–6 a new opportunity for missionary enterprise presented itself. A fund for temporal relief in Ireland was already in existence and Ashley made his own domestic economies to try to help the Irish: thus he gave orders that no more potatoes should be bought for his house.[9] But spiritual matters were also at stake, and, in December, 1846, a special fund 'for the spiritual exigencies of Ireland' was launched by the Society for Church Missions to the Roman Catholics of Ireland. The Society felt that to remedy physical calamities in Ireland should be the task of the government. To assist with filling the spiritual wants and necessities of the country should be left to individual benevolence, and it sought to raise £20,000 for the purpose.[10] The money was to go partly towards grants to existing missionary societies. Thus an agreement was reached with the Irish Society that it would direct its efforts towards the Irish speaking population: the Society for Church Missions would appeal chiefly to English-speaking Roman Catholics. The Society for Church Missions also sponsored its own scripture readers and school masters. Ashley was a Vice-President of the Society –

he gave £10 to the Fund and was keenly interested in its work. He felt that in the circumstances of the late 1840s in Ireland, there was 'a wonderful opening for the admission of the Gospel'.[11]

The situation in Britain at this time was no less urgent, and Ashley was more than ever convinced of the pressing need to strengthen Christian influences. He was concerned to provide more Church of England teacher-training schools. He took the chair at a meeting in 1849 which set up the Church of England Metropolitan Training Institution. Its object was to train 'pious persons as masters and mistresses of Juvenile schools, connected with the Established Church, in principles, scriptural, Evangelical and Protestant.'[12] The College was situated at Highbury and was financed partly by private contributions and partly by the Committee of the Privy Council on Education, although this carried no rights of inspection. Ashley took an interest in a similar institution set up in Cheltenham in 1849.[13] He was also extremely anxious to increase the number of clergymen. He was Patron of the Clerical Education Aid Fund, instituted in 1845 with the object of giving financial assistance to young men who wished to enter holy orders. Between 1845 and 1850, the Fund helped to complete the education of sixteen young men of 'decided piety, Evangelical sentiments . . . and attachment to the Established Church,' and ten others were in the process of completing their education.[14] But he knew that it was extremely difficult to provide a sufficient number of clergy to examine – as he put it in 1847 – 'all the dark corners and bring under scriptural tuition the many hundreds of thousands who seemed to be almost shut out from the very shade of the Gospel.'[15] Thus he continued to support the work of the Scripture Readers Society and, above all, that of the Church Pastoral Aid Society. He told its annual meeting in May, 1847, that the Society had done invaluable work in the twelve years since its creation – he wondered what would have been 'the issue of things' had not God 'put it into the hearts of certain people . . . to raise up this great dam against that flood of impiety and ignorance that was on the point of desolating the country.'[16] But, in the circumstances of 1848–9, when revolutions swept Europe and disturbance threatened in Britain, there was an even greater need for the agencies of Evangelical religion to work at full stretch. In 1848, Ashley told the Society that, if the country were to stand erect during the present difficulties, it would only be through the diffusion and reception of Evangelical principles; religion alone could provide the firm and lasting stability of the time; and the Church, acting on pure and Evangelical impulses, would be the 'police and standing army of the great empire'.[17] In 1849, he returned to similar, if somewhat broader, themes. He told the Society that the existence of the realm and all its institutions would be decided in the next ten years. And, he continued:

it is not by might or by arms, by science, by commercial prosperity, or by secular education that this country can be saved. It is only by the evangelicalization of her people – it is only by giving to them . . . the internal principle of self-control that will enable them in some measure, to use their privileges so that they may be enabled to govern themselves. . . .[18]

The Church Pastoral Aid Society – 'the very best Society, to my mind, that ever existed in these realms,' as Ashley said in 1849[19] – was uniquely qualified to carry out this task: its lay agency provided a means to 'penetrate and percolate those large masses to which access (was) very often denied to the ordained minister.'[20]

Ashley thus retained and strengthened his links with the Evangelical societies during these years. He did not, indeed, always play an active role in the day-to-day workings of them. He told the London Jews Society in 1850 that he had not been able to give time or attention to the detailed affairs of the Society,[21] and he said to the Church Pastoral Aid Society in 1849 and again in 1850 that he was able to praise the work of its committee because he had taken so little part in its labours.[22] But his yearly appearances on the platform gave him an opportunity to review the year's work and to urge the society in question to continue its efforts.

Further, in parallel with his activities in matters of social concern, Ashley used his renewed membership of Parliament after 1847 to promote ecclesiastical measures which were of an Evangelical nature. In April, 1848, he supported a proposal that the distinction between Episcopal and common funds be discontinued. This distinction had limited the application of surplus revenues of Archbishops and Bishops to Episcopal purposes and had disallowed any part of such a surplus to be applied to the relief of needy parishes. In his speech, Ashley urged the pressing need for an increase in the number of working clergy. He, more than most, had seen the wants of the population, and – echoing his remarks to the Church Pastoral Aid Society – he told the House that if another ten years were to elapse before attention was given to the grievances of the people, he believed that 'the evil would require the faith – ay, and the inspiration – of a David to tear down that monstrous and almost unassailable Goliath. . . .'[23] He returned to such themes in 1849, when he put forward a motion for the appointment of a Commission to inquire into the practicability of subdividing the larger parishes, so that no parish contained more than four thousand souls. This scheme also took up points which he discussed in these years at the Annual Meetings of the Church Pastoral Aid Society. Ashley constantly referred to the need for work being done at the parish level. Only under the parochial system could the clergyman have daily access to his flock and his flock to him – it was a 'great supervisory and parental system which tended to the security of the Church and the welfare and security of the people.'[24] But with very large parishes, this was quite impossible. A division into more manageable units would make the task of the clergyman easier, although – as he assured the Church Pastoral Aid Society – it would not dispense with the need for lay assistance.[25] Thus the subdivision of parishes would allow greater opportunities for the work of mission, and, by so doing, it would add the finishing touches to efforts which had been made for social reform: it would, as Ashley put it, be a 'glorious winding up of (his) several schemes for social improvement.'[26] Now that some progress had been made in the things of the body, there would be increased scope for attention to the things of the spirit and the gathering in of the harvest.

There were, however, difficulties to be encountered. The Archbishop of Canterbury, Sumner, who succeeded Howley in 1848, was not unsympathetic to his ideas but was cautious. The Archbishop wrote to Russell on 5 February, 1849,[27] that Ashley's scheme was 'rather of a revolutionary character', but, he added, 'the world is not standing still; and it might produce a great reform.' He pointed out that Ashley's plan was, in many ways, an extension of Peel's measure of 1843.[28] Some two hundred 'new' parishes had been created under the terms of that measure, containing about four or five thousand people, but lack of money had prevented the process being taken any further. 'No doubt,' wrote Sumner, 'one thousand more such parishes might be formed, with excellent effect, if we had the means . . .' and, he added, 'Lord Ashley has succeeded already in difficult enterprises. . . .' One difficulty, however, was that Ashley's scheme went further than Peel's, since it would give to each new parish its own poor rate and overseers. This might be an improvement but, Sumner wrote, it would raise a storm, and, however beneficial the measure, it would be difficult to execute. However, Ashley met the Archbishop on 20 February and said that he had given up his original intention of touching the temporal concerns of parishes, and this, wrote Sumner to Russell,[29] removed the greatest practical difficulty and left his plan virtually an extension of Peel's. 'Such subdivision of parishes,' he added, 'leading to better pastoral super-intendence, is the great desideratum;' and it might well be assisted by the Commission which Ashley had in mind. The way, therefore, seemed clear, and, on 28 February, Ashley noted that Russell had said that he would not oppose his motion.[30] There was one last-minute difficulty when Russell wrote again on 1 March, asking Ashley to postpone his motion on the grounds that it would be opposed by the Dissenters, but finally, on the same day, Russell changed his mind and asked Ashley to proceed.[31] Ashley thus put forward his motion that a Commission be appointed.[32] He mentioned the faulty distribution of responsibility and labour. Some clergymen had an impossible task to superintend the highly populated parishes committed to their charge.

They would never get to know their people, and working people would abandon church-going, if they ever had the habit. The number of children attending schools connected with the Church was too small, and there was also the fact that very large parishes gave vicars and rectors undue power over their curates. Smaller parishes would, therefore, be much more effective units. The Commission, Ashley said, would respect all vested rights and existing incumbents – any arrangements for subdivision would not take place until vacancies occurred. Touching on the financial aspects of his plan, he said that the division of larger livings would yield some funds for the endowment of smaller benefices, and he looked for increased liberality from the members of the Church. The number of parishes with a population exceeding four thousand was two hundred and seventy nine; an addition of five hundred clergy would meet this need and, at £300 each per year, £15,000 would be required to provide the necessary funds. This, he argued, was not a large sum to ask 'from the pious and patriotic members of the Church of England.' After Ashley's speech, there were some criticisms that his motion did not take regard of the efforts of the Dissenters,[33] but Ashley denied that he was being unfair to such efforts.[34] His motion was successful: on 9 March, Grey announced that the Commission would be appointed.[35] Ashley was delighted at the success of his scheme; 'by this means,' he had written on 1 March, 'the Church can and will, God blessing us, recover her just position and "conservatise" the Kingdom.'[36]

A further Evangelical cause which Ashley attempted to assist after his return to Parliament concerned Sunday labour. Since the late 1830s, the Sunday question had lain relatively dormant: the advocates of Sabbatarianism had been concerned with small and local issues and had lacked any real cause to bind them together in a national effort. This, however, they received in the late 1830s by a re-opening of the issue of Sunday labour in the London Post Office. The first mention of the scheme was in October, 1847, when the press carried a notice to the effect that, owing to pressure of business in the Post Office, it had become necessary for the authorities to give careful consideration to the question of Sunday labour.[37] This alerted the Sabbatarians. A special meeting of the Committee of the Lord's Day Observance Society was held at Exeter Hall on 5 March, 1847, 'to confer with Lord Ashley in reference to the desecration of the Lord's Day by the Post Office.'[38] Ashley took the chair and it was agreed to address a memorial to the government 'deprecating any despatch of letters from London on the Lord's Day and further urging the suspension of the transmission of mail and of the delivery of letters throughout the Kingdom during the 24 hours of that day.'[39] This was a much more ambitious plan than that of the late 1830s,[40] when the London Post Office had been the only matter of concern. Three thousand one hundred persons signed the memorial, which was presented to Russell in May, 1848, by a group of Evangelicals, with Ashley as one of its leaders.[41]

Russell was non-committal about the future plans of the government, but the plans were being made. These involved the closure of provincial branches of the Post Office for an average of three-and-a-half hours more on a Sunday, but letters were to be forwarded through London on a Sunday so that they might be delivered the following day, and this demanded a larger staff for Sunday work in the London Post Office. This plan was formulated in February, 1849, and it was to be introduced in October, but kept secret until then. In late September, however, news of the government's policy got out in the London press. The Lord's Day Observance Society was furiously active: meetings were held and memorials composed objecting to the arrangements. And the whole campaign was organised on a nationwide basis. Deputations waited on the government, but Russell was unwilling to abandon the scheme, which was finally announced on 11 October. Provincial offices throughout England and Wales were to be closed on Sundays from 10 a.m. to 5 p.m. and Sunday mail deliveries were to be restricted to one. Forward letters were, however, to be sent through the London Office and were to be dealt with on a Sunday so that they might arrive the following day.

Ashley first heard rumours of the government's plans to introduce firm proposals on 28 September when he received a letter about them from Seeley: 'well this is strong indeed,' he wrote, and he commented on how inappropriate such plans were in the immediate aftermath of the abatement of cholera – it was a proof, to his mind, that 'heavy judgments' were impending over the country.[42] On 6 October, he wrote in his Diary that the movement to increase Sunday labour was 'the fruit of a self-seeking Mammon-serving spirit; and the more difficult to encounter as it is hypocritically based on a pretence of reducing the labour of the provincial offices.'[43] The same day, he wrote to Russell.[44] He had, he said, always been most anxious to support Russell's government and, in this spirit, wrote to warn the Prime Minister that he had no notion of the strong and determined resistance that would be made to the arrangement. 'It will expose you, I suspect,' Ashley wrote, 'to some personal and political annoyance.' On 28 October, as the scheme began, Ashley hoped that God would 'blow upon it' and 'bring to confusion this vile attempt.'[45]

It is certainly true that the reaction to the government's plan was extremely strong. The Lord's Day Observance Society was active in organising Anglicans of a Sabbatarian frame of mind throughout the country. There was also a more widely-based Metropolitan Committee, composed of Anglicans and Dissenters, and the Dissenters had their own Committee. All energies were bent on achieving the entire cessation of Sunday postal labour. Faced with this storm, the government did make certain concessions, such as the earlier closing of post offices on Sundays, but the Sabbatarians were not satisfied and wanted the complete closing of offices. Ashley himself thought that the remedy lay in closing all Post Offices, provincial and metropolitan, from midnight on Saturday until 2 a.m. on Monday. Numerous petitions were organised, and, on 30 May, 1849, Ashley gave notice in the House of an Address to the Queen requesting the cessation of Sunday collection and delivery of letters throughout the Kingdom. In his speech,[46] Ashley stressed the 'scriptural character of the institution of the Sabbath' and the religious obligation to observe it, and he also mentioned the beneficial effects which greater rest and relaxation would have on those who worked on a Sunday. 'If relaxation was necessary for those who lived in great measure of ease,' he said, 'how requisite it must be for those sons of toil who laboured from morning to night.' And, referring to the feeling on the subject, he rejoiced that, here, 'vox populi' and 'vox dei' were in strict harmony.

Ashley introduced his motion on a morning session of the House, and the attendance was thin. The government opposed him – it was pointed out that other persons worked on a Sunday, like policemen and coastguards, and that the government had done its best to reduce Sunday postal labour. But the motion was carried.[47] Thereupon, the government decided to act upon it, without consulting the Lords, and the Queen was asked to accede to the government's decision. She did so: and thus from 23 June, all Sunday labour in the post offices throughout the Kingdom and all Sunday collections and deliveries were to cease.

But opposition to the new arrangements was not long in expressing itself. The metropolitan press denounced it: merchants and underwriters associated with Lloyds protested against the inconvenience to commerce which would result. Ashley himself was widely criticised. *Punch* portrayed him as Lord Sackcloth-in-Ashleys. He was well aware of the hostility towards him: 'well be it so,' he wrote; 'if the cause is God's. I am the gainer in the long run. And all this because certain aristocratical people will not have their gossip in the country every Sunday.'[48] At this particular time – the summer of 1850 – Ashley had also to bear the criticism of the factory reformers, and he noted on 22 June that the factory bill and the postal resolutions taken together had brought on him 'a variety, universality and bitterness of attack quite original'.[49] Faced with mounting opposition, the government in July appointed a Commission to inquire whether Sunday labour could be reduced, but letters still delivered. This reported on 10 August: it recommended a return to the arrangements in London introduced before Ashley's resolution and one Sunday delivery outside London, unless local feeling was clearly against it. This was accepted. Ashley noted that the government had reversed the Post Office resolution: 'Much joy manifested by the "anti-Saint" party and much grief, I doubt not, by those who are once again brought under Egyptian bondage.'[50] He was not, in fact, surprised by what had happened – he knew that he had stirred a hornet's nest[51] and even as the Post Offices closed felt that 'every trick, scheme and juggling' would be adopted to 'render the measure odious.'[52] Nevertheless, he felt it a source of satisfaction to reflect that he had 'laboured for the repose of these poor men.'[53]

In 1851, however, the Sunday question was overshadowed by another cause into which Evangelicals poured their energy, and Ashley was prominent among them. This was precipitated by the publication of a papal brief in Rome in September, 1850, creating a Roman Catholic hierarchy in England, based on twelve new sees. The following day, Nicholas Wiseman was made a Cardinal and Archbishop of Westminster and, on 7 October, 1850, Wiseman issued a pastoral letter 'out of the Flaminian Gate of Rome', ordering it to be read in the Churches of his diocese. The letter exalted papal claims, and Wiseman did not make it clear that his jurisdiction extended only over Catholics. The pastoral letter was read in the Churches on 17 October. These events provoked a highly unfavourable reaction in England. Russell himself was indignant. He was already irritated with the Pope for refusing to acknowledge his attempts to advance higher education in Ireland by means of mixed colleges – this, Russell felt, was poor reward for his past willingness to further Catholic causes. Russell was also on edge over relations between Church and State in England. These had been highlighted by the Gorham Case of 1850. The Bishop of Exeter, Phillpotts – a noted High Churchman – refused to present a clergyman, Gorham, to a living in his diocese on account of Gorham's views on Baptism.[54] Gorham had appealed to the Privy Council, and the judgment, given in 1850, was that the Bishop had no right to refuse to present him. This clearly implied the control of the Church by the State and was not to the liking of the Tractarian party. Russell, however, welcomed the decision – he regarded the Tractarians as little less than Roman Catholics and would have been prepared to see them follow the example of Newman and secede, if this was the only way in which the Church could remain Protestant.[55] Russell was, therefore, in no mood to receive what he regarded as an aggressive step in the shape of the Roman Catholic Church's plans for re-establishing a territorial hierarchy, and, on 4 November, gave vent to his feelings in a letter to the Bishop of Durham, which attacked the measures of the Pope 'as a pretension of supremacy over the realm of England and a claim to sole and undivided sway. . . .'[56] But if Russell was antagonistic to the Pope, he was even more so to the Tractarians. He attacked them bitterly as 'enemies within the gate, indulging in their mummeries of superstition.' The

Durham Letter was an injudicious act on Russell's part. The Tractarians were not responsible for encouraging the Pope's action, and the Letter exposed Russell to the charge that he was abandoning his past professions of tolerance towards Roman Catholicism and attempting to strike a popular cause to strengthen the position of his government.[57]

The Durham Letter was, however, greeted with acclaim by the Evangelicals within the Church of England and outside it, and, in particular, by Ashley. Ashley had, from 1846, sought to give advice to Russell over religious matters. He had had two interviews with Russell in October, 1846, to talk over the state of the Church.[58] He was anxious to warn Russell of the continuing dangers of Puseyism and he wished to advise him on Church appointments which would avert these dangers. He asked Russell if he might send him a list of names, adding that the Prime Minister might 'throw it behind the fire or consult it' as he saw fit. Russell had agreed to this and had expressed his dislike for Tractarianism, and Ashley had left the interview satisfied that he had done his duty, having 'testified to this Prime Minister, as to the last.' He did not think Russell to be a man with 'much spiritual knowledge of religion', and, although he preferred Russell as a man to Peel, he doubted if his efforts would bear fruit. The postal matter divided Ashley from Russell, and, in November, 1849, Ashley wrote that it was manifest that Russell held his opinions ecclesiastical and religious in 'supreme contempt'.[59] Russell denied this, replying that he had often acted in accordance with Ashley's ideas, but must reserve some liberty of judgment to himself.[60] In the light of this reply, Ashley asked to be allowed to qualify the words 'supreme contempt', adding that he saw that it was 'not quite so bad'.[61] In fact, he continued to offer Russell advice over appointments to bishoprics, and both men saw the question of 'Papal Aggression' in very similar terms. Ashley strongly approved of the Durham Letter: he regarded it as 'bold, manly, Protestant and true'. It was, indeed, 'ten times more imbued with religious Protestantism' than Ashley had expected, and he regarded it as 'the finest thing in 300 years of our history. . . .'[62] Ashley also took a very active part in the meetings held in the country on the subject. He took the chair at a conference for clergy and laity in November to devise a way of meeting the crisis. The meeting lasted for five hours and ended with the appointment of a committee to 'stir (the) country'.[63] This was the Protestant Defence Committee, the purpose of which was to encourage the presentation of petitions to Parliament and to assist with their preparation and drafting.[64] On 5 December, 1850, Ashley made a powerful speech at the Freemasons Hall where a meeting was held, attended by lay members of the Church of England.[65] He condemned the 'monstrous audacity' of the Pope and asked for the Queen's help in suppressing Romish innovations in the Church of England, which, he claimed, had encouraged the Pope to take the step. It was, as he put it in his Diary, a meeting of laity 'against Popery and Puseyism'[66] and he was well satisfied with the reception which he was given. He thought it more than merely 'boisterous' but 'deep and sincere' with 'all the character of being permanent and religious'.[67] Again, throughout the early months of 1851, Ashley was extremely active in meetings of the Protestant Defence Committee, and, on 20 March, presented an Address to the Queen against 'the aggression of the Pope and the Tractarian innovations lately introduced into the service of the Church of England.'[68] He wrote to Russell that such a step was 'indispensable for the health and safety of the Church'.[69]

Further, when Wiseman claimed that the setting up of the Jerusalem Bishopric was a parallel case, Ashley wrote to Russell that 'the Cardinal abounds in mis-statements.' He pointed out that Britain had diplomatic permission from the Sultan to establish the Bishopric, that the title was 'Bishop of the Church of England and Ireland *in* Jerusalem' and that the jurisdiction was limited to the Church of England congregation there and was not universal, like that of the Cardinal.[70] In January, 1851, he reminded Russell that, as Prime Minister, he had 'much to do' and, he added, 'you have great means and will have much to answer for. May God give you strength.'[71] The following month, on 7 February, Russell did, indeed, introduce legislation, the Ecclesiastical Titles Bill, which pronounced all ecclesiastical titles, except those of the Church of England, illegal and declared void all donations and bequests given to Catholic Bishops under their unlawful titles under pain of forfeiture to the Crown. The bill was to have a long and complicated passage through Parliament. Its progress was briefly interrupted by the resignation of Russell in February, 1851; and, on his return, its terms were made less stringent. When it finally passed in July, the penalty of forfeiture was dropped and a fine of £100 was the only penalty to be exacted for disregarding the Act. Ashley was very anxious about these events. He was appalled by the prospect of Russell's resignation, and, when he heard rumours of it, he counselled Russell that he must not 'abandon hastily a charge to which God (had) specially called (him) in this resistance to the Papacy;' he also reminded Russell of the words of God to Joshua : 'Be strong and of a good courage. . . .'[72] He noted in his Diary his dislike and distrust of those who opposed Russell's bill, who included the prominent Peelites. Thus a speech by Gladstone showed 'much intellectual power' but 'no patriotism or Protestantism'.[73] He disapproved of the watering down of the bill, although he recognised Russell's difficulties in adhering to its earlier provisions. But the most positive part which Ashley played was to deliver two long speeches on the subject in February,[74] and March,[75] 1851. In his first speech, Ashley rebutted the various charges that had been made against the government's original proposals, in particular the charge that it was a restriction on religious liberty and took back the concessions granted by Catholic Emancipation in 1829. The measure of 1829 had, indeed, made it clear that Roman Catholics should have full rights and privileges to develop their religion, but there was no reason why a Bishop should have a territorial title – it was a purely spiritual office. Indeed, the possession of a territorial title by a Roman Catholic Bishop – such as Wiseman's title of Archbishop of Westminster – gave him rights and privileges which interfered with the rights of the Crown and the civil and religious liberties of British subjects. Protestants must resist this; if they did not, an 'ecclesiastical empire' would be set up in the heart of the British metropolis and it was very questionable how far canon law could co-exist with civil law. In his second speech in March, Ashley ranged over similar points. He regretted the changes made in the government's original proposals and felt that the bill was mutilated; nevertheless, the residue was 'exceedingly valuable as a solemn, national and Parliamentary protest against this Papal aggression.'

There was, then, in the pursuit of Ashley's Evangelicalism in the late 1840s, much continuity with his activities in the first half of the decade. He remained concerned with matters of 'Prophecy and Protestantism'. In terms of belief, too, the old 'hallmarks' were still there. He remained intensely concerned with sin and salvation, especially at the time of death. On Melbourne's death in 1848, Ashley wondered if he had died 'in the faith of his Lord and in sure and certain hope. God only knows.'[76] Ashley clearly had doubts. As Melbourne had died, those who stood about his bed said 'not a prayer, not a syllable about repentance, mercy, the Almighty Judge, the only Saviour.' It was not the death of a heathen, Ashley wrote, for he would have had the image of a ceremony – it was the death of an animal. And yet Ashley's 'dear, kind mother-in-law' wrote complacently that Melbourne was in heaven. To say this of any 'modern man', Ashley wrote, was bold; to assert it of any one who had never sought it by turning his paths to righteousness was 'perilous presumption'.[77] The death of Peel in 1850, the result of a riding fall, came as a great shock to Ashley, bringing back memories of past dealings with him. And the circumstances of his death could not escape Ashley. It was, he wrote to Evelyn, a solemn lesson for a heedless race, for Peel, in the full height of his physical and intellectual capacity, had been 'plucked like a branch and cast on to the bed of death.'[78] And to Ashley's constant questionings as to the strength of Peel's religious commitment in life was added his further query about Peel's spiritual state in death: 'did he die in perfect peace?' Ashley asked.[79] This was also a matter of supreme importance to Ashley when his own son, Francis, died in 1849.[80] And, looking beyond the life of individuals, Ashley maintained his firm belief in the Second Coming. He wrote in December, 1847, that every hour of reading, every hour of reflection, strengthened him more and more in the conviction that the Second Advent was the hope of all the lands of the earth,[81] and in August, 1849, wrote that the Second Advent was 'more and more necessary for the peace of mankind'.[82]

But if continuity with past practices and profession is evident in these years, it has also been argued that Ashley's religious commitment and outlook became more rigid and uncompromising at this time; and that the years 1850 and 1851 saw the 'hardening of Ashley's Evangelical zeal into something very near bigotry.'[83] This has been linked to the death of his friend Edward Bickersteth in 1850. Bickersteth had exercised a great influence on Ashley and, although a staunch Evangelical, he was a kindly and gentle person. His place as counsellor and friend to Ashley was, in large measure, to be taken by Alexander Haldane, owner of *The Record* newspaper. In the past[84] Ashley had dissociated himself from the newspaper's extreme Evangelical views, but it may be maintained that, as his friendship with Haldane developed from 1849–50, Ashley was exposed to an Evangelicalism more harsh and strident than that of Bickersteth.

All this has, indeed, some truth, although it should be noted that over 'Papal aggression' – as over Maynooth in 1845 – Ashley stopped short of an extreme position. Before the meeting of December, 1850, at the Freemason's Hall, Samuel Wilberforce, Bishop of Oxford, wrote to Ashley urging him to concentrate his attack on genuine Romanising tendencies in the Church and not to brand as Romanisers all those, such as himself, who 'were of the school of Andrews, Hooker, Beveridge etc.'[85] Ashley replied that this was not his intention – his movement, he said, was 'against Popery without and Popery within' and Wilberforce could rest assured that he would not 'say a word to limit that fair latitude of opinion that must always be permitted within certain points.'[86] Again, in his speech of March, 1851, on the Ecclesiastical Titles Bill, he was careful not to attack the Catholic laity, but only the priesthood; indeed, he said that the most mischievous effect of the matter was the disturbing and unsettling effect it had had among 'one of the most orderly, most loyal and most respectable portions of Her Majesty's subjects – English Roman Catholics.'[87] He noted that he had heard that Catholics had expected a violent attack on them, but they had not received one.[88] But although Ashley still did not indulge in the most violent manifestations of Evangelical sentiment, it is true that he displayed a growing impenetrability in these years. He admitted in 1848 that he never refreshed his mind with new stores;[89] his intellect, 'small at all times, is blunted,' he wrote, 'because never sharpened by thought or reading.'[90] Thus, as Ashley grew near the age of fifty, the old traits, understandably, grew deeper; and he became further entrenched in his beliefs by what he saw as the exigencies of the times, religious, moral and social. He could find no sympathy with others who had remedies for these problems which were different from his own, even although they were inspired by Christian conviction. Thus he disliked and distrusted the outlook of the Christian Socialists – men like F. D. Maurice and Charles Kingsley – who were active in the late 1840s and early 1850s and who sought to bring Christianity to bear on the social problems of the time and urged the need for cooperation in society rather than competition. Ashley's dislike was partly founded on 'secular' differences: his belief in hierarchy and rank could not co-exist with what he saw as the Christian Socialists' tendency towards 'liberty, equality, fraternity (brotherhood they call it) as the principle of the Gospels'.[91] But there was also antagonism on religious grounds between himself and Maurice. In 1843, Maurice had addressed a pamphlet to Ashley *On Right and Wrong Methods of Supporting Protestantism* in which he had urged Ashley to refrain from attacking Tractarianism in the interests of the unity of the Church.[92] There were, then, clear differences between Ashley and Maurice, and to expect them to have worked together is somewhat unrealistic. Moreover, Ashley was more practical in his approach than Maurice, and had much more capacity, for example, for the grinding work of committees in the cause of his objectives. But his failure to see any good in Christian Socialism was a sign of his increasing unresponsiveness to new ideas.

On Christmas Day and Boxing Day, 1850, Ashley set himself the task of reviewing his past career in all its aspects.[93] For the public he had, as a member of Parliament, laboured on many issues: lunacy, employment in factories, mines and printworks, public health, subdivision of parishes. Outside Parliament, he had spared no trouble or expense – and both, he noted, had been excessive – for Ragged Schools, Model Lodging Houses, the Malta College, Emigration, in addition to 'meetings by day and by night on every imaginable subject'. He also asked what had been gained 'for the cause of our blessed Master'. Possibly here, he conceded, there was an 'awakened attention, though but partially so, to the wants and rights of the poor; to the powers and duties of the rich;' perhaps a 'freer, safer use of religious sentiment and expression'. He also asked what he had gained for himself. He had, in these years, continually developed the theme that every man was against him and that the public were tired of him. 'The business of a philanthropist,' he noted in 1849, '(is) a heavy and despicable one.'[94] And he reverted to these thoughts in his review in 1850. He had no friends in State or Church, Press or Public – even the factory operatives had turned against him. He had gained neither power nor patronage, influence nor fame.

It was a sad catalogue, showing Ashley in the depths of self-pity. What was, perhaps, surprising was his claim that all he had achieved for his efforts was 'peace of mind'. For, despite his deep religious beliefs, this was something which Ashley never enjoyed, and, at this period of his life, it was notably absent. These years were, indeed, ones of considerable personal strain, anxiety and sadness. His own health was far from good. Writing at the end of 1849,[95] he commented that since August, 1848, he had scarcely enjoyed a week of consecutive health and had passed through every form of nervous symptom. These had, indeed, taken various forms. As in the past, he complained of noises in his ears – 'roarings', as he called them; sleeplessness, broken and restless nights, vibration of the body during the night, dreams. He took medicine and was careful with his diet, but there was little relief: the symptoms recurred and he sometimes wondered if he would ever be well again. It seems that no clear cause could be established for the 'roarings' in his ears: he wrote that 'they come and they go and no cause can be traced.'[96] But part of the cause for these and the other disorders from which he suffered was almost certainly over-work. His doctor in 1849 ascribed his symptoms to 'over-toil, over-anxiety, over-sensitiveness to . . . subjects handled during many years,' and he also advised him that he must be 'more moderate or utterly disabled.'[97] Ashley did, indeed, take autumn holidays in Scotland and he went to Paris in the spring of 1850 and 1851. But, for the most part, these were years of immense activity: of time 'broken into bits by letters, interviews boards.'[98] Even on holiday, Ashley did not completely relax. When in Scotland in 1850, he visited Glasgow to make speeches and 'to stir up the wealthy on behalf of Lodging Houses;'[99] he also visited Edinburgh and attended meetings and committees.[100] In Paris in 1850 and 1851, he visited Ragged Schools and, indeed, part of his purpose there was to examine the homes of the working classes and make comparisons between them and those in London. Thus, over-work contributed to his ill-health, and there was also the emotional strain and frustration of not always achieving what he wanted. 'Toil, toil, toil,' he wrote in April, 1850, 'nor should I lament, could I say fruit, fruit, fruit,'[101] and he felt that his work on the Board of Health and all the difficulties which he encountered there contributed in no small measure to his 'disorders'.[102]

A further source of the nervousness and tension which Ashley suffered in these years – and which must surely have contributed to his 'roarings' and other physical symptoms – may be traced to financial and family matters. He complained in March, 1848, that his condition was approaching that of a 'brat' in a Ragged School. He bought nothing for himself and he was getting daily deeper and deeper into difficulties: nine children could not be supported and fed 'by a trifle'.[103] He wrote in August of the same year that things were 'very black' – his expenses were increasing as his children and private and public efforts demanded much more.[104] Ashley's responsibilities, in fact, increased with the birth of a sixth son and tenth child, Cecil, on 8 August, 1849. His eldest son, Anthony, moreover, continued to cause him great anxiety. In January, 1848, Ashley wrote of a debt of £75 which Anthony had incurred for clothes, having already received nearly £40 for them, and more bills were to follow. 'The boy is weak and childish, below his years,' Ashley wrote, 'without a particle of restraining principle . . . I see nothing in him to please or comfort me, but his good temper.'[105] In January, 1848, indeed, Ashley and Minny finally decided that Anthony should go to sea and in March, Ashley took him to Sheerness and signed him on to the *Havannah*. It was a sad parting: they would not see him for three years. But it seemed to be for the best – life at home or at College, Ashley felt, would not be good for Anthony, with his amiable but feckless ways and his interest in amusements and clothes.[106] Ashley and Minny received letters during the voyage. Sometimes Ashley seemed to detect signs of improvement, but, at other times, these proved to be illusory: a letter from Sydney in January, 1851, spoke of debts and also of regret at having incurred them and promises for the future. Ashley wrote that he would do his best to pay the debts, but he was not very hopeful of improvement: 'I fear,' he wrote in January, 1851, 'that with all his amiable qualities, he is set for my grief and dishonour.'[107]

Worries of this kind, however, by no means completed the scope of Ashley's anxieties – others were considerably worse. The health of his third son, Maurice, had given anxiety for some time, but, at Easter, 1848, a few months after Anthony's departure, it became clear that the boy had epilepsy. And, as the doctors had warned, there were other attacks to come. Thus in August, 1848, while in Scotland, Ashley was roused by a maid to say that Maurice was seized by another bad fit, and they were constantly to recur. A great number of doctors were employed, at considerable expense, but there was no improvement. Maurice's condition deteriorated and, in September, 1849, the doctors advised that he must leave home and live a life of solitude and tranquillity – this, they said, might bring about an improvement by the time the boy was twenty-one. His age at the time was fourteen. Ashley had doubts about this, but he had to agree and Maurice went abroad, spending much time at the Hague. But there was very little sign of recovery: on 23 August, 1850, Ashley noted that he had received 'melancholy accounts' that Maurice was unwell – 'solitude and separation,' Ashley wrote, 'have done nothing for him.'[108] Moreover, Ashley had worries about the health of his daughters, Victoria, Mary and Constance and the newly born baby, Cecil, was sickly at first.

But the greatest blow to Ashley in these years was the death of his second son, Francis, in May, 1849. On 19 May, 1849, Ashley received word from

Harrow that Francis was unwell with what was clearly pleurisy. Ashley and Minny went at once and, for the next ten days, one or both of them were almost constantly at the boy's bedside. At one time, there seemed to be some hope of recovery, but, on 31 May, Francis died. Ashley's accounts of his son's illness and the last days of his life – preserved in great detail in his Diary – show the intensity of his faith.[109] He read the Bible to Francis; he talked with him of the 'free and full mercy of God in Christ Jesus'; he prayed with him; he felt deep consolation in the boy's calmness and composure, in the gratitude which Francis expressed for his religious training. And, when he died, Ashley affirmed his own trust in the love and mercy of God: 'The child, we doubt not, is with Christ, which is far better.' The Diaries also show – very movingly – the intensity of Ashley's loss. Francis had been the opposite of Anthony in his father's eyes, showing respect and love, piety and unselfishness; and entering into all Ashley's interests. Minny wrote to the Duchess of Beaufort that Francis had 'the most gentle and loving spirit and it would be vain to say that the loss is not heart breaking; and to Ashley the greatest deprivation of sympathy, interest and affection; for he was almost as much interested as he is, in all the objects in which Ashley loves to work. . . .'[110] Ashley himself wrote that 'no pen, no tongue' could 'set forth the charms and perfections of that blessed boy;' he had been '(his) companion . . . co-adjutor, nay half (his) very soul.'[111] The loss was, indeed, irreparable and a sense of it remained with Ashley to the end of his life. And Francis's death made him fearful for the other members of his family: 'every trifle, if it be sudden,' he wrote, 'makes me expect some sad intelligence – a knock at the door, a footstep, a letter, an unusual expression of countenance.'[112] Thus, as he admitted, he had become more nervous and apprehensive; delayed shock at Francis's death certainly exacted its toll. 'It was,' he wrote, 'a blow of which the internal results were not exhibited when it was struck.'[113]

A further family death was to occur two years after that of Francis. On 1 June, 1851 – a Sunday – at 5.30 a.m., Ashley received news that his father was dangerously ill. He travelled to St Giles by the 9 a.m. train: 'how wonderful,' he wrote, 'that I shall be compelled (for so it is) with all my objections to travel on Sundays!'[114] The following morning his father died without recovering consciousness. Ashley was glad that he was present to commend his soul to God and 'to close his eyes,'[115] and he was grateful that, at the last, there were no harsh or angry words. Ashley's thoughts dwelt on his father's besetting sin of self-satisfaction,[116] and he regretted that many good things in him had been thrown away and lost. But if there was regret that his father's life was not what it might have been, of true grief at its ending there was none: the contrast with Ashley's feelings on Francis's death could not have been more marked. Thus Ashley was now to bear a new name and enter a new career, and, as he contemplated the future, he prayed for guidance and sanctification.[117]

The review of his career – already noted – which Ashley had carried out at Christmas, 1850, had, therefore, been made at an appropriate time: on the eve of his translation to the Lords. His years in the Commons had, indeed, coincided with a period of considerable disturbance in the country's affairs, when the old order had been challenged by new forces. Advocates of the manufacturing interest had sought to breach the domination of the landed interest, whether by parliamentary reform, as in 1831–2, or later by repeal of the Corn Laws. Working-class radicals had also been active, prompted by a sense of injustice not only at an exclusive political system – and for them the reformed Parliament was little better than the unreformed – but also at social grievances such as hours in factories or the introduction of the new Poor Law of 1834. Chartism provided ample evidence of the strength of such feelings.

Faced with such threats and pressures, the ruling classes may be said to have adopted four policies to meet and contain them. The first was so to reform the country's political institutions as to grant the propertied contenders for political recognition some degree of representation. Moderate institutional reform would, it was felt, stabilise the country's political system and make it less amenable to radical attack. This – broadly speaking – was the Whig approach to the situation, adopted primarily in 1831–2. The second approach was to encourage business activity and economic growth and thus to induce greater prosperity: this was consistent with maintaining the interests of the landed classes, but would help to take the edge off the demands of middle- and working-class radicals. Such was the hallmark of Peelite Conservatism in the 1840s. The third approach was to promote legislative measures of direct social improvement. This was a policy which neither Whigs nor Tories ignored, but one to which neither party gave high priority. Rather it was a policy canvassed by individuals, both inside Parliament and outside it. Finally, the fourth approach lay wholly outside Parliament – in private acts of paternalism and philanthropy to meet specific social needs.

As a Tory, Ashley could have no dealings with the Whig approach in 1831–2: nor, despite his support for Corn Law repeal in 1845–6, was he in sympathy with the free trade policies followed by Peel in the 1840s. His role lay in the adoption of the third and fourth policies; and – even allowing for his marked tendency to exaggerate his isolation and to discern a universal hostility towards himself and his works – it was one which led him to an independent and sometimes idiosyncratic position. Within the Tory party, he was clearly adrift of the mainstream of Peelite thought and practice, and yet he could not identify with the 'Young England' group, with its overtones of High Churchmanship. Outside the Tory party, he could see nothing good in the egalitarian sentiments to be found in Christian Socialism, and, despite his strong associations with the Ten Hours Movement, there were political and class differences between himself and many of its supporters. On occasion, moreover, he became impatient with the tendency of some in the Movement to regard him as little more than a delegate. Again, Ashley's paternalism found room for a considerable measure of state intervention when he felt that this provided the only effective remedy for a social problem: the state, he remarked, could play the role of the 'faithful and pious parent'.[118] He was willing to cooperate with Chadwick, with all his Benthamite assumptions, to secure a centralised system of public health. This, however, cut him off from others who favoured private paternalism but disliked the bureaucratic and centralising tendencies of the state.[119] On the other hand, Ashley's advocacy of state intervention was not all-embracing: especially in the field of education, he felt that it was bound to introduce secular principles and could not be harmonised with religious objectives. Further, he was unsympathetic to any extension of state activity which sapped individual energy and initiative: the state should only help those who could not help themselves. Outside Parliament, too, his role was distinctive and difficult to categorise. His willingness to work with Dissenters in such ventures as Ragged Schools was not always to the liking of fellow-Anglicans, and his readiness to support philanthropic effort separated him from certain fellow-paternalists, who regarded such activity as diffuse and wasteful of effort.[120] Yet underlying the considerable variety of Ashley's endeavour was his simple and overriding belief in his duty to act as a faithful steward of his God-given talents and possessions, and to use them to enlarge the area of freedom and opportunity open to the less fortunate so that they might develop their physical, moral and spiritual potential. And as himself a member of the old order, he felt that his role was conducive to its survival: it would remove the grievances which fed the movements menacing it. The moral, social and political overtones of Evangelicalism had been amply evident in Ashley's parliamentary and public activities, although he had developed them in his own individualistic and distinctive way.

The old order did, indeed, survive. Despite all the threats and pressures which had faced it since Ashley's entry to the Commons, it remained remarkably intact when he entered the Lords in 1851. The mere fact that the House of Lords still existed in 1851 belied many of the dire predictions which had been made about its future twenty years earlier. The country had overcome its difficulties and social bitterness was giving way to social harmony. In assessing the reasons for this, the political adjustments made by the Whigs in the 1830s must be duly noted, as must the role of Peel during his Ministry of 1841–6 in stimulating economic activity and recovery. It can be argued that these outweighed Ashley's role: and Professor Gash has suggested that Peel's budgets 'did more for the working classes ... than all (Ashley's) reforms put together.'[121] It is, clearly, impossible to measure the effect of Ashley's efforts with any precision. Nevertheless, it can reasonably be said that they did contribute to the increasing awareness of social problems discernible during the 1830s and 1840s and to the measure of remedial provision made for them. His claim in 1850 that his work had 'led to an awakened attention, though but partially so, to the wants and rights of the poor: to the powers and duties of the rich' was not without foundation. What, however, is certain is that his accession to the title opened up for him a private and immediate sphere for the exercise of his sense of social responsibility: the improvement of the conditions of those who lived on the Estates which now passed into his possession.

NOTES

1. A. L. Tibawi, op. cit., pp. 86–105.
2. *The Record*, 8 May, 1848.
3. N.R.A., Shaftesbury (Broadlands) MSS, SHA/PD/5, 12 Dec., 1848.
4. *The Record*, 9 May, 1848.
5. N.R.A., Shaftesbury (Broadlands) MSS, SHA/PD/5, 5 May, 1851.
6. ibid., SHA/PD/6, 17 May, 1851. Ashley did, however, approve of a plan whereby boys from Ragged Schools were employed as 'shoeblacks' at the Exhibition. (Hodder, II, 341–2). And he did modify his ideas later: in Sept., 1851, he wrote, after a visit to the Exhibition, that, at one time, he regarded it as the 'triumph of Materialism, the Deification of Sensuality; at the next, as a type of the Millenium, when "all kindreds and tongues and nations" shall flow together to the Holy City in peace and worship, to hear and see the wonderful works of God.' (N.R.A., Shaftesbury (Broadlands) MSS, SHA/PD/6, 27 Sept., 1851).
7. ibid., SHA/PD/4, 14 Oct., 1846.
8. ibid., SHA/PD/5, 5 Nov., 1849.
9. ibid., SHA/PD/4, 7 Oct., 1846.
10. *The Record*, 31 Dec., 1846.
11. ibid., 24 May, 1849.
12. ibid., 26 Apr., 1849.
13. ibid., 2 May, 1849.
14. ibid., 12 Dec., 1850.
15. ibid., 3 June, 1847.
16. ibid., 13 May, 1847.
17. ibid., 13 May, 1848.
18. ibid., 9 May, 1849.
19. ibid.

20. ibid., 10 May, 1850.
21. ibid., 7 May, 1850.
22. ibid., 9 May, 1849, 10 May, 1850.
23. Hansard, *Parl. Debates*, 3rd ser., XCVII, 1269.
24. *The Record*, 16 May, 1851.
25. ibid., 10 May, 1850.
26. N.R.A., Shaftesbury (Broadlands) MSS, SHA/PD/5, 22 Feb., 1849.
27. Russell MSS, 30/22/7 E, fos 266-7.
28. See above pp. 153-4.
29. Russell MSS, 30/22/7 E, fos 306-7.
30. N.R.A., Shaftesbury (Broadlands) MSS, SHA/PD/5, 28 Feb., 1849.
31. ibid., SHA/PD/5, 1 Mar., 1849.
32. Hansard, *Parl. Debates*, 3rd ser., CIII, 11 ff.
33. ibid., 25-35.
34. ibid., 46-7.
35. ibid., 464.
36. N.R.A., Shaftesbury (Broadlands) MSS, SHA/PD/5, 1 Mar., 1849.
37. G. M. Ellis, op. cit., pp. 204-5.
38. L.D.O.S. Minutes, III, 214.
39. ibid.
40. See above p. 110.
41. G. M. Ellis, op. cit., p. 206. See also pp. 206-18.
42. N.R.A., Shaftesbury (Broadlands) MSS, SHA/PD/5, 28 Sept., 1849.
43. ibid., SHA/PD/5, 6 Oct., 1849.
44. Russell MSS, 30/22/8 B, fos. 3, 4.
45. N.R.A., Shaftesbury (Broadlands) MSS, SHA/PD/5, 28 Oct., 1849.
46. Hansard, *Parl. Debates*, 3rd ser., CXI, 466-75.
47. ibid., 484.
48. N.R.A., Shaftesbury (Broadlands) MSS, SHA/PD/5, 12 June, 1850.
49. ibid., SHA/PD/5, 23 June, 1850.
50. ibid., SHA/PD/6, 20 Aug., 1850.
51. ibid., SHA/PD/5, 2 June, 1850.
52. ibid., SHA/PD/5, 23 June, 1850.
53. ibid., SHA/PD/5, 2 June, 1850.
54. Phillpotts had attempted to show that Gorham did not believe the teaching of the Prayer Book concerning Baptismal Regeneration.
55. J. Prest, op. cit., pp. 320-21.
56. Quoted in E. R. Norman, *Anti-Catholicism in Victorian England* (1968), p. 57.
57. J. Prest, op. cit., p. 322.
58. N.R.A., Shaftesbury (Broadlands) MSS, SHA/PD/4, 31 Oct., 1846.
59. Russell MSS, 30/22/8 B, fos. 214-15.
60. N.R.A., Shaftesbury (Broadlands) MSS, SHA/PC/88. Ashley did not, however, join in the general condemnation of Russell's appointment of the liberal theologian, Dr Hampden, as Bishop of Hereford in 1847. Russell did not consult him about it, but asked him later what he thought of it. Ashley said that, had he been Prime Minister, he would not have made it himself, but now that it was made, more good than evil would come of it. Hampden's views had, he felt, recently become more orthodox. (ibid., SHA/PD/5, 13 Dec., 1847).
61. Russell MSS, 30/22/8 B, f. 241.
62. N.R.A., Shaftesbury (Broadlands) MSS, SHA/PD/6, 7 Nov., 1850.
63. ibid., SHA/PD/6, 11 Nov., 1850.

64. *The Record*, 6 Mar., 10 Apr., 1851.
65. Hodder, II, 331–4. *The Record*, 9 Dec., 1850, carries a slightly different version of this speech.
66. N.R.A., Shaftesbury (Broadlands) MSS, SHA/PD/6, 5 Dec., 1850.
67. ibid., SHA/PD/6, 5 Dec., 1850.
68. *The Record*, 24 Mar., 1851.
69. Russell MSS, 30/22/9 B(ii), fos. 254–5.
70. ibid., 30/22/8 F, fos. 253–4.
71. ibid., 30/22/9 A, fos. 288–9.
72. ibid., 30/22/9 B (Pt I), fos. 115–16.
73. N.R.A., Shaftesbury (Broadlands) MSS, SHA/PD/6, 26 Mar., 1851.
74. Hansard, *Parl. Debates*, 3rd ser., CXIV, 300 ff.
75. ibid., CXV, 147 ff.
76. N.R.A., Shaftesbury (Broadlands) MSS, SHA/PD/5, 1 Dec., 1848.
77. ibid., SHA/PD/5, 25 Nov., 1848.
78. H.R.O., Shaftesbury (Broadlands) MSS, 27M60, 4 July, 1850.
79. N.R.A., Shaftesbury (Broadlands) MSS, SHA/PD/5, 3 July, 1850.
80. See below pp. 323–4.
81. N.R.A., Shaftesbury (Broadlands) MSS, SHA/PD/5, 26 Dec., 1847.
82. ibid., SHA/PC/15.
83. Battiscombe, pp. 217–18.
84. See above pp. 167.
85. Hodder, II, 329–30.
86. Wilberforce MSS, C 10, 93–5.
87. Hansard, *Parl. Debates*, 3rd ser., CXV, 149.
88. N.R.A., Shaftesbury (Broadlands) MSS, SHA/PD/6, 18 Mar., 1851.
89. ibid., SHA/PD/5, 8 July, 1848.
90. ibid., SHA/PD/5, 9 Apr., 1848.
91. ibid., SHA/PD/6, 1 July, 1851.
92. O. J. Brose, *Frederick Denison Maurice* (Ohio U.P., 1971), pp. 163–5. See also P. R. Allen, 'F. D. Maurice and J. M. Ludlow: A Re-assessment of the Leaders of Christian Socialism' (*Victorian Studies*, IX, No 4, 461–82).
93. N.R.A., Shaftesbury (Broadlands) MSS, SHA/PD/6, 25, 26 Dec., 1850.
94. ibid., SHA/PD/5, 24 July, 1849.
95. ibid., SHA/PD/5, 2 Nov., 31 Dec., 1849.
96. ibid., SHA/PD/5, 2 Sept., 1850.
97. ibid., SHA/PD/5, 30 Jan., 1849.
98. ibid., SHA/PD/5, 11 July, 1849.
99. ibid., SHA/PD/5, 26 Sept., 1850.
100. ibid., SHA/PD/5, 31 Oct., 1850. During his visit to Scotland in 1849, however, Ashley was made a freeman of Tain: the first public honour which he had ever had. He confessed that he was 'not indifferent to the goodwill and esteem of a body of Citizens, though small and remote.' (ibid., SHA/PD/5, 17 Oct., 1850).
101. ibid., SHA/PD/5, 22 Apr., 1850.
102. ibid., SHA/PD/5, 31 Jan., 1850.
103. ibid., SHA/PD/5, 25 Mar., 1848.
104. ibid., SHA/PD/5, 1 Aug., 1848.
105. ibid., SHA/PD/5, 8 Jan., 1848.
106. ibid., SHA/PD/5, 25 Jan., 1848.
107. ibid., SHA/PD/6, 12 Jan., 1851.
108. ibid., SHA/PD/6, 23 Aug., 1850.

109. ibid., SHA/PD/5, 21, 22, 25, 28 May; 1–7 June, 1849.
110. ibid., SHA/PC/14/1/2.
111. ibid., SHA/PD/5, 3 June, 1849.
112. ibid., SHA/PD/5, 11 Oct., 1849.
113. ibid., SHA/PD/5, 11 Oct., 1849.
114. ibid., SHA/PD/5, 1 June, 1851.
115. ibid., SHA/PD/6, 6 June, 1851.
116. ibid., SHA/PD/6, 7 June, 1851.
117. ibid., SHA/PD/6, 10 June, 1851.
118. Quoted in D. Roberts, *Paternalism in Early Victorian England* (1979), p. 190.
119. ibid., p. 206 ff.
120. ibid., pp. 34–5.
121. N. Gash, *Aristocracy and People. Britain 1815–1865* (1979), p. 4.

13
A New Name, A New Career, 1851-1855

Despite the distant relations which had existed between the Sixth Earl and his son, all the family property was left to Ashley, with the exception of Richmond, in Surrey, which was left to the Earl's widow.[1] Thus, as Ashley put it in June, 1851, his father had 'left nothing away' from him and had thus tried to make some compensation for the past.[2] By his own admission, he entered on this new career as landlord and proprietor with few, if any, qualifications. 'Land, rent, etc. etc., are as Arabic to me!' he wrote. Parliamentary business and 'city duties' had been his calling and he wondered how, at fifty years of age, he could learn other things.[3] He was greatly perplexed by what he found. He inherited a considerable debt and immediately had to undertake fresh obligations by raising mortgages to meet the interests of his family in the settled Estate.[4] A further problem was the condition of the Estates. Shaftesbury found them in a state of great disarray and disrepair and it was clear to him that the debt had not been incurred in improving conditions but, rather, had been mounted up by extravagance and waste.[5] Even the main house at St Giles was in a very poor condition: the walls were sinking, the roof was giving way and the house seemed to be in danger of falling in.[6] The position elsewhere on the Estates was equally bad – farm cottages and buildings were in a deplorable condition. Some twenty years later, in 1870, Shaftesbury recalled that every item on the Estates seemed to be on the road to ruin.[7] And all his impressions written down at the time of his succession suggest that this was not an exaggeration. His early inspection of the cottage accommodation prompted such comments in his Diary as 'Filthy, close, indecent, unwholesome'; or, again, 'many ... dangerous, many more disgraceful, all unsatisfactory'.[8]

Shaftesbury's problems as proprietor were, therefore, manifold but basically they reduced themselves to two. In the first place, he had to reduce the debt; in the second, he had to repair and improve the property. In the case of St Giles's House itself, repair was almost a matter of necessity, and, understandably, he also wanted to make the house 'tidy and comfortable'.[9] Improvement of the Estates was not, perhaps, a matter of necessity, but it was one of obligation. For, as Shaftesbury well realised, he had spent his life 'rating others for allowing rotten houses and "immoral" unhealthy dwellings'; he had now come into Estates so rife with such 'abominations' as to make his flesh creep.[10] But this could not be done without expenditure, and expenditure was the one thing which Shaftesbury could not afford. He was constantly aware of his dilemma. 'Much to be done and little to do it with':[11] this was a comment constantly echoed in his Diary as he visited different parts of the Estates in the autumn of 1851 and saw the full extent of the improvements which, he felt, had to be undertaken. In January, 1852, he wrote to Chadwick from Dorchester while on a further tour of inspection.[12] He had, he wrote, just read a report prepared by the Board of Health official in the town. He felt that the report had dealt with conditions there 'very gently' – they were worse than he himself had ever thought. And, he added, among the worst houses were some of his own; but what could he do? 'Debt upon debt swallows up every grain as it is yielded by the rent.' He was 'the most perplexed of men'. What would be thought of the sincerity of his 'preachments'? He could only take comfort in the thought that he had been the first to urge the 'forcible introduction' of the Health Act into the town. And the need on his Estates was not only one of buildings and accommodation. He found that several farms had been undercultivated and were not, in his view, employing half the proper numbers of labourers. He gave his thoughts to agricultural improvements, but, again, lack of money dogged him and he also met resistance from some of the farmers. He was determined, for example, to stamp out the system of truck, which he had known had been practised and for which he himself – as has been seen[13] – had suffered criticism in the past. Then he had been 'tongue tied'; now that he was master, things would be different. Very soon after succeeding to the title, he visited various farms and made his views known. But this, of course, caused difficulties. When he told one farmer that the system of truck must stop, the man 'flew into a towering passion and *resigned* his farm.'[14] Thus Shaftesbury wrote that every hour that passed confirmed him in the belief that the old class of farmers were 'pig-headed and hard-hearted'.[15]

The difficulties of the situation did not, however, deter Shaftesbury from trying to deal with them. Thus, to reduce the debt, he sold his properties at Dorchester, which had proved uneconomic in the past and for which a great deal of money would be required to put into good repair.[16] He also sold half his plate.[17] For a time, he closed St Giles. And he constantly pleaded the necessity for economies: 'every economy must be practised,' he wrote in 1851; 'everything turned into money for the liquidation of debt.'[18] But he also undertook improvements. Characteristically, one of his first efforts in this direction was with the church at St Giles. He felt that it had the appearance of an old ballroom and was glad, as he wrote in January, 1852, to have made it look like a church once again.[19] Again characteristically, he appointed Scripture Readers to certain parishes, and he built schools and carried out repairs to cottages and homesteads. He planned rewards for well-kept gardens and allotments, and evening classes for young men and cricket clubs for the cottagers were started. He also began cultivation improvements and carried out repairs and alterations to St Giles's House. At times, he felt satisfied with his efforts: thus in October, 1853, he noted that all the men employed in the House desired a holiday and they had it 'with cricket, football, quoits etc.; bread, cheese, meat, beer and apples in just quantity.' He was well satisfied with their conduct – they behaved 'admirably well and went home perfectly sober.' And, he continued: 'I confess it did my heart good to see them sharing with me, in due time and proportion, the enjoyment of the old park of my ancestors.'[20] But a few months later, he was depressed. He complained of a lack of energy among the people and an indifference to advancement.[21] On Easter Sunday, 1854, he felt that his people were going back. The congregation at the church was smaller in number and thefts and small crimes were frequent. In June, 1854, he wrote of his distress that his people were not showing greater signs of moral improvement, especially when more was being done for them than ever before.[22] And over and above everything was the worry over the financial problem. Economies were painful, for, as he admitted, 'ancestral feelings' were still strong within him. He managed to part with Dorchester with few qualms, but he could not bring himself to sell estates at Purton in Wiltshire and Swine in Yorkshire. He felt that these represented assets with which it would be wrong to part, but there was also the point that to have sold them would have meant breaking family ties and severing long-standing connections. And, if the existing debt was reduced, other debts were incurred. In 1856, Shaftesbury estimated that repairs to cottages and homesteads had cost £3,000, the church repairs almost £1,000, the schools over £1,000.[23] Thus, at the very time that Shaftesbury was struggling to reduce the inherited debt by sales and economies, he was undertaking fresh expenditure which tended to cancel out his efforts.[24]

It was, perhaps, an irreconcilable financial problem with which Shaftesbury was faced. Further, Shaftesbury was constantly approached with requests from charitable organisations. He complained that people assumed that he was rich and wrote to him 'in all the fervour of meritorious need to one blessed by God with abundant wealth.'[25] It is not surprising that he felt constantly harassed by demands for outlay and, as he put it, knew not which way to turn.[26] But, if his difficulties were intractable, it can be argued that he made them worse than they need have been. Understandably, he was very reluctant to withdraw money from his charitable activities, and, although he did find it necessary to refuse appeals, he admitted that he had given away more than he ought.[27] And he also confessed to making mistakes in the handling of his money. Thus he planned to sell pictures to pay for the reconstruction of St Giles, but he began the work before selling the pictures. He then discovered, to his dismay, that the National Gallery would not, at that time, buy any picture from him and this left him in need of money. He had, he wrote, been 'embarrassed by (his) own haste' in his determination to 'prop up the crazy, falling mansion of (his) ancestors.'[28] He wished he had done no more than shore up the house and leave it to his successor, or, at least, that he had effected the picture sales before beginning the work. Again, however praiseworthy his desire to improve the Estates, there was, perhaps, an element of rashness in it for one in his position: 'must build cottages, cost what it may,' was his comment on one occasion.[29] He started a scheme to reduce the building costs by the development of a brick machine and wrote enthusiastically to his son, Evelyn, about this in October, 1851. Three thousand bricks were to be produced 'in a day of *ten* hours', he wrote: this would soon be eight thousand and Shaftesbury hoped to be able to supply the whole county at a cheap rate and thus encourage the building of cottages.[30] But the scheme was a costly failure. Shaftesbury was dissatisfied with the conduct of the person whom he engaged to manage it; the kilns which were built proved to be unsuitable and had to be altered; and, even so, two of them burned out. While all these difficulties were being encountered, Shaftesbury himself was at Ems on holiday and could not be at St Giles to supervise the work. He wrote sorrowfully to Chadwick, who had suggested the manager to him, about the problems of the scheme. 'The whole thing,' he wrote in August, 1852, 'seems an utter failure; and I *am far worse off* than when I began.'[31] Lack of adequate supervision, indeed, was apparent over a wider area than this particular project. Shaftesbury was not as vigilant as he might have been. He complained in 1854 that he was ill served, that there was a want of 'zeal and sympathy' in those whom he employed.[32] He thought that the steward whom he inherited from his father, Robert Waters, honest, but neglectful; and yet, over the years ahead, he did not apply himself sufficiently to correct the latter fault. And, when he did, he was to discover that Waters's sins extended beyond those of omission.[33] On his succession to the title and Estates, Shaftesbury complained of 'much confusion and little worldly help'.[34] It was, in many ways, a just complaint, but some of the confusion thereafter was of his own making. He did not have a head for business and never really applied himself to acquiring one.

One reason for Shaftesbury's difficulties in making economies lay in the continuing needs of his family. Anthony remained a great source of anxiety. In November, 1851, Shaftesbury was worried about two bills which his son had drawn the previous August without his captain's signature, and this prompted the sad thought that Anthony's spendthrift ways might prove to be an obstacle to the plans for improving the Estates.[35] Anthony returned from his first voyage in December, 1851 : Shaftesbury was pleased with his state of health and found him, as usual, 'simple, dear and affectionate'.[36] But he thought that absence of moral discipline would induce the return of old habits, and, indeed, no sooner had Anthony returned to his ship in February, 1852, than there was a demand for money from one of his messmates. At the end of the year, in December, Shaftesbury and Minny set out for the Continent to see Anthony, whose ship was in the Mediterranean – they wanted to spend time with him at Nice 'to endeavour by renewed intercourse, to do him good and maintain our influence.'[37] But, when Anthony returned for a further visit in 1854, more financial difficulties were revealed. Shaftesbury noted sorrowfully that Anthony confessed to still larger expenditure and this meant, for himself, 'still larger necessity for loans, sales, exhaustions of every kind'.[38] Shaftesbury's feelings for his eldest son remained a compound of affection and despair. Anthony was amiable, kind and good humoured but thoughtless, and, when he promised amendment of life, Shaftesbury knew that this resolution would not last. During the Crimean War, Anthony's ship was sent to the Dardanelles and Shaftesbury was anxious for his safety, but he always thought that he had done right to send Anthony to sea. Any other course would have been ruinous. Even as it was, Shaftesbury was haunted by the fear that Anthony would have no feeling of responsibility for the Estates which he was so painfully trying to improve; when Anthony succeeded, he would 'convert the ancient acres of St Giles into top boots, cigars, jewellery and all the paraphernalia of a profligate and useless life.'[39] For different reasons, Maurice, too, worried Shaftesbury greatly. The boy remained abroad : Shaftesbury visited him in Lausanne in September, 1853, but found no improvement. There had, indeed, been a regression in Maurice's state and the only consolation was that he was happy. A year later, the news was no better – a new remedy had been tried but to no effect. Thus there seemed no hope of a cure and Shaftesbury knew that the boy could never work for a livelihood and could never enter a profession; he would have to make personal provision for him. This was something which his financial situation made it hard to contemplate with any peace of mind, but a more harrowing thought was what might happen to Maurice if his parents died before him. Shaftesbury knew of the sufferings of such persons once parental care and affection were removed. 'Fits are treated as madness,' he wrote, 'and madness constitutes a right, as it were, to treat people as vermin. . . .'[40] Shaftesbury's other children, however, were a source of greater happiness. He found Constance a delight and joy: indeed, at one point, he commented that of Victoria, Evelyn and Lionel, Constance alone exhibited 'a relish for divine things'.[41] But, at other times, he felt more satisfied with the others. Lionel reminded him of Francis and made excellent progress at Harrow, where he started in 1853. Evelyn, too, was showing good qualities: 'a noble fellow,' Shaftesbury wrote in September, 1853, 'full of zeal and heart and sympathy, rejoicing in good, eager to do it, enthusiastic to hear of it. . . .'[42]

Shaftesbury's own health over these years remained indifferent. In June, 1851, there seemed to be some signs of improvement, and, on the advice of his doctor, he was using a new shower bath, which proved beneficial. But by the end of the year, there were complaints of returning ill-health: stomach trouble, noises in the head and ears, pressures in the throat and stomach and racing of the pulse. And this was a pattern which was to recur. His doctor recommended several remedies, among them, yearly visits to take the waters at Ems. Shaftesbury did not like these 'exiles', as he often called them, and was never sure of their value. In July, 1852, he wrote to Evelyn from Ems to say that the relaxing climate was neutralising the benefit of the springs.[43] And he felt bored and restless: 'the labour of idleness is excessive,' he told Chadwick during the same visit to Ems.[44] As for reading books, he continued, he had 'lost the art'. He could not fix his attention for half an hour — his mind ran 'instantly to something *practical* such as drains, hollow bricks and liquid manure.' And any benefit which such enforced rest induced did not last long; the old symptoms of palpitations, 'roarings', headaches and billiousness returned. And, if this was not bad enough, there was the thought of the expense of it all. In October, 1851, Shaftesbury complained that he had spent a fortune on physicians and was no better,[45] and this, unhappily, was to be his experience in the years ahead.

If Shaftesbury's new 'name' provided fresh proprietorial occupations, it also occasioned a change of residence in London. He left his house at Upper Brook Street in February, 1852, and moved into the London family house in Grosvenor Square. He was, he told Evelyn, very sorry to leave the old house, where he had 'passed so many years and done so many things,'[46] and where — as he put it in his Diary — he had 'prepared for nearly all his public labours in study, thought and prayer.'[47] At first, he told Evelyn, the smell of paint in the new house was 'very great' and disorder reigned everywhere — his own room was like a 'broken down Diligence'. But the new house was 'excellent',[48] and it was to be the centre of his London sojourns. There was, of course, another change in London connected with Shaftesbury's 'new career'. And this change of parliamentary status was much less pleasing to him, for he did not like the House of Lords. He had, indeed, decided not to take his seat in the Lords: he felt that his previous career had caused such ill feeling towards him in the Upper House that he would be out of place there.⁴⁹ However, he changed his mind⁵⁰ and decided to take his seat, grumbling about the various documents which were demanded of him, including a patent of peerage: what folly, he thought, when his father had been recognised there for so many years.⁵¹ He was not reassured by his reception in the Lords on 23 June. His greeting, he wrote, reminded him of the chapter in Isaiah in which the King of Babylon goes down to Hades: 'Hell from beneath is moved at his coming; "art thou become one of us?"' '⁵²

Shaftesbury thus viewed the political events of the day from a new vantage-point. There was, indeed, considerable political activity to view, for politics were now increasingly dominated by the groupings – Whig, Radical, Irish, Peelite and Protectionist – into which the broad party allegiances of the 1830s and 1840s had dissolved. Governments found themselves at the mercy of various alignments, which made political stability very hard to achieve. Thus Russell's Whig administration was defeated in the Commons in February, 1852, and resigned. It was succeeded by a minority Protectionist ministry led by Derby and Disraeli, but, despite some accession of strength in the General Election of 1852, it, too, was defeated in the House in December of that year and resigned. Some re-alignment of the groupings was required before stability could be restored, and the Ministry which came into office in December, 1852, gave some promise of this, for it was a coalition of Whigs, Radicals and Peelites under the premiership of Aberdeen, a Peelite. Thus, in Shaftesbury's first years in the Lords, political life was eventful as Ministry succeeded Ministry, and he followed it all with interest. But he felt quite out of touch with political events. Just a few days after taking his seat he commented that one of the most striking effects of his removal from the Commons was his 'absolute ignorance of the political movements, thoughts and facts of the day'. Everything of importance, he wrote, revolved round the Commons, and 'unless you be there to see it, hear it, feel it, you get it at second hand, and then only half.'⁵³ And such comments were to recur: he might as well, he wrote, be removed to 'the Pampas or Timbuctoo: know nothing, see nothing, hear nothing.'⁵⁴ He found it hard to get used to being 'shut out of the medley.'⁵⁵ In May, 1853, he concluded that it was impossible to be an *effective* man out of the Commons: 'you may experience much social civility, but no one accords you a hairs-breadth of political influence.'⁵⁶

At times Shaftesbury felt tempted to think that his position in the Lords was a barrier to any possible political advancement or reward. When the Aberdeen coalition was being formed in December, 1852–January, 1853, he wrote that his political value was much reduced by his being in the Lords.

He recalled that he had been offered office in the past, yet, within the previous two years, two governments had been formed – Derby's and Aberdeen's – and neither had invited his cooperation.[57] But, as he recognised on other occasions, his detachment from political life was only very marginally explained by his presence in the Lords; it had long been a feature of his public career and was, indeed, to remain so. Shaftesbury's attitude to public honours retained a certain wistfulness at what might have been, but he also realised that his position of aloofness and independence was now well-established. In late 1852, there were rumours that he might be offered the Chancellorship of Oxford University, vacant on the death of Wellington. But this, he felt, would be an added burden, and he would not surrender one of his existing burdens for it. There would be candidates enough for the position; he would rather retain those places for which there were no candidates, such as the Chair of the Ragged School Union: 'This is clearly my province,' he wrote, 'I am called to this and not to any political or social honours.'[58] Again, in 1854, he was offered the Order of the Garter by Aberdeen. It was not offered as a political appointment, but to mark Aberdeen's admiration for Shaftesbury's 'unwearied exertions in the cause of humanity and social improvement'.[59] Minny felt that Shaftesbury should accept the offer as an acknowledgement of his deserts. But Shaftesbury himself was much less sure; he turned the matter over in his mind for a day and prayed for counsel and guidance. One objection was the fees, which amounted to over £1,000. This was a sum which, he noted,[60] he did not have and could not command, and which, if he had possessed, he should have devoted to his children and his responsibilities on the Estates. But there were also several other objections. He felt, for example, that ignorant and malicious people would 'decry all public virtue and say that "every man had his price" '; that he would attract criticism for accepting such an offer; that those for whom the decoration was principally intended would be offended by its being awarded for services such as he had given. But possibly the strongest objection was that he did not wish to put himself under any obligation to the Minister who had offered it: he wished to be free from all party and other ties. Thus he finally decided to refuse the offer. He wrote to Aberdeen and acknowledged the honour which he had been offered, but, he continued:

> In the public career I have to maintain, and to secure the objects I pursue, it is essentially necessary that I should not only be, but that I appear to be, altogether independent. You, I know, would impose no conditions; but were your offer accepted, I should impose them on myself, and feel bound, by my own act, to limit somewhat my own discretion....[61]

Thus, if Shaftesbury's career was 'new' in some senses, the substance remained the same: the advancement, at his 'own discretion', of evangelical and paternalistic causes.

The Sabbatarian controversy over the opening of the Post Office had, indeed, been overshadowed by the question of 'Papal Aggression', but another issue arose in 1852 which was to occupy the attention of Evangelical Sabbatarians. The royal warrant which had authorised the building of the Crystal Palace in Hyde Park had stipulated that the building must be removed and the site restored to its original condition by 1 June, 1852. As the time for this approached, various voices were raised to retain the Crystal Palace structure for recreational purposes, and it was in this light that Evangelicals first considered the matter. After the government had announced that the royal warrant must be adhered to and the Palace removed from Hyde Park, a large meeting was held in April, 1852, at Exeter Hall under the chairmanship of Shaftesbury. In his speech, Shaftesbury dwelt on the need for recreation for the working classes. Buildings such as the Crystal Palace – if used for good and wholesome purposes – performed a valuable function: they humanised men's spirits, abated discontent and tended to unite the classes. Working men would be impressed if they saw 'wealth and station engaged on (their) behalf' by the Crystal Palace being devoted to purposes of recreation and instruction.[62] A memorial was sent to the Queen, urging delay in any decision over the Palace. But the government remained firm, and, in May, 1852, several individuals, many of whom had business interests in railways, formed a company to buy a site at Sydenham for the transference of the Palace, which would be converted into a permanent exhibition hall. It was at this point that the Sunday question arose, for there were reports that the company intended to open the building on a Sunday afternoon. This aroused Evangelical protests and, for two years, Evangelical groups and societies displayed great energy in attempting to combat such plans. The Lord's Day Observance Society played an active role, urging the presentation of memorials to the government, and many were submitted by Evangelical societies such as the Scripture Readers' Society and the Religious Tract Society. Outside the ranks of the Established Church, too, Dissenters were vocal in their condemnation of Sunday opening. Shaftesbury contributed to the activity: he was consulted by the Lord's Day Observance Society and presented petitions in the Lords.[63] In the event, the company produced a plan in 1854 to open the Palace on Sunday afternoons to its shareholders, but it dropped this when the Solicitor General stated that such a course might endanger the validity of the charter granted to it in 1853, which had forbidden the admission of any person to the building or grounds on a Sunday without the consent of Parliament. The episode, in one sense, ran parallel to the Post Office issue, for both witnessed the activity of highly organised Evangelical opinion – in which Shaftesbury was involved; but, in another sense, there was an important difference. For the efforts of the Evangelicals over the Post Office had been directed towards the cessation of Sunday work: those over the Crystal Palace were concerned with the curtailment of Sunday recreation. To the Evangelical mind, the difference was not, perhaps, a real one, for recreation implied spiritual re-creation, not secular enjoyment. Thus Sunday work should be stopped to make way for the former but not for the latter, which, it was supposed, would prevail at the Palace. But to the non-Evangelical, this was too subtle a point, and, if understood, not an acceptable one. Indeed, the efforts of the Evangelicals over the Crystal Palace were challenged by various groups, among which working-class secular opinion was present, represented fleetingly by Henry Mayhew. This aspect of the controversy was of significance for the future, and Shaftesbury was to be involved in it in later years.[64]

If Shaftesbury continued his support of Evangelical Sabbatarianism in the early 1850s, he also showed that he had lost none of that dislike of Tractarian influences in the Church which he had displayed so energetically at the time of 'Papal Aggression'. He regretted the resignation of Russell in February, 1852: the reasons for his regret were principally religious, since he had approved of Russell's Church appointments. He wrote to Russell, thanking him for 'many excellent and invaluable appointments'. 'No Prime Minister,' he wrote, 'has ever surpassed you; nay, I do not believe has equalled you. There may have been an exception or so; but I speak of the mass of your nominations.'[65] With Derby in office, Shaftesbury thought that the High Church party would be promoted, and, indeed, during Derby's short-lived Ministry of 1852, he had two notable skirmishes with the Tractarians. One arose from a speech which he made at the annual meeting of the British and Foreign Bible Society on 5 May, 1852. It was a stinging attack on Tractarianism, which, he said, was offensive, deceitful and hypocritical. Further, he claimed that Tractarianism was in alliance with Infidelity against Evangelicalism: a phrase which caused considerable offence.[66] The second episode, in November, 1852, arose from rumours circulating that the Derby government had given leave to Convocation – consisting of an upper house of Bishops and a lower house of elected clergy – to transact business. Since 1717, meetings of Convocation at the beginning of each Parliament had been purely formal and had consisted of the presentation of an Address to the Crown before dissolution by the Archbishop of Canterbury. But, since the early nineteenth century, there had been demands that Convocation should be given more power and allowed to legislate for the Church. These demands did not come exclusively from Tractarians, but many Tractarians had voiced them in their desire to assert the independence of the Church from the State. In the late 1840s, especially in the wake of the Gorham case, the volume of this demand notably increased. To Evangelicals, this was a sinister development: their suspicions were aroused by the rumours about Derby's intentions and were still further sharpened by the fact that on the opening of Parliament after the Election of November, 1852, Convocation met for three days – longer than ever before – and appointed committees. All this, moreover, came on top of a decision made by Bishop Phillpots in favour of the incumbent of a Church near Plymouth who, it was said, had introduced the practice of compulsory confession among girls attending an orphanage in his parish.

Shaftesbury was on the alert to probe these developments. On 22 November, 1852, he put a question to Derby in the Lords 'on a subject of great interest': Convocation. He wished to know what were the intentions of the government. Would Convocation, which stood adjourned until February, 1853, be allowed to assemble again and proceed to its business and would the committees appointed by the Lower House be allowed to sit?[67] But this parliamentary question was the least part of Shaftesbury's activities over the matter. Since 'Papal Aggression', Protestant Defence Committees had remained in existence, and Shaftesbury had, from time to time, mentioned in his Diary his continuing association with them. The question of Convocation was another issue for these Committees to espouse, and a meeting was arranged by them to take place at the Freemason's Hall to protest against Convocation and Confession. As had happened before the meeting at Freemason's in 1850 to condemn Popery – when Wilberforce had written to him – Shaftesbury received a letter asking him to restrain any extravagance or excess at the meeting. This time, it was from Gladstone, who was much in favour of the restoration of Convocation, but wanted to reform its constitution to give greater representation to the laity. Gladstone wrote on 8 November[68] of his desire to reconcile the various procedures of the Church of England and to invigorate the parochial system of the Church. He asked Shaftesbury not to lend his name, abilities and influence to any course which would aggravate 'the wounds and scandals of the Church of England and place beyond all hope of remedy the utter feebleness and insufficiency that now mark her ordinary contact with the dense masses of human souls for whom she has to render an account.' Shaftesbury replied on 11 November[69] saying that Evangelical fears of the revival of Convocation had been very great; but there was no denying that it might be expedient for the Church to have some form of synodical meeting or some means of self-regulation. In any such arrangement, however, the laity should hold the principal share. This, indeed, was the theme of Shaftesbury's speech at the Freemason's on 15 November. There could be no revival of Convocation, he said, as it had been when its full sitting had been terminated in

1717, 'animated by the worst sentiments and views of priestly despotism and priestly ambition'. There could be no submission to any clerical Parliament that would make the laity of the Church and of the country mere 'hewers of wood and drawers of water' to a 'select knot of sacerdotal dignitaries'. Although a form of Church government on a reasonable and moderate basis was well worthy of consideration, this would have to be one in which the laity had not only a great but a dominant share.[70]

If Shaftesbury continued to support Evangelical causes and fight Tractarianism at home, he proved to be a zealous defender of Protestants and Protestantism abroad. In August, 1851, he successfully moved that an Address be presented to the Queen praying that Her Majesty would be 'graciously pleased' to have a circular addressed to British Ministers and Consuls abroad, instructing them to report on the facilities which different countries offered for the erection of Protestant Chapels and the establishment and regulation of Protestant burial grounds, and also on the laws which prevailed in Roman Catholic countries affecting the exercise of the Protestant religion.[71] In 1852, he took up the cause of two small shopkeepers, Francesco and Rosa Madiai, who lived in Florence and had broken away from the Roman Catholic Church to spread the Protestant faith. For their efforts, they were sentenced to five years' imprisonment by the Grand Duke of Tuscany. Their cause found sympathy in Europe generally, and, in Britain, Shaftesbury became associated with it. He approached Prince Albert on the subject, although the Prince – and the Queen – were already aware of the fate of the Madiai and were exercising what influence they could. A deputation set out in October, 1852, and Shaftesbury received it on its return. He felt that the blessing of God had been on the enterprise and all the other deputations which had been involved; it was, he felt, a 'proof of the latter days that when two small shopkeepers (were) persecuted by the hand of tyranny for righteousness' sake, all Europe (was) in commotion. . . .'[72] The deputations did not, however, succeed, and in January, 1853, while he was in Italy, Shaftesbury himself had plans to visit Florence and seek out the Madiai. In the end, he decided not to do so, but, in March, 1853, the Madiai were released and, while he was abroad in September, 1853, Shaftesbury called on them: 'May God bless them in time and eternity,' he commented, 'and raise up many such to "witness before" Kings, Judges and dukes.'[73] Further, while in Italy in January, 1853, Shaftesbury *did* visit the Waldensians and was inspired by their witness: he wrote to Cavour to express his interest in the progress towards religious and constitutional liberty in Sardinia and to raise the case of a Mr Mazzinglia, who had been sentenced to three years' imprisonment for having a copy of St Paul's Epistle to the Ephesians. Cavour's reply stressed the gradual nature of his reforms towards civil and religious liberty in Sardinia and expressed the hope that Shaftesbury would approve of 'cette marche prudente'.[74] Shaftesbury also wrote to other prominent figures in the same cause. In 1854, he had an exchange of letters with Napoleon III on the subject of the Protestant Churches in the French Empire, which, Shaftesbury claimed, were suffering 'many grievous vexations'.[75]

Further, the traditional Evangelical preoccupation with mission also claimed Shaftesbury's attention in the early 1850s. The Taiping rebellion in China between 1850 and 1853 seemed to offer the prospect of Christianity being established in the Chinese Empire and Shaftesbury was greatly excited at this. The rebellion was, he felt, due to the direct interposition of God, and he foresaw the Gospel being offered 'where, in truth, it has never yet been fairly offered, in China and Japan.' It would then have been 'preached for a witness to all nations,' and this would usher in the Second Coming.[76] The British and Foreign Bible Society decided to send to the people of China a million copies of the New Testament in their own language, and the London Missionary Society sought to raise funds to send out more missionaries. It held a fund-raising meeting in November, 1853, and Shaftesbury was invited to take the chair. He accepted the invitation, although he knew that, in thus cooperating with Dissenters, he would give offence to his friends in the Church of England. He was, he wrote, 'sorry for it', but the cause was 'too holy, too catholic, too deeply allied with the single name of Christ, for any considerations of Church system and Episcopal rule. . . .'[77] In his speech, he spoke of the recent events in China. The old wall of superstition was broken down; the empire of China was opened to missionary effort; 'The citadel (was) to be stormed, not by the potentates and armies of Europe, but by Protestant agents, by a noble rivalry of Protestant missions from every part of the civilised globe and of every evangelical denomination.'[78]

China thus greatly interested Shaftesbury in the early 1850s, and so too did America, and, in particular, American slavery. He was much touched by Mrs Harriet Beecher Stowe's *Uncle Tom's Cabin:* 'marvellous work! What a power of Christian intellect!' he wrote of it in November, 1852, and he decided to draw up an Address from the women of England to the women of America to 'try to stir their souls and sympathies.'[79] This he did and sent a copy of it to the newspapers. In it, he acknowledged that it was with great reluctance that he ventured to suggest a course of proceeding to his 'fair fellow-subjects', but he was 'impelled to do so by a feeling almost irresistible.' Public opinion, he wrote, and appeals to the 'great sympathies of mankind' could achieve more than force or statute laws, and if his Address were undertaken by local committees, numerously signed and sent to America, it could not fail 'under God's blessing, to produce a deep and fruitful impression.'[80] The Address asked the women of America to consider how far the system of slavery accorded with the word of God and with the 'inalienable rights of immortal souls and the pure and merciful spirit of Christian religion'. It acknowledged that there were difficulties and dangers in the abolition of a longstanding system and admitted that preparation would be necessary, but, it ran, 'we appeal . . . to you, as sisters, as wives and mothers, to raise your voices to your fellow-citizens and your prayers to God for the removal of this affliction from the Christian world.' It was not that Britain was guiltless in the matter – Britain had started the system in the past, but she was now anxious to avow her complicity and to join with America in expunging their common guilt.[81] In the months after Shaftesbury took this initiative, the matter continued to occupy his mind. He marvelled that a country could so flout the laws of God by its practices, customs and laws and yet prosper; it was, he wrote, 'wonderful to contemplate the long-suffering of God towards the American Republic.'[82] The next day, he wrote that the United States slavery harassed his 'very soul'. He could think of nothing else: 'breathe a prayer for them minute after minute.'[83] He wondered if his 'crusade for the Niggers' would prosper: would he attain the praise of Wilberforce or of Don Quixote?[84] He received support from the Duchess of Sutherland, who formed a committee of ladies to adopt the Address, and, in December, he wrote to Mrs Stowe to express admiration for her work and his gratitude to God who had put it in to her heart to write it. In May of the following year, he met Mrs Stowe when she was received by the Duchess of Sutherland at Stafford House – he entertained her to dinner at his house in Grosvenor Square and, after dinner, invited a number of people to meet her. Two weeks later, he took the chair at an anti-slavery meeting at Exeter Hall: 'zeal tremendous,' he wrote of it.[85] His activities met with some criticism. *The Times* commented unfavourably on his speech at Exeter Hall. It took up remarks which he had made about the impossibility of justifying slavery on religious grounds: these had been to the effect that any clergyman who rested American slavery on the Bible desecrated his pulpit 'by doctrines better suited to the synagogue of Satan'.[86] *The Times* wondered if Shaftesbury had not heard of slavery in the Bible? Were slaves not told to remain content with their lot?[87] Shaftesbury answered these points. There was, he wrote, a wide distinction between Hebrew and American slavery – protection had been given to the first group, but the latter was utterly helpless. And he defended his comments about the impossibility of reconciling slavery with religion. Any man who could mount the pulpit and defend the sale of human beings on the authority of Holy Scripture seemed to him 'either not to know Christianity or to promulgate doctrines diametrically opposed to it.'[88] The Address to the American women was also criticised. Letters to the press pointed to social abuses in Britain which might be dealt with before attention was focused on America, and when the Address was sent, Mrs Tyler, widow of a former President, adopted a similar tone: 'leave it to the women of the South to alleviate the suffering of their dependents, while you take care of your own. The negro of the South lives sumptuously, in comparison with a hundred thousand of your white population in London.'[89] Shaftesbury was distressed by such responses to his efforts, but one comment made in the press in the United States amused him. It was written by the editor of a religious paper in the South, who asked:

> And who is this Lord Shaftesbury? Some unknown lordling; one of your modern philanthropists suddenly started up to take part in a passing agitation. It is a pity he does not look at home. Where was he when Lord Ashley was so notably fighting for the Factory Bill and pleading the cause of the English slave? We never even heard the name of Lord Shaftesbury *then*.[90]

But if Shaftesbury had interests which extended to the internal conduct of other countries, he did not neglect the condition of his own – he continued to 'look at home'. There, admittedly, the situation was in some respects more hopeful than it had been in the 1840s. Shaftesbury was aware of the improvement in economic well-being and social relations. In March, 1851, he visited Lancashire and met the factory operatives once again. It was his first visit since his 'betrayal', and, although admittedly it was an occasion organised by those who had remained loyal to him at that time, he was given a warm reception and gratitude was expressed for the part which he had played over factory reform. In reply, he dwelt on the benefits of the Act of 1850 and also mentioned the effects of the repeal of the Corn Laws. These two measures, he said, 'had left little bad feeling behind. The effect had been to improve the condition of all classes . . . from the highest to the lowest.'[91] After his visit, he wrote to Russell that 'often as (he had) seen this people, (he) never saw them so ardent, so affectionate, so enthusiastic.'[92] And he returned to similar themes in 1853 when he commented that England in all her history had never combined before so many elements of material prosperity. The Monarchy and the Lords were well esteemed, and there was 'a singular union and mutual respect, of all classes, the highest, the middle, the lowest. . . .'[93] Yet Shaftesbury was by no means satisfied that no more could be done. Factory reform had, in his view, given more time for leisure and self-improvement and there might be a greater 'diffusion of wealth' than ever before, but there were many areas where there was still need for improvement: among ragged children, in housing conditions; over juvenile crime and chimney sweeping; in the treatment of lunacy; in provision for public health. Thus, despite the economic progress of the 1850s, Shaftesbury remained faithful to the cause of social improvement. Although there had been evidence of a slackening in his interest in factory reform at the end of the forties, there was no sign of lack of intensity in his attitude to other issues in the early fifties: in June, 1853, he wrote of being 'harassed by public and private business' – his heart went 'so completely into every question' that he felt like 'one possessed'.[94]

Ragged Schools remained a major concern in those years. Shaftesbury made frequent visits to individual Ragged Schools and took an interest in all the other activities which were started under the auspices of the Ragged School Union in London: the shoeblacks brigades[95] and also the refuges and dormitories which the Union assisted to receive children for board and lodging.[96] In January, 1852, he took Anthony to see the Field Lane Refuge: 'Ah, what things there are within a walk of Palaces, Luxuries, Comforts, wholly unknown, wholly unimagined,' he commented.[97] He gave farewell addresses to emigrant children who were sent abroad under the auspices of the Union: these remained privately financed, since a further attempt to secure government funds in June, 1852, failed. In September, 1851, Shaftesbury presided at the leave-taking of emigrants on board the ship *Athenian* for Melbourne and he warned the boys and girls to be on guard against the gold mania.[98] He also presented prizes to children whom the Ragged School Union had placed in employment – the Union offered such prizes to every pupil who retained a place for a specified period as an inducement to good conduct. And, every May, he took the chair of the Union. His speeches ranged over familiar themes: the contribution which Ragged Schools made to public order and the prevention of crime; the habits of economy and self-discipline which they had inculcated; the extent to which laymen were active in the work of the Union. He also urged his hearers to persevere in their efforts, for, although much had been achieved, much remained to be done. He always insisted that the work of the Schools lay among children who were truly humble in intellect and origin. He was opposed to periodical exhibitions and displays in Ragged Schools – this encouraged teachers to spend time on the more intelligent children and sacrifice children of less ability. And he warned against accepting children into Ragged Schools who were not truly destitute: 'You must keep your Ragged Schools down to one mark: you must keep them ... in the mire and the gutter, so long as the mire and the gutter exist.'[99] Further, he became more and more convinced that the root cause of the 'mire' lay in the domiciliary condition of the working classes. Abodes of 'filthiness and vice' caused the destitution of the children who found their way into Ragged Schools, and, once they returned to such abodes, they were virtually certain to be disabused of the lessons they had learned. Thus Shaftesbury told the tenth meeting of the Union in 1854:

You make one step in advance and two other steps are made in arrear
and such will be the case until you can prevail upon the Government of
the country . . . to rise to a sense of their duty and take care that all those
noxious, those pestiferous, those destructive influences, be altogether
removed from the presence and from the sufferings of the people.[100]

And, despite his new parliamentary status, Shaftesbury was still concerned to prevail on governments to 'rise to a sense of (their) duty' in these matters. In his first few weeks in the Lords, he took up two bills on the subject of lodging houses which he had proposed in his last months in the Commons. Indeed, the knowledge that these bills had still to be completed was one consideration which made him overcome his reluctance to take his seat in the Lords, and he told his new political colleagues that it was only his sense of the urgent need for legislation on this subject which induced him to address the Lords so early after his entry to the Upper House.[101] The Society for the Improving the Condition of the Labouring Classes had built Lodging Houses, and Shaftesbury – when still Ashley – had, in 1847, written on the subject in *The Quarterly Review*.[102] In April, 1851, he had introduced a bill in the Commons to encourage the establishment of Lodging Houses for the working classes. This proposed that towns with a population of ten thousand or more inhabitants should be empowered to build Model Lodging Houses and raise money to defray the expenses. In June, 1851, he had introduced a further measure for the regulation and inspection of Common Lodging Houses. Both measures were much in accordance with his ideas on public health and owed much to Chadwick's practical experience – bad housing, whether permanent or temporary, was a rabid breeding ground for disease and was also an inducement to intemperance and vice. Both bills passed the Commons, and Shaftesbury successfully steered them through the Lords. The Act provided for the inspection and registration of Lodging Houses was to be quite widely adopted. There was little expenditure involved in its implementation and lodging house keepers showed a readiness to cooperate with the police, who had the task of inspecting their premises under the Act. No doubt they felt that it was in their interest to do so, in order to keep in business, and attention to the physical surroundings of their premises might divert the notice of the police from any criminal pursuits which took place within them.[103] Shaftesbury himself was pleased with the operation of the Act. He mentioned it in his speech to the Annual Meeting of the Ragged School Union in 1853 and drew the attention of his audience to a Report made by Captain Hay, the Superintendent of the Police, which showed that improvements had taken place.[104] Hay's Report, however, suggested that there was a need for an amendment to the 1851 Act to give the police more powers to remove sick persons to hospital, to punish offenders under the Act and to arrange for reports on the lodging of beggars and vagrants. A further measure was, indeed, introduced by Shaftesbury in May, 1853,[105] a few days after his speech to the Ragged School Union. It reached the Commons on 6 June and went on to the statute book on 4 August. It had the effect of strengthening and widening the scope of the earlier Act. There were, indeed, still defects which reduced the effectiveness of legislation on this subject. There was a need for a tighter definition of a Common Lodging House; and whereas the lodging house keeper had to attend to improvements, the owner of the premises was not forced to make structural alterations, which would have brought greater benefits. Nevertheless, the two Acts of 1851 and 1853 went a considerable way towards the improvement of Lodging Houses.

The other Act of 1851, however, permitting the establishment of Lodging Houses by local councils, was to have little effect. It was only permissive, and, if implemented, offered the prospect of considerable expenditure, with very little return. And other measures which Shaftesbury introduced – in 1853 – were also to be of limited effect. In March, 1853, he expressed concern over the consequences of the demolition of property by Improvement Companies to make way for railway or dock development or the construction of new and wider streets.[106] Parliament, Shaftesbury argued, should take steps to stop this; he was taking the initiative in this matter, he said, mostly on behalf of the 'humbler classes', but there was also the danger that epidemics might start in such poor areas and spread to richer ones. He proposed that there should be a standing order to the effect that before any power was given to demolish houses, proof would be required as to which of the houses were used wholly or partly as working-class accommodation, and, further, whether such houses could be demolished without involving pecuniary or other injury to those who had lived in them and without causing overcrowding of other houses. But the Lords were wary of such a standing order; critics of the scheme argued that it was unworkable and would stand in the way of improvements for sanitary purposes. A select committee was appointed and its Report, of 9 May, suggested a weakening of Shaftesbury's standing order. It simply proposed that companies should report any schemes involving the demolition of thirty or more houses in any one parish; the Report had to be deposited in the office of the clerk of Parliament and had to include a statement of the number of houses, and, if possible, the number of persons, affected by any proposed development; and also, if provision were made in the bill for remedying the inconvenience that was likely to arise. Although it was not what he had wanted, this was accepted by Shaftesbury – he acknowledged that their Lordships had 'gone far towards instituting the very best relations between capital and labour that were capable of being made' on the subject.[107]

A further area of Shaftesbury's activity in the Lords in 1853 was that of juvenile crime, and, here again, he did not secure complete success. The extent to which young persons were involved in criminal activities in cities and towns was a matter to which Shaftesbury had frequently referred in his speeches to the Ragged School Union. On 17 June, 1853, he introduced a measure in the Lords to deal with the problem; it was given its second reading on 27 June and Shaftesbury's main speech on it was delivered at the committee stage on 5 July.[108] He drew on his own knowledge of the subject; on the reports from magistrates and police inspectors; on statements and confessions of thieves; on the testimony of city missionaries. Shaftesbury argued that the origins of much crime of this kind lay not so much in the children themselves as in their parents: children were often sent out by their parents and told that they must not return without money, however this was obtained. This was the starting-point of a life of crime. Thus Shaftesbury's measure proposed that the police might have greater powers to arrest all children found in a state of vagrancy in the streets and bring them before the magistrates. They would then be put into a workhouse and educated, the cost being borne, if possible, by the parents; if not, by the ratepayers. The scheme illustrated Shaftesbury's belief in the need to discipline and restrain the wrong-doer in addition to 'reforming' him, and somewhat to his surprise, it proved substantially acceptable to the Lords and went to the Commons. On 1 July, Shaftesbury had written to Palmerston,[109] the Home Secretary in the Aberdeen Coalition, enclosing the bill which, he said, was 'intended to strike at the source of half the crime and pauperism of the country.' The only difficulty, he wrote, might be the expense, but he felt that two-thirds of the parents could afford to contribute to the upkeep of the children once detained, and, indeed, the very publication of the Act would drive half the young mendicants off the streets. But by the time the bill reached the Commons, it was late in the session and was dropped. Shaftesbury was deeply disappointed and wrote to Palmerston expressing his feelings.[110] He also wrote to Chadwick from Ems in August, 1853, saying that he had just heard that Palmerston had given up his Juvenile Mendicancy bill: 'The House it is said,' Shaftesbury wrote, 'refused to listen; this, if it be so, is a sad omen for my future exertions. I have not time before me, as I had many years ago when I moved my factory bill; nor have I the same strength and fire to endure disappointment.'[111] But in 1854 a measure on youthful offenders was passed under Palmerston's auspices and with Shaftesbury's assistance. This made greater use of Reformatory schools, which had been set up in various parts of the country by voluntary initiative. On conviction, children were to be admitted, after a short imprisonment, to such schools and remain in them for a number of years. The cost of this was to be borne by the Treasury and recovered, if possible, from the parents. And powers were given to counties and boroughs to build Reformatory schools.

There were, however, other areas where not even such limited success was to be gained. One was in relation to chimney sweeps. The effects of previous legislation on the subject which had come into force in 1842 had been patchy, and, in many places, the practice of using children for sweeps continued. The late 1840s and early 1850s witnessed further developments. There were revelations of cruelty practised by master sweeps on children, leading to injury and death: one particularly notorious case occurred in Manchester in 1847 and led to the trial and sentencing of a Master Sweep, John Gordon. This case and others of a similar nature prompted the establishment of a Climbing Boys' Society, of which Shaftesbury was chairman. This gathered information about breaches of the law and, where possible, brought prosecutions. It was, however, difficult to obtain convictions – to do so, it was necessary to show that a boy had been seen going into a flue or coming out of it, but since master sweeps locked a boy into the house on entering, such evidence could not be easily obtained. A further defect was that, under the existing legislation, no child under sixteen could be apprenticed to the trade of chimney sweeping, but masters had then started to employ children who were not apprentices, ostensibly to carry the brushes and tools. Once inside the house, they were forced up the chimneys. After an unsuccessful attempt to remedy these defects in 1851, Shaftesbury introduced a bill on the subject in May, 1853.[112] It provided that every master who allowed any person under sixteen to engage or assist in the trade should be liable for punishment; and any boy employed to carry the tools would not be allowed to go beyond the door of the house where the sweeping was to take place. The proposal, however, ran into strong opposition in the Lords. Lord Beaumont was critical of the Act of 1840 which, he argued, had only had the effect of burning more houses. If it were not for the 'high character of the noble earl who introduced the bill,' said Beaumont, he would call it the 'pityful cant of pseudo-philanthropy',[113] and he objected to the constant interference of the legislature in matters of this kind. Shaftesbury sprang to the defence of the earlier legislation which, he argued, had brought considerable benefits. Nevertheless, it was agreed to appoint a select committee to inquire into the expediency or otherwise of the regulations in the bill. Shaftesbury himself was a member of the committee. In the course of its investigations, damaging evidence was given about the chimneys of two members of the committee, Lords Beaumont and Hardwicke, but despite this, the committee recommended that no further action should be taken.

In April, 1854, however, Shaftesbury tried again[114] and this time Beaumont dropped his opposition, although Lord Clancarty, who had been chairman of the select committee, remained hostile to the bill and proposed an amendment that it be read in six months' time.[115] The bill, however, survived this opposition and went to the Commons, where the second reading was proposed in May.[116] But criticisms were expressed in the Commons. The bill proposed that a master who compelled any person under sixteen to 'use or assist' in the trade of chimney sweeper should be liable for a fine not exceeding £10. Russell pointed to the difficulties of ensuring that a boy was not taken into a house and forced to sweep the chimney. Unless the doors of the house were left open, no conviction for an offence of this kind could be obtained, and, since sweeping sometimes took place at 3 or 4 a.m., doors could not be left open without danger of burglary. On the other hand, a chimney sweeper, who employed a boy to ride his donkey or carry his sack, might be convicted of an offence. There would, therefore, be no means of convicting the guilty but the innocent might be convicted; further, in the absence of a public prosecutor, the law would be inoperative.[117] Such arguments won the day and the House accepted the motion that the bill should be deferred for six months. Shaftesbury was, as he wrote, 'very sad and low' about the loss of the bill. All the horrors of the system had been perpetuated 'in a light and saucy way',[118] and he did not forgive Russell for his part in this. He was uncertain whether to move an Address to the Crown and revive the whole matter, or to let it rest and take it up the following session. He decided on the latter course and, in May, 1855, introduced a further measure, but again, it did not succeed and was dropped after its first reading.

Two further areas of activity and concern for Shaftesbury during these years related to his extra-parliamentary position on the Lunacy Commission and the General Board of Health. Despite the increased safeguards in the procedure of certification of persons to be admitted to asylums, criticism that undue detention could still take place continued virtually unabated, and this was vocally expressed by the Alleged Lunatics' Friend Society, which was founded in 1845 with the object of protecting the individual from unjust confinement. This was a matter of great anxiety to Shaftesbury. In November, 1847, he had spent a great deal of time investigating the case of Mrs Henry Howard, who had been detained as a lunatic: when he and three other Commissioners investigated the case, they had come to the conclusion that Mrs Howard was 'as sane as any woman in England'[119] and that she had been improperly detained. Mrs Howard was released, but Shaftesbury wrote that he trembled when he contemplated the facility which still existed of incarcerating a victim. In September, 1851, he referred in his Diary to another case of a lady considered insane. This case, he wrote, proved what his experience had long indicated: 'the sad ignorance of medical men; the awful imperfection of evidence, whereon people are shut up.' And he reflected sadly on the 'prodigious cruelties' which would be inflicted if the Commissioners were 'either annihilated or sleepy' and of the 'vast amount of it that exist(ed) notwithstanding (their) activity.'[120] Shaftesbury felt that there was need for revision of the legislation of 1845, and he cooperated with Derby's government in 1852 in preparing the necessary amendments. The fall of the government before the legislation was passed was a disappointment to him,[121] but the matter was taken up by Lord St Leonards in the subsequent government and in the course of 1853 amending legislation was passed. A new Act, amending the Act of 1845 for the regulation of the care and treatment of lunatics, introduced more stringent safeguards into admission procedures. Further details were now required: thus medical certificates had to distinguish between facts indicating insanity which had been observed by the certifying doctor personally and those communicated to him by others; and the certifying surgeon had to state his qualifications to practise in that capacity.[122] Another new Act replaced that of 1845 concerning the provision of asylums in counties and boroughs: it established various methods in which a county or borough asylum might be set up and also ways of financing this, whether public or private, or a combination of both. Shaftesbury took no part in the early debates on these bills, but at the third reading, he expressed his views. He reiterated the theme that no control or superintendence could be fully effective so long as private asylums were permitted to exist and a proprietor derived gain from insufficient treatment or prolonged detention. But the public was not ready for radical change, and, meantime, he expressed his gratitude to St Leonards and felt that the benefits of the new legislation would be great.[123]

Shaftesbury could not say the same, however, of developments in public health in these years. His removal to the Lords caused Chadwick some alarm. The Board, Chadwick felt, would be greatly weakened by Shaftesbury's absence from the Commons, and he told Shaftesbury that Russell also thought that his place could not be easily filled. Nevertheless, Chadwick continued, Shaftesbury would still be free to initiate measures and would be in a position to influence public opinion.[124] An immediate concern was the Board's attempt to buy out the private burial companies, authorised by the Treasury in March, 1851: the Board had served compulsory purchase orders on the Brompton and Nunhead cemeteries. It seemed that no further trouble would be encountered but this was a misleading impression. One difficulty was in finding the money required. Two insurance companies were approached and refused to lend, on the basis that the Board's limited term of existence – five years – did not afford sufficient security. A further difficulty arose from the activities of a newly-formed cemetery company, the

Necropolis Company, which proposed to open a cemetery on the fringes of the Metropolitan Burial district; and the competition which this clearly involved was felt to be a threat to the Board's claim to monopoly within that district. The Board was anxious to assert its position on both issues. It asked the Treasury to supply the money required for the purchase of the two cemeteries immediately and also proposed clauses to amend the Act of 1850 which would have completed its monopoly and safeguarded it against the activities of the Necropolis Company or others of a similar nature. Shaftesbury took part in the negotiations with the government in the summer of 1851 and had various conversations with the Chancellor of the Exchequer. But the Treasury took a very unaccommodating line, claiming that the Board had started negotiations with the Cemetery companies before being sure that money would be available to buy them out; moreover, it refused to advance the money and ordered the Board to take no further steps. All that it would do was to grant money to buy the two cemeteries which the Board was already committed to purchasing and this was incorporated into the Metropolitan Interments (Advances) bill introduced by Grey on 25 July, 1851. Shaftesbury was furious. At one point, he had thought that all would be well, but this seems to have been based on a misunderstanding and, when the government's hostility to the Board became evident, Shaftesbury wrote angrily to Chadwick of the Chancellor's 'insolence'.[125] When the matter was debated in the Lords on 31 July, 1851, he was bitterly critical of the Treasury's conduct.[126] He also reverted to the theme that a separate, permanent and independent Board was much preferable to the existing Board, with its state of dependence and impermanence.

It had been a sadly mismanaged business on both sides. The Board overestimated its capacity to command loans and overstretched its claims to monopoly; on the other hand, the Treasury did not realise until too late the implications of the Board's plans. Moreover, it was clear that the government was planning the abandonment of the Act of 1850: Seymour was, indeed, preparing an alternative measure. Chadwick wanted to retain the scheme for closing the two cemeteries and favoured a remonstrance on the subject.[127] Shaftesbury, however, was opposed to this. He could see that the Board was in too weak a position to put up a struggle, and, in any event, he could see no point in taking a stand on the two-cemetery plan, with which he did not agree and which, indeed, had not been the Board's original suggestion. He felt that since the government had taken responsibility, this was where responsibility should remain. The Board should not be pledged to anything except its own first plan, and he advised Chadwick that the only course was to cooperate with the government. 'Say that, in deference to the Ministerial authority,' he wrote, 'we will, while holding our own opinions, do our utmost as a Board, to carry theirs into effect.'[128] But by December, 1851, it was clear that the Board was to lose all executive power over interments, whether their own schemes or those of the government, and that cemeteries were to be left where they were. Thus 1851 closed on a note of total failure: legislation was awaited which would clearly remove all power from the Board in this area.

The water question had likewise come to nothing.[129] The government measure introduced by the Home Secretary, Sir George Grey, on 29 April, 1850, had been quite at variance with the proposals put forward by Chadwick and reflected the views of Sir William Clay, Chairman of the Southwark and Vauxhall Company. Clay was anxious that there should be cooperation between the Board of Health and the private companies along the lines of greater consolidation, but his plans stopped far short of the buying out of the Companies which the Board desired. The bill of April, 1850, thus proposed a compromise: existing companies were to be amalgamated and placed under the supervision of the Home Secretary and dividends would be limited to a lower level of 5% and an upper level of 6%. If the proprietors did not comply with the provisions of the Act, the Home Secretary might stop the dividends. There was, therefore, an element of government supervision and control, but the service was left in private hands and, indeed, these now enjoyed a legal monopoly. Further, the service would be little different in practice from that previously offered. The government refused to enforce a constant supply, justifying this on the grounds that existing equipment could not be superseded. And there was to be no universal supply – many Londoners would remain without water. The supply, moreover, was not to be filtered; no immediate use was to be made of the purer sources until the matter was further investigated. And there was to be no consolidation of drains and water under a single authority.

Chadwick had known of the government's proposals before they were announced and he had submitted a memorandum to the Home Secretary in protest: in this, Shaftesbury had fully concurred. But if the government's proposals could find no friends in this quarter, they could find no friends in any quarter. Clay's advocacy of consolidation did not commend itself to all the proprietors and many vestrymen wanted a much looser form of control. The bill thus suffered attack after attack in the House, and, although it passed its second reading, it was referred on 5 June to a select committee, which would have the task of settling the question of the new supplies and devising the best administrative arrangements. The committee sat for weeks and concluded its hearings at the beginning of August. They were dominated by the various interested parties and, although the committee favoured consolidation, it did not make a Report. Finally, in July, 1851, after further delay, Russell announced that the government did not intend to legislate on the water supply that year,[130] and the matter was dropped.

The new year 1852, therefore, started with both the burials and the water questions undecided. Legislation on each was, however, clearly foreshadowed and Seymour was entrusted with this task – the Board was completely ignored. But before Seymour could do anything, Russell's Ministry was defeated and the Derby Ministry replaced it. On 29 April, 1852, Shaftesbury moved a resolution in the Lords 'that the sanitary state of the Metropolis requires the immediate interposition of Her Majesty's Government.' He supported this in a long speech[131] and he called on the government to 'institute sound measures for the benefit and safety of the great mass of the working people.' Derby came down clearly on the side of doing as little as possible. He stated all the classic objections to intervention and centralisation and argued that morality, decency and cleanliness could not be enforced by legislation : a statement which drew 'No, No' from Shaftesbury.[132] Shaftesbury changed his resolution to read that the sanitary state of the Metropolis required the immediate 'attention' of the government rather than 'interposition' and this was accepted,[133] but Derby's attitude clearly betokened measures which would do little in the way of introducing effective control over burials or water supply. And, indeed, the two bills on the subject introduced by Manners, Seymour's successor, were of this kind. The Interments bill repealed the 1850 Act: the new bill simply empowered the Home Secretary to close any Metropolitan burial ground and the parishes, either singly or jointly, could provide new grounds or enter into a contract with the commercial cemeteries. The Water bill allowed the private companies to continue their separate existence; even the measure of consolidation envisaged in the previous year's bill was abandoned. There were certain conditions laid down over the quality of the water and its distribution, but these were to come into existence gradually, over a period of five years. Both bills passed the Houses and reached the statute book, and both represented a great setback for the Board.

Shaftesbury surveyed these and other developments with a deepening sense of gloom. In May, 1852, *The Times* published an article critical of the Board. Shaftesbury commented that the newspaper had taken up

> the note of the undertakers, the water companies, the Parliamentary agents and the whole tribe of jobbers who live on the miseries of mankind and are hunting the Board of Health through brake and briar, and hope to be 'in at the death'. Be it so (he continued): if we fall, not a body will be left to shout 'unclean, unclean', and form, and guide, and impel, public opinion. . . .[134]

He was fearful for the future. He had taken a walk in his 'old haunts' in

Westminster and Pye Street: 'sick, sick, sick to see how little years of labour had done,' he wrote.[135] Further, he felt personally aggrieved by a speech by Seymour, who, in the course of the debate on the Interment bill, had taken the opportunity to complain about the composition of the Board. He recalled that, although he had been responsible for the proceedings of the Board, he had been outvoted by two civil servants, Chadwick and Southwood Smith, and thus had finally stopped attending. This was a strongly personal view of the proceedings, and it left out of account Shaftesbury's labours at the Board. Shaftesbury wrote to Seymour contrasting Seymour's very frequent absences from the Board with his own regular attendance.[136] Moreover, resistance had been offered to Seymour on only one occasion, and this had been by Shaftesbury and not by Chadwick or Southwood Smith. Seymour wrote in reply and apologised, claiming that his speech had been incorrectly reported,[137] but he did not retract his statements in public and his speech was greatly resented by Chadwick and Shaftesbury. Further, when the Water bill reached the Lords in late June, Shaftesbury felt that it was so late in the session that nothing effective could be done about it. The bill had to be passed 'without their Lordships knowing more of it than if it were a Chaldean manuscript.'[138]

When the legislation which made such a mockery of his hopes had been passed, Shaftesbury was at Ems. He wrote to Chadwick, looking back bitterly to the proceedings of the year. The weather was hot in Ems; he had heard that it was even hotter in London. Thus Shaftesbury had 'pictured ... the sufferings of *our* clients in their crowded alleys, Courts, Lanes and houses of the Metropolis with poisonous and deadly water. ...' He could not, he wrote, describe the pain of his disappointment – it came between him and his 'cure'.[139] He also reflected on the progress made in these respects by Louis Napoleon in Paris: 'he has proclaimed war against all courts, alleys, lanes and culs de sac,' Shaftesbury wrote. Thus working men would have cause to shout 'Vive le Despotisme: à bas les gouvernements libres!': and he continued:

> Why our Vestries, Boards of Guardians, paving Boards and all the apparatus of what is called 'local' and 'Self' government, have only been so many obstacles in the way of physical and Social amelioration.[140]

After his return to London, Shaftesbury's spirits were still very low. Indeed, he knew that the Board's existence was in danger: 'The Board is to be destroyed,' he wrote, 'its sin is its unpardonable activity.'[141] In December, on the defeat and resignation of the Derby government, Shaftesbury felt that there was little to be gained by a return to 'our old Masters', as he put it to Chadwick.[142] Public men, he reflected, 'know nothing, want to know nothing, hate to be told anything, which does not openly and directly affect their political position and safety.'[143] The new President of the Board was not, in fact, to be Seymour but Sir William Molesworth, but, like Seymour, he preferred to act independently of the Board. Shaftesbury was depressed at the prospect: on the last day of December, he recalled the 'mortifications' which he had undergone in the Board's service, and he wrote that it would 'vex (him) beyond expression to see Chadwick and Southwood Smith sent to the right-about and the Board, which, under God, (had) done and ... conceived so many good things, broken up.'[144]

In the course of 1853, Shaftesbury, indeed, continued to be quick to defend measures designed to improve health. Thus he supported a measure brought in by Lord Lyttelton to extend the practice of vaccination — he regarded vaccination as 'one of those manifold and gracious measures that (God) be pleased, from time to time, to reveal for the alleviation of suffering in this fallen world.'[145] But he was more than ever convinced that the Board of Health could not last another year. While at Ems in August, he saw a newspaper cutting that the Board would terminate the following year, and mused that, had the members of the Board been less careful of the public interests and considered its own popularity rather than the general welfare, it might have neutralised many enemies.[146] He made a list of all the interests which the Board had offended: Dissenters, parliamentary agents, civil engineers, in the last case because the Board had chosen its own men to carry out its ideas over drainage at a smaller salary, the College of Physicians, because of the Board's initiative and success in dealing with cholera, the Boards of Guardians, the Treasury, the water companies, the Commissioners of Sewers. He admitted that the Board had not always helped its own cause; it had not always been on its guard. Chadwick had attracted unpopularity by his 'overbearing manners and modes of action too Doctrinaire', and he himself had been imprudent, 'smarting under a sense of insult and injustice'.[147] But the damage was done, and he wrote to Chadwick on 28 August that he could not doubt that the Board's dissolution had already been decided.[148]

One bright prospect offered to the Board in late 1853, however, lay in the activities of Palmerston at the Home Office. Shaftesbury was certainly disappointed at first that Palmerston did not take up his Juvenile Mendicancy bill, but he rejoiced that his father-in-law took up several of the Board's proposals. Thus, acting under the Interment Act of 1852, Palmerston closed various cemeteries. Shaftesbury could not help but reflect how easy progress was if such action were taken by the government. The Board had laboured hard in the cause of interments and had borne the heat and burden of the day but, lacking support from the government, had failed; Palmerston 'having borne and done nothing of the kind, but being the Secretary of State, succeeds!'[149] He thought that Palmerston avoided difficulties with which the Board had tried to deal over such matters as compensation for the clergy's fees and was not concerned with the cost of extra-mural burials for the poorer classes. Nevertheless, Shaftesbury felt that the cause had at last a friend in high places: he had never known any Home Secretary equal to Palmerston 'for readiness to undertake every good work of kindness, humanity and social good'.[150] Thus there seemed to be some hope that the Board might be saved from immediate destruction. A further cause for hope – paradoxically, in a sense – seemed to be offered by an outbreak of cholera. There were already outbreaks on the Continent in August, 1852, and Shaftesbury wrote in that month to Disraeli, then in office, asking for permission to send out 'spies' to see the state of the cholera which was 'manifestly advancing towards our shores.' Indeed, there was reason to believe that it was in England already: 'we ought to be prepared,' Shaftesbury wrote.[151] The threat receded at that point, but it recurred in 1853, and this offered the prospect that the Board might be called upon to resume its previous activity. But this time, the lessons of the past must be learned. Shaftesbury wrote to Chadwick urging him to be cautious in his dealings with the Treasury – he must take care that, in all instances where additional intelligence of the progress of cholera was received, fresh application was made for powers to the Treasury: 'but be very respectful,' Shaftesbury wrote, 'for be assured that the slightest suspicion will be magnified into a crime by men who are resolved to remove us from our places and tarnish us in reputation.'[152] In September, cholera broke out in Newcastle and Gateshead: in the first two weeks of the month, there were two hundred and fourteen deaths. The Nuisances Act was put into effect and the Board issued regulations and carried out house-to-house visitations. Throughout the episode, Shaftesbury continued to do his best to protect the Board. In addition to urging on Chadwick the necessity of adopting a conciliatory tone with the Boards of Guardians, the Treasury and all authorities,[153] he wrote to Palmerston asking that the Board should not be turned out during the epidemic. He reminded Palmerston that the Board has passed through the whole of the 1848–9 epidemic and no one had disputed the zeal, skill and judgment with which it had discharged its duties. It would be an insult to remove men

> against whom [as he wrote] there is not even a shadow of an accusation; and surely it would be hazardous to the Public Service to break up, in the very midst of the Cholera, a tried and approved system, banish the functionaries who have carried it into practice and introduce new and probably inexperienced men with new plans and new opinions.[154]

The Board did survive the epidemic, and this time its efforts in preventing a worse outbreak received praise. The outbreak was contained in Newcastle and died out by November.

Nevertheless, the future of the Board could not long remain in doubt – it had to be decided in 1854. On 28 January, 1854, Shaftesbury wrote to Palmerston[155] recounting an interview which he had with Molesworth. Molesworth had asked for Shaftesbury's opinion on two matters: whether a new Board of Health should be appended to some existing Department or whether it should be an independent Department, with a chief of its own sitting in one or other House of Parliament. Shaftesbury had no hesitation in stating his decided preference for the latter. But he also told Palmerston that he was equally convinced that, for the sake of the public good, the Board should remain as it was. Chadwick and Southwood Smith – 'in whom,' he wrote, 'great knowledge, experience and indefatigable zeal are so combined' – would be very hard to replace, and they far outmatched the services which could be offered by a President aided by two secretaries, to be replaced at every change of government. Shaftesbury had also told Molesworth that it was desirable to keep the present Board until the end of the session – cholera might well recur and, by being retained, the members of the Board would be saved from unnecessary pain and insult. There was, indeed, the threat that cholera would recur: in March, Shaftesbury referred to this in the Lords[156] in answer to a point raised by Harrowby. He explained what the Board had been doing – it had, for example, with the aid of the College of Physicians, produced a manual to help people remote from medical treatment to administer aid to themselves. But, looking to the future, Shaftesbury said that these were only temporary expedients. What was necessary was the institution of permanent works: good drainage, widened streets, plentiful supplies of water and good ventilation. Shaftesbury thus tried all he could to justify the need for the Board to continue in existence; and the government did, indeed, state that it would continue until November. In July, Palmerston asked the House for a grant to keep it going until April, 1855, but, along with this, was to go a change in its composition. This would involve the appointment of two paid members and one unpaid, all directly under the control of the Home Secretary. The Board would thus be brought under ministerial control and its anomalous position of virtual independence would end.

Such proposals did not, however, satisfy the Board's critics, who wanted a wholly new Department to be created, with a new Minister, a President of the Board of Health. In the debates on the matter, the Board in general, and Chadwick in particular, were subjected to harsh criticism. It was clear that, if Palmerston's proposals were to succeed, the new Board would have to be composed without Chadwick, and he was persuaded to retire on a pension. Shaftesbury received this news at Ems: he wondered what Southwood Smith would do and whether he himself could remain. 'We have been, I feel,' he wrote, 'so utterly lacerated that we have neither shape nor strength. To hold our place would be, probably, useless; certainly, burdensome to excess.'[157] In fact, Shaftesbury and Southwood Smith also decided to resign.[158] Palmerston was unwilling to accept Shaftesbury's resignation, but Shaftesbury was unwilling to remain 'unless on grounds very intelligible'.[159] But the matter was decided when Palmerston proposed the second reading of his bill on 31 July. The critics of the Board – in particular, Seymour – returned to the attack and insisted that the present Board be removed before any proposal to reconstruct it was accepted. He thus moved a three-month adjournment to the debate and this was accepted. This amounted to a dismissal of the Board. As Shaftesbury put it on 31 July, 'No choice of resigning or remaining; the House of Commons threw out the Bill this day . . . thus after five years of intense and unrewarded labour I am turned off like a piece of lumber! Such is the public service. . . .'[160]

The experience had been a bitter and wounding one. In the course of the debates in mid-July, Shaftesbury had vigorously defended the activities of the Board.[161] He refuted the allegation that sanitary measures had been carried out by the 'despotic interference' of the Board rather than by the free will of the inhabitants of the towns; he also denied the suggestion that the Board had indulged in any kind of jobbery or corruption in its dealings with local Boards of Health and in the appointments which had been made to undertake sanitary improvements. And he praised his colleagues, Chadwick and Southwood Smith. As has been seen, Shaftesbury did realise Chadwick's shortcomings. He wrote in his Diary that Chadwick had 'done many things in a stiff, self-willed and arrogant spirit' and that his resolute and unwearying prosecution of his conclusions had brought him into frequent and almost personal conflict with those from whom he differed; his 'air and manner' had doubtless 'aggravated the mischief'.[162] But he had a very high respect for him and for Southwood Smith. He said in the Lords that he had never met with 'more diligent, zealous and efficient men of business'. Shaftesbury was also at pains to contradict the charge which Seymour had revived that he had ceased to attend the Board because of opposition to his plans. A rancorous dispute developed between Shaftesbury and Seymour on the issue. On 31 July in the Commons, Seymour once more challenged Shaftesbury's statements[163] and the following day in the Lords, Shaftesbury defended himself at length against these renewed attacks.[164] But he ended on a note of disdain: he said that he did not care for the opinion of his contemporaries, nor for that of posterity; what he did care for was the conviction that he had, by God's blessing, done his duty in that state of life to which it had pleased God to call him, and that conviction could not be taken away either by Seymour or the House of Commons.

As in the past, Shaftesbury had the better of the argument with Seymour, but – also as in the past – it was to no avail. On 1 August, a bill was introduced by Molesworth to make new arrangements. The Board was to be replaced by a new Health Department, with a President, Secretary and Under Secretary. This passed on 12 August. Meanwhile, on 5 August, Shaftesbury had given a farewell dinner to all connected with the Board: commissioners, doctors, engineers, clerks, secretary – a total of seventeen persons. And, when the Board was finally extinguished on the 12th, he reflected on the close of six years of hard and gratuitous service. There had, indeed, been achievements. The Board itself, in an attempt at self-defence, had produced a statement of these. Thus, by the end of 1853, two hundred and eighty four towns had applied for the intervention of the Board: two hundred and forty three of these had been examined by the Board's inspectors and in some half, steps were being taken towards schemes of improvement. But in London, there had been almost total failure, and it was on these and the attacks to which he had been subjected that Shaftesbury tended to dwell. Despite his disclaimer in the Lords, he felt the attacks keenly. Chadwick, he reflected, was not the object of attack: he could not forget the observations of Seymour and was sure that this showed a more general feeling of hatred towards himself. 'Lord Seymour,' he wrote, 'surpasses all conception in malice, gossip and cool lying . . . but not a voice raised on my behalf.'[165]

It was an understandable comment, but not an altogether accurate one, for, in the debates, Russell paid him generous tribute[166] and even Seymour said that he had great respect for Shaftesbury's personal character;[167] it was his policies which he disliked. Here, as so often in the past, Shaftesbury found it impossible to make the distinction, and indeed, he often gave way in these years to his habitual feeling that he was universally disliked and despised. Further, he felt increasingly neglected and ignored; the public were tired of him, his day was over and his enemies were beginning to laugh at him.[168] Here again, Shaftesbury saw things in highly personal terms, but it is true that, in the early 1850s, the cause of social improvement did not occupy a very high place in the attention of the public or the politicians. With the more relaxed conditions of the period, with radicalism less of a threat, measures for social improvement had less urgency. Further, on the outbreak of the Crimean War in 1854, much attention was focussed on foreign affairs. Shaftesbury was depressed and dismayed at the lack of concern: when he looked at the Metropolis and great towns, he found 'everything that should not be, in full abundance, everything that should be, totally wanting,' and yet 'not a hand is stirred!' All this, after so many years of labour, made him 'sorrowful and desperate in (his) days of approaching feebleness and decline of life.'[169]

If Shaftesbury was increasingly pessimistic about his own future role, he was also gloomy about the future on wider political grounds. It was certainly true that the old landmarks, the Monarchy and the Aristocracy, had survived and that there were more harmonious relations between the classes. Yet Shaftesbury detected what he regarded as sinister influences at work. Radicalism was, he felt, still a force to be reckoned with in the persons of Cobden and Bright, for whom he retained his hearty dislike. And he also sensed the existence of a desire for the redistribution of property. In a letter to Russell in November, 1851,[170] he wrote that socialist doctrines and principles were 'far more rife in the great towns of this country than most people are aware of.' They were to be found principally among the artisans and skilled workmen, especially in London, and they aimed at a distribution of all the property of those above them, particularly landed property. The mass of the people would be content with the social order if they were left alone, but, Shaftesbury wrote, 'an active and factious minority, bent on mischief and revolution' would eventually carry its purpose. He was anxious to reduce the turmoil and expenditure surrounding parliamentary elections and to create quieter conditions for voting. Thus he proposed a bill in 1853[171] which would have involved a stricter control of expenditure at elections and the replacement of the existing system of 'viva voce' voting by one whereby names were written on slips of paper which would be collected from house to house. This was not the ballot system, and, on these grounds, the bill incurred the criticism of Cobden. He wrote to Shaftesbury[172] to say that he could not support the bill; he himself was 'fanatical for the ballot not only as a cure for the moral evils which we all deplore, but as a means of elevating the political character of the electors.' He felt that any scheme which exempted voters from attendance at the poll would lead to frauds. For Shaftesbury, however, the ballot would be the very means whereby sinister influences could exert themselves in secret and the process which he so dreaded would be assisted. His own plan kept a system of open voting, but, he felt, would tempt moderate and respectable voters; for they were deterred from political involvement by the rowdiness and bribery which accompanied the present system to register their votes. The scheme came to nothing and was dropped,[173] but it was illustrative of Shaftesbury's desire to strengthen the quiet and orderly forces in the country.

Further, Shaftesbury was anxious to strengthen the role of the Lords. He was extremely dispirited by its existing role. The system was, he felt, bound by tradition and few members had any experience of business. The House was little more than a 'registration office' for bills from the Commons.[174] Already in 1849 – before his accession to the peerage – Shaftesbury had written to Russell stressing the desirability of recruiting new peers from men of trade and commerce. This would be in the interests of strengthening and adapting aristocratic institutions 'to the wants and character of the times'.[175] After his succession to the title, he brought up the need for a reform of the system of business in the Lords and approached Russell and Derby on the subject. Unless this were speedily done, Shaftesbury felt, the Lords would lose all effective share in legislation,[176] for, with such a menial role in the constitution as the existing one, the Lords – 'essentially the guardians of property', as he once put it[177] – were unable to perform any useful service. And Shaftesbury had little confidence in the Commons itself. He felt that its behaviour in constantly opposing the government of the day and forcing it into a weak position was irresponsible and self-seeking. He was also of the opinion that the calibre of the members was deteriorating. They were, he wrote, 'of inferior order in heart and mind, worse bred in their manners and more coarse in their language and feelings.' And this, he added, aided 'the movement'.[178]

The political system, therefore, did not fill Shaftesbury with confidence, nor did the men at the top of it. Although Russell was acceptable on religious grounds, he was very suspect politically. Thus Shaftesbury was very doubtful of his wisdom in preparing a measure of parliamentary reform in late 1851 which involved a lowering of the borough franchise to £5. Well-disposed people, Shaftesbury felt, did not require any measure of this kind; ill-disposed people would accept it as an instalment towards revolution.[179] He wrote to Russell urging caution. The existing institutions would not bear a 'rude shock'; the temper of the country at that moment might be 'loyal, aristocratical and conservative' but it might pass 'as a morning cloud'.[180] In November, he warned Russell once again of the dangers of lowering the franchise without extending it at the other end – thus he urged the enfranchisement of fund holders, annuitants and lawyers in chambers as persons with an interest in the welfare of the country, whose admission to the political system would strengthen the ranks of property and order.[181]

Russell's scheme did not, indeed, commend itself to all Whigs and came to nothing on his defeat in February, 1852. The accession of the Protectionists to office did not greatly reassure Shaftesbury. The talent at their disposal was meagre: 'not a man who is known to office,' Shaftesbury wrote, 'scarcely one who is known to the country!'[182] Moreover, he was afraid that their adherence to Protection would give ample opportunity for attacks on the landed aristocracy. In March, he commented that Derby had done more to sustain and promote Cobden and Bright than a thousand Leagues could have done,[183] and in April, wrote further that the Protectionists by their 'foolish adherence to what is either perilous or impossible, have revived the republican feeling and effort.'[184] It is true that Protection was quietly dropped by the Protectionist Tories in the course of their short-lived Ministry and, once this was done, there were clearly fewer political barriers in the way of Shaftesbury making his peace with them. He wrote that, had he been in the Commons, he would have supported Derby's government and would have attempted a reconciliation with those who, despite their faults, were 'natural friends and allies' in a way that Whigs and Radicals were not. But, when the Derby Ministry was defeated, Shaftesbury felt that this was retribution for an over-long attachment to Protection, a cause which, in his view, they had taken up 'to "make themselves a name", to coax the farmers, to disturb the government. The whole thing was "the party" and not the Country. . . .'[185] The Whigs were, therefore, too democratic; the Tories, for the moment, a spent force; and Shaftesbury viewed the Aberdeen Coalition with deep distaste. Part of this was based on personal considerations, for, although the reorganisation of the political groupings in the Coalition did offer greater hopes of stability, it also involved the promotion of men like Gladstone and Graham whom Shaftesbury regarded as antagonistic to him. He was disheartened, he wrote to Evelyn, to see his 'bitter enemies installed in office.'[186] And there was also the return of Russell in the Coalition, his plans for reform once again in preparation. Shaftesbury noted this in November, 1853: the £5 borough franchise which Russell proposed was, he wrote, 'the nearest form to universal suffrage, the next door to a mere rabble! May God avert this pestilence.'[187] And a few weeks later, he wrote fearfully of the steady advance of Democracy, 'or, what is in result the same, the spirit of yielding to it.'[188]

Shaftesbury thus still saw the institutions of the State and the social order as under attack. What was worse, he could detect in those at the head of State no will to meet the threat – indeed, by their actions, they were actually encouraging it. A similar situation, he felt, existed in the Church. The evidence of the 1851 Census showed a deplorable state of affairs: the Church of England, he commented, did not contain a majority of those who attended worship on the Sunday of the census. Further, there was the growing pervasiveness of liberal theology, or, as Shaftesbury called it, 'Neology'. He had been critical of it soon after its first real appearance in Britain under German influence in the late 1820s and 1830s[189] and he became increasingly impatient of persons who professed to be Christians and members of the Church of England and who yet questioned the inspiration of the Scriptures. If they were not inspired, Shaftesbury argued, they were of no value; if they were inspired, they were *all* inspired. There could be no middle way of choosing parts which were and parts which were not inspired. The Church was, then, under various threats and its ability to meet them was, Shaftesbury argued, being eroded by Tractarianism. He attributed much of the poor attendance which the Census of 1851 showed to Tractarianism which, he wrote, had driven many away from the established Church and had shed 'a chilling, hostile and nauseating sentiment over the people'.[190] He complained in 1852 that Tractarianism was in alliance with Neology to attack and weaken Evangelicalism.[191] This precipitated an acrimonious correspondence with Pusey,[192] who asked Shaftesbury to substantiate or withdraw it. Shaftesbury refused to do either, and, although he admitted that he had no one person in mind when he used the phrase, he did, in subsequent letters, criticise Pusey and the Divinity Professors at Oxford for failing to attack works such as those of H. H. Milman, whose *History of the Jews*, published in 1829, had marked 'the first decisive introduction of German theology into England, the first palpable indication that the Bible could be studied like any other book. . . .' Shaftesbury told Pusey that he had not yet heard 'that any learned or leisurely Professor had as yet discharged his public duty' and expressed the 'abominations' of such works. Pusey rebutted these charges, and the acrimony was made the worse by the fact that Pusey published his letters to Shaftesbury on the ground that Shaftesbury had delayed answering the first letter. Shaftesbury objected to only half the correspondence being published: 'it is for you,' he wrote to Pusey, 'to judge how far such a course is becoming.' These comments on the exchanges with the Tractarians further indicate the hardening of Shaftesbury's attitudes. His explanation of the Census figures of 1851 as being attributable to Tractarianism was, to say the least, dubious, and, in the correspondence with Pusey, it seems that Shaftesbury used a phrase without thought and then justified it in a way that gave further unnecessary offence. And he was unrepentant. In a letter to his new friend, Alexander Haldane, Shaftesbury referred to Pusey's letters and to a critical article on the episode which had appeared in *The Christian Remembrancer*: 'I have no disposition to notice the opprobrious fellows: I care not what they say or what they do.'[193]

Shaftesbury's judgments on contemporary political and religious events did, of course, betray his prejudices which were, indeed, becoming deeper. He often wrote in these years of the 'March of the Intellect', which he defined as a compound of 'infidelity, insubordination, pride and good intentions',[194] and, as he saw this make strides, he could only be fearful for the survival of old traditions and attachments. His definition of the 'March of the Intellect' was idiosyncratic, but his sense of the existence of such a phenomenon was not without discernment. The material prosperity of the 1850s and early 1860s and the increasing intellectual confidence also apparent in these years[195] were, in time, to be erosive of the old order. In detecting a 'March of the Intellect' in the early 1850s, Shaftesbury was an acute and perceptive observer. But he was also one whose increasing inflexibility made him likely to be overtaken by it.

Thus, on a variety of grounds, Shaftesbury's first years under his 'new name and career' were scarcely happy. He was burdened with proprietorial and personal difficulties; he felt ignored and neglected in public life; his public concerns, most notably over the Board of Health, ran into severe difficulties; he could feel little confidence in public men; the temper of the times seemed to be running against him. But in the midst of his depression, events were to turn to his advantage. The disasters which Britain suffered in the Crimean War exposed the Aberdeen Coalition to the criticism that its handling of the War was grossly inefficient, and, in January, 1855, a motion for a select committee to inquire into the conduct of the war was passed and the Coalition resigned. Shaftesbury was appalled at the political confusion which followed: 'is it nothing,' he asked, 'in the midst of a fearful crisis, an army perishing, a nation sinking, a war at its height, to stop the very machine of government?'[196] But the situation was finally resolved when, on 5 February, Palmerston was entrusted with the task of forming an administration. He succeeded and held office until 1858, when he resigned after suffering defeat in the Commons. But he was not out of office for long; the minority Tory government under Derby which succeeded him held office briefly. On its defeat in 1859, Palmerston returned and remained Prime Minister until his death in 1865. Thus Palmerston held the Premiership for virtually ten years, and during that period, his son-in-law was to enjoy the unaccustomed and unfamiliar experience of influence in high places.

NOTES

1. N.R.A., Shaftesbury (Broadlands) MSS, SHA/EST/2.
2. ibid., SHA/PD/6, 4 June, 1851.
3. ibid., SHA/PD/6, 2 June, 1851.
4. It is very difficult to obtain reliable figures of the inherited debt. According to one account written by Shaftesbury in 1862 (ibid., SHA/EST/7), the debt was £100,000 and £30,000 was the extent of his own personal debts, giving a total of £130,000. Another estimate, given in 1870, was £133,000 (SHA/EST/8). For the general problem of meeting the interests of family in a settled estate, see F. M. L. Thompson, *English Landed Society in the Nineteenth Century* (1963), pp. 66–70.
5. N.R.A., Shaftesbury (Broadlands) MSS, SHA/PD/6, 4 June, 1851.
6. ibid., SHA/PD/6, 29 Mar., 1853, 22 June, 1853.
7. ibid., SHA/EST/8.
8. ibid., SHA/PD/6, 22 Aug., 1851, 3 Jan., 1852.
9. ibid., SHA/PD/6, 14 Nov., 1851.
10. ibid., SHA/PD/6, 14 Jan., 1852.
11. ibid., SHA/PD/6, 2 Nov., 1851.
12. Chadwick MSS, 14 Jan., 1852.
13. See above p. 198.

A NEW NAME, A NEW CAREER, 1851–1855   367

14. N.R.A., Shaftesbury (Broadlands) MSS, SHA/PD/6, 7 Oct., 1851.
15. ibid., SHA/PD/6, 14 Oct., 1851.
16. Shaftesbury estimated that £10,000 would be required to be spent on it. It was sold for £48,500 (ibid., SHA/EST/7).
17. ibid., SHA/PD/6, 2 Mar., 1852. He retained a few articles of ancient family plate because money could never replace it.
18. ibid., SHA/PD/6, 30 Aug., 1851.
19. ibid., SHA/PD/6, 27 Jan., 1852.
20. ibid., SHA/PD/6, 5 Oct., 1853.
21. ibid., SHA/PD/6, 9 Dec., 1853.
22. ibid., SHA/PD/6, 6 June, 1854.
23. ibid., SHA/EST/7.
24. See below pp. 430–1 for some of the improvements in drainage etc. which Shaftesbury tried to implement.
25. N.R.A., SHA/PD/6, 22 Sept., 1851.
26. ibid., SHA/PD/6, 1 Apr., 1854.
27. ibid., SHA/PD/6, 22 Sept., 1851.
28. ibid., SHA/PD/6, 21 Dec., 1854.
29. ibid., SHA/PD/6, 6 Sept., 1851. Shaftesbury noted that a pair of Cottages cost him £400 and the rent which he received from them was at most £3 for each cottage, garden included. (ibid., SHA/PD/6, 29 June, 1853).
30. H.R.O., Shaftesbury (Broadlands) MSS, 27M60, 22 Oct., 1851.
31. Chadwick MSS, 12 Aug., 1852.
32. N.R.A., Shaftesbury (Broadlands) MSS, SHA/PD/6, 17 Feb., 1854.
33. See below pp. 430–1.
34. N.R.A., Shaftesbury (Broadlands) MSS, SHA/PD/6, 4 June, 1851.
35. ibid., SHA/PD/6, 17 Nov., 1851.
36. ibid., SHA/PD/6, 5 Dec., 1851.
37. ibid., SHA/PD/6, 15 Dec., 1852.
38. ibid., SHA/PD/6, 4 July, 1854.
39. ibid., SHA/PD/6, 6 Feb., 1855.
40. ibid., SHA/PD/6, 5 Sept., 1851.
41. ibid., SHA/PD/6, 1 Jan., 1854.
42. ibid., SHA/PD/6, 14 Sept., 1853.
43. H.R.O., Shaftesbury (Broadlands) MSS, 27M60, 9 July, 1852.
44. Chadwick MSS, 29 July, 1852.
45. N.R.A., Shaftesbury (Broadlands) MSS, SHA/PD/6, 7 Oct., 1851.
46. H.R.O., Shaftesbury (Broadlands) MSS, 27M60, 17 Feb., 1852.
47. N.R.A., Shaftesbury (Broadlands) MSS, SHA/PD/6, 6 Feb., 1852.
48. H.R.O., Shaftesbury (Broadlands) MSS, 27M60, 17 Feb., 1852.
49. N.R.A., Shaftesbury (Broadlands) MSS, SHA/PD/6, 16 June, 1851.
50. See below p. 347.
51. N.R.A., Shaftesbury (Broadlands) MSS, SHA/PD/6, 16 June, 1851.
52. ibid., SHA/PD/6, 24 June, 1851.
53. ibid., SHA/PD/6, 25 June, 1851.
54. ibid., SHA/PD/6, 7 July, 1851.
55. ibid., SHA/PD/6, 20 Feb., 1852.
56. ibid., SHA/PD/6, 3 May, 1853.
57. ibid., SHA/PD/6, 3 Jan., 1853. In 1851—as in 1849—Ashley's name was considered for office by the Protectionists: but the idea was rejected partly because his views on religion were considered impracticable. Again, as in 1849, it seems

unlikely that Ashley was aware of this episode. (J. R. Vincent (ed.), op. cit., p. 48 and p. 356, n. 35).
58. N.R.A., Shaftesbury (Broadlands) MSS, SHA/PD/6, 24 Sept., 1852.
59. Add. MSS, 43, 253, f. 69.
60. N.R.A., Shaftesbury (Broadlands) MSS, SHA/PD/6, 5 May, 1854.
61. Add. MSS, 43, 253, fos 74-5.
62. *The Times*, 28 Apr., 1852. See also G. M. Ellis, op. cit., p. 225 ff. for a full examination of this subject.
63. Hansard, *Parl. Debates*, 3rd ser., CXXVII, 650. This was a petition on behalf of the Chaplains of H.M. Prisons in and near the Metropolis against the opening of the Exhibition on any part of a Sunday.
64. See below pp. 392-3.
65. Russell MSS, 30/22/10 B, fos 264-5.
66. See below p. 365.
67. Hansard, *Parl. Debates*, 3rd ser., CXXIII, 277.
68. Add. MSS, 44, 300, fos 11-12.
69. ibid., fos 13-14.
70. Quoted in Hodder, II, 406-7.
71. Hansard, *Parl. Debates,* 3rd ser., CXVIII, 1956.
72. N.R.A., Shaftesbury (Broadlands) MSS, SHA/PD/6, 12 Nov., 1852.
73. ibid., SHA/PD/6, 18 Sept., 1853.
74. Quoted in Hodder, II, 435.
75. Quoted ibid., II, 468-73.
76. N.R.A., Shaftesbury (Broadlands) MSS, SHA/PD/6, 3 Sept., 1853.
77. ibid., SHA/PD/6, 1 Dec., 1853.
78. Quoted in Hodder, II, 441.
79. N.R.A., Shaftesbury (Broadlands) MSS, SHA/PD/6, 6 Nov., 1852.
80. *The Times*, 9 Nov., 1852.
81. ibid.
82. N.R.A., Shaftesbury (Broadlands) MSS, SHA/PD/6, 20 Nov., 1852.
83. ibid., SHA/PD/6, 21 Nov., 1852.
84. ibid., SHA/PD/6, 9 Nov., 1852.
85. ibid., SHA/PD/6, 17 May, 1853.
86. *The Times*, 21 May, 1853.
87. ibid., 18 May, 1853.
88. ibid., 21 May, 1853.
89. Quoted in Hodder, II, 438.
90. Quoted ibid., II, 439.
91. *The Manchester Examiner and Times*, 22 Nov., 1851.
92. Russell MSS, 30/22/9 H, fos 212-13.
93. N.R.A., Shaftesbury (Broadlands) MSS, SHA/PD/6, 16 Aug., 1853.
94. ibid., SHA/PD/6, 29 June, 1853.
95. The committee of the Union found that it could not keep pace with the demand for shoeblacks and encouraged the formation of branch societies for different parts of London. Red-coated shoeblacks worked in central London; blue coats in east London and yellow coats in the area south of the Thames. Between March 1854 and March 1855, a grand total of 346,404 pairs of boots and shoes had been cleaned by the boys of the three brigades and the total earnings for the year were £1,433/7/-. (*Ragged School Union Magazine* (1855), p. 108).
96. The committee of the Union was doubtful about the desirability of assisting Dormitories and Refuges for the Destitute on the grounds that these might

pauperise the pupils rather than encourage habits of industry and self-reliance. But it found the demand so great that it could not refuse assistance. A grant of £3 a year was made for every boy sent from a Ragged School to a Refuge and boarded and lodged there to the satisfaction of the Committee.

97. N.R.A., Shaftesbury (Broadlands) MSS, SHA/PD/6, 31 Jan., 1852.
98. ibid., SHA/PD/6, 22 Sept., 1851. Most of the emigrants sent under the auspices of the Union went to Canada because the committee was afraid that the gold mania would induce bad habits.
99. Quoted in Hodder, II, 410.
100. *Ragged School Union Magazine* (1854), p. 113.
101. Hansard, *Parl. Debates,* 3rd ser., CXVII, 1140.
102. *The Quarterly Review,* LXXXII, 142–52.
103. E. Gauldie, op. cit., p. 246.
104. *Ragged School Union Magazine* (1853), p. 110.
105. Hansard, *Parl. Debates,* 3rd ser., CXXVII, 294.
106. ibid., CXXV, 400–408.
107. ibid., CXXVI, 1292.
108. ibid., CXXVIII, 1202–15.
109. N.R.A., Shaftesbury (Broadlands) MSS, GC/SH/23.
110. ibid., GC/SH/24.
111. Chadwick MSS, 3 Aug., 1853.
112. Hansard, *Parl. Debates,* 3rd ser., CXXVII, 198–9.
113. ibid., 497.
114. ibid., 132, 364.
115. ibid., CXXXII, 1283–6.
116. ibid., CXXXIII, 650–51.
117. ibid., 654.
118. N.R.A., Shaftesbury (Broadlands) MSS, SHA/PD/6, 21 May, 1854.
119. ibid., SHA/PD/5, 4 Nov., 1847.
120. ibid., SHA/PD/6, 19 Sept., 1851.
121. H.R.O., Shaftesbury (Broadlands) MSS, 27M60, 28 Dec., 1852.
122. W. Ll. Parry-Jones, op. cit., p. 302.
123. Hansard, *Parl. Debates,* 3rd ser., CXXVI, 1221.
124. Chadwick MSS, 9 June 1851 (copy). There were two letters. The first, a rough draft, is simply dated June 1851 and is very gloomy about Shaftesbury's elevation. The second, copy of 9 June, is more composed. See also R. A. Lewis, op. cit., p. 268.
125. Chadwick MSS, 28 July, 6 Aug., 1851.
126. Hansard, *Parl. Debates,* 3rd ser., CXVIII, 1174 ff.
127. Chadwick MSS, 9 Dec., 1851.
128. ibid.
129. See R. A. Lewis, op. cit., p. 268 ff.
130. Hansard, *Parl. Debates,* 3rd ser., CXVIII, 835.
131. ibid., CXX, 1283–99.
132. ibid., 1306.
133. ibid., 1315.
134. N.R.A., Shaftesbury (Broadlands) MSS, SHA/PD/6, 14 May, 1852.
135. ibid., SHA/PD/6, 14 May, 1852.
136. R. A. Lewis, op. cit., p. 326 (Shaftesbury to Seymour, 22 June, 1852).
137. ibid. (Shaftesbury to Seymour, 24 June, 1852).
138. N.R.A., Shaftesbury (Broadlands) MSS, SHA/PD/6, 24 June, 1852.

139. Chadwick MSS, 16 July, 1852.
140. ibid., 18 July, 1852.
141. N.R.A., Shaftesbury (Broadlands) MSS, SHA/PD/6, 17 Nov., 1853.
142. Chadwick MSS, 18 Dec., 1852.
143. ibid.
144. N.R.A., Shaftesbury (Broadlands) MSS, SHA/PD/6, 31 Dec., 1852.
145. Worcester Record Office, Cobham Archives, Shaftesbury to Lord Lyttelton, 5 Mar., 1853. Under the Vaccination Act of 1841, the Boards of Guardians were authorised to defray the expenses of vaccination in their Unions. Vaccination was, however, voluntary and large numbers were not vaccinated.
146. N.R.A., Shaftesbury (Broadlands) MSS, SHA/PD/6, 8 Aug., 1853.
147. ibid., SHA/PD/6, 9 Aug., 1853.
148. Chadwick MSS, 28 Aug., 1853.
149. N.R.A., Shaftesbury (Broadlands) MSS, SHA/PD/6, 9 Aug., 1853.
150. ibid., SHA/PD/6, 14 Dec., 1853.
151. British Library of Political and Economic Science, Hughenden MSS, R (Microfilm). Film 131. 31 Aug., 1852.
152. Chadwick MSS, 28 Aug., 1853.
153. ibid., 17 Sept., 1853.
154. N.R.A., Shaftesbury (Broadlands) MSS, GC/SH/25.
155. ibid., GC/SH/26.
156. Hansard, *Parl. Debates,* 3rd ser., CXXXI, 530 ff.
157. N.R.A., Shaftesbury (Broadlands) MSS, SHA/PD/6, 25 July, 1854.
158. R. A. Lewis, op. cit., p. 365.
159. N.R.A., Shaftesbury (Broadlands) MSS, SHA/PD/6, 29 July, 1854.
160. ibid., SHA/PD/6, 31 July, 1854.
161. Hansard, *Parl. Debates,* 3rd ser., CXXXV, 234 ff.
162. N.R.A., Shaftesbury (Broadlands) MSS, SHA/PD/6, 13 July, 1854.
163. Hansard, *Parl. Debates,* 3rd ser., CXXXV, 987 ff.
164. ibid., 1079 ff.
165. N.R.A., Shaftesbury (Broadlands) MSS, SHA/PD/6, 3 Aug., 1854.
166. Hansard, *Parl. Debates,* 3rd ser., CXXXV, 1001.
167. ibid., 990.
168. N.R.A., Shaftesbury (Broadlands) MSS, SHA/PD/6, 6 and 7 Sept., 1854.
169. ibid., SHA/PD/6, 1 Apr., 1854.
170. MSS Eng. Lett., d. 198, f. 166 ff.
171. Hansard, *Parl. Debates,* 3rd ser., CXXVIII, 1410–12; CXXIX, 261–3.
172. University of California, Los Angeles, Research Library, Department of Special Collections, Collection 1040, Richard Cobden Letters, Cobden to Shaftesbury, 19 July, 1853.
173. Hansard, *Parl. Debates,* 3rd ser., CXXIX, 268.
174. N.R.A., Shaftesbury (Broadlands) MSS, SHA/PD/6, 10 Apr., 1853.
175. Quoted in Hodder, II, 302.
176. MSS Eng. Lett., d. 198, f. 168. Shaftesbury to Russell, 18 Nov., 1851.
177. N.R.A., Shaftesbury (Broadlands) MSS, SHA/PD/6, 15 Aug., 1853.
178. ibid., SHA/PD/6, 28 July, 1852.
179. ibid., SHA/PD/6, 15 Oct., 1851.
180. Russell MSS, 30/22/9 G (Pt 1), fos 177–8.
181. MSS Eng. Lett., a. 198, f. 167.
182. N.R.A., Shaftesbury (Broadlands) MSS, SHA/PD/6, 23 Feb., 1852.
183. ibid., SHA/PD/6, 16 Mar., 1852.

184. ibid., SHA/PD/6, 1 Apr., 1852.
185. ibid., SHA/PD/6, 24 Dec., 1852.
186. H.R.O., Shaftesbury (Broadlands) MSS, 27M60, 28 Dec., 1852.
187. N.R.A., Shaftesbury (Broadlands) MSS, SHA/PD/6, 21 Nov., 1853.
188. ibid., SHA/PD/6, 1 Dec., 1853.
189. See above p. 51.
190. N.R.A., Shaftesbury (Broadlands) MSS, SHA/PD/6, 1 Apr., 1854.
191. See above p. 340.
192. N.R.A., Shaftesbury (Broadlands) MSS, SHA/PC/71-82.
193. Quoted in Hodder, II, 402.
194. N.R.A., Shaftesbury (Broadlands) MSS, SHA/PD/6, 15 Oct., 1851.
195. See also p. 423.
196. N.R.A., Shaftesbury (Broadlands) MSS, SHA/PD/6, 14 Feb., 1855.

14
Near the Fountain Head 1855–1865

On Palmerston's accession to office, Shaftesbury's political future was once again raised. In February, 1855, Palmerston offered him the Duchy of Lancaster, with a seat in the Cabinet. Shaftesbury's presence in the Cabinet, Palmerston wrote, would be 'useful' to his government and also 'gratifying to large bodies of the people'.[1] Palmerston, however, was forced to suspend the offer[2] owing to difficulties in forming his Cabinet and, to satisfy the Whigs, the place went to Carlisle. But, the following month, on a re-shuffle of ministers, the place was once more offered to Shaftesbury. In the course of the two episodes, Shaftesbury showed his old characteristic of half wanting and half not wanting office. At one time, he wrote in March, he shrank from the post 'on the score of incapacity'; at another, he was attracted to it 'as a position of interest, usefulness and temporal assistance'.[3] But, on the whole, his inclination was decidely against acceptance. Apart from his 'incapacity', there were all the 'important occupations' which he would have to sacrifice[4]: such thoughts re-echoed those of earlier years, when Shaftesbury had been in a similar position. He also felt that there were points of difference between himself and Palmerston which would make it difficult for him to accept office. He thought that there might be a further endowment of Maynooth College, which he could not support; he was also opposed to the appointment of Roman Catholic chaplains to jails; there was the possibility that the Ministry might support a Jewish Relief Bill, to which he was opposed; and a further point concerned a proposal to open places of amusement on a Sunday. This, too, the Ministry might favour, but Shaftesbury could not.[5] He mentioned all these points at the time of the first offer in February,[6] but Palmerston's difficulties in forming a Cabinet closed the matter without any real discussion of them. But when the offer was renewed in March, there was a long negotiation between the two men. Shaftesbury once again rehearsed the obstacles in the way of his acceptance and Palmerston tried to overcome them.[7] Shaftesbury was strongly encouraged to accept office by Minny and her mother. He wrote of the first offer in February that his first impulse was to refuse it, but he was 'overruled by the importunities of Minny'[8] and persuaded to put to Palmerston the various matters on which reassurance would be necessary. On the second occasion, Minny kept up her insistence that Shaftesbury should accept the offer. She asked him to reflect how much weightier would be the support he could give to all his projects as a Cabinet Minister.[9] Lady Palmerston also tried her best to soothe Shaftesbury's scruples.[10] She reminded her son-in-law that he had already turned down office in the Queen's Household and refused the Garter. If he refused a third offer, the Queen would be 'quite offended'.[11] Amidst all this, Shaftesbury was distraught, the more so since he heard from Lady Palmerston that her husband was displeased and vexed at his conduct.[12] Shaftesbury wrote to Palmerston to explain his behaviour and ask his forbearance[13] and to Lady Palmerston, expressing his grief and agony.[14] His private and domestic peace, he wrote, had been broken, and he was fearful that he had lost the affection and good will which he had always enjoyed from Minny's parents, that family ties would be disrupted and, even if 'patched up', could not be as they were before.

In fact, Lady Palmerston treated Shaftesbury very kindly. She assured him that she entered fully into all his difficulties and felt that he was not at all to blame; that Palmerston also understood his predicament, but was still hopeful that a way would be found of releasing him from his objections. Whatever the result, she wrote, 'pray never imagine that either Palmerston's confidence and affection or mine can ever alter – on the contrary, it is greater than ever and we most fully appreciate your excellent qualities.'[15] Shaftesbury replied, expressing his gratitude, but he told Lady Palmerston that there must be no delay in filling the Duchy through any hope of finding a way for him.[16] In fact, there was a further delay, and it did seem that Shaftesbury would accept the office. He received a letter from Lady Palmerston conveying the message that Palmerston would meet all his points and requesting him to be at the Palace that afternoon to be sworn in.[17] Lady Palmerston also told Minny[18] that Shaftesbury would think this a very hurried proposal, but he had lost so much time in giving his answer that Palmerston was very anxious for the Queen's sake that he should be sworn in without further delay, and she repeated that Palmerston would make Shaftesbury's mind '*quite* easy upon *all* (the) points'. It appears that Shaftesbury was finally persuaded, went to dress for the occasion and, while waiting for the carriage, knelt down and prayed for 'counsel, wisdom and understanding'.[19] But, at the very last moment, he received a note from Palmerston telling him not to go to the Palace. Thirty years later, Shaftesbury recalled the occasion: 'I dance with joy at the remembrance of that interposition, as I did when it happened. It was, to my mind, as distinctly an act of special providence as when the hand of Abraham was stayed and Isaac escaped.'[20] The place was taken by Harrowby, and Shaftesbury was excused. There was one further episode in the autumn of 1855, when Palmerston once more offered Shaftesbury office, but, this time, it was firmly turned down. Shaftesbury wrote[21] that he felt Palmerston's kindness very deeply in the renewed offer of a post, but the difficulties in the way of acceptance were precisely the same as they had been earlier in the year. Palmerston, he felt, would see this, 'were he not biased by his friendship to such an extent as to *undervalue* many of the objections and to *overvalue* the service I could render to his Government.' Shaftesbury was 'decidedly of opinion' that he could give more effectual assistance by being outside the government than by being inside it.

Shaftesbury thus retained his independence and freedom from any official restraint on his conduct. Yet he did enjoy a position of closeness in relation to Palmerston's governments which he had never previously enjoyed with any other government. One mark of this was his decision finally to accept the Garter in 1861. Palmerston wrote on 10 December, 1861, offering him a vacant Garter – he was sure, he said, that its conferment on Shaftesbury would 'gratify the whole country'[22] and, although Shaftesbury had turned it down on an earlier occasion, there was no reason against his taking it now. Shaftesbury wanted a day to consider the offer,[23] but Palmerston pressed the point and tried to reassure Shaftesbury over the expenses of accepting the honour. He said that he could see his way to overcoming this difficulty and commented that it was a 'gross abuse that honours given by the Crown as marks of approbation should have the operation of personal taxes.'[24] Shaftesbury was pleased with the offer: it was, he wrote,[25] another of the friendly acts which he had so often received at Palmerston's hands and it was only because it had come from Palmerston that he had not refused it at once. He also recognised the honour and value of the Garter 'in the general working of society', but he felt that, in his case, it was not appropriate. Such services as he had been able to give were not considered 'public' by most of the better classes, at least, in the sense of deserving public recognition. The fees were too great and he could never consent to Palmerston undertaking such a large expenditure on his behalf 'merely to invest (him) with a Ribbon.' But Palmerston persisted and finally Shaftesbury conceded the point, yielding to Palmerston's judgment that the grant should be made 'somewhat out of the common line' in recognition of 'unofficial labours'.[26] He was especially grateful to Palmerston over the matter of the fees; he had reason to believe that Palmerston had paid the entire expenses himself – 'this is, indeed, truly generous and friendly,' Shaftesbury wrote.[27]

Palmerston's influence on Shaftesbury was thus displayed in this episode, but there were other areas where Shaftesbury's influence on Palmerston was to be felt. He approached Palmerston from time to time about miscellaneous items of patronage. In August, 1859, he sent a memorial on behalf of the daughter of Robert Southey, 'one of the greatest of our literary men,' he wrote, 'but, like most of them, very poor.' Palmerston would, Shaftesbury said, gratify a vast number of Southey's friends and admirers by placing this lady on the pension list.[28] The pension was clearly given, for, in 1864, Shaftesbury enclosed a letter from the Revd. Robert Hill, who married the second daughter of Southey; she was 'in some need' and asked, through Shaftesbury, that the pension vacant on the death of her sister might be paid to her. A note on the front of the letter recorded that Palmerston had approved of £100 a year being given.[29] The plight of two women descended from Daniel Defoe also engaged Shaftesbury's sympathy. They were needlewomen, earning from three shillings to five shillings a week, but with 'excellent characters', and the fact that they were descended from Defoe helped their case in Shaftesbury's eyes – his 'literary services,' Shaftesbury wrote, 'are unrivalled by anything, except his political services (for he did more than any man to uphold William III and the Revolution of '88).' Thus in 1860 Shaftesbury asked Palmerston to give the women an annuity on their joint lives and that of the survivor.[30] Or again, in 1862, Shaftesbury wrote to Palmerston saying that it would be a highly popular act to confer a Baronetcy on David Baxter of Fife, who had expended a great deal of money in constructing parks and had done 'many other things for the education and improvement of the working classes.' The honour was duly granted.[31] Shaftesbury thus had close access to Palmerston and he used it to press on him the claims of persons whom he felt to be deserving of help or honour. And Palmerston proved amenable to Shaftesbury's requests. Recalling this aspect of his relationship with Palmerston in 1865, Shaftesbury wrote that he had kept no record of the various cases he had brought before Palmerston for aid from the 'Bounty Money'. But applicants 'in abundant instances' had approached the Prime Minister through him and, since he never undertook any except deserving cases, he never met with 'anything but ready acquiescence'.[32]

The area in which Shaftesbury felt the most pressing need for Palmerston's support was, however, that of ecclesiastical appointments. For Shaftesbury to give advice on such matters to a Prime Minister was, of course, no new thing, but there was an added urgency in the circumstances of the time. It was now a question not only of countering Tractarian influences in the Church: there were other enemies who presented a threat, not only to the Church, but to the Faith itself. For these years were vitally important in the theological debate of the nineteenth century, in that they witnessed various attempts by English theologians to come to terms with the school of Biblical criticism. *Essays and Reviews*, published in 1860, represented a feeling shared by various Anglican clergymen that the time had come to expose to honest and open debate the whole question of the relevance of modern scholarship to the Bible. The tenor of the book was that Christians should not fear such scholarship and should not regard their faith as undermined by it. All truth was of God, and any investigation of it could not but lead to Him. Further, if investigations tended to throw doubt on the literal accuracy of the Bible, this did not matter. Christianity did not depend for its truth on a rigid interpretation of miracles and prophecies; it had a moral content, which far transcended such considerations. A work of a similar kind was that by Bishop Colenso: his *Critical Examination of the Pentateuch*, published in 1862, cast doubt on the literal truth of the Mosaic books of the Bible. Another notable contribution to the subject was *Ecce Homo*, published in 1865. This was written by J. R. Seeley, the son of the Evangelical book publisher who had been a friend of Shaftesbury before their difference, albeit short-lived, over the Corn Laws. In France, Renan's *Vie de Jésus*, published in 1863, was a further work which attempted to strip the life of Christ of some of the myths and mysteries which, the author held, had accumulated around it. The controversy engendered by the work of such 'Broad Churchmen', as they were called in England, was intense. Two of the contributors to *Essays and Reviews* were tried and convicted of heresy and Colenso was deprived of his see as Bishop of Natal, although, in all these cases, the Judicial Committee of the Privy Council reversed the decisions.

Shaftesbury thoroughly deplored all such Broad Church attempts to take account of modern trends in scholarship. He felt that no part of the Bible could be rejected without the whole being abandoned.[33] Once inspiration was taken from the texts and infallibility from their writers, the supernatural was eliminated and the 'record' brought down to the level of man's comprehension. The Neologists thus reduced the Bible to the same value as that of any other religious book. 'How,' he asked, 'does it differ from the Koran?'[34] Again, he admitted that the Neologists might have admiration for the person of Christ: 'doubtless,' he wrote, 'there are many phrases of Love, many of reverence, many of enthusiastic admiration.' But, he asked, could not these be applied to 'Heroes, Martyrs, Patriots and Orators?'[35] Thus to Shaftesbury, the Neologists stripped the Bible of inspiration, Christ of His Divinity, but, worst of all, God of His power and man of his hope. Man must acknowledge God as 'omnipotent, or as nothing at all. A God limited in power, and open to resistance is all but an absurdity;

this is the pitfall of the Neologist,' he wrote.[36] The very efforts of the Neologists to question the biblical texts were a sign of resistance to God – indeed, they were a clear manifestation of what many of them, in his view, ignored: man's sinfulness and corruption and his 'unqualified inability to do, or even to think, a good thing of himself.'[37] And, having ignored man's depravity, the Neologists also ignored God's salvation, the Atonement of the Cross: 'the great fundamental turning-point of our religion'.[38] Christ and His Apostles, Shaftesbury wrote, assert the 'full necessity and merit of an expiatory sacrifice to wipe away our Sin.' The Neologists in 'cold and calculated homage, allow Him no more than the virtue of unprecedented generosity and unparalleled self-Denial.' So to reduce the significance of the Cross was, in Shaftesbury's eyes, to deny the basic belief that Christ's sacrifice was 'the only basis of all morality, of all hope, of all escape from sin and everlasting condemnation' and was thus to remove from Christianity 'its grand distinction from all other Creeds' and from the Bible that without which it was 'of little more value to suffering generations than Homer or Ivanhoe.'[39]

When Palmerston came into office in February, 1855, all this was in the future. But already, Shaftesbury feared the worst. In 1856, he wrote that the progress of rationalism was 'rapid, fearful, resistless';[40] the inspiration of Scripture was being steadily assailed in sermons and books and he could foresee nothing but mischief. Shaftesbury, however, did not expect to be consulted by Palmerston. He wrote in 1855 that people would begin to expect that Palmerston's Church appointments would be influenced by his (i.e. Shaftesbury's) opinions. 'There could not be a greater error,' Shaftesbury commented. . . . It is not very likely that he will consult anybody; but, if he does, it will not be one connected with the Evangelical party.'[41] Three weeks later, Shaftesbury wrote to Evelyn that he much feared that Palmerston's ecclesiastical appointments would be 'detestable'. In theological matters, Palmerston did not know Moses from Sydney Smith. The vicar of Romsey, where he went to Church, was the only clergyman to whom he ever spoke, and the views of the religious part of the country were as 'strange to him at the interior of Japan'. It was only a short time ago, Shaftesbury commented, that Palmerston heard for the first time of the 'grand heresy of Puseyites and Tractarians'.[42] Shaftesbury thought that if anybody would advise Palmerston it would be William Cowper, Minny's brother, whose views, at this point, were of a liberal nature and would thus be acceptable: Palmerston's ear, Shaftesbury wrote, was 'always ready to be tickled by liberal flourishes' and thus Neology would carry the day in every future appointment.[43] There had already been a case, Shaftesbury claimed, where Cowper had succeeded in reversing a promise which Palmerston had made to him. Cowper had 'stepped in' and warned Palmerston that the clergyman in question was a Sabbatarian and the benefice had been obtained for another: 'so here is the rule of the minister,' Shaftesbury wrote, 'and this the spirit of his advisers.'[44] The vacant Bishopric of Gloucester and Bristol also caused Shaftesbury great anxiety. Palmerston had 'the adherents of Christ on one side; of Belial on the other.' One set called for an Evangelical, the other for a Neologist to fill such vacancies, and more might well occur, since several Bishops were ill. If Cowper's influence prevailed and appointments of Neologists made, it must be taken as a sign, wrote Shaftesbury, that 'God is wrath unto us: and He will most justly, tho' fearfully, cast us off as a filthy rag.'[45]

But Shaftesbury would not give in without a struggle: he would do his best to match and outmatch the influence of Cowper. He felt that the human resources available for preferment were somewhat limited. Although it was desirable to have a learned bench of Bishops, learned men were, in his view, very suspect: 'so piteously unsound that they could hardly speak a sentence without mischief in it.' Again, he wondered where men were to be found capable of public statement and debate in the Lords – political and polemical Bishops were to be avoided, but there was a need for men who could 'stand up for the Church's rights, expose evil, sustain what is good and maintain their fair position.' There were, indeed, men who were good, pious, active, clever, persuasive and true. Such were to be found in abundance, but 'of men of profound and varied acquirements, hardly an instance.'[46] But choices would have to be made from what was available, and, in Shaftesbury's view, it was the good, the pious, the active and the true who should be promoted to Bishoprics rather than the clever or the persuasive. Professors, tutors and dons of Colleges were not, on average, fitted for episcopal duty; knowledge of mankind and experience of parochial life were not, Shaftesbury wrote, acquired in 'musty libraries and easychairs'.[47] Shaftesbury conveyed such thoughts to Palmerston. He wrote to the Prime Minister in December, 1856, saying that the country required Bishops drawn from the larger parishes: men of activity and experience, who could live on friendly terms with their clergy and busy themselves in everything which had to do with the temporal and spiritual interests of the working classes – men, in fact, who 'as Bishops, (would) work with no less vigour and effect than they did as Parish-priests' and who would be able to be on good terms with Dissenters. This excluded a learned Bench in the sense of 'profound and minute research, detailed scholarship and the power of keeping pace with the theological literature of the times.' They must, indeed, have a full knowledge of all that was 'primarily necessary', but this would have been acquired before they were thirty years of age; they could not contend with the heresies and theological problems of the day and 'manifest all the specialities and precision that would be exhibited by a

German Professor.' In Shaftesbury's view, Bishops elevated on these principles would 'rivet the Church in the affections of the people . . . secure the Establishment and promote true and sound religion.' Learned and scholarly men could, however, be appointed as Deans: a man might study as a Dean, 'keep watch and ward in his Library; read and write without interruption; eat deservedly of the bread of the Church, and defend her and the truth against all Assailants.' Shaftesbury thus advised Palmerston, as a general rule, to reserve Deaneries for learned men and Bishoprics for active men: 'be assured,' he wrote, 'that, thus, you will please the Country; do honour to yourself; and good to the Church.'[48]

Despite his early expectations to the contrary, Shaftesbury found Palmerston a ready listener, for Palmerston's views on the role of Bishops were similar to his own. A Bishop, Palmerston told the Queen, should supervise the clergy in the performance of parochial duties, preserve harmony between clergy and laity and 'soften the asperities between the established Church and the Dissenters.' He required a practical knowledge of parochial functions and should not be overbearing or intolerant. He should engage himself in diocesan duties rather than in theological disputes: 'much mischief has been done,' Palmerston wrote, 'by theological bishops.'[49] From the start of Palmerston's Ministry, Shaftesbury did all he could to take advantage of this unexpected affinity of views between Palmerston and himself. He could not, as he said, foresee the duration of Palmerston's power. The Prime Minister was old; he might die or be turned out and nothing could be expected from his successor: 'if Palmerston fail us, all is lost,' Shaftesbury wrote.[50] He was, therefore, resolved to do all he could to advance men to Bishoprics who met his requirements. The first Bishops were, indeed, as he put it, 'decidedly of the Evangelical School';[51] it was, of course, men of this school who possessed the qualities which Shaftesbury desired. The Bishopric of Gloucester and Bristol over which he had been so anxious, was disposed as Shaftesbury desired: Baring was elected to the see, and Shaftesbury hoped that God would grant many such.[52] Another appointment, in 1856, for which Shaftesbury was responsible was that of Villiers to Carlisle and this was against other possible candidates favoured by the Queen and the Whigs; and further elevations from the Evangelical party were those of Bickersteth[53] to Ripon in 1856 and Pelham to Norwich in 1857. And the appointment of Close to the Deanery of Carlisle in 1856 also gave Shaftesbury cause for pleasure – it was, he wrote, 'just, right'.[54]

There were, however, certain anxieties. Shaftesbury knew that he could not quite have it all his own way and that, in making appointments, Palmerston had to take into account various considerations. This had been true of the vacancy at Ripon. Palmerston had felt that he ought to appoint a Cambridge man, since all his early appointments had been from Oxford, and he had recommended Dawes, Dean of Hereford.[55] 'Never was I so dumb founded,' wrote Shaftesbury,[56] and he was the more distressed that his own nominee, Brodrick, Canon of Wells, had been rejected. Shaftesbury did succeed in stopping the appointment of Dawes, and the appointment of Bickersteth, whose name he suggested after further consideration, gave him great satisfaction. But, to the last moment, he was fearful that William Cowper had dropped 'a word *out* of season',[57] and the incident illustrated the fears, always present to Shaftesbury, that Palmerston, knowing little of such matters himself, would be a ready and easy prey to this influence.[58] Further, the Bishopric of London gave Shaftesbury cause for disquiet. There were rumours that Palmerston would appoint Waddington, Dean of Durham, to the Bishopric. Shaftesbury admitted that Waddington might have some learning, but he was suspect on the Sunday question: 'ah what anxiety these appointments give me,' Shaftesbury wrote.[59] But Waddington was not, in fact, appointed. The see went to Tait, Dean of Carlisle. This was due partly to personal circumstances. In the spring of 1856, Tait had lost five of his small daughters in a scarlet fever epidemic and the Queen suggested that the Dean should be moved away from Carlisle. Shaftesbury saw Tait's sister, Lady Wake, who later wrote to her brother, telling him of her interview with Shaftesbury.[60] She remembered that Shaftesbury gave great attention to what she had said on the subject of her brother's 'powers of arranging and classifying, and getting things to work and influencing men's minds,' and she felt that her brother owed it to the Queen that he was a Bishop at all and very probably to Shaftesbury that he was Bishop of London. Shaftesbury did, indeed, mention Tait's qualifications to Palmerston, but he would have preferred to see Tait appointed to a smaller Bishopric than London: he told Lady Wake that he had her brother in mind for the Westminster division of the Diocese of London when it was divided. He would have liked to have seen Pelham appointed to London itself.[61] But London was not divided at the time and Tait was appointed. He was a Broad Churchman and, although Shaftesbury regarded him as the mildest of that school, he looked on him with certain misgivings. These seemed to be confirmed when Tait appointed A. P. Stanley, who had been elected Regius Professor of Ecclesiastical History of Oxford in 1856, as his Examining Chaplain. Shaftesbury felt that many of Stanley's views smacked overmuch of Neology, and he wrote to Lady Wake, expressing his anxiety at the appointment and asking her to interpose as a 'Guardian Angel'.[62] Tait, however, would not accept any interference, but Shaftesbury was soon reassured. He attended Tait's first sermon and was, he told Lady Wake, 'much gratified'. He had not expected 'to hear the Second and personal Advent of our blessed Lord preached by the Metropolitan Bishop in the Pulpit of St James.'[63]

Tait's appointment and, indeed, that of Stanley to the Chair of Ecclesiastical History at Oxford, show that not all appointments in Palmerston's first ministry of 1855-8 were of the Evangelical school, and another exception was the appointment of Longley, a High Churchman, to Durham in 1856. Further, Shaftesbury suffered great disappointment over the Deanery of Westminster, vacant in 1856 on the death of Buckland. He was extremely anxious to promote the cause of McCaul, a staunch supporter of the London Jews Society; his appointment, Shaftesbury wrote, would 'accomplish a long-cherished desire.'[64] But Palmerston refused to appoint McCaul, giving as his reason that many names had been suggested to him. Shaftesbury was not satisfied at this: he was 'deeply and painfully disappointed'.[65] Trench was appointed to Westminster; Shaftesbury did not know who had been influential on this occasion.[66] Trench was regarded as Broad Church, and a further appointment made from this school was that of Alford to the Deanery of Canterbury in 1857. On this occasion, Palmerston passed over various names which Shaftesbury had put to him as persons preferable, in his eyes, to Alford.

It is, therefore, wrong to suggest that Shaftesbury was in complete control of the ecclesiastical appointments. Palmerston could show a mind of his own and he also took into consideration other points of view. But, although these qualifications have to be made, Shaftesbury's influence was strong. He would, indeed, have preferred another appointment to the Deanery of Canterbury, but he had mentioned Alford to Palmerston as a possibility for the Deanery. He wrote to the Prime Minister saying that if he desired to 'enter on a new line and name one of the Broad Church' – as Palmerston had once said to him – Alford would be an acceptable choice: 'a deep Greek scholar, fit to be a Dean and very unfit to be a Bishop.'[67] Alford's appointment was, therefore, in accordance with Shaftesbury's remarks to Palmerston about suitable candidates for Deaneries, and he was, in fact, very mildly Broad Church and had certain affinities with the Evangelicals.[68] Further, although Shaftesbury did not like Tait's appointment of Stanley, Stanley's views were not fully developed at the time, and, despite his original misgivings about Tait himself, Shaftesbury got on well with him: he later wrote that 'we got from him, as Bishop of London, ten times as much as ever was obtained from one, or all, of his predecessors.'[69] Longley was regarded with suspicion by Shaftesbury, but he was only moderately High Church, and it may be that, having succeeded in 1856 with Villiers and Baring, Shaftesbury felt that he could not press the case of another Evangelical.[70] The fact that the majority of the appointments were from the Evangelical school was, perhaps, more noticeable in view of the previous exclusion of Evangelicals from preferment, but the upsurge of the fortunes of the Evangelical party in these years owed a great deal to Shaftesbury.

In 1859, on the formation of Palmerston's second Ministry, a certain change may be detected. This Ministry marked the final merging of the Whig and Peelite political forces: an alliance which formed the parliamentary basis of the Liberal party and gave the political system a degree of stability which it had not enjoyed since the repeal of the Corn Laws. But many of the Peelites were High Churchmen, and Palmerston told Shaftesbury that he would have to be rather more cautious in the selection of Bishops so that he would not, as Shaftesbury reported his comments, 'unnecessarily . . . vex (his) colleagues, some of whom (were) very high.'[71] And Shaftesbury himself recognised this. He knew that after 1859, it would be necessary to justify the selection of 'worthy, qualified . . . men, if they were altogether unknown;'[72] questions were now more likely to be asked about them. And he also felt that, the longer Palmerston's power endured, the more expedient it would be to draw from a wider section. In a letter to Palmerston in 1862, he agreed with a view which Palmerston had expressed that the Church should reflect various shades of opinion, and he went on to suggest that, since 1855, Palmerston had acted on this principle. He noted Evangelical appointments to Bishoprics and Deaneries; he admitted that there had been no ultra High Church appointments, but suggested that men of moderate High Church views had been elevated; and he also indicated certain Broad Church appointments. 'A fairer distribution,' Shaftesbury wrote, 'could not have been made.'[73] A number of the appointments which Shaftesbury noted as 'non-Evangelical' had been made since 1859, and there were to be some further appointments of this nature after 1862, notably that of Stanley, as Dean of Westminster in 1863. This, then, could be taken to indicate that after 1859, the earlier 'Evangelical appointments' were balanced, in some measure, by appointments of moderate High Churchmen and Broad Churchmen.

It is certainly true that in the course of Palmerston's second Ministry, there were cases where Shaftesbury's views were set aside. Thus in 1860, he wrote to Palmerston that the Bishop of Worcester was 'in extremis' and suggested that the best man for the see was Brodrick, Canon of Wells, who would, Shaftesbury argued, command the respect of both High and Low Church.[74] But Brodrick was not appointed and Worcester went to Philpott, whom Shaftesbury regarded as a moderate High Churchman. Again, in 1863, the Deanery of Westminster was vacant on the appointment of Trench as Archbishop of Dublin. This gave Shaftesbury a further opportunity to put forward McCaul, but, as in 1856, he was disappointed. Palmerston showed Shaftesbury a letter which he had received from the Queen requesting Stanley's appointment and asked Shaftesbury if there was any good reason for refusing the Queen's wishes.[75] Shaftesbury had, indeed, told Lady Wake in 1856 that he would be prepared to appoint Stanley to a Deanery,[76] but, in 1863, he did not favour the appointment. Nevertheless, Stanley was appointed. Another instance where it can be held that an influence other than that of Shaftesbury prevailed was in the appointment of Jacobson as Bishop of Chester in 1865. Shaftesbury had suggested Prest, Archdeacon of Durham, for this vacancy and Palmerston, it appears, had accepted it. But shortly after this, Palmerston wrote to Shaftesbury, enclosing a letter from Gladstone which asked that Jacobson be appointed to the vacant see on the grounds that he was chairman of Gladstone's election committee in Oxford, and that the nomination of Jacobson, a Professor at Oxford, would strengthen his interests.[77] Prest was set aside and Jacobson appointed.

Yet the argument that there was a major change in appointments after 1859 can be exaggerated. In the first place, even in the period before 1859, there had been non-Evangelical appointments, and, in this earlier period, Shaftesbury had, more than once, noted that Palmerston was anxious to see all sections of the Church represented. This was not a wholly new development after 1859. Again, the persons whom Shaftesbury mentioned as 'moderate High Churchmen' in his letter to Palmerston in 1862 could, indeed, only be described as men of very moderate views and it seems probable that Shaftesbury was exaggerating the views of some of the Bishops to convince Palmerston that a fair distribution had been made.[78] Again, there were – as is clear from Shaftesbury's 'list' of 1862 – several Evangelical appointments and translations made to more important Bishoprics after 1859, and the period ended with the appointment of Payne-Smith to the Regius Chair of Divinity at Oxford. This was Palmerston's last appointment, and, to Shaftesbury, there could hardly have been a better one than that of a man who was an exponent of Messianism in his interpretation of Isaiah. 'A glorious appointment', Shaftesbury wrote. 'The finger of God is manifest in it.'[79] It would, therefore, be a mistake to conclude from the appointments of the second Ministry that Shaftesbury's position as ecclesiastical adviser to Palmerston had been wholly usurped. And he did, at least, acquiesce in the appointments of Stanley and Jacobson. He was given the opportunity to dissuade Palmerston from appointing Stanley but felt, in the circumstances, that he could not do so: the Queen's wishes had to be taken into account and he thought that Stanley might even do less harm in London than among the young men in Oxford.[80] And Palmerston fully consulted Shaftesbury over the appointment of Jacobson. Shaftesbury would certainly have preferred Prest and thought Jacobson a 'cold comfortless preacher ... with few Episcopal qualities,' but he told Palmerston that he could safely appoint Jacobson as 'thoroughly respectable and beyond any hostile criticism,'[81] although Jacobson's stormy relations with the Dissenters after his appointment changed Shaftesbury's opinion in this respect.[82] Again, Shaftesbury's influence was felt in the appointment of Jeune to the Deanery of Lincoln in 1864[83] and he favoured his appointment later in the year to the Bishopric of Peterborough. Shaftesbury put forward the name of Jeremie to succeed Jeune at Lincoln,[84] and, in 1864,[85] suggested to Palmerston that Browne was a suitable choice for the Bishopric of Ely. Jeremie and Browne were duly appointed. Thus Palmerston still consulted Shaftesbury very extensively. He had always disapproved of the Queen's interference and continued to do so. When Jeremie was recommended for Peterborough, the Queen suggested other candidates. Palmerston wrote to Shaftesbury that he did not intend to give way. 'She fancies poor woman,' he wrote, 'that she has peculiar Prerogatives about the Church because she is its Head, forgetting that she is equally Head of all Institutions of the Country.'[86] And of Gladstone, Palmerston wrote to Shaftesbury that he did not feel that 'either as a colleague or as a Member for Oxford, (Gladstone) had any further claim on (him) as to Ecclesiastical Patronage than the right of sending (him) names for consideration....'[87]

Thus too sharp a break should not be made in 1859, either with regard to Evangelical appointments or Shaftesbury's influence. The period from 1855 to 1865 is better seen as a unity, in which a greater number of Evangelical appointments was made than ever before in a comparable period, and, for the first time, the Evangelical party was to enjoy, in numerical terms, a 'position of respectability' in the Church.[88] In 1865, Shaftesbury looked back on the previous ten years,[89] and, although he did acknowledge a change of emphasis but not of principle in 1859, he wrote of the whole period as one in which Palmerston consistently consulted him before any other person, lay or clerical. He recalled that every letter which Palmerston received from a Bishop was passed to him for remarks, and, on one occasion, when Shaftesbury offered to obtain some Bishops' names to support a candidate, he claimed that Palmerston had replied: 'No, No, you are quite enough. I had rather take your advice than that of all the bishops put together.' This is not, of course, first-hand evidence of Palmerston's remark and, in retrospect, Shaftesbury tended to exaggerate the extent of his influence and forgot the remarks which he himself had made from time to time about other influences making themselves felt. Again, Shaftesbury himself almost certainly consulted others, in particular Haldane. Nevertheless, Shaftesbury's was the most important voice throughout these years: 'it was no slight interest,' he wrote in 1865, 'to be near the centre of all action in politics, the fountain-head of all information.'[90] Others might be in the vicinity of the centre, but, in matters ecclesiastical, Shaftesbury was nearer than anyone else.

Despite such new-found influence, Shaftesbury still retained his commitment to all his Evangelical societies. The activities of Gobat in Jerusalem still gave rise to disquiet in some circles and, in 1853, the Archbishops had felt it necessary to defend him when he was criticised for exceeding the proper objects of his mission and for introducing schism into the Eastern Churches by his aggressive policy towards the Greek Orthodox Church.[91] In a sense, this was another victory for Gobat, but further criticisms were aired in two pamphlets published in 1858.[92] This time, it was not the general policy of the Bishop which was under attack; rather, it was his conduct in the Diocese. The pamphlets alleged that various scandals had taken place. One concerned Gobat's willingness to assist a Roman Catholic convert who had been convicted of living on immoral earnings and who, after a third marriage – arrangements for which Gobat had made in the face of opposition – was found guilty of robbery with violence and was sentenced to life imprisonment. The other accusation alleged that the Diocesan Boys School was inefficiently run. The headmaster was himself ill-educated – he had been a soap boiler and a member of a mission of workmen before being appointed to the school. It would seem that he owed his appointment to his marriage to Gobat's head nurse. But worse allegations were made than inefficiency in the running of the school: these were that immorality had been practised among the boys. There were demands for a judicial inquiry, and McCaul, who had long been a critic of Gobat, joined in these demands. But Shaftesbury had always been quick to defend Gobat, and, on this occasion, he was unwilling to take action to investigate the allegations. The Jerusalem Diocesan Missionary Fund, which had been set up in 1852–3 under his chairmanship to finance the Bishopric, issued what has been called a 'very vague reply'[93] to the charges made against Gobat; its tenor was to vindicate the Bishop. Further, Shaftesbury expressed his disapproval of any public discussion of the matter at the meeting of the London Jews Society in 1857.[94]

Shaftesbury was, indeed, much concerned to uphold all Evangelical societies at this time, since he saw in them secure bastions in the face of the threats to orthodox belief. In 1856, he told the fifth annual meeting of the Protestant Alliance that there was as much need to stand out against the 'Neology of Germany' as against the 'vile superstition of Rome'. The original reason for the foundation of the Protestant Alliance was to resist the 'Pope of Rome'; the need now was to resist the 'errors of Neology' and to ally for 'the propagation of the truth as it is in the Lord Jesus Christ.'[95] In 1861, at the meeting of the Bible Society, he turned his attention to *Essays and Reviews*, compiled, as he put it, by 'seven gentlemen, conscientious no doubt, in their own views, but holding a belief and a faith antagonistic in the extreme from that which we hold,'[96] and, in 1863, he attacked Colenso's book as a 'puerile and ignorant attack on the sacred and unassailable Word of God'.[97] He told the London Jews Society in 1864 that Renan's *Vie de Jésus* had been written for 'the most iniquitous purposes',[98] and, in 1866, he was to lambast *Ecce Homo* as 'the most pestilential book ever vomited from the jaws of Hell'.[99] The only good, Shaftesbury felt, that might come from such publications was that they provoked interest in religion and gave its true defenders in the Evangelical societies an opportunity to uphold it. He told the Bible Society in 1863 that, the greater the number of attacks on the Bible, the more determined and zealous the Society should be: it should redouble the number of its issues, reduce the price and increase circulation.[100] And Shaftesbury felt that he could take refuge in the Evangelical Societies against the Neologists. He told the London Jews Society in 1865 that 'amidst those gigantic heresies' that were affecting the whole world and, he was ashamed to say, especially the Church of England, he cleaved 'more and more to this Society, which rests on the simple assertion of Evangelical truth.'[101] To the Church Pastoral Aid Society, also in 1865, he said that he thought the time not far distant when the Society might 'for some purposes be almost the only depository of religious truth in this country.'[102]

If, at one level, the Church of England seemed threatened in the 1850s and 1860s by intellectual attack, at another level, the threat arose from its failure to reach the masses. Shaftesbury was certainly aware of this. Indeed, one of his earliest parliamentary efforts in the decade had this matter at its heart. The Religious Worship bill had passed the Commons without difficulty between 4 and 11 May, 1855. Its purpose was to repeal the provisions of an Act of 1812 which had prohibited more than twenty persons from assembling in a hall or house for purposes of religious worship. Shaftesbury introduced the first reading of the bill in the Lords on 14 May, 1855, but, by contrast with its smooth passage through the Commons, it was strongly opposed in the Upper House. Shaftesbury justified it in terms of the increased opportunities which it would give for the work of evangelism, and, at the Report stage on 12 June, when it was clear that opposition would be expressed, spoke at some length on the subject.[103] He reminded their Lordships that there were thousands of thousands, and possibly even millions, in the country who were 'absolutely without the pale of Christianity'. Many efforts were, indeed, being made to reach them, by the use of halls and other premises, but, Shaftesbury claimed, these were technically illegal, since it was always the practice to close the meeting with a hymn or a prayer. It was true that the law had not been generally enforced, but there were instances where it had been enforced and, if these became widespread, many efforts to evangelise those outside the Churches would be curtailed.

The bill was, therefore, an opportunity to remove all barriers to the work of mission, and as he put it, to 'untie the hands of the laity'. But the objections which had been anticipated were, indeed, made. Both Bishop Wilberforce[104] and Derby[105] criticised Shaftesbury for over-eagerness in presenting a bill which, they argued, had not been fully discussed in the Commons, and they denied the need for legislation on the subject. Existing legislation imposed no practical limitations on evangelical activity: Dissenters could already obtain licences without any difficulty. But, more basically, both argued that the bill would be disruptive of the order and discipline of the Church and would lead to the parishioners of one parish calling upon the incumbent of another to preach, and also to the unauthorised intrusion of laymen into clerical functions. On 15 June, Derby proposed that the bill be referred to a select committee; this was accepted and the committee produced another bill to replace the first. This was introduced by Derby in July and involved tighter control by the clergy over the activities of the laity. But finally, by various compromises, the matter was settled. Derby withdrew his bill, and Shaftesbury made certain modifications to the original bill. He had found that the existing Act of 1812 allowed places of religious worship to be registered, not as Dissenting but as Protestant places of worship. This met most of the requirements which the original bill had sought, and thus the modified bill claimed only for private houses the privilege of being protected for the purpose of worship for more than twenty persons.[106] This modified bill passed at the end of July, 1855. Shaftesbury wrote to Disraeli to ask for his help in securing the passage of his bill through the Commons. He had, he said, reason to believe that opposition would be forthcoming from 'the Gladstonian clique' and he urged Disraeli to resist their efforts 'to injure, or even delay, this healing enactment.'[107]

The struggle had aroused all Shaftesbury's antagonism to the High Church party. Bishop Wilberforce and Derby incurred his severe criticism. Derby's ignorance and disregard for the state of the people were, he wrote, 'painful' and he commented that, although Derby would refuse permission to hold public worship in his house or barn, 'he would maintain the full privilege to use them, at discretion, for a cock-pit or betting-room! Such is the result of a racing life, and many a jovial hour passed at Tattersall's.'[108] He was greatly distressed by the opposition voiced at the Report stage: it was, he wrote of the occasion, 'one of the most, perhaps the most unpleasant evening I recollect in public life,' and it brought on thoughts about his incapacity for business and loathing for the House of Lords. 'In that House,' he wrote, 'I stand alone . . . hated for my opinions, and despised for my inability. . . .'[109] When the select committee was appointed, he felt that the Bishops had exhibited great ignorance, bigotry and opposition to evangelical life and action. He spoke vigorously against Derby's proposals and moved that they be deferred for three months; tightening the reins of clerical control would, he argued, achieve nothing towards reaching out to the millions at present beyond the influence of religious teaching – the Church must be free to act as a missionary church.[110] Final success did, of course, revive his spirits; the bill, he felt, contained everything which he had asked for and, when it finally passed, he was given a dinner by the persons with whom he had cooperated in the cause: 'friendly, cordial and Christian,' he wrote. 'Speeches after dinner, very religious in their tone and such as we require in these times of secret "rebuke and blasphemy".'[111]

Further, Shaftesbury was well pleased with the working of the Act. It was decided to use Exeter Hall for the services, and, at the end of May, 1857, a series of twelve special services began there on Sunday evenings. They were advertised for all-comers, but especially the working classes 'who were not habitual Church or Chapel goers.'[112] The first service was conducted by the Bishop of Carlisle, Villiers, for whose appointment, the previous year, Shaftesbury had been largely responsible. Shaftesbury was delighted with the result. It was, he wrote, 'a glorious triumph for religion and the Church of England'. He reported an attendance of more than three thousand; it had been an orderly, attentive and reverent gathering and among it, he claimed, were persons who had never in their lives been in any place of public worship.[113] Shaftesbury attended all twelve services and was much gratified at the response to them. After the series was over, a further number of meetings was planned for October. This, however, ran into difficulties.[114] Before it began, the incumbent of the parish in which Exeter Hall was situated, the Revd. A. G. Edouard, issued an inhibition to the clergyman who was to have taken the first service. Even under the new Act, it was necessary for a clergyman to obtain the permission of the incumbent of a parish in which a special service was to be held before he could take part in that service. The Bishop of London, Tait, was much in favour of the services and Edouard himself had given permission for clergy to take part in the first series. But he had done so with considerable misgivings and had said that it was only for a trial period. Once this had expired, he refused to permit the second series, giving as his reasons that the services were not attracting the working classes and were emptying the 'ordinary' Churches. In fact, these charges had little justification[115] and Edouard was simply trying to find a pretext for withdrawing his permission. Shaftesbury was doubtful if Edouard was entitled to do this and advised that the services should continue. But he was mistaken and was overruled by the committee organising the services, and they ceased. An application was made for the use of St Martin's Hall, but that, too, failed, and finally the Dissenters agreed to assist and supply a hall. Shaftesbury was deeply grateful for this assistance,[116] but he felt that there was need for revision of the 1855 Act.

Thus in December, 1857, Shaftesbury explained the principles of a revision which he proposed in the Lords. In his long speech in support of his principles,[117] he rejected the criticism which had been made of the special services. They *were*, he claimed, attended by the working classes, and, since they started at 6.30 p.m., they could not intefere with the normal services, held at 11 a.m. and 3 p.m. Further, Shaftesbury now clearly felt that the parish system, in which he had previously placed staunch faith, was no longer adequate in itself. The population of large towns – and especially the metropolis – had outstripped the parochial system, and some relaxation of it was necessary so that the 'mighty masses' might be cared for. Any such relaxation would be ultimately to the advantage of the parishes. As things stood, the people who attended Exeter Hall would not attend any other place of worship. They would never go to Westminster Abbey or St Paul's. But if they went to Exeter Hall, they would, in time, go to the established places and finally to their own parish churches, although then it would be necessary to treat them with proper respect and not exclude them from certain pews, as was the present practice. But meantime, no further infringement of parochial rights would be made than was absolutely necessary, and Shaftesbury stressed that the sanction of the Bishop of London and the incumbent of the parish had been obtained before the first series of Exeter Hall services had been held. He was not prepared to comment on the power of the incumbent to ban such services, but, accepting that it existed, he now proposed to change it. Thus his bill proposed that the power of the incumbent should not extend to parishes with a population of over two thousand. If under two thousand, the power might be exercised, but only on the authority of the Bishop, who would be able to view the matter in the light of the overall necessities of his diocese. Shaftesbury urged that he was doing no more than was essential and was leaving the parochial system untouched, wherever it was unnecessary to interfere with it.

The proposal, however, encountered opposition; it was criticised by Bishop Wilberforce and others, and Shaftesbury was persuaded to postpone it. Before he could proceed further with it, the Archbishop of Canterbury, on 5 February, 1857, introduced the Church of England Special Services Bill which, he said, was in agreement with the object which Shaftesbury aimed at, but in disagreement with its methods.[118] The bill made it necessary for the Bishop's permission to be sought before any special services could be held. If the Bishop thought that such services were desirable, he could convey his opinion to the incumbent of the parish in which the services were to be held, and, if the incumbent were of the same mind, the services would take place. But, if the incumbent disagreed with the Bishop, an appeal could be made to the Archbishop. The bill, it was argued, enabled the Bishop – and the incumbent – to supply in some degree the spiritual wants of large and populous districts. Hearing that the prevailing episcopal opinion was overwhelmingly against his bill, Shaftesbury dropped it in favour of the Archbishop's: he felt that his own was better, but conceded that it would be impossible to carry it without a long and angry argument.[119]

The bill passed to the Commons, but, in fact, it never reached the statute book. In these circumstances, the committee responsible for organising the services wrote to Edouard and guaranteed that none of the Litany would be used. They felt that, in this way, the objection to the services would lapse. But Edouard was not satisfied and passed the matter to Tait. Tait could not give the services official approval, but he did not stop them, and the services were resumed, although without official sanction.[120] Shaftesbury frequently took part in them, often reading the lesson. Again, he was well satisfied with their effects and felt that attendance at such services would, in the long run, bring people to Church. There were, however, still criticisms to meet. In February, 1860, Lord Duncannon, a High Churchman, moved a resolution that services in the theatres were irregular and inconsistent with order.[121] Once again, Shaftesbury rose to the defence of the services, stressing the necessity of taking action when not two per cent of the working men in London ever attended any place of worship. He also refuted the arguments put forward by Duncannon that there had been ginger beer bottles opened and oranges peeled, and he quoted evidence from Sir Richard Mayne, chief of police, that the meetings had been orderly. He cited letters from clergymen who had taken part in the services to show that there was no threat to the established Church; indeed, the reverse was true. And, in words which were reminiscent of his days in the Factory Movement, he asked if it is

> nothing to find that if we only speak to the people in a kind, straightforward, sincere open and earnest manner, we may be given their affections and keep them in obedience and good order? My Lords, what the people of England want is not patronage but sympathy; the bringing of heart to heart, the acknowledgement on the part of the person ... of all degrees of wealth, that they are men of like passion with themselves, with the same hopes, the same aspirations, the same fears and the same destinies....[122]

Shaftesbury received support in the debate and Duncannon withdrew his motion. Thus the services continued, although it is true that some of those who took part in them tended to give them a bad name in certain quarters, and even Shaftesbury himself was doubtful about one preacher, who was too bombastic.[123] Nevertheless, he still felt that they were successful: they had 'affected many stiff, cold, hard and hostile Peers' and had 'warmed even Derby into approval:' that, wrote Shaftesbury, was 'akin to a miracle'.[124]

The theatre services thus gave increased opportunities to the Church to bring people within its doors on a Sunday, and Shaftesbury continued to devote his exertions to prevent other distractions from taking up their time and attention on that day. The Sunday question was, indeed, a live one in the mid-1850s. The opening of the Crystal Palace on Sundays had been averted by the decision of the Company not to proceed with its plans, but, in 1854, Evangelicals had attempted to restrict the hours of Sunday opening of public houses and put up resistance to efforts to open institutions such as the British Museum on a Sunday. Such activity, however, was increasingly seen as hostile to the enjoyment and leisure of the working classes, and suspicion of the Sabbatarians was largely responsible for the reception given in the summer of 1855 to a bill introduced the previous April by Lord Robert Grosvenor to restrict Sunday trading in the metropolis. This was not, in fact, a Sabbatarian measure, but was more in harmony with earlier efforts to relax work on a Sunday on recreational, rather than on spiritual, grounds. It was, however, regarded as a further effort to harm the interests of the working classes, this time by depriving the poor of their livings. A series of demonstrations took place in Hyde Park, which resulted in some violence and disorder, and the bill was withdrawn. Shaftesbury deplored these demonstrations. 'Sedition and infidelity' were manifested in them and he had no doubt that Russian agents had inspired them.[125] Further evidence of anti-Sabbatarianism was apparent in the formation in September, 1855, of the National Sunday League, which grew out of the views of those who advocated a secular approach to Sunday. The League campaigned for the opening of the Crystal Palace and the British Museum on a Sunday. Shaftesbury was much disturbed at this. He addressed a large meeting of Sunday School teachers in Exeter Hall in February, 1856, protesting against proposals to open the Crystal Palace, but, on another occasion also in February, he experienced considerable difficulty at the hands of opposing groups which attended a meeting of the North London Sunday Rest Association. Shaftesbury took the chair, but, when he called for prayer to open the meeting, he was interrupted and a proposal was put and seconded that the business should proceed without prayer. Shaftesbury said that he had never heard such a resolution before and refused to put it: this was greeted with uproar and Shaftesbury had to leave the meeting with the assistance of the police.[126] The meeting then went on to express strong support for the adoption of a more relaxed attitude to the Sabbath, and, in particular, thanked the government for authorising the Life Guards to play on Sundays in Kensington Gardens after Church – this had been done in 1855.[127]

In the spring of 1856, permission was once more given to the bands to provide concerts in the park, and this raised further contention between Sabbatarians and anti-Sabbatarians.[128] At first, it appeared that the National Sunday League, which wanted to extend the concerts, would triumph; Sir Benjamin Hall, Commissioner of Public Works, appeared before a National Sunday League meeting and announced that additional concerts would be given. Yet, in May, 1856, the government ordered the suspension of the bands. Shaftesbury certainly played a part in this. He objected to the practice of Sunday bands and did his best to persuade Palmerston to withdraw the permission. At first, Palmerston refused to listen. Then Shaftesbury spoke to the Archbishop of Canterbury and obtained a letter to Palmerston; this he took to Palmerston, persuaded him to accept it and discontinue the bands. Shaftesbury thus once more acted from the Sabbatarian point of view – a view which was shared by the Queen, who also brought some influence to bear. He expected that the decision would be unpopular and that there would be a repetition of the disturbances of the previous year. Indeed, he kept the windows of his house in Grosvenor Square closed and the blinds down for two successive Sundays in expectation of rioting and disturbance.[129] His fears proved groundless.

Shaftesbury, however, was always conscious of the difficulties and dangers of appearing to deny recreation and amusement to the working classes by an extreme Sabbatarianism. Partly in this connection, he had already shown an interest in the Early Closing Movement. This had its origins in the 1830s and had certain associations with the Factory Movement: both sought to provide more time and leisure for those who worked in factories and shops. In 1842, a more formal organisation, the Metropolitan Drapers' Association, had been set up in Chelsea and Shaftesbury had presided at a meeting of the Association in 1846.[130] As its activities spread, it changed its title to the Early Closing Association. Closely connected with this movement was the Young Men's Christian Association. Founded in 1843, its purpose was to provide libraries, reading rooms and religious instruction for young shop assistants whose hours were curtailed because of early closing on a certain day of the week.[131] Shaftesbury also supported this movement, and, in March, 1856, addressed a meeting which it held in Manchester. His speech showed the connection between such movements and the Sunday question. He said that he saw the 'immense value' of early closing, and he expressed his belief that there was no other way in which the observance of the Sabbath could be improved so effectually as by giving 'time for amusement and repose on every Saturday afternoon'. If recreation were refused on a Sunday, it must be allowed on some other day.[132] In 1856, Shaftesbury took the chair of the Early Closing Association; he referred to the improved condition of the working classes since the introduction of the Ten Hour system and felt that this formed a good precedent for a half-holiday for others. Further, in 1857, a new body was set up – the National Lord's Day Rest Association, which, in 1861, became the Working Men's Lord's Day Rest Association. This was formed partly to counter the National Sunday League. Unlike the Lord's Day Observance Society, it was inter-denominational. It was also designed to appeal to the working classes more widely than the Lord's Day Observance Society. It had a lower subscription and met at times when working men were able to attend, and it included early closing and a Saturday half-holiday among its objects.[133] Shaftesbury retained his links with the older body and was, indeed, chairman of its metropolitan committee. It was also active in the struggle against the secularists in the 1850s. But he was to forge closer links with the newly established organisation and, in time, was to become its President.

During the years after 1855, Shaftesbury's Evangelical endeavours were, therefore, exercised in many and varied forms. They embraced the new position of influence which he enjoyed as 'adviser' to Palmerston and the older position in the Societies, which he had long occupied. It is arguable that his attitudes and activities in these years betrayed a further hardening of his Evangelicalism: that his mind became more tightly closed to any points which could not be accommodated to his views. His conduct over the Gobat affair adds weight to this point. He was unwilling, it would seem, to consider the possibility that the accusations made against Gobat had any substance and was not prepared even to investigate them. Further, his criticisms of Neology were, in many cases, ill-conceived and, indeed, ill-advised. He was less than fair to Seeley in his denunciation of *Ecce Homo*. Seeley did not enter the field of textual criticism, but was more concerned to see the texts in a new light as portraying moral principles which Christ taught and the way in which these had influenced subsequent history. To some, it was a refreshing and invigorating book.[134] Further, the extreme denunciation was unwise and Shaftesbury himself realised that it would have been better not used. He admitted that it escaped in 'the heat of declamation, justifiable and yet injudicious,'[135] and he later wrote that his comments had merely drawn publicity to the book. It had been seen by Seeley as a piece of good fortune, and had, Seeley claimed, sold ten thousand copies and put £1,000 into his pocket.[136] Shaftesbury also adopted a very extreme point of view towards biblical criticism. The questions which he posed about Divine inspiration were by no means unimportant or lacking in penetration, but to claim that no part of the Bible could be subjected to scrutiny without the whole being abandoned was to take a stance which exposed him to attack. He was, indeed, excessively distrustful of an intellectual approach: 'with the heart man believeth and not with the intellect,' he told the Young Men's Christian Association. 'The intellect is very well in its way, but the heart is God's special province.'[137] He was extremely wary even of new versions of the Bible. He wrote to Bishop Wilberforce in January, 1864, expressing dismay at a rumour that the Archbishop of Canterbury had convoked the Bishops to consider an amendment of the Authorised Version. He hoped that Wilberforce was not of the same mind: 'what a fearful declaration, in these days,' he wrote, 'to pronounce the blessed old version unworthy of credit!'[138]

Nevertheless, Shaftesbury was not alone in expressing opposition to the intellectual developments of the time. His old antagonist over some issues, Bishop Wilberforce, was also vehement in his denunciations of Neology. The Scriptures, he felt, were either supernatural or false; if Christ's miracles were refuted, Christ himself was refuted. It was morally dishonest to put forward views such as those in *Essays and Reviews* and to continue in the service of the Church. When the Privy Council Judicial Committee upheld two of the Essayists against their conviction, Convocation, largely on Wilberforce's prompting, condemned the book, and Pusey, along with allies in the Evangelical school, drew up a declaration upholding the inspiration and Divine authority of the Bible. This was signed by half the clergy in England and Ireland.[139] Pusey and Wilberforce, indeed, joined forces with Shaftesbury over the issue. When the Judicial Committee dismissed the case against the Essayists, Pusey wrote to *The Record* asking all Christians to overcome their minor differences in combined resistance to the doctrinal errors of the time. Shaftesbury wrote to Pusey, complimenting him on the letter and agreeing earlier differences must be set aside to 'contend earnestly for the faith once delivered to the Saints.'

> We have to struggle [he continued] not for Apostolical Succession or Baptismal Regeneration, but for the very Atonement itself, for the sole hope of fallen Man, the vicarious sacrifice of the Cross.[140]

Pusey replied that the 'soul-destroying judgment' of the Privy Council might be brought to good account if it bound 'as one man all who love our blessed Lord, in contending for the faith assailed.' Wilberforce also wrote to Shaftesbury after the judgment of the Privy Council to say that it was his earnest desire that it should be the means of healing 'the wound which the separation of High and Low Church inflicts upon us, by bringing together all who believe simply in the Bible and in the plain language of our Creeds.'[141] Shaftesbury took up the offer. He replied on 2 March, 1864, that he would be happy to talk with Wilberforce on the subject. He wrote that it was now a grand and undeniable necessity that all, who are earnest for the Faith and its fulness and purity, should lay aside subordinate differences and join heart and soul, to combat the common enemy.[142]

Further, Shaftesbury's attitude towards another aspect of the intellectual developments of the 1850s and 1860s, that of scientific discovery, was a good deal more liberal than that of many of his contemporaries. Scientific advances, especially in the fields of geology and biology, cast doubt on the age of the world to be found in Genesis and on the Biblical view of the role of man as a being created in the image of God. As with Biblical criticism, this was by no means new, but came within a long tradition of positivist thought, and, in terms of the nineteenth century, Lyell's *Principles of Geology* (1830–33) and Chambers' *Vestiges of the Natural History of Creation* (1844) had already pointed towards an evolutionary process in the creation of the Universe. But, once again, the 1850s and 1860s brought much of this to a head. Darwin's *Origin of Species* of 1859 may not have been original in the sense of putting forward the idea of evolution for the first time, but it did put it forward with a wealth of evidence – and hence with an authority – which had hitherto been lacking. Darwin disclaimed any intention of saying anything which bore on theological matters and, at the time he wrote the *Origins*, had a belief in a personal God. His aim was not to refute theology, but to correct earlier evolutionists such as Chambers. But the implications of his work were seen as damaging from a theological point of view. He was held by many to have substituted 'Chance' for 'Design' in the creation of the Universe, and man now appeared as no more than the highest stage of evolution, rather than as a special creature with unique God-given gifts. Certainly, Darwin's work called down on him the widespread opposition of Churchmen. The most famous attack came from Bishop Wilberforce,[143] and Pusey, too, was in the forefront of Darwin's critics. But, on this occasion, there was no alliance between them and Shaftesbury, who adopted a much more tolerant line. It is certainly true that he deprecated any attempts of scientists to unsettle faith, and he also felt that scientists could be guilty of audacity, conceit and ignorance. But, from a letter which he wrote to Richard Owen – admittedly a scientist to whom he did not attribute such characteristics – it is clear that Shaftesbury did not distrust science in the way that so many of his contemporaries did. Although he was, as he told Owen,[144] convinced that in the great pursuit of salvation, the heart was 'everything' and the intellect 'scarcely anything', he had no wish to place any constraints on the activity of scientists. He would 'check no enquiry ... suppress no fact, nor shrink from any just inference ... offer no shifts, nor suggest such weak and fanciful explanations as have increased, rather than have abated doubt.' And in 1863, he wrote that he would encourage the study of science in the most liberal way: it was not the knowledge but the ignorance of scientific men that did mischief. Although for a long time to come, there might seem to be discrepancy and even collision between science and the Scriptures, Shaftesbury had complete confidence that 'Science in a more extended compass ... will be the surest, stoutest, most irresistible "Apology for the Bible" in the whole history of facts and arguments since Controversy began.' The Mosaic Creation, the authenticity of the Pentateuch, the Deluge and Noah's ark would all be established.

> I do not object to any research into Nature and her deepest secrets [he continued]. I do not say 'no' to anyone who wishes to announce that he has discovered a fact inconsistent with Scripture. Let him do so, and push his discoveries further; but let him not, in the arrogance of half-informed persons, assume and declare that the puling infancy of Science has flooded the manhood of the Bible.[145]

And, as discoveries were extended, the faith which had seemed to be in danger would be built up.

In the Church of England's response to Biblical Criticism, it can, therefore, be argued that Shaftesbury did not adopt a uniquely negative role, and, in his attitude towards scientific developments, his attitude was, for his time, enlightened. In facing the other great challenge of the time, that of winning over the working classes to the Church, Shaftesbury was not by any means alone in realising the extent of the challenge and in trying to meet it. The years 1858–9 witnessed an Evangelical revival in Ulster, Scotland and Wales, although it has been argued that this had relatively little influence in England.[146] But the 1850s and 1860s *did* see an outburst of missionary activity in England. Various methods of appealing to the masses were tried: open air preaching, the establishment of special missions in the poorer parts of cities, tract delivery. Shaftesbury's work was part of all this effort, and, even in the work of theatre services, many others were involved. There were also the efforts of men of various persuasions in the Church of England and outside it. Thus Tait, Bishop of London, who, as has been seen, could not be described as an Evangelical, took part in out-of-doors preaching, and there were, too, the activities of the Congregationalist, Samuel Morley, the Baptist, Charles Spurgeon, and the early efforts of William Booth, later to be channelled into the Salvation Army. Shaftesbury did not, in fact, always approve of everything that was done. He never liked or trusted Booth and his methods, and he wrote to Morley complaining of Spurgeon's 'coarse language'.[147] But Shaftesbury's efforts did show an awareness of what he called the 'peculiar and dangerous character of the times'.[148] His 'nominations' to Bishoprics were designed in part to ensure that the Church was on good terms with the working classes and the Dissenters, and part of his complaint against Spurgeon was that his language would endanger union between Churchmen and Dissenters. Again, he was perfectly prepared to praise the special services run by Dissenters in these years: he preferred evangelical religion to be preached by the Church of England but he wished any Church well which preached it.[149] It may be argued that, in his enthusiasm for theatre services, Shaftesbury showed too little regard for the rights of the incumbent clergy and his 'impetuosity in pressing the Evangelicals' case'[150] aroused opposition which hindered the success of the venture. Shaftesbury did, admittedly, take an outspoken line on these matters. In 1864, he wrote to the Archbishop of Canterbury over the case of two clergymen who were threatened with the Archbishop's displeasure because they had delivered a religious address at a public meeting and offered prayers in a private house without the permission of the incumbent of the parish. Shaftesbury strongly objected to the threat, for he felt that it would affect the special services which, he wrote, 'under God's grace (had) done more for the most wretched classes of the Metropolis than all the preachments in St Paul's and Westminster Abbey put together.' Shaftesbury admitted the necessity of forbidding a clergyman to disturb the ecclesiastical rights of another: thus he must not administer the Sacraments, use the liturgy and officiate in any Parish without permission from the incumbent. But, Shaftesbury insisted, 'to expound the Word of God, to offer up prayer, whenever and wherever he pleases, whether to persons disposed to hear, or to ten thousand, is a right inherent in every Christian man. . . . It is higher than a right; it is absolutely a duty. . . .'[151] In upholding this 'duty', Shaftesbury was, indeed, prepared to sit loose to strict ecclesiastical discipline, but, equally, it can be argued that such flexibility was essential for the Church of England at that time. He told the Church Pastoral Aid Society in 1857 that if the Mountain would not go to Mohamed, Mohamed must go to the Mountain, and he urged on his hearers the need to experiment with the 'great principle of adaptation in the Church of England'.[152] He was not, indeed, alone in this and much credit must go to Tait, but Shaftesbury was its most consistent and outspoken lay champion. The theatre services have been described as 'the first real appreciation of the problems forced upon the traditional ecclesiastical structure and methods by the growth of the new, less than Christian proletariat in the country as well as town.'[153]

But despite all his efforts, Shaftesbury was gloomy about the future of Evangelicalism within the Church and in the religious practice and observance of the country. In 1865, he thought the state of the Church 'singularly alarming'. The Evangelical party once so powerful was, he wrote, 'fast disappearing'. He ascribed this partly to a compliance with Neology on the one hand, and High Churchmanship on the other; partly to a 'defective supply from the youth of the country'; and partly to a lack of communication and cooperation within its own ranks. Thus he felt that the Church would go to High Church or Broad Church extremes: was it, he asked, to become a 'mass of bigotry, superstition and sacerdotal tyranny, a tissue of forms, ordinances and ceremonies' or a 'creedless, empty, system of ethics, without dogmas, without the supernatural, without the knowledge and confession of sin, without repentance, without prayer, without God's certain and unmistakable word and without Divine Sanction?' He wondered which was the worse. 'I know not,' he wrote. 'But one or the other (unless our Lord interfere with such a flood of His grace as never was before) is inevitable.'[154] Shaftesbury was also uncertain whether the work of the theatre services would be followed up. Already in 1860, he had written that he could see little evidence that Churchmen – or Dissenters – were doing anything to accommodate the new converts in their Churches.[155] And he was increasingly doubtful of the willingness of the country to accept Evangelical beliefs and practices. In 1864, he wrote to Morley that the country is 'not what it was in respect of Evangelical or Protestant feeling.'[156] In July, 1865, he wrote that he foresaw in the country a 'general Infidelity, cold, ignorant, saucy, self-satisfied'.[157] But the event which gave him most cause for depression was the death of Palmerston in October, 1865. He felt that Dean Stanley's influence and that of the Queen would now prevail. 'Be it Russell or be it Gladstone,' he wrote, 'the Dean will rule all things, and both he and she will rejoice to reverse the policy of a Minister they so feared and hated.'[158] In December, 1865, he noted that he had received a letter from the incumbent of St Mary's, Bryanstone Square, whose appointment he had obtained from Palmerston: 'and excellent was the issue.' But ill-health had compelled the incumbent to retire. 'The great work of *"undoing"* is begun,' wrote Shaftesbury. '. . . The appointment lies with . . . Russell. Rejoice, ye Neologians and Tractarians, all who hate the truth as it is in Christ Jesus.'[159] And, as he noted the new appointment – one of which he disapproved – he wrote that the 'reaction in spirituals has indeed begun.'[160] Thus, with the death of Palmerston, Shaftesbury felt that a 'great and mighty door for good is now closed upon me so far as I can see for ever:' but, he added on another occasion, 'our wonder and gratitude must be that it was for so long open.'[161]

Shaftesbury's gloom was not without justification. Despite the events of the decade, in 1865 the Evangelical party within the Church was not in a strong position. It had always been hampered by internal divisions and lack of unity, and this remained true in this period. Some of its members took a very rigid line on practice and belief; others were less rigid and even, as Shaftesbury noted, made a certain accommodation with High Church practices or Neological beliefs. Thus it presented an ineffective force in the face of High and Broad Church, especially when, as happened later in the century, High and Broad Church tended to draw closer together. Then, the temporary alliance of the 1850s and 1860s between High and Low Church over matters of belief broke down and the sharp divergences between them in matters of practice, never altogether obscured in this period, became clear once again. Another cause of Evangelical weakness in future years was somewhat fortuitous – many of the clergy who had been advanced in these years did not live very long. By 1875, only four were still alive.[162] This deprived the Evangelical party of leadership. But it must also be asked if the quality of that leadership, even when exercised to the full, was equal to the times and, in particular, to the intellectual challenge of the times. The 'Shaftesbury Bishops' have suffered considerable criticism as being unlearned and untutored. *The Saturday Review*, in 1861, wrote that the members of the Church of England were not required to be 'profound and recluse students', but they were required 'at such a juncture as the present, to be on a level with their age in point of knowledge, liberal-minded and capable of sympathising with different schools of thought, to the full extent of the range which a Church avowedly comprehensive permits within her pale.' The Bishops created under Palmerston did not pass this test: they were not noted for 'largeness of sympathy.'[163] It could be argued, in reply, that few men among the Bishops as a whole would pass the test. In 1861, Archbishop Sumner of Canterbury issued a general declaration of all the Bishops, condemning *Essays and Reviews*; and, as has been seen, probably the most outspoken criticism of both Neology and Science came not from a 'Shaftesbury Bishop' but from Wilberforce. Again, it cannot justly be said that all the Bishops recommended by Shaftesbury were unlearned men. Palmerston himself refuted this view. He told the Queen that several of the new men had distinguished themselves by their 'classical and academic attainments' and he cited Baring, Longley, Tait, Wigram and Waldegrave.[164] Three of these – Baring, Wigram and Waldegrave – could be said to have been of the Evangelical School.[165]

But the remarks made in *The Saturday Review* have some point. On the whole, the men promoted under Palmerston were 'parish men', who became good pastoral Bishops. This is in no way to their discredit – indeed, in this sense, they assisted the pastoral and 'social' role of the Church. But they were not well equipped to meet the intellectual challenge of the day. Even those who were learned were not learned in this respect. Shaftesbury, it will be recalled, advised Palmerston against the advancement of men who were 'learned' in the sense of having the power of 'keeping pace with the theological literature of the time.'[166] This meant that, in coming to terms with Neology, they were at a disadvantage; here, even the fact that few could read German made them less able to deal with the 'threat' than, for example,

Pusey, who had an excellent command of the German language.[167] Thus the 'Shaftesbury Bishops' made little intellectual contribution to the life of the Church in a period of considerable intellectual challenge, and, once the High Church party made an accommodation with the Broad, Evangelicalism as a system of belief within the Church was left isolated and weak. Shaftesbury had realised that his resources were limited and was, indeed, thankful that he had been enabled 'to raise up so many in every gradation of the Church to protest and testify against the various and terrible aggressions of Anti-Christ.'[168] But the tide was flowing against him, and such men as he was able to 'raise up' could not turn it. Like Shaftesbury himself, they lacked the resilience of mind even to accommodate to it.

Further, in the wider mission of the Church, the theatre services were, indeed, well attended: Shaftesbury claimed in 1860–61 that over a quarter of a million persons had attended them. No doubt, many were regular church-goers elsewhere, but, undoubtedly, many were not. How far all this had any permanent effect is impossible to say. What can be said is that, after 1865, the Evangelical impetus was not sustained and the work of mission to the working classes was increasingly undertaken in the later part of the century by other groups in the Established Church and outside it.[169] Shaftesbury's forward-looking plans and willingness to experiment were not sustained by those who followed in the Evangelical tradition. And if, by 1865, Evangelicalism was a waning force within the Church of England, its activities in other directions were also to come increasingly under attack in the years that followed. There were signs of this in the efforts of the National Sunday League in the fifties to resist Evangelical views on Sunday observance. The extent of the League's appeal and, indeed, that of secularist societies in general, should not be exaggerated, but it is arguable that a more secular mood, antagonistic to Evangelical values and opinions, was discernible in the later part of the nineteenth century.[170] Shaftesbury himself was already conscious of it and was to become ever more so. It now remains to be seen if the same might be said of the social and philanthropic endeavours in which he was also involved in these mid century years.

NOTES

1. St G.H., Shaftesbury MSS, C 25021/7th Earl.
2. ibid., C 25021.2/7th Earl.
3. N.R.A., Shaftesbury (Broadlands) MSS, SHA/PD/6, 2 Mar., 1855.
4. ibid., Palmerston (Broadlands) MSS, GC/SH/29/1/2.
5. This was a motion proposed by Sir Joshua Walmsley, M.P. for Leicester in Mar., 1855, for the opening of the British Museum on a Sunday. Palmerston was

approached by the L.D.O.S. and said that the government would oppose the motion, which it did (G. M. Ellis, op. cit., p. 264), and the motion was defeated by a large majority. Thus Shaftesbury's misgivings were groundless. He wrote of the 'abominable motion' and blessed God that it was rejected. (N.R.A., Shaftesbury (Broadlands) MSS, SHA/PD/6, 13 Mar., 1855).
6. ibid., Palmerston (Broadlands) MSS, GC/SH/29/1/2.
7. ibid., GC/SH/31, GC/SH/32.
8. ibid., Shaftesbury (Broadlands) MSS, SHA/PD/6, 8 Feb., 1855.
9. St G.H., Shaftesbury MSS, C 25021.16/7th Earl.
10. ibid., C 25021.19/7th Earl.
11. ibid., C 25021.18/7th Earl.
12. ibid., C 25021.10/7th Earl (copy).
13. N.R.A., Shaftesbury (Broadlands) MSS, GC/SH/33.
14. St G.H., C 25021.11/7th Earl.
15. ibid., C 25021.18/7th Earl.
16. ibid., C 25021.12/7th Earl.
17. ibid., C 25021.17/7th Earl.
18. ibid., C 25021.19/7th Earl.
19. Quoted in Hodder, II, 510. On 10 Mar., Palmerston had himself asked Shaftesbury to attend that afternoon at the Palace, but this was deferred by Shaftesbury's objection. It would seem that the occasion referred to by Lady Palmerston was later than the 10th, but her letters over this episode are not dated.
20. Quoted in Hodder, II, 511.
21. St G.H., Shaftesbury MSS, C 25028.1/7th Earl; C 25021.15/7th Earl (copy).
22. Quoted in Hodder, III, 132.
23. N.R.A., Palmerston (Broadlands) MSS, GC/SH/44.
24. Quoted in Hodder, III, 132.
25. N.R.A., Palmerston (Broadlands) MSS, GC/SH/45/1/2.
26. ibid., Shaftesbury (Broadlands) MSS, SHA/PD/7, 17 Jan., 1862. See also ibid., Palmerston (Broadlands) MSS, GC/SH/47.
27. ibid., Shaftesbury (Broadlands) MSS, SHA/PD/7, 29 June, 1862. The fees amounted to £608/4/6 and were sent to Palmerston. No account was sent to Shaftesbury nor any application made for payment. (H.R.O., Shaftesbury (Broadlands) MSS, 27M60, 13 Sept., 1862).
28. N.R.A., Palmerston (Broadlands) MSS, GC/SH/39.
29. ibid., GC/SH/65.
30. ibid., GC/SH/43.
31. ibid., GC/SH/48/1.
32. ibid., Shaftesbury (Broadlands) MSS, SHA/PD/8, 30 Oct., 1865.
33. See above p. 364.
34. N.R.A., Shaftesbury (Broadlands) MSS, SHA/PC/6. (This comment was made in a letter to the Duchess of Argyll).
35. ibid., SHA/PC/6.
36. ibid., SHA/MIS/2.
37. ibid., SHA/PC/6.
38. Quoted in Hodder, III, 165.
39. N.R.A., Shaftesbury (Broadlands) MSS, SHA/PC/6.
40. ibid., SHA/PD/7, 28 May, 1856.
41. ibid., SHA/PD/6, 6 Feb., 1855.
42. Quoted in Hodder, II, 505.
43. N.R.A., Shaftesbury (Broadlands) MSS, SHA/PD/7, 28 May, 1856.

44. ibid., SHA/PD/7, 28 May, 1856.
45. ibid., SHA/PD/7, 8 June, 1856.
46. ibid., SHA/PD/7, 20 Aug., 1856.
47. ibid., SHA/PD/8, 2 Nov., 1865.
48. ibid., Palmerston (Broadlands) MSS, GC/SH/34/1/2.
49. Quoted in Battiscombe, pp. 249–50. For Shaftesbury's appreciation of Palmerston's attitude, see E. Ashley, *The Life and Correspondence of Henry John Temple, Viscount Palmerston* (1879), 2 vols., II, 315–24.
50. N.R.A., Shaftesbury (Broadlands) MSS, SHA/PD/7, 23 Nov., 1856.
51. ibid., SHA/PD/8, 2 Nov., 1865.
52. ibid., SHA/PD/7, 30 June, 1856
53. Shaftesbury commented on Robert Bickersteth's election: 'We now have some Bishops ... who will declare and exalt the name of Christ.' (ibid., SHA/PD/7, 23 Nov., 1856).
54. N.R.A., Shaftesbury (Broadlands) MSS, SHA/PD/7, 14 Oct., 1856.
55. B. E. Hardman, 'The Evangelical Party in the Church of England, 1855–1865' (Ph.D., Cambridge, 1963), p. 26.
56. N.R.A., Shaftesbury (Broadlands) MSS, SHA/PD/7, 3 Oct., 1856.
57. ibid., SHA/PD/7, 23 Nov., 1856.
58. ibid., SHA/PD/7, 8 Sept., 1856.
59. ibid., SHA/PD/7, 20 Aug., 1856.
60. Lambeth Palace Library, Tait MSS, 79, 18 Sept., 1856.
61. ibid., 22 Sept., 1856.
62. ibid., 12 Nov., 1856.
63. ibid., 1 Dec., 1856.
64. N.R.A., Shaftesbury (Broadlands) MSS, SHA/PD/7, 20 Aug., 1856.
65. ibid., SHA/PD/7, 26 Aug., 1856.
66. ibid., SHA/PD/8, 2 Nov., 1865.
67. ibid., Palmerston (Broadlands) MSS, GC/SH/35.
68. B. E. Hardman, op. cit., p. 28.
69. N.R.A., Shaftesbury (Broadlands) MSS, SHA/PD/8, 2 Nov., 1865.
70. B. E. Hardman, op. cit., p. 25.
71. N.R.A., Shaftesbury (Broadlands) MSS, SHA/PD/8, 2 Nov., 1865.
72. ibid., SHA/PD/8, 2 Nov., 1865.
73. ibid., Palmerston (Broadlands) MSS, GC/SH/50.
74. ibid., GC/SH/42.
75. B. E. Hardman, op. cit., p. 37.
76. Tait MSS, 79, 12 Nov., 1856.
77. N.R.A., Shaftesbury (Broadlands) MSS, SHA/PD/8, 2 Nov., 1865.
78. ibid., Palmerston (Broadlands) MSS, GC/SH/50. Shaftesbury had described Dr Goode, appointed Dean of Ripon in 1860 and Dr Wigram, appointed to the Bishopric of Rochester in 1860, as 'Moderate High Church'. In fact, they would be better described as Evangelical.
79. ibid., Shaftesbury (Broadlands) MSS, SHA/PD/8, 29 Aug., 1865.
80. ibid., SHA/PD/8, 2 Nov., 1865.
81. ibid., SHA/PD/8, 2 Nov., 1865.
82. B. E. Hardman, op. cit., p. 42.
83. N.R.A., Palmerston (Broadlands) MSS, GC/SH/59.
84. ibid., Shaftesbury (Broadlands) MSS, SHA/PD/8, 2 Nov., 1865.
85. ibid., Palmerston (Broadlands) MSS, GC/SH/61. Browne was Professor of Divinity at Cambridge and thus broke Shaftesbury's rule about academics not

being suitable for Bishoprics. But Browne had been a contributor to *Aids to Faith*, a response to *Essays and Reviews*. (B. E. Hardman, op. cit., p. 33).
86. N.R.A., Shaftesbury (Broadlands) MSS, SHA/PC/68.
87. ibid., SHA/PC/66/1.
88. B. E. Hardman, op. cit., p. 16.
89. N.R.A., Shaftesbury (Broadlands) MSS, SHA/PD/8, 30 Oct., 2 Nov., 1865. A list of ecclesiastical appointments during Palmerston's Ministries, 1855–65, is given ibid., SHA/PD/8, 2 Nov., 1865: it is there described by Shaftesbury as 'a list quite unprecedented in the history of an Administration'. A slightly corrected list is given ibid., SHA/PD/8, 14 Dec., 1865.
90. ibid., SHA/PD/8, 30 Oct., 1865.
91. A. L. Tibawi, op. cit., pp. 113–14.
92. ibid., pp. 117–21.
93. ibid., p. 120.
94. G. F. A. Best, *Shaftesbury*, p. 71.
95. *The Record*, 14 May, 1856.
96. Quoted in Hodder, III, 162.
97. Quoted ibid., 163.
98. Quoted ibid.
99. N.R.A., Shaftesbury (Broadlands) MSS, SHA/PD/8, 12 May, 1866.
100. Quoted in Hodder, III, 163.
101. *The Record*, 8 May, 1865.
102. ibid.
103. Hansard, *Parl. Debates*, 3rd ser., CXXXVIII, 1835–48.
104. ibid., 1848 ff.
105. ibid., 1939 ff.
106. B. E. Hardman, op. cit., p. 245.
107. Hughenden MSS (on microfilm). Film 131, 21 July, 1855.
108. N.R.A., Shaftesbury (Broadlands) MSS, SHA/PD/7, 22 May, 1855.
109. ibid., SHA/PD/7, 13 June, 1855.
110. Hansard, *Parl. Debates*, 3rd ser., CXXXIX, 503–4.
111. N.R.A., Shaftesbury (Broadlands) MSS, SHA/PD/7, 1 Aug., 1855.
112. Quoted ibid., SHA/PD/7, 31 May, 1857.
113. ibid., SHA/PD/7, 31 May, 1857.
114. B. E. Hardman, op. cit., pp. 254–7.
115. It is true that some observers claimed that few members of the working classes were present: this is, for example, what *The Times* claimed (10 Nov., 1855). But others said that this was not the case and that the services attracted a widely based congregation. The Bishop of Ripon preached at one of the services and said in the Lords that there was a strong working-class element in the congregation: in his opinion, the congregation included persons who had never attended any Church at all (Hansard, *Parl. Debates*, 3rd ser., CXLVIII, 345–6). Lord Panmure said that many more men than women attended. (ibid., 347–8).
116. ibid., 327.
117. ibid., 321 ff.
118. ibid., 755.
119. ibid., 853–4.
120. B. E. Hardman, op. cit., pp. 266–7.
121. Hansard, *Parl. Debates*, 3rd ser., CLVI, 1662–3.
122. ibid., 1679.
123. N.R.A., Shaftesbury (Broadlands) MSS, SHA/PD/7, 13 Feb., 1860.

124. ibid., SHA/PD/7, 31 Mar., 1860.
125. ibid., SHA/PD/7, 6 Nov., 1855.
126. *The Record*, 13 Feb., 1856.
127. Shaftesbury gave a somewhat different version of this meeting. (N.R.A., Shaftesbury (Broadlands) MSS, SHA/PD/7, 11 Feb., 1856).
128. G. M. Ellis, op. cit., pp. 298–9.
129. N.R.A., Shaftesbury (Broadlands) MSS, SHA/PD/7, 17 May, 1856.
130. C. Binfield, *George Williams and the Y.M.C.A. A study in Victorian social attitudes* (1973), p. 125.
131. G. M. Ellis, op. cit., p. 193.
132. *Speeches of the Earl of Shaftesbury*, p. 299.
133. G. M. Ellis, op. cit., p. 304–5. See also: Office of L.D.O.S., London, First Annual Report of Working Men's Lord's Day Rest Association (1858), pp. 14–15.
134. Battiscombe, p. 269.
135. N.R.A., Shaftesbury (Broadlands) MSS, SHA/PD/8, 12 May, 1866.
136. ibid., SHA/PD/9, 1 Oct., 1869.
137. See *Speeches of the Earl of Shaftesbury*, pp. 302–3 for further comments on this subject.
138. Wilberforce MSS, C 14, p. 94.
139. O. Chadwick, op. cit., II, 84.
140. Quoted in Hodder, III, 166–7.
141. Quoted ibid., III, p. 168.
142. Wilberforce MSS, C 14, p. 103. Hodder (III, 168) says that Shaftesbury did not take up the offer: this is an error.
143. This was at a meeting of the British Association at Oxford in 1860: and Wilberforce also attacked *The Origin of Species* in print. (See A. Symondson (ed.), *The Victorian Crisis of Faith* (1970), pp. 19–20).
144. N.R.A., Shaftesbury (Broadlands) MSS, SHA/PC/60.
145. ibid., SHA/PD/7, 30 Aug., 1863.
146. B. E. Hardman, op. cit., p. 319 ff. See also J. Kent, *Holding the Fort, Studies in Victorian Revivalism* (1978), pp. 71–131, which also expresses this view.
147. N.R.A., Shaftesbury (Broadlands) MSS, SHA/PC/53. In time, Shaftesbury was to become very friendly with Spurgeon.
148. ibid., SHA/PC/53.
149. *The Record*, 6 Aug., 1859.
150. G. F. A. Best, *Temporal Pillars*, p. 402.
151. N.R.A., Shaftesbury (Broadlands) MSS, SHA/PC/22/1 (copy).
152. *The Record*, 13 May, 1857.
153. B. E. Hardman, op. cit., p. 294.
154. N.R.A., Shaftesbury (Broadlands) MSS, SHA/PD/7, 6 Apr., 1865.
155. ibid., SHA/PD/7, 11 Mar., 1860.
156. ibid., SHA/PC/53.
157. ibid., SHA/PD/8, 19 July, 1865.
158. ibid., SHA/PD/8, 2 Nov., 1865.
159. ibid., SHA/PD/8, 4 Dec., 1865.
160. ibid., SHA/PD/8, 14 Dec., 1865.
161. ibid., SHA/PD/8, 2 Nov., 1865.
162. B. E. Hardman, op. cit., p. 27.
163. *The Saturday Review*, XI, 286. Disraeli commented in 1863 that some of the recent appointments to Bishoprics had been 'mean and insignificant' and that Shaftesbury 'for several years (Palmerston's) guide on Church matters had scandalised

the country by some of his late low Church appointments'. (H. M. and M. Swartz (eds.), *Disraeli's Reminiscences* (1975), pp. 111, 112).

164. A. C. Benson and Viscount Esher (eds.), op. cit., III, 530.
165. *The Record,* 14 Dec., 1865, also claims that several of the Bishops were distinguished academically.
166. N.R.A., Palmerston (Broadlands) MSS, GC/SH/34/1/2.
167. B. E. Hardman, op. cit., pp. 120–21.
168. N.R.A., Shaftesbury (Broadlands) MSS, SHA/PD/8, 2 Nov., 1865.
169. B. E. Hardman, op. cit., pp. 293–5.
170. See E. Royle, *Victorian Infidels* (Manchester, 1974), p. 287 ff. for an assessment of Secularism. Royle concedes that Secularism was small and of little influence as an organised movement, but that, as a pressure group, it had considerable importance in moulding opinion.

15

Unprofitable Labours, 1855–1865

Shaftesbury's close attention to ecclesiastical matters in the ten years after 1855 did not mean that he neglected other areas where he had long been active. It will be recalled that one of his reasons for declining office in 1855 was his unwillingness to surrender his 'important occupations', and, thereafter, he continued to give time to sponsoring or supporting legislation in the Lords conducive to social improvement. He was also extremely active in lunacy administration, and he still took his accustomed role in the work of extra-parliamentary movements concerned with philanthropic causes. With all his many burdens, he constantly complained of lack of time. In 1859, he wrote that he did not have a vacant hour. His time seemed to be more occupied than it was in the House of Commons, or else, he was less capable of managing it.[1] Whatever the reason, his days were 'cut into shreds'.[2]

A major aspect of Shaftesbury's parliamentary activities during these years lay in his attempt to extend protection to children and young persons in trades and factories not protected by existing legislation. This was, in fact, a continuation of the work which he had first taken up in 1840, when he had moved for a Commission to inquire into the condition of such children and young persons.[3] The Mines Act of 1842 and the Print Works Act of 1845 had been fruits of this investigation. In 1861, Shaftesbury returned to the question.[4] He recalled his efforts of 1840 and mentioned the recent efforts of others, which had taken the process of protection further,[5] and he argued that the matter must now be subjected to further thorough investigation. His motion for a new Commission to carry out this task was accepted, and two years later, in 1863, Shaftesbury drew attention[6] to its first Report, which covered six trades.[7] He called for a remedy of the situation which the Commission had found to prevail in them. Legislation did, indeed, follow in 1864, when the Factory Acts Extension Bill became law and placed these six trades under the provision of the Factory Acts.[8]

Shaftesbury welcomed the Act and he hoped that it would be the first of a series of measures which extended protection to all children and young persons.[9] In 1865, indeed, he took up the practice of hiring and employing Agricultural Gangs.[10] These were groups of children and young persons, between the ages of five and sixteen, who were hired from their parents by a 'gang driver' and then let out to farmers to carry out farm labour. They frequently had to walk long distances to work, they were out in all weathers, and the rough state in which they lived gave rise to undesirable practices. Here was another group, hitherto unregulated and about whom little was known, and Shaftesbury successfully requested that the Commission should include the gangs in its continuing inquiries.

In addition to children whose conditions had previously been uninvestigated and unregulated, there were those who *had* been protected by legislation, but the legislation had proved to be inadequate and, indeed, inoperative. This was true of the chimney sweeps, and, after his efforts of the early 1850s, Shaftesbury returned to their defence in the years after 1855. In 1855 he did – as seen – introduce a further bill to improve the effectiveness of earlier legislation, but it was dropped after its first reading and the matter rested there for a number of years. In 1861 however, Shaftesbury secured the inclusion of the climbing boys in the Children's Employment Commission; and in his speech of 1863, dealing with its first Report, he made special reference to the findings which it made on these boys.[11] He mentioned the violations of the legislation, which were especially flagrant in the country districts and graphically described the suffering of the children involved in the trade. In 1864, in a speech[12] in support of a further bill on the subject, he once again rehearsed the evidence of witnesses who had appeared before the Commission: evidence which, he said, was 'revolting and disgusting'. Children between the ages of six and eight – and even sometimes as young as four-and-a-half – were made to work long hours: between eight and nine hours and up to sixteen hours in certain places. Work was begun at 2, 3 and 4 a.m. and the climbing boys ran the risk of suffocation and death. He admitted that this was not, on the whole, the fault of the master sweeps, the vast majority of whom were anxious to get rid of climbing boys and use a machine. It was the householders – 'and especially the great people' – who were anxious to keep the boys; magistrates were lax in their enforcement of existing legislation; and many builders did not construct houses to make the flues accessible to cleaning machines, as they were supposed to do under the Act of 1840. Shaftesbury thus asked for more stringent legislation: 'I ask you,' he said in the Lords, 'to protect not adults, who can take care of themselves, but the helpless young, many of them orphans, and some of them the offspring of cruel and unnatural parents.' The bill which Shaftesbury proposed passed the Lords and the Commons. It forbade a sweep to employ a child under the age of ten on any premises except his own; and to allow any child under sixteen to enter a house or accompany a sweep while sweeping a chimney. Once again, however, Shaftesbury's efforts were to be thwarted by the difficulties of enforcement.

Various other measures which Shaftesbury sponsored or supported in the Lords during these years were concerned with vagrancy, housing and health. In 1857, he moved[13] the second reading of a bill to encourage the establishment of industrial schools, to which vagrant children could be admitted. These schools, if properly certified, would be entitled to the receipts of a grant from the Privy Council, although parents might be called upon to contribute towards the maintenance of their children while they were in the schools. The bill was passed – it was permissive in nature, but the hope was that, if adopted, it would help to reduce vagrancy. Less successful was a bill which Shaftesbury also proposed in 1857,[14] to extend the Common Lodgings Act of 1851 to houses and rooms occupied by large numbers of persons who claimed that they belonged to the same family. The bill passed the Lords, but was withdrawn after opposition in the Commons. In 1861, he took up[15] the question which he had previously raised in 1853 of the demolition of working-class accommodation by schemes of improvement, and, in particular, railway projects. He claimed that the system of reporting on such schemes established in 1853 had proved useless. He had visited the threatened districts. When the notice to quit came in, it gave rise to the overcrowding of other districts and thus to physical and moral evils. He moved an addition to the standing order agreed in 1853: this was to the effect that the report made by the promoters of railway and other bills of the number of houses and inhabitants displaced should be referred to the select committee inquiring into each bill. This was accepted. He felt that the problems of overcrowding, especially in London, might be overcome by the construction of suburban villages, which would move people away from the centre, but this would take time as well as zeal and energy. As an immediate measure, the addition to the standing order might act as a check to extensive demolition, and the overcrowding which it caused.

Shaftesbury thus ranged over many areas in which he had long shown interest. And the motives behind this activity remained the same as they had been at earlier periods. It is true that, with the country in a state of greater tranquillity, there was less urgency than there had been previously to spread 'healing' influences among the working classes. The working classes, he said in 1861,[16] had become more reconciled to their position in life: they were no longer so disaffected towards other orders of society; they were no longer so hostile to property. Finding that persons of station and wealth in both Houses of Parliament were ready to examine their grievances and supply remedies, they were more content to leave those remedies to be supplied by the legislature than they had been at an earlier period. But this, Shaftesbury argued, was no reason for complacency – it was an opportunity to consolidate what had already been done, for this could well be undone by sinister forces. Even more than this, however, the religious considerations in Shaftesbury's social concern were still clearly evident. Thus, in connection with the chimney sweepers, he asked if the cruelties perpetrated on the children could be permitted to continue. 'Are we to call ourselves a Christian country,' he said in 1863, 'knowing that 2,000 of our fellow creatures, just as good as ourselves, are doomed to the most excruciating and intolerable agony . . . ?'[17] In 1864, he begged the Lords to ensure that the children should have repose, leisure and opportunity to enable them to prepare for a life of 'industry, honesty and comfort in this world and, above all, to attain that religious knowledge which alone can make a man just and wise.'[18] Similarly, Shaftesbury clearly stated his ideas in the speech which he delivered to the annual meetings of the Social Science Congress. Thus, as president of the Section on Sanitary Improvement at the Liverpool Congress in 1858, he spoke of the opposition aimed at the progress of public health. One argument which was put forward was that more thought should be given to the soul and less to the body. His reply was that the same God who made the soul made the body also. The body might be an inferior work, 'but nevertheless it is His work and it must be treated and cared for according to the end for which it was formed – fitness for His service.' The body was the temple of the Holy Ghost, and it ought not to be 'corrupted by preventable disease, degraded by avoidable filth, and disabled for His service by unnecessary suffering.' Society must do all it could to

> remove difficulties and impediments; to give to every man . . . full, fair and free opportunity so to exercise all his moral, intellectual, physical and spiritual energies, that he may, without let or hindrance, be able to do his duty in that state of life to which it has pleased God to call him.[19]

A clearer statement of Shaftesbury's basic ideas on social improvement could scarcely be given. And such ideas impelled him to keep to the task: he wrote in 1861 that he must continue his work, as long as God gave him strength, while there was work to be done.[20]

One area in which he had long been active was lunacy, and it was open to considerable public attention and controversy in these years. This involved Shaftesbury in very considerable effort. Despite the further safeguards over admission procedures in 1853, disputed cases of admissions still occurred. One such case, in 1858, concerned a Mrs Turner, who had been kept by the proprietor of Acomb House, York; she had escaped but had been recaptured. Her solicitor applied to the Commissioners for access to her and an inquiry was held at York, which returned a majority verdict that she was sane. Whether this was a valid verdict or not is open to question, but considerable irregularities over procedure had been revealed and these gave the opponents of the Commission an opportunity for criticism. A select committee of the House of Commons was, therefore, set up in 1859 to inquire into the operation of the various laws and regulations for the care and treatment of lunatics and their property.

Shaftesbury was called as a principal witness to this inquiry and his evidence ranged over a wide variety of matters connected with lunacy.[21] On the general incidence of lunacy, he agreed that statistics showed an increase in the numbers admitted to the various institutions in existence.[22] But this did not necessarily indicate a large increase in insanity, since many institutions had only recently been established and, before this, numbers were quite unknown: in 1845, there were vast numbers for whom no provision was made and, when institutions had been set up, they tended to admit many chronic cases of long-standing rather than fresh cases. Thus the statistics required some modification, and, indeed, Shaftesbury felt that insanity was not increasing in proportion to the population as a whole. This was especially true among the working classes. Here, Shaftesbury felt that efforts at education and temperance movements were helping to offset the effects of drink and intoxication, which he regarded as the most common cause of insanity.[23] Among the higher classes of society, however, Shaftesbury felt that insanity *was* increasing, and he attributed this to the quickening pace of life and especially methods of transport: this, he argued, kept persons in a state of great nervous excitement.[24] Apart from questions on such general matters, however, Shaftesbury was called upon to answer points about the Commission and its procedures, and he was at pains to defend the Commission from any charges of neglect. It was true that the order requesting that a person be admitted as a patient to an asylum could be signed by anyone, not necessarily a relative or friend, and this was something to which considerable objection had been made. But Shaftesbury pointed out that there were many people who had no near relatives and, indeed, some who had no friends. Thus it would not be possible to restrict the signing of the order to a relative or friend[25] in this way, and Shaftesbury argued that any person who knew the circumstances should be able to sign the order. There was, after all, the safeguard that this person had to provide a statement giving various details about the proposed patient: and this statement had to be signed by that person and counter-signed by another. Further, there was the check provided by the Commission in scrutinising the admission document.[26] It was the duty of the Secretary of the Commission to examine this document, a copy of which was sent to him, and he did this very carefully, bringing the slightest defect to the attention of the Board.[27] On occasion, certificates were sent back for correction, and these had to be returned duly corrected, within fourteen days. Shaftesbury felt that there *was* a case for reviewing the documents after three months and going through the admission procedure again at that point,[28] but, on the whole, he felt that the procedures worked satisfactorily and resulted in very few irregular detentions. He also argued that any further stringency in safeguarding the patient might not be in the best interests of the safety of the public; nor might it be in the interests of the patient, since it would postpone the opportunity of corrective treatment. He quoted medical opinion to the effect that fully seventy-five per cent of cases could be cured within three months, but probably not three per cent could be cured if more than twelve months elapsed before a patient was admitted. Thus, if there was sometimes a danger in admitting a person to an asylum, there was also a danger in not admitting him, in an attempt to safeguard his liberty.[29] This point, indeed, Shaftesbury claimed, was the most delicate the Commissioners had to handle: in taking action against an individual, they deprived him of his liberty and fixed the taint of insanity on him and his family; by not taking any action, they ran the risk of his becoming incurable.[30]

One further aspect of this question was over the detention of patients beyond the time when they might be set at liberty. Shaftesbury admitted that over-long detention did take place in private, although not in public, asylums. It was caused by various circumstances: the fact that proprietors had a financial interest in keeping patients on the premises; and the fact, too, that friends and relatives lost interest in a person once he was detained. 'Such is the melancholy condition of patients,' said Shaftesbury, 'that from the moment a patient is struck by this effect of Providence, from that hour, he becomes civilly and morally dead in respect to his relatives.'[31] He would have liked to see a revival of the obligation contained in an earlier Act that friends of the patient should visit him periodically.[32] But, again, Shaftesbury was at pains to defend the Commissioners' efforts to alleviate this problem. There were the regular visits paid by the Commissioners or the visiting justices:[33] on their visits, the Commissioners had to see every patient and examine the possibility of a discharge, and the Commissioners received the reports of the Visiting Justices on the same matters. Further, every patient had full opportunity to state any complaints to the Commissioners, and, if a complaint were made about improper detention, this was fully investigated.[34] If the complaint were deemed to be just, two visits were made at an interval of seven days and a discharge was ordered – although the discharge was carried out, if possible, by writing to the relatives.[35] Sometimes, the Commissioners recommended trial periods of discharge.[36] Thus Shaftesbury felt that the powers of discharge vested in the Commissioners were ample and that no further powers were necessary.[37]

If Shaftesbury argued that existing procedures for admission and discharge were adequate and had been carried out conscientiously, he also pointed out that the Commissioners could exercise control over conditions in the private asylums in the Metropolis by their power of issuing licences. This was especially true in the case of newly established houses in the Metropolis, since, before issuing a licence for a new house there, the Commissioners inspected it;[38] they had to see the plans and had the power to enforce that adequate space was provided for the patients,[39] and they also had power to control the diet.[40] Further, in all Metropolitan licenced houses, the Commissioners' power to refuse to renew a licence, which ran for not more than thirteen months, provided a certain check on cruelty and ill-treatment. Revocation of a licence could only finally be carried out on appeal to the Lord Chancellor and was not, in fact, often done,[41] but a proven case of malconduct could be punished in this way. In the localities, these powers lay with magistrates at Quarter Sessions, and it appeared that they were following a stricter policy in this respect than they had done previously. Further, the visits of the Commissioners or the Visiting Justices were a safeguard against abuse. The Commissioners tried to make their visits as unexpected as possible: thus they might visit at the very end of one quarter and at the very beginning of the next.[42] Shaftesbury also argued that the methods of treatment themselves had enormously improved. The system of mechanical restraint, prevalent in 1828, had been virtually eliminated. This had been largely due to the work of Dr Connolly and the authorities at Hanwell, who had courageously undertaken the reform: it was now the established rule elsewhere.[43] The non-restraint system, with the greater freedom which it gave to patients – allowing them, for example, to be employed out of doors in the grounds of the asylum – was, Shaftesbury said, 'without any exception the greatest triumph of skill and humanity that the world ever saw.'[44] When he started visiting asylums, he had 'never beheld anything so horrible and miserable': a large proportion of the inmates were chained to the wall, and there was noise and roaring. The women were virtually naked. Now, the position was greatly improved and in most asylums, conditions were clean, decent, orderly and quiet.[45]

In pointing to the improvements in the present position, Shaftesbury was not, however, uncritical of various aspects of it. Although he felt that the procedures for admission were adequate and acceptable, he admitted that everything turned on the accuracy of the two medical certificates on which the patient was admitted.[46] And this, in turn, raised the competence of those who provided them. It is true that, under the 1853 Act, doctors had to state their qualifications and the Commissioners did try to make further inquiries when they were in doubt,[47] but Shaftesbury's view was that the knowledge of lunacy was very limited and had never been made a subject of general study. He was convinced that a sensible layman 'conversant with the world and with mankind' could give 'not only as good an opinion, but a better opinion than all the medical men put together.'[48] It was true that doctors could point to any functional disorder, but Shaftesbury had a low opinion of the expertise of doctors in the field of lunacy.[49] Shaftesbury, therefore, hoped that a real school for the study of lunacy would be established, so that, in time, doctors would be able to give a properly informed opinion.[50] He also thought it necessary to have proper statistics on insanity drawn up and put on a sound footing.[51] Further, Shaftesbury realised that what determined the well-being or otherwise of an asylum was the quality of the attendants and the nurses, and, especially with the system of non-restraint, it was necessary to increase the number of nurses to supervise the patients.[52] At present, the number of attendants was insufficient and their calibre not sufficiently high, and Shaftesbury argued that it was necessary to pay considerably higher wages to attract suitable persons – in particular men – to the task.[53] At the moment, many female nurses were paid only twelve guineas a year, the wages, as he pointed out, of a housemaid.[54]

Shaftesbury was also much concerned about the condition of single patients. As has been seen,[55] the Act of 1845 set up a private committee of the Commission, composed of three members, including the chairman, to deal with private or single patients and to visit them once a year. But this was found to be unsatisfactory. The Commissioners had been unable to carry out the duty and it was very awkward, as Shaftesbury put it, to have 'secrets within secrets'.[56] Thus, in 1853, the power had been extended to the whole Commission. But there were still deficiencies in the system. The Commissioners had no right to visit single patients unless they were under certificate, and it was the duty of the person taking charge of the single patient to inform the Commissioners and adhere to the procedure for obtaining a certificate. There were one hundred and twenty four cases of this description, and some – mostly the wealthy – were well looked after. But the responsibility for obtaining the certificate was often evaded and patients were taken in under various pretexts: that they were, for example, 'nervous patients', since it was always the wish of their families to avoid going through the process of certification.[57] The Commissioners had no power to visit them and, indeed, no knowledge of them, and Shaftesbury believed that there was a vast number of actual lunatics in this position who ought to have been under certificate.[58] The condition of some of these was likely to be very bad; they would be very much better looked after, Shaftesbury felt, in a good private licensed asylum.[59] One of the great objects of the Commission, he said, was to obtain knowledge of cases where patients were kept in single houses and ought to be certified;[60] he thought that the Commissioners should have powers of compelling anyone who received a patient for profit to notify the Commissioners; and the Commissioners would then have the right to say whether that patient should or should not be put under certificate.[61] This would expose the system of keeping 'nervous patients' under private restraint. This was one area, indeed, where Shaftesbury felt that the Commissioners had erred on the side of leniency. They had tried to do things by persuasion. But they were now losing patience.[62]

Other groups about whom Shaftesbury was concerned were pauper and criminal lunatics. Pauper lunatics were often detained in workhouses, since it was thought cheaper to keep them there than to send them to the county asylum. Shaftesbury strongly condemned this practice. In some workhouses there were 'lunatic wards': but in most, no special provision was made for lunatics and mechanical restraint was still used.[63] Shaftesbury argued that it was essential that a pauper lunatic should be transferred from a workhouse to a county or borough asylum or a private house[64] and that relieving officers and overseers should be forbidden from putting any pauper lunatic into a workhouse on their own authority. The intervention of a magistrate to determine whether or not the individual should be sent to a county asylum should be made obligatory.[65] With regard to criminal lunatics, the majority were in Bethlem Hospital, placed there under the orders of the Home Secretary. After 1853, the Commissioners had powers to visit this institution. But there were many criminal lunatics spread over the country in private asylums, and, over these, the Commissioners had no jurisdiction.[66] Shaftesbury had long thought that the presence of such persons in private asylums alongside other patients was very unsatisfactory – it exposed non-criminals to corrupting influences. He had, for some years, urged the need for a State Asylum for criminal lunatics. In 1859, he expressed similar views, but noted, with satisfaction, that such an asylum was shortly to be built – this, he felt, would represent a great improvement.[67]

Shaftesbury's major criticism of the existing system, however, was that, in the private sector, it still rested on profit: and he thus returned to points which he had made in 1845 and 1853. There were, admittedly, good private asylums. Such houses were, indeed, the best that were available.[68] It was also true that, through the power to issue licences, the Commissioners had tried to ensure that only the best persons who could be found were given the authority to establish a private house, and the Commissioners did not issue licences even to good people unless some need for it was established, since they did not feel it desirable to multiply private houses.[69] Nevertheless, the principle of receiving profit from patients had been recognised by the legislature and Shaftesbury felt this to be wrong;[70] and, unless something of a very infamous nature came to light, it was difficult to refuse the renewal of a licence. Persons in possession of a licence depended on it for their livelihood, and, if they were not guilty of an actual offence, they could not be deprived of it.[71] Despite their shortcomings, medical men would, Shaftesbury argued, have made the best proprietors, but they often did not have the necessary capital – £5,000 or £6,000 – to open a house and run it;[72] and, although the Commissioners insisted that a medical man should be in attendance if the number of patients was large, he was not the owner and could be influenced by the owner.[73] Again, the Commissioners had to take account of the fact that conditions could not be imposed on proprietors which would eat up their profit,[74] and this restrained them from doing all that they would have liked. Shaftesbury felt that the profit motive was damaging even to those who were conscientious and well-disposed[75] – if only it could be removed, a great blessing would be conferred on the patients, half the lunacy legislation could be abandoned and an 'admirable, sound and efficient treatment of lunacy' could be established.[76] Although he felt it desirable to reduce the number of private asylums, he did not wish to abolish those already in existence,[77] and he suggested that encouragement should be given for the endowment of hospitals for lunatics under the control of the Commission. This could be done by private subscription – in Scotland, such a system was quite widely in operation,[78] but in England and Wales only eleven hospitals along these lines had been founded, visited once a year by the Commissioners, and none had been founded recently.[79] In 1845, indeed, Shaftesbury himself had appealed for funds for the establishment of such an institution for the middle classes, but had received little support.[80] Thus the voluntary principle had achieved only very limited success; and Shaftesbury suggested, as an alternative, that counties should build such institutions, obtaining money by loan on the security of their rates.[81] The patients resident in these hospitals would be almost entirely from the richer classes, and the payments which they made would not go to the profit of any individual – as they did under the private system – but would be used to repay the initial costs of the building and to meet running expenses. Thus a choice would be open to the public as to which kind of asylum they wished to enter: a private licensed asylum run for profit, or a house run on a public footing, either for paupers, or, under the proposed system, for 'persons in a better condition of life'.[82] Shaftesbury felt that, in the course of time, public feeling would run so much in favour of the new type of establishment that a large number of the private houses would cease to exist.[83]

Shaftesbury's evidence before the committee, therefore, provided an extremely full statement of his views on lunacy and at the same time, showed his great mastery of the subject. In the light of the investigations by the committee, further legislation was passed in 1862. One Act, the Lunacy Regulation Act, dealt with lunatics under the care of the Court of

Chancery and was an extension of an Act of 1853 on the same subject. It provided for more effective supervision and more economical application of their property in inquisitions, and Shaftesbury declared his support for these principles.[84] The other Act was concerned with a number of points regarding admission. It introduced further safeguards against improper admission. Thus the person signing the order for the admission of private patients had to have seen the patient within one month prior to the signing and had also to attach a statement of the time and place where the patient had been seen, and every order, where possible, had to contain the name and address of one or more relations of the patient. Any person who had a financial interest in the payments which a patient received into a licensed house would make was prohibited from signing any certificate or order. All the admission documents, except the statement of the medical superintendent, had to be forwarded to the Commissioners within twenty four hours instead of within seven days, as previously. The Act also made provision for more frequent visitations by the Commissioners or Visitors. In these ways, stricter control was established,[85] but not as strict as had been urged by some witnesses before the Committee. It had been suggested that a magistrates' order should be required before private patients were admitted to a licensed house, as was the case with paupers. This would, indeed, have been a further safeguard against improper admission, but it would have delayed treatment and the possibility of a cure and it was an idea to which, as has been mentioned, Shaftesbury was always rigidly opposed. The committee did, indeed, reject the suggestion. But if the outcome of the inquiry favoured Shaftesbury rather than those who called for more stringent safeguards on this issue, on the more far-reaching proposals which he had made, the committee and the Act had little to offer. Public asylums on the basis of private subscriptions were encouraged, but this did not extend to the plan that these might be financed from a loan on the rates. In 1861, Shaftesbury again tried to win support for an asylum for the middle classes, but nothing came of it for lack of support. Thus the private system continued, although, in fact, Shaftesbury was to become less critical of it with the passing of time and the introduction of more effective control. And a welcome development came in 1863, with the opening of Broadmoor for criminal lunatics: this was certainly in accordance with long-standing views expressed by Shaftesbury.

If parliamentary and official duties thus occupied Shaftesbury during these years, there was no diminution in his concern for extra-parliamentary and unofficial activities. Ragged Schools, shoeblack brigades, cripple homes, the Society for the Improvement of the Condition of the Labouring Classes, refuges for Homeless Families, Reformatories, orphanages: all these were a constant preoccupation, whether in London or in other towns and cities to which he was frequently invited to open such institutions. He was presented with a picture and an address by the Ragged School Teachers and with a bust by the Northern operatives. Both were, he wrote, 'affecting celebrations'.[86] In 1861, he was, however, saddened and angry at a Report of the Educational Commissioners which was critical of Ragged Schools. In May of that year, his whole address to the Ragged School Union was a rebuttal of these criticisms[87] and he also spoke at length in the Lords on the same subject in June, moving for the evidence on which the criticisms had been based.[88] He argued that the Commissioners had produced inaccurate figures about the number of Ragged Schools in existence, and he denied the criticism that Ragged Schools did not observe discipline and cleanliness. He also argued that the Commissioners showed great ignorance of the parents of ragged scholars by their suggestion that clothes and shoes should be supplied to the scholars to enable them to attend ordinary day schools; if this had been done, 'in the twinkling of an eye, every particle of clothing would have gone into the pawn brokers' and the money would have been spent in a gin shop. Finally, he denied the conclusions of the Report that no beneficial effects had been produced by Ragged Schools. They had reduced juvenile delinquency and crime, and, more positively, had taken the children off the streets and sent them to gain an honest livelihood in the colonies. Thousands had been put into service or other situations; penny banks had encouraged savings; industrial classes had encouraged skills and good habits. Again, there had been no word in the Report on the better understanding between rich and poor which the schools had, he claimed, brought about. And he assured the Lords that Ragged Schools would always exist as long as a ragged class existed, and a ragged class would always exist as long as the lower class of the population were left in their domiciliary condition. He spoke of the 'miserable and foetid atmosphere' in which the working classes lived: 'the disgusting and filthy courts whence they may never emerge into the light of day.' From this population, a ragged class was to be expected, and, he concluded: 'if you have Ragged Schools, you should cease to decry those who are doing without fee or reward that work from which you shrink with so much dignity and abhorrence.'

The criticisms of the Education Commissioners were thus angrily denounced, but they certainly helped to induce in Shaftesbury feelings of despondency and pessimism. For all his activities, such feelings were, in fact, very pronounced in these years. He continued to dislike the Lords. In 1860, he wrote that the atmosphere of the Lords 'or the inmates, I know not which, seem to deprive me of all courage, force or even desire to say or do anything.'[89] He was conscious of animosity towards him: that, as he once put it, 'wealth and luxury and indulgence and sloth, treated (him) as a

Gracchus, or a Tribune, speaking on behalf of the People and loathed (him) and showed their loathing accordingly.'[90] His speech on the Ragged School issue showed his contempt for the indifference which he encountered, and even on lunacy, after all the 'prodigious number of hours given to secret work, without fee or reward,'[91] there were no thanks. In 1865, he recalled that the committee before which he appeared for three days in 1859 'under close and vigorous examination' never said 'well done'.[92] And such points apart, there was, he felt, much to depress him in the progress of his work. On occasion, there were revelations of personal misconduct on the part of those who took part in such societies. It was discovered, for example, that the superintendent of the London Reformatory was a long-standing homosexual. This horrified Shaftesbury. For six years, he wrote in 1855, a body of 'pious, praying Christian men, not pursuing philanthropy for mere sentiment or natural feeling, as Unitarians might do, but in the depths and fervour of Evangelical life' had been allowed to go in 'blindness, ignorance and delusion'.[93] The young criminals would be ten times worse when they went out than when they came in, and, on this occasion, Shaftesbury even permitted himself to wonder at the mystery of God's Providence. He also heard in 1856 that the Secretary of the Society for the Improvement of the Condition of the Labouring Classes had embezzled £1,700. This catalogue of misdeeds saddened him: they were all men by whom he 'could have sworn, the most evangelical, professing and austere Christians to eye and ear' he had ever known. 'What a discovery!' he wrote. 'What an overthrow of all confidence!'[94] Shaftesbury was also dispirited that his efforts did not receive more financial support. In March, 1857, he was disappointed by a response to an appeal for Ragged Schools: 'very small as compared with our wants, nothing as compared with the wealth of the Kingdom,'[95] he wrote. This, indeed, was a regular complaint during these years. In 1858, he wrote that the difficulty of raising money for good causes increased every day. The number of givers remained as it was and had not grown with the increase in national and private riches. 'It is starvation for the present, and death for the future.'[96] In 1860, the London Reformatory was wound up: Shaftesbury wrote that efforts to sustain it had been long and arduous, but unavailing. Year by year support had declined, and there was now nothing to face except difficulty and debt.[97] The disclosures about the superintendent may have had their effect here, but Shaftesbury also felt that it was another manifestation of the public apathy which he discerned during these years towards such ventures. In 1855, he wrote that philanthropy was 'at a low figure in the market';[98] ten years later he echoed the same theme when he commented that indifference was the 'growing characteristic of the age'.[99] The country was bent on materialistic pursuits and was deaf to appeals for philanthropic effort based on religious principles.

Further, Shaftesbury felt that considerable assistance to this process was given by those secular influences which he had previously discerned, but which now seemed to be gathering strength. The 'March of the Intellect', he felt, was ever more inexorable and was striding into all areas of life. In 1859, he was present at the Social Science Congress at Bradford. It had been a busy conference, with essays, proposals and discussion: he noted that there had been no lack of ability in writing or in talk and there had been much evidence of desire to do good. But, to his mind, it was all 'hollow'. There had been no reference in any debate to a Supreme Being. Thus education was debated at length; and debated in purely secular terms. Moral training was kept out of view and in all

> the consideration of the material on which Education has to work, the corrupt heart of fallen man; and the special tools which, in consequence, are alone available ... were never mentioned or even thought of.[100]

And all this made him more than ever convinced that his 'day' was over. He still complained of his isolation in public life. In March, 1857, he wrote that no man was with him, for him, behind or before him: 'all is isolation'.[101] In May, 1860, he mentioned all his 'Chairs', then in high season. They were, he supposed, his 'calling' – he could not be useful in any other way. But, while a few thanked him, many misunderstood him and very many calumnated him.[102] The following month, he gave full rein to thoughts on the sacrifice which he had made of health, time, mind, political connections, domestic life and money. 'Labour and anxiety,' he wrote, 'have been my portion.'[103] If philanthropy was at a low figure in the market in 1855, he himself as an 'eminent Philanthropist' was at a lower one still.[104] In 1859, he wrote that, for the past two or three years, he had found meetings over which he presided less well attended and his appeals vain: he had 'beaten the air like a Mill ... without grist in the hopper.'[105] In 1860, he was depressed by a report in *The Times* which traced Ragged Schools to Dr Guthrie of Edinburgh. Shaftesbury claimed that Guthrie had only been occupied with his own school in Edinburgh. He would have thought that Ragged Schools were a speciality with him and lamented the denial of his achievement because it crippled his influence and dried up public liberality towards him.[106] In June, 1865, he wrote that every day gave him fresh evidence that his public career was nearing a close. All that he had ever said or done was forgotten; young and new men were taking his place. 'I have been too long before the Public,' he wrote, 'they have had enough of a "good thing".'[107] And he wondered who would take his place and 'stand in (his) shoes.'[108] Without him, all his cherished societies and projects would perish. And the work of the Lunacy Commission would be impaired. He felt that an unpaid Chairman was necessary, and he had for years tried to get a layman to join the Commission, but to no purpose. Thus there would be no one to take his place.[109]

The wider political prospects of the country also continued to depress him. He still deplored the lack of discipline and order in the Commons; the members had 'no occupation but to decry public men collectively and individually, make and unmake Governments...'[110] When the first Palmerston Ministry was forced to resign in February, 1858, he despaired of the conduct of the Commons: it had lost all organisation and would never return to the systematic support of any Minister. 'The truth is,' he wrote, 'that the House of Commons is conscious that it, and it alone, is, in fact, Minister; and it plays with officials as boys do with peg-tops.'[111] And this instability would give an impetus to the democratic tendency in the country which he still discerned. The country, he wrote, was 'insensibly and unwittingly drifting from all its ancient moorings and sliding into views, forms, modes of a character especially democratic.'[112] When the minority Conservative government of Derby-Disraeli sponsored a Reform Bill in 1859, Shaftesbury felt that it could have been worse and it was less than he expected, but a Conservative party ought never to have 'touched the accursed thing.'[113] He had a low opinion generally of the calibre of the Conservative party – it had, he felt, no persons of ministerial quality. And few of the Whig leaders inspired any confidence. Russell still incurred his stern displeasure. At the time of the General Election of 1857, he dreaded the prospect of the return of Russell. He could not forget his 'cruel overthrow' of the relief given to the Sunday postmen and his 'yet more cruel and saucy rejection of the Chimney Sweepers bill. . . . Keep him, Lord, from power, place and the House of Commons.'[114] And when the Derby-Disraeli Ministry sponsored its Reform Bill, Shaftesbury – somewhat unfairly ignoring the fact that Russell had himself introduced a bill in 1851-2 – commented that Lord John seized the opportunity 'to do something for himself' by arousing the working classes and representing them as 'ignored, despised, forgotten, trampled on' in the bill. Thus, he wrote, 'we may anticipate uproar and vexation,' and Russell would be 'borne on the billows, drunk with selfishness, treachery and ambition.'[115]

Public issues and public men thus filled Shaftesbury with alarm and apprehension. He felt that the future was bleak 'unless the Second Advent step in, and bring on the full, final and blessed revolution in all human affairs.'[116] A more human source of comfort was, however, to be found in Palmerston. In addition to the affinity between the two men on personal and ecclesiastical grounds, there was a closeness on other issues. Palmerston was not, indeed, an ardent social reformer, but he was not as indifferent in these respects as has been often said and Shaftesbury always found his father-in-law ready to give some support and sympathy over legislation of an improving kind.[117] And, on wider political issues, Shaftesbury found Palmerston a reassuring figure, with his attachment to conservative principles and resistance to organic reform. In 1858, Shaftesbury had commented that Palmerston was wonderful for his years in body and mind: but change could not be far distant and who would take his place? 'No one,' was Shaftesbury's answer.[118] This was, perhaps, a somewhat premature judgment in 1858, but, in the 1860s, Shaftesbury became ever more a prey to fear at the prospect of Palmerston's death. When Palmerston became ill in the spring of 1865, Shaftesbury grew frantic with anxiety, and Palmerston's recovery in the summer did not abate his fears. Palmerston might, he wrote, have many faults before men and 'very many (as doubtless he has) before God,' but Shaftesbury was convinced that he was the 'only true Englishman left in public life'.[119] Palmerston was able to take part in the Election in the summer of 1865, but, by October, he was gravely ill and Shaftesbury went at once to Brocket Hall where he lay dying. As ever, Shaftesbury was deeply concerned for the soul of the departing, and his Diary gave a full account of Palmerston's death bed.[120] Shaftesbury prayed over him and was assured by the doctor that he had heard and understood the words. Thus Shaftesbury was confident that his father-in-law had 'joined in the confession of sins, and trusted in the merits of the All-powerful Redeemer.' This was a comfort: but there was little comfort in the future prospects of the country. 'Thus goes the "Ultimus Romanorum",' Shaftesbury wrote to Haldane, 'and now begins, be assured of it, the greatest social, political, and religious revolution that England has yet endured.'[121]

In all his comments about his own position, the state of society, and the conduct of politics, Shaftesbury's views have, of course, always to be approached with care. In this period, as in others, his mood could change rapidly, and these years were not without his own periodic and painful self-assessments: 'My temperament,' he wrote in 1859, 'is painfully susceptible: I am very soon elated and as rapidly depressed, both in extremes, at one moment in the highest joy, then in the deepest despair.'[122] As was always the case, he exaggerated the opposition and animosity towards himself and underrated the regard in which he was held, and he could be buoyed up by some small token of recognition. He was delighted by letters to *The Times* in 1865, praising his efforts over Ragged Schools – these, no doubt, made up for the earlier neglect. 'I am far from indifferent to these things, if spontaneous,' he wrote, '... They are Capital and Stock in Trade for further exertions.'[123] Again, he almost certainly over-dramatised the extent to which the springs of philanthropic effort were drying up. It is true that the Ragged School Union found it difficult to finance all its ancillary activities, such as refuges and emigration,[124] and the Union did, from time to time, complain that its finances were reduced. Thus, in 1856, its Report stated that the committee had been forced to draw on the Union's deposit fund to make up for a fall in income,[125] and in 1863 it also reported that its finances had dropped and attributed this to the distress in the country caused by the American Civil War: 'every religious and philanthropic society has felt its means reduced,' it wrote.[126] But special appeals were made to meet the difficulties, and although, as has been seen, Shaftesbury was disappointed with the result of the appeal made in 1857, the Report of the Union for 1858 felt that it had been 'on the whole encouraging'.[127] The Report of 1864 also commented favourably on the proceeds of an appeal made to offset the losses of 1863 – an appeal which, indeed, Shaftesbury himself assisted by a letter to *The Times*. 'That name,' commented the Report, 'which in every Christian work is a tower of strength, lifted the Society in two months from a state of poverty to one of comparative wealth and greatly relieved the anxiety of the Committee.' It also wrote of the 'cheering letters' which had been received in large numbers in answer to the appeal; these were encouraging and 'showed that the work had taken a deep hold on the sympathies of a large body of Christians throughout the United Kingdom.'[128] Such comments may, of course, have been intended to boost morale, but they suggest that Shaftesbury was being over-pessimistic about the measure of support which such a body as the Ragged School Union could command.[129]

Nevertheless, Shaftesbury's observations cannot be wholly discounted. Intellectual confidence and faith in material progress, already discernible in the early 1850s, were increasingly apparent in these mid-century years, and the effects of the more widely diffused economic prosperity of the period were, in time, likely to induce the demand and strengthen the case for political change. It could, indeed, be argued that forces in the social and political world – as in the religious – were gradually eroding the evangelicalism and paternalism which Shaftesbury upheld. And he had some reason to tremble, as he contemplated the future after Palmerston's death. 'We must now be prepared for vast and irrevocable changes,' Shaftesbury wrote:

> Palmerston [he continued] was the grand pillar appointed, under God's Providence, to which all the vessels of the State were linked, and so the fleet was held to its moorings. It is now cast down; the ships are set afloat without rudder or compass and will drift in every direction over the broad sea.[130]

It was a graphic, and, no doubt, over-graphic prophecy, but it was not without substance. Palmerston's conservatism had been an obstacle to the forces of change; his death removed that obstacle and opened the way for those forces to express themselves.

Amidst Shaftesbury's public interests and concerns over these years, personal and family worries were also constantly present. Apart from deaths amidst his friends and acquaintances – Bunsen in 1860 and Southwood Smith in 1861 – this was a very sad period in Shaftesbury's family life. His brother, Henry, died in 1858 and his mother in 1865. His mother had become a convert to Evangelical religion in later life: Shaftesbury noted in 1861 that all he had seen for some time made him believe that 'by God's grace, her heart is right towards Him.'[131] In these years, he was, in fact, on better terms with his mother than he had ever been previously and he frequently visited her at her house in Richmond. She became very deaf. Shaftesbury noted that she could not hear one word in twenty, but would not use a trumpet, nor would she use glasses, despite her failing eyesight. But he was glad that, apart from these frailties of age and a tendency to be 'wandered', she suffered little illness and pain – he often commented that, for her age, she was 'wonderfully well'. Much more grievous, however, were losses which Shaftesbury sustained in his own family. Maurice died in 1855 and Mary in 1861. Maurice had remained at Lausanne. Between 1853 and 1855, Shaftesbury had been able to see him only twice and was, in fact, on his way to Lausanne to visit him when he received news of Maurice's death. He was greatly saddened by the fact that he was not with Maurice when he died, as he had been present with Francis. But he knew that, had the boy lived, he would have been greatly handicapped, and, he wrote, if God 'in His wisdom, resolved to deprive him of reason and self-government, He resolved also in His Mercy to remove him from evil.'[132] He was also comforted that Maurice had been under the charge of a 'pious woman, who ever talked to him and heard him talk about Jesus Christ,'[133] and, when he went with Minny to Lausanne for the funeral, all that he heard of Maurice was 'consolatory and assuring'.[134] The death of Mary in 1861 was, perhaps, a more severe blow. There had been anxiety about Mary's health for some time, and Shaftesbury had noted in his Diary that she suffered from severe attacks of bronchitis and that she was, as he put it, a 'frail plant'.[135] In 1861, her condition became acute and she was taken to a home in Richmond. As she grew steadily worse during the summer of 1861, Shaftesbury and Minny were constantly with her and Minny nursed her night and day – the girl could not endure to be left alone for an instant. Her father, deeply distressed at her suffering, could only wonder at her 'gentleness, meekness (and) goodness' amidst all her trials.[136] On her death in September, he permitted himself to wish that God would reveal to him 'before the time when all things will be known, His purpose, in such awful severity.'[137] The death of his second daughter was a great shock: 'The gap made in this family is very wide,' Shaftesbury wrote to Haldane, '. . . I stagger under the blow.'[138]

But he was comforted by the belief that Mary 'truly, purely and solely believed, and trusted in her Lord and Saviour.'[139]

The health of two of Shaftesbury's seven surviving children also gave cause for concern. In 1860, he noted that Constance, 'the jewel of temper, simplicity and unselfishness, my precious child',[140] was showing signs of ill health. The doctors were puzzled, but suspected that her lungs were the cause of the trouble – in time, the diagnosis was to prove correct. Cecil started school in 1862. Shaftesbury was very sorry to see him leave home and was anxious at news that he had become ill, with headaches. In February, 1863, he had to be brought home from school and the doctors said that only a 'listless life' would do for him.[141] In 1864, Shaftesbury wrote that he could make little of Cecil: the good qualities which he had shown were neutralised by lack of discipline and regularity and his illness had induced everyone to let him have his way.[142] Other aspects of his children's lives also gave Shaftesbury cause for anxiety. He was worried that his two daughters of marriageable age, Victoria and Constance, were showing few signs of attracting suitors. They were duly 'launched' into society by Minny, a task which Shaftesbury regarded as possibly necessary but disagreeable. But there was, as yet, no success. In 1864, Shaftesbury wrote that he would deeply like to see his daughters happily married and settled in life, and he wondered if his own personal character and career discouraged potential suitors and their parents; it might be that he himself averted 'young men and the Parents of young men from a near connection', he wrote.[143] Evelyn and Lionel were, he thought, 'good honest lads',[144] but both seemed to be showing signs of drifting away from their parents and, although Shaftesbury realised that this was natural, he was distressed at some of their views and habits. He complained that his sons did not attend family prayers regularly: he noted that on Christmas Day, 1857, not one was present. 'I have spoken, as I felt, with indignation,' he wrote: 'but cui bono?'[145] And Evelyn at one point caused him some pain by arranging a breakfast with some friends on a Sunday and often, it seems, dined at his Club on a Sunday. Anthony, moreover, continued to be a source of great anxiety to his father. Adverse reports from his captain in the mid fifties confirmed in Shaftesbury the feeling that there was nothing ahead but 'indolence, sensuality and extravagance'; the family would be distressed during his life and beggared at his death.[146] In 1855, Anthony did finally pass his naval examinations and Shaftesbury hoped that this might be the 'beginning of usefulness and service in Christ Jesus',[147] but, only a few days later, there were still further bad reports from Anthony's captain, indicating neglect of discipline and debts: 'What a Son! What an infliction,' wrote Shaftesbury. And yet he was to inherit the titles, estates and legislative functions: 'Such a man does more to destroy an aristocracy than an army of

Radicals' was Shaftesbury's comment.[148] A further distressing episode was in 1856, when Anthony was arrested in Portsmouth and Shaftesbury had to pay £500 to secure his release. Anthony showed contrition and Shaftesbury felt that he might have learned a providential lesson,[149] and, as always, Shaftesbury was touched by expressions of regret by Anthony but sceptical about any real change of heart.

In 1857, however, two events of importance in Anthony's life occurred. He stood for Parliament in the General Election of that year. Shaftesbury was anxious about it at first, but hoped that a parliamentary career was one of the best 'secular and secondary modes of saving (Anthony) from mischief'.[150] Anthony was adopted at Hull. Shaftesbury told him to avoid all bribery and keep down expense,[151] and Anthony's election – assisted, it appears, by Evelyn's canvassing – made his father hope that this might be the beginning of a new and more honourable career.[152] The second event was Anthony's marriage: this was in April, 1857. Neither Shaftesbury nor Minny knew the girl – Harriet, daughter of the Marquis of Donegal. But everyone spoke well of her, and, at first, Shaftesbury was pleased with his daughter-in-law and hoped that the marriage would have a good and settling effect on Anthony. But, within a few years, he had changed his views about Harriet – he felt that he had been deceived by the good reports about her. Anthony was 'feeble', he wrote in 1860, but Harriet was 'spiteful'. Both, moreover, were worldly, she by choice and he through infirmity.[153] He could foresee nothing but shame and sorrow from the marriage. Anthony's native defects were being accentuated by Harriet's 'example, practice, language'[154] and, in the summer of 1860, he wrote that every day gave him fresh reason to deplore Anthony's marriage with that 'daughter of Heth'.[155] He recounted with severe disapproval how she had gone to Ascot in a 'crowded carriage called a "drag", had descended from it and before the crowds had played at "Aunt Sally" '; she did what 'no girl in any tradesman's shop pretending to only the elements of moral training, would have condescended to do.'[156] She behaved in a similar way at the Goodwood races in July – she and Anthony stayed at the races for a week and, much to Shaftesbury's chagrin, returned on a Sunday.[157] Shaftesbury could find nothing good to say of Harriet: she was 'ignorant in mind, vulgar in manner, proud and selfish in heart'. She had neither the 'modesty of a girl nor the dignity of a matron'. She lacked 'every requisite of a Lady'; she truckled to rank and fashion, but was insolent and contemptuous to all in an inferior position. The marriage was, then, a 'heart-breaking thing' to him. A good and sensible wife, he felt, might have kept Anthony on the right course, but Harriet had done the very reverse: she had exercised no control, except what was for her own immediate and personal gratification. It was all, Shaftesbury admitted, a 'great mystery'. The marriage 'seems to be (I say "it seems" for God only knows) a full and direct contradiction of all my prayers, my hopes, my aspirations.'[158]

Shaftesbury had, therefore, great worries with his family during these years. In 1864, he wrote that he had no child left who, in any respect, realised his prayers or even his hopes.[159] In these areas of his life, too, his mood could change. Thus in 1865, he felt that he detected a change for the better in Harriet, and Anthony himself showed more promise. As in the past, his hopes were illusory, and, more often than not, he was critical of his son and daughter-in-law. To add to his troubles, his own health was variable. On occasion, he felt well and strong, but the 'roarings' recurred from time to time and there were also frequent complaints of indigestion and biliousness. Minny, too, was often unwell – her nursing of Mary in 1861 took a very heavy toll of her strength. There were, indeed, yearly visits abroad to spas to restore their health, but these, too, were another regular cause of complaint. Shaftesbury wrote in 1855 that it was a 'sad prospect to be doomed every year, to two months of this tedious, idle, monstrous, unprofitable life.'[160] He grudged the time and often doubted if the waters were improving his health. The visits were, indeed, undertaken very much at Minny's prompting and caused some tension between the two. Shaftesbury wrote in 1865 that it was a 'sad thing' that he and Minny differed so much in some of their tastes. All she wanted was to reside abroad: what he wanted was to stay at home. She argued that it was only for a short time every year, but, he wrote, 'if it were prolonged to the twelve month, there would be no objection on her part.' He would have much preferred to vary their foreign tours with residence at home or a holiday in Scotland, always the place which he enjoyed above all others. And there were the Estates: 'some time,' he wrote, 'must in duty be given to one's people and one's estate.'[161]

The Estates, indeed, remained a major worry. Shaftesbury constantly complained of mounting debts. In 1856, he noted that the mortgagers had demanded an increase in interest and there was also an increase in Income Tax during the Crimean War. In 1856, too, there was a demand for several thousand pounds for extra labour at St Giles's House. Shaftesbury felt 'deeply responsible for this', but the architect, he claimed, had misled him and he had been charged five times the amount which had been estimated.[162] Further, the pictures which he had hoped to sell for £6,000 had fetched nothing.[163] He loved the 'dear old saint' and wanted it as a 'rallying point' for his children and to make them love it, and he dreaded being forced to shut it up. But to live there was, he found, almost impossible. He could not spend a few weeks at St Giles without an outlay that – as he put it in 1859 – was 'fearfully, insufferably, ruinously' beyond his means and obligations.[164] He thus had insufficient means to live in the house in any comfort and he could not do a fraction of what he felt would be for his people's good. He tried to be economical and spent nothing on himself, not even to the extent of buying a horse. But there was always the expenditure on his charities, and one which was especially burdensome at this time was the Malta College. It had to be wound up in 1865 because of insolvency. Shaftesbury, in an effort to rescue it, had promised to put some £2,000 towards it and, although Haldane and others wished to share the burden, most of this sum fell to him. He had incurred it, as he admitted, 'foolishly, perhaps, for what (he) believed to be for the temporal and spiritual good of a large portion of the human race.'[165] There were also numerous requests – many of which he had to refuse – which came to him on the assumption that he was rich, and there were his children. There was the expense of his daughters' 'entrance to the world'. There was also the expenditure involved in a career for Lionel. In 1863, Lionel was admitted to a partnership in a commercial house and, to meet the expense, Shaftesbury drew £2,000 from the Estate account set apart for mortgages. He then found that he could not replace the sum.[166] And, in addition to the nagging worry of Anthony's debts, Shaftesbury always felt that, even if he did so some good on the Estates, dissipation and neglect in those who came after him would undo it all.

It was, then, a sad and sorry catalogue of good intentions and insufficiency of means. But there was also something more culpable than this: on the one hand, the activities of Robert Waters, Shaftesbury's steward, and, on the other, Shaftesbury's own undue neglect in supervising these activities. Waters had been steward to the Sixth Earl since 1845 and Shaftesbury had confirmed him in his position in May, 1852. Waters lived in some style. He occupied a farm of two hundred and forty acres, had three maids and a groom and bred horses, having built stables for the purpose. Shaftesbury did not approve of his steward's racing activities and, in 1854, raised the matter with Waters, who had promised to abandon them.[167] This appears to have satisfied Shaftesbury and, indeed, until 1863, Waters retained Shaftesbury's confidence. Shaftesbury thought Waters neglectful,[168] but did not doubt his honesty. But others were less sure and, in 1861, Palmerston wrote to his son-in-law, expressing misgivings about the management of the Estates.[169] He had, he said, heard people talk, and he feared that Shaftesbury, from kindness and generosity and from a desire to improve every part of his large Estates, had been led by his steward to devote a much larger part of his income to such local expenditure than would normally be given to such purposes. Palmerston also pointed out that it was common knowledge that every servant or agent would, if he could, absorb the largest possible amount of his employer's income and needed a very watchful hand to keep him within bounds. Palmerston admitted that he himself had suffered in this respect and, although Shaftesbury's agent might be better than his own had been, even the best agent sometimes thought himself entitled to percentages on his employer's expenditure and was tempted to make it as large as he could. And reports suggested that Waters kept race horses, bred mares, was connected with racing men and was a betting man. All these things, Palmerston wrote, 'if they do not lead a man astray, infuse into his mind habits of restlessness not very suitable to accurate economy.' Palmerston thus suggested that his son-in-law might do well to supervise his Estates more closely, and, in particular, that he might employ one of his London solicitors to make a minute examination of the accounts of his agent and make a report.

It was an extremely tactful letter. Palmerston felt justified in writing and sending it on the grounds, as he put it, of his 'great regard and friendship' for Shaftesbury and his sense of duty towards Minny's children and grandchildren.[170] Further instances of Palmerston's generosity towards Shaftesbury followed in 1863, when he sent Minny £5,000 to pay for half of Lionel's apprenticeship.[171] Shaftesbury and Minny were deeply grateful for this assistance. Minny wrote to Palmerston that it was impossible for her to explain what she felt about his kindness and to tell him of the relief which it had brought to the 'miserable anxiety' she had recently felt at the state of Shaftesbury's affairs and the effect she feared it must have on his health. 'He has been passing sleepless nights,' Minny wrote, 'turning over in his head a way out of his difficulties without finding it.' And the letter concluded with the remark that the money for Lionel was 'only a continuance of the constant goodness you have always shown to me.'[172] Palmerston thus showed Shaftesbury great sympathy and understanding, and yet another tangible sign of this was his appointment of Evelyn as his private secretary. His advice over Waters finally bore fruit, for, in 1863, Shaftesbury dismissed his steward 'under pretence of allowing him to resign.'[173] Once again, he received offers of financial help. Samuel Morley wrote expressing sincere regret at his pecuniary difficulties and offering a loan of £10,000 'as the private offering of a few attached and earnest friends'.[174] Shaftesbury was very reluctant to accept it, but, in the end, did so, and an increased sum of £12,500 was placed at his disposal by Morley and his friends.

Shaftesbury was thus well served by his relatives and his friends. He was much gratified by their response: he wrote to Morley that nothing could be 'more delicate . . . kind and generous' than what had been done for him – it had kept his eyes from tears and his feet from falling.[175] But he was also deeply hurt by what he regarded as gross betrayal by Waters and as carelessness on the part of his auditors, Messrs Nicholl, Burnet and Newman. Robert Burnet, the partner who dealt with the Estate accounts, earned Shaftesbury's criticism for failing to inform him of the true position of his finances. There can, indeed, be little doubt that Shaftesbury was ill-served by those on whom he relied to administer his Estates. Waters's role had been an extensive one. He had the responsibility of collecting rents and profits, the latter coming from the sale of timber, bricks and tiles – an average of £21,300 was said to have passed through his hands from these sources annually.[176] He was also authorised to negotiate the terms of leases and to superintend the improvements to the Estates and the expenditure which these involved: improvements and expenditure directed not only to the building of new cottage accommodation but also to the land drainage schemes which Shaftesbury instituted. Drainage had started in 1853, with the assistance of the Enclosure Commissioners, who advanced £5,000 for the purpose. In 1857 and 1862, contracts were made with the General Land Drainage and Improvement Company, which advanced some £27,000.[177] But, wide-ranging as these responsibilities were, Waters added to them very considerably. Thus he granted leases on longer terms than those approved by Shaftesbury.[178] In 1856, he opened accounts at Swindon, Salisbury and Hull. These were ostensibly intended to make the remission of rents from the estates in Wiltshire and Yorkshire more convenient, but they were opened without Shaftesbury's authorisation.[179] In other respects, however, Waters signally failed to carry out his responsibilities. No proper accounting system was devised for the money which Shaftesbury himself put into the drainage schemes.[180] No accounts at all were kept between 1855 and 1863 for the sale of timber, bricks or tiles.[181] In these circumstances, Shaftesbury's auditors were placed in a difficult position. Burnet had few accounts to audit, although, admittedly, he does not appear to have tried very hard to come to terms with the situation, and, in that sense, he may have deserved Shaftesbury's censure.[182] How much money Shaftesbury lost by these defalcations and irregularities is very hard to say. He admitted that he himself would never know the whole loss which he had suffered by 'mismanagement, peculation, trickery and direct fraud'.[183]

It must, however, be conceded that Shaftesbury allowed such things to happen. Waters's extravagant style of life – it was said that he lived at the rate of £2,000 with an income of £500[184] – was well known locally and, as has been noted, even reached Palmerston's ears, but Shaftesbury refused to draw the obvious conclusion until 1863. He himself came to realise that he could and should have been more vigilant. In 1863, he commented that he had entrusted too much to his steward and had omitted much of his 'special duty'. In looking after other people's interests, he had neglected his own. He had laid down what he regarded as 'admirable rules' but had neglected to see that they were properly observed.[185] And it must be admitted that some of his rules were scarcely likely to prevent mischief. In 1855–6, he had instituted new banking arrangements. But they were extremely complicated, involving, at one point, five separate accounts.[186] Such a scheme was almost a temptation to improper usage, or, at least, provided a good screen behind which it could take place. The drainage arrangements made in 1857 were also exceedingly complex. They involved Shaftesbury himself, Waters and the General Land Drainage and Improvement Company. Waters was to be in charge of the work and was to be paid for it by the Company on its completion, but Shaftesbury was to pay Waters all expenses incurred in the execution of the work and was to indemnify him against loss. Despite Palmerston's warnings about Waters, these arrangements were repeated in the second contract in 1862.[187] And there was always Shaftesbury's overriding desire to improve his Estates. As he himself admitted, this led to too great and too hasty expenditure. It also gave Waters his chance, and, as Shaftesbury put it, 'he saw his harvest and reaped it.'[188]

Even after he had parted with Waters, Shaftesbury was far from finished with him. Waters had extorted money from a tenant farmer, William Targitt. He had refused a request from Targitt for remission of rent and, in obtaining the money, forced Targitt to give up the farm. Shaftesbury took proceedings against his former steward on the grounds that Waters had embezzled the money. Waters was committed for trial at Dorchester; there, he was indicted on charges of embezzling £14,361.[189] But Waters's counsel applied for and was granted permission to take his case to the Central Criminal Court. Shaftesbury realised that the proceedings were likely to be troublesome and costly. 'And yet,' he wrote, 'it is a positive duty; nay a demand of conscience, to prosecute this cool, calculating, persevering, hardened, villain.'[190] Meantime, however, Waters had filed a bill of complaint against Shaftesbury, claiming money due to him: in particular, he demanded repayment of £3,827, a sum which, he argued, he was due from Shaftesbury for expenditure incurred over the drainage plan. The demand was based on the claim that, under the agreements of 1857 and 1862, Waters was entitled to be treated and remunerated as an agent of the General Land Drainage and Improvement Company and not merely as steward of Shaftesbury.[191] So complex had been the arrangements which had been made in these contracts that such a claim had some validity. The bill of complaint also asked that Shaftesbury be restrained from instituting any proceedings at law against Waters. And, if this suit was not enough, Shaftesbury was involved in another. This concerned one of his tenants, Edward Lewer, who had rented various farms since 1858, one of these being occupied by his son, Frederick. In 1864, Shaftesbury's solicitors, now more active in his interests, claimed that Lewer owed arrears of rent and of interest arising from drainage improvements carried out on his farms. When this was not forthcoming, a notice to quit was served on Lewer. Lewer, however, claimed that his lease had been granted for twenty-one years, and he thus countered actions taken against him by Shaftesbury in the Court of Exchequer, to secure his ejection and recovery of arrears, by a bill of complaint in Chancery.[192]

In December, 1864, Shaftesbury gloomily noted both cases, referring to them as 'fresh annoyances in law suits'. He foresaw a 'pretty waste ... of time and spirits and money. A successful suitor in the Court of Chancery is nearly always a ruined man, always a loser – even by victory.' He also reflected bitterly that such were the results of his 'weak, foolish, almost criminal confidence in Waters': and further, that Frederick Lewer had been a timber merchant who, he suspected, in conjunction with Waters, had defrauded him of 'immense sums' in his dealings in timber.[193] Waters and Lewer had certainly shared business dealings, and it will be recalled that no accounts were kept of the timber sales. Shaftesbury's suspicions of Lewer may well have been correct. The two suits were to drag on for some years: as will be seen, it was not, indeed, until 1868 that they were finally resolved. Shaftesbury was to pay dearly for the activities of his 'unjust steward' and for his own past negligence. In 1865, he wrote of his 'sad misgivings' that his enemies would triumph over him. 'Be it so,' he wrote, 'if such be the will of God.' Yet it was a sad close to his life to be 'thus harassed, defrauded and then dishonoured' in his old age. And he returned to the thought that he himself was largely at fault. He had thought too much of the affairs of others and spent too largely on affairs near his heart; he had 'omitted to consider that, after all, a man must be his own Guardian. . . .'[194]

The decade after 1855 had been one of varying fortunes for Shaftesbury. There had been the satisfaction of being close to Palmerston in matters of Church and State, but there was also the frustration of feeling that his efforts were doomed to ultimate failure and extinction. On a personal level, the years were shot through with trials and tribulations. Yet, Shaftesbury also found time and energy to devote attention to other matters. The decade was remarkable for the cluster of foreign and imperial issues which took place within it: the Crimean War, relations with China after the seizure of the *Arrow*, the Indian Mutiny, the cause of Piedmont-Sardinia, the American Civil War, the Polish Rebellion. Shaftesbury thus had ample opportunities to indulge his habitual interest in such issues, and, despite his domestic and private preoccupations, he took full advantage of them.

NOTES

1. N.R.A., Shaftesbury (Broadlands) MSS, SHA/PD/7, 27 Feb., 1859.
2. ibid., SHA/PD/7, 15 June, 1859.

3. See above pp. 125,127.
4. Hansard, *Parl. Debates*, 3rd ser., CLXIV, 1875.
5. Bleach (except open-air bleaching) and dye works were placed under the Factory Acts in 1860. (There was further legislation to close loopholes in 1862, 1863 and 1864 and a consolidating Act was passed in 1870). Legislation affecting lace-making was passed in 1861. (See B. L. Hutchins and A. Harrison, *A History of Factory Legislation* (1903), pp. 139–40, 145).
6. Hansard, *Parl. Debates*, 3rd ser., CLXXII, 1331.
7. Pottery, lucifer matches, percussion caps and cartridges, paper-staining, fustion cutting, and lace and hosiery. (Certain subsidiary aspects of bleaching and dyeing were also covered). See B. L. Hutchins and A. Harrison, op. cit., p. 150.
8. ibid., pp. 154–5.
9. Hansard, *Parl. Debates*, 3rd ser., CLXXVI, 1448.
10. ibid., CLXXIX, 174–6.
11. ibid., CLXXII, 1335–8.
12. ibid., CLXXV, 1123–32.
13. ibid., CXLVII, 435–6.
14. ibid., CXLVI, 1542–6.
15. ibid., CLXI, 1069; CLXII, 716.
16. ibid., CLXIV, 1879.
17. ibid., CLXXII, 1336.
18. ibid., CLXXV, 1132.
19. *Speeches of the Earl of Shaftesbury*, p. 308.
20. N.R.A., Shaftesbury (Broadlands) MSS, SHA/PD/7, 3 Feb., 1861.
21. P.P., 1859, III. Shaftesbury answered 922 questions put to him in the course of three days.
22. ibid., Qs 49, 51.
23. ibid., Qs 51, 55.
24. ibid., Q, 59.
25. ibid., Q. 161.
26. The Admission document was divided into five parts:
    (i) Notice of admission, signed by the proprietor and superintendent of the asylum.
    (ii) Statement of the medical man in the asylum which received the patient.
    (iii) Order of the person who had put the patient into the asylum, with a statement of the particulars: history of the patient etc. This order could be signed by any person.
    (iv) A medical certificate from one medical man who had seen the patient.
    (v) A second medical certificate from another medical man. The certificate had to state the qualifications of the doctors, who had to have examined the patient not more than seven days before the date of the certificate, and had to distinguish between facts observed by the doctors themselves and other signs indicating insanity. One certificate was kept by the superintendent of the asylum (as his security against subsequent legal proceedings); the other had to be lodged with the Commission within seven days.
    (ibid., Qs 157–65).
27. ibid., Q. 172.
28. ibid., Q. 201.
29. ibid., Q. 185.
30. ibid., Q. 315.
31. ibid., Q. 187. See also Q. 220.

32. ibid., Qs 226, 271.
33. ibid., Qs 113, 208, 212.
34. ibid., Q. 217.
35. ibid., Qs 217, 241, 258, 259.
36. ibid., Q. 242.
37. ibid., Q. 254, 5.
38. ibid., Q. 149.
39. ibid., Q. 400.
40. ibid., Q. 461.
41. ibid., Qs 116–17.
42. ibid., Q. 245.
43. ibid., Q. 569.
44. ibid., Q. 395.
45. ibid., Q. 569.
46. ibid., Q. 182. It is true that the statement of the medical superintendent of the asylum was a 'third' certificate and would bring any irregularities to the attention of the Commissioners. (ibid., Qs 174, 5, 6).
47. ibid., Q. 85.
48. ibid., Q. 192.
49. In 1862, indeed, in a debate in the Lords, Shaftesbury returned to this point and quoted the case of a doctor with whom he had disputed a matter of lunacy. The doctor had stated—seemingly to prove beyond doubt that the lady in question was insane—that she subscribed to the Society for the Conversion of the Jews. It was not a question calculated to arouse Shaftesbury's confidence in the man's judgment. Had the doctor been 'acquainted with what was going on in the world,' Shaftesbury commented, 'he would have known that hundreds and thousands of persons of the most sane and solid description' were subscribers to this Society. (Hansard, *Parl. Debates,* 3rd ser., CLXV, 1291).
50. P.P., 1859, III, Q. 195.
51. ibid., Q. 263.
52. ibid., Q. 419.
53. ibid., Qs 375, 6, 88.
54. ibid., Q. 392.
55. See above p. 230.
56. P.P., 1859, III, Qs 274, 292.
57. ibid., Qs 275, 298.
58. ibid., Q. 11.
59. ibid., Q. 308.
60. ibid., Qs 334, 5.
61. ibid., Qs 315, 6.
62. ibid., Q. 301.
63. ibid., Qs 641,
64. ibid., Q. 664.
65. ibid., Q. 690.
66. ibid., Q. 439.
67. ibid., Q. 442.
68. ibid., Q. 308.
69. ibid., Qs 77, 82.
70. ibid., Qs 88, 101.
71. ibid., Q. 102.
72. ibid., Q. 107.

73. ibid., Q. 82, 88, 94.
74. ibid., Q. 88.
75. ibid., Q. 494.
76. ibid., Q. 507.
77. ibid., Q. 508.
78. ibid., Q. 510.
79. ibid., Q. 527.
80. ibid., Q. 524.
81. ibid., Q. 519.
82. ibid., Q. 508.
83. ibid., Q. 521.
84. Hansard, *Parl Debates,* 3rd ser., CLXI, 2146 ff; CLXV, 780 ff, 1289 ff.
85. See D. H. Tuke, *Chapters in the History of the Insane in the British Isles* (1882), pp. 195–6.
86. N.R.A., Shaftesbury (Broadlands) MSS, SHA/PD/7, 17 Sept., 1859.
87. *Ragged School Union Magazine* (1861), pp. 138–9.
88. Hansard, *Parl. Debates,* 3rd ser., CLXIII, 916–19, 928, 929. He withdrew the motion. There was also an acrimonious correspondence published in *The Record* (17 May, 1861) between Shaftesbury and the Commissioner who had made the comments, Cumin. Shaftesbury claimed that the Report had been based on Cumin's investigations in Plymouth, which were insufficient for the wide-ranging criticisms which were made. This was denied by Cumin.
89. N.R.A., Shaftesbury (Broadlands) MSS, SHA/PD/7, 26 Jan., 1860.
90. ibid., SHA/PD/7, 1 May, 1860.
91. ibid., SHA/PD/8, 3 Aug., 1865.
92. ibid., SHA/PD/8, 3 Aug., 1865.
93. ibid., SHA/PD/7, 25 May, 1855.
94. ibid., SHA/PD/7, 28 May, 1856.
95. ibid., SHA/PD/7, 18 Mar., 1857.
96. ibid., SHA/PD/7, 13 June, 1858.
97. ibid., SHA/PD/7, 13 Aug., 1860.
98. ibid., SHA/PD/7, 30 Dec., 1855.
99. ibid., SHA/PD/8, 28 July, 1865.
100. ibid., SHA/PD/7, 20 Dec., 1859.
101. ibid., SHA/PD/7, 1 Mar., 1857.
102. ibid., SHA/PD/7, 9 May, 1860.
103. ibid., SHA/PD/7, 14 June, 1860.
104. ibid., SHA/PD/7, 30 Dec., 1855.
105. ibid., SHA/PD/7, 24 Dec., 1859.
106. ibid., SHA/PD/7, 2 Oct., 1860.
107. ibid., SHA/PD/8, 19 July, 1865.
108. ibid., SHA/PD/8, 28 July, 1865.
109. ibid., SHA/PD/8, 3 Aug., 1865.
110. ibid., SHA/PD/7, 23 May, 1855.
111. ibid., SHA/PD/7, 20 Mar., 1858.
112. ibid., SHA/PD/7, 20 Mar., 1858.
113. ibid., SHA/PD/7, 2 Mar., 1859.
114. ibid., SHA/PD/7, 28 Mar., 1857.
115. ibid., SHA/PD/7, 2 Mar., 1859.
116. ibid., SHA/PD/7, 20 Mar., 1858.
117. D. Southgate, *The Most English Minister. The Policies and Politics of Palmerston*

(1966), pp. 414-15. See also Hon. E. Ashley, op. cit., II, 261-9. It appears, for example, that, on occasion, Palmerston accompanied the Lunacy Commissioners on their visits.
118. N.R.A., Shaftesbury (Broadlands) MSS, SHA/PD/7, 3 Jan., 1858.
119. ibid., SHA/PD/8, 11 July, 1865.
120. ibid., SHA/PD/8, 20 Oct., 1865.
121. Quoted by Hodder, III, 185.
122. Shaftesbury (Broadlands) MSS, SHA/PD/7, 30 July, 1859.
123. ibid., SHA/PD/7, 28 Apr., 1865.
124. *Ragged School Union Magazine* (1857), pp. 109-10: (1859), p. 107.
125. ibid. (1856), p. 111.
126. ibid. (1863), p. 129.
127. ibid. (1858), p. 109.
128. ibid. (1864), p. 126.
129. See also B. Harrison, 'Philanthropy and the Victorians' (*Victorian Studies*, IX, No. 4, pp. 372-4).
130. N.R.A., Shaftesbury (Broadlands) MSS, SHA/PD/8, 2 Nov., 1865.
131. ibid., SHA/PD/7, 26 May, 1861.
132. ibid., SHA/PD/7, 21 Aug., 1855.
133. ibid., SHA/PD/7, 21 Aug., 1855.
134. ibid., SHA/PD/7, 22 Aug., 1855.
135. ibid., SHA/PD/7, 12 June, 1860.
136. ibid., SHA/PD/7, 1 Sept., 1861.
137. ibid., SHA/PD/7, 3 Sept., 1861.
138. Quoted by Hodder, III, 131.
139. N.R.A., Shaftesbury (Broadlands) MSS, SHA/PD/7, 3 Sept., 1862.
140. ibid., SHA/PD/7, 12 June, 1860.
141. ibid., SHA/PD/7, 28 Feb., 1863.
142. ibid., SHA/PD/7, 14 Sept., 1864.
143. ibid., SHA/PD/7, 19 Nov., 1864.
144. ibid., SHA/PD/7, 5 Feb., 1860.
145. ibid., SHA/PD/7, 25 Dec., 1857.
146. ibid., SHA/PD/6, 13 Apr., 1855.
147. ibid., SHA/PD/7, 13 Oct., 1855.
148. ibid., SHA/PD/7, 17 Oct., 1855.
149. ibid., SHA/PD/7, 15, 17 Nov., 1856.
150. ibid., SHA/PD/7, 17 Mar., 1857.
151. ibid., SHA/PD/7, 18 Mar., 1857.
152. Anthony was returned for Cricklade in 1859 and remained its Member until 1865.
153. N.R.A., Shaftesbury (Broadlands) MSS, SHA/PD/7, 31 Mar., 1860.
154. ibid., SHA/PD/7, 10 Apr., 1860.
155. ibid., SHA/PD/7, 14 June, 1860.
156. ibid., SHA/PD/7, 14 June, 1860.
157. ibid., SHA/PD/7, 30 July, 1860.
158. ibid., SHA/PD/7, 2 July, 1860.
159. ibid., SHA/PD/7, 14 Sept., 1864.
160. ibid., SHA/PD/7, 9 Aug., 1855.
161. ibid., SHA/PD/8, 14 Sept., 1865.
162. ibid., SHA/PD/7, 29 Feb., 1 Mar., 1856.
163. ibid., SHA/PD/7, 14 May, 1860.
164. ibid., SHA/PD/7, 28 Feb., 1859.

165. ibid., SHA/PD/8, 24, 25 Nov., 1865.
166. ibid., SHA/PD/7, 10 June, 1863.
167. B. Kerr, *Bound to the Soil. A Social History of Dorset, 1750–1918* (1968), pp. 208, 215.
168. See above p. 354.
169. Quoted by Hodder, III, 146–7.
170. Quoted ibid., III, 147.
171. N.R.A., Shaftesbury (Broadlands) MSS, SHA/PD/7, 19 July, 1863.
172. H.R.O., Shaftesbury (Broadlands) MSS, 27M60, 17 July, 1863.
173. N.R.A., Shaftesbury (Broadlands) MSS, SHA/PD/7, 30 Aug., 1863.
174. H.R.O., Shaftesbury (Broadlands) MSS, 27M60, 23 Nov., 1863.
175. ibid., 27M60, 20 July, 1864. (Copy).
176. P.R.O., C/16/242. W 176. See also B. Kerr, op. cit., p. 208.
177. P.R.O., C/16/242. W 176.
178. B. Kerr, op. cit., p. 209.
179. P.R.O., C/16/242. W 176.
180. This sum amounted to £40,000 between 1851 and 1863. (P.R.O., C/16/242. W 176).
181. P.R.O., C/16/242, W 176.
182. N.R.A., Shaftesbury (Broadlands) MSS, SHA/EST/8. Shaftesbury claimed that Burnet would sometimes say that Waters's accounts were satisfactorily kept; at others that they were not all that he could wish, but, nevertheless, asked Shaftesbury to sign them. Shaftesbury, pressed by business and trusting Burnet, did so.
183. The estimates of this loss vary. In 1863 Shaftesbury himself estimated it at £12,000 but he thought that this was too low (ibid., SHA/PD/7, 20 Aug., 1863); later at £80,000 (ibid., SHA/EST/8); B. Kerr (op. cit., p. 221) estimates it at £20,000.
184. B. Kerr, op. cit., p. 214. His salary from Shaftesbury was £430 p.a.
185. N.R.A., Shaftesbury (Broadlands) MSS, SHA/PD/7, 20 Aug., 1863.
186. P.R.O., C/16/242. W 176.
187. Hammonds, p. 176.
188. N.R.A., Shaftesbury (Broadlands) MSS, SHA/PD/7, 20 Aug., 1863.
189. B. Kerr, op. cit., pp. 217–18.
190. N.R.A., Shaftesbury (Broadlands) MSS, SHA/PD/7, 29 Mar., 1865.
191. P.R.O., C/16/242. W 176.
192. P.R.O., C/16/217. L 134.
193. N.R.A., Shaftesbury (Broadlands) MSS, SHA/PD/7, 12 Dec., 1864.
194. ibid., SHA/PD/8, 21 Nov., 1865.

16
Righteousness Exalteth a Nation, 1854–1865

Politicians, wrote Shaftesbury in May, 1853, were 'busy about Turkey and Russia',[1] and, as events developed which were to lead to the outbreak of the Crimean War, his sympathies were in no doubt. He recognised the decay of the Turkish Empire and felt that Britain could not 'prop up' the Sick Man indefinitely. Nevertheless, for reasons of obligation and also of interest, Britain must resist any Russian designs which would lead to the unilateral dismemberment of Turkey. There were, he felt, long-standing attachments between Britain and Turkey: 'she has been to us, in peace and war, in commerce and in politics,' he wrote, 'a firm and faithful friend.'[2] Moreover, British interests would not be served by Russian domination of Asia, and, in particular, the possession of the Danube by Russia would have a damaging effect on British trade.[3] Thus, when Russia and France disputed the custody of the Holy Places in Palestine, Shaftesbury, fearing that the Russian claims to custody would, if granted, constitute a regular right to interference in Turkey, adopted a strongly anti-Russian outlook, and he maintained this in the face of the subsequent Russian invasion of the Danubian Principalities in the summer of 1853, the Turkish declaration of war against Russia in October, 1853, and the final involvement of Britain and France in the war on the Turkish side in March, 1854. The Tsar had, in his opinion, been guilty of aggression against Turkey, and that aggression had to be resisted.

In taking this point of view, Shaftesbury was at one with most of his fellow countrymen. But his own particular outlook was illustrated by the strong exception which he took to a statement, issued by the Tsar in February, 1854, that Britain and France had taken the side of the enemy of Christianity and were fighting the upholder of the Orthodox Faith. He wrote to Clarendon, Foreign Secretary in the Aberdeen Coalition, that he did not wish to take any step which might lead to public debate on foreign affairs unless Clarendon felt that this would not be prejudicial to British interests, but he felt that the Tsar's manifesto demanded some comment: 'many are uneasy, many are actually misled thro' ignorance of the real state of the case,' he wrote.[4] And, on 10 March, Shaftesbury spoke at some length on the subject in the Lords.[5] He refuted the Tsar's comment that Turkey was the enemy of Christianity. On the contrary, his experience had been that the Turk had been liberal in the freedom given to Christian missionaries and efforts to circulate the Scriptures. Russia, on the other hand, had been intolerant in these respects. Again, whereas Russia had resisted efforts to obtain justice for Protestants and had forbidden Jewish subjects to possess the Hebrew Scriptures, Turkey had brought about 'a great development of knowledge and liberal sentiment'. Here, no doubt, Shaftesbury had in mind the permission which had been granted to create the Jerusalem Bishopric. In sum, therefore, Shaftesbury felt that Britain had ample justification for going to war against the aggression and despotism represented by Russia. She did so 'in no spirt of ambition, covetousness, or pride, but for her own defence and the maintenance of great principles. . . .' And he had no fear of the outcome of the war:

> Let us have no fear for the issue [he said], but, offering a humble and hearty prayer to Almighty God, let us devoutly trust that His aid will not be wanting to bless our arms with success, and a speedy peace, in this just and inevitable quarrel.

Shaftesbury was also anxious to take the opportunity offered by the French alliance to promote the cause of Protestantism in France. This was a cause in which he had already shown interest,[6] and, in April, 1854, he wrote to Napoleon III reviving it in the context of the alliance between the two countries.[7] Protestant Churches in the French Empire, he claimed, did not enjoy the freedom or rights enjoyed by Protestant seceders from the Greek Church in the Turkish dominions; they were, indeed, suffering many 'grievous vexations'. The Emperor denied that this was the case, but Shaftesbury would not be put off and wrote once again to suggest that Napoleon had been misinformed.[8] He would not, he said, write in such a vein to any other potentate, but he 'cherish(ed) from (his) heart' the alliance with France and could not endure the thought that the people of England should connect the Emperor's name with the 'odious name of Persecution'.

Another cause which Shaftesbury felt the War might advance was that of the Jews. His anti-Russian sentiments, indeed, derived partly from this consideration; Russia, he noted, was the Jews' 'principal, powerful and inhuman oppressor in body and soul'.[9] His earlier efforts in 1840 for the colonisation of Syria had yielded no results: the present crisis provided another opportunity to pursue the matter. In July, 1853, he had written to

Aberdeen, pointing out the dangerous state of affairs which would arise on any dissolution of the Turkish Empire. The vast provinces, he wrote, must be assigned to neutral powers. Syria, he commented, was a 'country without a nation'; to match it, a 'nation without a country' must be sought. 'Is there such a thing?' he asked. 'To be sure there is, The ancient and rightful Lords of the soil, the Jews!'[10] He also suggested to Clarendon that the Sultan should be induced to issue a firman, granting to the Jewish people power to hold land in Syria or any other part of the Turkish dominions, and he sounded out Jewish reaction to such a plan.[11] He did not think that this was running too far ahead of events – the Turkish Empire was clearly in decay. Nor did he think that the plan was precipitating prophecy; its requirements seemed very near fulfilment.

The Crimean War was, then, a 'just war' in Shaftesbury's eyes, undertaken for legitimate reasons of self-interest in resistance to 'a perilous ambition, a fearful tyrant, a cruel and grasping Despot',[12] and it offered opportunities for the pursuit of worthy objectives. But, if Shaftesbury's attitude to the War was enthusiastic, it was not bombastic. He felt that many of his fellow-countrymen entered the War in too light and frivolous a spirit. A banquet give to Sir William Napier on his departure for the Crimea was, Shaftesbury felt, out of place: 'prayer and hope,' he wrote, 'not wine and laughter' should have accompanied such events.[13] Shaftesbury also disapproved of the attitude of Lord Raglan, the Commander-in-Chief. His despatches were 'cold and thankless to Almighty God', and Shaftesbury wondered if Raglan was thinking more of the Clubs of St James' Street than the audience of the Heavenly host.[14] And not only were victories in the War such as Inkerman and Balaclava passed over by Raglan without acknowledgment of Divine assistance; they were not properly followed up. They had involved great loss of life and yet the main objective of Sebastopol eluded the grasp of the allies, and the outbreak of cholera among the troops made matters considerably worse. Shaftesbury followed these events with great anxiety. Victory after victory, he noted in November, 1854, still left Britain crippled. Reinforcements were slow and, as the winter set in, Shaftesbury felt that there was 'every danger and every cause of alarm'.[15] Reports of storms and wrecks on the Black Sea made him fearful of the future. No doubt anxieties for the safety of Anthony entered into his mind,[16] but he also wondered how the sea could be controlled in such weather – how the armies could be supplied and Sebastopol blockaded.[17] Thus what he called the 'terrors of the Crimea'[18] were much in Shaftesbury's mind at the close of 1854, and, to his earlier criticism of Raglan's lack of concern for religion, he added the charge of lack of experience and competence to command a large army. Raglan did not 'exercise ... all the energies and callings of a General.' All the 'mismanagement, loss, neglect, suffering' had been 'perpetrated under his eyes and reported to his ears,' and, although he might have the 'merit of feeling sympathy . . . he must also bear the charge of incompetency. . . .'[19]

As 1855 began, news from the Crimea got steadily worse, and Shaftesbury noted, with increasing despair, that disease, cold and hunger were taking their toll. Raglan and his staff incurred his continuing criticism, but he was no more satisfied with events at home. He was appalled by the political uncertainty on the resignation of the Aberdeen coalition in 1855.[20] The domestic confusion would, he felt, make the French suspicious of their ally and deter the Austrians from entering the War on the allied side. Palmerston's assumption of office in February, 1855, was, of course, a comfort, and, for some time after this, Shaftesbury was preoccupied with the offers of office which he received.[21] But his mind soon returned to the War and to the gross lack of a proper religious outlook and of prudent human planning which, he thought, had been displayed. He was soon to apply himself to remedy both defects. Thus he attempted to secure official approval for a national day of prayer. He had already written twice to Aberdeen on the subject in 1854 and had been critical of Aberdeen's refusal to agree to it.[22] In February, 1855, he took the matter up again: 'have been running about to stir up Prelates and Ministers to a day of prayer,' he wrote.[23] This time, he was successful and he was especially grateful to find Palmerston not only ready but willing to urge that a special day – and not a Sunday – should be set aside. 'This is very good,' Shaftesbury wrote; 'it looks serious and reverent.'[24] The other project was the appointment of a Sanitary Commission to go to the Crimea to combat the disease which wrought such havoc among the troops. On 14 February, 1855, Shaftesbury noted that he had been to see Panmure, Secretary of State for War, about some sanitary arrangements for the Crimean hospitals, but, he wrote, 'all in vain: a "Philanthropist" is always a bore.'[25] But the next day he recorded success. Panmure had listened to the scheme for a Sanitary Commission to go to Scutari and Balaclava with full powers to 'purify the Hospitals, ventilate the ships and exert all that Science can do to save life where thousands are dying, not of their wounds, but of Dysentry and Diarrhoea, the result of foul air and preventible mischiefs.'[26] The authorship of the idea of a Sanitary Commission is open to doubt. Shaftesbury received a letter from the War Department saying that Panmure had decided to appoint the Commission and would like to discuss it with him,[27] and Shaftesbury's Diary entry of the same day – 15 February – refers to 'my' scheme.[28] Further, the following day, Palmerston wrote to Panmure sending him a memorandum which Shaftesbury had given him on the subject.[29] On the other hand, it has been attributed to Florence Nightingale – whom Shaftesbury knew – and also to Dr Hector Gavin, who, for three years, had held the post of Government Commissioner for the prevention and cure of cholera in the West Indies. Gavin and Shaftesbury had, indeed, been in touch with each other about it, and Shaftesbury received a letter from Gavin to say that Panmure had adopted *his* (i.e. Gavin's) proposition and thanking Shaftesbury for all that he had done to bring about 'this most important result'.[30] And, in later years, Shaftesbury himself gave full credit to Gavin – in 1872, he wrote that it was Gavin who suggested the Commission to him and that he urged it on Panmure.[31] No doubt, too, the good offices of Palmerston helped to smooth the way, and Shaftesbury's influence was important in this respect.

Whatever the precise origin of the Commission, Shaftesbury set himself to implement it with great energy. The Commission consisted of Gavin himself and seven others. They were men of experience in public health, much of it acquired in Liverpool; they had, Shaftesbury told Panmure, 'cheerfully surrendered their personal comforts ... to aid the public in this crisis.' He urged on Panmure the necessity that the Commissioners should have freedom to carry out their task without delay. They could be trusted to advise nothing that was needless or extravagant, but, if their hands were 'bound with red tape and their shins broken by a succession of official stumbling blocks,' they would be useless and indeed ridiculous. 'We cannot,' Shaftesbury wrote, 'in these matters trifle with time; minutes here are as valuable as years.'[32] At Panmure's request, Shaftesbury drew up the instructions to the Commissioners:[33] it was their duty 'to state fully, and urge strongly' all that they considered necessary for the preservation of health and life. This received the government's continuing support and active approval; the Commission was despatched and reinforcements were sent out.[34] Shaftesbury received reports from Gavin and from another of its members, Sutherland, about its progress. Gavin wrote from Constantinople in March, 1855, that the work proceeded satisfactorily. All the hospitals at Scutari and the floating ships had been examined and reported on, although he added that it was difficult to say how much of 'all this ill conditioned state of things' could be easily and speedily remedied: there was not that 'energy and dedication to work which should characterise Englishmen.'[35] Sutherland also wrote of difficulties with the labour force at Balaclava, but, thanks to the efforts of the Commission's inspectors, sanitary conditions had improved.[36] Shaftesbury thus made an important contribution to the work of sanitary improvement in the Crimea. As has been seen, this was recognised by Gavin and also, indeed, by Florence Nightingale. Shaftesbury noted her comment that the Commission had 'saved the British Army.'[37] In 1858, she wrote to Shaftesbury enclosing with her letter a copy of her report to the War Office on army sanitary matters. The report was strictly confidential: 'but,' she commented, 'as Lord Shaftesbury has, for so many years, been our leader in Sanitary Matters (as in so many other wise and benevolent things) it seemed to me but right to send him a Report which contains much of what was done by himself viz the work of the Sanitary Commission in the East. . . .'[38] And in 1863, she sent Shaftesbury a copy of the report and evidence of the Indian Army Sanitary Commission: she did so, as she put it, 'always remembering that to you first we owe the giving of sanitary hope to our poor army. . . .'[39]

Shaftesbury was grateful for the larger measure of success enjoyed by the allies in the summer and autumn of 1855, and, after the fall of Sebastopol, he wrote to Clarendon expressing his thanks to God for the success and offering Clarendon and his colleagues congratulations on the event. There had been heavy loss of life, but this was less than would have been sustained by disease had the troops been forced to spend another winter outside Sebastopol.[40] But he also constantly urged the desirability of making an honourable peace. He did not want peace at any price, but he felt that Britain should 'desire peace . . . seek peace and not protract the war one moment beyond necessity.'[41] He was afraid that, the longer the War went on, the more the French alliance would become subject to strains and stresses. And when the War did finish and Clarendon set out for the peace conference in Paris in February, 1856, this thought was still in his mind. England and France, 'one in making war, would be two in making peace.'[42] He feared that France would draw near to Austria and that both might be sympathetic to Russia: 'It is the real, tho' unavowed, alliance of despotic and persecuting Governments against political freedom and liberty of conscience,' he wrote.[43] But, in the event, he was satisfied with the terms which were finally agreed upon. Turkey might not have much life left in her, but she had been saved from Russian aggression and thus Shaftesbury's initial considerations about the justice of the War had been met. He wrote to Clarendon in April, 1856, thanking God for the peace. The nation, he wrote, was 'quite ready for another brush with the Czar and had even a sly desire that he should reject the terms; but the Christian principle prevailed: and the people, one and all, declare that it would have been both wicked and foolish to prolong the war for the sake of somewhat improved conditions.'[44] But his other objectives were still unfulfilled. He added in his letter to Clarendon that the persecution of Protestants in France was still 'in full activity'; he did not ask Clarendon to interpose, but he ought to know about it, 'for as soon as the peace is secured and the country has breathing time, it will give vent to its long-suppressed indignation.'[45] And the hopes which he had for the Jews had not been realised. He wrote in his Diary in March, 1856, expressing the wish that it might 'pity us to see the stones of Zion in the dust' and her children in darkness and exile. 'May we sigh more, pray more, labour more,' he wrote 'that our enemies may cease to have power to say "My Lord delayeth His coming".' And, he added: 'Hasten Thy Kingdom, Hasten Thy Kingdom, Hasten Thy Kingdom, oh Lord Jesus.'[46]

The following year, 1857, witnessed two further episodes in foreign and imperial history, both of which were of great interest to Shaftesbury. They related to China and to India. The seizure by Chinese coastguards in 1856 of a small ship, or lorcha, the *Arrow*, engaged in piracy in the Canton River, precipitated a major diplomatic incident. The *Arrow* was, in fact, a Chinese ship owned by a Chinese pirate, but had been registered as a British ship to escape arrest: under the treaty of Nanking of 1842, the Chinese authorities were prevented from interfering with vessels flying the British flag in Chinese territorial waters. On its seizure, the British consul at Hong Kong, Parkes, accused the Chinese of insulting the British flag and demanded the release of the seamen – the British would investigate any charges to be made against them. Eventually, the men were released, but Bowring, the Governor of Hong Kong, ordered the Navy to bombard Canton as a reprisal for the original seizure and, when the Chinese retaliated, war broke out in the Canton area. The British government were embarrassed by the unilateral action which Parkes and Bowring had taken. There were, indeed, many legal complications involved, such as the fact that the British registration of the *Arrow* had expired three weeks before the seizure of the ship by the Chinese. Nevertheless, Palmerston felt that the British authorities in Hong Kong had to be supported: for the government to take any contrary action would be to undermine the British position in China. Palmerston's government, however, encountered severe opposition – a vote of censure was proposed in both Lords and Commons. It was lost in the Lords but carried in the Commons, whereupon Palmerston obtained a dissolution from the Queen and the General Election of 1857 took place.

Shaftesbury had long been interested in Chinese matters and was a long-standing opponent of the Opium Trade.[47] In this, he differed from Palmerston, who took the view that the trade should be legalised by the Chinese Emperor; if this were done, a tax could be levied on it, but the frictions over smuggling and piracy would cease. Before the seizure of the *Arrow*, Shaftesbury had decided to raise the matter of the trade once again in the Lords and to express his continuing opposition to it, but, when the *Arrow* was taken, he deferred it. The whole incident, he felt, had in large measure derived from the illicit trade in Opium: 'it is a painful question,' he wrote. 'The Chinese are, doubtless, insolent, irritating, aggressive and false. We, on the other hand, give abundant provocation in the pertinacity and outrage of our opium smuggling.'[48] Yet he supported the government in its handling of the incident involving the *Arrow*. On the vote of censure in the Lords, he wrote that 'in the present case . . . we had law and right on our side . . . and even had the right been less clear, the vote proposed – a vote of censure – was extreme.'[49] He felt that the motion derived from self-seeking and partisan considerations. When the government was defeated in the Commons, it was, he said, a 'sad result'. 'Right or wrong,' he continued, 'the Government must be supported to bring these matters to a satisfactory close; but now they are crippled in the eyes of the Chinese. . . .'[50] Nevertheless, having supported Palmerston over the *Arrow*, Shaftesbury reverted to his former intention to condemn the Opium Trade. On 9 March, 1857, he proposed his motion and, in the course of his speech,[51] attacked the trade as 'one of the most flagitious instances of unscrupulousness in the pursuit of wealth that mankind had ever witnessed. . . .' It was evil from a commercial, financial and political point of view, and, above all, it was immoral – a disgrace to the character of England and an impediment to the progress of Christianity. He moved that the opinion of the judges be taken as to whether the East India Company was legally entitled to derive a revenue from the Opium monopoly and to sell Opium for the purpose of being smuggled into China. The motion was, in fact, withdrawn on the understanding that the government would take the opinion of the law officers of the Crown on the matter. Shaftesbury was not especially pleased with his performance: 'weak, unconvincing, unimpressive,' he wrote of it, and he once again expressed his dislike of having to address the Lords: 'no sign of life,' he wrote; 'no sympathy, no indication of approval or disapproval.'[52] Nevertheless, despite his stand with the government over the *Arrowe*, he had carried out his previous intention to raise the Opium question.

Shaftesbury's conduct over the matter has been the subject of criticism. The Hammonds appear to suggest[53] that the influence which Shaftesbury enjoyed with Palmerston over ecclesiastical appointments interfered with his principles; that it was only through fear of losing that influence that Shaftesbury supported the government over the *Arrow*. But this cannot be substantiated. Shaftesbury had, it is true, hoped and believed that 'God having employed (Palmerston) as an instrument for good, would maintain him.'[54] He was, therefore, displeased and surprised at Palmerston's defeat in the vote of censure in the Commons: he could only attribute it to the inscrutability of God's ways. But he was careful to avoid any impression that, in supporting Palmerston in the Lords, he was acting in collusion with the government. This was, indeed, one reason why he reverted to the motion against Opium Trade. It appears that he was asked not to do so by Granville, who, according to Shaftesbury, pointed out that it would 'embarrass the government, raise inconvenient debate and do much mischief.'[55] Shaftesbury replied that 'the belief of "collusion for electioneering purposes" would do ten times more harm and that withdrawal was impossible.'[56] He would only withdraw the motion if Granville would state in the Lords that the discussion would be detrimental to affairs in China. Granville would not do this, but agreed to grant the motion if Shaftesbury would keep to the legal points, and, to this, Shaftesbury agreed. Further, Shaftesbury felt that, even if Palmerston survived and remained in power, his influence over ecclesiastical appointments would end, for, in his view, the coalition against Palmerston had been caused by antagonism to his influence over Church appointments.[57] Such a comment may indicate a considerable exaggeration of the effect of his role in this respect, but it does not suggest that he looked to the perpetuation of his influence. A more substantial charge which may be made against Shaftesbury is one of inconsistency. It may be argued that Shaftesbury's opposition to the Opium Trade should have led him to oppose the government for upholding the rights of pirates and, thereby, in some measure, supporting the trade. As has been noted, he himself admitted that the Opium Trade and the *Arrow* incident were connected. Nevertheless, Shaftesbury felt that, over the *Arrow*, Britain had 'law and right', as he put it, on her side: he always felt that, when this was the case, British authority must be upheld, even by forcible measures. On the Opium issue, he did not consider Britain to be so placed: thus Britain must stand condemned. He himself would have seen no inconsistency in the two attitudes which he adopted.

The Indian Mutiny was, however, the more notable event of 1857. News of the mutiny among the Sepoy troops in the area of Delhi, Lucknow and Cawnpore filtered through to Britain in mid-June, 1857, some five weeks after the outbreak had taken place. As the summer months passed, reports increased and gave more and more cause for alarm. At first, Shaftesbury felt inclined to discount many of these reports. In July, he wrote that there was, as yet, little or no authentic intelligence from the East – there were only 'endless rumours, one more terrible than another, but in fact based on imagination, designed or diseased'. He also felt that the Mutiny was to some degree the result of mismanagement and justifiable grievance among the native troops.[58] In August, 1857, while abroad, he noted 'a number and variety of things to be prayed for'. These included an early end to the Mutiny; 'the commencement of a new order of things; of a wiser and more vigorous government; of justice and judgment; of greater knowledge and greater zeal for man's real good; of fresh openings for the advance of the Gospel; of enlarged missionary operations; of increased opportunity to promote and invite the Second Advent.'[59] And to his son, Evelyn, he wrote that the Mutiny of the Sepoys had given Britain a right and an opportunity to initiate reforms, which she would never have had if they had remained loyal – such reforms would otherwise have been long delayed.[60] But, despite his initial scepticism of the reports of the savageries perpetrated during the

Mutiny, he came to take an extremely serious view of them. Later in August – and while still abroad – he prayed that God would 'protect, shield and deliver from their unspeakably ferocious enemies, the helpless women and children, outraged, tortured, murdered by the incarnate fiends of Hindustan.' He felt that history nowhere presented anything at all equal to the 'bloody and refined tortures, mental and bodily that (had) been inflicted by the mutineers on Europeans of both sexes and all ages, even on babies at the breast.' It seemed, he continued, as if a temporary licence, the power of a plenipotentiary had been given to Satan himself and all his crew: 'one is aghast in reading the events.'[61] He wrote to Evelyn that he thought of such things day and night: 'what a worse than devil is man unsoftened by Christianity and left to himself!', was his comment.[62] But he was also filled with admiration at the conduct of the British. He felt that every one of them in India had shown coolness, judgment and patriotism in the crisis.

Shaftesbury also urged that the most severe measures should be taken to put down the Mutiny. He wrote to Palmerston, Panmure and others counselling the levy of African regiments,[63] and he also wrote at length to Clarendon on the same theme.[64] Africans would make first-rate soldiers, could bear the climate, would be cheaper than Europeans and would show no sympathy for the natives. He urged the total destruction of Delhi – in his view, the extinction of a place defiled by the unprincipled cruelties of Hindus and Mohammedans would be an act of justice and judgment. Delhi was also the memorial and centre of the Mogul Dynasty, and the Mohammedans of India looked to it as the exiled Jews looked to Jerusalem. So long as Delhi stood, he continued, so long would Mohammedan intrigues prevail. 'Destroy it,' Shaftesbury wrote, 'and you will altogether destroy a great part of their confidence and a still greater part of their means to raise their fanatical people.' Further, Shaftesbury favoured stern reprisals and retribution on those who had been involved in the murders and the massacres. There should be no outright vengeance, he told Clarendon, but 'every line of God's Book demands that those to whom He has confided the rule of this lower world should execute Judgment and Justice.' Unless retribution were carried out, the assertion of law and order would be undermined and all the hopes of isolated Europeans living in peace and security under the Queen's rule would vanish. Women and children and the private property of the poor must be held sacred, but every man directly or indirectly implicated in the massacres should die on the gallows and every other 'untainted by blood' should be sentenced for life to penal servitude in the West Indies. There should also be extensive rewards offered to those who had remained loyal: 'Let there be no stint to white men and black,' he advised Clarendon, 'of crowns, ribbons, promotions, titles, money payments. Let every true, courageous, faithful man have, if possible, his heart's desire.'[65]

On his return to Britain, Shaftesbury continued to develop these themes, but now he gave public expression to them. On 30 October, at Wimborne Minster, he told a meeting to raise funds for the relief of the sufferers in the Massacre that atrocities had been committed on a scale unprecedented since the days of the early Christians. He deprecated silence or reserve about these events, and he urged on his hearers the importance of justice and retribution in very similar terms to those which he had used to Clarendon. If severe measures were not taken, British tenure of India and all the advantages which it brought with it, would be lost. But there must be action beyond this. Having executed justice on the culprits, everything should be forgotten and every effort concentrated on advancing the country's 'temporal and eternal interests'. This, Shaftesbury trusted, would be 'the beginning of a new order of things of freedom, of judgment, of knowledge, of good government for all those mighty myriads confided to our care.' He also spoke of a 'far higher consideration' which should occupy Britain's attention. She must declare that the government of India was a Christian government, resting on Christian principles, and, although she must be prepared to allow the Hindus and Mohammedans the same countenance and protection as the Christians, she must bend every missionary effort to spread the Gospel. Everything proved, he concluded, that Britain was reserved as a nation to advance the civilisation of 'these millions of the human race and to be the agents in the promulgation of the Gospel of His Blessed Son. . . .'[66] Shaftesbury also voiced his views on such matters at the meetings of the missionary societies with which he was connected. He urged on the British and Foreign Bible Society the need for activity in sending out missionaries and copies of the Bible, pointing out that the scriptures were not allowed to penetrate to Bengal, where the outbreak had occurred. He wished to show, he said, that the principle of the diffusion of the scriptures was in India, as everywhere, 'the only true, lasting and conservative principle for empires and nations'.[67]

If Shaftesbury spoke at length on platforms in the country on the Indian Mutiny, he also addressed the Lords on the subject. One notable occasion arose from a proclamation addressed by Lord Canning, Governor-General of India, to the chiefs and peoples of Oudh, confiscating the property of the native landowners who had not remained loyal to the British government, although, if no crime had been committed against them, there was the possibility of restoration. Derby's minority government of 1858-9, however, disavowed this proclamation and Ellenborough, President of the Board of Control, issued a despatch censuring the Governor-General for his harshness. The despatch aroused unfavourable comment, and, in both Houses, votes of censure were moved. The vote in the Lords was moved by Shaftesbury.[68] He acknowledged that, in so doing, he was speaking against the party which represented his political sympathies, but this did not deter him from taking a critical attitude. And, although a long-standing critic of Ellenborough, he denied that he was actuated by personal animosity. He did, however, recall that Ellenborough, when Governor-General, had confiscated the territories of the Ameers of Scinde: an action which had not been considered by everyone as 'just, righteous and becoming'. But the subsequent government had not reversed this policy – it had simply restored the Ameers to liberty without restoring their territory. It was, indeed, an impossibility for one government to renounce the policy of its predecessor, and, in the present case, could it be wise, he asked, to announce to a people in arms against Britain that they were not rebels, but warriors fighting for their own country and their own rights? The Proclamation issued by Canning had, in his view, been thoroughly commendable: it was not only the best policy, but 'the most solemn Christian duty' to put down the rebellion, punish the specific insurgents and then do all that could be done for the moral and physical welfare of the peoples of India. Ellenborough had claimed that Canning's proclamation would make the restoration of peace more difficult. On the contrary, Shaftesbury argued, it was Ellenborough's despatch which would do this, for it would make the people of Oudh believe that they had been unjustly treated. Shaftesbury thus called on the House to express its disapproval of the despatch on the grounds that it was calculated to weaken the authority of the Governor-General and encourage those now in arms against Britain. His motion was, however, lost by nine votes.

Shaftesbury's role over the Indian Mutiny was, therefore, an extremely active one, but some of his comments aroused an acrimonious controversy. In his speech at Wimborne Minster on 30 October, he had claimed that he had seen a letter from 'the highest lady now in India' – Lady Canning – stating that day by day ladies were coming into Calcutta with their ears and noses cut off and their eyes put out.[69] Very young children had been put to death 'under circumstances of the most exquisite torture' before the eyes of their parents; the parents had been made to swallow portions of the flesh cut from the limbs of their children and they themselves had then been burned over a slow fire 'to gratify the malignity of the hellish temperament of those creatures who bore the human form.' Shaftesbury repeated these points in another speech later in November.[70] But such accounts of the atrocities were challenged in a letter published in *The Times* on 29 January, 1858,[71] and a further letter of 2 February asked Shaftesbury to substantiate his assertions or withdraw them. Shaftesbury's statements, the letter claimed, had 'harrowed the feelings and excited the passions of thousands,' coming as they did avowedly with all the authority of one who by his high connections, claims to be near the source of correct information, and who by his position as the head of a great religious party ought to be especially careful not to deviate from accurate truth nor needlessly to inflame uncharitableness, hatred and violence, even against heathens.[72]

The matter was taken further by a third letter to *The Times* published on 3 February,[73] which looked forward to Shaftesbury's reply, especially since well-informed persons now denied that Lady Canning had written any such letter. Shaftesbury duly replied on 4 February.[74] He said that someone in whom he had 'entire confidence' had told him that there was a letter from Lady Canning about mutilated ladies arriving in Calcutta. But in his speech, he had meant to say that he had *heard* of this letter. The papers reported 'saw', but he had corrected it in his speech and had circulated the correction. He acknowledged that he should have been more careful, but he still held to the view that children had been put to death in cold blood. Another letter to *The Times* on 6 February[75] thanked Shaftesbury for clarifying the matter, but still argued that he had implied a further correction: to say that children had been murdered in cold blood was different from his original statement that they had been subjected to the 'most exquisite torture'. Shaftesbury, moreover, not only incurred the criticism of the letter writer – or writers – to *The Times*: he was also warmly criticised by Lady Canning herself. On Christmas Eve, 1857, she wrote to Lord Granville that 'truth was not a flourishing plant anywhere just at present.' She continued that the 'highest lady in India' felt much inclined to call out Lord Shaftesbury. 'What *can* he have said that he saw in her letter?' she asked. And she continued that she had certainly *heard* of one lady without nose and ears, but never *believed* in her existence, and she could only have named it as a story she had heard. And she had never written that such mutilated visitors had arrived in Calcutta day after day.[76] At the end of February, 1858, she wrote that the stories of mutilated people were 'wholly and entirely untrue' in so far as they were told of Calcutta and she had never heard of them at any other place. 'I am more than indignant at Lord Shaftesbury's abominably untrue speech,' she wrote. 'I wish he would learn that it is wrong not to ascertain the truth of what he asserts.'[77]

Shaftesbury thus emerged from the episode under considerable criticism. Greville also struck a critical note of Shaftesbury's activities. Noting in his Diary that he had received a letter from Lady Canning complaining of the exaggeration of the atrocities in the newspapers, he added that Shaftesbury, 'who is a prodigious authority with the Public, and who has all the religious and pseudo-religious people at his back,' was doing his best to 'make the case out to be as bad as possible and to excite the rage and indignation of the masses to the highest pitch.' Shaftesbury, Greville claimed, was not satisfied with the 'revolting details' contained in the press, but felt that the 'particulars of mutilation and violation' had not received sufficient attention. Greville could not understand Shaftesbury's motives for taking such an attitude, 'but,' he wrote, 'it is no doubt something connected with the grand plan of Christianising India, in the furtherance of which the High Church and the Low Church appear to be bidding against each other. . . .' Their joint efforts, Greville added sardonically, would probably be irresistible, and this would make any government in India impossible.[78]

The matter, however, did not rest there. Shaftesbury's continuing insistence that atrocities had not been fully reported was challenged in a letter from a Mr Hargreaves on 11 March, 1858.[79] He wished to know Shaftesbury's sources for this, since it had come to his knowledge that the Relief Committee in Calcutta had not found any such cases, nor had the Directors of the East India Company. There followed a correspondence[80] between Hargreaves and Shaftesbury, in which Shaftesbury adhered to his belief that atrocities had taken place but refused to give evidence for this belief. Hargreaves, for his part, kept up his questioning. Shaftesbury terminated his side of the correspondence on 17 March, 1858, by advising Hargreaves to write to someone in India; he would then easily ascertain the facts. Hargreaves retorted two days later, asking how anyone in India could know what was alone known to Shaftesbury, and, again, he asked Shaftesbury to prove his points or retract them – they had, he claimed, 'stimulated to a frightful degree the vindictive passions of our countrymen.' Shaftesbury was further criticised by *The Saturday Review* of 27 March, 1858, which gave an account of the whole proceedings: the original speech made by Shaftesbury, the subsequent correspondence in *The Times* and the correspondence with Hargreaves. Shaftesbury was condemned for carelessness and inaccuracy unworthy of a religious leader. He dwelt 'in a serene atmosphere, far above the motives or appeals of this common, vulgar, truth-seeking, accurate world. He contemplates only his own perfections and the interests of religion.'[81]

Shaftesbury had clearly made an error in his original speech over the letter from Lady Canning: this brought on him, as he put it, a 'world of troubles'.[82] Granville wrote to Canning that Shaftesbury had been obliged to 'eat dirt' about Lady Canning's letter and was much abused for his 'inaccuracy and thirst for feeding the popular delusion, whatever it may be.' And, he added, 'he deserves it.'[83] When Shaftesbury himself reflected on the incident many years later, in 1873,[84] he realised that he should have said that he had, a few days earlier, heard a lady whom he knew well[85] say that she had just come from a house where she had heard a letter from Lady Canning read out, recounting many and fearful mutilations. But, although the error was one which should have been avoided, Shaftesbury did at least try to correct it at the time and conceded his mistake on 4 February. Again, as far as Lady Canning was concerned, relations between her and Shaftesbury were healed by Shaftesbury's defence of her husband in the vote of censure debate. Lady Canning wrote expressing her delight at Shaftesbury's 'admirable speech': it was, she said, 'a very great comfort in such anxious and troubled times to find that the cause, in which one is so deeply interested, is so ably and heartily defended. . . .' She also mentioned the controversy in which Shaftesbury had been involved. She was sure that he would find it 'nearly hopeless' to get at the truth of the Indian stories in England, and, if there was any truth in the stories she read from England, she felt that they must relate to persons who had returned *via* Bombay, of whom she had no knowledge.[86] But if Shaftesbury's original comments were more ill-judged than ill-intentioned, his conduct towards his questioner, Hargreaves, is less easy to defend. He himself complained that, whereas the first phase of his troubles arose from those who treated him as a 'wilful misrepresenter of Lady Canning' – a charge of which he could scarcely be condemned – the second phase – with Hargreaves – arose from efforts to prove that he was 'bloodthirsty and false, a savage and a liar'. And, he added: 'they have not proved it to my satisfaction, but they have to their own, and to that, I doubt not, of many others.'[87] But such an interpretation of the points made by Hargreaves is scarcely tenable, and, in any event, Shaftesbury himself did nothing to clarify the matter. He disdainfully refused to be drawn into discussion with Hargreaves and laid himself open to the criticism which he received. The whole episode was, indeed, a further illustration of the way in which Shaftesbury could allow firmly held opinions to lead him into ill-advised remarks: in a sense, his conduct over the matter suffered from the same weakness as his wholesale condemnation of *Ecce Homo*. Nevertheless, the more constructive remarks of his ill-fated Wimborne speech should not be forgotten – those which dwelt on the future of India after the Mutiny. And immediately after the Mutiny, Shaftesbury took an active role in the foundation of the Christian Vernacular Education Society for India, which sought to lay the foundation of a general system of Christian education in India by establishing training schools in which missionaries might be taught the vernacular language. The Society also published educational material which would be of assistance to missionaries. Shaftesbury, speaking at one of its annual meetings in 1865 mentioned the particular importance of raising up a 'native agency'. He believed that without this, no effect whatever could be produced.

> Your mission [he said] is not simply to send out a body of men who are to be the guides and governors of that country but you are to train that

whole people, religiously, socially, politically and civilly, so that hereafter they may be their own masters. . . . What is the vernacular language that you use but a native agency?[88]

These sentiments were much in harmony with the ideas on India which Shaftesbury had held in the 1820s[89] and which, after the Mutiny, he continued to support. In 1876 he was to say that a time might come when

> after a long course of happy rule, we may surrender India to natives, grown into a capability of self-government. Our posterity may then see an enlargement of the glorious spectacle we now witness, when India shall be added to the roll of free and independent Powers that wait on the Mother Country and daily rise up and call her blessed.[90]

Certainly, in his view, this could not be done without training the natives to harbour 'British sentiments', infusing them with 'British principle' and imbuing them with 'British feeling'. But his ideas were far-seeing. And, more immediately, Shaftesbury supported plans in 1861 for the extension of irrigation and internal navigation in India. These would prevent the recurrence of a famine which had recently struck North West India. It is true that Britain had an interest in this: the outbreak of the American Civil War was clearly to threaten British cotton supplies. Britain, Shaftesbury argued, should learn the lesson of relying on one source of cotton. The plans which he supported would prevent this. Nothing came of them, but they were positive and would have brought benefit to India in addition to Britain.[91] Thus Shaftesbury's remarks about the atrocities of the Mutiny, hasty and ill-judged as they were, should not be allowed to obscure the constructive and visionary plans which he had long entertained and to which he remained faithful.

A further area of long-standing interest for Shaftesbury was Italy. It will be recalled that, in 1834, he had written that the millenium of European policy would be the establishment of a 'Kingdom of Italy',[92] but, at that time, it was only a dream. As the dream seemed to have more chance of being transformed into reality, Shaftesbury's interest became keener. He wrote to Clarendon in 1855, expressing his dislike of Austria. This was on a number of grounds. There was, for example, her 'dependence on the Papacy and that of the Papacy on her', and he also mentioned Austria's oppressions in Italy and, in particular, in Piedmont-Sardinia

> We admire, beyond measure [he wrote] the character and attitude of that noble little state: and there is hardly an Englishman in the three Kingdoms who would not call upon the Queen to sustain, *with her whole Power*, the people of Piedmont against the Emperor of Austria. . . .[93]

Once war had broken out in 1859 between Austria on the one hand and Piedmont-Sardinia in alliance with France on the other, Shaftesbury's sympathies were unequivocally on the side of Piedmont-Sardinia, and he explained his reasons in a letter to *The Record*. Sardinia, he wrote, had declared and proved herself to be the defender of civil and religious liberty in Italy. She had assisted the Waldensians and permitted the 'free preaching of God's word in public and in private'. Where in Europe, Shaftesbury asked, was the circulation of the Scriptures 'so open, so wide, so countenanced by the authority of the state?' Her policy was to resist the encroachments of the Roman Catholic Church, whereas Austria was the declared enemy of civil and religious liberty and was the 'chief, perhaps sole, support of Papal tyranny in Central Italy'. Shaftesbury added that, with Parliament not in session, there could be no expression of the public voice, but, he wrote:

> Let us all, singly or unitedly . . . implore Almighty God that the nascent cause of 'Truth, Justice, Religion and Piety' may, by His blessing, speedily and universally prevail in lands so long in thraldom to ignorance and oppression.[94]

Shaftesbury suffered some criticism for expressing such positive support for one party in a struggle in which Britain was not officially involved. One of his critics was Clarendon, who wrote that he shared Shaftesbury's hatred of the Austrian system of government, but he feared that the eviction of Austria from Italy would result in its replacement by French influence, and France, he argued, had no desire to promote the cause of liberty.[95] Shaftesbury, however, was unrepentant, and, in a speech to the Bible Society in May, 1859, he stated his position. He had not concealed his sympathies 'upon this great question' and did not intend 'at any time, or in any place, or under any circumstances to conceal them.' He took up a point – somewhat related to that which Clarendon made – that in denouncing Austria, he had been defending the conduct of the Emperor and the French. This he strongly denied. His letter had only been concerned to point out the contrast between Sardinia and Austria: 'between merit and demerit . . .' And, even if he had felt obliged to defend the conduct of Napoleon III, he could have pointed out that 'the word of God, under his rule, has a free circulation throughout the whole of the French Empire.' And he repeated his earlier plea that all who cared for religious liberty and for the revival of religion in 'these benighted regions of the earth' should come forward and express sympathy for the Sardinian cause.[96]

In addition to his efforts in the press and on the platform, Shaftesbury had personal contacts by interview or letter with individuals in official positions. He was on very friendly terms with Emanuele d'Azeglio, the

Sardinian minister in London, and, on occasion, passed on information from d'Azeglio to Palmerston.[97] Before the war broke out, he was invited to meet Emanuele's uncle, Massimo, whose literary and political efforts on behalf of Sardinia were renowned. Shaftesbury was pleased with the invitation issued by Malmesbury, Foreign Secretary in the Derby-Disraeli Ministry of 1858–9, while Massimo d'Azeglio was on a special visit to Britain in 1859. 'My known sentiments towards Sardinia,' Shaftesbury wrote, 'are thus recognised by the Minister as those he is not afraid to countenance; and I may, too, have an opportunity of dropping a word in season.'[98] A few days later, Shaftesbury arranged a dinner for Massimo d'Azeglio and Delane, editor of *The Times* – this, he felt, might lead to 'ten thousand truths towards the defence of Sardinian freedom and European Peace.' The fact that these two occasions took place in Holy Week shows the importance which Shaftesbury placed on them: they were, he wrote, two things which he should ordinarily have refused.[99] In June, 1859, moreover, Shaftesbury was consulted by the French ambassador, de Persigny, as to the feeling of Britain towards France. Shaftesbury took the opportunity once again to express British support for Sardinia and for Italy. He wrote of an 'earnest, deliberate and lasting sympathy for the revival of Italy and its deliverance from the many and various oppressions of its peoples' and he assured the ambassador that Sardinia was regarded with the 'greatest affection and hope'. As far as France was concerned, he told de Persigny that there was a certain suspicion of France in Britain. Experience of the first Empire led British people to fear that Napoleon III's campaign in Italy might be a scheme for territorial aggrandisement in Europe and the wisest course for the Emperor would be to take the first opportunity – as, for example, after a great victory – to publish a proclamation to assure Europe that he had no objective except the liberation of Italy, and that, having achieved this, he would retire within the French frontier without taking anything for himself.[100] In August, 1859, there was another exchange of letters.[101] Shaftesbury wrote that the feeling towards the Emperor was now more calm and there was greater confidence in his intentions towards Italy and Europe. He still stressed, however, the importance of Italy being left to manage her own affairs: any foreign intervention would be regarded as 'cruel, tyrannical, wicked and foolish.' The British people would not believe that Napoleon III contemplated such intervention, nor did they think that he would permit the Emperor of Austria to do it. He added that the only thing which kept alive suspicion was the fact that the French troops had been in Rome since 1849 and remained there: this, he wrote, 'none of us like or understand.' But there were other reasons for suspicion, as rumours grew in 1860 that Napoleon III was demanding the surrender of Savoy and Nice. Shaftesbury again used his official connections to express his point of view. He wrote to Palmerston in January, 1860,[102] that such an action would gravely discredit Napoleon III. It would make it appear that 'other motives than those of generosity prompted his action.' He also felt that there would be deep public antipathy in Britain if the British government did not protest against such an action. The country would consider the act 'a return to the old system of dealing with nations like flocks of sheep and handing them over as articles of barter and exchange.' It would lead to the apprehension that France was seeking 'natural boundaries': the acquisition of Savoy might be followed by an effort to obtain the Rhine. In February, 1860, Shaftesbury rehearsed the same points when speaking in the Lords in support of an Address to the Queen, asking her to direct her government to use their endeavours to prevent the transfer of Savoy and Nice to France.[103] But it was to no avail. After plebiscites, Savoy and Nice went to France – 'Savoy and Nice,' Shaftesbury wrote in March, 1860, 'are handed over like sheep to the Usurper of France.'[104]

Shaftesbury was in contact, moreover, not only with officials and ministers in Britain. He also had links with persons in Sardinia and in Italy directly involved in the struggle. He wrote to Cavour in February, 1860, congratulating him on his return to office after his period of retirement following the ending of the war by the Peace of Villafranca. The feeling in England, among all who desired the welfare of Italy, he wrote, was one of joy and gratitude to God for Cavour's return, and no one could entertain that feeling more strongly than he did himself. He also took the opportunity to mention the possibility of the separation of Savoy and Nice and urged Cavour never to listen to any such scheme. He said that it would 'tarnish very much the motives and conduct of the Emperor of the French, and, not a little, the motives and conduct of the Sardinian Government. It would throw a stain on the whole efforts for National Independence, and entirely alienate the affections of Englishmen.' He asked Cavour to excuse him for writing in these terms: 'it (was) forced on (him) by the very deep respect (he felt) for the honour and welfare of Italy.'[105] After Cavour's death in 1861, Shaftesbury was in touch with his successor, Ricasoli. Ricasoli wrote in 1862 of his gratitude for British support and sympathy for Sardinia and of the further need for Rome to be freed from the presence of French troops. He ended his letter asking Shaftesbury to 'continue to wish us well; for the Italians will ever imitate the English in their love of independence and liberty.' In sending his 'best wishes and esteem', he signed himself 'your devoted Ricasoli'.[106] Shaftesbury also developed close links with Garibaldi. In November, 1859, he received a letter from an Italian resident in London, G. F. Avesani, asking that Shaftesbury might take an interest in forming an English committee to assist Italian independence.[107] A second letter[108] from Avesani explained that several British people had expressed the desire to respond to an appeal made by Garibaldi to the Italian people and had promised contributions for the purchase of muskets for Central Italy. Avesani had been entrusted by Garibaldi to open subscriptions in Britain and had replied to the offers through the medium of an open letter in the *Daily News*.[109] Shaftesbury was anxious to help Garibaldi. No one, he wrote, could be more anxious than he to show respect to Garibaldi. 'He seems to me,' was his comment, 'to be one of the noblest fellows that ever lived; just the sort of man that the English ought to reverence and support.'[110] And he wrote a long and sympathetic letter to Avesani.[111] He would not accept the Chairmanship of the Committee until its function was more clearly defined and, in fact, the Committee was not formed: its association with subscriptions for Garibaldi had met with criticism. But his letter to Avesani had appeared in the press and caused considerable enthusiasm in Italy. Garibaldi wrote to him in 1859, expressing gratitude for his support and urging him to maintain his active assistance.[112] Answering this in January, 1860, Shaftesbury urged Garibaldi to come to Britain to receive assistance himself from the British people.[113] This proved impossible at that time – Garibaldi was preoccupied with his progress north through Italy. Shaftesbury followed his exploits with the greatest interest. He noted in June, 1860, that Garibaldi had achieved wonderful results: 'It seems to me,' he wrote, 'that God's protecting and accompanying power has repeated for him the miracle of Gideon and his 300 ... My heart has been with him all along. It is now with him more than ever. ...'[114] In October, he wrote that he earnestly prayed for Garibaldi 'that great man, that noblest hero and champion since the days of Gideon or the Maccabees'.[115] When Garibaldi did finally visit Britain in 1864, Shaftesbury played a prominent part in meeting and accompanying him on his various engagements. At a banquet given in Garibaldi's honour, Shaftesbury said that 'of that name no man can speak without emotion. He is a man that represents, in himself, the best qualities that adorn mankind.'[116] On Garibaldi's departure, Shaftesbury gave him a New Testament in Italian as a gift, and Garibaldi's portrait hung in Shaftesbury's library in Grosvenor Square. This was a lasting testimony of the enthusiasm with which, from the first, Shaftesbury had regarded the cause of Italian Unity.

The other foreign issues which occupied much of Shaftesbury's attention in the first half of the 1860s were the American Civil War and the Polish Rebellion. His attitude towards the American Civil War was entirely consistent with the sentiments which he had expressed in the 1850s on the subject of slavery. He was, at that time, active in various anti-slavery projects,[117] and, later in the 1850s, he returned to similar themes in his thoughts and writings. In 1856, he wrote that America baffled his judgment, disturbed his faith and left him 'at a nonplus as to the character of right and wrong, of wisdom and folly, in the conduct of men and nations.' And he went on to explain the reasons for his bewilderment: 'A people of democratic freedom and license keeps, in subjection the most ... cruel and degrading, in slavery the most frightful, some millions of their fellow men. ...' This, he felt, would have been hideous and disgusting in ancient Rome or 'among the Bechuana or in the Feegee (sic) Islands':

> But [he continued], what is it in a Country which calls itself Christian? Which has the light of the Bible? Which has declared the equality of all mankind? Which sends out missionaries to convert the Heathen? It is not the unauthorised career of a few, of a section of the people. It is the law of the land, the lawful custom of the Country....[118]

He felt, too, that, for ignoring basic Biblical teaching, retribution must be at hand. In 1861, when addressing the British and Foreign Bible Society, he used the American issue to prove the relevance of the Bible. He asked if the Bible could be unsuited to the present times, for, had its precepts and commands been heeded:

> we should not have before us those gigantic cruelties that pervade the continent of America, the non-observance of which precepts has now led to that great and astounding issue, the severance and demolition of the largest Republic that ever figured upon the face of the earth.[119]

Thus, in the War, there could be no doubt where Shaftesbury's sympathies would lie. He was a strong supporter of the North. He wrote to *The Times* at the beginning of the War that 'the triumph of the South meant the consolidation of slavery.'[120] He felt that the best solution would be the separation of North and South. 'A quiet and peaceful severance would prove best for America and the world,' he wrote. 'The severance will take place at last.'[121] Such comments were, indeed, over-dramatic: and his view of the War as a struggle between freedom and slavery was over-simplified. But on that issue, he knew no compromise.

The same was to be true of Shaftesbury's attitude towards the Polish uprising of 1863 and the Russian subjection of it. There was considerable sympathy in Britain for the fate of the Poles and, at a public meeting in March, 1863, in the Guildhall, Shaftesbury spoke at length on the subject.[122] It was, he said, not a rebellion: it was a 'great and glorious uprising of a wronged and abused nation, driven to despair by a series of cruelties unprecedented in history.' And he gave full rein to his anti-Russian sentiments urging that it should go forth from the meeting that the English nation condemned in the strongest manner the violence, the cruelty, the savagery to which, to an extent unparalleled . . . the Czar and his myrmidons lent their sanction. Let them be told that by such acts they disgraced themselves in the eyes of the world and violated every principle of Christianity.

He also followed these efforts by a long and strongly worded speech in the Lords on 8 May, when presenting the petition for the Guildhall and other meetings.[123] But he was distressed by the fact that nothing could be done to assist the Poles. He wrote to Edward Beales in February that he 'wanted words' to express 'how deep, how constant, how burning' were his feelings towards the Poles. This, no doubt, was not of material importance, but would anything further be of any avail? There was, he felt, too little international interest in the matter to make any assistance to the Poles a realistic proposition, and it could be that an exhibition of sympathy could encourage prolonged and hopeless resistance in the face of 'all the horrors that the insolence and cruelty of their atrocious Rulers can invest and inflict.'[124]

Thus, between 1854 and 1865, Shaftesbury showed a keen and continuing interest in the various foreign issues which marked the period. Many of his reactions were instinctive and impetuous, and sometimes – as over the Indian Mutiny – this could lead him to judgments and courses of action which might have been prevented by more patience and prudence. On other occasions, as with Sardinia and Garibaldi, he could be led by his impetuousness to embrace a cause to an extent which went beyond the limits of diplomacy. His admiration for Garibaldi may, indeed, have owed something to the element of impulsiveness which Garibaldi displayed in the service of a cause in which he believed – an element also to be found in Shaftesbury himself. Nevertheless, there were certain consistent principles to be discerned in Shaftesbury's attitudes. One was his support for the Jewish cause and his desire to further it whenever the opportunity arose. The affairs of countries such as China or America would not, he wrote, 'hasten (or) retard the final development of man's destiny on earth.' Prophecy was 'busy with these empires only that affect His ancient people. . . .'[125] Thus the affairs of the Turkish Empire were always of special concern to him, and, throughout the Crimean War, he tried to assert and assist the cause of the Jews. He wrote to Clarendon in 1855, thanking him for his patience in listening to his propositions: he rejoiced that he had been instrumental in persuading a Minister at the Foreign Office to undertake the cause of the Jewish people.[126] A further constant concern of Shaftesbury was his desire to promote missionary endeavour and the circulation of the Bible and to secure the advancement of religious liberty and Protestantism. Memorialists approaching him on behalf of French Protestants in 1854 wrote of him as the 'steady advocate of religious Liberty in every part of the world',[127] and his approaches to Napoleon III during the Crimean War, his urging of missionary work in India and his attitude towards Italy bear out this description. He did not, indeed, favour such a direct approach as some of his co-religionists. Thus, in March, 1861, he refused to accept office as President of a society to spread the Gospel in Italy. He felt that its activities in seeking 'the Evangelisation of Italy' were likely to arouse indignation: a nation of 'intellectual men, with high traditions (and) ancient history' would, understandably, react unfavourably to the implication that they were 'utterly ignorant of the fundamentals of Christianity and need the instruction of a Protestant people.'[128] Nevertheless, he was President of the London Committee of a Society for the Reformation of Religion in Italy. This was a Society based in Italy. In 1861, one of its members, Signor Gavazzi, visited London and asked for the support of British Christians to assist with various measures to spread the Gospel in Italy, including the provision of a good supply of books, especially commentaries on the Bible, and the establishment of a printing office to publish a daily Evangelical paper. The London Committee commended this work and asked for contributions towards it.[129] And, if religious considerations permeated Shaftesbury's views on the foreign issues of the period, moral concern was also amply evident. Thus there was his continuing opposition to the Opium Trade and his support for what he saw as 'righteous causes': the punishment of wrong-doers in the Indian Mutiny, the anti-slavery movement, the claims of small nations and oppressed people – Italians or Poles – against despotic or arbitrary rule.

Finally, in international, no less than in personal, affairs, Shaftesbury had a strong sense of the Providence of God. He admitted that the idea of 'Special Providences' was a difficult and delicate one: 'to allow it fully, in almost every trifling instance,' he once wrote, 'seems to cripple man's free agency, and supersede secondary causes; to deny it, is to deny God's goodness and mercy and His moral government of mankind!'[130] But, despite the difficulties, Shaftesbury was firmly convinced that, on several occasions in her history, Britain had been specially favoured by God. This belief reinforced his view that, if Britain proved unworthy of God's goodness, she must repent and seek forgiveness, and, more positively, that Britain should behave in a way which accorded with the 'moral government' of God. He was not afraid or ashamed to advance British interests if he felt that they did accord with God's purposes. Britain, indeed, had a duty to use her influence to promote good and resist evil, and force might be used if it were necessary to 'back any right or redress any wrong.'[131] Shaftesbury regarded those who looked on foreign policy in purely material and commercial terms with scorn and contempt. The policy of the free traders would, he felt, reduce

Britain's influence to nil and would mean that nothing approaching chivalry or sentiment could ever again stir her to action. Such an attitude was, he felt, evident in Britain's reaction to the war conducted by Prussia and Austria against Denmark in 1864 over the Schleswig-Holstein issue. Britain had been a party to the Treaty of London in 1852, which had made a settlement of the duchies of Schleswig and Holstein, and, although Shaftesbury conceded that Britain could not go to war alone on behalf of Denmark in 1864, he felt that the justification of her neutrality made by Russell, the Foreign Secretary, was an announcement to the world that Britain henceforth 'can form no alliances, guarantee no treaties and give no active expression in support of any principles whatever.'[132] If the greater powers had nothing to fear and the weaker powers nothing to hope for from Britain unless her commercial interests were directly affected, it was, he argued, hard to see 'on what grounds her influence (would) be based.'[133] This materialistic approach to foreign issues was, he felt, also evident in what he regarded as the meagre financial provision made for the war effort in the Crimea and the poor response to appeals launched on behalf of those who suffered in the Indian Mutiny and in the Indian Famine: on behalf, too, of the Poles and the Danes. And all this was, in Shaftesbury's view, a further manifestation of that preoccupation with wealth and material enjoyment which he saw – and so deplored – in the 1850s and 1860s. 'The love of money and its cohesive power,' he wrote, 'increase with its bulk.'[134] And, as in domestic, so in foreign affairs, Shaftesbury regarded Palmerston as the only guarantor of his ideas – after Palmerston, he wrote, the free trade school would 'rule all things'. Then British foreign policy would be shamefully stripped of honour, righteousness and any sense of – or claim on – God's guiding hand.

NOTES

1. N.R.A., Shaftesbury (Broadlands) MSS, SHA/PD/6, 30 May, 1853.
2. ibid., SHA/PD/6, 30 May, 1853.
3. ibid., SHA/PD/6, 6 June, 1853.
4. Bodleian Library, Clarendon MSS, Dep. c 19, fos 196–7.
5. Hansard, *Parl. Debates*, 3rd ser., CXXXI, 591–604.
6. See above p. 343.
7. Quoted in Hodder, II, 468.
8. ibid., 469–72.
9. N.R.A., Shaftesbury (Broadlands) MSS, SHA/PD/7, 5 July, 1855.
10. The correspondence is referred to ibid., SHA/PD/6, 30 July, 1853.
11. ibid., SHA/PD/6, 7 May, 1854.
12. ibid., SHA/PD/6, 12 Nov., 1854.
13. Quoted in Hodder, II, 484.

14. N.R.A., Shaftesbury (Broadlands) MSS, SHA/PD/6, 27 Nov., 1854.
15. ibid., SHA/PD/6, 17 Nov., 1854.
16. See above p. 335.
17. N.R.A., Shaftesbury (Broadlands) MSS, SHA/PD/6, 29, 30 Nov., 1854.
18. ibid., SHA/PD/6, 23 Dec., 1854.
19. ibid., SHA/PD/6, 23 Dec., 1854. Shaftesbury slightly modified his views on Raglan's death in 1855. 'He was a fine specimen of a soldier and a gentleman,' he wrote: but also added 'nothing would ever induce him to recognise in his despatches, the superintending providence of Almighty God.' (ibid., SHA/PD/7, 1 July, 1855).
20. See above p. 366.
21. See above pp. 373-5.
22. Add. MSS, 43, 252, fos 155-6, 309.
23. N.R.A., Shaftesbury (Broadlands) MSS, SHA/PD/6, 14 Feb., 1855.
24. ibid., SHA/PD/6, 15 Feb., 1855.
25. ibid., SHA/PD/6, 14 Feb., 1855.
26. ibid., SHA/PD/6, 15 Feb., 1855.
27. St G.H., Shaftesbury MSS, C 25067/7th Earl.
28. N.R.A., Shaftesbury (Broadlands) MSS, SHA/PD/6, 15 Feb., 1855.
29. Sir George Douglas and Sir George Dalhousie Ramsay (eds.), *The Panmure Papers* (2 vols., 1908), I, 68.
30. St G.H., Shaftesbury MSS, C 25070/7th Earl.
31. ibid., Shaftesbury MSS, C 25074/7th Earl. See also Battiscombe, p. 247.
32. St G.H., Shaftesbury MSS, C 25072/7th Earl. (copy.)
33. ibid., Shaftesbury MSS, C 25073/7th Earl. (copy).
34. Palmerston wrote to Panmure in June, 1855, saying that Shaftesbury had told him that he (i.e. Shaftesbury) had been in touch with Panmure and had recommended that other doctors should be sent out to assist those originally appointed. They would make arrangements for the general health of the troops and organise a system of tent to tent visitation to check cholera. 'This,' writes Palmerston, 'would be a very judicious step and the sooner it was adopted the better.' (Sir George Douglas and Sir George Dalhousie Ramsay (eds.), op. cit., I, 230).
35. Chadwick MSS, 19 Mar., 1855. (Gavin to Shaftesbury).
36. ibid., 21 June, 1855. (Sutherland to Shaftesbury).
37. Battiscombe, p. 248.
38. St G.H., Shaftesbury MSS, C 25026.8/7th Earl.
39. Quoted in Hodder, III, 145.
40. Clarendon MSS, Dep. c 19, f. 487.
41. N.R.A., Shaftesbury (Broadlands) MSS, SHA/PD/7, 13 Nov., 1855.
42. ibid., SHA/PD/7, 16 Feb., 1856.
43. ibid., SHA/PD/7, 18 Feb., 1856.
44. Clarendon MSS, Dep. c 54, fos 201-2.
45. ibid.
46. N.R.A., Shaftesbury (Broadlands) MSS, SHA/PD/7, 31 Mar., 1856.
47. See above pp. 174-6.
48. N.R.A., Shaftesbury (Broadlands) MSS, SHA/PD/7, 27 Feb., 1857.
49. ibid., SHA/PD/7, 27 Feb., 1857.
50. ibid., SHA/PD/7, 4 Mar., 1857.
51. Hansard, *Parl. Debates*, 3rd ser., CXLIV, 2027-33.
52. N.R.A., Shaftesbury (Broadlands) MSS, SHA/PD/7, 9 Mar., 1857.
53. Hammonds, p. 244.

54. N.R.A., Shaftesbury (Broadlands) MSS, SHA/PD/7, 4 Mar., 1857.
55. ibid., SHA/PD/7, 8 Mar., 1857.
56. ibid., SHA/PD/7, 8 Mar., 1857.
57. ibid., SHA/PD/7, 4 Mar., 1857.
58. ibid., SHA/PD/7, 21 July, 1857.
59. ibid., SHA/PD/7, 29 Aug., 1857.
60. Quoted in Hodder, III, 56.
61. N.R.A., Shaftesbury (Broadlands) MSS, SHA/PD/7, 29 Aug., 1857.
62. Quoted in Hodder, III, 56.
63. N.R.A., Shaftesbury (Broadlands) MSS, SHA/PD/7, 29 Aug., 1857.
64. Clarendon MSS, Dep. c. 80, fos 299–300.
65. ibid., Dep. c. 80, fos 301–3. See also N.R.A., Shaftesbury (Broadlands) MSS, SHA/PD/7, 12 Oct., 1857.
66. *The Times*, 2 Nov., 1857.
67. *The Record*, 7 May, 1858.
68. Hansard, *Parl. Debates*, 3rd ser., CL, 579–600.
69. *The Times*, 2 Nov., 1857.
70. Quoted in *The Saturday Review*, V, 315–17 (27 Mar., 1858).
71. *The Times*, 29 Jan., 1858. Letter signed by 'Judex'.
72. Ibid. 2 Feb., 1858. Letter signed by 'Lover of Truth'.
73. Ibid. 3 Feb., 1858. Letter signed by 'Lover of Accuracy'.
74. Ibid. 4 Feb., 1858.
75. Ibid. 6 Feb., 1858. Letter signed by 'Lover of Truth'.
76. Lord Edmond Fitzmaurice, *The Life of Lord Granville, 1815–1891* (2 vols., 1905), I, 284.
77. A. J. C. Hare, *The Story of Two Noble Lives. Being Memorials of Charlotte, Countess of Canning and Louisa, Marshioness of Waterford* (3 vols., 1893), II, 422–3.
78. L. Strachey and R. Fulford, op. cit., VII, 300. Greville also commented (ibid., VII, 329–30) that Shaftesbury was 'stirring up all the fanaticism of the country and clamouring for what he calls the emancipation of Christianity in India.'
79. *The Daily News*, 24 Mar., 1858.
80. Reprinted ibid., 24 Mar., 1858.
81. *The Saturday Review*, V, 316 (27 Mar., 1858).
82. N.R.A., Shaftesbury (Broadlands) MSS, SHA/PD/7, 28 Mar., 1858.
83. Lord Edmond Fitzmaurice, op. cit., I, 289.
84. N.R.A., Shaftesbury (Broadlands) MSS, SHA/PD/10, 5 Nov., 1873.
85. The lady seems to have been his sister-in-law, Fanny Jocelyn. In a letter to Clarendon (Clarendon MSS, Dep. c 80, f. 302), Shaftesbury wrote that his sister-in-law, Fanny Jocelyn, had read this letter at Broadlands. Two or three persons had said to him that the details were too frightful for publication. Shaftesbury had disagreed and advised her to speak to Delane and get them published.
86. Quoted in Hodder, III, 62.
87. N.R.A., Shaftesbury (Broadlands) MSS, SHA/PD/7, 28 Mar., 1858.
88. *The Record*, 19 May, 1865.
89. See above pp. 38–9.
90. Quoted in Hodder, III, 370.
91. Hansard, *Parl. Debates*, 3rd ser., CLXIV, 371–89.
92. See above p. 96.
93. Clarendon MSS, Dep. c 27, f. 235.
94. *The Record*, 23 Apr., 1859.

95. See Hodder, III, 86.
96. *The Record*, 6 May, 1859.
97. N.R.A., Palmerston (Broadlands) MSS, GC/SH/46.
98. ibid., Shaftesbury (Broadlands) MSS, SHA/PD/7, 22 Apr., 1859.
99. ibid., SHA/PD/7, 22 Apr., 1859.
100. Quoted in Hodder, III, 89–90.
101. St G.H., Shaftesbury MSS, C 25010/7th Earl. (copy).
102. N.R.A., Palmerston (Broadlands) MSS, GC/SH/41.
103. Hansard, *Parl. Debates*, 3rd ser., CLVI, 591.
104. N.R.A., Shaftesbury (Broadlands) MSS, SHA/PD/7, 31 Mar., 1860.
105. Quoted in Hodder, III, 97.
106. Quoted ibid., 126.
107. St G.H., Shaftesbury MSS, C 25079/7th Earl.
108. ibid., c 25080/7th Earl.
109. *The Daily News*, 8 Oct., 1859.
110. St G.H., Shaftesbury MSS, C 25081/7th Earl.
111. Hodder, III, 93–4.
112. St G.H., Shaftesbury MSS, C 25082/7th Earl.
113. See Hodder, III, 95–6.
114. N.R.A., Shaftesbury (Broadlands) MSS, SHA/PD/7, 12 June, 1860. In September, 1860, Shaftesbury did, however, urge Garibaldi to be cautious in his plans for an advance on Rome and Venetia: 'You have now the sympathies of our whole nation, not only for your courage and magnanimity, but for your discretion,' he wrote to Garibaldi. 'Pray do everything to retain it. . . .' (Add. MSS, 37, 772, fos 86–7).
115. N.R.A., Shaftesbury (Broadlands) MSS, SHA/PD/7, 12 Oct., 1860.
116. Quoted in Hodder, III, 175.
117. See above pp. 343–4.
118. N.R.A., Shaftesbury (Broadlands) MSS, SHA/PD/7, 12 Aug., 1856.
119. *The Record*, 3 May, 1861.
120. Quoted in Hodder, III, 136.
121. Battiscombe, p. 277.
122. See Hodder, III, 141–3.
123. Hansard, *Parl. Debates*, 3rd ser., CLXX, 1369–83.
124. Huntington Library MSS, HM 23367, Shaftesbury to Edward Beales, 13 Feb., 1864.
125. N.R.A., Shaftesbury (Broadlands) MSS, SHA/PD/6, 15 Aug., 1852.
126. Clarenden MSS, Dep. c. 42, f. 331.
127. N.R.A., Palmerston (Broadlands) MSS, GC/SH/28/1/2.
128. Quoted in Hodder, III, 124.
129. *The Record*, 7 June, 1861.
130. N.R.A., Shaftesbury (Broadlands) MSS, SHA/PD/5, 7 Nov., 1848.
131. ibid., SHA/PD/7, 8 Sept., 1864.
132. ibid., SHA/PD/7, 8 Sept., 1864.
133. ibid., SHA/PD/7, 8 Sept., 1864.
134. ibid., SHA/PD/7, 8 Sept., 1864.

17
Doubt, Darkness, Discouragement, 1866–1873

Shaftesbury's prophecy that change would soon follow Palmerston's death was to prove strikingly accurate. Within two years, the Second Reform Act was on the statute book. The reasons for this rapid development are complex. Palmerston's death did, indeed, remove a determined opponent to further parliamentary reform, and his successor as Prime Minister, Russell, had, for many years, been an advocate of reform. The leader of the Liberal government in the Commons, Gladstone, was a more recent convert, but, by 1866, was enthusiastically of the opinion that an extension of the franchise should be carried out. This, however, was not true of all Liberals, and the Liberal bill, introduced by Gladstone in March, 1866, ran into considerable opposition, expressed in celebrated terms by Robert Lowe. Similarly, it was opposed by the Conservatives. Nevertheless, it was the Conservative Ministry under Derby and Disraeli, coming into office on the resignation of the Liberals in June, 1866, which carried the second Reform Act the following year. The precise motives which led the Conservatives to take this course of action have long been a matter of debate among historians. One point of view puts weight on an outburst of popular agitation which broke out in the summer of 1866: in particular, there was a demonstration in Hyde Park in July, when the railings of the Park were beaten down and struggles with the police took place. This, it has been argued, formed a background of violence which made the politicians amenable to accepting a measure of parliamentary reform. Another point of view sees the eventual passing of reform more in terms of the political opportunism of Disraeli. It was, it has been argued, Disraeli's desire to extract political credit for himself and the Conservative party which made him ready to sponsor reform and, more particularly, to accept a number of amendments to the bill which made it much more extensive than the measure originally introduced. But, if there is room for argument about the reasons for the introduction of the measure,[1] there is no doubt as to its effects: the introduction of what was virtually household suffrage into the boroughs and the creation of a 'mass' urban electorate.

Shaftesbury was very unhappy about many of these developments. He noted in December, 1865, that the desire of Russell and Gladstone seemed to be to proceed in a direction diametrically opposite to that of Palmerston.[2] The following month, he wrote that the prospect of the new year was 'frightful' – it was 'pregnant with Revolution'.[3] After the Liberal bill was introduced by Gladstone in March, 1866, it seemed to Shaftesbury that events were heading in one way – the way to democracy and revolution – and he greatly admired Lowe's speech. It was, he felt, a 'masterpiece of sustained and consecutive logic' and doubted whether a speech 'better adapted to place, persons and circumstances, was ever delivered in any country or in any age.'[4] He did not, however, favour the resignation of the Liberal government in June, thinking that the situation at home and abroad was too dangerous for such a course of action.

Shaftesbury's general disenchantment with the Liberal Ministry after Palmerston's death was noted by Derby. Writing to Shaftesbury on his accession to office, Derby suggested that Shaftesbury's displeasure with the Liberals since 1865 might induce him to assist with the formation of the Conservative Ministry which Derby was constructing. He assured Shaftesbury that, if he accepted office as Chancellor of the Duchy of Lancaster, he would have leisure for his ordinary engagements.[5] But Shaftesbury refused. He was, he noted in his Diary,[6] anxious to be of use to 'stem the tide of Democracy', but acceptance of office would, he felt, be a self-sacrifice without any adequate compensation. He thought that all Derby wanted was to have him as 'a sort of picture to present to the Country ... the picture of a friend of the working classes!' This might strengthen Derby for a time, but it would confer nothing on himself. If the Home Secretary were unfriendly, Shaftesbury's interest in socially remedial measures would be thwarted and he would be forced to resign. Only the Home Office would give him a sufficiently powerful status, and his lack of official experience was, he felt, an obstacle to his fitness for that office. It does, indeed, appear that Derby offered Shaftesbury the Home Office and the Presidency of the Council.[7] But it was to no avail. Shaftesbury felt that he could be of little assistance to Derby in an official capacity, and, as in the past, he expressed his unwillingness to withdraw himself from the varied pursuits which had occupied so large a portion of his life.[8]

Shaftesbury thus retained his independent position. But he recognised that the popular agitation and interest in reform did pose problems for the Conservative government, and he was willing to use his influence to 'put the Government and Derby right with the working classes.'[9] He took the opportunity of a visit to the Social Science Congress in Manchester in October, 1866, to make a number of speeches on social issues and also carried out various engagements while he was in the north: he laid a stone for the founding of a Ragged School and met delegates from the cotton districts of Lancashire. He had not looked forward to the visit; he wrote that he regarded it as probably his final visit to 'those places and peoples whose affairs (had) occupied so large a portion of (his) life.'[10] But he was well pleased with the result. His visit to Manchester was, he wrote, 'providential from first to last . . . It was all the finger of God.'[11] He was less pleased that the London newspapers did not report his activities more fully. This made it look as if the whole thing had been a failure, and yet, he noted, 'it was mainly to affect the Ministers and the Legislature that I undertook the fearful toil.'[12] Shaftesbury also corresponded with Disraeli to suggest various ways in which the reform question could be met. He sent Disraeli two copies of a publication entitled the *Working Man*, which contained an essay on reform by an operative, so that Disraeli might see the 'predilection that respectable men have for "fancy franchises" . . . founded on solid possessions.' There were many such franchises, Shaftesbury wrote, which would be 'satisfactory to the honest and *diligent* portion of the working class.' This portion was 'specially hostile to Mr Bright and his school . . . being in fact conservative.'[13] Shaftesbury also put forward the idea that halls should be constructed to house public meetings. The dangers of open air meetings were apparent from the incident in Hyde Park, and, in any event, such meetings in the Park were technically illegal. The building of halls might multiply public meetings, but, Shaftesbury felt, it would also multiply 'safety values'. He wrote to Disraeli urging the desirability of the scheme, but Disraeli was too busy to take it up. Shaftesbury told Disraeli's secretary, Montague Corry, that he had suggested the halls because he believed such a system to be useful and popular: it would have prevented monster meetings. He recognised that Disraeli had many other important matters to attend to and that the matter had to wait, but he felt that the idea had presented the opportunity to deal with the question of public meetings in a 'Conservative' way.[14] Thus Shaftesbury felt that the difficulties and dangers of the situation could be handled with safety. Although he did not, intrinsically, favour reform, he felt that the Conservative Ministry could not avoid some action on the subject. In February, 1867, he wrote that it was not now possible to adopt Lowe's attitude: however impeccable the logic of Lowe's opposition to reform, it was not based on an 'estimate of men and things'.[15] The matter had to be settled, and he ventured to suggest to Derby the 'expediency (and) wisdom' of introducing a Reform Bill.[16]

Shaftesbury's general support and sympathy for the Derby-Disraeli Ministry did not, however, extend beyond the introduction of the bill by Disraeli in February, 1867. He commented that, had he joined the Cabinet the previous July, Disraeli's bill would have forced him to resign from it.[17] The measure was, he felt, too extreme, and it was dishonest for the Conservatives to introduce such a bill having denounced that previously introduced by the Liberals. Had they decided that an extreme measure was necessary, they should have 'surrendered their places to the men who had always enforced Reform principles.' But all was determined by 'the "Desire of place" '.[18] Shaftesbury had previously regarded Disraeli with some favour as one interested in schemes of social improvement: as recently as August, 1866, he had written that Disraeli was 'decided and true to the cause' and that he had always found him so.[19] But, after February, 1867, Shaftesbury became convinced that Disraeli was merely an adventurer, who had 'not a thought beyond his own immediate person'.[20] In this respect, he was the same as Gladstone: both were 'governed by the greed of place and salary and power.' They were, Shaftesbury wrote, like 'two tigers over a carcase; and each one tries to drive the other away from the titbits.'[21] He noted that even Derby, whom he felt less to blame than Disraeli, had told his friends that, if they passed his bill, they would occupy office for many years. All, then, were alike – '. . . equally carnivorous'. It was not the welfare of the realm nor the security of institutions which were the primary considerations, but the 'certainty of place'.[22]

Shaftesbury's interpretation of the episode is, therefore, broadly in line with that which places emphasis on the importance of political and party interest. And, although he included Gladstone and Derby in his strictures, it was Disraeli who, in his eyes, was the real villain – the 'author of all the mischief'.[23] Shaftesbury may have attributed rather too far-reaching ideas to Disraeli: to argue that Disraeli was the 'wilful and astute promoter' of Revolution and that he saw the 'attainment of his long cherished hope, the triumph of Democracy'[24] is to exaggerate the extent to which Disraeli was influenced by long-term ideas and also the extent to which Disraeli wished to embrace democratic forms of government. But the view that Disraeli was actuated by immediate political and party considerations in sponsoring the bill and, more especially, in accepting amendments which made it more extensive, has much to be said for it, and Shaftesbury was shrewd enough to grasp this in its essence. It should also be remembered, however, that he did not discount the pressure of popular demand and external circumstances. In his view, this had made some measure inevitable by the time the Conservatives took office; it was the *nature* of the measure which he attributed to party machinations, and which, he felt, would lead to disastrous consequences.

Such themes were, indeed, present in a long speech which he made on reform in the Lords in July, 1867.[25] Contemplating his speech, he was afflicted by doubts and nerves. He could hardly, he wrote, 'muster up courage to speak.' The longer he was in the Lords, the less he got used to it. He was more 'in terror of it' than he had been earlier.[26] Nevertheless, he overcame his doubts; he felt he had to speak. He repeated his view that some reform, although not necessary for good government, had become indispensable and inevitable and could not be postponed much longer. But he would have wished 'to hold up the suffrage as a great object of ambition to the working man . . . the reward of thrift, honesty and industry.' He would have reduced the £10 household qualification in the boroughs to £7: this would have meant the addition of thousands of men to the electorate who 'would be an honour and a security to the kingdom.' In that respect, he had always been 'a very considerable radical', for what he most rejoiced to see was 'the working man rising by his own industry and character from the lowest point in the scale of society to the very highest point.' But, he continued:

> to proceed, as is done by this Bill, to lift by the sudden jerk of an Act of Parliament the whole residuum of society up to the level of the honest, thrifty, working man, is, I am sure, perilous to the state, and, I believe, distasteful to the working men themselves. I am sure it dishonours the suffrage, and that you are throwing the franchise broadcast over the heads of men who will accept it, but who will misuse it.

Moreover, the democratic influence which the bill would introduce to the Commons would 'speedily act in a most dangerous way against the old-established and organised institutions of the country.' The House of Lords and the Church of England would be threatened; the existing distribution of property would come under critical scrutiny; and there would be a revival of 'that hazardous and angry feud between the House of Want and the House of Have'.

The speech was, indeed, an exposition of Shaftesbury's paternalism, and he was satisfied with it. He felt that he had set forth 'the dangers to be feared from the People' and yet he had also spoken of them with 'kindness and respect' and had not given cause for offence.[27] He was also much gratified by favourable comments which he received. Lowe wrote to him in praise of his 'noble speech', which had displayed 'commanding ability': honesty and courage which had led Shaftesbury to 'tell the exact truth about classes to whom (he) had devoted (his) life, and whom everyone but (him) has combined to flatter with a fulsome hypocrisy. . . .'[28]

But pleasure at the success of his speech was overshadowed by gloom at future prospects. Shaftesbury wrote in 1868 that the Reform Act had removed all check to the 'voice of the Multitude'. If it remained where it was, it would exhibit 'an autocratic Public Will'; if it were pushed further, it would 'burst like a Deluge on every institution, social, political and religious. . . .'[29] He continued to look on the leading politicians with extreme disfavour. He commented that Disraeli, who succeeded to the Premiership in March, 1868, was a 'Hebrew' – that was 'a good thing'. He was also a man 'sprung from an inferior station' – that was another good thing in these days as showing the 'liberality of our institutions'. But, Shaftesbury continued, he was a 'leper': he was 'without principle, without truth, without feeling, without regard to anything human or divine, beyond his own personal ambition.' He had 'dragged and . . . (would) continue to drag, everything that is good, safe, venerable and solid through the dust and dirt of his own selfish objects.'[30] Had Disraeli been an honest man, he would have been, with his various qualifications, a 'heaven-sent Minister'. As it was, he seemed to have accepted the 'Condition of Satan': ' "All these things will I give thee if thou wilt fall down and worship me".'[31] Gladstone was no better. He was 'impetuous and revolutionary',[32] 'utterly untrustworthy'.[33] There was, then, no difference between the leaders of the two parties. Shaftesbury wrote that he was 'totally indifferent' to both; there was 'not a pin to choose between them.'[34] Nevertheless, a Liberal Ministry under Gladstone was an alarming prospect. The Conservative government had been an 'express train'. A Liberal Ministry would be a 'special train for purpose and velocity'.[35]

Thus when the Liberals *did* come to power in December, 1868, after the General Election of that year, Shaftesbury was filled with apprehension. He already felt that the House of Lords was of little use as an institution. In March, 1866, he had written that it stood 'like a candle flickering in the socket: if it be not snuffed out, it will go out of itself.'[36] In June, 1867, he proposed in the Lords that the House should start its business at 4 p.m. instead of 5 p.m. This, he argued, would enable younger men to take part in its proceedings and would add to its efficiency.[37] But, after the Reform Act, he felt that the future of the Lords was bleak – now, indeed, it would be 'snuffed out' by a Commons elected on so wide a suffrage. There was, however, no need to hasten the process. In May, 1868, Shaftesbury wrote to Gladstone rebuking him for remarks which Gladstone had made to the effect that he would not take a word of command from the House of Lords. Gladstone, Shaftesbury wrote, had given 'to that weak and tottering Institution another shove towards the fatal precipice;' he urged Gladstone to 'let our Institutions in Church and State go down, so far as possible, to their graves in peace.'[38] And, if rash and extreme sentiments on the Liberal side might complete the interment with undue haste, so too might dogged resistance on the part of the Upper House itself. Shaftesbury felt that it was necessary for the peers to accept its inferior status, and he restrained himself from violent opposition to certain of the measures proposed by the Liberal Ministry on the grounds that this could only expose the Lords to attack and, indeed, the threat of extinction.

A notable instance of Shaftesbury's sentiments on public men and public institutions was over the disestablishment of the Irish Church, proposed by Gladstone in March, 1869.[39] Gladstone first raised the matter in March, 1868, when Disraeli was still in office. His proposal was that a suspensory bill should be passed to prevent new appointments until the matter had been settled. This was rejected by the Lords. Shaftesbury was prepared to admit that the Irish Church did contain certain anomalies and abuses which, he felt, were largely due to the neglect of the Church itself,[40] but he had severe misgivings about Gladstone's proposal. If the foundations of the Protestant Church of Ireland were overthrown, he told the Lords,[41] the foundations of Britain's 'national existence' would be broken up and the first step taken towards national apostasy. But he also felt that resistance by the Lords to the measure would only bring censure and calumny – thus he abstained from voting, a fact which exposed him to attack in certain Evangelical circles. At the General Election of 1868, the question of Irish Church Disestablishment was a very prominent one. Resistance was organised by groups in which Anglican Evangelicals were active, who argued that the establishment of the Church of England was greatly endangered by the proposed disestablishment of its Irish arm. The meetings and demonstrations which were held stressed the Protestantism of the Church of England and numerous anti-Roman tracts were issued. It was a cause to which Shaftesbury might well have been expected to give a lead, but he stood aloof from it. The defects which he acknowledged in the Church of Ireland made the task of defending it difficult, and he considered that there was too much indifference among 'all forms and shades' of Protestants both in England and Ireland to launch an effective campaign. Further, the Establishment attracted the hostility of the Nonconformists. The meetings that were held were, he argued, not well organised and had insufficient lay representation – they gave the impression that the public could be 'bishopped . . . into a submissive line of thought,'[42] and simply injured the cause. And, in any event, resistance was pointless. If the Conservatives were returned to office, Disraeli could not be trusted to defend the Establishment. 'He was and he is,' Shaftesbury wrote, 'believed to be as ready as Gladstone, should it serve his purpose to annihilate the Church, and even outbid him in concessions to the Papists.'[43] And if the Liberals returned under Gladstone, the fate of the Irish Church was sealed.

When the Liberals did come into office and a measure for disestablishment and disendowment was introduced, Shaftesbury's depression and sense of hopelessness deepened. He wrote in June, 1869, that the bill had a 'very terrible appearance' and was founded on the 'despoliation of all rights and laws', extinguishing 'a light shining in a dark place'.[44] Once it had passed the Commons, he was very unsure how to vote at the second reading in the Lords. He could not vote for it. He would, he wrote, vote against it if, by doing so, he would save the Church or even prolong its existence. But that was 'beyond all power and beyond all hope'. By bringing the Lords into collision with the Commons and the country, he would only add to the ruin of the Church and the degradation of the Lords, which would disable it for the defence of the land settlement in Ireland and the Establishment in England. The only course seemed to be to abstain in the division. He also wondered if he should speak and asked plaintively how the scriptures could guide him in this perplexity: 'there are numerous political questions,' he wrote, 'which the Bible does not solve.'[45] He was, indeed, in a state of great depression. This was partly caused by the death of his sister, Caroline, in early June,[46] but, personal matters apart, the Irish question weighed heavily on him. Never before, he wrote, had he been in such uncertainty.[47] He finally decided that he should speak but, to his distress, did not, in fact, get the opportunity to do so, and, like many other peers, abstained in the division in which the bill passed its second reading by a majority of thirty-three. He felt it necessary to defend his conduct and wrote to *The Record* to explain that he had been kept away from the Lords by the death of his sister and that then he did not get a chance to speak.[48] He was thus 'shut out from making a protest . . . against the most momentous measure that, except in times of revolution, was ever submitted to the deliberation of a Legislature.'[49] But his view was that the Lords could do no more than register a protest and take up minor matters in Committee. He felt that he might speak on some of these, but, once more, did not get the opportunity to do so. On one occasion, he failed to stake his claim to speak and complained of the way in which rival speakers in the Lords got up and struggled to be heard: the matter was settled by 'roars of preference for one peer or the other.' He could not expose himself to this.[50] On another occasion, an amendment which he planned to introduce to devote the surplus funds of the Irish Church to small loans for the labouring population of Ireland was submerged in a larger issue, and, again, all his trouble and anxiety came to nothing.[51] But he was, in fact, almost relieved that he was prevented from speaking: never before, he wrote, had he had 'a period of doubt, darkness and discouragement' so long on him.[52] When he *did* speak on 21 July,[53] it was simply to record his repugnance to the measure and its implications – it was 'calculated to produce, and that shortly, still larger changes in the existing relations between Church and State, in religion and in property, than any measure that (had) been laid before this country since England was a nation.' But the Commons and the nation had approved it, and the Lords could do no more than accept it. Any attempt at rejection would simply lead to conflict and the overthrow of other institutions. All that he felt it right to do was to give the Lords the benefit of 'true, necessary, wise, painful counsel'.[54]

Other occasions for such advice were, indeed, soon to follow. Two bills which passed the Commons in 1870 ran into opposition in the Lords. One was to legalise marriage between a widower and the sister of his late wife and the other to remove religious tests at Universities which placed disabilities on non-Anglicans. Shaftesbury felt that there was no scriptural barrier to such marriages as the first bill proposed to legalise,[55] but he feared that the bill might lead to marriages being allowed in every case of affinity and he was apprehensive of the domestic and social implications of such a development.[56] But, he wrote, 'the tendency, no doubt, is all in the direction of removing every prohibition: and if the House of Commons, elected as it is by universal suffrage, persist, we must give way.'[57] He voted against the second reading of the bill, but offered no further resistance. Shaftesbury also disapproved of the bill to remove the tests at the Universities: 'a vile bill' was his description of it.[58] But again, nothing could or should be done by the Lords and he did not vote on it. The Lords, then, could not 'in sense or safety, resist the persistent will of Universal Suffrage.'[59] All that the Upper House could do was to act in such a way as to give time to the Commons to re-consider a measure. If it kept to this, it might, indeed, perform a useful role. Shaftesbury wrote to Salisbury that if the Lords kept 'within the bounds of Public Opinion', it might recover some of its former position. If the nation had confidence in its 'judgment and moderation' it might 'yet be reserved for vigorous and real defence of our Institutions.'[60] But it must be seen to be acting with 'judgment and moderation': and consistently to oppose the Commons and the country was 'foolish and perilous'.[61]

Shaftesbury was, therefore, prepared to concede that all effective power lay in the Commons and ultimately in the Country. He felt that further electoral changes were inevitable. Thus, if female suffrage were desired, it was bound to come. He himself would not stimulate the desire for such a change, but there could be no point in resisting it. He told a lady, who wrote asking his opinion on the subject of female suffrage, that the people held the power and were 'considered to be the best judges of social and political proprieties' – their 'fiat' had to be obeyed 'except in cases where the principle of a change might be so strong as deeply to affect the conscience.'[62] One such change *did*, however, provoke Shaftesbury's conscientious resistance: the proposal for the introduction of the Secret Ballot. In November, 1871, he wrote that he had one ambition left and this was to speak against the Ballot. He knew that it was 'hopeless ... to turn the hateful system aside: but (he wished) to denounce it, as everything that is dangerous in politics, mean in morale, and cowardly in the discharge of duty.'[63] He was as good as his word. In August, 1871, a bill introducing the Ballot reached the Lords, having passed the Commons. Shaftesbury proposed that it be deferred for six months, claiming that the bill had been introduced too late in the session to allow proper discussion of it. He rejected the view that this was merely a matter for the Commons – he knew of no question in the whole history of legislation 'so completely an imperial one'.[64] His motion was carried and the matter deferred. But, once more, this was as much as the Lords could and should do. Writing in December, 1871, to Gladstone, Shaftesbury commented that his motion had been 'tantamount to a call for the opinion of the country'. But this had not been forthcoming. He felt that the majority of people were opposed to the Ballot, but they would not stir. His call had been met by silence and the country had thus acquiesced in the proposal. The Lords could not, therefore, put up any further resistance.[65] When the bill for the Ballot was reintroduced in June, 1872, and reached the Lords, Shaftesbury did not oppose it. But he did take the opportunity to state his objections to it.[66] He denied that any intimidation of voters had taken place under the open system of voting: the Ballot was, therefore, unnecessary in this respect. It would not reduce bribery and corruption; it would, indeed, increase it. Under the Ballot, 'briber and bribee,' he said, 'would have every facility.' Moreover, honest voters would be deterred from exercising their vote, since it could never be proved that they had voted as they said they would, and they would, therefore, always be subject to suspicion and doubt. But the heart of Shaftesbury's objection was that the Ballot removed 'the noble sentiment of public responsibility'. He had always, he said, urged on working people the need for a sense of responsibility to God and man; they must be 'proud to discharge that responsibility in the eye of day and in the face of the whole community.' The Ballot would enable and, indeed, 'force a man, like a creeping animal, to slink away with his tail between his legs.' The Ballot thus struck at the roots of one of Shaftesbury's cherished beliefs: accountability to God and to man.

The political prospects were, then gloomy and dismal. In 1871, Shaftesbury had written that he had 'grown resigned to Politics and almost indifferent to them.'[67] He deplored the listlessness of 'men of station and property': all were afflicted by indifference and a 'desire for enjoyment and a fear of disturbance . . . Après Moi le Déluge is the spirit.'[68] These were not new complaints, but, after 1867, they had added point as Shaftesbury saw politicians and parties bent on courting the popular will. Any attempt to resist the transition to far-reaching change would only make things worse by weakening the forces which might still restrain the worst excesses. As so often with Shaftesbury, it was an over-dramatic diagnosis, but also one which contained elements of truth and discernment.

When Shaftesbury received Derby's offer of office in 1866, he mentioned that there still remained a large number of women, children and young persons to be brought under the protection of the Factory Acts, and one of his reasons for rejecting the offer was that he wished to have time and opportunity to devote to this task.[69] Throughout these years, indeed, he maintained his long-standing interest in social matters, in particular those concerning conditions of employment, housing and public health. Thus, in 1866[70] and again in 1867,[71] he drew attention to the fact that further Reports of the Commission on Child Employment had been issued, and he wished to know what action was to be taken, in the first place by the Liberal government and in the second by the Conservative. In 1867, two measures were, indeed, introduced by the Conservative Ministry of Derby and Disraeli and reached the statute book: the Factory Acts Extension Act and an Act for the regulation of workshops. The former Act was to apply to larger establishments employing over fifty employees. These were to be subject to the Factory Acts and to the inspectorate. Under the latter Act, workshops with fewer than fifty employees were also to come under the Factory Acts, but the hours to be worked were spread over a longer period[72] and inspection was to be carried out by the local authority. The two Acts extended protection to many workers hitherto unprotected and Shaftesbury was satisfied with them. In August, 1867, he wrote that the 'two bills about to receive the Royal Assent, shall have closed 34 years of labour on behalf of the industrial classes of the country.'[73]

Nevertheless, there were still many exceptions to this legislation, and Shaftesbury did not shrink from the effort of bringing them to light. Thus, in 1871, he took up the question of child employment in brickyards.[74] He told the Lords that such children were excluded by a technicality from the protection given to other occupations. There were some three thousand such children, ranging from the ages of three-and-a-half to seventeen, and there were also many female workers who were employed. Long hours were worked in miserable conditions and he asked the Lords if it could be denied that, in such employment, men, women and children – especially female children – were 'brought down to a point of degradation and suffering lower than the beasts of the field.' No man, he said, 'with a sense of humanity or with the aspirations of a Christian, could go through these places and not feel that what he saw was a disgrace to the country and ought not for a moment be allowed to continue.' He also felt that Parliament owed it to the great majority of employers who had accepted the Factory Acts to extend their protection to persons employed in brickyards. As a result of his efforts, this was, indeed, brought about.

Further, Shaftesbury was extremely anxious to bring the agricultural worker within the scope of protective legislation. It will be recalled that, in 1865, he had been responsible for having the system of agricultural gangs referred to the Commission on Child Employment.[75] In 1867, he asked when the Commission was likely to report: the matter, he said, was especially important, in the light of the two measures which applied to factories and workshops.[76] Two months later, when the Report had been issued, he brought the matter to the notice of the Lords, reminding his fellow peers that it was their duty to show that they were mindful of the agricultural community and so to rebut the charge levelled against landlords that they had no concern for their poorer tenants. In a long speech,[77] which evinced many similarities in style with his earlier speeches on factories and mines, he drew extensively on extracts from the Report which illustrated the long hours worked and long distances walked in all weathers by children employed in gangs. These might be 'public' gangs, where the employer was a master, or 'private' gangs, employed by a farmer. 'When a system like this exists,' Shaftesbury said, 'it is obvious that the legislature ought not to hesitate a moment in applying a proper remedy.' Since he had heard that the government did not propose to introduce legislation on the subject that session, he gave notice of his intention to introduce a bill after the Easter recess – this would be the 'crowning stroke to the various efforts made for many years to bring all the industrial occupations of the young and defenceless under the protections of the law.' Shaftesbury moved the second reading of this bill in July, 1867[78]: it would have excluded boys under eight and girls under thirteen from hired employment in agricultural labour, and girls under eighteen would have been debarred from working in a public gang. In the event, Shaftesbury dropped the bill in the expectation of government legislation being introduced the following session. This was, indeed, done and duly passed. It prohibited the employment of any child in a gang under the age of eight and any woman or child in a gang where men were employed. Gang masters were to be licensed. The legislation controlled the activities of public gangs, but, as a result, an increase in private gangs took place. It was not until 1873 that a further bill was passed on the subject and this closely followed Shaftesbury's proposals of 1867.[79]

Shaftesbury thus still took the initiative in proposing legislation to extend the scope of protection to the 'young and defenceless' in various areas of employment hitherto unregulated, and he readily supported any other initiatives which were made in this direction. Thus, in 1872, he supported the second reading of a bill which sought to protect young children from being compelled to take part in acrobatic performances.[80] This bill was, in fact, withdrawn, as was a further bill on the subject in 1873, and Shaftesbury well realised that it was difficult to prevent such practices by legislation. Nevertheless, he felt that public opinion must be brought to bear on the subject. In this way such 'abominable and degrading exhibitions' which were 'a disgrace to the age and to the progress of our refinement' might be exposed and abolished. Shaftesbury also supported legislation which widened the measure of protection given to employment already regulated by legislation. Thus, in 1872, he spoke in favour of a Mines Regulation bill. This raised the age at which boys could be employed in mines from ten to twelve and proposed a ten-hour day or fifty-four-hour week for boys between twelve and sixteen. It also increased the number of inspectors and introduced more stringent safety regulations. Shaftesbury recalled[81] that, when he first introduced legislation on the subject thirty years earlier, Parliament and the country were not ripe for the remedial measures that were required and thus he had to confine himself to less than he ought to have done. He felt that the present proposals still did not go far enough, but he thanked the government for 'what he trusted the bill would do in elevating the character and improving the condition of a class who, with all their faults, were amongst the most generous, honest and single-minded of our people.' As in 1842, various amendments were moved in the interests of the coal industry – thus it was proposed that the fifty-four-hour week for boys under sixteen should be extended to fifty-six. Shaftesbury said that the moral effect of the Lords going beyond the Commons in imposing work on coalminers would be 'the worst possible'. But – again as in 1842 – his protests were unavailing, and, once more, the mining interest was able to exercise its influence in reducing the amount of protection given by the measure when it finally reached the statute book in August, 1872.[82]

These years also witnessed legislation which dealt with the problems of working-class housing. Here, Shaftesbury did not so much initiate legislation, but he did support that which was introduced. In 1866, the Labouring Classes Dwelling Houses Act was passed. This was designed to assist persons put out of their houses by the construction of railways and public improvements. The Public Works Loan Commissioners were authorised to advance sums of money to public companies and private individuals for the purpose of providing dwellings for the working classes; these sums would not exceed half the value of the premises and would bear interest at the rate of 4%. This was a matter which Shaftesbury had taken up in the 1850s,[83] and he gave the principle of the measure his warm support. He did not think, however, that it would have any marked effect. He thought the interest rate too high to encourage many borrowers – it would need to be reduced to $1\frac{1}{2}$ to 2%. Further, the rents to be charged for such accommodation were likely to be beyond all but the skilled artisan. His prophecies as to the limited effect of the legislation were to prove substantially correct,[84] but he felt that the measure was useful and would lead to the acquisition of valuable information: every experiment in this field, he said, was desirable. Shaftesbury also supported the Artisans and Labourers Dwellings Act, passed in 1868, which made provision for the demolition of insanitary premises. The Act was weakened by a number of amendments imposed by the Lords, and its permissive nature meant that it was ignored in many places.[85] Shaftesbury feared that it would, indeed, be ineffective, but he supported the bill as 'an honest and wise endeavour to remedy one of the most terrible evils that ever afflicted any large community.'[86]

Public health likewise received parliamentary attention in the late 1860s and early 1870s: these were, indeed, years of great importance in this field. After the dissolution of the ill-fated Board of Health, public health had been advanced by local, rather than central, effort and by voluntary initiative rather than compulsion. This pattern was established by the Local Government Act of 1858 and the Public Health Acts of 1858 and 1859, and considerable progress was made, which owed much to the efforts of John Simon, Secretary of the Medical Department of the Privy Council, created under the legislation of 1858-9. Simon's flexible approach and his powers of persuasion – attributes markedly different from those of Chadwick – built up great influence for the Department and his own post.[87] But the system was far from perfect: it was haphazard in structure and operation. Simon's regular reports pointed to the deficiencies and, gradually, the need for tighter central control and greater expert advice became more widely recognised. As had happened in the past, the cause of public health was advanced by an outbreak of cholera in London in 1866, and, in that year, a further Public Health Act was passed. It was introduced by the Liberal government and completed by the Conservatives on the change of administration. The Act did little to rationalise the multiplicity of local bodies responsible for various aspects of public health, such as sewage disposal, water supply and the removal of 'nuisances'. But it did enjoin rather than permit them to take action and widened their scope: a 'nuisance', for example, might now include insanitary and overcrowded houses. Further, central control was more firmly established and provision was made for the Home Secretary to act if local authorities did not. There were, however, to be many difficulties in connection with the operation of the Act, and the whole question was investigated by a Royal Commission on sanitation which sat between 1868 and 1871. The recommendations of its Report were embodied in further legislation in 1871 and 1872. The Local Government Board, set up in 1871, coordinated the activities of the old Poor Law Board and the health functions of the Privy Council, Home Office and Local Government Act Office, and the Public Health Act of 1872 helped to reduce the chaos of local public health authorities by setting up new urban and rural bodies for sanitary purposes. In practice, the Local Government Board frustrated many of Simon's efforts and the Act of 1872 left many issues unresolved, but the legislation of 1866 and 1871-2 did help to consolidate much of what had been done during the previous thirty to forty years in the field of public health.

There was, indeed, much here that Shaftesbury could and did welcome. He supported the Act of 1866, and he expressed his gratitude to the Liberal government for having brought in the measure and to the Conservatives for having completed it.[88] No doubt in the light of his earlier experience, he stressed the need for strengthening the power of the central government in such matters. Again in 1871, he supported the need for further legislation: the earliest attention of the government, he said, should be directed to social and domestic questions, which 'had a far greater effect on the morals, the health, the happiness and the tranquillity of the people than political measures.'[89] Further, he maintained his earlier interest in the question of London's water supply. In 1866, he wrote to Disraeli and urged the appointment of a Commission on the subject. It was, he wrote, 'essentially a matter affecting the *working classes*.' The wealthy might be able to look after themselves. The poor could not do so, for, in terms of quantity, quality and time of supply, they were 'utterly helpless'. And, he continued:

> No one, but a person who has studied, as it were, the question can form a notion of the physical, moral and domestic losses and suffering which the Poor have to endure, by consequence of this denial of this one great necessity of life.

He felt that the instructions to be given to the Commission should be ample and specific. It should examine and investigate the sources of supply, the possible causes of pollution and the conduct of the several water companies, and urgent inquiry should be made as to the feasibility of a regular and constant supply. A full investigation must, therefore, be made of the circumstances which led to a 'sickly and, consequently, immoral population', and, Shaftesbury added: 'it is not necessary to say more to Mr Disraeli, who has always exhibited a real desire to consider and promote the welfare and comfort of the working people.'[90] As yet, Shaftesbury was not disillusioned with Disraeli.

A Commission on London's water supply was, indeed, set up in December, 1866, to consider new sources. When told in advance of the government's intentions, Shaftesbury wrote to Derby to say that he 'sincerely rejoiced' at this news. The government, he felt, would do well to extend it to the whole country, since the increase in population and the extensive use of water in modern manufacturing processes would soon make the ordinary sources quite insufficient. He also suggested that the public document announcing the Commission should indicate that it had reference to the 'masses of the population'. In addition, Shaftesbury advised Derby about persons whom he might consult over the appointment of the civil engineers and chemists which the Commission would need. Derby, he wrote, could not do better than approach three men already in the public service, Robert Rawlinson, Dr Farr – 'the admirable man at Somerset House' – and John Simon. He had known them for many years and could answer for their capacity and zeal.[91] On receipt of Shaftesbury's letter, Derby sent it to the Lord President of the Council, the Duke of Buckingham. Derby wrote that he had known it would please Shaftesbury to be told of the government's intention to issue a water supply Commission, and he also felt that Shaftesbury's idea that reference should be made in the Commission to the sufferings of the working classes, especially because of the inadequate supply of water in the large towns, well worthy of consideration. And, he added: 'Shaftesbury is, as you will see, very friendly, and it will be well to keep him so.'[92] The Commission did, indeed, carry out its task under the chairmanship of the Duke of Richmond, and reported in 1869. It recommended that London's water supply should be removed from the control of the existing water companies and given to a public body. Little was immediately done to implement the Report, and, in 1871, Shaftesbury complained about this. There was an urgent need, he said, for a much larger supply of water and the 'corruption and mischief' in the existing supply must be eliminated. The water supply of four million persons was 'most questionable' in many cases and 'deadly' in others.[93] In 1871, indeed, the Liberal government did attempt to bring about the compulsory purchase of the companies by the Metropolitan Board of Works. But the plan failed, and, as in the past, Shaftesbury's hopes were not realised.

Shaftesbury, therefore, maintained his interest in social questions which had occupied so much of his life for the past thirty years: the same concern for the physical and spiritual well-being of persons who, in his view, were being exploited and could not look after themselves, was still amply evident. It was also to be seen in a new context in his support for the Married Women's Property bill, proposed in 1870. He did, it is true, have misgivings about the bill, especially as it applied to the wealthier classes; in enabling a married woman to hold property, the bill might strike 'at the very root of domestic happiness'; it might introduce 'insubordination, equality and something more'. In these remarks, Shaftesbury showed his social conservatism, but, in others, he showed his paternalism. For, among the poorer classes, he recognised the need to protect a woman's earnings – the wife of the working man was, he said, the 'moving principle of the whole family'. She was much superior to a man in 'tact, sound judgment and economy' and it was quite wrong for her to have her savings from employment wasted by a dissolute and spendthrift husband. The bill would, therefore, greatly assist a 'most meritorious and defenceless class of women'.[94]

Further, if Shaftesbury was still active in such matters at the parliamentary level, he retained and, indeed, extended his 'unofficial' pursuits. In April, 1866, he took the chair of a workman's club in Pye Street, Westminster; in June, the chair of a Society for the Medical Education of Women. Much effort in 1866 went into a scheme to assist homeless boys in London.[95] A supper for such boys was arranged and held in St Giles' Refuge, Lincoln's Inn Fields. Shaftesbury addressed the boys, asking them who had been in prison and how often; whether they roamed the streets by day and slept outside at night; and how they obtained a livelihood. He put forward the idea – which owed much to a long-standing friend, William Williams – that a ship on the Thames might be used for housing homeless boys and training them for trades or for naval service. 'It has been a dream of fifteen years or more,' Shaftesbury wrote.[96] Finally, the government granted a gun frigate, the *Chichester*, to be used for such purposes, and, in December, 1866, Shaftesbury himself made the inaugural speech. In 1868, his interests took another turn: to the Costermongers – or wandering street traders – of London. His attention had been drawn to them by W. J. Orsman, who, since 1861, had devoted considerable energy to the task of mission among the Costermongers and had established the Golden Lane Mission. Shaftesbury replied to a letter which he received from Orsman in November, 1868, saying that he would be glad to assist his 'admirable efforts' and to accept the office of President of the Mission.[97] He subscribed to the Mission's Barrow & Donkey Club: a barrow was bought with his contribution and bore the Shaftesbury arms and motto; later, he was presented with a donkey.[98] Earlier pursuits, however, were not forgotten. In 1869, a visit to Bradford to unveil a statue to Oastler recalled old causes and associates in them. In 1871, Shaftesbury opened a Lodging House for

Newsboys in Grays Inn Road – 'what a rough, unwashed, uncombed lot!' he wrote. 'But there is good material in them; and by God's blessing, we can work it into shape.'[99] And, in 1872, he laid the Memorial Stone of a number of dwelling houses erected by the Artisans Labourers and General Dwellings Company Ltd in Wandsworth Road, London. The Company had been formed in 1867 for the purpose of enabling working men to construct buildings and become their eventual owners by the payment of a small additional rent. The houses were well built, thoroughly drained and supplied with running water; there was ample school accommodation, recreation space and a hall for public meetings and lectures. Shaftesbury said that he was delighted with what he saw. The development was established on wise principles: that every man should have a house to himself and be the master of that house and head of a moral and industrious family. There was nothing so economical, he said, as 'humanity'. Whatever it might cost at the outset, good air, good water and no overcrowding would be found to be the most thrifty and best means of developing the physical and moral energies which God had given. Moreover, the domiciliary condition of the people affected their contentment, and people who were contented always gave a government less trouble than those who were not. Further, the experiment was a notable example of self-help and independence – it had been achieved without any assistance other than that which every man had a right to receive from his fellow man: sympathy and kind aid. He had, he said, been active in charitable work for thirty years. But it was not by reliance on charitable means that the work could be effected, nor was it by the speculative efforts of capitalists. 'It must be done,' Shaftesbury told his audience, 'by the exertion of your own hearts and hands. You may say "We are Christians and will live like civilised men".'[100] The speech, indeed, well illustrated the various aspects of Shaftesbury's social concern.

There were, then, many achievements in these years to give Shaftesbury cause for satisfaction. In 1868, indeed, he wrote – in relation to one such achievement – that the question of labour were all settled, since almost all forms of labour had been brought under regulation and control: he only had to watch the progress.[101] Nevertheless, gratification on these grounds was offset by other considerations which made him feel increasingly despondent and discouraged. There was his old dislike of the House of Lords. In 1866, when he spoke on the Labouring Classes Dwelling Bill, he wrote that the House was 'cold, comfortless, unsympathising; and more than usually inattentive'. He was vexed by the 'manifest disregard of so important a subject', and by the 'equally manifest disregard' of himself.[102] When speaking on the same subject in 1868, he wrote of the 'old inevitable spell' which always beset him in the Lords,[103] and in 1871 that, whereas he could always count on some supporters in the Commons, there were none in the Upper House.[104] There was also the long-standing complaint that schemes for social improvement met with indifference from the wealthy. He wrote in April, 1866, that charity was 'growing sleepy';[105] in 1871, after distributing prizes to Ragged School children, that he had never been able to excite an interest for such children among 'the fine and wealthy folks'.[106] He still felt that matters such as public health aroused insufficient interest and support. In 1872, he wrote to Playfair, a leading spokesman for public health in the Commons thanking him for a speech on the subject, but adding that it was

> melancholy and humiliating that, after so much experience, so much research and so much proof, a vast proportion of the educated people of this country do not perceive that the Public Health ranks among the very first of physical, financial and *moral* questions.[107]

But to these old sources and dissatisfaction and complaint were added newer ones, and these related to his pessimism over the effects of the Reform Act of 1867. As he contemplated the passing of the Act, he reflected on the ways in which it would undermine one aspect of his paternalistic and evangelical concern. He had, he wrote, long entertained a 'fond belief' that while making 'the welfare, physical, temporal and spiritual, of the working classes (his) primary object, a secondary one might be obtained in the contentment of the people; the repression of Democracy and the maintenance of our ancient Institutions.' He had partially gained the first, but he had totally failed in the second. Democracy would be established by the Conservative government, and he could see nothing but 'darkness, gloominesss and speedy extinction'.[108] Later, he returned to such themes. He wrote in November, 1867, that the Act would abate some of his labour 'for the People can now do everything for themselves;' but it also abated a good deal of his interest, 'for all, manifestly, is fruitless and is tending to speedy Revolution.'[109] The People were, then, beyond his reach – 'neither collectively nor by classes, had (they) any need of an Advocate.'[110] Even satisfaction that causes which he had long upheld still commanded some support was overlaid with pessimism. In March, 1869, he wrote of a great gathering of London workmen held to resist the opening of museums on a Sunday. This gave him hope that there would be a 'residue of Christian men in this land', but it gave him no hope that they would uphold the institutions of the country in Church and State. 'The new spirit is amongst them as elsewhere.'[111] In 1870, he wrote of a Temperance gathering which had taken place at St Giles. He was glad to see the 'venerable place' the source of enjoyment to so many hundreds, but he wept to think how soon all such things would pass away into republican sentiment.[112] The people had no reverence. They had it once, but no longer: 'they have no reverence for men, or things, past or present. They estimate everything by its power of instrumentality for their purposes.'[113] There were, it is true, occasions when he felt more optimistic. In 1872, a day of National Thanksgiving was held to mark the recovery of the Prince of Wales from a serious illness. Shaftesbury rejoiced in this manifestation of feeling – it was 'something gathered out of the wreck of all hereditary attachments' and might be the 'seed plot of better things in this ancient Kingdom'.[114] But such moments of optimism were rare, and he became increasingly certain that, in the social, as in the political world, the country was beyond control and could not be guided and restrained. Indeed, the popular demand would only be fanned by self-seeking politicians courting the popular will and the popular vote. In 1871, Shaftesbury wrote that Gladstone was an 'Instrument, not ... a leader: the People had taken him not because they had confidence in the man but because they had confidence in themselves' and wished to use him as a 'good tool'.[115]

Shaftesbury's prediction of the social consequences of the Reform Act were, like his views on its political implications, exaggerated and extreme. But, again, his analysis did have some validity. The Reform Act of 1867, with its injection of democracy into the political system, did mean that social improvement might well become a more lively issue. Yet Shaftesbury was not alone in sensing the dangers of this situation to the established order; a paternalistic concern for social improvement as a means to social stability might, indeed, be seen as more urgent in the light of 1867, if more difficult to practise. It was partly in this context that the question of education became more widely debated in the late 1860s, for there was a feeling that, now that considerable numbers of the working classes had the vote, they should be subjected to the influence of education. This could be a means of containing their demands and preserving social order. It might be thought that Shaftesbury would have found comfort and consolation in such an attitude, for it had not been absent from his ideas on the subject of education in the 1840s. But, although the principle of 'containment' might appeal to him on such grounds, the difficulty lay in its practice, for education in such circumstances could only mean state education, and this carried the danger of secular education. Shaftesbury thus found no consolation in the renewed interest in the subject in the late 1860s – indeed, it only served to deepen his pessimism. In 1868, he warned of the future as he addressed the Ragged School Union at its May meeting. He spoke of the danger that was looming; the system of compulsory education. He warned his audience to watch this 'with much care and jealousy; for recollect this ... that if the state is to impose a compulsory system of education, it must impose also a *secular* system of education.' No school could impose a system which involved the teaching of dogmatic truth – the school must be left 'entirely to the teaching of these things which concern man's lower life.' The establishment of state education would, moreover, undermine the position of the Ragged Schools. The role of those whose duty and pleasure it was 'to promote amongst the poorest of mankind a Knowledge of the Gospel of Christ' would clearly be threatened, for it would be even more difficult to raise funds for the schools from the public than it had been previously.[116] In 1869, after distributing prizes to Ragged School children, he wrote that it was a 'heart-cheering, heart-comforting sight. The result of 25 years of anxiety, labour and prayer.' But he 'wept to think how soon it must pass away.' The 'national' system of education was inevitable and it must 'eliminate all religion and freeze up the flow of genuine, simple, evangelical life.' The moment children became the object of state care, they would cease to be the objects of private compassion, and when 'ten thousand are taught to read, not one hundred will be taught to know that there is a God.'[117]

Shaftesbury thus prepared for the battle which lay ahead over education in a resigned frame of mind. Battle lines were clearly drawn in 1869 with the establishment of two bodies with opposing views: the National Education League, supported by many radicals and Dissenters and campaigning for free, universal, compulsory and non-sectarian education; and the National Education Union, which sought to preserve the religious and moral basis of education and to retain, if also to supplement, the denominational and voluntary system. It was, in fact, towards the latter view that the bill, introduced in February, 1870, by W. E. Forster, inclined. For the bill did not propose to destroy the existing system. The state would intervene and compel the establishment of schools in districts where, after inquiry, education was found to be lacking, and, even then, voluntary organisations would be given a year's grace to fill the need. Where state schools were set up, they would be administered by School Boards which would have authority to levy a rate, make attendance compulsory and pay fees for poor children. They would also decide on the religious training to be given and a conscience clause would give the parent the right to withdraw his child from such teaching. The bill was not unfavourable to the Church of England, and, for that very reason, it aroused the fierce antagonism of the Dissenters. They argued that it gave the Established Church an unfair advantage in allowing it to 'catch up' by means of the year of grace, and, even if Boards were established, they might, if dominated by Anglicans, prescribe Anglican religious teaching and support it from the rates. The battle which the Education bill aroused was not, therefore, so much one between the secularists and those who advocated religious education; rather it was one between Anglicans and Dissenters.

Despite his gloomy prognostications, Shaftesbury had not, in fact, been altogether dissatisfied with the bill. It is true that there were certain aspects of it which he did not like. One was compulsory attendance. He thought that this would be difficult to enforce in a mobile population. He also disliked the age range within which children were to be required to attend school: five to thirteen. He would have preferred four to ten. He pointed out in the Lords that Ragged Schools took in very young children, whose mothers were working. If this were not done in the new system, young children of working mothers would not be properly looked after, especially since older children would be at school. Again, at the other end, to keep children at school until thirteen would be to deprive parents of their earnings, and Shaftesbury felt that this was not altogether just.[118] Nevertheless, he was prepared to admit that, despite its imperfections, it was the best bill which the government could have produced.[119] It had due regard for what had been done by members of the Church of England and the various denominations. He also praised Forster, describing him at the annual meeting of the Ragged School Union in May, 1870, as an 'admirable and excellent man' who had introduced his bill in 'the very best possible of spirits and with great ability and earnestness'.[120]

Shaftesbury, however, thoroughly deplored the denominational rivalries to which the bill gave rise. The religious difficulty, he said, was simply a 'euphonious term for the assault and defence of the Established Church'. It presented no difficulty to those who were banded together to teach the 'great and saving truths of the Gospel' and who did not devote time to advancing denominational issues – such persons were to be found in the Ragged Schools.[121] He knew that it was not possible to insist on the introduction of the Catechism and Prayer Book, as some Church of England clergy wanted; this would be reckless and would endanger the Established Church. But equally, he condemned the opposition of the Dissenters to the bill. They were, he argued, jeopardising all religious teaching and playing the game of the secularists. When speaking in April, 1870, to the National Education Union, he stressed that he was anti-secularist, not pro-denominational. In a rousing speech, he asked simply that the Bible and the teaching of the Bible should be 'an essential and not an extra'. And he stressed the importance of 'the checks and restraints of religion' at a time when so wide an extension of the franchise had been granted. 'Is this a time,' he asked, 'to take from the mass of the population, in whom all power will henceforward reside, that principle of internal self-control . . . ?'[122] Shaftesbury was pleased with the speech: he blessed God that he had been 'enabled to stand up in defence of His holy word for this and for all the generations of children.'¹²³ Forster was also gratified at his speech, writing to Shaftesbury that it would do a great deal of good and would cause a reaction among Dissenters who would 'shrink in fear from their position.'¹²⁴

But denominational difficulties did not, in fact, abate, and, in the face of pressure from the Dissenters, the government in June accepted various amendments to the bill. One provided that, in Board Schools, no catechism or formulary distinctive of any particular denomination was to be taught. The amendment was proposed by William Cowper-Temple, Shaftesbury's brother-in-law, who was chairman of the National Education Union. Cowper-Temple was not opposed to sectarian education, but his amendment was designed to overcome the objection that the use of denominational material for religious instruction implied acceptance of that particular denomination. Another amendment provided that School Boards should not assist voluntary schools from the rates, although the government grant to denominated schools was increased; and yet another reduced the 'year of grace' to six months. Gladstone, it appears, explained these proposals in advance to Shaftesbury in general terms and he told him that he was willing to communicate with Shaftesbury 'freely in regard to the prospects and provisions of the measure.' He himself had assented to the changes reluctantly, but he felt that the measure was a reasonable compromise and that it would be acceptable to 'men of moderation'.¹²⁵ Shaftesbury replied that he would be ready to support the amendment of his brother-in-law – indeed, he would gladly have accepted this provision in the original bill. The other amendments he did not like, fearing that the increased grant to denominational schools would 'raise up annually a "Maynooth Debate" and terminate as disastrously.'¹²⁶

Thus Shaftesbury was always at pains to counter secular influences rather than to score denominational points. And this was true once the Boards were set up. A section of the Act made it possible to remit the fees of children whose parents could not afford to pay them, but, until the Board schools were actually built, the only way in which this could be done was to make the fees for such children payable to the existing denominational schools. This, however, raised a storm of protest against the use of money from the rates to finance voluntary schools. Dissenters held a conference at Manchester in 1872 and urged the repeal of the relevant section of the Act. Shaftesbury, addressing a Meeting of the National Education Union, argued strongly against this. The clause was a poor man's charter, and, again, he urged Dissenters to cease such squabbles and defend the Bible.¹²⁷

In a sense, the Bible *had* been defended as part of the new system: education was not wholly secular and Shaftesbury told the Ragged School

Union in 1871 that he did not intend to disparage the arrangements which had been made. He believed that the law did all that was possible to provide for the Christian education of children. Again, he praised Forster as a 'good and true man', who had done his best and saved the country from national apostasy.[128] But, although Shaftesbury's worst fears had been confounded, his gloom was not dispelled. He wrote that the new schools 'founded on rates and fierce hatred of "denominational" teaching (would) prove to be, in nine cases out of ten, vast factories for Infidelity.'[129] Where the Boards *did* prescribe religious instruction, little time would be given to it, and, in practice, it would make a very small contribution to the development of a Christian life. He urged Ragged School teachers to do all in their power to redress the balance: 'If your schools subsist,' he told them, 'you must give them more and more of a religious character; you must endeavour to catch the children when they come out of the secular furnaces and bring them under the influence of the Gospel.'[130] He also did his best to press the cause of Ragged Schools. He had written to *The Times* in October, 1870, requesting that subscriptions to them should be continued. The Education Act would take some time to come into effect, and, if Ragged Schools were broken up in the interval, some thirty thousand children would be thrown back into their former state of 'wretchedness, ignorance and neglect'. And he pointed to what Ragged Schools had done in encouraging emigration, domestic service and employment.[131]

But Shaftesbury had known in his heart that the Ragged Schools were, as he put it in 1870, a 'dying Patient'.[132] He noted towards the end of 1871 that, as he had foreseen, the schools *were* being broken up,[133] and, in early 1872, that it would be a waste of time, health and strength to attempt to prolong their existence.[134] Their buildings were already being surrendered to the London School Board.

> These Buildings [he wrote] were raised by monies, sought on behalf of distinctive Evangelical Religion to the poorest classes. They are to be made over to the Board, which will not tolerate us more than a dot of time, and a spark of truth to these poor children. . . . All this will greatly abridge my labours, but it will half break my heart.[135]

In the face of all such discouragements, Shaftesbury did not give up. He had written, in 1868 that while life and strength were accorded to him, he would set himself to see how he might

> institute and diffuse the constant and universal preaching of Christ and His Second Coming, and so elevate the Residuum, even in this world, by the forcing pump of the Gospel.[136]

Yet he became more than ever convinced that his day was over. He often reverted in these years to earlier thoughts that his career had raised up many enemies: the factory question and 'all the kindred questions' had severed him from politicians and their friendship and had engendered 'among a very numerous class a contempt and hatred which, in such men's minds, must ever attach to "Philanthropy". . . .' Perhaps he had come forward too often and spoken too freely, but he could not help it – such was his nature: it was 'all or nothing'. He was, then, every day becoming more alone without advisers, assets, friends and co-adjutors: he was 'an ancient weather-beaten rock with the sea daily receding from it.'[137] Moreover, his place as a spokesman on social matters was being taken by others. Matters such as health, sanitation and dwellings for the working classes were 'seized upon and assigned to other "Experts".' Many had been his own, but time had forced them into the hands of men who had 'vastly superior opportunities, resources and public favour'.[138] In 1872, he reflected that there had been a time when he had been an authority on many social questions, but he was no longer, for many had 'risen up in the various walks and have a good deal to say for themselves.' He considered, moreover, that his course had always been 'tainted . . . by the intermixture of Religion.' This was endured so long as there was no other. But now the secularists had entered the field of Philanthropy ('the dreadful word', he added) and they were held in favour by the public and the press.[139] A symbol of this declining influence was, he felt, the fact that a volume of his speeches on various social matters[140] attracted little attention. He received two or three 'kind notices', but, he wrote, the world at large had ignored them – a third of the edition remained unsold.[141] Thus any influence he might once have had was extinct. Another sign of this was the fact that he was not invited to stand for election to the new School Boards. He reflected that many sympathetic to the cause of religion had been invited to stand, but he was not: 'Not a Deputation, not a request, not an expression of sympathy have I had,' he wrote. He would not, in fact, have accepted the post, being too 'pressed by business and age.' But – reverting to thoughts expressed earlier in his career – he would have liked the tribute to his services.[142] He even felt that he was coldly received at the Ragged School Union. He wrote in May, 1871, that 'even on (his) own dung-hill, (he was) no longer the true Chanticleer,'[143] and, a year later, that audiences were tired of him and he of audiences, for he could get no response. He could 'move no hearts, raise no money and advance no interests.'[144]

There were, indeed, certain occasions in these years when Shaftesbury felt some measure of inner consolation. In 1867, he felt that his career – 'dry, dreary and secretly despised by the world' – had surely been ordained to him by God, and he added: 'I therein do rejoice: yea and will rejoice.'[145]

And there were other occasions when he felt less 'despised'. His volatility of temperament was still amply evident, to no one more than himself: 'oftentimes in high spirits and oftentimes exceedingly low,' he wrote at the end of 1871, when he surveyed the 'three score years and ten' which he had completed in the course of that year.[146] Old complaints, such as his 'fastidious stomach' had, indeed, troubled him during these past few years, and he once wrote that his nerves were so highly strung that they felt like 'the twang of a Jew's Harp'.[147] Nevertheless, at the age of seventy, he felt that there were many reasons for gratitude. His eyesight was good, he required glasses only for reading and he was only 'somewhat deaf'. He slept well and walked easily, although not very far without getting tired; he was 'tolerably erect' and had few grey hairs. And, although he suspected that his memory was 'a little weakened', he thought that 'whatever mind' he ever had, he still retained. His feelings were 'as vivid and as keen' as in his youth. He did, indeed, admit to many faults and defects. He was behind his contemporaries in knowledge of all kinds; he had no pretence to literary attainments, although he had a great fondness for them; he was 'intellectually not strong'; he was 'over-anxious for success, over-fearful of failure, easily exalted, as easily depressed, with a good deal of ambition, and no real self-confidence.' He was 'weak in debate, and incapable of any effort, without some preparation; a poor and ineffective orator, though foolishly desirous of being a great one.' But, despite all these handicaps, there had been successes, and he admitted that qualities which he *did* have were 'feeling, perseverance and conviction'. These, under God, had brought him to the position which he now held – 'a position of notoriety and even of reputation'.[148]

Even this assessment was somewhat too self-critical and disparaging, but it had more truth in it than the view, to which he so often gave way, that all persons looked on him with secret or open loathing. At the age of seventy, Shaftesbury *had* reached a position of great public eminence and was widely respected; he himself noted 'birthday presents of laudatory passages in newspapers'.[149] Another mark of this was the presentation of the freedom of the City of Glasgow made to Shaftesbury during a visit which he made to the city in August, 1871. In making the presentation, the Lord Provost said that citizens of Glasgow recognised in the 'long course of public work' in which Shaftesbury had been engaged 'something which merited the highest approval at their hands,' and the freedom was given in testimony of the City's appreciation of Shaftesbury's

> long-continued and valuable services in the promotion of all measures having for their object the amelioration of the condition of the great body of the people, and their intellectual and religious progress.

In reply, Shaftesbury said that it would have been a great honour to himself and his family to have been enrolled among any body of free and independent citizens. But when he found that he was to be enrolled a citizen 'of the second City of the empire, whose name is in every country, whose ships cover the ocean, whose products are known in every soil and in every climate', he felt that he had attained an honour which was a full reward for any 'humble labours' which he might have performed.[150] And in London, the fact that the site of the houses erected by the Artisans Labourers and General Dwellings Company was called the 'Shaftesbury Park Estate' was another recognition of his past endeavours.

And yet there was some truth in Shaftesbury's pessimistic observations. The very fact that public honours were being conferred on him indicated that he was now something of a 'monument to the past'. Few men of seventy can, of course, be anything else, and it was also inevitable that others should take his place in initiating further developments. But it is also true that the forces of democracy, collectivism and secularism were increasing, and with these, paternalism, evangelicalism and an advocacy of individual responsibility and self-betterment were to be uneasy bedfellows. As so often in the past, Shaftesbury felt that opposition to his 'causes' was tantamount to opposition to and disapproval of himself. The truth was that he himself was held in high regard; his 'causes' were gradually, but increasingly, being overtaken or being advanced in other ways. He had been accurate in describing himself as a weatherbeaten rock with the sea receding from it. A further simile which, if somewhat over-dramatic, also contained a good deal of truth, was his comparison of his position to an old tree in a forest 'half submerged by a mighty flood' : he remained where he was, while everything was passing beyond him.[151]

If domestic affairs darkened Shaftesbury's outlook in these years, he found little comfort in the momentous events which took place on the Continent of Europe : the Austro-Prussian war of 1866 and the Franco-Prussian war of 1870. The victory of Prussia in both wars did, admittedly, bring him some satisfaction on religious grounds. He wrote of the Austrian defeat in 1866 that it was the 'hand of God falling on Popery' and 'resting on Protestantism',[152] and the war of 1870 was, he felt, one between the 'Papal Champion and the Protestant in Continental Europe'.[153] Further, he was glad that the Italian cause was assisted in both wars. It is true that the Italian participation on the Prussian side in the war of 1866 ended in her defeat at the hands of Austria, but Shaftesbury felt that this was no dishonour. Italy had fought against fearful odds and with immense courage and her effort had raised her reputation. Further, Venetia was added to Italy in 1866 and her unification completed by the acquisition of Rome in 1870. Of the latter, he noted that the march of the Italians on Rome followed immediately the declaration of the Pope as infallible: 'first goes the temporal power, to be destroyed by man: then, though perhaps with an interval, his spiritual power, to be destroyed by Christ only!'[154]

Nevertheless, there were aspects of both wars which were not to Shaftesbury's liking. His long-standing admiration for Prussia was tempered by the fact that Neology owed much to German scholarship. Thus, if Austria was the 'Romanist Idolator', Prussia was the 'Protestant Infidel'[155] – she had 'departed from the Living God.'[156] The Franco-Prussian war was a 'fearful thing'. It was 'Anti-Christ on both sides: the Papal and the Infidel Anti-Christ.'[157] Further, although his sympathies were with Prussia – for he felt that both wars had been precipitated by her enemies – he did have some misgivings about the implications of German unification under Prussian leadership. He wrote in 1866 of the dangers of being

> landed in a new set of principles, justifying aggression, annexation, extinction of smaller states, denial of all rights to the weak, provided that you can show that political symmetry will be the result.[158]

The Protestantism of Prussia was certainly 'antagonistic to the Man of Sin in the Vatican and subversive of him,' but it was also a 'cold, political, selfish form of faith'.[159] Shaftesbury was also deeply distrustful of Bismarck. He wrote of him in 1866 as 'ambitious, deceitful, grasping, violent, the ne plus ultra of Politicians',[160] and, in 1870, as 'too unscrupulous, too dishonest'.[161] He also feared the military strength of Prussia, armed with the breech-loading needle Musket: until other powers were properly armed, Prussia was the 'Arbitress of Europe'.[162] He deeply deplored the loss of life involved in both wars – in 1870, he took part in efforts to assist the sick and wounded and recommended that representations should be made to the government on the question of exporting arms to either of the belligerents.[163] And he could not but reflect on the cruelly false hopes of universal peace and concord which had been held out by the Manchester school. Free trade, commercial treaties and all the trappings of material progress were to 'rule mankind, subdue the passions, regenerate society and render tumults (and) bloodshed impossible!' The Gospel had gone for nothing. But one had only to look at events. 'What a satire is all this war and Horror on the wisdom of this world' Shaftesbury wrote.[164]

The wars were, then, a clear sign of the folly of man's self-confidence and conceit, and the Prussian victories were by no means wholly to be welcomed. And Shaftesbury was appalled by the state of France after her defeat in 1870. He had little sympathy, it is true, for Napoleon III, whose conduct, he felt, had done much to provoke the war with Prussia, and, in the fall of Paris in September, 1870, he saw the judgment of God – 'the external beauties of that Capital of all the Vices, Luxuries and Enjoyments of mankind are destroyed for at least half a century.'[165] He also found little to praise in the resistance of the republican régime which replaced that of Napoleon III – it was 'vanity called valour and pride called patriotism'.[166] But there was worse to come when the republican government of Thiers, having negotiated a settlement with Germany, was itself overthrown by the Commune. Shaftesbury noted in March, 1871, that 'terrible intelligence' of a Revolution in Paris had been received: Thiers had been deposed and a 'Red Republic' set up.[167] Never since 1793 had extreme democrats achieved such power, and Paris had been wilfully destroyed by the 'hands of her own children'.[168] Shaftesbury reflected, more in sorrow than in anger, that the fate of his own country was little different; such, indeed, was his pessimism about the direction of events at home that he was moved to comment that, although France was in an 'awful condition', her future was brighter than that of Britain.[169]

Public affairs thus gave grounds for gloom and depression, and private affairs offered no relief. The law suits in which Shaftesbury was involved with Lewer and Waters were an anxiety and a burden. 'These suits are wearisome,' Shaftesbury wrote in 1866, 'they demand a very large proportion of my time, a serious amount of my money and no end of thought and attention. And what will issue? . . .'[170] The case involving Lewer was heard in Chancery in March and April, 1866, and the decision given against Lewer. Shaftesbury was much relieved, but he heard that Lewer threatened to appeal: thus, he wrote, he had as yet gained nothing and must wait on the process of the law to recover the rents which had been withheld. In June, Shaftesbury noted that Lewer had, indeed, appealed – this increased his expenses and prolonged his anxieties.[171] But in February, 1867, Lewer's appeal was dismissed: 'I bless the Lord,' wrote Shaftesbury.[172] The suit involving Waters was more intractible. The case which Waters brought against Shaftesbury for payment in connection with the drainage works came up for trial in Chancery in March, 1866. The decision was to the effect that Waters was entitled to be regarded as an agent of the Drainage Company and that settlement with Shaftesbury in his favour would, therefore, have to be made. Waters had thus won his point, and Shaftesbury was dismayed and perplexed. He could not but reflect how the result had 'gainsayed and annihilated so many ardent, continuous, faithful prayers; such earnest supplications to be delivered . . . from sorrow and disgrace.' Had prayers 'deep, intense, sincere,' ascended from the other side? If so, it might be that those, in God's wisdom, were more acceptable: 'He only can read men's hearts.'[173] Had Shaftesbury won the case, he would have dropped the criminal charge against Waters for embezzlement, but the decision clearly made this impossible. The criminal suit was, in fact, postponed so that accounts could be drawn up, and Shaftesbury decided to take the Chancery decision against him to appeal. The appeal was heard in January, 1867, and, on 11 January, Shaftesbury heard that it had gone in his favour: Waters's case was dismissed with costs. It was, wrote Shaftesbury, a 'deliverance'.[174] Nevertheless, it was still necessary for an account between Shaftesbury and Waters to be made up and this caused further delays. In June, 1867, Shaftesbury noted that there was no hope of closing Waters's accounts that year. Thus Waters still had power to 'harass, annoy and insult' him. Waters was 'beaten and exposed in everything', yet he stood erect in court with the means and the will to protract his former employer's distress. 'Lord, how long?' wrote Shaftesbury.[175] Later, in the summer of 1867, Shaftesbury noted that the taxing Master in Chancery had assigned to him £260 in costs, but Waters had appealed against it.[176] Waters's next move was to declare himself a bankrupt, and this closed the examination of the accounts. 'What a successful villain,' wrote Shaftesbury. 'Not a single decree of the Law reaches him . . .'[177] Waters's trial for embezzlement was due to begin in May, 1868. It was further delayed by the illness of Waters – just before the trial started, he became ill with smallpox. Shaftesbury could scarcely believe that an illness could strike at so opportune a moment. But it was clear that Waters's bankruptcy made it very unlikely that any settlement in Shaftesbury's favour could produce any tangible result, and through the good offices of a neighbouring landowner in Dorset, Lord Portman, an 'agreement' was reached between the parties in July, 1868. This stated that the investigation of the accounts in Chancery had shown that they were 'multifarious, intricate and badly kept', but it was agreed that no further proceedings should be taken in these matters by either party. All proceedings in bankruptcy and all criminal proceedings by Shaftesbury against Waters were to end, and all transactions between Shaftesbury and Waters were considered as terminated.[178] Waters thereupon went abroad. Some months later, Shaftesbury noted that his former steward was safe from all financial troubles – he had married a rich woman. 'Will he now repay me one farthing of the thousands of which he has robbed me? I trow not.'[179]

The whole episode thus had a bitter sequel for Shaftesbury, and, although he was glad to be rid of the case, he looked back on the matter with great anguish. He felt that his lawyers ought not to have allowed him to plunge into the criminal suit: 'plain, manifest, tangible as was the double-dyed guilts of Waters,' he wrote, 'the Solicitors ought to have known . . . that a matter of account was no subject for a Penal Court.'[180] He would have been spared years of vexation, wasted time and expense. Thus – as in the past – Shaftesbury felt that he had been badly served, but – as also in the past – he knew in his heart that he should never have allowed the trouble to arise in the first place. Even before all the complexities and delays of the case, he noted in 1866 that he had reposed unlimited and unjustifiable confidence in Waters: it was the 'duty of a proprietor . . . to be more regular, attentive and less incautious in exposing his agents to temptation.' And he blamed himself for failing to see 'the labyrinth of darkness, difficulty, errors and treachery' which he was entering when he had opened so many accounts and had made such complicated arrangements, all under the care of one man. 'Here is Mr Waters's loophole,' he reflected, 'here his one means of escape . . . in the impossible and unprecedented intricacy of facts and figures.'[181] Shaftesbury's knowledge that the intricacy was of his own making can only have increased his sense of frustration.

In this sad review of his dealings with Waters, Shaftesbury also explored the related theme of his financial difficulties. He admitted that he had spent too much money on his various interests and projects. The purposes might have been good, but the end – at least financially – did not justify the means. Ever since he began the factory question, he noted, he had laid out on that and all 'kindred movements' much more than he had proposed. Debt – heavy debt – had been the result of 'an impetuous entry into many religious and charitable undertakings'. There was, he felt, 'occasionally an excuse' and it was one which he had put forward in the past: that parsimony would have brought his outward profession into contempt among persons who did not know about his 'contracted means'. And he also reflected that the management of the Estates since 1851 had acted in a similar way. He was eager to improve them 'for the sake of the working men' and had ' "rushed into cottage building", hoping to rejoice in the benefits, tho' ignorant of the "ways and means" to pay for it.' The large drainage works had been instituted on the same principle. He never contemplated any pecuniary return to be enjoyed by himself: he did it to employ labour, elevate the whole farming system and the people with it. But the effect had, by mismanagement and peculation, proved ruinous, and years would need to elapse before matters could be put right. The whole matter had meant that he had lost any reputation for 'sense and administration', and now, far less money was entrusted to him than had been done previously for religious and charitable purposes. The impression had got about that he could not manage money well and it might also be that some people feared that, in his distress, he might misappropriate it. He concluded from all this that he had acted 'on feeling'; he had not realised that there was 'no promise of miracles to be wrought to supply what might be done by common sense; and that mere warmth of heart is a very deceptive guide in the details of life.'[182]

It was a painful – and, in large measure, a truthful – assessment of his position. And yet the years that followed saw little improvement. The Lewer and Waters cases, of course, continued to drain his finances: he noted in May, 1870, that his legal expenses were still unpaid.[183] Demands for money for religious and charitable activities continued to tax his resources. He wrote in October, 1867, that such demands were made daily. If he complied, he ran into debt; if he refused, no one believed that he could not afford it and discredit was thrown on the profession of Christianity.[184] The ill-fated Malta College still plagued him. He noted in March, 1868, that, in addition to the sum which he had already paid for the debts of the College, he had to pay a further £250. Such was the issue, he wrote, of the efforts of his fellow-workers in the cause; although professing the highest principles of Evangelical religion, they were 'utterly reckless of the things they do and the counsel they give.'[185] And, if Shaftesbury could not escape from this aspect of his financial problem, he could not, in conscience, ignore the other aspect which he had stressed in March, 1866: his Estates. In October of the same year, he wrote that there was still much to be done on his Estates: cottages to be built and repaired, roads to be made, education to be improved and people to be induced to accept it. All required time, strength and labour. This he would readily give, but it also required 'money and much money' and that he did not have to give.[186] He maintained and increased all his old efforts at economy. His estate in Yorkshire, Swine, was sold in August, 1866: 'I was finally severed from my People,' he wrote. 'God's will be done. It is a sad grief to me.'[187] The sale realised £125,000, a sum which Shaftesbury considered much below its value,[188] and it was not of as much assistance as he had hoped. In December, 1866, he decided that he could not live at St Giles for at least a year – he must shut it up and 'sneak there occasionally to look after the people.'[189] In the autumn of 1867, he wrote that all was cut down to the lowest point[190]: in 1868 that economies had to be pushed to the utmost.[191] In 1869, he sold the greater part of a diamond tiara: 'it was pain and grief thus to dispose of hereditary Jewels.' Minny, however, made no difficulty: 'nay she was cheerful and urged it. Such is a good woman and an affectionate wife. God be praised for His "unspeakable gift"!'[192] But money was still urgently required to carry out such repairs to cottages as Shaftesbury felt he could afford – or, rather, which he felt he must afford. Thus he noted in April, 1871, that, to counterbalance the presents of laudatory passages in the newspapers on his seventieth birthday, he received 'terrible demands' for repairs,[193] and his comments became ever more desperate and despairing. In October, 1871, he wrote that cottages and farms were greatly in need of repair, tenants refused to pay their rents, and every resource was 'dry'. He had sold, for the benefit of the Estates, everything of his own with which he could part: 'Economies!' he declared. 'What economies are practicable in my state?'[194] He felt that his new steward, Turnbull, was, unlike Waters, a good and profitable servant, but wondered how he could meet Turnbull's requests for more money for the Estates – 'the thing is simply impossible' he wrote on one occasion.[195]

Shaftesbury was thus constantly harassed by financial worries, and there were also other grounds for anxiety and discouragement. In June, 1867, indeed, he wrote that he had had sixteen years of occupation of the Estates, and yet it had not 'pleased God to bless any one project' which he had set on foot. Schools and a careful selection of clergy had 'availed nothing'; the people were 'no better in knowledge, morality or a life of prayer.' He had made great efforts to bring about increased employment and higher wages with good cottage accommodation at nominal rents, and yet his tenants had not taken advantage of the opportunities offered to them: 'it is their own fault,' he wrote; 'they will not turn to account the blessings of Providence.'[196] His efforts, then, had gone unrecognised, even by his own people, and unacknowledged, too, he felt, in other quarters. Shaftesbury was saddened by the findings of the Commission on the Employment of Children, Young Persons and Women in Agriculture, appointed in 1867. The evidence which related to Dorset was contained in the Appendices to the second Report of the Commission published in 1869.[197] The Commissioner who had visited Dorset was Edward Stanhope, and his Report did, of course, extend to the whole county and not only to Shaftesbury's Estates. Stanhope, however, commented on the low rents for cottages charged on Shaftesbury's Estates,[198] and he drew particular attention to what he called the 'redeeming feature of rural life'.[199] This was the amount of land held by the labouring classes in the form of gardens and allotments, and, again, Shaftesbury's Estates merited a favourable mention: there were three hundred and ninety six allotment gardens and one hundred and sixty five of these extended to half an acre. All were let out at low rents.[200] Again, Stanhope referred to considerable improvement in cottage accommodation in the county[201] – a point which the Revd Sydney Godolphin Osborne, who gave evidence to the Commission, also mentioned.[202] But Stanhope gave the credit for this to Osborne himself, and he also mentioned the lead which had been given by Mr Sturt at Crichell[203] – Shaftesbury's efforts were not specifically mentioned. Moreover, even allowing for such improvements as had taken place, Stanhope was still very critical of existing cottage accommodation in the county. In the absence of adequate bedroom space, overcrowding was common, and sanitary arrangements were also minimal.²⁰⁴ Shaftesbury's Estates did not escape such condemnation,²⁰⁵ and Shaftesbury was thrown into gloom and despondency. He wrote that he was 'grieved by a disingenuous and malevolent report' on the state of his property. Some facts were true, but others had been suppressed. He would have hoped that the Report would have indicated some progress in wages and cottage accommodation. But Stanhope had given 'a picture of the county as though it were the same as thirty years ago'; he had taken everything from Godolphin Osborne, 'who to maintain his own character blinds the eyes of his wretched pupil.'²⁰⁶ Such comments were, in fact, unfair to Stanhope and to Godolphin Osborne – the Report *had* indicated some progress. But, to Shaftesbury, it was a great disappointment:

> I had hoped for a juster issue for the sake of the Aristocracy; I had hoped it for the honour of the County; I had hoped it for the proof of my own consistency and that thus an occasion might be avoided for charging professors of religious life with selfishness and hypocrisy.²⁰⁷

Even accepting, however, that progress had been made over the condition of the Estates, Shaftesbury felt that it was all doomed to extinction. On the eve of the passing of the Reform Bill he wrote that he had hoped to make his Estate 'a model Estate, almost a garden for cultivation and comfort of the Peasantry'. It had been his 'desire to do, thereby, some good to the Constitution, and show the benefit of hereditary Property, and large surfaces of land in single hands.' But now 'the Revolution was at hand;' the effect of the Reform Bill would upset and reverse all his work.²⁰⁸ In August, 1867, he asked himself if he should labour to improve his Estates and benefit his people. 'Certainly because it is right,' was his answer: but, he added, he would not transmit them to another generation. He would view 'dear old St Giles' as the inheritance of his father, 'to be broken up and partitioned among aliens and Democrats.'²⁰⁹ He wondered if Anthony would be allowed to succeed to the title and the ancient lands. If so, there did, at last, seem to be signs that Anthony himself was improving. Shaftesbury noted in March, 1866, that Anthony had undergone 'a mighty change'. His letters to Victoria were 'quite rich in piety and scriptural truth'.²¹⁰ And Shaftesbury was pleased at the birth of a son to Harriet and Anthony, now living on the Estate in Dorset, after four daughters. The birth and christening in 1869 were a cause for rejoicing on the Estate; Shaftesbury wrote that the tenantry had 'exhibited something of former days when real affection subsisted between Peasant and Proprietor, Landlord and Tenant.'²¹¹ The tenantry showed delight that a son and heir had been born in their midst and plate was presented to Anthony. Shaftesbury noted with pleasure that Anthony had made himself deservedly popular with them. But he could only reflect that all inheritances were gone:

> The Radicals and Residuum . . . have extinguished all but the 'Inheritance of the Saints in Light', a thing which they do not covet, and which, therefore, they do not care to deny to others.

The demonstration of loyalty on the birth of Shaftesbury's grandson was the 'last trace of the ancient sympathies. The Age of Calculators and Economists is at hand.'[212]

Moreover, Shaftesbury was by no means sure that Anthony's change of heart would last, and, even if it did, the influence of Harriet could be counted on to liquidate the Estate, even if the 'Calculators and Economists' did not. In 1867 Shaftesbury noted that he had received an account for £1,000 to pay for Anthony. He, 'poor boy', was not to blame, but Harriet had been extravagant over the purchase of furniture.[213] Anthony's marriage to Harriet continued to be a source of sadness and displeasure. Shaftesbury mentioned at the end of December, 1869, that they had presented 'a series of wretched and forged excuses to cloak their refusal to give us either the season of Christmas or New Year's Day.'

> Well be it so! [he continued]. I should have liked their company as a mark of kindness and respect to my advanced life; but I shall desire it no more; and I shall content myself by doing my duty towards them without the hope of their society or the reward of esteem and affection.[214]

But he could not shrug it off as easily as that. Early in January, 1870, he wrote that there was still no sign of Harriet and Anthony, and no message of courteous regret. 'What have we done to deserve such insolence?' he asked.[215] Later in the month, Shaftesbury mentioned rumours that Anthony might be asked to stand for the county. He was, however, 'most unfit for such a duty and such a life': he had offended both constituencies which he had represented – Hull and Cricklade – by inattention and neglect of duty.[216] Shaftesbury was 'cut to the quick' when he thought of those who were to come after him. Meanness and oppression would reign where kindness and liberality were required; prodigality would be practised when the expenditure was calculated 'for an ample return in aristocratic and social grandeur.' He believed that, within twelve months of coming into the Estates, Anthony and Harriet would be odious to everyone on them. Delighted as he was at the birth of a grandson, he 'trembled' for his grandchildren, especially Margaret, the eldest of the family.[217] Harriet's behaviour to her – and indeed to Minny, Victoria, Caroline and Hilda – made Shaftesbury 'grieve that such a woman (was) a member of (his) family and was to inherit (his) substance.'[218] In 1872, Shaftesbury was greatly offended that Anthony and Harriet undertook enlargements to their house on the Estate without his approval and had issued 'something like orders' to his steward to provide the bricks, slates and lead. 'What have I done to be thus hated by them,' he asked.[219] Anthony finally wrote and apologised – Shaftesbury was glad of this and attributed much of his son's objectionable conduct to Harriet. But, as in the past, Shaftesbury felt that the letter of contrition did not betoken a permanent change of heart: it was 'a bright bubble and soon bursts.'[220] He wished to talk to Anthony on Estate matters, but it was impossible. Thus Shaftesbury's dealings with his son and daughter-in-law could only make him feel that, despite all his sacrifices, his Estates would pass into 'unworthy hands' which would consume them by 'neglect, grasping, hardness and vulgar ostentation'.[221]

Shaftesbury also had worries about his third surviving son, Lionel. The commercial company in which Lionel had started work failed in 1866 owing to over-speculation. Shaftesbury was glad that Lionel had not been implicated; indeed, he had behaved with courage and principle. But his future was 'confiscated' wrote Shaftesbury; he was 'without a shilling unless I can find one to give him.'[222] Here, then, was yet another financial problem. Other events concerning his sons, however, gave cause for greater pleasure. Evelyn was married in 1866, and Lionel himself in 1868. Shaftesbury was well pleased with his new daughters-in-law. Evelyn's wife was Sybella Farquhar: 'a charming girl,' wrote Shaftesbury, 'and I much like the family.'[223] It was one of Evangelical stock. Lionel married Fanny Hanbury-Leigh. It was, Shaftesbury wrote, 'a wonderful event, *a Special Providence* . . .' The girl had preferred Lionel, poor as he was, to Lord Mahon, who had title and estate.[224] Fanny was a 'good dear girl with every charm of body and every quality that can give dignity and truth to a woman.'[225] Shaftesbury thus had 'deep and unspeakable reason to bless God that He (had) given (him) two such wives for (his) sons as Sissy and Fanny. They (were) thorough Darlings, in every sense of the word.' He could not resist remarking how different Harriet was: 'hard-hearted, insolent, mean, tyrannical and ungrateful'.[226]

If Shaftesbury was glad to see Evelyn and Lionel married to such suitable wives, he dearly wished to see his daughters married to suitable husbands. This was a constant theme in his Diary entries during these years: 'is there no hope,' ran one such entry in 1868, 'that, before I close my eyes, I may see these unhappy, friendless girls joined to true, pious and faithful husbands?'[227] He trembled at the prospect of 'departing this life and leaving them unprotected.'[228] So long as he had three unmarried daughters, he felt that he had to keep a carriage for them and a house in London, although he also knew that this was an expense which he could ill afford.[229] He was overjoyed when, in August, 1872, Victoria announced her engagement to Lord Templemore, and it was a suitable marriage. Templemore was a 'truly kind, amiable, gentleman like and sensible man, who (had) everything to make himself and her happy.' He would 'render her life joyous, joyous . . . in Christ Jesus,' and Victoria would repay him. The circumstances, Shaftesbury wrote, were 'wonderful, singular, Providential, wholly unforeseen, wholly beyond all human possibility. But is anything too hard for the Lord? Nothing!'[230]

There were, then, some events which brightened these years for Shaftesbury, but others were deeply distressing. He was saddened by the deaths of many long-standing friends and associates: Sir James South in 1867; the Duchess of Sutherland and Archbishop Longley – who had tutored him in Oxford – in 1868; Judge Joseph Payne, who had closely collaborated with him in many Evangelical pursuits and especially in the Ragged School Union, in 1870. Such deaths increased his sense of isolation. Worse still, there were many family deaths. His brother, John, died in 1867; his sisters, Harriet and Caroline in 1868 and 1869 respectively. Shaftesbury had always felt a particular closeness to his sisters, and the deaths of Harriet and Caroline moved him greatly. There was the consolation in the case of Harriet that she had been ill for a number of years and paralysed for the previous four – existence, Shaftesbury felt, had become burdensome for her and death could be looked on as a relief to herself as well as to others. 'Poor Darling,' he wrote, 'she truly and tenderly loved me and, I am sure, I returned it!'[231] Caroline had also proved to be a staunch sister and friend: she had helped her brother considerably with money and had financed many of the alterations in St Giles's House.[232] She was, Shaftesbury wrote, 'kindness itself',[233] and, when she died in June, 1869, he mourned the death of 'a most affectionate, true and generous friend, and one who loved (him) with a depth and sincerity seldom manifested or felt.'[234] A further death in 1869 removed another relative who had been a good friend to Shaftesbury: Lady Palmerston. Shaftesbury and Minny received news of her illness in September, 1869, while they were abroad. Before they were able to return, Lady Palmerston had died and they were able only to attend the funeral in Westminster Abbey. Shaftesbury always realised that his own attitude to his mother-in-law was ambivalent: he was truly grateful for her kindness and liberality. She was, as he put it, his and Minny's 'main source of aid'.[235] But he also wished that she would mend her worldly ways. 'Would that her heart was as true towards God, as it is towards us' was his comment on one occasion in 1868 after further financial assistance. But at her death, he wrote that, until he lost her, he hardly knew how much he loved her.[236] He told Minny's brother, William Cowper-Temple, that, in the forty years of his marriage, he had never once seen 'a cloud come over the face of that dear woman to mark any change in her unceasing thoughts and acts of kindness, generosity and affection. Poor, dear, beloved Mum, it is a very terrible thing to have lost her.'[237] She had been to him a 'well-spring of tender friendship and affectionate service'.[238]

Overshadowing all the events in Shaftesbury's personal life at this time, however, was worry about the health of Constance and also that of Minny herself. Shaftesbury regarded Constance with a special affection,[239] and her health, for some years, had given cause for concern. In 1867, the lung disease, which had previously been suspected, was confirmed when she began to spit blood. From that point onwards, her state was a ceaseless source of anxiety to Shaftesbury and to Minny. Medical advice was regularly sought, in particular, the advice of the well-known Dr Gull. This was at very considerable cost – Shaftesbury noted in 1868 that he had paid Gull seventy guineas for a consultation.[240] The treatment which Gull advised for Constance was also expensive: visits abroad to warmer climates. The advice was followed, although the cost which it involved was a further crippling burden to Shaftesbury. 'All my economies, savings, cheese-parings are swallowed up by such gigantic doings' he wrote on one occasion,[241] and, on another,[242] that he was at his 'wits end' to know how to pay for these sojourns at places such as Nice, Cannes and Mentone. Apart from the expense, he found – as in the past – residence abroad wearisome and oppressive, and sometimes he remained at home, or returned early, leaving Minny and Constance to stay longer. But then he disliked the separation and tried to overcome it by writing regularly to Minny, giving her news of his activities.[243] No doubt it would all have been more bearable had the visits helped Constance, but, although there were, from time to time, signs of improvement in her condition, there were as many of relapse and deterioration. 'Who can calculate?' Shaftesbury wrote in 1871. 'She has been better and worse for nearly four years.'[244] His numerous Diary entries on the subject show the intensity of his anxiety for 'Conty', as he called her: he was 'deeply harassed' by her suffering.[245] He was also increasingly worried about Minny. Minny's health had never been strong since Mary's death in 1860. The strain of nursing Mary had told on her, and, during Mary's illness, she had suffered from headaches and dizziness. These recurred in later years. In 1867, Shaftesbury noted that Minny had been ill every winter for the past four years.[246] He called in doctors to see her, and it was hoped that the journeys abroad for the sake of Constance would help her mother. But Constance's illness took its toll on Minny's strength. And in the summer of 1871, there was also great anxiety over Cecil's health. This had, indeed, caused concern in the past,[247] but Cecil had recovered and, in 1868, had gone to Cambridge. In 1871, however, he became acutely ill with typhoid fever, and, again, Minny bore much of the brunt of the illness. In July, 1871, Shaftesbury noted that her 'anxieties and watchings' about Cecil and Constance had been too much for her.[248] Cecil, rather unexpectedly, recovered from his illness, but Minny's condition became progressively worse. In September, 1872, Shaftesbury wrote that Minny was seriously ill. 'Long labour, long anxiety and long neglect of herself' had brought her to a dangerous state of weakness.[249] She was losing her appetite and growing thin, and, in October, Shaftesbury became desperately anxious. It was, he wrote, 'heart-rending to witness poor Minny's sufferings. My own dear, true and precious wife.'[250] A week later, on 15 October, she died. Shaftesbury was distraught. He mourned the loss of 'the purest, gentlest, kindest, sweetest and most confiding spirit that ever lived. Oh my God, what a blow!' He regretfully recalled how, in his 'excitable temper', he had said 'unjust and cruel things' to her; he could only wonder at and be thankful for her 'placable spirit' and her power to forgive and forget. 'Somehow or other her heart could not retain the impression of an affront or a harshness.'[251] He received many letters of condolence: 'warm religious letters', he called them.[252] To one of these, from Lady Gainsborough, he replied that he was 'astounded and dazed' to find himself without Minny:

> She was [he continued] my earthly mainstay, and cheered almost every moment of my existence by the wonderful combination of truth, simplicity, joyousness of heart and purity of spirit. She was a sincere, sunny and gentle follower of our Lord; and almost the last words that fell from her lips were, 'None but Christ.'[253]

There was at least consolation that she had died in peace, and Shaftesbury wrote that now that God had taken her, he must believe that it was 'a continuance and not a withdrawal of His mercy....'[254]

Constance, then, survived her mother; but not for long. On the advice of the doctors, she went once again to Mentone in October, and Shaftesbury joined her there in mid-November. 'Journey very tedious and very sorrowful,' he wrote. 'Arrived ... still more sorrowful. I could admire nothing, enjoy nothing, for she was not here to share it with me.'[255] Constance seemed to be better, but there was another relapse and, on 16 December, she died. Shaftesbury's Diary entries from mid-November to mid-December show his anguish and distress, but they also suggest that he knew his daughter had not long to live and was almost resigned to it. '... My flesh cries stay, stay, stay,' he wrote at the beginning of December. 'No not she; she is ready, nay almost desirous to be gone.'[256] And when Constance did die, he was deeply comforted by the manner of her death: 'never was a death so joyous, so peaceful. Heaven itself opened before her eyes.'[257] As on the occasion of Francis's death, he wrote at length of Constance's dying moments. She had said 'Christ is very near': she must, thought Shaftesbury, 'have perceived something that we did not.' And this, he wrote, was 'a striking and special mercy vouchsafed by Almighty God, not only to mitigate our sorrow, but positively to raise us in to joy.'[258] He wrote to Tait, who, in 1868, had succeeded Longley as Archbishop of Canterbury and who had written to offer his and his wife's condolences, that Constance's last minutes were 'such as by God's Grace gave me, if possible, more than *assurance* of the everlasting safety.'[259]

In early January, 1873, Victoria was married to Lord Templemore. Shaftesbury wrote that it would be very private and, for a wedding, very sad. 'And yet it may be accompanied by Hallelujahs in heaven, while we are weeping on earth.' He was, he continued, lost sometimes, in floods of tears, but not of grief; almost of joy . . . What a band is now in heaven, not a band of hope, as on earth, but a band of bliss. My own dear Minny, Francis, Maurice, Mary, Constance . . .'[260] Such comments point to the intensity of Shaftesbury's faith, but there were others which indicated the depth of his sense of loss. In April, he wrote that they were never out of his mind and hardly out of his sight: 'as the days lengthen the solitude seems to increase.'[261] At St Giles, a few days later, he wrote that the place was 'solitary and sad; the charm of one to share it with me is gone.'[262] He confessed that Minny's loss was 'more and more keen every day. God alone knows what I feel and suffer. May He watch over and subdue me.'[263] There were many such comments in the months ahead. A visit in August to Scotland, where he stayed with his old friend, John Burns, at Castle Wemyss helped to restore his spirits, and, at the end of the month, he visited Victoria and Lord Templemore at their home at Dunbrody in Ireland. He corresponded regularly with Victoria, and the letters inevitably contained many references to the loss which he had sustained. 'They are ever in my mind,' he wrote in July, 'and I love to sit and think over their last and assuring words. . . .'[264] In January, 1874, he wrote to Victoria that he missed Minny and Constance more and more every hour. He told her that Pusey had written to him at the time of their death and said that he would be a changed man – 'and so I am in many respects,' he wrote.[265]

Victoria was, indeed, a great source of comfort to him at this time. Shaftesbury was sad that he could not say the same of Anthony and Harriet. He invited them for Christmas in 1873, but they made an excuse and did not come. He was, then, 'utterly disappointed in (the) hope and almost belief that the death of Beloved ones would have softened their spirit and brought a change of conduct.'[266] The normal letter from Anthony followed, full of regrets: 'Ah poor Boy,' wrote Shaftesbury, 'when has he ever been a son to me? When has he ever conformed to my wishes, done me honour, or comforted my heart?'[267] He greatly regretted that he had been allowed to see so little of Anthony's children: Margaret – or Poppy as she was called – had been kept away from him since she was eight. But other younger members of the family were pleasing to the old man. Cecil was 'so dear, so gracious, so kindly, so companionable, so honest and so good... He is my "Seth" whom God gave me when He took Francis (my Abel) and he is too my Benjamin, for he is the youngest born of his beloved and blessed Mother!'[268] Hilda, too, 'racked her precious little heart to make (him) happy.' They were all, he continued, 'kind and loveable and loving', and Sissy and Fanny were, with Evelyn and Lionel, 'full of feeling and attention'.[269] His grandson Wilfred, the son of Evelyn and Sissy, was a great joy. He saw him regularly and could only wish that he had been allowed to exercise a similar supervision over the grandson who would ultimately inherit his title and Estates.

A few days after Minny's death, Shaftesbury had written to Tait thanking him for his prayers and his sympathy. 'Had I been younger,' he wrote, 'the blow would have been almost beyond endurance. But at the age of 71, the world is really closed to me and the separation will be but short.'[270] Shaftesbury did not, however, carry out this threat to retreat into himself. He told Victoria in January, 1874, that he must

> find refreshment in the duties of London life; some distraction from thoughts of former days; something to keep out of sight the vacant chair; something to keep my ears from always listening to catch that dear, beautiful, silver voice.[271]

Thus Shaftesbury kept himself busy. And 1874 was to be an active year, especially in connection with Church matters. Not, indeed, that such matters had been absent from Shaftesbury's life since 1866, for there had, in these years, been much in the Church which attracted his attention and vigilance.

NOTES

1. For the various points of view on this, see, for example, R. Harrison, *Before the Socialists. Studies in Labour and Politics, 1861 to 1881* (1965), pp. 78–136, F. B. Smith, *The Making of the Second Reform Bill* (Cambridge, 1966), *passim*, and M. Cowling, *1867: Disraeli, Gladstone, and Revolution* (1967), *passim*.
2. N.R.A., Shaftesbury (Broadlands) MSS, SHA/PD/14, 5 Dec., 1865.
3. ibid., SHA/PD/8, 5 Jan., 1866.

4. ibid., SHA/PD/8, 30 Apr., 1866.
5. Quoted in Hodder, III, 210–11.
6. N.R.A., Shaftesbury (Broadlands) MSS, SHA/PD/8, 30 June, 1866.
7. See P. Smith, *Disraelian Conservatism and Social Reform* (1967), pp. 38–9.
8. See Hodder, III, 212.
9. N.R.A., Shaftesbury (Broadlands) MSS, SHA/PD/8, 8 Aug., 1866.
10. ibid., SHA/PD/8, 30 Sept., 1866.
11. ibid., SHA/PD/8, 2 Nov., 1866.
12. ibid., SHA/PD/8, 10 Oct., 1866.
13. Hughenden MSS (on microfilm). Film 131, 19 Sept., 1866.
14. ibid., 18, 19 Jan., 1867.
15. N.R.A., SHA/PD/8, 9 Feb., 1867.
16. ibid., SHA/PD/8, 9 Feb., 1867.
17. ibid., SHA/PD/8, 25 Feb., 1867.
18. ibid., SHA/PD/8, 4 Mar., 1867.
19. ibid., SHA/PD/8, 8 Aug., 1866.
20. ibid., SHA/PD/8, 4 Mar., 1867.
21. ibid., SHA/PD/8, 9 Mar., 1867.
22. ibid., SHA/PD/8, 9 Mar., 1867.
23. ibid., SHA/PD/8, 6 June, 1867.
24. ibid., SHA/PD/8, 23 May, 1867.
25. Hansard, *Parl. Debates*, 3rd ser., CLXXXVIII, 1917–22: 1923–34.
26. N.R.A., Shaftesbury (Broadlands) MSS, SHA/PD/8, 17 July, 1867.
27. ibid., SHA/PD/8, 26 July, 1867.
28. Quoted in Hodder, III, 223.
29. N.R.A., Shaftesbury (Broadlands) MSS, SHA/MIS/3.
30. ibid., SHA/PD/8, 5 Mar., 1868.
31. ibid., SHA/PD/8, 5 Mar., 1868.
32. ibid., SHA/PD/9, 22 July, 1871.
33. ibid., SHA/PD/9, 5 Oct., 1871.
34. H.R.O., Shaftesbury (Broadlands) MSS, 27M60. Shaftesbury to Hon. William Cowper Temple, M.P., 30 Oct., 1868.
35. N.R.A., Shaftesbury (Broadlands) MSS, SHA/PD/7, 25 Mar., 1867.
36. ibid., SHA/PD/8, 1 Mar., 1866.
37. Hansard, *Parl. Debates*, 3rd ser., CLXXXVII, 1928–9.
38. Add. MSS, 44, 300, fos 24–5.
39. See A. Bentley, 'The Transformation of the Evangelical Party in the Church of England in the late Nineteenth Century' (Ph.D. Durham, 1971), pp. 23–30.
40. N.R.A., Shaftesbury (Broadlands) MSS, SHA/PD/8, 8 Sept., 1868.
41. Hansard, *Parl. Debates*, 3rd ser., CXCVIII, 210 ff.
42. N.R.A., Shaftesbury (Broadlands) MSS, SHA/PD/8, 8 Sept., 1868.
43. ibid., SHA/PD/8, 8 Sept., 1868.
44. ibid., SHA/PD/9, 14 June, 1869.
45. ibid., SHA/PD/9, 14 June, 1869.
46. See below p. 303.
47. N.R.A., Shaftesbury (Broadlands) MSS, SHA/PD/9, 18 June, 1869.
48. *The Record*, 19 June, 1869.
49. N.R.A., Shaftesbury (Broadlands) MSS, SHA/PD/9, 22 June, 1869.
50. ibid., SHA/PD/9, 3 July, 1869.
51. ibid., SHA/PD/9, 7 July, 1869.
52. ibid., SHA/PD/9, 6 July, 1869.

DOUBT, DARKNESS, DISCOURAGEMENT, 1866–1873 509

53. Hansard, *Parl. Debates*, 3rd ser., CXCVIII, 281–2.
54. N.R.A., Shaftesbury (Broadlands) MSS, SHA/PD/9, 21 July, 1869.
55. ibid., SHA/PD/9, 21 May, 1870. See also Hodder, III, 278.
56. N.R.A., Shaftesbury (Broadlands) MSS, SHA/PD/8, 21 May, 1870.
57. Quoted in Hodder, III, 278.
58. N.R.A., Shaftesbury (Broadlands) MSS, SHA/PD/9, 15 July, 1870.
59. ibid., SHA/PD/9, 2 May, 1870.
60. St G.H., Shaftesbury MSS, C 25026.72/7th Earl.
61. N.R.A., Shaftesbury (Broadlands) MSS, SHA/PD/9, 1 Apr., 1871.
62. Quoted in Hodder, III, 285–6.
63. N.R.A., Shaftesbury (Broadlands) MSS, SHA/PD/10, 23 Nov., 1871.
64. Hansard, *Parl. Debates*, 3rd ser., CCVIII, 1264.
65. Add. MSS, 44, 300, fos 56–9.
66. Hansard, *Parl. Debates*, 3rd ser., CCXI, 1447 ff.
67. N.R.A., Shaftesbury (Broadlands) MSS, SHA/PD/9, 1 Apr., 1871.
68. ibid., SHA/PD/9, 13 May, 1871.
69. Quoted in Hodder, III, 211.
70. Hansard, *Parl. Debates*, 3rd ser., CLXXXII, 1503.
71. ibid., CLXXXIV, 781.
72. The hours were 6 a.m. to 8 p.m. for children; 5 a.m. to 9 p.m. for women and young persons.
73. N.R.A., Shaftesbury (Broadlands) MSS, SHA/PD/8, 17 Aug., 1867.
74. Hansard, *Parl. Debates*, 3rd ser., CCVII, 1401 ff.
75. See above p. 408.
76. Hansard, *Parl. Debates*, 3rd ser., CLXXXV, 906.
77. ibid., 1465 ff.
78. ibid., CLXXXVIII, 1661.
79. Hammonds, pp. 182–3. An Act of 1876 raised the age below which children might not be employed to ten.
80. Hansard, *Parl. Debates*, 3rd ser., CCXII, 621.
81. ibid., 1600–1.
82. See P. Smith, op. cit., p. 173.
83. See above p. 409.
84. E. Gauldie, op. cit., p. 260.
85. ibid., pp. 270–71.
86. Hansard, *Parl. Debates*, 3rd ser., CXCII, 907; CXCIII, 987–8.
87. For Simon's biography, see R. Lambert, *Sir John Simon, 1816–1904 and English Social Administration* (1963).
88. Hansard, *Parl. Debates*, 3rd ser., CLXXXIV, 2072–3.
89. ibid., CCVIII, 307.
90. Hughenden MSS (on microfilm). Film 131, 16 Aug., 1866.
91. Huntington Library MSS, STG Box 118 and 129 (Shaftesbury to Earl of Derby, 10 Nov., 1866).
92. ibid. (Edward, Earl of Derby to Duke of Buckingham and Chandos, 12 Nov., 1866).
93. Hansard, *Parl. Debates*, 3rd ser., CCVIII, 1761–2.
94. ibid., CCII, 609.
95. Hodder, III, 205–8.
96. N.R.A., Shaftesbury (Broadlands) MSS, SHA/PD/8, 6 Nov., 1866.
97. Hodder, III, 271.
98. ibid., 272–3.

99. N.R.A., Shaftesbury (Broadlands) MSS, SHA/PD/9, 18 Mar., 1871.
100. ibid., SHA/MIS/35.
101. ibid., SHA/PD/8, 19 Nov., 1868.
102. ibid., SHA/PD/8, 5 May, 1866.
103. ibid., SHA/PD/8, 26 May, 1868.
104. ibid., SHA/PD/10, 31 Dec., 1871.
105. ibid., SHA/PD/8, 20 Apr., 1866.
106. ibid., SHA/PD/9, 15 Mar., 1871.
107. Imperial College of Science and Technology, London. Playfair MSS, 15 Apr., 1872.
108. N.R.A., Shaftesbury (Broadlands) MSS, SHA/PD/8, 2 Mar., 1867.
109. ibid., SHA/PD/8, 14 Nov., 1867.
110. ibid., SHA/PD/8, 19 Nov., 1868.
111. ibid., SHA/PD/9, 19 Mar., 1869.
112. ibid., SHA/PD/9, 11 June, 1870.
113. Quoted in Hodder, III, 252.
114. Quoted ibid., 303.
115. N.R.A., Shaftesbury (Broadlands) MSS, SHA/PD/10, 19 Jan., 1871.
116. *Ragged School Union Magazine* (1868), 129.
117. N.R.A., Shaftesbury (Broadlands) MSS, SHA/PD/9, 17 Mar., 1869.
118. Hansard, *Parl. Debates*, 3rd ser., CCIII, 1187, CCIV, 1851.
119. ibid., 843.
120. *Ragged School Union Magazine* (1871), 129.
121. Hansard, *Parl. Debates*, 3rd ser., CCIII, 844.
122. Hodder, III, 264-5.
123. N.R.A., Shaftesbury (Broadlands) MSS, SHA/PD/9, 9 Apr., 1870.
124. Quoted in Hodder, III, 266.
125. St G.H., Shaftesbury MSS, C 25024.5/7th Earl.
126. ibid., C 25024.6/7th Earl (copy).
127. A. Bentley, op. cit., p. 67 ff.
128. *Ragged School Union Magazine* (1871), 129.
129. N.R.A., Shaftesbury (Broadlands) MSS, SHA/PD/9, 27 Apr., 1871.
130. *Ragged School Union Magazine* (1871), 130.
131. *The Times*, 18 Oct., 1870.
132. N.R.A., Shaftesbury (Broadlands) MSS, SHA/PD/9, 8 Mar., 1870.
133. ibid., SHA/PD/9, 5 Aug., 1871.
134. ibid., SHA/PD/10, 6 Jan., 1872.
135. ibid., SHA/PD/10, 10 Jan., 1872.
136. ibid., SHA/PD/8, 19 Nov., 1868.
137. ibid., SHA/PD/8, 18 Jan., 1867.
138. ibid., SHA/PD/8, 19 Nov., 1868.
139. ibid., SHA/PD/10, 6 Jan., 1872.
140. *Speeches of Lord Shaftesbury upon subjects having relation chiefly to the Claims and Interests of the Labouring Class* (1868).
141. N.R.A., Shaftesbury (Broadlands) MSS, SHA/PD/8, 7 Oct., 1868.
142. ibid., SHA/PD/9, 18 Nov., 1870. For a similar attitude, see above Chapter 6.
143. ibid., SHA/PD/9, 9 May, 1871.
144. ibid., SHA/PD/10, 9 May, 1872.
145. ibid., SHA/PD/8, 20 Jan., 1867.
146. ibid., SHA/PD/10, 22 Dec., 1871.
147. ibid., SHA/PD/8, 29 May, 1868.

148. ibid., SHA/PD/10, 22 Dec., 1871.
149. ibid., SHA/PD/9, 24 Apr., 1871.
150. *Speeches of the Earl of Shaftesbury in Glasgow* (Glasgow, 1871), p. 7.
151. N.R.A., Shaftesbury (Broadlands) MSS, SHA/PD/8, 17 Nov., 1868.
152. ibid., SHA/PD/8, 17 Aug., 1866.
153. ibid., SHA/PD/9, 16 July, 1870.
154. ibid., SHA/PD/9, 14 Sept., 1870.
155. ibid., SHA/PD/8, 26 June, 1866.
156. ibid., SHA/PD/9, 26 Aug., 1870.
157. ibid., SHA/PD/9, 19 July, 1870.
158. ibid., SHA/PD/8, 4 July, 1866.
159. ibid., SHA/PD/8, 17 Aug., 1866.
160. ibid., SHA/PD/8, 17 Aug., 1866.
161. ibid., SHA/PD/9, 9 Aug., 1870.
162. ibid., SHA/PD/8, 7 July, 1866.
163. ibid., SHA/PD/9, 31 Aug., 1870. See also Hodder, III, 280–81.
164. N.R.A., Shaftesbury (Broadlands) MSS, SHA/PD/9, 25 Dec., 1870.
165. ibid., SHA/PD/9, 14 Sept., 1870.
166. ibid., SHA/PD/9, 5 Jan., 1871.
167. ibid., SHA/PD/9, 19 Mar., 1871.
168. ibid., SHA/PD/9, 2 June, 1871.
169. ibid., SHA/PD/9, 31 May, 1871.
170. ibid., SHA/PD/8, 17 Feb., 1866.
171. ibid., SHA/PD/8, 7 June, 1866.
172. ibid., SHA/PD/8, 23 Feb., 1867.
173. ibid., SHA/PD/8, 19 Mar., 1866.
174. ibid., SHA/PD/8, 11 Jan., 1867.
175. ibid., SHA/PD/8, 7 June, 1867.
176. ibid., SHA/PD/8, 27 July, 1867.
177. ibid., SHA/PD/8, 28 Nov., 1867.
178. Hammonds, p. 180.
179. N.R.A., Shaftesbury (Broadlands) MSS, SHA/PD/9, 13 Feb., 1869.
180. ibid., SHA/PD/8, 22 June, 1868.
181. ibid., SHA/PD/8, 1 Mar., 1866.
182. ibid., SHA/PD/8, 1 Mar., 1866.
183. ibid., SHA/PD/9, 19 May, 1870.
184. ibid., SHA/PD/8, 23 Oct., 1867.
185. ibid., SHA/PD/8, 1 Mar., 1868.
186. ibid., SHA/PD/8, 27 Oct., 1866.
187. ibid., SHA/PD/8, 11 Aug., 1866.
188. ibid., SHA/EST/8.
189. ibid., SHA/PD/8, 13 Dec., 1866.
190. ibid., SHA/PD/8, 24 Oct., 1867.
191. ibid., SHA/PD/8, 19 May, 1868.
192. ibid., SHA/PD/9, 6 Feb., 1869.
193. ibid., SHA/PD/9, 24 Apr., 1871.
194. ibid., SHA/PD/9, 5 Oct., 1871.
195. ibid., SHA/PD/9, 15 June, 1871.
196. ibid., SHA/PD/8, 11 June, 1867. Shaftesbury wrote to the Revd. George Davis in 1873 that the people of Dorset were 'good, civil, well-disposed': but they had no energy, no sense of thrift, no value for education, no desire to accept any

means of advancement, if it demanded an exertion on their part. He added that if they had the enterprise of the northern peasantry, they would be thriving. (St G.H., Shaftesbury MSS, C 25014.29/7th Earl (copy).
197. P.P., 1868–9, XIII.
198. ibid., Q. 15.
199. ibid., Q. 16.
200. ibid.
201. ibid., Q. 17.
202. ibid., Pt II, Q. 4.
203. ibid., Pt I, Q. 17.
204. ibid., Pt I, Qs 18–19.
205. ibid., Pt II, Q. 156.
206. N.R.A., Shaftesbury (Broadlands) MSS, SHA/PD/9, 29 Nov., 1869.
207. ibid., SHA/PD/9, 29 Nov., 1869. See also letter to *The Times* (6 Dec., 1872) in which Shaftesbury rebutted renewed charges that he was only interested in factories and not in agriculture. In the letter, Shaftesbury laid out his priorities for improvement on his estates: cottage accommodation, allotments, payment of wages in money.
208. N.R.A., Shaftesbury (Broadlands) MSS, SHA/PD/8, 12 June, 1867.
209. ibid., SHA/PD/8, 27 Aug., 1867.
210. ibid., SHA/PD/8, 19 Mar., 1866.
211. ibid., SHA/PD/9, 23 Oct., 1869. See also letter to Alexander Haldane, quoted in Hodder, III, 253.
212. N.R.A., Shaftesbury (Broadlands) MSS, SHA/PD/9, 23 Oct., 1869.
213. ibid., SHA/PD/8, 28 Feb., 1867.
214. ibid., SHA/PD/9, 31 Dec., 1869.
215. ibid., SHA/PD/9, 5 Jan., 1870.
216. ibid., SHA/PD/9, 13 Jan., 1870.
217. ibid., SHA/PD/9, 13 Jan., 1870.
218. ibid., SHA/PD/9, 19 May, 1870.
219. ibid., SHA/PD/10, 26 Mar., 1872.
220. ibid., SHA/PD/10, 10 Apr., 1872.
221. ibid., SHA/PD/9, 5 Oct., 1871.
222. ibid., SHA/PD/8, 7 Apr., 1866.
223. ibid., SHA/PD/8, 28 July, 1866.
224. ibid., SHA/PD/8, 14 July, 1868.
225. ibid., SHA/PD/9, 12 Dec., 1868.
226. ibid., SHA/PD/9, 13 Dec., 1869.
227. ibid., SHA/PD/8, 2 Apr., 1868.
228. ibid., SHA/PD/8, 19 Nov., 1868.
229. ibid., SHA/PD/8, 24 Oct., 1867.
230. ibid., SHA/PD/10, 6 Aug., 1872.
231. ibid., SHA/PD/8, 26 Mar., 1868.
232. ibid., SHA/EST/8.
233. ibid., SHA/PD/9, 3 Feb., 1869.
234. ibid., SHA/PD/9, 11 June, 1869.
235. ibid., SHA/PD/9, 23 Oct., 1869.
236. ibid., SHA/PD/9, 22 Sept., 1869.
237. H.R.O., Shaftesbury (Broadlands) MSS, 27M60, 12 Sept., 1869.
238. N.R.A., Shaftesbury (Broadlands) MSS, SHA/PD/9, 22 Sept., 1869.
239. See above p. 336.

240. N.R.A., Shaftesbury (Broadlands) MSS, SHA/PD/8, 30 Nov., 1868.
241. ibid., SHA/PD/8, 16 Nov., 1867.
242. ibid., SHA/PD/9, 3 Feb., 1869.
243. Quoted in Hodder, III, 304-8.
244. N.R.A., Shaftesbury (Broadlands) MSS, SHA/PD/9, 23 May, 1871.
245. ibid., SHA/PD/9, 28 Dec., 1869.
246. ibid., SHA/PD/8, 14 Nov., 1867.
247. See above p. 425.
248. N.R.A., Shaftesbury (Broadlands) MSS, SHA/PD/9, 28 July, 1871.
249. ibid., SHA/PD/10, 6 Sept., 1872.
250. ibid., SHA/PD/10, 7 Oct., 1872.
251. ibid., SHA/PD/10, 15 Oct., 1872.
252. ibid., SHA/PD/10, 30 Nov., 1872.
253. Quoted in Hodder, III, 315.
254. ibid.
255. N.R.A., Shaftesbury (Broadlands) MSS, SHA/PD/10, 13 Nov., 1872.
256. ibid., SHA/PD/10, 1 Dec., 1872.
257. ibid., SHA/PD/10, 16 Dec., 1872.
258. ibid., SHA/PD/10, 18 Dec., 1872.
259. Tait MSS, 92, 7 Jan., 1873.
260. N.R.A., Shaftesbury (Broadlands) MSS, SHA/PD/10, 7 Jan., 1873.
261. ibid., SHA/PD/10, 1 Apr., 1873.
262. ibid., SHA/PD/10, 10 Apr., 1873.
263. ibid., SHA/PD/10, 14 Apr., 1873.
264. Hodder, III, 341.
265. ibid., 341-2.
266. N.R.A., Shaftesbury (Broadlands) MSS, SHA/PD/10, 29 Dec., 1873.
267. ibid., SHA/PD/10, 3 Jan., 1874.
268. ibid., SHA/PD/10, 13 Jan., 1874.
269. ibid., SHA/PD/10, 4 Mar., 1874.
270. Tait MSS, 90, 21 Oct., 1872.
271. Quoted in Hodder, III, 342.

18

The Juggernaut of Rationalism and Ritualism, 1866–1874

Even before the death of Palmerston in 1865, Shaftesbury had prophesied that the Church of England would drift into extremes of Broad Churchmanship or High Churchmanship,[1] and that the strength of the Evangelicals, which he had tried so hard to establish during the ten years after 1855, would be eroded. In December, 1866, he returned to such thoughts. Many, he wrote, fell spiritually 'under the Juggernaut of Rationalism' because it enlarged, elevated and emancipated the intellect; many under that of Tractarianism and Ritualism because it pleased the fancy, made religion easy and lulled the conscience.[2] And in February, 1867, he wrote that the two forces of Neology and Tractarianism – or Rationalism and Ritualism – were 'rife, ready and riotous'.[3]

Shaftesbury's opposition to Neology – 'Christianity without Christ', as he called it[4] – remained as fierce and uncompromising as it had always been. He was still deeply distrustful of an intellectual approach to religion. God, he wrote, cared 'comparatively little for man's intellect. He cares greatly for Man's heart. Satan reigned in the intellect: God in the heart of Man.'[5] But a liberal theology, shot through with intellectual reservations, seemed to be increasingly the order of the day. On Good Friday, 1867, he wrote that Christ crucified was the Christ of the Bible, and yet He was either 'shut out of His own world, or shorn of all His claims.'[6] He wrote in 1869 that the authors of *Essays and Reviews* were regarded as religious men 'in their own way' – they were 'believers with a large view'.[7] Moreover, such men were now receiving increasing recognition. The process had started with Russell, after Palmerston's death; it was to be continued by Gladstone. Shaftesbury was, indeed, grateful to Gladstone for the elevation in 1871 of Payne Smith to the Deanery of Canterbury: a 'first rate appointment', he wrote of it.[8] But other appointments left him aghast. In 1869, Seeley, the author of *Ecce Homo*, was appointed by Gladstone to the Professorship of

Modern History at Cambridge. Shaftesbury noted that, as far as he could make out, the appointment had been received with indifference, and Gladstone might now take 'any plunge he please(d) into this Ocean of Neology, for there are very few in private, and none in public, who, like Elijah, "are very zealous for the Lord God of Hosts".'[9] But worse was to follow. Dr Frederick Temple, one of the contributors to *Essays and Reviews*, was elevated by Gladstone in 1869 to the See of Exeter; 'so the admirer of and Patron of *Ecce Homo* had passed the Rubicon and has raised Temple . . . to the office of a Bishop,' was Shaftesbury's comment.[10] Temple had, in fact, withdrawn his essay from subsequent editions of *Essays and Reviews*, but this did not satisfy Shaftesbury – Temple had not, he felt, retracted the spirit of the essay. He regarded his appointment to a Bishopric as a significant stage in the disastrous progress of the Church of England towards Arianism: 'Such an issue has long been in preparation,' Shaftesbury wrote. But it was 'the turning point in English Ecclesiastical and Theological history.'[11] Another blow fell the following year, with the election of Benjamin Jowett as Master of Balliol. Shaftesbury had not been willing to lend his support in 1864 to a move to block the endowment of the Chair of Greek at Oxford, held by Jowett. Replying to Archdeacon Denison, who had approached him on this subject, Shaftesbury wrote that, much as he loathed Jowett's theology, the move which was proposed would dishonour his Chair. The efforts of those who held 'the fundamental truth' would, he wrote, have 'ten times more effect if . . . separated altogether from movements of this character.'[12] On this occasion, as on others, Shaftesbury had shown his willingness to dissociate himself from the most extreme and intolerant wing of Evangelicalism. But he despaired of Jowett's election as Master of Balliol. Thus the 'heretical opinions' which Jowett had displayed in *Essays and Reviews* were seemingly countenanced by 'perhaps the first College in Oxford'.[13]

Shaftesbury felt, however, that he had to be careful in expressing too violent opposition to such developments. He had, as he said, to 'mind (his) ps and qs.'[14] He did not forget that his violent denunciation of *Ecce Homo* had drawn attention to the book: his 'disapprobation', he wrote, was 'an assurance of the approbation of the reading world'.[15] Thus the less he said the better. He did, however, present a Memorial to Gladstone over Temple's appointment, asking the Prime Minister not to advise the Queen to exercise her royal prerogative in Temple's nomination. He had, he told Gladstone, every respect for Temple's talents and personal character, but he felt that a share in the composition and publication of works such as *Essays and Reviews* was an 'absolute disqualification for the profession and responsibilities of so sacred an office.'[16] But it was to no avail. Gladstone replied that the appointment had been made in the firm conviction that it would tend to promote the true interest of religion.[17]

Opposition offered by Shaftesbury to Neology thus seemed unavailing, and this was also true of his efforts to prevent a new translation of the Bible. He had already expressed his opinions on this matter when it had been broached in the past,[18] and he returned to the cause when, in 1870, Bishop Wilberforce, then Bishop of Winchester, proposed that steps should be taken to produce a revised version of the Old and New Testaments. Shaftesbury wrote to *The Times*, expressing his view that a new version would create confusion and uncertainty,[19] and he also wrote to Gladstone on the subject. The Authorised Version, he said, had 'rested in the hearts of men for 250 years and has mainly formed the thought and language of the masses.' They had lost all reverence for the Church, the Lords, even the Monarchy. 'Remove this single remnant,' he warned, 'and the English People, they may be better or they may be worse, will not continue the same.'[20] Shaftesbury received a number of letters on the stand which he took. One, from a Rector in Bridport, thanked him for his 'seasonable letter' to *The Times* and stated that a new translation would undermine the Faith.[21] Another letter, from the Bishop of St Davids, was also in sympathy. The world, the Bishop wrote, was made up of 'Doubters, Cavillers, literary Coxcombs, half-Scholars but thorough Infidels, hands ever itching to find fault and fingers ever itching to write.' A new translation would provoke dissatisfaction; revision would follow revision, unless, as was more likely, indifference set in.[22] Other letters – for example, one from William Selwyn – expressed gratitude to Shaftesbury for stating so fully the argument against the proposed revision: it strengthened the need for caution and restraint in the execution of the work. Nevertheless, Selwyn was convinced that a large number of biblical passages could be rendered more correctly 'and so show more fully the mind of the Spirit that speaks in the Holy Scriptures.'[23] Such sentiments prevailed, and so was set on foot the process which was, in time, to lead to the publication of the Revised Standard Version of the Bible in 1885.

Shaftesbury thus fought hard to preserve the integrity of the Bible in the face of attempts to strip it of the mysterious and the miraculous and to alter the familiar and time-honoured words of the Authorised Version. And, as in the past, he maintained a sharp distinction between attempts of this nature and those of scientific investigation. In 1866, he took the Chair at the founding meeting of the Victoria Institute, the purpose of which, as he put it, was to show the 'necessary, eternal and Divine Harmony between Science and Religion'.[24] In 1871, he presided over Payne Smith's lecture on the Harmony of Science and Religion. In 1874, he wrote of the address of the President of the British Association for the Advancement of Science: it was, he noted, heavily secular and 'atheist'. And yet, he continued, he would give enormous sums for the promotion of Science. His only complaint against the pursuit of Science was that it was too slow. The more rapidly Science advanced, the more rapidly the conclusion would be reached that the God of Revelation and the God of Nature were one and indivisible: 'thus should we be *spared* a fearful amount of mis-used Intellect, of blasphemous Vanity; of ignorance under the impudent guise of knowledge, and of souls perverted and irrevocably lost.'[25] Scientists, moreover, would, in time, 'come to maturity and to faith': but

> what if these critics, full of learning, research, discriminating and puzzling power, declare that *you have not the word*; *the true text*, urge the number, variety and discrepancy of Mss; the errors, omissions and interpolations! This is puzzling, harassing, annoying ... Various translations are embarrassing above all; and specially to the Old Testament, where sometimes versions give a totally different sense; or one diametrically opposite.[26]

But there were many and persistent agencies to spread this approach: the School Boards, the Universities, the Press. All, Shaftesbury felt, were deeply affected by Rationalism. 'The whole tone, tendency and complexion of all society,' he wrote, '... is of the free, enlarged, broad and liberal character.'[27]

Rationalism was one Juggernaut which seemingly carried all before it. The other was Ritualism. In a sense, this was a further manifestation of Tractarianism. Tractarianism had, it is true, originally been concerned with matters of doctrine and discipline, rather than practice, but an emphasis on ritual had always been inherent in it.[28] The doctrine of the Real Presence demanded that Communion Services should be surrounded with rich ceremonial. Another impetus to Ritualism had been the Camden Society, founded in Cambridge in 1839, to promote Church building on mediaeval Gothic lines. Such ideas and practices had, of course, encountered strong opposition at the time of 'Papal Aggression' in 1851 and were also disliked by moderate High Churchmen; and the Evangelical dominance of the Church of England during Palmerston's tenure of office had prevented their official advancement. But, even in the 1860s, the Ritualists were far from dormant.[29] The English Church Union, founded in 1860, provided an organisation and focal point for the Ritualistic party and it quickly gained numbers – in 1862 it had 780 enrolled members, in 1866 over 3,000, and, in 1870, 7,895. The appeal of the party was primarily to clergy and wealthy laity, but it also made efforts to reach the working classes in the city slums, where the elaborate ceremonial of the Church services might act as a welcome contrast to the drabness of the surroundings in which most people lived. The English Church Union was, in part, also a defensive organisation, setting out to defend Ritualistic clergy who encountered opposition or persecution. And its expectation of opposition was well-founded. In 1865, the evangelical Church Association was founded. Its purpose was to counteract what it regarded as the Romish practices being introduced into the services of the Church of England by the Ritualists.

There could be no doubt as to where Shaftesbury would take his stand in the controversy which was to embroil the Church of England in the later years of the nineteenth century. The Ritualists aroused that particularly severe anger which he always reserved for those whom he regarded as crypto-Catholics within the Anglican tradition. All his worst suspicions were confirmed when he attended a service along with Haldane at St Albans, Holborn, a noted centre for Ritualism, in 1866. 'In outward form or ritual,' he wrote, 'it is the worship of Jupiter or Juno.' He noted with strong disapproval various aspects of the Ritualistic building and service: the high altar; the grill separating the chancel from the body of the Church; the number of servitors dressed in 'Romish apparel'; the intoning of the service, except the Lessons, by priests dressed in white surplices and green stripes. The sacramental part of the service earned his especially severe censure: he described it as

> such a scene of theatrical gymnastics, of singing, screaming, genuflections, such a series of strange movements of the priests, their backs almost always to the people, as I never saw before even in a Romish Temple.

There were also 'clouds upon clouds of insense'. An hour and three quarters were given to the 'histrionic part'. The communicants, he noted, went up to receive the elements to the accompaniment of soft music, 'as though it had been a melodrama, and one was astounded, at the close, that there was no fall of the curtain.' He concluded his remarks by wondering if 'our blessed Lord' was obeyed in such ceremonies: 'Do we thus lead souls to Christ or to Baal?' he asked.[30]

In the course of the years which followed, Shaftesbury made various attempts in the Lords to repress such practices by legislation. In March, 1867, he introduced a Vestments bill, the purpose of which was to correct, as he put it, 'certain ritualistic abuses which (had) crept in to the Church of England.'[31] The bill proposed to give the force of law to long-established usage regulating the ceremonials of public worship, in particular the fifty-eighth of the Canons of 1603, enjoining the clergy to wear a 'decent and comely surplice with sleeves' and the academic dress to which they were entitled while administering the sacraments. Shaftesbury would have preferred the initiative in this matter to have been taken by the Bishops. He had written to the Bishop of Peterborough earlier in March disclaiming any desire to score a triumph for himself or any party, and had he been certain that a measure was to be introduced on the authority of the Bishops, he would have withheld his own bill.[32] But, although it was rumoured that a bill was to be introduced by the Archbishop, Shaftesbury felt that it might be delayed, and thus he felt it necessary to take action. By the end of March, it had, indeed, become clear that the Bishops had abandoned their bill in preference to the appointment of a Royal Commission to inquire into Ritualistic practices. This, indeed, appears to have been a device largely intended to head Shaftesbury off. Shaftesbury was not, however, deterred. Although he did not wish to offer any impediment to the Commission, he felt that one aspect of Ritualistic activities – that concerning vestments – should be dealt with without delay. Thus in May, 1867, he proposed the second reading of his Vestments bill, supporting it in a long speech.[33] He stressed that the laity had looked for the support of the Bishops, but nothing had been done. Thus the laity must take the matter into their own hands, and they had determined – with the assistance of the Bishops or without it – to 'make every attempt in their power to remove this abuse from the fair face of the Established Church.' But Shaftesbury's efforts were defeated by a motion by the Archbishop, Longley, to the effect that no action should be taken until the Royal Commission on Ritualism had reported, and, in 1867, Shaftesbury told the Lords that, although he would not withdraw the bill, he would allow its life to expire with the session.[34]

The first Report of the Commission was presented in August and was largely concerned with vestments. The second Report appeared in April, 1868, on the subject of incense and lighted candles.[35] Shaftesbury was dissatisfied with the first Report on the grounds that it did not pass any specific judgment on the Ritualists. And when the second Report was presented, he expressed his impatience that nothing had been done about either Report. The time, he told the Lords, was ripe for legislation.[36] Again, he took the initiative by introducing the Uniformity of Public Worship bill. At its second reading in July, 1868, he argued that some restraint must be employed to prevent certain practices.[37] His unsuccessful bill of the previous year had related only to vestments; this bill included incense and lighted candles. These must be pronounced illegal. He admitted that many of the Ritualistic party were sincere and conscientious in their conviction that their practices were essential to meet the exigencies of the time. But he must say that 'a more grievous error never entered the minds of men.' He referred to St Albans: a decent, wealthy, orderly congregation gathered there simply to gratify their curiosity and see what was going on. There were no 'poor working people' present. On the other hand, at Field Lane Ragged School, there was a large congregation on a Sunday morning of 'persons in the most destitute, abject and miserable condition', who positively enjoyed a very humble and simple service. At the special Theatre Services, there were twenty to twenty-five thousand persons in the poorest condition in life. The poor, he argued, were not attracted to Church 'by incense, lights, coloured vestments and everything which can delight the eye and ear.' He also felt that Ritualistic practices alienated the general body of Nonconformists: even the Wesleyans, hitherto friendly to the Church of England, were being turned into enemies. And those who remained within the Church of England would become indifferent. They would come to the conclusion that the Church of England and the Church of Rome were so nearly identical that it was of little importance which party got the upper hand. The speech was, therefore, an exposition of Shaftesbury's objections to Ritualism, but again, it was countered by the Archbishop of Canterbury. He was, he said, as anxious as Shaftesbury to restrain Ritualistic practices, but he was also anxious not to cause convulsion in the Church. Thus he refused to support the bill, and it was not even put to the vote.

Having failed to make any progress in these directions, Shaftesbury gave his attention over the following years to an attempt to reform the procedure of the ecclesiastical courts. The courts assumed special importance in the light of the current controversies within the Church. That Shaftesbury should undertake their reform had been suggested to him by A. J. Stephens, a noted ecclesiastical lawyer, and Haldane,[38] and, in 1867, he had given notice of his intention to raise the matter.[39] In March, 1868, while at Nice, he wrote to Bishop Tait that he proposed to move for a Commission to inquire into and report on the system, conduct and working of the courts.[40] But instead of a Commission, it was, in fact, a bill which Shaftesbury proposed, and he moved its second reading in April, 1869.[41] He argued that the Church courts were badly in need of reform. There were, he said, long delays in the hearing of cases, and very heavy expenditure was involved. He also felt that the judges – almost always clergymen – were lacking in legal qualifications. The bill thus sought to make procedure cheaper and more expeditious. It also provided for the appointment of a superior Judge for the two principal Courts of Appeal. At present, each Archbishop had a Judge or Chancellor for his own province. But Shaftesbury argued that there was not enough business for the two Judges. It was desirable to have one superior Judge for the two courts and he should be a man learned and experienced in the law – a barrister of fifteen years' standing or a Judge in one of the superior civil courts. The bill also sought to improve the administration of justice at the level of the diocesan courts. It provided that a Bishop might appoint a barrister of seven years' standing as Chancellor of the court. Chancellors, Shaftesbury said, had for a long time been almost exclusively clergymen and they did not possess the confidence of the public, since they lacked specialised knowledge. Further provisions of the bill established Juries to try issues of fact, admitted solicitors to practise in the courts, gave the laity the right to institute proceedings in the courts without the permission of the clergy and improved the practice of the Registries in giving safe custody to important documents. The bill thus aimed to provide for greater efficiency and economy, and to promote a greater degree of lay professionalism and participation. Its object was, as Shaftesbury explained on another occasion, to assimilate the courts to the Common Law Courts, to make their processes cheap and expeditious and to render them accessible to the community at large.[42]

Even before he introduced the bill, Shaftesbury knew that a long and tedious struggle lay ahead. He had told Haldane that it would be extremely difficult for a private member to introduce a bill on 'so wide and deep a subject as the Ecclesiastical Courts'. Such measures, he felt, must be introduced on the authority of the Government. 'I should be left,' he wrote, 'at the mercy of law lords, bishops, ritualistic peers, and a hostile Cabinet to fight the battle alone.'[43] And – as he had told Tait – he felt that a Commission should be first appointed. He was no more hopeful of success in his own private thoughts. He wrote in March that, if he could do any service by persisting in anti-ritualistic legislation, he would endure any amount of 'toil and obloquy'. But, he asked, 'why for no issue except abuse, vexation and fruitless labour, renew a career of public abomination and private contempt?'[44] The following month, he wrote that he wished he had never undertaken the bill: it was long, intricate and on a subject with which he was not at all conversant. Moreover, he knew that he would be opposed by the Bishops who secretly detested the measure 'as touching their dignity and their patronage'. He wished it was over and settled, and never again would he 'touch so hopeless, so thankless, so fruitless a work, as the reform of Church abominations.'[45] When he introduced the bill in April, 1869, he told the Lords that he was 'fully aware of the arduous character of the question but still more so of its wearisomeness.' It would, he feared, be 'inexpressibly tedious'.[46]

The experience of the next three years amply bore out such prophecies. The bill was given a second reading in April, 1869, but it was referred to a select committee. By the time that committee's report was available, it was too late in the session to make any progress and Shaftesbury agreed to withdraw the bill, announcing his intention to take it up again the following session.[47] In 1870, he did, indeed, revert to the matter,[48] but again there were delays. Questions were asked about the sources of the income which would be necessary to pay for the agencies which Shaftesbury's bill envisaged, and it was necessary to obtain returns of the money received – from sources such as fees for marriages – in the diocesan courts. This took a considerable amount of time, and thus Shaftesbury put the matter off for another session. When he once more spoke on his bill in 1871,[49] he announced that he would remove a clause which had caused opposition: that giving the laity the power to institute suits without the concurrence of the Bishops. He said that he proposed to bring this forward as a separate bill the following year. Again his bill – shorn of this clause – passed its second reading, but, such was the accumulation of business in the Commons, that there was no hope of getting it passed that session. In 1872, therefore, Shaftesbury made another attempt.[50] His separate bill to allow laity to initiate a prosecution without the intervention of the Bishop was defeated, but the main bill passed the Upper House. Once it reached the Commons, however, it was rejected. Shaftesbury had, then, persisted in his efforts to curb ritualism by reforming the courts, but, by 1872, his comments of three years earlier about the prospect of 'fruitless labour' had proved strikingly accurate.

Equally unsuccessful was an effort which Shaftesbury made in 1872 to reform Convocation, a body always suspect to Evangelicals. Here, indeed, Shaftesbury took up a cause which he had first championed twenty years previously when Convocation had been revived,[51] but it had an added urgency in the context of the emergence of Ritualism. He wrote to Gladstone in May, 1872, expressing the view that the two Houses of Convocation were 'alienating the clergy by hundreds and the laity by whole sale.' Gladstone, as Prime Minister, should either forbid their sitting or insist on a thorough reform.[52] Gladstone replied that the proceedings of Convocation were open to criticism, but its sittings had now had the sanction of eight successive governments and, on the whole, this policy had been wise. Convocation, Gladstone argued, had supplied a vent for opinion and complaint. It had prevented discontent from growing to extremes and had helped to mitigate the violence of controversy and party spirit. Also, Convocation had a certain – if rather feeble – moral influence, and, Gladstone urged, it was by moral influence of many years standing that the Church of England must be guided and held together rather than by penal and coercive proceedings. He admitted that a reform would be desirable, but this would best come under the auspices of the Archbishop of Canterbury.[53] Shaftesbury commented in reply that Convocation could not reform itself without parliamentary aid: the initiative must come from the Queen's Minister. And the 'leading details' of such a measure should be that the Lower House must rest entirely on election. Moreover, the clergy and laity – who required to be there in great numbers – could be returned only on an extended suffrage. If this were done, Convocation, Shaftesbury argued, might acquire the confidence of the Church.[54] But, once more, his views did not win official approval.

Thus there seemed to be little to show for all Shaftesbury's efforts to combat both Rationalism and Ritualism. In February, 1871, he wondered if the Church of England could go on – indeed, he wondered if it ought to go on. Rationalism and Ritualism were 'running riot'.[55] Moreover, the fact that the Ritualist controversy had reached such proportions meant that Shaftesbury could not achieve the kind of cooperation with High Churchmen over doctrine which he had found possible in the 1850s and early 1860s. As in the earlier period, there remained much in common between Shaftesbury and Pusey on such matters. At the annual meeting of the London Jews Society in 1866, Shaftesbury raised the question of the role of the Society – 'the great preacher and avower of simple, pure, unmixed Evangelical truth' – in relation to the 'heresies' which abounded. He advised all members of the Society to read two works: one was by Payne Smith on Isaiah, the other by Pusey on Daniel. He admitted that it might startle some of his audience that he should recommend a work written by Pusey, and there were certainly differences between them on 'ecclesiastical points'. Nevertheless, Shaftesbury affirmed his view that it would be difficult to find 'a man of greater intellect, of more profound attainments, or of a more truly pious heart than Dr Pusey.' He warmly praised Pusey's work on Daniel: it had 'not left a single scrap of reasoning, a single shred of fact, to bring to bear against the volume of Revelation.'[56] Because of the Ritualist conflict, however, Shaftesbury found it difficult to act along with Pusey and others of a similar disposition in resisting Neology. Thus, on the appointment of Temple to the See of Exeter in 1869, a move was set on foot to organise a joint protest from High Churchmen and Evangelicals, but, although Shaftesbury affirmed harmony of sentiment with the High Church party, he withheld active cooperation. To have presided over a joint effort would, he wrote, have been impossible: 'we should have spent our time and strength in struggles and disputes.'[57] As has been seen, he did present a Memorial on the subject to Gladstone, but this was on behalf of the evangelical Church Association: 'I have disclaimed all connection with the High party,' he wrote.[58]

Again, the Ritualist question brought Shaftesbury into conflict with Wilberforce, with whom he shared many sentiments over Rationalism. Wilberforce was not, indeed, a Ritualist, but he opposed Shaftesbury's attempt in 1867 to introduce a Vestments bill, and Wilberforce's membership of the Royal Commission on Ritualism, appointed the same year, provoked Shaftesbury's wrath. Shaftesbury himself declined membership of the Commission on the grounds that his known commitment to one side of the issue would impair its authority and impartiality.[59] He urged that extremists on the other side should also be excluded, and he put Wilberforce in this category. This provoked a strong denial from Wilberforce that he was an extremist on the issue and he accepted membership of the Commission.[60] But Shaftesbury was not reassured. He felt that the Commission was biassed: 'as unfair, partial and prejudging as it well could be,' he wrote of it in 1867,[61] and, in 1871, he denounced its 'shortcomings and treachery'.[62] And, although Shaftesbury appears to have come to realise that Wilberforce was not as extreme as he had branded him, the Ritualist question still bulked large in his dealings with the Bishop. When Wilberforce became Bishop of Winchester in 1869, Shaftesbury wrote to him promising support in his new Bishopric, and he mentioned, in particular, the difficulty of attracting the working classes to the Established Church. He suggested various people who could help and advise Wilberforce on this matter; there were, he wrote, few clergy who had the 'power of entering into the real feelings and intimate social life of these seething masses.' But Shaftesbury warned Wilberforce of the dangers of introducing ceremonial. He might have little difficulty at first in doing this 'in due amount', but he would later have great difficulty in preventing it from going to extremes. Wilberforce must not, moreover, be led to the assumption that the people liked such things. They loathed them. If crowds gathered in St Albans and other places of 'Papist Revival', Shaftesbury wrote – repeating his earlier point – it had been to 'indulge their curiosity and not to satisfy their devotion.'[63]

Similarly, the conflict with the Church on matters of Ritual placed Shaftesbury in a somewhat difficult position over the issue of the Athanasian Creed. The Creed was strongly disliked by the Broad Church party on intellectual grounds. They questioned its credentials; they disliked its precise definition of such matters as the Incarnation and the Trinity; and they particularly objected to its 'damnatory clauses' as morally offensive.[64] High Churchmen, on the other hand, were ill-disposed to this rationalist approach and felt that the Creed should be stressed as part of the Prayer Book. The Royal Commission on Ritualism considered the rubric governing the use of the Creed in 1870, and petitions were sent to it for and against change. In terms of combating rationalist thought, Shaftesbury should have been on the side of the High Churchmen and against the Broad. But again, the Ritualist controversy made this difficult, and the laity were strongly against the Creed. Thus Shaftesbury supported the view that the Creed should not be made compulsory in Church, and he headed a lay protest in 1872 to try to secure this. He felt that the Creed should be kept in the Prayer Book as an embodiment of faith, which might, indeed, be authorised by Scripture; nevertheless, he wrote: 'a document, however sublime and true, yet human, must not be forced on unwilling ears.'[65] He sent Archbishop Tait a memorial with some 7,000 signatures asking that the Creed should not be made compulsory.[66] It is not, then, altogether surprising that Pusey, who would still have liked to form an alliance with the Evangelicals to combat Neology, should have expressed his perplexity: 'I don't understand Shaftesbury now,' he wrote.[67]

Shaftesbury thus found it increasingly difficult in these years to join forces with High Churchmen in resisting the threat of Rationalism. Equally, there were difficulties in cooperating with Neologists to combat the threat of Ritualism. 'So London is going to Canterbury,' Shaftesbury wrote in 1868 on Tait's appointment to the Archbishopric. 'A Broad Churchman to replace a Churchman high and dry. It is a day of glory for Stanley and the Neologians.'[68] Shaftesbury thus retained his old suspicion of Tait as a Broad Churchman, although there had always been a certain rapport between the two men on other grounds.[69] But this became harder to maintain. Tait shared many of Shaftesbury's views on the activities of the Ritualists. Like Shaftesbury, he felt that they were stretching over-far the comprehensiveness of the Church of England, weakening its position as the National Church and even endangering its Establishment.[70] He was not unsympathetic to Shaftesbury's initiative in 1867 over vestments, and, when this failed, he was prepared to use the ecclesiastical courts to clarify the law. And, like Shaftesbury, he was anxious to reform the procedure of the Courts. But, such was the internal conflict in the Church that it was difficult for Tait to cooperate with Shaftesbury. To choose such an undoubted Evangelical ally would be to threaten the very unity of the Church which Tait sought to promote. And Shaftesbury also found it hard to cooperate with Tait. In 1868, Tait, when still Bishop of London, wrote to Shaftesbury telling him of his intention to bring in a measure to reform the courts at the earliest opportunity.[71] Shaftesbury replied saying that he could not defer his bill on the grounds that Tait was preparing a measure. He was, he wrote, under an 'honourable obligation' to the Church Association, which had borne the entire expense (some £1,000) in the preparation of the bill. It was understood that it would be produced in the present session and he could not inform the Association that another course would be taken. He had, however, no objection to Tait's bill being presented in due course and running *pari passu* with his own, so that the Lords might be enabled to consider their respective measures.[72]

The developments in the Church thus wedded Shaftesbury ever more firmly to the Evangelical party. But this is not to say that he approved of its conduct. He felt strongly that the Evangelicals were quite unable to present a united and effective resistance to the challenges of the times. 'How resist the flood of Ritualism and Infidelity?' he wrote in 1868. 'The thousand efforts that are made seem disjointed, inadequate, temporary.' Those who made them were not wanting in 'sincerity and zeal but in knowledge and conduct.'[73] Opposition to Neology was, he felt, totally ineffectual. Some Evangelicals, indeed, were not opposed to it at all. Shaftesbury continued to deplore the fact that they had lapsed from the faith of their fathers. *Ecce Homo* was the work of one who came from 'a right good Evangelical stock':

Jowett was the son of Shaftesbury's collaborator in the Ten Hours Movement. There were also Bickersteth, the nephew of Shaftesbury's close friend of the 1830s and 1840s, and Venn, son of the Secretary of the Church Missionary Society. All were in the 'full bloom of arrogant unbelief', and he wondered how so many descendants of Evangelicals were 'deep-dyed in this foul insult to our Lord'.[74] He was shocked when he found that the Secretary of the organisation to promote the Special Services – a 'correct, active and pious man' – was a great admirer of *Ecce Homo* and had told Shaftesbury that the book exalted his view of the human character of Christ. 'Come Lord Jesus,' was Shaftesbury's comment: 'this alone will solve all doubts and give us assurance and peace.'[75] And such opposition as was expressed to Neology was hampered by internal rivalries and dissensions – the Evangelicals were 'scattered, ignorant of each other and without power of concerted action.'[76] The Temple affair, he noted, was a case in point, revealing the coldness and insincerity of the bulk of the Evangelicals, their disunion, their separation in place and action.'[77] Some, he felt, went too far in their opposition to Temple – they had, for example, urged the Chapter of Exeter Cathedral to oppose their new Bishop. Others did not go far enough and were even admirers of and apologists for Temple. The movement against Temple had thus been 'rash, violent, undignified and abortive',[78] and he felt sure that Gladstone would have noticed the internal divisions. The way would now be open for the appointment of 'even a Colenso'.[79]

Given such internal disunity, Shaftesbury felt that it was impossible to give a lead to any Evangelical movement. 'Who is to lead a regiment like that?' he wrote to Haldane after the Temple episode. 'Even Falstaff would not march through Coventry with them.'[80] The Evangelicals had no 'germ of true, vital self-surrendering Protestantism'; they were actuated only by personal antipathies.[81] And Shaftesbury also often felt that much antipathy was shown towards him. For some Evangelicals he was too extreme. Thus he was not at first asked to be President of the Church Association, because its founders felt that this would make it too partisan a body and would frighten off High Churchmen who were anti-Ritualist.[82] Again, in 1866, controversy over the Confessional caused feelings against Ritualism to run high and there were demands that a lay Evangelical movement should be founded in protest. Shaftesbury, however, was not asked to join the Committee which was formed on the subject. He was greatly offended. He wrote in December that he was 'deposed from the leadership of the Protestant Party.' He reflected that, at the time of the contest for the Oxford Professorship of Poetry, he had received hundreds of letters of congratulations and everyone seemed anxious to follow his guidance. Again, at the time of Papal Aggression, he was the natural choice to be 'chairman everywhere and spokesman in the House of Commons'. But now he was told that his opinions were too extreme and that the Protestants wanted another sort of man.[83] But, if to some, he was too extreme, to others, he was not extreme enough. His speech in favour of Pusey's work on Daniel did not meet with approval in certain Evangelical circles, and he wrote that his support for a High Churchman – even on a matter of doctrine – condemned him for ever in their eyes. Some Evangelicals were 'obsessed simply by anti-Ritualism and hatred of Dr Pusey' and would prefer 'two Temples' to 'one Pusey'.[84] Shaftesbury did, it is true, act on behalf of the Church Association in presenting the Memorial to Gladstone protesting against Temple's appointment, and over the promotion of the bills for the reform of the ecclesiastical courts. But he did so somewhat half-heartedly, believing that Evangelicals were not united behind either project nor prepared to give him unanimous support.

Thus as in matters of State, so in those of Church, Shaftesbury felt increasingly isolated. He steered clear of Church Congresses, bodies held since 1861 to provide a forum for discussion and debate.[85] Evangelicals had, in fact, been uncertain whether or not to attend these gatherings, but in 1869, the Church Association decided, by a small majority, that it should do so and made preparations for its members to attend the following meeting, to be held in 1871 at Southampton. At first, Shaftesbury was to speak on matters connected with the Church and the working classes, but he decided against this. He felt that, had he spoken, he could not have refrained from touching on the dangers which beset the Church and, as he told Haldane, 'first and foremost among them, the apathy or connivance of our Bishops.'[86] When the Congress was over, he felt that it had been useless. It had come to 'no conclusions, made no suggestions, promised no action, and exhibited no unanimity.' The clergy had expressed a desire for the cooperation of the laity, but felt that they could not be admitted to Convocation; the 'abominations of Ritualism' had not been attacked and were barely mentioned.[87] Shaftesbury thus was heartily glad that he had not attended the Congress and refused to attend others held in the future. He was suspicious of the Mildmay Conferences, which had been started in 1856 as focal points of Evangelical effort with the aim of spiritual regeneration. He did, on occasion, take part in them, but, despite the enthusiasm of his brother-in-law, Cowper-Temple, he never gave them wholehearted support.[88] And to his feeling of isolation was added that of rejection: 'it is clear that I have nobody's confidence and certainly nobody has mine,' he wrote in 1868,[89] and, as has been seen, this was true, he felt, even among Evangelicals. All he could hope for was the Second Advent, and, even on this matter, he could find distressingly little interest. On Christmas Day, 1868, he wrote that, amidst all the celebrations of the first Advent, little was said or thought of the Second. It was an 'unpalatable prospect' even among 'good people'.[90] In 1870, he referred to a correspondence which he himself had initiated in *The Record* on the Second Advent. The result, he wrote, was an admission on the part of the clergy that they did not preach it and, such was its unpopularity with the laity, that they would not preach it.[91] He returned to the matter in 1873, referring to a letter which he had written to *The Record* to rebuke the clergy of the Church of England for their silence on the Second Advent.[92] A few days later, he wrote that, to his mind, the strongest proof that the Second Advent was near was the 'almost universal inattention to it'.[93]

Shaftesbury's comments on his role in the religious – as in the secular – world in this period must, of course, be treated with caution. As ever, he was guilty of exaggeration and over-dramatisation. In the first place, he did imply a wider acceptance of his 'leadership' of the Evangelical movement in the 1840s and 1850s than, in fact, had been the case. Even over Maynooth and 'Papal Aggression', he had taken a line of which not all Evangelicals had approved.[94] Similarly, in 1856, he had firmly disclaimed the title attributed to him by Haldane as 'Leader of the Evangelical Party'.

> This [he wrote] is a position too perilous, too uncertain and too useless for anyone to accept. No one can be an effective leader unless those who follow him are prepared to repose confidence in his judgment and guidance, not during smooth and easy times alone, but in times of doubt and perplexity. No one in these days has such a sentiment. . . .
> Besides though there are very many points, indeed most points, in which I concur theologically with the Evangelical party, there are some in which, as friends and counsellors etc., etc. I think several of them very far from charity and justice. Let them catch me tripping (and who can always walk upright?) and there would be as much real spite (though veiled under regret) and pleasure, as among the editors of newspapers or the congregation of Puseyism.[95]

Shaftesbury was not, therefore, 'deposed' from the leadership of the Evangelical party – he had never occupied this role and had not sought to do so. Nor was the role which he *had* occupied entirely changed. On two occasions in the early 1870s, he offered to resign from the Presidency of two Societies with which he had a long association, but his offers were rejected. In 1870, he had an exchange of letters with the Secretary of the British and Foreign Bible Society over the proposed translation of the Bible.[96] The Society took the view that its task was simply the production and distribution of the Scriptures. On the merits and demerits of a new translation, it took a neutral stance. Shaftesbury, however, could not accept this, and committed himself strongly to opposing the translation. He realised that this affected his position as President of the Society and was prepared to accept the Committee's judgment on the matter. The Committee reaffirmed its neutrality, although it did not wish to interfere with Shaftesbury's freedom of speech and action on the question of revision, nor with that of any committee member; and it could not entertain the thought of Shaftesbury demitting office as President. It hoped that God would spare him long to work in the cause. Shaftesbury, on his side, refrained from commenting on the subject of revision from the Chair of the Society in May, 1870. The second occasion on which Shaftesbury felt that his views might be too strong to be acceptable was in 1873, when he made up his mind to address the Church Pastoral Aid Society on the subject of Church Reform. He told Haldane that 'previously to passing into regions of twaddle not far distant,' he longed to 'deliver (his) soul on Church Reform.' He was sure that his views would give great offence, but he felt that he could not remain at the head of Church Societies and conceal them. He proposed to speak out openly at the Society and then resign his Presidency on the grounds that the position ought to be held by someone in harmony with the views of the members.[97] His speech was, indeed, a strong appeal for various reforms[98]: a reform of the Liturgy, of the patronage of livings, of the system of administering Ordination and admitting men to Holy Orders. On the last subject, Shaftesbury argued that Ordination must no longer be the exclusive prerogative of the bishops. He also spoke against any increase of the Episcopate: 'I am not such a lover of Episcopacy as to think it necessary to salvation,' he said. If there were to be an increase, it would have to be done by subdividing the dioceses and revenues into two, and this might involve removing Bishops from the House of Lords. Such a step would be a serious one and would involve careful consideration as to its effects on the Lords; 'but,' Shaftesbury said, 'our duty at the present moment is to consider the safety of the Church of England and not how to perpetuate the House of Lords.' In all of this, his great object was to make the Church acceptable to the great body of the people, and the speech showed the extent to which Shaftesbury was willing to go to obtain reform.[99] In his comments on his speech, he wrote that his propositions were, no doubt, 'large, sweeping, with a certain amount of hazard'. But less would not bring 'one element of safety'.[100] Nevertheless, he felt that such expressions, coming from the President of a Society, would tend to compromise it and lose its support and finance. Thus he had written immediately and given in his resignation. It was not accepted.

Shaftesbury thus retained his Presidencies in the Evangelical world, and each May brought with it the accustomed round of chairs and speeches. He noted in 1870, 'last week as usual very heavy,' and he listed the societies which he had addressed: the British and Foreign Bible Society, the London City Mission, the Church Pastoral Aid Society, the London Jews Society, the Christian Blind Relief Society.[101] Some days later,[102] he added the Society for Vernacular Education in India and the Lord's Day Working Men's Society to the tally. While in Glasgow in 1871,[103] he visited societies concerned with evangelical effort in addition to those involved in social improvement. He spoke to the Glasgow Working Men's Sabbath Protection Association, and he attended and addressed a large meeting at which representatives from the Y.M.C.A., the Young Men's Society for Religious Improvement, the Sabbath School Union and the Foundry Boys' Religious Society were present. At another meeting, he heard of missionary enterprise, and supported the point of view put forward that churches were required in Glasgow in which a working man could go and sit where he liked. This, said Shaftesbury, was perfectly consistent with his experience in London, and, drawing on his experience of theatre services, he argued that religious services should be held in places suited to the needs of the people. At the same conference, Shaftesbury welcomed the efforts of societies concerned with Bible and Tract Circulation and Colportage. The visit to Glasgow, was then, almost a microcosm of the causes into which Shaftesbury had put the effort of some thirty years.

Further, Shaftesbury was asked to undertake fresh offices and labours. In 1868 he was approached by the British organisation of the Evangelical Alliance and asked to become its President.[104] One of its members wrote personally to him and stressed the position which Shaftesbury occupied 'in relation to the great Religious and Philanthropic interests and societies of our own country and in the view of Christendom.'[105] In 1871, he was asked if he would become the President of the Church Association.[106] He declined these offers, telling the Evangelical Alliance that he dared not, at his time of life, 'plunge into any more.'[107] Nevertheless, the fact that the offers were made indicates that he was held in much greater esteem than he himself allowed. Although not officially connected with the Church Association, he did act, even if somewhat reluctantly, on its behalf, and it was said that he 'represented the whole body of Protestant and Evangelical Churchmen, of whom a considerable section never sympathised with the methods of the Church Association.'[108] His guidance and support were indeed sought on many issues. A notable instance of this was on the question of education in the early 1870s. In 1873, the National Society asked him if his name might be added to a list of supporters of its efforts to sustain the voluntary system which, it felt, was essential to the maintenance of religious instruction.[109] Shaftesbury agreed to this, adding, in his normal style, that he had 'so many enemies' that a cause was often injured by the part which he took in it.[110] And, although he was critical of the sectarianism shown by the Dissenters over the Education Act, he had many contacts with Dissenters and was held in great respect by them. He had a full correspondence with Spurgeon over the Act. Both men were agreed on the need for Education which, as Spurgeon put it, was 'unsectarian but not unreligious',[111] and Spurgeon expressed his admiration for Shaftesbury – 'I greatly venerate your Lordship and have you near to my heart in deep respect,' he wrote.[112] In 1873, Shaftesbury was asked by the Wesleyan Education Committee to take the Chair at the Annual Meeting on behalf of Wesleyan Education in Training Colleges, Day Schools and Sunday Schools. He agreed to go, subject to a declaration being made that God's Word was the 'one thing needful' in all public and private Education. This condition was fulfilled.[113] Further, on the Ritualist controversy, Shaftesbury was consulted about the formation of various new bodies and unions. He did, it is true, despair of such things being of any avail. But, in 1871, he took the chair of a meeting at which the Clerical and Lay Union was formed as a branch of the Church Association, and, in 1873, was nominated President of the Evangelical Union of the Church of England, a body initially designed to press for Church reform, although it soon became embroiled in the Ritualist controversy and did not, it would seem, have a very long life.[114]

Despite his feelings of isolation and rejection, Shaftesbury, therefore, continued to occupy an important role within many strands of Evangelical effort. It may, of course, be argued that – as in secular matters – he was increasingly regarded as a 'figure-head' and an object of veneration rather than as a new and invigorating force. There is certainly some truth in this. To take a small example: he was asked to become Vice-President of a Committee of the Islington Shoe Black Brigade, formed for the purpose of fighting School Board Elections,[115] but it will be recalled that he did not – to his chagrin – receive any invitations to stand in an election himself.[116] But even this argument can be taken too far, for Shaftesbury was, in fact, to play a central part in the Ritualist controversy in 1873-4. In mid and late 1873, anti-Ritualist sentiment reached considerable proportions.[117] This was partly the result of the failure of earlier efforts – including those of Shaftesbury himself – to stop Ritualist practices by reforming the courts, and of anger that the Bishops seemed to be so inactive in stopping what was seen as a drift to Rome. What gave this added point in the summer of 1873 was a petition presented on 9 May to Convocation, signed by four hundred and eighty three clergymen of the Church of England, asking that, in the light of the increasing practice of sacramental Confession, Convocation might consider the advisability of providing for the education, selection and licensing of duly qualified confessors. The practice of Confession was a grave affront to Evangelical consciences, and the issue united Evangelical efforts in protest against it. It also brought Shaftesbury to the forefront of these efforts. He presided over a meeting held at Exeter Hall on 30 June to protest against the introduction of the Confessional in the Church of England. Shaftesbury delivered a powerful speech, reported as lasting for an hour.[118] He referred to the 'unholy and wicked attack which had been made on the purity of the Church of England.' He castigated the Bishops in Convocation for receiving the Petition in 'soft and delicate language': they had pronounced it a 'serious error', but had referred it to a committee. Such faint condemnation of what was a 'degradation of God's law' and a 'scandal to Holy Scripture' was lamentable, and, when such a weak position had been assumed by the clergy, it became the duty of the laity to take the matter into their own hands. He had, he said, written to the Archbishop of Canterbury to say that the laity were in alarm – they turned to their Bishops and wanted to know the intentions of the Episcopal Bench. The Archbishop had replied that the matter had been considered by the Bishops, who had now gone into their dioceses and would meet again in early July. 'This,' said Shaftesbury, 'was the balm for the comfort of the troubled English Churchman, the soothing syrup for his pain.' After attacking the practice of the Confessional, Shaftesbury concluded by declaring that

> the people of England would maintain the true principles of the Reformation in all their integrity, honour and efficiency, and that they would maintain the Church of England while she was true to her allegiance to the Holy Scripture; but if she wavered in her allegiance, if she abandoned the Reformation, then ... let her go and all the Bishops with her. ...

He was pleased with the mood of the meeting: 'the enthusiasm prodigious,' he noted in his Diary, 'and sustained to the very last.'[119] He also took the chair of a meeting of Churchmen at which common action was planned to ensure that the Church of England be kept a Protestant Establishment.[120]

Shaftesbury thus once again assumed a position of great prominence at a moment of crisis in the Evangelical world. Moreover, the storm which he helped to raise shaped future events. As has been seen, Tait was already sensitive to the activities of the Ritualists and the effects which they were having on the unity of the Church, and the presentation of the Petition over the Confessional, followed by the outburst of militant Protestantism at Exeter Hall, made the situation even more difficult. Tait had not greatly approved of Shaftesbury's speech at Exeter Hall. 'I think your language as reported stronger than was required,' he wrote.[121] But the mood of the meeting had been equally strong, and, if Tait did not take prompt action, Shaftesbury, with the backing of the Church Association, might introduce legislation which would divide the Church even more.[122] Further, Tait was under strong pressure from the Queen to curb the activities of the Ritualists, and thus he finally decided that legislation was required to tighten Church discipline. The situation was complicated by the dissolution of Parliament in 1874 and the General Election which followed it. The prospect of forthcoming legislation in the Church was, indeed, one reason why Gladstone decided to dissolve – he wished a fresh mandate before he dealt with the matter. He was not destined to get it, for, on the defeat of the Liberals at the polls, Disraeli and a Conservative government came into office. Undeterred, Tait kept to his plans to proceed with legislation. He sent Disraeli a memorandum of his proposals. They were, in fact, moderate in substance and amounted only to a request for legislation to set up a quick and inexpensive process for ensuring obedience to the laws governing public worship. The Bishops were to act as the agency to which disputes over ceremonial should be directed. This was not new; what *was* new was that they should be given coercive power, exercised on the advice of diocesan boards, composed of equal proportions of clergy and laity.

The proposals – subsequently released by Tait to *The Times* – had, of course, to run the gauntlet of ecclesiastical opinion, and this Tait well knew. He also knew that he would have to deal with Shaftesbury as a prominent representative of Evangelical opinion. He told Disraeli that Shaftesbury and his following would need to be convinced that there was 'no danger of weapons intended for other purposes rebounding against themselves, unless in such cases as are obvious violations of the law.'[123] Indeed, Tait went out of his way to consult Shaftesbury, supplying him with a copy of the memorandum which he had sent to Disraeli.[124] He wrote that he had been anxious to see Shaftesbury for some time 'on the subject of legislation to check the lawlessness which is abroad in the matter of our Church service,' and he asked for any suggestions that Shaftesbury could make to help the Archbishop of York and himself in drafting a bill. His hope was that a mixed body of clergy and laity, elected from the Diocese, might be able to counteract the irresponsible power claimed by each incumbent, and that, thus, many practices might be stopped. As to Confession, what was done privately by clergymen might be beyond legislation, but any open introduction of it would be stopped. He added that the Bishops almost unanimously wished the Archbishop to prepare a bill; the wider question of Ecclesiastical law reform was independent of it.[125] But the fact that the bill came from the Bishops did not endear it to Shaftesbury. Further, he was not well disposed to a proposal which increased the power of the bishops, and the board which was designed to give advice was, he felt, very unlikely to introduce any effective lay voice. Further, the measure did nothing to reform the abuses of the ecclesiastical courts.[126] Tait, however, still tried to conciliate Shaftesbury, sending him a second memorandum.[127] He took up the point about the reform of the courts and expressed his willingness to cooperate with Shaftesbury by asking Parliament to consider their reform along with his proposed measure. Such a reform, he said, was certainly in the interests of efficiency and economy, but even reform would not eliminate costs altogether, since counsel would still have to be engaged. Tait's proposal was, therefore, designed to introduce a simpler procedure which would settle disputes which were not taken to court: it was a complementary measure to a more far-reaching reform of the courts. Thus the two could go forward together. But Shaftesbury was still dissatisfied with Tait's measure. It did not, he replied,[128] make the mode of electing clergy to the board clear, and, in any event, the board amounted to a new court. If it did not, why was the aid of Parliament invoked? He also did not feel that the new bill and the old one for reforming the courts which he himself had proposed for four years, could run *pari passu*, and, he wrote, 'even were the thing within the compass of human power, I could not consent to undertake it. My experience of lawyers, laymen, Bishops and Chancellors,' he added, 'is not agreeable as to the past, nor encouraging for the future.' Further, Shaftesbury felt that the bill would not deal with the Confessional. Shaftesbury showed his increasing preoccupation with the Confessional by an exchange of letters with Archbishop Manning of Westminster in April. He was on good terms with Manning, having previously corresponded with him about their common interest in social matters and also on their common desire to 'keep the name of our Blessed Lord afloat upon the waters.'[129] Now he asked Manning to explain what regulations the Roman Catholic Church imposed in relation to the Confessional, and whether it was held to be necessary to salvation.[130] Thus Shaftesbury showed his willingness to acknowledge what he regarded as Roman Catholic practices for the Roman Catholic Church. But his letter to Tait showed his ever present desire to denounce such practices in the Church of England. The Confessional, he wrote, was now of greater importance than Ritualism and 'all its mischievous trumperies'. It had got 'fearfully ahead' and unless the Church could 'cleanse herself of the foul thing, she and all her Children will sink in to the dust.'[131]

Shaftesbury was not, then, well disposed to Tait's proposals, and he maintained his critical attitude once these proposals came to Parliament. The Public Worship Regulation bill was given its second reading on 11 May, 1874. Shaftesbury announced that he did not intend to oppose the second reading, but he spoke at length on various aspects of the bill which he did not like.[132] These echoed the points which he had already made privately to Tait. He felt that the bill gave too much power to the Bishops. The composition of the advisory board had, in fact, been changed twice since Tait had outlined his original proposals. In the first place, on the prompting of the Lord Chancellor, the Evangelical Lord Cairns, it was to be made up of the Dean or Archdeacon or Diocesan Chancellor, a barrister of seven years standing and a nominee of the Bishop. Then Tait had shown himself willing to accept a second change, suggested by Convocation, that it should be limited to the Diocesan Chancellor. But, even under Cairns's plan, it only *advised* the Bishop, and, moreover, it was for the Bishop to decide whether a complaint initiated against an incumbent – which could only be for an illegality – should be referred to it at all. It was, therefore, for the Bishop to enforce, or not to enforce, the legislation as he pleased. He acknowledged that he was a 'Low Churchman', but, even if he were sure of Low Church Bishops for half a century to come, he would not confer on them the discretion contained in the bill. Moreover, Shaftesbury disliked the fact that, if the Bishop *did* initiate proceedings and the offending incumbent refused to obey the monitions of the Bishop and his 'Board', the incumbent would be inhibited from ministering in his parish until such time as the monitions were reversed on appeal.[133] Shaftesbury asked if it was consistent with the spirit of the law of England that a sentence, though appealed against, was to be executed. The Bishop would seize the income of the parish and use it for making alternative provision for the parish, even while the appeal was being heard. It was, then, a penal measure which placed almost irresponsible power in the hands of the Bishops. Further, Shaftesbury objected to it on the grounds that it would not touch the worst abuses in the Church. Ritualism had now got very far ahead and it would not be possible to do more than lop off some of its excrescences. Moreover, even Ritualism was now of secondary importance. The appearance of Altar Cards gave ample proof that the worship of the Virgin, Invocation of the Saints, prayers to the Apostles were taught by Ministers of the Church. The Confessional was not an 'idle phantom'. It was spreading. How could the provisions of the bill touch these? Shaftesbury asked. One way to stop them was to create a strong, persistent and united sentiment of disgust. This was difficult, since there was a powerful party in favour of such practices and the bulk of the nation was thinking of other things and living 'in a state of utter indifference'. The other way to stop these practices was to promote a 'wide and deep and searching reform of the Church of England'. But, Shaftesbury said, no one would listen to that.

Shaftesbury had, indeed, decided to wash his hands of the bill altogether – but he was approached by Cairns, promising him government support if he introduced as amendments a large part of his previous Ecclesiastical Courts bill. 'We shall make a good bill,' Shaftesbury reported Cairns to say, 'and the amendments as coming from you will have great weight.'[134] Shaftesbury suspected that Cairns might take the credit for the measure himself, but he agreed to his request and, on 4 June, 1874, moved in Committee the most important amendment, which provided for the appointment of a single judge for the two Provinces of Canterbury and York, to whom ecclesiastical questions arising under the bill would be referred.[135] This, Shaftesbury said, relieved the Bishops of great anxiety and also from any charge of partiality. Tait did not favour the substitute of a judicial for an ecclesiastical authority, but, once he learned that it had government approval, he had little alternative but to accept it. Were he to drop his bill, a more drastic solution might be sponsored by the Church Association. He thus voted reluctantly for Shaftesbury's amendment, which was carried by 112 to 13. Shaftesbury, on his side, proved to be amenable on another matter. He had wished to remove from the Diocesan Bishop the power of deciding whether or not a case should go ahead and be referred to the judge for the ecclesiastical provinces: a safeguard against frivolous complaints would be that the complainant would require to give security for the costs. But he yielded on this point, and suggested the compromise that the Bishop must give him reasons why he refused to allow a case to proceed.[136] One further way in which Shaftesbury exercised a moderating influence was in helping to persuade Bishop Magee to drop an amendment which the Bishop had intended to introduce – this would have exempted from the bill certain practices which deviated from a strict observance of the rubric. Some of these were in accordance with Evangelical practice, in particular, the celebration of Holy Communion at the Evening Service. But one was a High Church practice – the stance of the priest in an Eastward direction. Evangelicals strongly disapproved of this – and of Magee's attempt to make it legal. Among others, Shaftesbury advised Magee to abandon his amendment, and he did so.[137]

The bill was introduced to the Commons on 9 July, 1874, by Russell Gurney, the Recorder of London. It was strongly opposed by Gladstone, but it passed its second reading without a division, having secured the personal support of Disraeli. Shaftesbury commented on these events.[138] He vigorously denounced Gladstone's contribution – an 'ultramontane' address he called it – and he noted that, at the second reading, Gladstone had 'slunk out of the House not daring to have, according to his own favourite phrase, "the courage of his convictions".' Shaftesbury was delighted when, in Committee, the House agreed to the appointment of the judge, the 'crux' of the bill, as he put it – 'the finger of God has been manifest all through,' he wrote. And, on this occasion, he expressed admiration for Disraeli: 'of all the clever men I knew, or ever have known, D'Issy is the chief. What a head he has for policy and practice.' He knew, however, that the battle was not over and, indeed, a number of amendments in the Commons threatened the bill. Shaftesbury, indeed, was deeply depressed when the bill passed back from the Commons to the Lords. The bill, he wrote, having come into the Commons like a lion went out like a mouse, 'eviscerated, emasculated, evaporated'.[139] He took exception, in particular, to two amendments: one had deferred the operation of the bill for twelve months to give Convocation time to suggest changes in the rubric and the second had altered the arrangements for the payment of the judge's salary but had put nothing in their place. Shaftesbury was exasperated at the delay in the bill's implementation. 'Gladstone and the Jesuits have delayed and neutralised the measure,' he wrote. 'It is a mere Eunuch on the face of the Statute Book.' And now Disraeli incurred his criticism: 'Dizzy, self-seeking like Peel, was weak and indecisive.'[140] And another amendment passed by the Commons was to pose problems for the Lords. This had been introduced on behalf of the Church Association and made it possible for an appeal to be made to the Archbishop if the Bishop used his veto to prevent a case being referred to the judge. Feeling in the Commons had run high over this, and Disraeli warned that, if the Lords rejected this amendment, the Commons would throw out the whole bill.[141] Tait appreciated the danger of the Lords tampering with the Commons' amendments and so too did Shaftesbury, for, despite his disappointment over the delay in implementing the bill, he did not want to lose it. 'Still in pangs about this Public Worship bill,' he wrote on 4 August. 'If the Lords disagree with any of the Commons' amendments, the Bill will be lost.'[142] Later the same day, his fears were realised when the Commons' amendment concerning the appeal was rejected by 44 to 32, some Bishops voting with the majority. This caused great resentment in the Commons and the situation was exacerbated by disparaging remarks which Salisbury made about the Commons. Shaftesbury, at Cairns's request, negotiated with members of the Commons to try to soothe the way to agreement: a task, he wrote, which would have been relatively easy had it not been for Salisbury's language. Nevertheless, Shaftesbury felt that there were 'hopes of safety',[143] and so it was to be, for the Commons accepted the Lords' rejection of their amendment. At 7 p.m. on 5 August, Shaftesbury noted that the bill was safe. 'I bless Thee, O Lord. The Commons gave way and all is peace and harmony.'[144]

Shaftesbury had thus played an active role over the whole question. He was by no means the sole instigator of the Act, but his strong denunciation of the Confessional in 1873 had helped to hasten the legislation and, once the details of a measure had been outlined, he was involved in the various stages through which it passed before it finally reached the Statute Book. The whole question had, moreover, carried him once more into a position of prominence in the Evangelical movement. As in the past – for example over the Oxford Movement – it may be argued that Shaftesbury played a role which accentuated the divisions in the Church. And yet – as also in the past – it may also be held that the divisions were as much caused by the opposing party, and Shaftesbury was not unamenable to compromise – as over the question of the episcopal veto. Partly, indeed, for this reason, the Act was to have relatively little effect; the veto was frequently to be used and thus many cases never went the length of being referred to the judge at all. Moreover, when cases *did* proceed to the judge and judgment was passed, many Ritualists proved to be unwilling to accept the jurisdiction of the court, and this resistance also contributed to the relative ineffectiveness of the Act in restraining Ritualism. Shaftesbury, indeed, had not expected very much from the Act, describing it as two halves of different bills joined together.[145]

The 'Juggernaut of Ritualism' was not, therefore, halted, nor was that of Rationalism. Indeed, in pouring such energy into resisting the first, Evangelicals, including Shaftesbury had, to some extent, been distracted from their struggle with the second, and distracted, too, from the task of mission, much of which was being undertaken by the Ritualists. Moreover, such unity as the Evangelicals had displayed in 1873-4 did not last – even the question of how rigidly the Act of 1874 should be enforced was to divide them. Thus Shaftesbury remained pessimistic about the future. Writing to Tait of a recent Church Congress in Brighton, he said that it had shown 'the power and determination of the Ritualistic Body and the impossibility of cohesion, common action and, tell it not in Gath, common sense among the "Evangelicals".' Thus, he told Tait, 'the horizon is very black.'[146] Future events were not to alter that judgment, nor, despite his activity of 1873-4, to change his opinion that his day was over.

NOTES

1. See above p. 399.
2. N.R.A., Shaftesbury (Broadlands) MSS, SHA/MIS/3.
3. ibid., SHA/PD/8, 9 Feb., 1867.
4. ibid., SHA/PD/8, 30 Mar., 1866.
5. ibid., SHA/PD/8, 7 Apr., 1867.
6. ibid., SHA/PD/8, 7 Apr., 1867.
7. ibid., SHA/PD/9, 21 Dec., 1869.
8. Add. MSS, 44, 300, fos 54-5.
9. N.R.A., Shaftesbury (Broadlands) MSS, SHA/PD/9, 1 Oct., 1869.
10. ibid., SHA/PD/9, 8 Oct., 1869.
11. ibid., SHA/PD/9, 13 Dec., 1869.
12. Quoted in Hodder, III, 169-70.
13. N.R.A., SHA/PD/9, 8 Sept., 1870.
14. ibid., SHA/PD/9, 1 Oct., 1869.
15. ibid., SHA/PD/9, 1 Oct., 1869.
16. Add. MSS, 44, 300, fos 28-9.
17. ibid., f. 30.
18. See above p. 395.

19. *The Times*, 14 Feb., 1870.
20. Add. MSS, 44, 300, fos 34-7.
21. H.R.O., Shaftesbury (Broadlands) MSS, 27M60. Undated.
22. ibid.
23. ibid.
24. N.R.A., Shaftesbury (Broadlands) MSS, SHA/PD/8, 25 May, 1866.
25. ibid., SHA/PD/10, 27 Aug., 1874.
26. ibid., SHA/PD/10, 26 Oct., 1874.
27. ibid., SHA/PD/10, 3 Sept., 1874.
28. P. T. Marsh, *The Victorian Church in Decline. Archbishop Tait and the Church of England, 1868-1882* (1969), p. 112 ff.
29. M. A. Crowther, *Church Embattled: Religious Controversy in Mid-Victorian England* (1970), pp. 190-91.
30. N.R.A., Shaftesbury (Broadlands) MSS, SHA/PD/8, 23 July, 1866.
31. Hansard, *Parl. Debates*, 3rd ser., CLXXXV, 1624.
32. MSS Eng. Lett., d. 193.
33. Hansard, *Parl. Debates*, 3rd ser., CLXXXVII, 478-501.
34. ibid., CLXXXIX, 1632.
35. A. Bentley, op. cit., pp. 138-9.
36. Hansard, *Parl. Debates*, 3rd ser., CXCII, 332-3.
37. ibid., CXCIII, 868-78.
38. Hodder, III, 234.
39. Hansard, *Parl. Debates*, 3rd ser., CLXXXIX, 1558-9.
40. Tait MSS, 84, 3 Mar., 1868.
41. Hansard, *Parl. Debates*, 3rd ser., CXCV, 808 ff.
42. ibid., CCVI, 1749.
43. Quoted in Hodder, III, 234.
44. N.R.A., Shaftesbury (Broadlands) MSS, SHA/PD/9, 17 Mar., 1869.
45. ibid., SHA/PD/9, 3 Apr., 1869.
46. Hansard, *Parl. Debates*, 3rd ser., CXCV, 808.
47. ibid., CXCVIII, 885.
48. ibid., CCIII, 614.
49. ibid., CCVI, 1746.
50. ibid., CCIX, 618.
51. See above pp. 340-1.
52. Add. MSS, 44, 300, fos 60-61.
53. ibid., fos 62-3.
54. ibid., fos 64-5.
55. N.R.A., Shaftesbury (Broadlands) MSS, SHA/PD/9, 16 Feb., 1871.
56. Quoted in Hodder, III, 229-30.
57. N.R.A., Shaftesbury (Broadlands) MSS, SHA/PD/9, 21 Oct., 1869.
58. ibid., SHA/PD/9, 23 Oct., 1869.
59. See Hodder, III, 229-30.
60. S. Meacham, *Lord Bishop. The Life of Samuel Wilberforce, 1805-1873* (Cambridge, Mass., 1970), p. 258.
61. N.R.A., Shaftesbury (Broadlands) MSS, SHA/PD/8, 7 June, 1867.
62. ibid., SHA/PD/9, 16 Oct., 1871.
63. Wilberforce MSS, C 17, fos 15-18.
64. P. T. Marsh, op. cit., pp. 42-3.
65. N.R.A., Shaftesbury (Broadlands) MSS, SHA/PD/10, 17 May, 1872.
66. Tait MSS, 91, 29 June, 1, 2, 4 July, 1872.

JUGGERNAUT OF RATIONALISM AND RITUALISM, 1866–1874   541

67. A. Bentley, op. cit., p. 112. H. P. Liddon, op. cit., IV, 226.
68. N.R.A., Shaftesbury (Broadlands) MSS, SHA/PD/8, 16 Nov., 1868.
69. See above pp. 382, 389–90.
70. P. T. Marsh, op. cit., p. 119.
71. Tait MSS, 85, 14 Dec., 1868.
72. ibid., fos 265–7. This was done: both measures were brought in in Apr., 1869 and both were referred to the select committee. Shaftesbury's measure was, however, preferred and Tait withdrew his proposals.
73. N.R.A., Shaftesbury (Broadlands) MSS, SHA/PD/8, 26 Jan., 1868.
74. ibid., SHA/PD/8, 22 Nov., 1866.
75. ibid., SHA/PD/8, 29 Mar., 1867.
76. ibid., SHA/PD/8, 27 Aug., 1867.
77. ibid., SHA/PD/9, 23 Oct., 6 Nov., 1869.
78. Quoted in Hodder, III, 256.
79. N.R.A., Shaftesbury (Broadlands) MSS, SHA/PD/9, 6 Nov., 1869.
80. Quoted in Hodder, III, 256.
81. N.R.A., Shaftesbury (Broadlands) MSS, SHA/PD/9, 23 Oct., 1869.
82. A. Bentley, op. cit., pp. 131–2.
83. N.R.A., Shaftesbury (Broadlands) MSS, SHA/PD/8, 31 Dec., 1866.
84. ibid., SHA/PD/9, 9 Nov., 1869.
85. A. Bentley, op. cit., p. 220 ff.
86. Quoted in Hodder, III, 282.
87. N.R.A., Shaftesbury (Broadlands) MSS, SHA/PD/9, 16 Oct., 1871.
88. A. Bentley, op. cit., pp. 383–400.
89. N.R.A., Shaftesbury (Broadlands) MSS, SHA/PD/8, 21 Oct., 1868.
90. ibid., SHA/PD/9, 25 Dec., 1868.
91. ibid., SHA/PD/9, 8 Jan., 1870.
92. ibid., SHA/PD/10, 16 Apr., 1873.
93. ibid., SHA/PD/10, 23 Apr., 1873.
94. See above pp. 167–8, 320.
95. Quoted in Hodder, III, 3.
96. H.R.O., Shaftesbury (Broadlands) MSS, 27M60, 16, 17, 18, 24, 28 Feb., 1870.
97. Hodder, III, 328–9.
98. Quoted ibid.
99. Shaftesbury struck a similar note in a letter to Disraeli in July 1873. 'Few things,' he wrote, 'would be so acceptable, and . . . so conservative, as the Removal of the Bishops from the House of Lords.' (Hughenden MSS (on microfilm). Film 131, 11 July, 1873).
100. N.R.A., Shaftesbury (Broadlands) MSS, SHA/PD/10, 9 May, 1873.
101. ibid., SHA/PD/9, 9 May, 1870.
102. ibid., SHA/PD/9, 12 May, 1870.
103. See above pp. 492–3.
104. St G.H., Shaftesbury MSS, C 25004/7th Earl.
105. ibid., C 25004.2/7th Earl.
106. ibid., C 25097/7th Earl.
107. ibid., C 25004.1/7th Earl.
108. Supplement to *The Record*, 2 Oct., 1885.
109. St G.H., Shaftesbury MSS, C 25014.34/7th Earl.
110. ibid., C 25014.35/7th Earl.
111. N.R.A., Shaftesbury (Broadlands) MSS, SHA/PC/92.
112. ibid., SHA/PC/97.

113. St G.H., Shaftesbury MSS, C 25014.47, 48/7th Earl.
114. A. Bentley, op. cit., pp. 181–7.
115. St G.H., Shaftesbury (Broadlands) MSS, C 25014.19/7th Earl.
116. See above p. 491.
117. P. T. Marsh, op. cit., p. 158 ff.
118. *The Times*, 2 July, 1873.
119. N.R.A., Shaftesbury (Broadlands) MSS, SHA/PD/10, 1 July, 1873.
120. A. Bentley, op. cit., pp. 140–41.
121. St G.H., Shaftesbury MSS, C 25014.17/7th Earl.
122. P.T. Marsh, op. cit., pp. 159–60.
123. Quoted ibid., p. 164.
124. ibid., p. 167.
125. Tait MSS, 203, 18 Mar., 1874.
126. P. Marsh, op. cit., p. 167.
127. ibid., p. 168.
128. ibid., See also Tait MSS, 203, 27 Mar., 1874.
129. St G.H., Shaftesbury MSS, C 25026.16/7th Earl.
130. N.R.A., Shaftesbury (Broadlands) MSS, SHA/PC/47–50.
131. Tait MSS, 203, 27 Nov., 1874.
132. Hansard, *Parl. Debates*, 3rd ser., CCXIX, 12 ff.
133. The appeal was to the Judicial Committee of the Privy Council, with the possibility of an intermediate hearing in the provincial court, if the Archbishop required it.
134. N.R.A., Shaftesbury (Broadlands) MSS, SHA/PD/10, 13 June, 1874.
135. Hansard, *Parl. Debates*, 3rd ser., CCXIX, 953–5.
136. P. T. Marsh, op. cit., p. 178. See also J. Bentley, *Ritualism and Politics in Victorian Britain. The Attempt to Legislate for Belief* (Oxford, 1978), pp. 57–8. Bentley says that, although Shaftesbury was willing to yield and acted as a teller, he became so irritated at his own leniency that he voted against his own proposal.
137. P. T. Marsh, op. cit., pp. 179–80. J. Bentley, op. cit., pp. 58–9.
138. N.R.A., Shaftesbury (Broadlands) MSS, SHA/PD/10, 18 July, 1874.
139. ibid., SHA/PD/10, 1 Aug., 1874.
140. ibid., SHA/PD/10, 1 Aug., 1874.
141. P. T. Marsh, op. cit., p. 189.
142. N.R.A., Shaftesbury (Broadlands) MSS, SHA/PD/10, 4 Aug., 1874.
143. ibid., SHA/PD/10, 5 Aug., 1874.
144. ibid., SHA/PD/10, 5 Aug., 1874.
145. Supplement to *The Record*, 2 Oct., 1885.
146. Tait MSS, 93, 12 Oct., 1874.

19
Notice to Quit, 1873–1878

If the problems of the Church helped to draw Shaftesbury back into public life after his personal losses in 1872, other interests were not neglected in the years that followed. One of his first actions after Minny's death was, indeed, to set up the 'Emily Loan Fund', designed to assist the Flower and Watercress Girls Mission. The plight of such women and girls, who made their living by selling fruit, cress and flowers, was a precarious one and could be especially harsh in winter. The Fund, administered by the committee of the Mission, provided loans to facilitate the purchase of produce and goods suitable for sale: flowers and fruit in the spring and summer and coffee stalls in the winter. Security had to be given for the money borrowed and it was paid back on a regular basis. Shaftesbury was thoroughly satisfied with the venture. In 1875 he wrote that to give help to 'hundreds of poor and friendless girls' had been 'one of the best undertakings' to which he had been called by God,[1] and, in the 1880s, he recalled that between eight hundred and a thousand loans had been made and almost all the money had been paid back. 'Of all the movements I have ever been connected with,' he commented, 'I look upon this Watercress Girl Movement as the most successful.'[2] Another cause which meant much to him – possibly also because of its association with Minny – was that of the Costermongers. He had specially asked for their prayers during Minny's – and Constance's – illness. 'Our Lord teaches us,' he had written to Orsman, 'that there is mighty power in the fervent supplications of the poor.'[3] He wrote in January, 1873, to thank them for their prayers and took great interest in the work of the Golden Lane Mission. On occasion, he visited the Mission to address a group, as, for example, a 'tea party of aged costers' in March, 1874.[4] He also wrote frequently to Orsman about individual costers who required assistance: 'do not forget the woman who made the Braces. We promised her something,' he wrote on one occasion, and, on another: 'Your Missionaries must talk to the poor cabinet maker and *pray* with him. He is not hardened. Let him have what he wants in his necessity.'[5]

Shaftesbury thus concerned himself with societies which performed individual acts of charity to deserving cases: acts which, he felt, did not erode the sense of responsibility of the recipient. At the same time, he was willing to temper strict justice with mercy. He had shown a similar attitude during the distress in Lancashire in the 1860s caused by the American Civil War. He had said in 1862 that he would not hesitate to invoke the Poor Law outdoor labour test for any man who was too idle to work, but to do this in the case of a man who was unable to find work owing to the economic crisis would be cruel and injudicious.[6] These attitudes meant that Shaftesbury could not wholly sympathise with the activities of the Charity Organisation Society, founded in 1869–70 to regularise the work of charitable agencies to ensure that charity went only to persons who were deserving and would put it to good use. In the view of the founders of the Society, indiscriminate alms-giving simply debased and demoralised those who received it – the worthy and deserving should, indeed, be the objects of charitable concern, but the unworthy should be the responsibility of the Poor Law authorities.[7] Shaftesbury showed an active interest in the early stages of the Society. He took the chair at a meeting in 1868, when a paper had been read on the need for stricter control of charitable endeavour, and this meeting was one of several from which the Society itself ultimately evolved.[8] He was also present at the first annual meeting of the Society. Its insistence that fraudulent applications should be rejected and that only the worthy should be assisted did attract his sympathy, and he felt that much good would come from the elaborate system of checking and individual case-work which the Society developed. At the same time, however, Shaftesbury felt that it tended to act with too great a severity and that it lacked a sense of mercy and humanity which might, on occasion, rescue a seemingly undeserving man from the consequences of his actions.[9]

One source of misery and destitution which could readily lead to dependence on relief was drink. Here, too, Shaftesbury displayed an attitude which was by no means extreme or fanatical. He himself was not a teetotaler. Once at a dinner, he said that the custom of drinking a glass of wine with one's fellow man was 'one of the wisest institutions which appears to have been formed for conviviality and for promoting good feeling one towards another. . . .'[10] He urged his hearers never to give it up, but to take it 'like you should every other means of enjoyment, in moderation.' The cause of temperance won his support, and, in February, 1873, he opened a 'temperance public house' in Stepney. This was the 'Edinburgh Castle', formerly a gin palace, in the vicinity of which the young Thomas Barnardo held mission services. Shaftesbury had shown interest in the mission work which Barnardo had carried out in the East End of London in the years immediately after his arrival in London in 1866. In later life, it would seem that Barnardo tended to exaggerate the impression which he had made on Shaftesbury in these early years of his career, and, indeed, Shaftesbury was soon to entertain doubts about Barnardo's judgment.[11] Nevertheless, he felt that the acquisition of the 'Edinburgh Castle' by Barnardo a worthwhile and meritorious enterprise. It was designed to act as a centre for mission and also as a coffee house, where non-alcoholic drinks could be obtained. It also provided recreational facilities. Shaftesbury at its opening said that he hoped that it would be the first of many such places to 'provide fellowship, recreation and social intercourse without the menacing atmosphere created by the sale of intoxicants.'[12]

Shaftesbury, therefore, showed undiminished readiness to help enterprises which would relieve destitution and restrain the excesses which might lead to it. He also remained loyal to the cause of Ragged Schools, encouraged, no doubt, by letters which he received from Canada, giving news of children who had emigrated there and had been found employment;[13] one letter, from a girl who had been given a home, expressed gratitude for the 'many comforts' which she enjoyed and which she would not have had in England.[14] Shaftesbury went on an extensive tour of the London Ragged Schools in 1873. He was depressed by what he saw: 'sin, ignorance, cruelty, vice, drunkenness, with thousands of squalid children.'[15] And, he asked, how was all this to be put right? 'By the exclusion of the Word of God from the Schools of the Nation' was his bitter reply.[16] He was especially saddened when he discovered that the Field Lane Ragged School had handed over their school to the Metropolitan Board and that the Bible had been virtually excluded.[17] But he kept up the struggle. In November, 1873, he attended a meeting in St James's Hall called by the National Society to put forward candidates for the London School Board, and, in 1875, wrote of a visit to the Ragged School Union to make plans for a 'fresh aggression, nay a new form of one, on the very lowest of London; be we driven by the School Board from our present ground, we must seek another standpoint.'[18] Another development of earlier interests was the opening in August, 1874, of a second Training Ship: the *Arethusa*, gifted by Baroness Burdett Coutts. In the Lords in 1876, he recited the benefits which, he felt, the *Chichester* and the *Arethusa* had brought: they had trained sailors for the navy and they had redeemed boys from the lowest depths of society.[19]

Thus there was no lack of work to do – in June, 1873, Shaftesbury wrote of 'an abundance of chairs'.[20] Nor was there any lack of inclination to do it. 'I must "make hay while the sun shines",' he wrote in March, 1873, 'while

I have a remnant of strength of mind and body.'[21] He continued to give his support to efforts designed to extend legislative protection to employment hitherto unprotected. One such was that of merchant seamen. In 1873, Shaftesbury became chairman of a committee founded in aid of Samuel Plimsoll, member for Derby, who had made revelations about the dangers of overloading ships and using ships which were unseaworthy. Plimsoll had demanded and secured the appointment of a Royal Commission, and, to keep up pressure, a public meeting was held at Exeter Hall in March, 1873, over which Shaftesbury presided. He told his audience that they had been called to 'protest against, to denounce and to do all that (they could) under the blessing of God, to put an end to one of the most terrible and diabolical systems that ever desolated mankind.' He acknowledged the assistance of shipping magnates who were supporting Plimsoll: such were his friends John and George Burns of Cunard. Shaftesbury emphasised the necessity of protection being extended to merchant seamen on the same principle as the protection which was already given to miners, factory children and emigrant ships. Parliament must ensure that no ship left a port without full and accurate inspection and also that overloading must be forbidden. 'I beg of you,' he said, 'to insist with one voice and with one unwearied cry that these provisions should be enacted.'[22] Shaftesbury was pleased with the meeting – 'full, singularly enthusiastic, and yet prudent and judicious,' he wrote of it.[23] Plimsoll himself was scarcely 'prudent and judicious'; he was given to exaggeration and misrepresentation.[24] He was greatly disappointed when a Merchant Shipping bill brought forward in June, 1875 – a year after the Royal Commission reported – was deferred for a further year, and he raged and stormed in the House. Shaftesbury grasped Plimsoll's strengths and weaknesses. He thought him earnest and courageous but, as has been mentioned, also rash: 'he will ruin himself and the cause by his violence,' he wrote.[25] As one well seasoned in such matters, he tried to guide Plimsoll. Thus he advised him to apologise to the House for his outburst, for this, he felt, would advance his interests.[26] Finally, in 1875, the Unseaworthy Ships Act was passed as a temporary measure, limited to one year, and in 1876, it was replaced by the Merchant Shipping Act. This gave the Board of Trade increased powers to stop unseaworthy ships, made greater provision for the holding of surveys and established that a load line, fixed by the owner, should be used. It fell short of what Plimsoll wanted – in particular, it did not introduce compulsory surveys and an official and obligatory load line. Nevertheless, some concessions had been wrung from the government, which had shown itself unwilling to take action.[27]

Another new venture which occupied Shaftesbury's attention was also concerned with the extension of protection: on this occasion to animals. The practice of vivisection did not suddenly become a controversial issue in the late nineteenth century. There was already a substantial body of opinion which opposed it, and the Society for the Prevention of Cruelty to Animals, founded in 1824, had for long been active in campaigning against vivesection and in trying to ensure that legislation in restraint of it, passed in 1822 and 1829, was observed.[28] The matter was, however, more keenly debated in the 1870s. In 1874, legal action was taken for the first time in connection with a demonstration carried out in Norwich at a British Medical Association meeting. The action – to the effect that the demonstration was unnecessary and wantonly cruel – was unsuccessful, but the case gave the subject considerable publicity. Again, in the 1870s, physiology was developing in the British medical schools, and the first handbook for the physiological laboratory in England was published in 1873, giving details of various experiments. In June, 1875, a memorial was sent to the R.S.P.C.A.[29] asking it to concern itself with obtaining 'suitable restrictions on this rapidly increasing evil', and, the following month, the first of several separate anti-vivisectionist movements came into being, committed to obtaining the total abolition of the practice. In the forefront of the movement was Frances Power Cobbe[30]; in November, 1875, she founded what was to be the largest Anti-Vivisectionist Society, the Victoria Street Society for the Protection of Animals from Vivisection. This had branches in many cities and published a great deal of literature, and it took part in the petitioning carried out by all such societies. With this Society, Shaftesbury became closely associated – indeed, Miss Cobbe claimed that, rather than Shaftesbury joining it, it joined Shaftesbury. 'It was around him and attracted in great part by his name, that the whole body eventually gathered,' she wrote.[31] The cause certainly aroused Shaftesbury's sympathy and support. In January, 1876, he noted with displeasure that *The Times* had published an article in favour of Vivisection. 'It is the worship of science,' he wrote, 'and science must have its victims, like Moloch or Chamosh.'[32] In addition to his efforts on behalf of the Victoria Street Society, he spoke on the matter in the Lords. Legislation had, indeed, been introduced in 1875, but was withdrawn when the government appointed a Royal Commission, and after its Report, urging more stringent safeguards, had been submitted, the government brought in a measure. Lord Carnarvon, introducing its second reading in the Lords, argued that total abolition was impracticable, but he acknowledged the need for greater restrictions. Dogs and cats were to be excluded by the bill from any experiments: licences were to be necessary for the practice of vivisection and so too was the registration of places where experiments were carried out. No public demonstrations of vivisection were to be allowed; anaesthetics were to be used for experiments performed for teaching purposes; special certificates were to be necessary to experiment without anaesthetics or to keep an animal alive after the anaesthetic had worn off. Provision was also made for a system of inspection and reports.[33] Shaftesbury contributed to the debate.[34] 'To speak on Vivisection,' he wrote, 'became a matter of inevitable duty.'[35] He expressed gratitude to Carnarvon for introducing the bill. It did not go as far as he would have liked – opinion in the country, he said, was in favour of total abolition. Nevertheless, he was prepared to accept limitations which mitigated the system. He noted that vivisection was justified on the grounds that experiments on animals would lead to knowledge which would prolong human life and alleviate human suffering, but he asked if science could have gained 'by a cold-blooded, systematic cruelty such as this one hair's breadth of knowledge for the use of mankind.' He gave detailed examples of experiments being carried out, all 'in the terrible pursuit of science'.

Shaftesbury felt that his speech had 'gone up like a rocket' and 'come down like a stick'. The House had first received him with favour and then grew weary of the details.[36] The speech was published by the Victoria Street Society, and he noted that he received some criticism from the clergy and the medical profession.[37] He foresaw trouble ahead and the necessity for further speeches. In Committee, he expressed great anxiety at an amendment to dispense with the system of registration; this, he felt, would greatly weaken the bill.[38] He deplored the lack of support from the Bishops in the face of such threats: 'Of what use are the Bishops in the House of Lords?' he asked.[39] When the bill reached the Commons, representations were made to Cross, the Home Secretary, on behalf of the medical profession, which regarded the bill as too restrictive of medical science. Shaftesbury also met Cross. He was prepared to admit that the Home Secretary was 'earnest, true, anxious'[40] and acknowledged that he was under pressure and had little time to devote to the matter. Various changes were, indeed, made. Dogs and cats could be used for vivisection, subject to certification; the system of registration was dropped: and prosecution for infringement of the bill, which reached the statute book in mid-August, 1876, could only be initiated with the consent of the Home Secretary. Shaftesbury, however, was willing to compromise:

> reverted to my old position [he wrote] that something was better than nothing, specially if that something gives a foundation on which amendments may hereafter be built. The thought of this diabolical system disturbs me night and day. God remember Thy poor, humble useful creatures.[41]

Shaftesbury's new-found concerns in the Lords did not, however, absorb all his time and energy. He remained faithful to older causes. In the early 1870s, there were further revelations of fatalities in chimney sweeping:

in October, 1872, Shaftesbury had written that he had been 'stirred, after a long interval, by (his) poor climbing boys.'[42] The particular incident had been the suffocation of a seven-and-a-half year old boy at Washington, county Durham. 'Years of oppression and cruelty have rolled on,' Shaftesbury wrote, 'and now a death has given me the power of one more appeal to the public thro' *The Times*.'[43] The letter was published,[44] but nothing immediately came of it, and, in March, 1873, Shaftesbury moved for the report of the Coroner's Inquest on the boy.[45] The master sweep was duly punished, but this did not end incidents of this nature. In 1875, another case came to light, that of George Brewster, a fourteen-year-old boy who died two days after sweeping a flue at a Lunatic Asylum, near Cambridge. Shaftesbury drew the attention of the Lords to the case in February, 1875, and demanded that an end be put to practices which led to such fatalities. He noted that in large places, such as Glasgow and London, there was no such thing as the employment of climbing boys. Why, he asked, was it resorted to in smaller places? It was clear to him that the law was not sufficiently strong, and it also appeared that magistrates were not enforcing it to the full.[46] Shaftesbury followed this with various letters to *The Times*, which revealed that, even in larger places such as Liverpool, climbing boys were still used.[47] Further legislation was clearly necessary. Shaftesbury himself prepared this, noting in his Diary that one hundred and two years had elapsed since the 'brutal iniquity' had first been brought before the public, and yet it still prevailed.[48] Shaftesbury moved the second reading of the bill in May, 1875.[49] He was concerned, he said, with the 'temporal and eternal welfare of some thousands of children, the most depressed, degraded and tortured creatures on the face of the earth.' Previous legislation had fallen short of the needs of the situation and had not been properly observed. There had been neglect of the sections in earlier Acts regulating the construction of chimneys, especially the expense of introducing 'soot holes'. There had also been lack of adequate machinery for putting the Acts into effect, and a disinclination on the part of magistrates to convict. He did not seek any new law but wished simply to make the existing legislation effective. Thus he proposed that no person should be allowed to carry on the trade of a chimney sweeper until he received a licence from a competent authority; this had to be renewed annually and could be confiscated for breaches of the earlier Acts of 1840 and 1864. The bill passed the Lords and also the Commons, where the good offices of Cross were of assistance, and it received the royal assent on 11 August, 1875. The police were given the task of enforcing the Act, and it did, at last, go a long way towards fulfilling Shaftesbury's desire for effective legislation.

Another aspect of social policy of even longer-standing interest to Shaftesbury also received attention from the Conservative government and, in particular from Cross: factory reform. The Factory Act of 1874 consolidated earlier Acts and, indeed, restored the ten-hour day of 1847 by adding half-an-hour to the daily intervals allowed for meals and rest. It also raised the ages at which protection was to come into effect. A Royal Commission of 1875-6 made various recommendations which led to further consolidating legislation in 1878. This extended the application of the Acts and abolished the distinction between factories and workshops made in 1867. Shaftesbury warmly welcomed these developments. In a long speech in 1874,[50] he reviewed all previous legislation on the subject. He recalled that, when he took up factory reform in 1833, he had very few millowners on his side; now, there was a great deal of cooperation from the employers, a fact for which he was deeply grateful. He also recounted the earlier arguments about foreign competition, loss of trade, reduced wages and universal distress, but this was now out of date. It was remarkable, he said, how little was heard about the 'political economy' aspect of the questions. Trade had flourished under the protection of labour and, in addition to economic development, there had been many other gains. By legislation, he told the Lords:

> you have removed manifold and oppressive obstacles that stood in the way of working men's comfort, progress and honour. By legislation, you have ordained justice and exhibited sympathy with the best interests of the labourers . . . By legislation, you have given to the working classes the full power to exercise, for themselves and for the public welfare, all the physical and moral energies that God has bestowed on them; and by legislation have given them means to assert and maintain their rights; and it will be their own fault, not yours, my Lords, if they do not, with these abundant and mighty blessings, become a wise and an understanding people.

In 1878, he returned to these themes.[51] He expressed appreciation of the efforts of Cross in bringing the whole of legislation, scattered over the previous fifty years, into 'one lucid and harmonious whole'. The general result of past legislation on this subject had been to 'introduce and establish a system of order, content and satisfaction.' Children were now hale and stout in their appearance, adults were grateful to Parliament for the improvement in their conditions. Further, the 'order and discipline' which had been introduced made 'revolutionary agitation against the ruling Powers throughout the country very difficult.'

The factory legislation of the 1870s thus saw the culmination of the process to which Shaftesbury had contributed so much time and effort since the early 1830s.[52] The same was true in the field of public health. The Public Health Act of 1875, which owed much to the efforts of Sclater-Booth at the

Local Government Board, promoted the much-needed consolidation of existing sanitary legislation and was to affect rural areas more significantly than earlier Acts.[53] Further, the decade was important for legislation relating to working class housing. The Artisans Dwelling Act 1875 was, it is true, permissive and ran into many difficulties in its implementation, but it was a notable step forward and has been described as 'the first major attempt to tackle the problem of working class housing in the great towns'.[54] It empowered local authorities in London and the larger cities to draw up plans for the improvement of areas designated as unhealthy by a medical officer of health. Such authorities might purchase the land, compulsorily if need be, undertake the provision of roads and sewers and grant or lease the land for development of working-class housing by private contractors under conditions which they laid down.[55] In drafting the bill, Cross was influenced in part by a report of a committee of the Charity Organisation Society, of which Shaftesbury had been a member,[56] and the partnership which it embodied between municipal initiative on the one hand and private enterprise on the other was similar to that contained in a measure privately sponsored in 1874, which Shaftesbury had piloted through the Lords.[57] Shaftesbury did have some misgivings about the 1875 Act. As in the past, he argued that the effect of demolishing property to make way for construction would displace many families and would promote further overcrowding, and, as on previous occasions, he expressed the opinion that reconstruction could not be carried out only by philanthropic effort. Recourse would have to be made to capitalist enterprise, and experience suggested that few would undertake the work at less than 10% on the outlay. Thus the promoters and the contractors would be at variance: the promoters would want to obtain accommodation for all classes temporarily displaced, whereas the contractors would seek to erect houses which would bear the highest rent by being adapted to the needs of the richer order of skilled artisans. A large proportion of the labouring population in London were unskilled. They had casual and irregular employment and the legislation would do little to help them. One way of overcoming this problem, Shaftesbury suggested, was to adapt, drain and ventilate old tenements, courts, alleys and culs-de-sac at far less an outlay than was required to construct anything new. This, he pointed out, had been done by the Society for Improving the Condition of the Labouring Classes and, more recently, by Miss Octavia Hill, in her housing projects. Nevertheless, despite such criticism – and advice that progress should be gradual – Shaftesbury supported the government in its introduction of the measure, expressing his admiration at its boldness and perseverance in undertaking it.[58]

There was, then, much to arouse Shaftesbury's interest and sympathy in the social legislation of the Disraeli Ministry. Lunacy was also a considerable preoccupation for Shaftesbury in the 1870s. Further agitation had arisen on the subject of improper detention in asylums and the cry was revived that a magistrate's order should be necessary before a detention could take place. This was led in Parliament by L. L. Dillwyn, member for Swansea, who, in February, 1877, moved for a select committee to inquire into the Lunacy laws in relation to the security which they afforded against violations of personal liberty.[59] Shaftesbury knew that, as in 1859, he would have to give evidence before the committee. He doubted his ability to do so — when he looked back on the evidence which he had given almost twenty years earlier, he was surprised to discover how much he knew then and how little he now seemed to know. He reflected that it was not lack of work, and he wondered if his memory was failing him.[60] He dreaded the prospect of appearing before the committee. 'My hour of trial is near,' he wrote in March. '. . . Well, then, shall fifty years of toil, anxiety and prayer crowned by marvellous and unlooked for success, bring . . . at the close only sorrow and disgrace?'[61] But, in fact, his gloom was quite misplaced: his evidence, although not so extensive as that in 1859, showed no less a command of the subject. The writer of an article in *The Journal of Mental Science* commented that 'his Lordship spoke with such a thorough mastery of every lunacy question about which he was asked, that his replies are the admiration of all his younger fellow countrymen who are interested in the welfare of the insane.'[62]

In answer to a question whether there had been an increase in lunacy, Shaftesbury gave a cautious answer — somewhat similar, in fact, to an answer which he had given when the same question was put to him in 1859. The returns, he pointed out, could not give a complete solution to this; they could only speak of the numbers that came under care and treatment. Again, there was no way of knowing whether the figures referred to recent or chronic ones. But there had been an increase of 115% in the number of asylums in 1877 compared with 1859, and calculations suggested that the number of admissions to every 10,000 of the population in each year from 1866 to 1875 showed a gradual increase of 4.6% in 1866 to 5.9% in 1875.[63] As in 1859, he expressed his satisfaction at the progress which had been made in the treatment of lunacy since he had first become associated with the subject.[64] He was still insistent on the need for early treatment, which was the 'one thing needful in the care and treatment of lunacy',[65] and he was once more full of praise for the system of non-restraint.[66] He was also to record an improvement in the standard of the attendants in asylums. This was especially true of women but also of men attendants, owing to the better wages that were being offered.[67] The profit motive in the running of licensed asylums once again incurred his criticism,[68] but he was much less critical of it than he had been in 1859.[69] There had, he said, been a great improvement in the standard of private licensed houses during the last twenty years.[70] This was partly attributable to an increase in the number of medical proprietors of such asylums, the greater interest shown by the public and the friends of the patient and the more exacting standards imposed by the visiting Commissioners.[71] He also recognised the fact that a great many persons would always prefer to send their relatives to a private licensed house,[72] and he conceded that any prohibition of such houses would mean the loss of asylums which offered treatment not obtainable in a public institution.[73]

As far as the administration of the Acts was concerned, Shaftesbury told the committee that he would have liked to see a consolidation of the existing legislation and had discussed this with the Home Secretary.[74] But he saw little need to change the present laws. It was, for example, unnecessary to enlarge the number of central Commissioners: this might lead to prolonged and disharmonious meetings.[75] The Commissioners in their present numbers had discharged their duties 'excessively well on the whole'.[76] There was no necessity for a greater number of visitations, except in the provinces, where one further medical visitation might be made.[77] And on the main issue which had prompted the inquiry, Shaftesbury did not feel that any changes should be made in admission procedures. He did not wish to make it necessary for a magistrate or police officer to sign the admission order – such a person might not be within reach and he did not feel that crime and insanity should be associated.[78] The existing system had worked well and he could not recall a single occasion on which a patient had been taken into an asylum for treatment on insufficient grounds.[79] The system of certificates had also been satisfactory. Very few defective certificates had been produced since 1859, although this was principally because the system came into operation only when the symptoms of lunacy were so evident that they could not be mistaken.[80] This was not desirable, and Shaftesbury repeated his plea of 1859 for better training for doctors in lunacy, although he did not favour the suggestion that only doctors who had specialised in this field should sign the certificates. This, he argued, would surrender everything to science and take away the leaven of common sense, and it would lead to people being shut up 'by the score'.[81] On the question whether patients were being detained too long, Shaftesbury did not feel that this was the case;[82] in this respect, too, he modified his views of 1859. It was, he said, a great responsibility to send a patient into the world, and, if anything, the tendency was to turn patients out too soon.[83]

The committee's Report dismissed the allegations of serious abuses in the admission and detention of prisoners. Rather, it pointed to the considerable improvement which had taken place in the treatment of lunacy. It did, it is true, suggest certain additional safeguards, such as that the original order should be made by a near relative or by a person who could be held responsible, and that it should last for not more than three years, after which a special report should be sent annually to the Commission by the Superintendent. Again, it suggested that the person who had signed the order should visit the patient every six months and argued that regular and frequent visitation was the best gurantee against undue detention. The Commissioners might also adopt more generally the system of probationary release.[84] Little, however, came of these suggestions, since the government did not act on the Report, and Dillwyn was far from satisfied and kept up his campaign for much more stringent safeguards. But Shaftesbury's views had carried the day, an indication that his authority on the subject was still held in high regard.

Shaftesbury's religious pursuits in the mid and later 1870s may have lacked the intensity generated by the Ritualist controversy of the early part of the decade, but they did not lie dormant. The revivalist activity generated by the visit of the American evangelists, Moody and Sankey, was a matter of considerable interest to him. After their arrival in 1873, elaborate preparations were made for a highly organised campaign, which started in 1874-5. Shaftesbury had spoken in 1870 of the need for a 'bold and vigorous attempt to carry the Gospel of Christ to the people'; this was the only way in which Britain could save herself from the horrors then breaking out in Paris. The means might be 'extrinsic to our present form of operations' and 'novel according to our existing system of organisation'.[85] He was, then, willing to be receptive to the efforts of Moody and Sankey and, freed of his efforts to curb Ritualism, followed their activities closely. He felt that, at a time of mass indifference, Moody might be the 'right man at the right hour'.[86] He did, it is true, have certain misgivings about revivalist preachers, thinking that their methods were somewhat too theatrical,[87] and, at first, he argued that Moody was too interested in mass audiences and loved 'the excitement of multitudes'. He felt that Moody should broaden his appeal and preach to varied types of audience.[88] Nevertheless, when he went to hear Moody preach on Good Friday, 1875, he was, he wrote, 'deeply impressed', the more so because of the 'imperfections of the whole thing.' The singing – provided by a solo voice – was simple and 'yet it went to the inmost soul, and seemed to empty it of everything but the thought of the good, tender and lowly Shepherd.' The preacher wore ordinary dress, his language was 'colloquial, free, easy and like common talk'. His voice was poor – he had 'volubility but no eloquence.' And yet the result was 'striking, effective, touching and leading to much thought.' Shaftesbury could not but reflect on the fact that these were two 'simple, unlettered men . . .', with no theological training, no denomination, no skill in delivery and no pretensions to rhetoric. They were 'calm, without an approach to the fanatical or even the enthusiastic.' And yet they were holding the attention of 'thousands of all degrees in station and mental culture.' Shaftesbury could only conclude that God had 'chosen the "foolish things of the world to confound the wise".'[89] When he took leave of Moody and Sankey in July, 1875, he remarked that they were as simple at the end as at the beginning; they were not puffed up nor were they elevated by their success.[90] And he felt that Moody had been sent with a message 'to awaken, to stir up, to make people think, feel and enquire.'[91]

One of the secrets of Moody's success had, Shaftesbury, felt, been the simplicity of his message: 'Christ crucified'. And he remained as vigorous as ever in his efforts to maintain this simplicity in the face of Rationalism. In 1877, he took exception to two books published the previous year by the Society for Promoting Christian Knowledge: *A Manual of Geology* by the Revd T. G. Bonney and *The Argument from Prophecy* by the Revd Brownlow Maitland. Bonney's work accepted various current scientific theories about creation, and Brownlow Maitland cast doubt on a liberal interpretation of the prophecies of the Old Testament.[92] Shaftesbury wrote to the Archbishop of Canterbury about these books. He felt that Bonney's book was of a 'most noxious character and leading to Neological views of the first Chapter of Genesis,' and Brownlow Maitland's work was also harmful.[93] So keenly did Shaftesbury feel that he withdrew his name from the S.P.C.K. 'All zeal for Christ seems to have passed away,' he wrote. 'The Ritualists have more of it than the Evangelicals.'[94] He felt that he was fighting a lone and losing battle against Rationalism, but fight it he would. 'It would be easier,' he wrote in 1878, 'for me to give up Revelation altogether, and reject the whole Scriptures, than accept it on the terms, with the conditions and the immediate and future limitations of it, imposed and exercised by "Higher Criticism".'[95] He retained his belief that there need be no conflict between Science and Religion. In correspondence with Bonney, he reiterated his faith that, in time, Science would 'bow, in grateful amazement, before the superhuman truths of the first Chapter of Genesis,'[96] and he maintained his interest in the Victoria Institute. Part of his opposition to vivesection derived from his belief that, on this issue, Science was being unduly elevated. He felt that the practice was blasphemous, since it was ascribing to man what belonged to God. 'This,' he told Cowper-Temple, 'is the mind and object of a large part of the vivesectionists. They are seeking to discover the *principle of life*, which they hope to separate from the Almighty Power and give it to some other cause.'[97] On this issue, the activities of scientists had to be curbed, but, more generally, Shaftesbury was optimistic that scientists would abandon such presumptuous claims;

the further Science advanced, the greater would be its harmony with revealed religion.[98]

Shaftesbury was, therefore, still active at many points and he constantly complained of overwork. He also undertook extensive travelling. This was partly on holiday – he visited Castle Wemyss regularly in the autumn and, in the summer of 1878, spent some time in Germany.[99] But many of his journeys were to carry out public engagements. While in Scotland in September, 1876, he was urged to attend a meeting in London to protest against Turkish atrocities in Bulgaria; then he had to return at once to Glasgow to attend a similar meeting. 'In vain I urged 400 miles of distance,' he wrote '. . . to be followed by a journey the same night (making 800 miles) to keep an engagement in Glasgow the next evening. . . .'[100] His willingness to do this shows his undiminished readiness to denounce arbitary rule. In April, 1878, he was in Edinburgh to receive the freedom of the City, the following month in Paris to open the Salle Évangélique at the Exhibition and a House of Refuge and Instruction for young English women.[101] In London once again, other engagements crowded in on him: 'May I, by His grace, die in harness,' he wrote, 'and may I, before I die, know when to desist from active share in public talking.'[102]

Yet, despite this activity, Shaftesbury did not lose the feeling that it was all to little purpose. In April, 1873, he had struck the familiar theme of his isolation. People were weary of him and almost fifty years of public life had taken away all the novelty and most of the 'shine' from his labours.[103] This theme recurred on numerous occasions in future years in relation to all his spheres of activity. He wrote in 1875 that there was no need for him any longer in the religious Societies such as the Bible Society, the Church Pastoral Aid Society and the London Jews Society – they were 'amply provided with active and efficient men and need no cooperation.'[104] He was hurt that he was not asked to join Moody and Sankey on their committees. The only request which he received was for money and this he gave according to his means, but his active cooperation with the evangelists was not sought.[105] In April. 1875, he wrote that his isolation was 'manifest'. He received no invitations to Conferences, prayer meetings, committees, councils or anything connected with religious movements.[106] And, if he did offer his help or advice, no one took any notice. There was no point in further attempts at Church reform. He wrote in 1874 that previous efforts at reform of the Courts showed the determination of the Bishops and dignatories to maintain the greatest abuses. 'Reform, the majority of the clergy will not admit . . . Reform, even now, might save the Church for a generation . . . but she will have none of it.'[107] In 1878, he wrote that he could not meet any one clergyman or any group of clergymen ('for the Broadism is now in all sections') without being aware of their dislike or, if he spoke, of their open aversion. It was, he wrote, a 'strange position'. Almost everyone was against him: the great majority of the clergy of the Church of England and the Dissenting Ministers and, he did not doubt, of the Church of Scotland, Established and Free.[108]

If this was true of Churchmen, Shaftesbury also felt it to be true of politicians and members of Parliament and of 'the great bulk of the Intellectual men'.[109] Even when he was in sympathy with certain events and developments, he felt ignored and neglected. Thus, although he approved of much of the social legislation of the Conservative Ministry after 1874 and thought well of Cross, he privately resented that his place was being taken by others. In January, 1875, he reflected that he had not been consulted at all on the Factory Act of the previous year nor on the forthcoming Artisans Dwellings bill. This, he felt, was a sign of how little his aid was esteemed.[110] The following month, he wrote of a meeting called by the Association for the Promotion of Social Science to consider the Artisans Dwellings bill. He had, he wrote, laboured in this cause for thirty years: now, when the government had taken it up and success was near, he received no invitation to preside at the meeting. The honour went to a younger man, the Earl of Rosebery. Shaftesbury could not but reflect that he was old enough to be his grandfather and the Earl's public labours had been confined to a committee on racehorses. This proved the point that he himself was the 'great Pis-aller of the three kingdoms'. People had accepted him because there was no other. Now there were many others.[111]

Nothing remained, therefore, but 'social efforts of the poorest kind'.[112] But here, too, avenues were being closed. Ragged Schools, on which, as he himself acknowledged, most of his labour had been expended, were drawing rapidly to a close, and, in areas such as these, other men were active. In 1874, he referred to a 'long and tedious correspondence with that excellent but somewhat presumptuous man, Dr Barnardo.' Barnardo had wanted to add a training ship to the work which he was already undertaking: 'my advice', wrote Shaftesbury, 'is, of course, regarded as proceeding either from ignorance, or decline of zeal in the cause,' and he added that the correspondence had changed his opinion of Barnardo's 'judgment and distinction'.[113] Even allowing for Shaftesbury's increasing doubts about Barnardo,[114] such comments may contain an element of resentment at the activities of newcomers. Later in 1874, while on a visit to Glasgow to carry out various engagements, he noticed a report in the *Glasgow Herald* which described him as 'tall, gaunt, ungainly, with a nose as prominent as Mr Disraeli's jaw and a voice which seems to come from some other world'. Shaftesbury felt this a 'coarse and personal remark', but he also felt that he must not enter into conflict with men young enough to be his grandchildren and have his 'ancient, time-worn and out of date principles and sentiments weighed in the balance with theirs, found wanting and turned to ridicule.'[115] He was also often discouraged over his work at the Lunacy Commission. He had a disagreement with the Lord Chancellor, Lord Selborne, in 1873 and resigned his seat: 'such is my recompense for 44 years gratuitous service, immense Labour and immense success in God's goodness,' he wrote.[116] In the event, he came to an agreement with Selborne and withdrew his resignation – he had made his point but, he felt, 'for the last time'.[117] In 1875, he recorded that, for the first time in forty-five years, his colleagues on the Lunacy Commission had rejected his advice on a point where his experience was, of necessity, better than theirs. 'Prestige once set aside,' he wrote, 'is not easily recovered.' But it was not worthwhile to have a conflict: 'I might as well try to stop the ebb tide.'[118] He was anxious to prepare a measure to consolidate the Lunacy Laws: 'lunacy was my first duty,' he wrote in 1876, 'let me make it the last.'[119] But he could get no answer from Cross and, without the Home Secretary's assistance, he could do nothing. And although he succeeded in answering the questions put to him by the select committee in 1877, he still felt that his efforts over many years had gone unrecognised:

> beyond the circle of my own Commissioners and the Lunatics that I visit [he wrote], not a soul, in great or small life, not even my Associates in many works of Philanthropy ... had any notion of the years of toil and care that, under God, I have bestowed on this melancholy and awful question.[120]

Shaftesbury thus readily gave way in these years to his habitual feelings of isolation and alienation. Symptomatic of this was his memorandum, written in 1873, stating his objections to a biography of himself being written.[121] He admitted that many people regarded biographies as the most profitable form of history, but his would be 'of small interest, and of smaller use, to anyone alive, or anyone to come.' Men of Literature, men of Science, politicians, theologians, Evangelicals: none would find his biography remotely interesting, nor even acceptable. Further, no one could write such a work, for only he himself could know

> the reasons on which (he had) acted, the labours, the difficulties, the sorrows, the vexations, public and private, that have attended (his) career; the friendships (he had) had to sever, the political temptations to resist and the wear and tear of (his) income and ... health.

The only thing of which he could be sure was that he had been appointed by God to do the work and had been blessed and sustained for more than forty years in it. 'He both assigned the measure and gave the means.'

Not only was Shaftesbury ever more convinced of his isolation; he was increasingly out of sympathy with most of the events which he observed. This, of course, was true of the Church, still beset by Ritualism and Rationalism, and it was also true of the political nation. He was rather surprised that Gladstone did not remain in office after the General Election of 1874. He 'neither admire(d) the man, nor approve(d) his measures,' but Gladstone's 'fulsome adulations of the People ought to have pleased them. . . .' Why, then, did he not secure a larger vote? The reason, Shaftesbury felt, was 'mere fickleness, mere desire of change; mere fancy; mere want of principles, mere indulgence of caprice, all excited, stimulated, and rendered safe by the Ballot.'[122] The return of a Conservative Ministry was no more proof that people were attached to the old order 'than that the present fashion of chignons will be the head-dress of the women of England for several generations.'[123] Disraeli still aroused his suspicion. He admired his abilities, but not the use to which he put them: 'there is nothing really to admire in him beyond the possession of talents,' Shaftesbury wrote.[124] And, if he had some sympathy for the Ministry's social legislation, he felt that this was virtually dictated by the need to placate the working classes. Shaftesbury repeated his earlier views that, in their newly established political position, they could — and did — fight their own battles; they had become patrons instead of clients;[125] anyone who sought to be 'well among them' had to be 'less a guide, than a follower of their opinions'.[126] And not only were they discovering their political power; they were also, to Shaftesbury's chagrin, severing themselves from their old advocates by joining Trade Unions.[127] He foresaw a 'great conflict between property and labour', in which property would finally succumb.[128]

Developments at home could only give grounds for ever-increasing pessimism, and Shaftesbury was no more reassured by events abroad. He was now convinced that Turkey was beyond reform and redemption. In November, 1875, he wrote that its collapse was coming 'so rapidly that we may almost count its days in Europe,'[129] and, as has been seen, he vigorously protested against Turkish repression in Bulgaria. The Russian aggression against Turkey, in 1877-78, did, of course, arouse his opposition, but he did not approve of every aspect of the Treaty of Berlin in 1878 which finally settled the crisis. He felt that the guarantee to maintain the Turkish Empire was one of 'broad and barefaced Impiety'. The promises of reform were known to be hollow, both by the Turk and by Disraeli. The Turkish Empire, Shaftesbury continued, rested on robbery, slavery and sin, and yet Disraeli had bound Britain to its defence.[130] Moreover, he did not feel that the arrangements of the Treaty were conducive to the cause of the Jews. The acquisition of Cyprus by Britain, he told Cowper-Temple, involved the loss of Palestine. The French knew this well — thus they agreed to the annexation 'as a precedent for a similar one on their part in Syria.' And, he continued; 'I much fear that the return of the Jews is, by our own act, left to be encouraged, or impeded, by Ultramontane Influences.'[131]

Shaftesbury's most concerted opposition to the foreign and imperial policy of Disraeli's government was, however, over the Royal Titles bill, which conferred the title of 'Empress of India' on the Queen. Two days after Disraeli moved the second reading of the bill on 9 March, 1876, Shaftesbury was summoned to Windsor. This was the first occasion on which he had been asked for twenty years and he was surprised by the command. He did not relish the prospect: 'I dread it,' he wrote, 'the cold, the evening dress, the solitude, for I am old, and dislike being far away from assistance should I be ill at night. . . .'[132] He recalled that the Queen had sent for him in 1848 to consult him, and he felt that the reason on the present occasion must be to sound him out over the Titles bill. He was told to meet the Lord-in-Waiting, Lord Torrington, at Albert's Mausoleum, and Torrington informed him that the Queen wished to know his opinion. He recorded in his Diary that he had told Torrington that nothing could be worse than the title. It would make Royalty ridiculous and that was more dangerous than being hated. 'What can add to the Dignity and position of the Queen of England, with the historical traditions of a Monarchy of a thousand years?' he wrote. He advised that the style should be 'Queen of England and India'.[133] The following day, he recorded that Torrington had written to say that he had been 'fiercely rebuked' by Disraeli for having passed on these opinions and he wondered if Torrington had exceeded his commission or, indeed, had a commission at all to sound him out.[134] But he adhered to his views. He wrote to Disraeli that the labours of his office might prevent him from seeing or hearing as much as he did about the Title. 'The repugnance to it is enormous,' he wrote, 'and if it be appended to the Royal dignity, it will be hated by one set and ridiculed by another.' The evil would be 'serious and irreparable'.[135] On 3 April, 1876, he moved – unsuccessfully – that an Address be presented to the Crown requesting that the Queen might be 'graciously pleased to assume a title more in accordance than the Title of Empress with the history of the Nation and with the loyalty and feelings of Her Majesty's most faithful subjects.'[136] In his speech, he developed his reasons for disliking the title. There were at present many things to 'gild' the title of Empress. It would be 'held by an illustrious Lady who has reigned for nearly 40 years, known and beloved'; it also bore an impression of 'feminine softness'. But, in time, there would be an Emperor, and this would change its whole aspect. It would then have 'an air military, despotic and offensive and intolerable, alike in the East and West of the Dominions of England.' The title was also unacceptable in England itself, and it would erode sentiments of loyalty to the throne. He asked what could be gained by India beyond a name repudiated by the English people, which would bring to India no increase in happiness or freedom. But if nothing was gained, something might be lost. A time might come when India became capable of self-government. 'Our posterity,' Shaftesbury said, 'may then see an enlargement of the glorious spectacle we now witness, when India shall be added to the roll of free and independent Powers, that wait on the Mother Country, and daily rise up and call her blessed.' But, he continued:

> to attain this end we must train them to British sentiments, infuse into them British principles, imbue them with British feeling, and rising from the vulgar notion of an Emperor, teach them that the deepest thought and the noblest expression of a genuine Briton is to fear God and honour the King.

The British invasion of Afghanistan in 1879 was, Shaftesbury felt, another example of Disraeli's – or, as he had become, Beaconsfield's – bombastic and aggressive foreign policy. Others were, indeed, of a similar mind and an 'Afghan Committee' was set up to protest against it. Shaftesbury was asked twice to join the Committee, but he refused to do so. He wrote of his hate for the war and distrust of the government, but he felt that he 'could not allow the F.O. (*sic*) to be decanted into Trafalgar Square, and mobs and committees to take the places of Secretaries of State; nay, more, practise the Imperialism they denounce in Disraeli.'[137] He also had no wish to associate himself with the Liberal party, also active in denouncing the war, and thus he refused to take any part in the proceedings either out of Parliament or in it. He explained his position in a letter to the Afghan Committee which was subsequently published in the press. He attended the Lords for the debate on the matter, which ended with the government being upheld, and he was depressed and dispirited by the speeches which he heard. They ignored all questions of right, justice and morality: 'all those deep and tremendous considerations, which must be present in every mind that is really Christian, were never alluded to,' he wrote. 'Four hundred professed infidels could not, more completely, have ignored the Gospel.'[138] And once again, he felt isolated and ignored: 'my own effort,' he wrote of his letter to the Afghan Committee, 'has fallen flat. It is simply ignored . . . by the Public at large.'[139] One particularly hurtful aspect of the war was the fact that Haldane supported it in *The Record*. Shaftesbury was shocked that he could bring himself to do so, and he also felt that Haldane had betrayed him by privately sympathising with his opposition to the war and yet publicly supporting the war in the press. Shaftesbury wrote bitterly that his only remaining friend was not to be trusted.[140]

As in the past, Shaftesbury's complaints about his isolation were exaggerated and only partly justified. He retained his Presidencies and still received many tributes to his past activities; and, to some degree, his isolation was, as it had always been, self-imposed – his refusal to join the Afghan Committee was matched by similar refusals in other fields. And, as he grew older, his sense of alienation became ever more intense; he withdrew more and more into himself and also grew more stridently self-righteous. Before he was examined by the select committee on lunacy in 1877, he wrote that no man could find fault with him: 'against Thee, Thee only have I sinned,' he added.[141] But, at the same time, the isolation of which he complained was becoming more real. This was partly, of course, the result of age and declining powers. He complained in April, 1878, that he felt languid and was also very deaf. There were sounds in his ears when he spoke as though his head 'were made alternatively of iron and cotton'[142] – whether or not there were the old 'roarings' is not clear. He was told by his doctor to take more rest: advice which he scarcely heeded. A further source of his isolation was, however, the continuing erosion of the causes which he had so long espoused. Voluntary, philanthropic and paternalistic effort was still far from extinct, and societies such as the Ragged School Union were, in future, to find new areas of activity as old ones were closed. Moreover, the policies of Disraeli's government should not be taken to denote a 'new' Conservatism, devoted to social reform, nor a willing commitment on the part of governments to large schemes of state intervention.[143] Nevertheless, the activities of the Ministry did imply a recognition – however grudging in some party circles – of the need to give attention to social questions, and although, as Shaftesbury suggested, this may well have been inspired by some degree of political calculation, it did result in 'one of the most notable instalments of social reform of the century'.[144] It was inevitable that these reforms should be mostly in areas in which Shaftesbury had long been active and, except in relatively novel matters such as vivisection, inevitable, too, that others should take his place. The influence of Evangelicalism was also becoming ever more tenuous. The intellectual challenge to an extreme fundamentalism was considerable, and, despite his continuing enlightened attitude towards Science, Shaftesbury's refusal to give any ground to Neology was increasingly marking him off as a die-hard, even to other Evangelicals. Thus Haldane tried to wean him away from his stand over the publication by the S.P.C.K. of the works of Bonney and Brownlow Maitland. He only succeeded in convincing Shaftesbury that he, like all others, had lost his zeal.[145] Again, despite the seeming success of Moody and Sankey, the task of mission was far from easy. Indeed, it seems likely that Moody and Sankey scarcely touched the great masses of the working classes outside the churches but had most effect on those in the middle ranks who were already Church-goers. To them, the campaign meetings were an occasion for holding on to values increasingly threatened by a secular world.[146] Other, longer-established Evangelical activities were also losing ground. At a Garden Party held in 1878 to raise funds for the continuation of the Theatre Services, one clergyman spoke of the 'enormous difficulty' in getting poor people to come to Church.[147] The effort to raise funds was, indeed, itself an indication that the project of the Theatre Services was running into difficulties. In his speech, Shaftesbury recalled that nineteen years had elapsed since the Association to run the services had been founded, 'and,' he continued, 'we begin to observe signs of decay – signs of decline in the public estimation of it, signs of a disinclination to give us that support without which our operations cannot be conducted.'[148] Also in 1878, Shaftesbury noted that the Church Pastoral Aid Society had ended the session in debt and must retract its efforts: 'yet,' he wrote, 'this Society is the great Evangelical Institution, the Boast, the Glory of that Section of the Church.'[149] The days of outward-going, aggressive Evangelicalism in the Established Church were passing and the tendencies towards disunity – always present – became more marked as the movement became increasingly defensive and introspective.

It is also true that Shaftesbury was becoming more and more isolated in his own personal life. These years witnessed the deaths of many former friends and associates. In 1873, he was shocked by the news of the death of Wilberforce as the result of a riding fall – 'absolutely thunder-struck with amazement and terror,' Shaftesbury wrote; '... We know not what an hour may bring forth.'[150] He had not, of course, always thought well of Wilberforce, but he told Haldane that 'every kind feeling' he ever had towards the Bishop was now revived: 'he was neither covetous nor hard, and he often times stood forward in the defence of the oppressed.'[151] In 1874, Dr Thomas Binney, a noted Congregationalist Minister, died. Shaftesbury had corresponded with him in the past and thought well of him. A more severe loss was that of John Forster, the historian and essayist, in 1876. He had been a close friend of Shaftesbury; indeed, when he had considered the possibility of a biography, Forster had been one person who had come to his mind. Shaftesbury was much concerned when Forster fell ill in 1875. He wrote to his wife telling her that he prayed for his recovery 'for his own sake, for yours; and for my own. I have very few friends left,' he continued, 'I could count them all on either hand and have a finger to spare. He is one of them.'[152] When Forster died, he wrote to Mrs Forster to express his sympathy. Her late husband's friendship had, he said, been 'happy and profitable' to him for almost twenty years.[153] In another letter, he wrote that Forster was almost the last of those on whom he could rely for counsel and sympathy.[154] Later in 1876, there was the death, as the result of an accident, of George Moore, with whom Shaftesbury had been associated in charitable and philanthropic work: 'he loved and maintained Christian men and Christian doings' Shaftesbury wrote, '... Cannot but think much of George Moore, he was ever so kind to me in manner and language.'[155] And in 1878, Shaftesbury's friend of many years, the Duchess of Argyll, died. He was greatly distressed at the loss of 'one of the dearest, truest, steadiest of all those who loved me,' as he put it. He had loved and regarded her as his daughter.[156] There was, then, ever-increasing loneliness. Shaftesbury wrote in 1878[157] that the only clergy whom he knew were Canon Reeve, of Portman Chapel, Baker Street, and Spurgeon, but they were seldom or never within reach. In politics, he knew 'not a soul'. In social matters, there were, he acknowledged, 'a host of noble, ardent, trustworthy, precious, inestimable friends', such as George Holland, missionary in Whitechapel and Joseph Gent, Secretary of the Ragged School Union, and, as has been seen, he developed a close association with Frances Power Cobbe. But, except perhaps for the Burns of Castle Wemyss, Shaftesbury had few intimate friends now alive, and, as has been perceptively observed,[158] the friends that he had were not from his own social circle. In many respects, of course, Shaftesbury had always been something of an 'outsider' in his own social world; now he was virtually without friends in it. This may well have helped to intensify his sense of isolation.

There were also further losses in Shaftesbury's own family during these years. Lionel's wife, Fanny, died in 1875. It was, Shaftesbury wrote, 'a fearful gap' – the 'precious girl' had passed months with him at St Giles.[159] Two years later, his brother, William, died. They had shared many common interests in religion and had been close to each other. 'It is a sad loss,' Shaftesbury wrote, 'but God's will be done. I do not suppose that a day will henceforward pass in which I shall not think of him.'[160] There was also the continuing – and deepening – solitude without Minny. Shaftesbury's satisfaction that Evelyn was returned to Parliament in 1874[161] was mitigated by the fact that Minny was not alive to share it. 'How glad would her dear heart have been in the success of her sympathising son!' he wrote.[162] Later in 1874, Shaftesbury wrote that Minny was never far from his mind, still less from his heart.[163] 'Why was she taken away?' he asked in 1878. 'God in His wisdom, alone can know.' The loss to him was 'beyond all power of language to express'. She had been 'a security and a refuge'. He reflected that they had often made plans for their declining years: how, once their children were 'settled in marriage or the engagements of duty,' they might retire to a small house and spend the rest of their lives 'in serving our most blessed Lord and comforting each other.' But God had decreed otherwise: 'four of the precious children are no more. *She* is gone and I am left almost alone....'[164] The loss of Minny's company and influence no doubt contributed to the increasingly shrill nature of Shaftesbury's complaints about his isloation. The departure of Cecil, who had been appointed to the staff of Sir Bartle Frere, Governor of Cape Colony, to the Transvaal in 1877 was also a great sorrow to him. He was glad at the honour of Cecil's appointment, but 'almost heart broken' that Cecil, his 'Seth' and his 'Benjamin' was to leave him.[165]

One consolation was that relations with Anthony and Harriet improved. There had been an apparent improvement when they and their three children had spent Christmas in 1874 with Shaftesbury: 'I rejoice and receive them heartily,' he wrote, 'tho they are all but strangers to me.' But, although he was sure that Anthony and Poppy felt pleasure in the visit, he was unsure of Harriet. She was 'silent and cast down' and he wondered if it was temper or dejection of spirits; he would, however, do his best to make her welcome and prove that he had forgiven the past.[166] But on New Year's Day, 1875, he wrote that all was in vain. They had departed that morning and Harriet was 'cold, proud, rejoicing to escape from a place where she (had) not absolute power.' Her character was 'that of an Incarnation of Satan'; she was preoccupied with the love of money and the pursuit of power which, once attained, was used to inflict pain on others.[167] A further misdemeanour on Harriet's part was to join the church of an 'arch Jesuit,' the Revd G. H. Wilkinson: it was, Shaftesbury wrote, no surprise. He had thought that 'Rome would catch her.'[168] But later in 1875, a change *did* take place. In October, Shaftesbury wrote that Anthony and Harriet and their family were at St Giles. The children were 'very dear' and Anthony always desired to be 'well' with his family. Further, Harriet seemed 'much disposed to be civil and friendly, externally at least.' He gave no explanation of this, and he wondered if it was sincere and would last.[169] It proved to do so, and the access which Shaftesbury now had to Anthony's children was a great source of joy to him. Another cause of satisfaction was that, in 1876, Shaftesbury finally succeeded in paying off the 'ruinous mortgage' on the St Giles Estate,[170] and there was an improvement in his financial position. But this was not to last. Later in 1876, while at Castle Wemyss, he received news from the Estate: 'my old Enemy, Debt, Debt, Debt, from which by God's mercy, I had extricated myself will re-appear,' he wrote. 'No one will pay me my dues and I must borrow money at ruinous interest to cultivate the land.'[171] The following month, in September, his fears were confirmed: 'once more plunged in to debt after a few years of happy freedom,' he wrote. A farm had been given up and in the present state of agricultural affairs, no one would take it. He had to manage it himself and had borrowed £6,000.[172] It was Shaftesbury's harsh misfortune that, just when the management of his Estates was improving, the consequences of the agricultural depression began to make themselves felt.

These were, then, years of considerable activity – years, too, which gave some grounds for satisfaction but, even more, grounds for dejection. He was constantly caught between two moods: on the one hand, that he must give up his public career and, on the other, that he must continue it as long as he had strength to do so. In 1876, he bemoaned the fact that little money had been raised in answer to an appeal which he had made on behalf of the Bulgarians. 'This, and other things of late,' he wrote, 'are a "notice to quit".' The public were tired of him and wanted 'material better suited to the age'. He would, therefore, bury himself in the dens and back slums of London, his 'first and fitting career', and appear little if at all in the Lords or on public platforms.[173] He did not, however, accept the 'notice to quit'; he waited for one from a higher authority. He prayed that God would give him a sign as to when he should give up his public career, such as that in the Book of Numbers: 'Go not up, for the Lord is not with you.'[174] But the sign had not come, nor, indeed, was it to come. Rather, even amidst the encircling gloom, he remained convinced that there was still work for him to do and strength for the doing of it.

NOTES

1. N.R.A., Shaftesbury (Broadlands) MSS, SHA/PD/10, 22 July, 1875.
2. Quoted in Hodder, III, 321-2.
3. Quoted ibid., 313.
4. N.R.A., Shaftesbury (Broadlands) MSS, SHA/PD/10, 7 Mar., 1874.
5. Quoted in Hodder, III, 352.
6. Hansard, *Parl. Debates*, 3rd ser., CLXVI, 1532-5.
7. See D. Owen, *English Philanthropy, 1660-1960* (Cambridge, Mass., 1965), pp. 215-46.
8. C. L. Mowat, *The Charity Organisation Society, 1869-1913* (1961), p. 16.
9. Hodder, III, 325.
10. Quoted ibid., 324.
11. G. Wagner, *Barnardo* (1979), pp. 48-51, 295-6, See also below p. 577.
12. N. Wymer, *Father of Nobody's Children* (1954), p. 80. See also Mrs. Barnardo and James Marchant, *Memoirs of the late Dr Barnardo* (1907), pp. 95-110 and G. Wagner, op. cit., pp. 61-3.
13. St G.H., Shaftesbury MSS, C 25014.38, 39, 40, 43, 45/7th Earl.
14. ibid., C 25014.41/7th Earl.
15. N.R.A., Shaftesbury (Broadlands) MSS, SHA/PD/10, 1 Apr., 1873.
16. ibid., SHA/PD/10, 1 Apr., 1873.
17. ibid., SHA/PD/10, 12 June, 1873.
18. ibid., SHA/PD/10, 16 Feb., 1875.
19. Hansard, *Parl. Debates*, 3rd ser., CCXXVII, 1780-86.
20. N.R.A., Shaftesbury (Broadlands) MSS, SHA/PD/10, 20 June, 1873.
21. ibid., SHA/PD/10, 29 Mar., 1873.
22. *The Record*, 24 Mar., 1873.

23. N.R.A., Shaftesbury (Broadlands) MSS, SHA/PD/10, 24 Mar., 1873.
24. See P. Smith, op. cit., p. 230.
25. N.R.A., Shaftesbury (Broadlands) MSS, SHA/PD/10, 22 Apr., 1873.
26. Quoted in Hodder, III, 327.
27. See P. Smith, op. cit., pp. 230–42.
28. For consideration of this matter, see M. N. Ozer, 'The British Vivesection Controversy' (*Bulletin of the History of Medicine*, XL, 158–67).
29. This Society became the 'Royal' Society in 1840.
30. Frances Power Cobbe (1872–1904). Writer on religious and social subjects: active in various philanthropic works, especially the anti-vivesection movement.
31. Quoted in Hodder, III, 372.
32. N.R.A., Shaftesbury (Broadlands) MSS, SHA/PD/10, 18 Jan., 1876.
33. See Hansard, *Parl. Debates*, 3rd ser., CCXXIX, 1001–13.
34. ibid., 1016–30.
35. N.R.A., Shaftesbury (Broadlands) MSS, SHA/PD/10, 23 May, 1876.
36. ibid., SHA/PD/10, 23 May, 1876.
37. ibid., SHA/PD/10, 3 June, 1876.
38. Hansard, *Parl. Debates*, 3rd ser., CCXXX, 121.
39. N.R.A., Shaftesbury (Broadlands) MSS, SHA/PD/10, 21 June, 1876.
40. ibid., SHA/PD/10, 12 Aug., 1876.
41. ibid., SHA/PD/10, 12 Aug., 1876.
42. ibid., SHA/PD/10, 9 Oct., 1872.
43. ibid., SHA/PD/10, 9 Oct., 1872.
44. *The Times*, 7 Oct., 1872.
45. See N.R.A., Shaftesbury (Broadlands) MSS, SHA/PD/10, 20 Mar., 1873.
46. Hansard, *Parl. Debates*, 3rd ser., CCXXII, 391–2.
47. *The Times*, 24, 25 Mar., 9 Apr., 10 May, 1875.
48. N.R.A., Shaftesbury (Broadlands) MSS, SHA/PD/10, 28 Apr., 1876.
49. Hansard, *Parl. Debates*, 3rd ser., CCXXIV, 437 ff.
50. ibid., CCXX, 1329 ff.
51. ibid., CCXXXIX, 947 ff.
52. See O. MacDonagh, *Early Victorian Government, 1830–1870* (1977), pp. 73–7.
53. P. Smith, op. cit., 223; E. Gauldie, op. cit., p. 47.
54. P. Smith, op. cit., p. 222. See also ibid., p. 260 for Smith's remarks on the limitations of this measure.
55. ibid., p. 221. See also E. Gauldie, op. cit., p. 276.
56. P. Smith, op. cit., p. 218.
57. ibid., p. 219. See also Hansard, *Parl. Debates*, 3rd ser., CCXX, 982.
58. Hansard, *Parl. Debates*, 3rd ser., CCXXIV, 453–8.
59. ibid., CCXXXII, 246–7.
60. N.R.A., Shaftesbury (Broadlands) MSS, SHA/PD/10, 26 Feb., 1877.
61. ibid., SHA/PD/10, 11 Mar., 1877.
62. *The Journal of Mental Science*, XXIII, 510–11.
63. P.P., XIII, 1877.
64. ibid., Q. 11252.
65. ibid., Q. 11603.
66. ibid., Q. 11330.
67. ibid., Q. 11336.
68. ibid., Q. 11504.
69. ibid., Q. 11505.
70. ibid., Q. 11357.

71. ibid., Q. 11378.
72. ibid., Q. 11351.
73. ibid., Q. 11501.
74. ibid., Qs. 11637-8.
75. ibid., Q. 11367.
76. ibid., Q. 11368.
77. ibid., Qs. 11358-9.
78. ibid., Qs 11522, 11524.
79. ibid., Q. 11254.
80. ibid., Q. 11345.
81. ibid.
82. ibid., Q. 11444.
83. ibid., Q. 11257.
84. D. H. Tuke, op. cit., p. 201.
85. Quoted in A. Bentley, op. cit., p. 340.
86. N.R.A., Shaftesbury (Broadlands) MSS, SHA/PD/10, 25 Mar., 1875.
87. See Hodder, III, 354.
88. N.R.A., Shaftesbury (Broadlands) MSS, SHA/PD/10, 7 Apr., 1875. See also J. Kent, op. cit., pp. 156-8.
89. ibid., SHA/PD/10, 31 Mar., 1875.
90. ibid., SHA/PD/10, 13 July, 1875.
91. ibid., SHA/PD/10, 24 Aug., 1875.
92. See A. Bentley, op. cit., pp. 114-15.
93. N.R.A., Shaftesbury (Broadlands) MSS, SHA/MIS/41.
94. ibid., SHA/PD/10, 8 Dec., 1877.
95. ibid., SHA/PD/11, 16 Feb., 1878.
96. ibid., SHA/MIS/41.
97. H.R.O., Shaftesbury (Broadlands) MSS, 27M60, 23 Oct., 1878.
98. N.R.A., Shaftesbury (Broadlands) MSS, SHA/PD/10, 7 Feb., 1875.
99. See Hodder, III, 309-90.
100. N.R.A., Shaftesbury (Broadlands) MSS, SHA/PD/10, 18 Sept., 1876.
101. Hodder, III, 387-8.
102. N.R.A., Shaftesbury (Broadlands) MSS, SHA/PD/11, 7 May, 1878.
103. ibid., SHA/PD/10, 1 Apr., 1873.
104. ibid., SHA/PD/10, 11 Jan., 1875.
105. ibid., SHA/PD/10, 23, 28 Feb., 1875.
106. ibid., SHA/PD/10, 22 Apr., 1875.
107. ibid., SHA/PD/10, 10 Feb., 1874.
108. ibid., SHA/PD/11, 16 Feb., 1878.
109. ibid., SHA/PD/11, 16 Feb., 1878.
110. ibid., SHA/PD/10, 11 Jan., 1875.
111. ibid., SHA/PD/10, 25 Feb., 1875.
112. ibid., SHA/PD/10, 11 Jan., 1875.
113. ibid., SHA/PD/10, 22 Aug., 1874.
114. See G. Wagner, op. cit., p. 168.
115. N.R.A., Shaftesbury (Broadlands) MSS, SHA/PD/10, 3 Oct., 1874.
116. ibid., SHA/PD/10, 6 June, 1873.
117. ibid., SHA/PD/10, 8 June, 1873.
118. ibid., SHA/PD/10, 14 Apr., 1875.
119. ibid., SHA/PD/10, 3 July, 1876.
120. ibid., SHA/PD/10, 22 July, 1877.

121. ibid., SHA/EST/9/3.
122. ibid., SHA/PD/10, 11 Feb., 1874.
123. ibid., SHA/PD/10, 11 Feb., 1874.
124. ibid., SHA/PD/10, 22 Apr., 1875.
125. ibid., SHA/PD/10, 11 Jan., 1875.
126. ibid., SHA/EST/9/3.
127. ibid., SHA/PD/10, 11 Feb., 1874.
128. ibid., SHA/PD/10, 15 Apr., 1874.
129. ibid., SHA/PD/10, 30 Nov., 1875.
130. ibid., SHA/PD/11, 17 July, 1878.
131. H.R.O., Shaftesbury (Broadlands) MSS, 27M60, 2 Sept., 1878.
132. Quoted in Hodder, III, 367.
133. N.R.A., Shaftesbury (Broadlands) MSS, SHA/PD/10, 16 Mar., 1876.
134. ibid., SHA/PD/10, 17 Mar., 1876.
135. Hughenden MSS (on microfilm). Film 131, 15 Mar., 1876.
136. Hansard, *Parl. Debates*, 3rd ser., CCXXVIII.
137. N.R.A., Shaftesbury (Broadlands) MSS, SHA/PD/11, 21 Nov., 1878.
138. ibid., SHA/PD/11, 11 Dec., 1878.
139. ibid., SHA/PD/11, 2 Dec., 1878.
140. Battiscombe, p. 321.
141. N.R.A., Shaftesbury (Broadlands) MSS, SHA/PD/10, 12 July, 1877. See also Battiscombe, p. 318.
142. N.R.A., Shaftesbury (Broadlands) MSS, SHA/PD/11, 25 Apr., 1878.
143. See P. Smith, op. cit., passim.
144. ibid., p. 322.
145. Battiscombe, pp. 320–21.
146. A. Bentley, op. cit., pp. 366–7. J. Kent, op. cit., p. 160. The increasing defensiveness of Evangelicalism in the Church of England in this period is thoroughly explored in Kent's book.
147. University of Durham, Dept. of Palaeography and Diplomatic, Pamphlet Collection. Pamphlet 1083. 'A Great Problem Solved: or How to Reach the Heathen in Great Cities' (Address by the Rt Hon. the Earl of Shaftesbury K.G. and others at the Garden Party held in aid of the funds of the United Committee for Special Services for the People at His Grace the Duke of Devonshire's, Chiswick House, 16 July, 1878), p. 22.
148. ibid., pp. 27–8.
149. N.R.A., Shaftesbury (Broadlands) MSS, SHA/PD/11, 13 Aug., 1878.
150. ibid., SHA/PD/10, 20 July, 1873.
151. Quoted in Hodder, III, 338.
152. Huntington Library MSS, Forster Collection, Shaftesbury to Mrs Forster, 7 Jan., 1875.
153. ibid., Shaftesbury to Mrs Forster, 2 Feb., 1876.
154. ibid., Shaftesbury to Mrs Forster, 7 Feb., 1876.
155. N.R.A., Shaftesbury (Broadlands) MSS, SHA/PD/10, 22 Nov., 1876.
156. ibid., SHA/PD/11, 25 May, 1878.
157. ibid., SHA/PD/11, 18 Dec., 1878.
158. Battiscombe, p. 322.
159. N.R.A., Shaftesbury (Broadlands) MSS, SHA/PD/10, 2 Aug., 1875.
160. ibid., SHA/PD/10, 22 July, 1877.
161. Evelyn was Member of Parliament for Poole from 1874–80 and from 1880–85 for the Isle of Wight.

162. N.R.A., Shaftesbury (Broadlands) MSS, SHA/PD/10, 27 May, 1874.
163. ibid., SHA/PD/10, 22 Aug., 1874.
164. ibid., SHA/PD/11, 2 Mar., 1878.
165. ibid., SHA/PD/10, 26 Feb., 1877.
166. ibid., SHA/PD/10, 25 Dec., 1874.
167. ibid., SHA/PD/10, 1 Jan., 1875.
168. ibid., SHA/PD/10, 25 Jan., 1875.
169. ibid., SHA/PD/10, 23 Oct., 1875.
170. ibid., SHA/PD/10, 18 Feb., 1876.
171. ibid., SHA/PD/10, 10 Aug., 1876.
172. ibid., SHA/PD/10, 18 Sept., 1876.
173. ibid., SHA/PD/10, 22 Sept., 1876.
174. Quoted in Hodder, III, 357.

20

The Few Things that Remain, 1879–1885

On 1 January, 1879, Shaftesbury wrote that the year opened with a 'dismal and terrifying aspect'. There was, he wrote, 'much distress by stoppage of trade' and there were also many commercial failures. Eastern Europe was still unsettled; there was war in India and South Africa. Further, the whole world was under the sway of 'atheism, infidelity and indifference, a powerful Triumvirate'. The only remedy was the Second Advent. 'Come Lord Jesus, come quickly,' wrote Shaftesbury.[1] The comments illustrate his habitual interests and concerns, but there was truth in their reference to considerable distress and disturbance at home and abroad as the decade closed. To talk of a 'Great Depression' is to exaggerate the domestic situation, at least for British industry, but the term is not inappropriate for British agriculture, bedevilled by a series of bad harvests and increasingly undercut by competition from North America. And industry was not without its problems. Here, too, foreign competition was felt and Shaftesbury was correct in pointing to commercial failures. Abroad, the situation was unsettled, with the Eastern Question still simmering and the Afghan and Zulu wars as yet unresolved.

The Conservative Ministry was, therefore, beset by many problems, and this meant that its interest in social reform – never to be exaggerated in any event – became increasingly weak.[2] Shaftesbury had, of course, already lost sympathy with it over its handling of foreign policy: he told Lord Granville in 1880 that the Anglo-Turkish Convention and the Afghan wars were 'national crimes',[3] and to Lord Sherbrooke, he described Beaconsfield as 'perhaps the most unwise, untrustworthy and pernicious Minister that ever held office in this realm of England'.[4] He also bemoaned its virtual abandonment of measures for social improvement, especially when this had – as he saw it – been done as a result of Beaconsfield's pride and self-seeking in his pursuit of glory and immortality in foreign policy.[5]

Nevertheless, despite the unfavourable circumstances, Shaftesbury maintained his interest in social matters. In 1879, he revived a question which he had first raised in 1875 – that of working conditions in Indian factories. In 1875, he had called attention to reports of long working hours in the cotton mills in Bombay, indicating that fourteen to sixteen hours a day were not uncommon. There could, he had said on that occasion, be no jealousy of a rising trade in India. But British manufacturers must not be exposed to competition based on such a system, and he asked that India herself might be saved from all the social problems to which it would lead and to which Britain herself had been subject.[6] He raised the question again in 1877, expressing the hope that inquiries which the government had promised in 1875 would soon lead to satisfactory assurances, and he asked that the 'claims of humanity might be respected alike in every part of Her Majesty's dominions.'[7] Again, he had had to be satisfied with an assurance that the matter was receiving attention, but, once more, he became impatient with the progress which was made. In April, 1879, he moved that an Address be presented to Her Majesty praying that she would instruct the Viceroy of India to give immediate consideration to the necessity of passing a law for regulating the labour of women and children in mills and factories throughout India.[8] He noted that half a century had passed since he had first undertaken the cause in Britain. He had hoped that his career was now over and that, his arms being 'stiff and weary', he would not again be compelled 'to resume weapons to which (he had) been so long unaccustomed.' But the system was cruel and oppressive and disgraceful to the character of the Imperial government. Thus he would make another appeal, and he implored the Lords to listen to it and have mercy on the children of India. There were further expressions of sympathy from the government and Shaftesbury withdrew his motion. Finally, in 1881, a measure was passed.[9]

Another concern which Shaftesbury supported – again with some success – in 1879 was the progress of the Habitual Drunkards bill. This had been privately sponsored in the Commons by Dalrymple, and, when it reached the Lords, Shaftesbury moved its second reading in May.[10] It was, he explained, an experimental and permissive system which was envisaged and also a novel one. It enabled retreats to be set up, funded by private initiative or charitable subscription, into which a patient might be admitted at his own request. These would be licensed and inspected. Drunkenness, Shaftesbury said, was customarily treated as a vice and it might be thought too strong to suggest that it was a disease; but, in his view, no other term could be found for a 'morbid appetite' and craving, which, moreover, was likely to be hereditary. He also thought it essential to make a clear distinction between habitual drunkenness and lunacy, and, in Committee, he was always anxious that the retreats should be kept entirely separate from lunatic asylums.[11]

The bill reached the statute book, and Shaftesbury became President of the Society for the Establishment of the Dalrymple Homes or Retreats for Inebriates.[12]

Less successful, however, was a further measure on the subject of Vivisection. This was introduced by Lord Truro in July, 1879, and called for the total abolition of vivisection. Shaftesbury felt that the Act of 1876 had failed. In July, 1878, he wrote to Miss Cobbe that it had been right to give Cross's Act a fair trial, but there was now little good in upholding it. 'We shall gain more by demanding . . . total abolition,' he wrote. 'The demand will, at least, keep public feeling alive.'[13] In September, he wrote again that they must now 'leap over' all limitations and go for total abolition of 'this vile and cruel form of Idolatry – for Idolatry it is: and like all Idolatry, brutal, degrading . . .'

> May God prosper us [he continued]. These ill-used and tortured Animals are as much His creatures as we are, and to say the truth, I had, in some instances, rather be the Animal tortured, than the Man who tortured it. I should believe myself to have higher hopes and a happier future.[14]

He appreciated, however, the extent of the opposition which faced the antivivisectionists, and, on occasion, he sought to restrain Miss Cobbe from making suggestions and demands – such as that all medical men should not only abstain from vivisection but should openly denounce it – which he regarded as extreme and unwise. He also warned her of the dangers of being accused of caring only for animals and not for human beings. She must not, therefore, ask for too much.[15] He realised, too, the need for evidence to counter opposition,[16] and, when contemplating the part which he would play in support of Truro's initiative, told Miss Cobbe that he would want some well authenticated facts of recent cruelty.[17] He would, he wrote, make a 'short, though a decided speech',[18] and this he did on 16 July, 1879.[19] He said that he had hoped for an improvement from the legislation which had been passed, but there had been none. Licences had been freely granted for painful experiments, for dispensing with anaesthetics and with the obligation to kill an animal in pain after the experiment had been performed. The Act had also been delusive: it had lulled many people into the belief that protection was afforded by its provisions. And, as in the past, he asked in what way Science was advanced by 'such . . . refined cruelty'; on what authority of Scripture, or any other form of Revelation did those who practised vivisection rest their right to 'subject God's creatures to such unspeakable sufferings?' But his efforts were unavailing. Truro's bill was heavily defeated. Shaftesbury did not think that Truro had made a very effective speech; his own speech, moreover, was, he felt, inadequately reported in the press.²⁰ It was a dispiriting experience: nothing had been achieved and little publicity gained.

Shaftesbury's disenchantment with the Conservative Ministry made him largely indifferent to its defeat in the General Election of 1880. He told Lord Sherbrooke that he had 'no political creed'.²¹ Nevertheless, the Election opened up many unwelcome prospects. The candidature of Charles Bradlaugh, the noted atheist, at Northampton filled Shaftesbury with alarm. He wrote in April to Morley referring to a rumour that Morley was advocating Bradlaugh's cause. This, Shaftesbury felt, was deeply shocking. Bradlaugh was no ordinary atheist: he was an 'Apostle, a Missionary, of Atheism' and his return would result in an unprecedented impetus to unbelief. To recommend Bradlaugh's return was to say

> to the whole nation, that Atheism, the most audacious, constant and vituperative, is not, and ought not to be, a bar to the highest honours the People can bestow.

This, especially when promulgated by religious men was, Shaftesbury continued, a complete reversal of all efforts that were being made in Churches, Chapels, Working Men's Institutes and Reading Rooms.²² Morley called on Shaftesbury and, it seems, expressed regret for what he had done, explaining that it had been in the interests of the Liberal party.²³ Bradlaugh's return in the Election – although he was not permitted to take his seat and did not, in fact, do so until 1886²⁴ – depressed Shaftesbury still further. It was, he said, 'an unmistakable test' of the heart of the country towards God. He still could not understand why certain people, including Spurgeon, regarded it as a triumph for religious liberty. Rather, it was a matter of 'terror and shame' that the electors of Northampton had considered Bradlaugh worthy of trust and authority. The same men who had returned him had rejected Christ, and yet the followers of Christ were 'exulting in their Master's rejection.'²⁵

The wider results of the Election were also a source of great anxiety to Shaftesbury. Gladstone's Midlothian campaign and the general success of the Liberals were, he wrote, 'not a defeat of the Government but a Revolution'.²⁶ The landed interest was doomed, for the spirit of Bright and Chamberlain, he felt, dominated the Cabinet.²⁷ And this was doubly sure in the light of the situation in Ireland. He viewed Gladstone's proposed land reforms – granting the Irish tenant the 'three Fs' of fair rent, free sale and fixity of tenure – with the greatest alarm. He wrote to Gladstone at length on the subject in November, 1880,²⁸ telling him that whatever was enacted for Ireland would be speedily enacted for England. It would be in vain to urge the difference between the two countries, for 'the reign of argument' had ceased and that 'of passion' had begun. The tenant farmers, he wrote, were now set on gaining parliamentary support to give them long leases, low rents and a form of tenure which would render the landlords pensioners on their own estates. The labourers had even stronger views. Worked on by agitators, they contemplated – once granted the suffrage and that could not be long delayed – the seizure of the houses in which they lived and the gardens which they cultivated. They would never submit to be inferior, as they would see it, to the Irish peasant. He told Gladstone that he spoke from knowledge of the people. The cottagers even at St Giles were 'fearfully changed', and the 'language of excitement and violence' used by those who addressed them from time to time was 'more truculent and threatening' than even that of Parnell and Dillon. It was clear that the leaders in the movement contemplated a social revolution. And, from the land, they would pass on to money. He was convinced, he said, that the working classes viewed with 'deep and permanent dissatisfaction, the accumulation, in single hands, of enormous amounts of money.' They desired and would soon endeavour to obtain a more powerful vote over the capital of the country. He ended his letter thus:

> Such are the changes and chances of mortal life that many, many foresee, in all this, great benefits to the Human Race – it may be so: an abatement of our modern civilisation and a return to primitive simplicity may make us all more happy. In that case, many of the existing generation will live to bless the day in which the Irish League discovered and enforced the true principle of the acquisition and enjoyment of property.

As in the past, however, Shaftesbury felt that resistance by the Lords to a measure which had secured the assent of the Commons – in this case the Irish Land bill of 1881 – useless and dangerous, and even although he detested the principle of the bill, he was relieved when it was passed without provoking a conflict. In February, 1882, he was alarmed when the Lords voted for a committee to investigate the working of the new Land legislation and he wrote to Cairns of the dangers to which this course of action would lead. The Lords would simply give strength to the radical party in the Commons: 'the joy with which they hail the opportunity will sooner or later be very serious,' he wrote.[29] In a further letter to Cairns – written on a Sunday, such was Shaftesbury's concern – he wrote of a visit paid to him by a leading radical member who had told him that he had been brought up to respect the Lords and to consider the Upper House essential to the Constitution, but his opinion was beginning to change and he and others were prepared to 'assert the non-necessity of a second Chamber.'[30] Shaftesbury also wrote to Gladstone, who, he felt, had done his best on this occasion to smooth the path towards a peaceful settlement, and he expressed his dismay at the dangerous tactics of the Lords – in particular, Lord Salisbury – in threatening to upset such harmony as had been achieved.[31]

It was, however, only a question of minimising the damage: there was no possibility of averting it. Already in 1879 he had written that the 'last days of Establishments and Institutions of all kinds were at hand;'[32] and, in 1880, he had told Evelyn that changes in the order of things were inevitable. But, he continued, 'the policy of such men as Beaconsfield and Gladstone turn these movements, which should, and which might, be gradual into sudden and violent Revolutions.' The Act of 1867 had torn up the political system and Gladstone was bent on uprooting the social system.[33] Further organic changes were, moreover, certain to come. 'Politics,' Shaftesbury wrote in 1882, 'are fearful. Gladstone is claiming the leadership of the Revolution in every form.'[34] He foresaw another measure of parliamentary reform in three or possibly six years: this would extend household suffrage to the counties and would bring about 'the coarsest, vulgarist House of Commons that England can produce.'[35] The prophecy came true even more quickly than Shaftesbury had allowed with the passage of the third Reform Act of 1884. And, once again, Shaftesbury, while deploring it, felt it necessary to accept it. The people, he told the Lords,[36] did not have the same reverence for institutions which they once had. Penny post and railways had brought about great changes in their affections and aspirations. Frequent change was sought after because people saw – or fancied they saw – something to be gained in every change. And such fancies were exploited by reckless agitators. Shaftesbury said that he had confidence in the working classes when left to their own instincts and judgments, but none when they were subject to harmful influences. There was, then, no possibility that the Lords could justify a struggle with the Commons, and, if the Lords gracefully gave way, they might survive for a few years at least.

Thus Shaftesbury witnessed the events of Gladstone's Ministry with a settled pessimism. Events in Ireland and the Home Rule issue served only to intensify his mood. He was appalled by the assassination of the newly appointed Irish Chief Secretary, Lord Frederick Cavendish, in Phoenix Park, Dublin, in 1882. 'The crime is shocking and cruel beyond all power of expression,' he wrote '. . . Is not Hell let loose in that country?'[37] And Shaftesbury had long been totally opposed to Home Rule. In 1869, he had written – with some foresight – that there were some, Gladstone probably among them, who would 'deny that any evil could arise from the severance of England and Ireland.' It was, he had continued, difficult to believe that anyone could entertain such an opinion,' but the attempt would soon be made.[38] Had Shaftesbury lived to see his prophecy come true with the introduction of the first Home Rule bill by Gladstone in 1886, there can be no doubt as to the stance which he would have taken on a measure which he had long regarded as destructive of the British Empire.

Political affairs thus gave Shaftesbury ever increasing cause for despondency, and various aspects of his personal life seemed to him to offer little relief. 'In private, as in Public things,' he wrote in 1879, sing a "De profundis".'[39] Some of his anxieties and apprehensions were, indeed, exaggerated and needless. On his eightieth birthday in April, 1881, he received many private letters of congratulation. They ranged from an affectionate greeting from his sister, Charlotte, to a poem composed by Miss Cobbe.[40] A meeting was also held in the Guildhall, organised by the Ragged School Union and held under the auspices of the Lord Mayor. It was a large meeting, addressed by the Lord Mayor himself and also by the Earl of Aberdeen, W. E. Forster and H. R. Williams.[41] Before the meeting, Shaftesbury told Miss Cobbe that she little knew how much he disliked the coming celebration. When the matter was first mooted, he had expected that there would be a 'humble meeting of humble persons in Exeter Hall, the lower Hall.' Now, there would, he feared, be a pretentious meeting, neither grand nor humble.[42] Once it took place, he was, it is true, pleased by the occasion and especially so by Forster's remarks that his efforts had spread moderating influences and contributed towards the good conduct of the population. 'I don't think, in the course of my life,' Shaftesbury said, 'any words ever gratified me more.'[43] But, in his private thoughts, he questioned how far the meeting could be representative of public feeling. No one, he reflected, was present from the literary and scientific sections of society; not a single ecclesiastical dignitary; none of the Liberal party, except Forster; not a peer, except Aberdeen. The excuses made for non-attendance were cold and he could see that, although he might be loved in Bethnal Green, he was despised in Belgravia – a Triton among the Minnows, but a Minnow among the Tritons. Those assembled were, indeed, 'warm, hearty, affectionate, true', but 'they no more represented the Nation than they represented the Man in the Moon.' He admitted that much of the press had written with approbation and even praise, but, he wrote, 'even the warmest of them has a tone of patronage and apology, so indispensable in speaking of "Philanthropy" and a "Philanthropist".'[44] Such thoughts confirmed him in his previous view that there was no justification whatever for a biography being written.[45] Thus Shaftesbury betrayed his old sensitivity to slights which existed more in his imagination than in reality. In fact, many tributes were made to him in these final years, culminating in the bestowal of the Freedom of the City of London in June, 1884, although it must be admitted that this honour did come very late in his life.

Other personal matters in these years, however, afforded more genuine grounds for disquiet. Financial difficulties became more acute. In 1879, Shaftesbury wrote of the problems afflicting his Estates.[46] Supplies of timber had dwindled and the revenue from the slate quarries had fallen off by almost 50%. As the agricultural depression deepened, farms were being given up and tenants who remained were paying only a portion of their rent: some, indeed, were paying none at all. His income had been halved, and yet all his obligations remained the same. In 1880, he wrote despairingly of the debts which he was incurring. Instead of being able to give his last days to all that he had laboured and prayed for, he had to give them to finding ways to preserve a decent name and not bring discredit on the profession of Christianity by doing things which were inconsistent with it.[47] In October, 1880, he wrote to Turnbull to authorise a 10% reduction in rent to the farmers – this, he reflected, would mean a 20% reduction, since he would have to borrow a sum equal to the concession.[48] He felt that he could no longer live at St Giles: the expenses of living there were greater than in London or at a watering place. There would, he wrote, be periodical 'visits of superintendence and care', but there could no longer be prolonged periods of residence. The duty, he wrote, would remain but much of the interest would be gone.[49]

As in the past, he received offers of help. George Williams sent him money – anonymously – in 1880. Shaftesbury guessed the source of the gift and replied that he must return it, although he would ask Williams for money if his difficulties became more severe.[50] They did not, indeed, abate. In August, 1882, Shaftesbury wrote that the farmers paid him only 25% of his due and commented that he was worse off than when Waters had despoiled him.[51] In 1882, he *did* ask Williams for a loan, and the money was given as a gift.[52] In 1885, he accepted a further gift of £4,500 which twelve of his admirers had contributed as a birthday present. They asked him to 'accept it for the relief of . . . pressing necessities' in any way he thought best.[53] Their letter, wrote Shaftesbury, was a 'model of kindness, good feeling and good taste'.[54] There were, then, instances of generosity to illuminate the gloom, and one further source of pleasure and consolation in these years was Shaftesbury's family life. Relations with Anthony and Harriet remained harmonious and he had access to his grandchildren, whose company did much to brighten his last days.

Even here, however, there were problems and difficulties. Shaftesbury recorded in 1879 that Harriet had written a 'somewhat imperious letter' demanding that their allowance be doubled,[55] and, in 1880, he noted that a new loan had to be taken out for the couple.[56] There were also other family worries. Evelyn's wife, Sissy, suffered an illness which necessitated residence abroad and Cecil's health gave rise for further alarm. Shaftesbury's own health also gave cause for concern. He wrote in March, 1879, that he had lost all his former buoyancy and contemplated effort 'with something akin to terror'. He lay down frequently for short intervals and 'so get strength and a whiff of courage'.[57] In December, 1879, he caught a chill and was thoroughly examined by Dr Henry Thompson, who advised Shaftesbury to stay in bed and take nourishing food. His fee for the consultation was £84: 'Was it justified' wrote Shaftesbury, 'I hope so.'[58] His illness was, in fact, quite protracted over the winter months of 1879–80, and, as he again noted, it was expensive.[59] He recovered, but there were recurrent complaints of discomfort. In 1881, he wrote that he often felt that his heart would never have another pulsation. The nerves of his head seemed to be made of leather and he occasionally felt giddy. When he spoke, his voice appeared to himself – but not, he was told, to others – as though he were speaking through all the cotton of Lancashire. He was never entirely free from pain, which was sometimes very severe in the region of the stomach. He ate very little and, in most instances, 'without relish'.[60] This was to be his state for much of the following four years: 'shall I ever be well?' he wrote in January, 1885. 'That is known only to the great Physician to the body as well as to the soul,'[61] and, the following month, he bemoaned the expense of 'doctors, druggists and nurses over and above the decreased and decreasing income'.[62]

A further cause of depression and sadness during these years was the continuing toll which death took of his contemporaries. The death of Beaconsfield in 1881 prompted some wry reflections. He was, wrote Shaftesbury, a 'wonderful man in his generation'. But, he asked, 'was he a useful one?'[63] Other deaths affected him more deeply. Despite their antagonism, he mourned the death of Dean Stanley in 1881. 'I trembled at the contemplation of his theology,' Shaftesbury wrote, 'but I loved the man. Another who showed me attachment and who always did me more than justice, is now gone.'[64] Shaftesbury wrote in a very similar vein of Pusey, who died in 1882. 'Intensely and fearfully as I differed from him in many points of unspeakable importance, I could not but love the man,' he wrote.[65] The death of Archbishop Tait in December, 1882, also saddened him: 'I mourn his loss as a private friend,' he wrote.[66] Above all, he was greatly distressed by the death of Haldane, also in 1882. The coldness which had come upon the relationship between the two men had passed, and, when Haldane became ill in the summer of 1882, Shaftesbury sat by his beside and joined in prayer with his family. 'We cannot but have full assurance of his salvation,' Shaftesbury wrote on Haldane's death. 'He believed intensely in the Lord Jesus, His power, His office, His work ... His sole hope was in the all-atoning blood of our blessed Saviour.'[67] This was a comfort, but his loss was, to Shaftesbury, 'a complete blank'.[68] Haldane, he wrote, was the only one left to whom he could speak of many things.[69]

A catalogue of woe, public and private, was, however, by no means the entire scope of Shaftesbury's final years. He did, indeed, have many troubles and sorrows and – inevitably – failing health, but he did not retreat from his public duties. In 1879, he prayed for 'strength to discharge the "few things that remain",'[70] and, despite his complaints, he felt that he was given it. When he consulted Dr Gull in 1881, he was told that his pulse was quite strong,[71] and he fully realised that, for his age, he was still able to do a great deal. On his birthday in 1884, he wrote that it was wonderful and miraculous that, with all his infirmities, he yet retained 'by God's mercy some power to think and to act.' And, he continued: 'May He grant, for Christ's sake, that to my last hour, I may be engaged in His service, and in the full knowledge of all that is around and before me!'[72] It was a prayer which in very large measure, was granted.

The last years of Shaftesbury's life were, therefore, marked by considerable public activity. In 1880, he had written that there was still room for effort. Individuals might still be instructed, comforted and saved in this world and the next.[73] His programme was, therefore, to 'run in the old groove, Chairs, Ragged Schools and all the minor and obscure work of Great Cities.'[74] And, with little abatement, he was to carry out this programme over the following five years. In November, 1883, he wrote – after a day of considerable activity – of his gratitude for the strength to carry out his engagements. 'I bless Thee, O Lord . . . He can, and He does, oftentime, make an iron pillar out of a bulrush.'[75]

Thus, despite his earlier feelings that his place in the major Evangelical Societies could be taken by younger men, he retained his Presidencies, and every May brought its crop of 'chairs' and speeches. There were also many special occasions on which he was active, such as the centenary of the Sunday Schools in 1880, an International Conference of Y.M.C.A.s at Exeter Hall in 1881 and the Luther and Wycliffe Commemorations in 1883 and 1884 respectively. Long-standing Evangelical causes such as Sunday observance still commanded his attention. In July, 1881, he wrote disapprovingly of Sunday dinner parties and lawn tennis,[76] and he deplored attempts which were made in these years to extend the practice of Sunday opening of museums and galleries in London. He wrote to Gladstone in 1880 asking him to consider the matter deeply: 'to grant it would be the beginning of sorrows,' he said.[77] The question was, indeed, repeatedly raised in the Lords, Lord Thurlow urging the cause in 1879 and 1885 and the Earl of Dunraven in 1881, 1883 and 1884. Shaftesbury strongly resisted them. His primary objection to the idea was, of course, religious. 'Sunday' he said in 1881, 'is a day so sacred, so important and so indispensable to man that it ought to be hedged round by every form of reverence.'[78] But he also offered other objections: that there was strong feeling in the country against it;

that it would not – as its sponsors claimed – reduce intemperance by attracting the working classes from public houses; and, what particularly concerned him, that it would mean an addition of labour for those involved in transport and in the actual opening of the museums. While he did not wish to stand in the way of innocent recreation on a Sunday, this should not be done by sacrificing the rights of others. Sunday, he said in 1884, was the 'great charter' of the physical and moral rights of the working classes and the safeguards of their private and social liberty.[79] He repeatedly met the attempts to extend Sunday opening with amendments in favour of every weekday opening, and he was successful. On the last occasion, in 1885, he was, in fact, unable to be present in the Lords to resist Thurlow's efforts to obtain authorisation for the opening of the Natural History Museum at South Kensington on a Sunday. He entrusted his usual amendment to Cairns. 'It is the last hope,' he wrote to Cairns, 'of keeping, in the hearts of the People, *any reverence for anything*, sacred or profane.'[80] After Cairns had successfully taken charge of the amendment, Shaftesbury thanked him warmly: 'You did it as a very able and a very good man would discharge a solemn duty,' he wrote.[81] It was, in fact, the last duty which Cairns performed in the Lords; a few weeks later, he died. It was fitting that Shaftesbury should preside at the opening of a house for the Y.M.C.A. at Bournemouth as a memorial to Cairns. At this, he urged all young men to follow his Christian example.[82]

Shaftesbury also maintained his interest in missionary work at home. He took an interest in Open-air preaching,[83] and – despite the difficulties which they had encountered – in Special Services, and, in 1884, spoke at the jubilee meeting of the London City Mission.[84] He thus retained his links with Dissenters, acting on the opinion that the demands of the times called for cooperative effort. This was a view which he had long held and which had been evident in the late seventies in his support for relaxing the Burial Laws in favour of Dissenters by allowing a religious service to be held at the graveside rather than insisting on a silent burial.[85] They were, he had told Cairns in 1877, surrounded by 'combustibles of all kinds, torpedos, political and ecclesiastical', and the question was 'not whether we shall blow up the Enemy and so make an end of him, but whether we can in this "Feu d'Enfer" on all sides, retain anything erect for ourselves.'[86] This, then, was no time for partisan squabbles with those whose Protestantism, at least, was beyond doubt. It was in this spirit that, in 1881, he laid the memorial stone of a new Baptist Church at Bethnal Green. 'Externals,' he wrote of the occasion, 'must now be secondary in consideration.' Forms of church government must give precedence to 'the Gospel of God in all its integrity and force', and, before laying the stone of the new church, he had assured himself that Christ and Christ alone would be preached there.[87] In 1883, he distributed prizes at a Methodist chapel and, in 1884, accepted an invitation to preside at a meeting held in honour of Spurgeon's fiftieth birthday. 'I should like you to come,' Spurgeon wrote, 'because I want old-fashioned Evangelical doctrine to be identified with the event. I am a fair representative of the old faith, even as you are....'[88]

Shaftesbury's all-embracing outlook stopped short, of course, of Ritualism, and equally, at the other end of the spectrum, of the newly established Salvation Army. In 1881, he was invited by Admiral Fishbourne to join the Army. He refused and maintained strong opposition to its efforts. He told Fishbourne that his opposition did not spring from 'any repugnance to novel and abnormal modes of proceeding.' On the contrary, he had spent his whole life in 'breaking down barriers and prejudices,' and, in his efforts to take religion to the masses of the people, he had, for years, disregarded 'every mere form of external Church government and (had) laboured to bring into action all the hearts and minds of the high and low, rich and poor, among the laity, for ardent and vigorous ministerial services.' But he had always endeavoured to keep within the limits of the New Testament and primitive Christianity. He could, however, find no authority in Scripture for the system and discipline of the Salvation Army: 'its constitution, framework and organisation . . . its military arrangements, its Hallelujah Lasses, its banners, their mottoes and a thousand other original accompaniments.' He also took exception to the language and conduct of the members of the Army – 'in action as extravagant and in expression as offensive, as any that ever disgraced the wildest fanaticism.' Shaftesbury also argued that there was no need of any *new* method of addressing the people. There were at least a hundred lay missions in London and as many elsewhere, and they conducted their activities with 'abundant zeal and yet with modesty and sobriety.' It was a multiplication of these agencies which was required, and, although he acknowledged the good intentions of Booth, he could not applaud his judgment, nor could he have any part in maintaining or extending the Salvation Army.[89] Shaftesbury's strong opposition to the Army may have owed something to that resentment at the arrival of newcomers in the field which he was apt to betray in his old age, but he had always been suspicious of extreme revivalist techniques. To him, missionary endeavour was something separate from revivalism which, he felt, placed an undue emphasis on excitement and emotion.

In these years, Shaftesbury also took a keen interest in religious affairs abroad. He showed great concern in 1879 for a movement to reform the Armenian Church.[90] And, as ever, the cause of the Jews evoked his ready sympathy. In 1882, he responded to an invitation to assist Jews who were victims of persecution in Russia, taking part in a meeting at the Mansion House and speaking in the Lords on the subject.[91] He became President of a Society, established in 1882, to help Jews seeking to escape Russian persecution. It was hoped that a colony might be founded in Palestine but, in the face of Turkish resistance, this was changed to Cyprus.[92] Money had to be raised, and Shaftesbury, eager as ever to involve – and over-involve – himself in such activities, had to be restrained by Evelyn from entering into too many commitments. When plans were put forward to attract more Jews to increase the settlement, Evelyn wrote advising his father to 'let those who like do this,' and, he added, 'surely you have too many responsibilities and anxieties to consent to remain and see this carried on.'[93] He had thought that his father would do no more than leave the work to others. 'I hope you will,' Evelyn wrote, warning that the idea to finance the project indefinitely would last as long as subscriptions came in, and then would come the crash.[94] Shaftesbury took his son's advice. It was well-founded; as it was, Shaftesbury was glad to record a gift of £640 from certain ladies to clear off the incumbrances and difficulties which had arisen from the scheme.[95]

Another issue which gave cause for anxiety in the 1880s was the Jerusalem bishopric. Gobat died in 1879 and Shaftesbury was asked by Beaconsfield for his advice over a successor, now to be named by Britain. Shaftesbury wrote that the first priority must be that he be the 'very reverse of a Ritualist'. Any introduction of a 'fussy and pompous ceremonial' into the 'true Protestant simplicity' of the public worship observed in Jerusalem would not only be a 'sad blow to the German and English Piety' that had founded the Bishopric, but would disturb the Jews and 'lead them to confound the Church of England (and deservedly) in the same category with the Greek and Roman churches.' The new Bishop, he continued, must also be a man of earnestness and sound judgment, with a true and deep zeal for the welfare and honour of the Jewish people', and he suggested Dr Tristram, Honorary Canon of Durham, who had travelled in the East and had written on the history of Palestine.[96] Tristram was approached, but refused the appointment, and it went finally to Joseph Barclay, who had served as a missionary of the London Jews Society in Constantinople.[97] Barclay, however, had only a very short period as Bishop – he died in 1881. The appointment, therefore, reverted again to the German Emperor. But German interest in the arrangement had long been declining, and objections were now put forward to its continuance on the grounds that the Archbishop of Canterbury exercised a veto over the appointment and that Lutheran clergy refused to accept Anglican re-ordination.[98] It was, therefore, virtually certain that no nomination to the vacant Bishopric would be made from the German side. This suited High Churchmen in England who wanted the suppression of the Bishopric, but Evangelicals were anxious for its continuance and Shaftesbury wrote to Archbishop Benson, Tait's successor at Canterbury, expressing concern at the German reluctance to continue the 1841 arrangement. Funds would be required to make up the money now lacking because of the German loss of interest: 'We want no fresh law,' Shaftesbury wrote. 'Nothing is wanted but funds.'[99] There was, in fact, to be a long delay before the matter was finally settled and Benson wrote that Shaftesbury and the other English Trustees of the Bishopric had repeatedly asked for news of an appointment.[100] Finally, in July, 1885, the Trustees came to the view that the original arrangement should be rescinded and this was carried out. Shaftesbury, however, was too ill at this time to attend the meetings of the Trustees, and he did not live to see the new arrangement which was made with the Greek Orthodox Church and the appointment of a new Bishop.[101]

To the end of his life, therefore, Shaftesbury concerned himself with Evangelical causes in the Church to which he had devoted some fifty years. And, in these last years, he was still to be found as the spokesman for moral causes similar to those which his Evangelicalism had always embraced. Having for many years been President of the Anti-Opium League, he became, in 1880, President of a new Society, the Anglo-Oriental Society for the Suppression of the Opium Trade. At a meeting at the Mansion House in October, 1881, he seconded a resolution proposed by the Archbishop of Canterbury which condemned the Trade as unchristian, immoral and inimical to the commercial interests of Britain. He recalled that he had first spoken on the subject in the Commons almost forty years earlier at a time when he had had little support and was 'looked upon in some measure as a fanatic and certainly as a fool.'[102] The Trade had since then grown in volume and was now 'a question affecting the welfare and stability of the British Empire.' He denounced the evils of the Trade: there was, he said, scarcely a single man who believed one word of Revelation who would not agree with the view that, in its religious aspect, it was 'altogether and unequivocally abominable'.[103] On another issue, he was asked in 1883–4 by the International Arbitration and Peace Association to become its President.[104] He accepted the invitation, although he realised that the effectiveness of the Association was likely to be limited. 'It is a Body full of good intentions,' he wrote, 'but probably, with little hope of success.'[105] At home, he was much concerned with the production of literature and of plays which he regarded as pernicious and likely to have a corrupting effect, especially on the young. He was President of the Pure Literature Society. In 1881, he wrote to Gladstone over the licensing by the Lord Chamberlain of 'La Dame aux Camelias'. He recognised that this was well-intentioned, but the same reasoning as had led to the licensing of 'La Dame' could lead to the authorisation of many more plays of a similar description. He could see no embankment to stop the flood of this 'new pollution of the English stage'.

It would be better that the Lord Chamberlain had no jurisdiction at all over theatres than that he should exercise it to give sanction and currency to 'such abominations'. Parents and guardians would be thrown off their guard by such official countenance, and such 'authorised condition of the Drama' would affect the integrity of social and domestic life.[106]

The religious and moral dimensions of Evangelicalism thus still preoccupied Shaftesbury, despite the fact that there were many forces working against them. And the same is true of the social implications of his beliefs. There were great difficulties in the way of Ragged Schools. Shaftesbury wrote in 1880 that many had perished – the voluntary teachers had dispersed and nothing could be raised in the way of a subsidy.[107] Yet he felt that the need for them was as great as ever and that he must watch over those that did remain.[108] He also continued his interest in the training ships, *Chichester* and *Arethusa*; a third ship was, in fact, added to them under the auspices of the Metropolitan School Board. It was appropriately named the *Shaftesbury*. He also concerned himself with other agencies of relief. In 1882, he presided at the dedication of George Williams's House of Health and Repose for Young Men,[109] and, in July, 1883, laid the foundation stone of a Refuge for Boys and Girls in Manchester. He was pleased with the reception which he received there; he had hoped that he might 'be able to do a little good and have a real and touching farewell in that city, the scene of so many successful labours.'[110] In the summer of 1883, he also attended a meeting of the Flower and Water Cress Girls Mission and was presented with a clock in gratitude for the Emily Loan Fund, and he was present at an anniversary meeting of the Costermongers' Donkey and Pony show. It was, he wrote, 'one of the happiest successes in all our London movements'. He felt that the examples of the Costers of 'Golden Lane' in the treatment of the animals that belonged to them had led to a universal improvement all over London.[111] He also continued to support the cause of Vivisection. He wrote to Mrs Cobbe in 1879 that he did not think a further bill prohibiting vivesection would be 'altogether useless'. It would 'affirm a great principle' and be the basis of effective legislation in the future.[112] In 1880, he sent a Memorial with numerous signatures to Gladstone entreating the Prime Minister to use his power to put down vivesection. This stressed that the Act of 1876 had been a failure and that more 'vivisectors' were licensed than had been at work before it passed. Shaftesbury enclosed a private note, begging Gladstone to give as sympathetic a reply as possible.[113] Gladstone's reply was, it seems, sympathetic and Shaftesbury asked if he might make public use of it. Gladstone, however, was unwilling to allow this – he was anxious, he told Shaftesbury, to avoid new subjects.[114] There was, then, no official support for the cause, and bills which were privately sponsored every year between 1881 and 1884 were dropped without success. Shaftesbury knew that the possibility of obtaining total abolition was remote. He told Mrs Cobbe that there was little hope of obtaining anything substantial before public opinion had become enlightened and 'expressive' on the matter.[115] He was angered by opposition from quarters where he felt he might have expected support. He wrote to Miss Cobbe that so many dignitaries of the Church and Members of Convocation had declared themselves on the side of Vivisection that 'we must have a new Article, making 40 in all . . . What good is produced by having such men, officially, in the House of Lords?'[116] Equally, he was grateful for any assistance. In 1885, he wrote to Ruskin, expressing the gratitude of the Victoria Street Society for support which he had demonstrated 'on behalf of the rights of God's creatures and their undeniable claims to the mercy and protection of Man.' Sentiments such as Ruskin's, he wrote:

> backed by a name of high reputation, will make men and women think. They may affect even some of those who, professedly, follow this hideous practice for the benefit of the Human Race, and of those who, confessedly, are bent on the infliction of a series of indescribable tortures for no other purpose than the addition of a few facts to the general amount of Human Knowledge.[117]

And, throughout the last years of his life, Shaftesbury kept up a steady correspondence with Miss Cobbe. He advised her on the phrasing of publications which she issued, holding it, as he told her, a 'great honour to be called to the service of the meanest (which I doubt) of His creatures.'[118] He also ranged over other topics, such as his earlier career[119] and his present activities. 'Heavens, our Earth . . . is filled with the exhibitions of cruelty,' he wrote in 1881, after taking the chair at a meeting to found a Refuge for homeless children.

> Some people say [he continued] . . . that they rejoice that by their efforts they 'leave the world a little better than they found it' . . . So far as I am concerned, every day blackens with fresh horrors and the revival of old ones.[120]

Despite such despair, however, Shaftesbury did not slacken his efforts to 'leave the world a little better'. In 1884, he became Chairman of the London Society for the Prevention of Cruelty to Children. He also spoke regularly in the Lords on topics concerned with the care of children and general social improvement. In 1881, he supported a motion – subsequently withdrawn – in favour of a consolidation of existing legislation relating to reformatory and industrial education for children convicted of crime. He expressed the view that such children should not be turned adrift after their period of education was over but should be placed in a position that would enable them to make a start in life.[121] Also in 1881, he supported a motion to appoint a select committee to inquire into the state of the law relating to the protection of young girls from ploys inducing them to lead an immoral life. There was, he said, 'nothing more cruel, appalling or detestable . . . in the history of crimes all over the world than that abominable traffic.'[122] When the Criminal Law Amendment bill came before the Lords in 1883-4, Shaftesbury was at pains to amend it so that it rendered men, as well as women, liable to punishment for loitering for immoral purposes.[123] In 1883, he supported a measure to prevent the payment of wages in public houses. He claimed that he was, in a sense, the author of this since he had included a similar provision in his Mines bill in 1842.[124] Also in 1883 Shaftesbury supported the Factories and Workshops Amendment bill, which provided for greater facilities for washing, refreshment and ventilation,[125] and the following month, in August, he took up the question of the employment of acrobat children. An Act had been passed in 1879, prohibiting the employment of children under fourteen to go through any performance which could, in the opinion of the magistrates, endanger life or limb. Shaftesbury had supported this, although he would have preferred to see the age raised to seventeen.[126] In 1883, he told the Lords that the Act had not been effective and he called once more for raising the age of performance to seventeen, and – as he had also done in 1879 – pointed to the fact that training of children was not done in public and could not easily be controlled. The whole practice was, he said, 'a disgrace to the age in which we lived.'[127]

Further, Shaftesbury was much concerned with the question of working-class housing during these years. In 1881, he reported in his Diary that, in extreme heat, he had visited Whitechapel. He noted the 'concentrated filth', the closeness of the Alleys, the decay and rottenness of the houses 'begrimed with stench and dirt that no care or effort could remove.' Every conceivable obstacle, he wrote, was thrown in the way of cleanliness, decency and health. 'There the People live, if such a state of things can be called "Life",' he concluded.[128] He wrote to Mrs Cobbe of the same visit to these 'filthy and disgraceful residences'. He admitted that the inhabitants had many faults, but was that not also true of the comfortable? And in the midst of such degradation, they were marvellously patient.[129]

There was, in fact, considerable interest in the subject of working-class housing in the early 1880s. In 1882, a bill was passed amending the Torrens and Cross Acts. It was concerned with matters of compensation and had relatively little effect; indeed, it diminished the re-housing which was to take place on displacement owing to improvements.[130] But public opinion was jolted by revelations which were made, especially by a pamphlet published in 1883 by Andrew Mearns, *The Bitter Cry of Outcast London*.[131] Various journals also carried articles on the subject of housing,[132] and to one of these, *The Nineteenth Century*, Shaftesbury contributed one of several articles on the general theme of 'The Dwellings of the Poor'. In this, he wrote that the

> sudden manifestation of public feeling in regard to the domiciliary condition of large portions of the working classes in our cities and great towns, and specially in London, is one of the healthiest signs of modern times.

He could not, however, resist the comment that this feeling had long lain dormant; forty years had passed since the evil had been disclosed and ever since that date individuals, companies and associations had been 'unremitting to proclaim the mischief, to devise remedies, and, in some instances, to apply them.'

A further impetus to the question came in 1884 when Lord Salisbury moved for the appointment of a Royal Commission to investigate the housing of the working classes. Shaftesbury expressed the fear that improvements already being made would be terminated by the fact that a Commission was in existence. Nevertheless, he felt that the Commission would gather together information on the subject and give it weight and authority.[134] He thus supported the appointment of the Commission, and, when it met, he was the first witness to appear before it. He dwelt on the evils of overcrowding. This, he said, had increased because of the displacement of population after recent public works such as the Embankment and the Law Courts.[135] He elaborated on the physical and moral effects of the 'one-room' and thus the 'one-bed' system; this was especially harmful to the morals and health of young persons. If, he said, he were to go into the details of the consequences of overcrowding, particularly in single rooms, very few persons would believe what he said.[136] He was asked on several occasions whether or not such deplorable conditions were the result of the intemperance and carelessness of the people who lived in them. One questioner referred to a recent pamphlet entitled 'Is it the Pig that makes the Stye or the Stye that makes the Pig?'[137] In answer, Shaftesbury said that he had heard a great deal to the effect that people were so sunken, so lost and so enamoured of filth that reform was impossible. But he did not take that point of view: it was often the stye that made the pig. He admitted that there were great difficulties in improving the condition of the 'migratory classes,' who stayed in one place only for some three months; but, apart from them, he was convinced that many persons could be rescued from their surroundings and enabled to lead decent lives.[138] It was the poverty of the people that led them to live in wretched conditions, not their habits,[139] and, although he attributed their poverty in great measure to drink, he argued that excessive drinking was indulged in as an escape and a relief from bad living conditions.[140] Here, indeed, Shaftesbury repeated the point which he had made in the Lords when supporting the appointment of the Commission that it was bad housing which caused immorality rather than immorality bad housing.[141]

When it came to remedial measures, Shaftesbury also echoed earlier his remarks: this time in his article in *The Nineteenth Century* as well as in the Lords. In his article, he had denounced the suggestion that the central government should undertake improvements. If the state, he wrote, were required to provide houses for the working classes and also to supply them at nominal rents, it would

> while doing something on behalf of their physical condition, utterly destroy their moral energies. It will, in fact, be an official proclamation that, without any efforts of their own, certain portions of the people shall enter into the enjoyment of many good things, altogether at the expense of others.[142]

All that the state should do was to give every facility by law and enabling statute, but the work itself should be done by voluntary effort. Only if that voluntary effort failed and it was clear that nothing would be done, would it be necessary for the state to intervene. This could not take place without many evil effects; it would be a blow to 'the spirit of healthy thrift'.[143] Shaftesbury returned to this theme in the Lords in 1884, and he reiterated it on several occasions in his replies to questions when giving evidence to the Royal Commission. All the evils, he argued, could be dealt with by private effort, by the existing housing societies and joint-stock companies.[144] And existing legislation was sufficient: in particular the Act of 1851, to encourage the establishment of lodging houses for the working classes. Under this Act, which, he claimed, was wider in its application than more recent Housing Acts such as the Torrens and Cross Acts, vestries were entrusted with powers to effect improvements and to borrow money on the security of the rates for the purpose. The Act had not been widely implemented, but if it were put into effect now that there was strong feeling on the subject, he believed that London would soon be covered with a cluster of agencies which could set in motion the work of improvement.[145] This might take the form of demolition and the construction of houses of several storeys, or, in many cases, improvements could be made to existing properties.[146] All this could be done by private enterprise under the umbrella of the enabling powers to vestries contained in the 1851 Act. The resulting accommodation was likely to be available at rents which put them beyond the means of the poorest classes, but, as has been seen, Shaftesbury had come to the conclusion that relatively little could be done for them, especially if they were migratory. The rents would be within the reach of the thrifty working man and would thus act as an inducement to him to improve himself. Here, then, Shaftesbury showed his continuing belief in the virtue of individual effort and enterprise; a belief held the more strongly in the face of state intervention which he now regarded as excessive. 'Hitherto,' he wrote in his article – which was entitled 'The Mischief of State Aid' – 'we have done too little; there is now a fear that in some respects we may do too much . . . It is a melancholy system that tends to debase a large mass of people to the condition of a nursery, where the children look to the father and mother, and do nothing for themselves.'[147]

It was, in a sense, fitting that Shaftesbury's last major concern had also been his first: that of lunacy. The subject had, indeed, already been raised in 1883, when Lord Stanley called the attention of the Lords to the increase of insanity and wondered if it was being caused by overwork in elementary schools. In reply, Shaftesbury questioned whether there had been an increase in insanity. In his view, it was now decreasing, owing to the efforts of Temperance Societies and Bands of Hope. But he admitted that a special kind of insanity did exist, arising from excessive study especially among those rising to adult life. Many people were beginning to see that what he called the 'forcing system in schools and burning competition for place and position among teachers' was harmful.[148] A more substantial point, however, arose the following year, and it raised the old question of the liberty of the subject in relation to the procedures for confinement in an asylum. In May, 1884, Lord Milltown proposed a motion to the effect that the existing state of lunacy legislation was unsatisfactory and constituted a serious danger to the liberty of the subject.[149] He called attention to the observations of the judge in a recent case, *Weldon v. Winslow*.[150] The judge had expressed astonishment at the arrangements for consigning a person to an asylum. If a pauper or a crossing sweeper should sign an order, Milltown had said, and another crossing sweeper should make a statement and if this were followed up by the signing of a certificate by two medical men who had never had a day's practice in their lives, then a person could be confined, and such procedures were, the judge had continued, a perfect answer to any action. In reply, Shaftesbury made a long speech denying such allegations.[151] He said that if the judge had known the law and read the select committee's report of 1878, he would never have made such a statement. In the first place, the Lunacy Act of 1862 had laid down stringent qualifications for those empowered to give such certificates. Whenever the terms 'physician', 'surgeon' or 'apothecary' were used in Lunacy legislation, this indicated a person registered under the Medical Act of 1858: he was, then, a person of professional fitness. It was true that this did not necessarily imply practice of or training in lunacy, but, if this were insisted on, not one in ten thousand of the medical profession would be so qualified. Shaftesbury also refuted the claim that the procedures for admission of a patient were an answer to any action. Had the judge, he asked, never heard of cases tried in the courts in which patients had prosecuted doctors for negligence and been awarded damages? There was also a similar power against persons who had signed an order of admission. He admitted that the order itself was a 'weak point' – it was undesirable that *anyone* could sign an order. But there had always been the difficulty of providing for persons who were suddenly 'seized' in hotels, lodging houses or apartments, and there had been very little abuse of the power to sign the order. In fact, probably not more than one in five hundred orders had been signed by a person other than a relative or friend. Thus Shaftesbury once again denied that the existing legislation had resulted in a deprivation of liberty and he called to his support the findings of the two committees of 1859 and 1877. There were, he held, fewer cases of mistakes being made in placing patients under care and treatment than there were miscarriages of justice in the Courts of Law.

For the remainder of his speech, Shaftesbury ranged over other aspects of the question. He reiterated his firm belief in the need for early treatment of lunacy, which, of course, was another argument for not restricting the signing of an order to relatives or magistrates, but he also admitted that early treatment ran the risk of mistaking transient eccentricity of habit or manner for incipient mental disorder. It was the old dilemma: to act too quickly was to fix the taint of insanity on a person; to act too slowly meant that the person might deteriorate and become incurable. He also dealt with the problem of single patients and, in particular, with the difficulty of tracing them so that they might be properly visited. Even if they were visited, there was no one to bear witness to their testimony and it was all too easy for any complaints to be attributed by the attendant to mental wanderings. Despite the improvements which had been brought about in their condition, they still required the utmost thought and attention. He repeated the points which he had made in 1877 about private licensed houses: his dislike of the principle of profit but his belief that considerable improvement in their management had taken place. Little had been done to put anything in their place, but he believed that the feeling of the country would run in the direction of the public principle and when that happened such institutions would require no small amount of care and supervision. Shaftesbury concluded his speech by calling attention to the vast improvements which had taken place since 1828 – the contrast between then and 1884 was 'well nigh incredible'. All that was required was care and caution and that legislation should follow and not precede the guidance of practical science; he advised strongly against any action being taken in the light of hasty and nervous agitation. He trusted that

> by investigation and patience they would be able, by God's blessing, to arrive at some alleviation, if not a full remedy, for the most mysterious affliction that has been permitted to fall on the human race.

Shaftesbury thus spoke – even at the age of eighty-three – with great force and authority. But opinion was clearly against him, and other speeches, while acknowledging his past efforts, called for new legislation. This was promised for the following session by the Lord Chancellor, Lord Selborne, and Milltown thus withdrew his motion for an inquiry. The Lunacy Act Amendment bill of 1885 did, indeed, propose the change which had been demanded: no order for admission was to be valid without the signature of a county court judge, a stipendiary magistrate or a justice of the peace. Shaftesbury felt that the only course was for him to resign from the Chairmanship of the Commission. On 24 March, 1885, he noted that he would attend the Board for the last time. Although he said nothing to his colleagues, he sent in his letter of resignation to the Lord Chancellor. He acknowledged that Lord Selborne had been civil and courteous and, as far as he could judge, wanted him to remain, but he could not accept the 'Magisterial' clauses of the bill.[152] Two days later, Shaftesbury recounted that Selborne had asked him to withdraw his resignation until after he had presented and printed his bill.[153] Shaftesbury agreed to this request, and thus said nothing in the House when Selborne introduced the measure. On 6 April, however, he submitted his letter of resignation and also sent it to *The Times*, where it was published on 9 April. In it, he expressed his 'absolute repugnance' to the introduction of a magistrate into the process of placing a patient under care and treatment, and he reiterated his objections: that it would lead to delay, expense and excessive prying into family secrets. All this would militate against early treatment and would be a 'complete overthrow' of all that he had laboured for. The following month, he wrote despondently in his Diary[154] that he had received no encouragement; he had stood up for the honour of the medical profession but no one stood up for him. He had had no friend to consult, no precedent to examine. But he had no alternative to resigning. He could not go to the Lords and sit through the passing of a measure to which he was opposed, nor could he oppose it while holding office under the Chancellor. Selborne had offered his permission to do so, but, Shaftesbury commented: 'he knew, as well as I did, the indecency of such a course.' Thus he resolved to resign his position and absent himself from the House. It seemed, then, as if fifty-seven years of service in the cause had come to an end, but, on the fall of the Liberal government in June, 1885, the bill lapsed, and it was not until 1890 that the proposal which he had so fiercely denounced was enacted.[155] His resignation had not been formally accepted and thus he remained in office; and one of his very last entries in his Diary in July[156] showed him still preoccupied with lunacy business.

'Truly, man is fragile, even in his best day, but at past four score, it is a wonder that he holds together for a half-second.' Thus Shaftesbury had written in January, 1885,[157] and his activity in these years – and, indeed, in the first six months of 1885 – was remarkable. In May, he took the chair at the British and Foreign Bible Society. His prayer, he told the Society, would always be that he might die in harness.[158] He was also present at a meeting when he was presented with an illuminated address by the Ragged Schools and six framed copies of Holman Hunt's *The Light of the World* for his family. As in the past, he spoke with pride of his long association with the Movement – he would rather, he said, be President of the Ragged Schools than President of the Royal Academy. He recounted the work which the Schools had done: they had taught children the Gospel, given them a sound education and a trade; and they had had a soothing influence on the population. If there were no agencies such as the Ragged Schools, it would be necessary to have twice as many troops and three times as many police.[159] Shaftesbury thus returned to old haunts – and old themes. But, for the most part he was absent from these May meetings. *The Record* commented that one marked feature of the 1885 meetings was that ' "the old hack", as the venerable Earl of Shaftesbury has often called himself, was compelled at last to disappoint many gatherings that could not be without his presence what they had been with it.'[160] Even so, there was still activity ahead. In June, Shaftesbury learned that a legacy of £60,000 had been left to him for distribution among the charities of London, and he gave meticulous attention to this task. He was determined, as he put it, 'to be more precise and careful in the distribution of *entrusted* money (for such it is) than I would be in my own.'[161] In July, there were public engagements: he met the London City Missionaries, distributed flower prizes in Dean's Yard, Westminster and attended a meeting of a society founded for the protection of children against cruelty.[162] On 25 July, in addition to lunacy business, he recorded a visit to the Home Office and to the House of Lords to discuss revelations of child prostitution made in the *Pall Mall Gazette*. But he also recorded 'great anxiety of state of health', and mentioned also plans to go to Folkestone in the hope that the air would restore him to health.[163] Once in Folkestone, he recovered from the troublesome diarrhoea from which he had been suffering, but he caught a chill which led to inflammation of the lung.[164] Finally, it became clear to his family – and to himself – that he was dying. To the last, his mind appears to have been calm and undisturbed: he dictated replies to letters which he received – his daughter Victoria acting as his 'secretary' – and he chose portions of the Bible to be read to him. It was a sorrow that he was too ill to be moved to St Giles and was confined to a 'lodging house', as he called it, but he made his wish clear that his final resting place should be at St Giles and not – as was suggested in a letter read to him from the Dean of Westminster – in Westminster Abbey.[165] The end came inevitably, but peacefully. On 1 October, 1885, he died, four score years and four.

NOTES

1. N.R.A., Shaftesbury (Broadlands) MSS, SHA/PD/11, 1 Jan., 1879.
2. See P. Smith, op. cit., p. 266 ff.
3. N.R.A., Shaftesbury (Broadlands) MSS, SHA/PC/208.
4. St G.H., Shaftesbury MSS, C 25025.2/7th Earl.
5. N.R.A., Shaftesbury (Broadlands) MSS, SHA/PD/11, 2 Apr., 1880.
6. Hansard, *Parl. Debates*, 3rd ser., CCXXVI, 209 ff.
7. ibid., CCXXXVI, 813 ff.
8. ibid., CCXLV, 349 ff.
9. This forbade employment under the age of 7; limited the hours of children to 9, with one hour for rest; prohibited the employment of children on certain dangerous work; provided for the fencing of machinery and made arrangements for the reporting of accidents and the appointment of inspectors. But, although the Act was to be operative throughout India, some discretion was to be left to local governments to make their own rules for the fencing of machinery, ventilation, inspection, the hearing of appeals and sanitary matters. Indigo factories and tea and coffee plantations were to be exempt. (ibid., CCLXIII, 1108). In practice, the measure was to have a limited effect.
10. ibid., CCXLV, 1945 ff.
11. ibid., CCXLVI, 389–91.
12. Hodder, III, 408.
13. Huntington Library MSS, CB 129–361, 17 July, 1878.
14. ibid., 3 Sept., 1878.
15. ibid., 6 Sept., 1878.
16. ibid., 17 Sept., 1878.
17. ibid., 8 July, 1879.
18. ibid.
19. Hansard, *Parl. Debates*, 3rd ser., CCXLVIII, fos 425–30.
20. Huntington Library MSS, CB 129–361, 8, 18 July, 1878.
21. St G.H., Shaftesbury MSS, C 25025.2/7th Earl.
22. N.R.A., Shaftesbury (Broadlands) MSS, SHA/PC/55 (copy).
23. ibid., SHA/PC/56.
24. See W. L. Arnstein, *The Bradlaugh Case* (Oxford, 1965), *passim*.
25. N.R.A., Shaftesbury (Broadlands) MSS, SHA/PD/11, 28 June, 1880.
26. ibid., SHA/PD/11, 7 Apr., 1880.
27. ibid., SHA/PD/12, 21 June, 1881.

28. Add. MSS, 44, 300, fos 96–7.
29. P.R.O., Cairns MSS, 30/51/8, 21 Feb., 1882.
30. ibid., 26 Feb., 1882.
31. Add. MSS, 44, 300, f. 106.
32. University of Durham, Department of Palaeography and Diplomatic, 4th Earl Grey's MSS, 22 Feb., 1879. (Shaftesbury to 4th Earl Grey).
33. Quoted in Hodder, III, 418–19.
34. Quoted ibid., 453.
35. Quoted ibid., 454.
36. Hansard, *Parl. Debates*, 3rd ser., CCXC, 1342–5.
37. N.R.A., Shaftesbury (Broadlands) MSS, SHA/PD/12, 7 May, 1882.
38. Quoted in Hodder, III, 252–3.
39. N.R.A., Shaftesbury (Broadlands) MSS, SHA/PD/11, 13 Dec., 1879.
40. Quoted in Hodder, III, 425–6.
41. See Hodder, III, 421–4.
42. Huntington Library MSS, CB 129–301, 26 Apr., 1881.
43. Quoted in Hodder, III, 423.
44. N.R.A., Shaftesbury (Broadlands) MSS, SHA/PD/11, 6 May, 1881.
45. ibid., SHA/EST/9/3. He did, however, change his views and allowed Edwin Hodder access to his papers to write his biography (Hodder, I, v–ix).
46. N.R.A., Shaftesbury (Broadlands) MSS, SHA/PD/11, 2 May, 28 Oct., 1879.
47. ibid., SHA/PD/11, 20 Sept., 1880.
48. ibid., SHA/PD/11, 20 Oct., 1880.
49. ibid., SHA/PD/11, 20 Oct., 1880.
50. H.R.O., Shaftesbury (Broadlands) MSS, 27M60, 16, 17 Apr., 1880.
51. N.R.A., Shaftesbury (Broadlands) MSS, SHA/PD/12, 3 Aug., 1882.
52. Battiscombe, p. 328.
53. N.R.A., Shaftesbury (Broadlands) MSS, SHA/PD/12, 24 Apr., 1885.
54. ibid., SHA/PD/12, 24 Apr., 1885.
55. ibid., SHA/PD/11, 2 May, 1879.
56. ibid., SHA/PD/11, 2 Feb., 1880.
57. ibid., SHA/PD/11, 29 Mar., 1879.
58. ibid., SHA/PD/11, 16 Dec., 1879.
59. ibid., SHA/PD/11, 2 Feb., 1880.
60. ibid., SHA/PD/11, 24 Aug., 1881.
61. ibid., SHA/PD/12, 22 Jan., 1885.
62. ibid., SHA/PD/12, 16 Feb., 1885.
63. ibid., SHA/PD/11, 19 Apr., 1881.
64. ibid., SHA/PD/12, 19 July, 1881.
65. ibid., SHA/PD/12, 23 Sept., 1882. Shaftesbury also wrote to Gladstone on this subject in virtually identical terms. (Add. MSS, 44, 300, f. 112).
66. N.R.A., Shaftesbury (Broadlands) MSS, SHA/PD/12, 4 Dec., 1882.
67. ibid., SHA/PD/12, 20 July, 1882.
68. ibid., SHA/PD/12, 20 July, 1882.
69. ibid., SHA/PD/12, 9 July, 1882.
70. ibid., SHA/PD/11, 29 Mar., 1879.
71. ibid., SHA/PD/12, 30 Nov., 1881.
72. ibid., SHA/PD/12, 28 Apr., 1884.
73. ibid., SHA/PD/11, 16 Oct., 1880.
74. ibid., SHA/PD/11, 16 Oct., 1880.
75. ibid., SHA/PD/12, 11 Nov., 1883.

76. ibid., SHA/PD/12, 16 July, 1881.
77. Add. MSS, 44, 200, fos 86–7.
78. Hansard, *Parl. Debates,* 3rd ser., CCLVIII, 1496.
79. ibid., CCLXXXVI, 436. This repeated a point made ten years earlier to the Working Men's Lord's Day Rest Association. Shaftesbury then had denied that the object of the Association was to make Sunday a day of rest for everyone. If people chose to devote the day to amusement and idleness, he would regret it, but he would not interfere, provided that no labour was imposed on others. He would not consent that labour should be imposed on a day given by God as a great Charter to men to ensure that they might have one day to themselves to be employed for the highest and holiest purposes. (*The Record,* 1 May, 1874).
80. Cairns MSS, 30/51/8, f. 34.
81. ibid., f. 29.
82. Quoted in Hodder, III, 508. See also *The Record,* 10 Apr., 1855.
83. Hodder, III, 427.
84. N.R.A., Shaftesbury (Broadlands) MSS, SHA/PD/12, 17 May, 1884.
85. See A. Bentley, op. cit., pp. 37–8. This was largely implemented by the Liberal Government in 1880.
86. Cairns MSS, 30/51/8, f. 10.
87. N.R.A., Shaftesbury (Broadlands) MSS, SHA/PD/12, 27 July, 1881.
88. ibid., SHA/PC/101.
89. Quoted in Hodder, III, 438. See also ibid., 438–40 for further letter.
90. Hodder, III, 412–13.
91. Hansard, *Parl. Debates,* 3rd ser., CCLXVI, 229.
92. N.R.A., Shaftesbury (Broadlands) MSS, SHA/MIS/66.
93. ibid., SHA/MIS/67/1.
94. ibid., SHA/MIS/68.
95. ibid., SHA/PD/12, 28 Apr., 1885.
96. Hughenden MSS (on microfilm). Film 131, 16 May, 1879.
97. A. L. Tibawi, op. cit., p. 215.
98. ibid., p. 218.
99. Lambeth Palace Libr., Benson MSS, 174, f. 30.
100. ibid., f. 49 (copy).
101. A. L. Tibawi, op. cit., pp. 218–24.
102. Quoted in Hodder, III, 430.
103. Quoted ibid., 431.
104. St G.H., Shaftesbury MSS, C 25145/7th Earl.
105. Duke University, Durham, North Carolina, William R. Perkins Libr., Manuscripts Dept., Malet Family MSS, Shaftesbury to Sir Edward Baldwin Malet, 13 Dec., 1884.
106. Add. MSS, 44, 300, fos 100–101.
107. N.R.A., Shaftesbury (Broadlands) MSS, SHA/PD/11, 10 Apr., 1880.
108. ibid., SHA/PD/12, 28, 30 Nov., 1881.
109. ibid., SHA/PD/12, 30 July, 1882.
110. Quoted in Hodder, III, 487.
111. N.R.A., Shaftesbury (Broadlands) MSS, SHA/PD/12, 3 July, 1883.
112. Huntington Library MSS, CB 129–361, 23 Dec., 1879.
113. Add. MSS, 44, 300, f. 88.
114. ibid., f. 90.
115. Huntington Library MSS, CB 129–361, 23 Dec., 1879.
116. ibid., 13 Jan., 1880.

117. Humanities Research Center, The University of Texas at Austin, John Ruskin MSS, Shaftesbury to Ruskin, 18 May, 1885.
118. N.R.A., Shaftesbury (Broadlands) MSS, SHA/PD/11, 24 Jan., 1881.
119. See above p. 17.
120. N.R.A., Shaftesbury (Broadlands) MSS, SHA/PD/12, 12 July, 1881.
121. Hansard, *Parl. Debates,* 3rd ser., CCLXI, 1602.
122. ibid., 1609.
123. ibid., CCLXXX, 1399, 1863; CCLXXXI, 416; CCLXXXVIII, 410.
124. ibid., CCLXXVI, 1569.
125. ibid., CCLXXXI, 1871-3.
126. ibid., CCXLVI, 1112.
127. ibid., CCLXXXVI, 1462-5.
128. N.R.A., Shaftesbury (Broadlands) MSS, SHA/PD/12, 16 July, 1881.
129. Huntington Library MSS, CB 129-361, 15 July, 1881.
130. E. Gauldie, op. cit., p. 285.
131. G. Stedman Jones, *Outcast London. A Study in the Relationship between Classes in Victorian Society* (Oxford, 1971), p. 282 ff.
132. E. Gauldie, op. cit., p. 285.
133. *The Nineteenth Century,* XIV, 934-9.
134. Hansard, *Parl. Debates,* 3rd ser., CCLXXXIV, 1694.
135. P.P., 1884-5, XXX, Q. 14.
136. ibid., Qs 15, 29.
137. ibid., Q. 39.
138. ibid.
139. ibid., Q. 151.
140. ibid., Q. 154.
141. Hansard, *Parl. Debates,* 3rd ser., CCLXXXIV, 1694.
142. *The Nineteenth Century,* XIV, p. 935.
143. ibid., p. 938.
144. P.P., 1884-5, XXX, Q. 23.
145. ibid., Q. 39.
146. ibid., Q. 24.
147. *The Nineteenth Century,* XIV, pp. 935, 938.
148. Hansard, *Parl. Debates,* CCLXXXI, 1471.
149. ibid., CCLXXXVII, 1268.
150. For details of this case, see Hammonds, pp. 212-13.
151. Hansard, *Parl. Debates,* 3rd ser., CCLXXXVII, 1271-81.
152. N.R.A., Shaftesbury (Broadlands) MSS, SHA/PD/12, 24 Mar., 1885.
153. ibid., SHA/PD/12, 26 Mar., 1885.
154. ibid., SHA/PD/12, 5 May, 1885.
155. K. Jones, op. cit., p. 40.
156. N.R.A., Shaftesbury (Broadlands) MSS, SHA/PD/12, 25 July, 1885.
157. ibid., SHA/PD/12, 22 Jan., 1885.
158. *The Record,* 8 May, 1885.
159. ibid., 22 May, 1885.
160. ibid., 8 May, 1885.
161. N.R.A., Shaftesbury (Broadlands) MSS, SHA/PD/12, 4 July, 1885.
162. ibid., SHA/PD/12, 10 July, 1885.
163. ibid., SHA/PD/12, 25 July, 1885.
164. *The Charity Record and Philanthropic News,* 15 Oct., 1885.
165. Hodder, III, 515-16.

21

Epitaph to a Saint

Shaftesbury's final wish to be buried in the family vault in the village church at St Giles was faithfully carried out, but not before a Memorial Service was held on 8 October, 1885, in Westminster Abbey. In his biography, Edwin Hodder provides a full account of this: the progress of the hearse from Grosvenor Square, watched by crowds of onlookers; the deputations from the societies with which Shaftesbury had been associated lining the route and then following the procession, carrying banners inscribed with such texts as 'Naked and ye clothed me', 'A stranger and ye took me in'. The scene inside the Abbey is also described and the hymn of Charles Wesley sung at the end of the service quoted:

> Let all the saints terrestrial sing
>   with those to glory gone.
> For all the servants of our King
>   In earth and heaven are one.[1]

Hodder's account is, perhaps, over-sentimental, but it may be excused for that – it was an emotional and evocative occasion. But Hodder also adds a purely factual Appendix, in which he lists the religious and philanthropic societies which were represented at the service and this takes four pages of double columns to print.[2] All eight pall bearers were, moreover, drawn from societies in which Shaftesbury had shown a life-long interest. They – and the list of deputations – are, indeed, almost a roll-call of Shaftesbury's life. Their presence was, in itself, a fitting epitaph to Shaftesbury. Others, moreover, were to follow: the statue erected in Westminster Abbey and the Eros Monument, with its telling inscription composed by Gladstone:

> During a public life of half a century
> he devoted the influence of his station,
> the strong sympathies of his heart,

and the great powers of his mind,
to honouring God
by serving his fellow-men,
an example to his order,
a blessing to this people,
and a name to be by them ever
gratefully remembered.[3]

There was, however, also a rather more private epitaph. This takes the form of a memorial tablet in the Church at St Giles, and inscribed on it are three verses from the New Testament. Two are from First Corinthians. The first reads: 'What hast thou that thou didst not receive?'; and the second: 'Let him that thinketh he standeth take heed lest he fall.'[4] The third is from the Book of Revelation: 'Surely I come quickly. Amen. Even so, come Lord Jesus.'[5] The texts were, moreover, chosen by Shaftesbury himself. In 1879, he left instructions about the form of the tablet and these included the three texts which finally appeared on it.[6]

Clearly, too much significance may be read into them. On the other hand, the fact that they were self-chosen justifies the view that they have something important to say about Shaftesbury's life and beliefs. The text 'Let him that thinketh he standeth take heed lest he fall' may, of course, be taken to indicate his belief in the frailty and sinfulness of man, but it may not be too fanciful to see it as an indication of Shaftesbury's personality. As has been evident throughout this work, Shaftesbury's Diaries convey a strong sense of anxiety, pessimism, even despair. Part of this, indeed, derived from unhappy and distressing external circumstances: his worries and losses as paterfamilias, his burdens as proprietor, his feeling of isolation and alienation in public life, ever more acute with the passing of the years. But it may also be argued that the darkness of spirit which Shaftesbury so often displayed sprang more fundamentally from an unstable personality. The 'dash of madness' which Henry Fox noted in 1821 was also hinted at by Florence Nightingale, when she commented that, had Shaftesbury not devoted himself to reforming lunatic asylums, he would have been in one himself.[7] It might be held that Shaftesbury's unhappy childhood – his distant relations with his parents – led to a feeling of uncertainty and lack of self-confidence in later life. Lack of parental affection, it may be argued, can cause a lack of self-esteem and a disposition to feelings of failure, disappointment and despair.[8] Or again, it may be argued that Shaftesbury gave evidence of some of the characteristics of the hereditary malady of Cyclothymia or Manic Depressive Insanity. This is marked by phases of excitement alternating with phases of depression. The various aspects of these phases have been described by Oliver Ransford in his study of David

Livingstone.[9] Ransford points out that during the 'excited' phase, the sufferer may display impulsiveness, unjustified optimism, unwarranted suspiciousness of and uncharitableness towards other people; he may be assertive, ruthless and, at his most exalted, may experience an intense religious sense of being in direct contact with God. On the other hand, when depressed, the sufferer feels pessimistic, guilty, unable to come to decisions and lethargic. Such a person might well be reminded of the text 'Let him that thinketh he standeth take heed lest he fall.'

If this text may be taken as a peg on which to hang reflections on Shaftesbury's personality, the other two texts on his memorial tablet may serve a similar purpose in relation to his personal beliefs and public life. His choice of the last verse in the Bible – 'Surely I come quickly. Amen. Even so, come Lord Jesus' – illuminates his overriding belief in and constant prayer for the Second Coming. It was this which – as has been seen – gave a particular urgency to the task of mission to which Shaftesbury devoted so much attention and energy: man must cooperate with God to fill the world with the knowledge of His glory, so that the 'last days' might not be delayed. The mission to the Jews had a special relevance to this task. Further, this belief was closely related to Shaftesbury's social concern. Men must be freed from physical and material incumbrances which hindered their spiritual development. They must be given every opportunity to prepare themselves to meet their Saviour with confidence and dignity.

Certainly in that social concern there was no room for the doctrine of works. Shaftesbury always wrote of this with the most severe scorn. 'Oh God', he wrote in April, 1868, 'Thou canst not confer on man a greater blessing than to make him see and feel how vile, weak, worthless and corrupt he is. What a fearful soul-destroying doctrine is the "doctrine of works".'[10] He wrote of his activities in this respect as springing from a sense of gratitude to God for the gifts and benefits with which he had been entrusted. He told Miss Cobbe in 1880 of his conviction that God had 'called (him) to devote whatever advantages He might have bestowed on (him) to the cause of the weak, the helpless, both man and beast, and those who had no one to help them.'[11] There was, indeed, always an element of the aristocratic 'noblesse oblige' about Shaftesbury – as the Hammonds have well put it, he had 'all the patrician readiness for responsibility of any and every kind.'[12] But added to this – and more important than it – was the Christian idea of stewardship: man must regard his time, talents and possessions as gifts from God to be used in His service. As the text which Shaftesbury chose inquires: 'What hast thou that thou didst not receive?'

Just as with the first text which has been considered, it is possible to use the others to point to the limitations and flaws in Shaftesbury's outlook. Thus in terms of his religious beliefs, it may be argued that he was a man of rigid, narrow and uncompromising Evangelical views, which sprang from an excessive reliance on the emotions and much too scant a respect for the intellect. In ecclesiastical matters, he may be characterised as a bigoted, intolerant Protestant, who closed his mind to the possibility that those of a different persuasion in Church matters might have any valuable insights to offer. On moral issues, many of the same criticisms may apply: that his moral outlook was constrained and puritanical; that it consisted of a series of negatives and thus removed much of the pleasure and colour from life. Further, it may be held that his social concern was shallow, in that it dealt only with creating conditions for self-improvement. 'Laws may remove obstacles,' he wrote in 1872, 'and sympathisers may give aid, but it is by personal conduct, by sobriety, by order, by honesty, by perseverance that a man, under God, becomes "the architect of his own fortunes".'[13] For Shaftesbury, then, legislation and paternalistic and philanthropic effort were designed to 'help the helpless': to bring the individual to the point where he could harness his own resources of character. If they went beyond that, they would destroy the individual's initiative and sense of responsibility. This outlook, it can be argued, did not take sufficient account of the volume of poverty which made self-improvement difficult, if not impossible. It offered no real challenge to the evils of Victorian society – it sought only to ameliorate its worst abuses, and, in so doing, was sentimental, patronising and moralistic. It was hostile to forces which sought to change society in the interests of the 'non-properted'. Another argument which may be set against Shaftesbury's social commitment is that it was essentially self-interested. Thus, in a personal sense, it could be held that it was adopted to ease a troubled conscience and afford greater peace of mind, and, in a public sense, that it was designed to stave off radical political or social demands and ensure the survival of his own class.

Shaftesbury, then, is an 'eminent Victorian' about whom it is possible to reach conclusions which are far from flattering. One notable instance of this is to be found in the assessment made by Charles Whibley in his book *Lord John Manners and His Friends*. Whibley wrote of Shaftesbury's introspection, and he quoted approvingly the Hammonds' comment that the time that other public figures like Fox or Peel or Gladstone spent with Homer, Plato, Cicero, Dante or Shakespeare, Shaftesbury spent talking to himself and about himself. While others looked outside themselves, Shaftesbury looked within and could find little of which he could approve: thus he became a slave of his own egoism. Whibley also wrote of Shaftesbury's lack of culture – although he had taken a first class at Oxford, he forgot what scholarship was. There was also a lack of humour. Any spark of joyousness, Whibley wrote, had to be extinguished as soon as it was perceived. Whibley seized on Shaftesbury's intolerance. He knew so little of toleration, Whibley argued, that he was ready to quarrel with everyone who refused to accept not one but all his fads. His social concern was dictated only by a barren sense of duty, and, in the end, his isolation was caused by his refusal to 'abate by a jot his stiff-necked, unconquerable pride.' Thus, although he 'never ceased to save from tragedy those who sought his protection, he will be remembered as the most darkly tragic figure of his generation.'[14]

Such an attack on Shaftesbury is, of course, so bitter and extreme as not to be worth taking seriously. It seizes and exaggerates all Shaftesbury's shortcomings and ignores all his merits. And even interpretations which concentrate less savagely on his flaws, may well be questioned. Despite their unfavourable comments about Shaftesbury's introspection, the Hammonds were not without a certain admiration for his social concern, and their biography does make some penetrating comments. But they lacked any real sympathy for the religious motives which lay behind Shaftesbury's social activities and failed to explore them; they exaggerated the extent to which he 'changed course' into philanthropy in 1846 on his resignation from the Commons and were unrealistically critical of his failure to do certain things – for example make common cause with Christian Socialism – of which they would have approved but of which Shaftesbury himself disapproved.

On the more general points, moreover, the psychological approach to biography clearly has its dangers. The historian who attempts it runs the risk of committing elementary mistakes in another discipline: the psychologist who carries it out may have an insufficient grasp of historical detail. And even a limited incursion into these areas in the case of Shaftesbury must be hedged around with caution. The school of thought which ascribes a sense of uncertainty in later life to early deprivation of parental affection does not appear to hold undisputed authority,[15] and, even if it is accepted, it may well be asked if enough is known about Shaftesbury's early life to make it a tenable hypothesis. There can, indeed, be no question that Shaftesbury's childhood had its harsh and unhappy aspects and that his relations with his parents were extremely cold and distant. But, as is almost inevitable, very little detailed information is available about his very earliest years. Further, the question may be posed whether others who had a similar experience in childhood exhibited the same characteristics of uncertainty and depression in later life: what, for example, of his brothers and sisters? If there are, then, pitfalls in the approach which attributes Shaftesbury's inner doubts to lack of parental affection, the thesis that he was a manic-depressive must also be treated with great care. Shaftesbury did, indeed, appear to exhibit some of the characteristics which have been described, a point which did not escape the notice of Mrs Battiscombe.[16] But there are other aspects of the complaint, as described by Ransford,[17] which are less easily applicable to Shaftesbury: that the phases average six months' duration; that they tend to become apparent during the thirties and are often brought on by strain and 'enforced celibacy'; that they are most marked after the age of forty and tend to occur most frequently during spring and early summer. Ransford points out that there are exceptions to all of these, and the fact that Shaftesbury's pattern of moods does not accord with them is not conclusive. But there are also other aspects of the phases themselves which lead to a certain scepticism. There is little evidence that Shaftesbury suffered from total apathy, indifference and inability to reach decisions during the depressed phase, nor that he was unduly ruthless or aggressive during an exalted one. Thus the evidence on this, as Mrs Battiscombe has recognised, cannot be regarded as incontrovertible.

On the other hand, it cannot be denied that – for whatever reason or reasons – Shaftesbury's personality was a complicated one. On occasion, it must be admitted that he gave way to excessive self-pity and a sense of persecution on the one hand, and to impetuousness and ill-considered judgment on the other. But it must also be remembered that he himself was well aware of his sensitivity and fluctuating moods and often commented on them. And when he did so, it was as much to bemoan a 'thorn in the flesh' as to luxuriate in morbid introspection. What is remarkable is the extent to which, in public, he succeeded in coming to terms with his inner self. For the most part, his doubts, questionings and harshness of judgment of himself and others were confined to his Diaries. When other public figures – notably Gladstone – read extracts from his Diaries in Hodder's *Life*, they were perturbed; Gladstone could never have guessed Shaftesbury's private thoughts from his public conduct towards him.[18] The Diaries did, then, provide a means of release and relief for the moods which afflicted Shaftesbury, and, although the discrepancy between his private and public attitude may expose him to the charge of hypocrisy, such a discrepancy is not uncommon. Certainly Shaftesbury regarded the Diaries as purely private. They were not intended for publication. 'They are of no value to anyone but myself,' Shaftesbury told Hodder. 'They have never been seen by anybody and they never will be. They are a mass of contradictions; thoughts jotted down as they passed through my mind, and contradicted perhaps on the next page – records of passing events written on the spur of the moment and private details which no one could understand but myself.'[19] They were, in fact, almost destroyed by Shaftesbury,[20] and it was only after careful thought that he allowed Hodder to use them.[21] The inner thoughts of persons who did not keep a Diary, parts of which were later quoted in print, remain unknown or, at least, less well known; but this does not mean that they did not exist.

Shaftesbury's public deportment thus concealed much of the private man.

In public, he appears to have given the impression of being completely in command of himself. An early description written of him in the 1830s ran as follows:

> The whole countenance has the coldness as well as the grace of a chiselled one, and expresses precision, prudence, and determination in no common degree. To judge from the set form of the lips, you would say, not only that he never acts from impulse, but that he seldom, if ever, felt an impulse in his life.[22]

He was a very impressive platform speaker and chairman. The writer of an appreciation in *The Record* commented that Shaftesbury's 'figure, as he stood on the platform of Exeter Hall, is stamped indelibly on the memory of the present generation.'

> The tall and slight form [he continued], thin face, iron-grey hair, strongly marked lines, the voice that at first sounded so cold and weak, and the expression which seemed at first so passionless, until the great spirit within aroused and warmed both in a glow which spread to everyone within reach of their influence; the hand used, as it were, to let off steam by periodic strokes on the platform rail, delivered when any unusually strong point had been made with an energy that could make the hall resound, all these and a hundred other characteristics of the man live, and will live, for many a year in thousands of British hearts in every part of the world.[23]

He could also display impatience with long-winded speeches, and imperiousness in stopping them. G. W. E. Russell wrote that it was a disconcerting experience to speak on a platform when Shaftesbury was chairman and, just as one was warming to an impressive passage, to feel a vigorous pull at one's coat tail and to hear a quick, imperative voice say, in no muffled tone, 'my dear fellow, are you never going to stop? We shall be here all night.'[24] Shaftesbury, then, had a mastery over audiences and speakers: it has been perceptively remarked that 'as a chairman he transformed the one faculty which he had inherited from his tiresome father.'[25] But Shaftesbury could also display gentler qualities. Although his public demeanour was serious and sombre, he was not without humour. The writer of the article in *The Record*, indeed, commented on his 'keen sense of humour and love of fun'.[26] He could, it is true, be somewhat overbearing with Minny, especially when preoccupied with a favourite cause, and he was, perhaps, excessively concerned to ensure that Anthony walked strictly in the paths of righteousness. Anthony was once described as 'charming, handsome, civil, with the sunbeamy character of his mother, not in the least shy, full of animal spirits'.[27] To such a nature, Shaftesbury's attitude may well have been somewhat oppressive. Nevertheless, he was a fond and devoted husband, father and grandfather and had a great liking for the company of children. His anxiety for the well-being – as he saw it – of his family may have sprung from the feeling that he must not be guilty of his own parents' neglect. And he was prepared to recognise Anthony's good points – indeed he saw in them the making of his son's problems.

Furthermore, although Shaftesbury was, admittedly, over-sensitive to criticism, he was also sensitive to the needs of others. He had a great and lasting capacity for sympathy and compassion and wrote in 1868 that he seemed to have little left but a power to feel: and that (shall I say unhappily?) is as acute as when I was five and twenty.'[28] He was generous, indeed over-generous, with money, and, as was said of him on one occasion, his 'zeal' sometimes 'appeared stronger than his judgment'.[29] He could, it is true, be awkward and cantankerous: he was a difficult person to work with, so individual and independent were his views. A word often used about him and his schemes was 'impracticable'. Again, he realised this. In 1868, he referred to a comment in the press which had remarked on the 'party' of which he was 'the type and Leader'. He disclaimed the terms. 'I am not a leader and never will be one. I have no party and I will not attempt to form one,' he wrote. '. . . I am a type of nothing and no man or set of men.'[30] This was a remark which had considerable self-discernment. On the other hand, he did inspire respect, loyalty and affection in others, often in persons of an entirely different social background, and he was loyal and generous in his friendships. One of the principal reasons why he eventually allowed Hodder to use his Diaries was to do justice to those who had laboured with him. 'I could never have done the few things I have, had I not been supported by true, zealous, earnest men, who gave me their time and their brains to help forward the different movements,' he said.[31] And although this is, of course, entirely true, it must be remembered that Shaftesbury himself displayed sterling qualities of determination and perseverance in the pursuit of his numerous causes.

Shaftesbury, then, cannot be said to have given in to himself nor, except in his Diaries, to have allowed the darker side of his nature to predominate. His public career may, indeed, be said to gain stature when viewed in the context of his private anxieties and personal tensions. Moreover, the criticisms which have been made of his beliefs and activities may also be questioned. There is no doubt that some of his religious beliefs were extreme and inflexible: such were those in the Second Coming – even if he avoided any precise mathematical dating of the event – and in the infallibility of the Scriptures. As has been seen, his adherence to these divided him even from some of his fellow Evangelicals who took a less rigid stance. On the other hand, he was quick to grasp the issues posed by Biblical criticism, and, if he refused to try to find answers to them and relied simply on denunciation of the whole exercise, he was not alone. Pusey, after all, joined forces with him in his struggle with the Neologists. And – as has also been seen – he was enlightened in his attitude towards scientific development: here, his stance was considerably in advance of that of many of his contemporaries. On ecclesiastical matters, he was, indeed, harsh and unyielding towards Tractarians and Ritualists, but attitudes on Church affairs in the nineteenth century were generally harsh and unyielding and Shaftesbury's were scarcely more so than many others. In some respects, they were, indeed, less so – he was more tolerant of Roman Catholics than many of his fellow Evangelicals. He was also urgently concerned to take the gospel into the highways and byways, and he was willing to adopt and approve of relatively unconventional methods, involving cooperation with Dissenters, to do so. But here again, he was not an extremist. He disliked and distrusted the emotional and fanatical overtones often associated with revivalism. He preferred the hard and unremitting work of mission to brief, and possibly ephemeral, revivalist campaigns, although here it must be admitted that he underestimated the contribution to be made – in religious and social activity – by the Salvation Army. On moral issues, Shaftesbury did not belong to the strictest school, as is shown by his belief in temperance rather than teetotalism, and, although he was an upholder of Sabbatarianism, he did not wish to obstruct harmless enjoyment and recreation on a Sunday, provided that this did not mean that other people had to work to make it possible. Further, he upheld many 'moral' and progressive causes abroad – his great interest in foreign affairs is, indeed, often overlooked. In social matters, he laid upon his heart and soul the obligations of the Christian towards his fellow men. His religion was never one of purely personal piety. In his philanthropic and charitable work, he did not, it is true, wish to erode a sense of responsibility in the individual in receipt of assistance, but this was not carried to extreme lengths and he was willing to temper strict justice with a sense of humanity. His concern was, indeed, always one which had to do with the needs of 'real' people, but, while this approach could be somewhat simplistic, it did also take seriously the demoralising effects of a deprived environment – whether in the hovels of cities or on his own Estates. The fact that his efforts at social improvement through legislation and state intervention were primarily directed at providing assistance for those who could not assist themselves should not obscure nor detract from his willingness to expend time and effort in causes which, certainly in his earlier years, were unfashionable: factory reform, mines reform, the plight of chimney sweeps, public health and, most of all, lunacy were issues which lacked glamour and political reward, and the same could be said of the interest which Shaftesbury took late in his life in animal welfare. Shaftesbury's willingness, moreover, to envisage legislative solutions for many social problems made his approach to these matters more realistic and effective than that of many other paternalists who distrusted the state and felt that little could be done to remove social ills by the intervention of government. He was by no means exclusively committed to the voluntary principle in social policy. Once again, this point should not be overshadowed by his feeling, in the last twenty years of his life, that government intervention was becoming too great and was in danger of destroying qualities of individual initiative and responsibility. Although Shaftesbury's social concern did have its limitations and its precise effects cannot be measured, charges of superficiality and impracticability are wide of the mark; his was no mere 'soup-kitchen philanthropy'. Nor was it so idealistic as to be devoid of realism. Finally, it cannot be said that Shaftesbury ever showed any sign of complacency or a soothed conscience – rather, he was always impelled to continue his exertions on the principle that, the more he did, the more he saw to do. He did, indeed, hope to assist his social class by his efforts, and his sympathies were unashamedly Conservative, if of a distinctive kind. In political, as in religious and ecclesiastical – and indeed most other – terms Shaftesbury defies strict definition. His independent views meant that he was no more a 'Conservative of Conservatives' than he was an 'Evangelical of Evangelicals'. He saw the political and social role of the aristocracy to be wedded to the ideals of service, duty and responsibility,[32] but it would be absurd to suggest that he urged these ideals *merely* to prop up his own order. It would, moreover, surely be strange if Shaftesbury's political and social affiliations had been other than they were. As, indeed, with his inner problems of personality and temperament, so too with his social background: the wonder is that he was not imprisoned by it and that he moved outside it as far as he did.

Many descriptions have been applied to Shaftesbury. The writer of an obituary in *The Morning Post* called him 'the greatest Christian philanthropist of our time';[33] a historian has suggested that he became the social conscience of England.[34] Such descriptions may well be argued for and justified. Shaftesbury occupied a remarkable position in Victorian England. Claims such as these, however, have their dangers. They may lead to an exaggeration of the contribution which any one person *can* make, even in a long life. Social amelioration in Victorian England was assisted by many persons of much lesser eminence than Shaftesbury, as, indeed, he himself readily acknowledged, and also by men and women of persuasions different from those which he held and who favoured different methods. The three texts which have been considered have the merit that they emanate from the man himself. One last statement of his views – once more attributable to Shaftesbury – is also illuminating. The occasion was a speech in Glasgow in October, 1874, to a Social Science Congress. Shaftesbury dealt with various social matters, but ended on a note of advice:

> Pray and labour [he urged] that by the grace of God, when the last hour shall have arrived for you to lay your head upon the pillow, each one of you may be enabled to say, in gratitude and in joy: 'I have done my duty in that state of life to which it has pleased God to call me.'[35]

It was a statement illustrative of Shaftesbury's profound belief in the Divine ordering of human affairs: an ordering which set men in a 'state of life'. But it was also one which stressed the need for 'duty in that state of life'. Shaftesbury laid the obligation on himself and took his own advice to heart. Dutiful service to God and to man: this was the daunting and demanding task which he set himself and which, driven by unwearying dedication, he faithfully discharged.

NOTES

1. Hodder, III, 516–20.
2. ibid., 525–8.
3. Quoted in Hammonds, p. 288.
4. The first text comes from 1st Corinthians, IV, 7: the second from 1st Corinthians, X, 12.
5. The text comes from The Book of Revelation, XXII, 20.
6. N.R.A., Shaftesbury (Broadlands) MSS, SHA/FH/5-6.
7. C. Woodham Smith, *Florence Nightingale, 1820–1910* (1956), p. 589.
8. A. Storr, *Human Aggression* (1968), p. 78.
9. O. Ransford, *David Livingstone. The Dark Interior* (1978), pp. 2–4.
10. N.R.A., Shaftesbury (Broadlands) MSS, SHA/PD/8, 28 Apr., 1868.
11. Huntington Library MSS, CB 129-361, 14 Apr., 1880.
12. Hammonds, p. 261.
13. *The Times,* 6 Dec., 1872.
14. C. Whibley, *Lord John Manners and His Friends* (2 Vols, 1925), I, 162–5. See also Hammonds, p. 123.
15. I am grateful to Dr A. J. Weir of the Department of Psychology at Glasgow University for a helpful discussion on this matter.
16. Battiscombe, p. 333.
17. O. Ransford, op. cit., p. 3.
18. Add. MSS, 44, 773 f. 13. See also Hammonds, pp. 277–88 for a full consideration of this subject.
19. Hodder, I, vi, viii.
20. ibid., x.
21. ibid., viii.
22. 'Random Reflections of Exeter Hall in 1834–7 by One of the Protestant Party' (1838) (Quoted by F. E. Hugget, *What they've said about ... Nineteenth Century Reformers,* Oxford 1971, p. 61).

23. Supplement to *The Record*, 2 Oct., 1881.
24. G. W. E. Russell, op. cit., pp. 31-2.
25. C. Binfield, op. cit., p. 253.
26. Supplement to *The Record*, 2 Oct., 1885. G. W. E. Russell (op. cit., p. 32) wrote that when Shaftesbury was in the company of close friends, the 'sombre dignity of his conversation was constantly enlivened by flashes of a genuine humour, which relieved, by the force of vivid contrast, the habitual austerity of his demeanour.' Sir George Burns stated that, when Shaftesbury made his annual visit to Wemyss Bay, 'it was proverbial that wherever the ripple of laughter was to be heard, and the most fun was going on, there Lord Shaftesbury was invariably to be found' (Quoted in E. Hodder: *The Seventh Earl of Shaftesbury K.G. as Social Reformer* (1897) p. 9).
27. S. H. Oldfield, *Some Records of the Later Life of Harriet, Countess Granville* (1901), p. 250.
28. N.R.A., Shaftesbury (Broadlands) MSS, SHA/PD/8, 24 June, 1868. See also G. W. E. Russell, op. cit., p. 22.
29. J. R. Vincent (ed.) op. cit., p. 118-19.
30. N.R.A. Shaftesbury (Broadlands) MSS, SHA/PD/8, 20 Aug., 1868.
31. *Hodder*, I, ix.
32. See D. Spring, 'Aristocracy, Social Structure and Religion in the Early Victorian Period' (*Victorian Studies*, VI, 1963, 270-71).
33. *The Morning Post*, 2 Oct., 1885.
34. C. Binfield, op. cit., p. 246.
35. N.R.A., Shaftesbury (Broadlands) MSS, SHA/MIS/40.

Bibliography

MANUSCRIPT SOURCES

APSLEY HOUSE, LONDON
 Wellington MSS.
 (Note: these MSS were consulted at Apsley House: they are at present at Stratfield Saye House, Reading)

THE BODLEIAN LIBRARY, OXFORD (Department of Western MSS)
 Clarendon MSS
 Graham MSS (on microfilm)
 MSS Eng. Lett.
 Wilberforce MSS

THE BRITISH LIBRARY
 Additional MSS 35,185; 37,184; 37,772; 56,368
 Aberdeen MSS (Additional MSS 43,252; 43,253)
 Gladstone MSS (Additional MSS 44,200; 44,300; 44,773)
 Peel MSS (Additional MSS 40,398; 40,400; 40,401; 40,407; 40,416; 40,425-7; 40,432; 40,443; 40,450; 40,483; 40,511; 40,512; 40,517; 40,616; 40,617)

THE BRITISH LIBRARY OF POLITICAL AND ECONOMIC SCIENCE
 Hughenden MSS R (Microfilms) Film 131

CALIFORNIA, UNIVERSITY OF, LOS ANGELES (Research Library; Department of Special Collections)
 Richard Cobden MSS (Collection 1040)

CARLISLE, THE RECORD OFFICE
 Lonsdale MSS

CASTLE HOWARD ARCHIVES
Carlisle MSS

DUKE UNIVERSITY, DURHAM, NORTH CAROLINA (William R. Perkins Library, Manuscripts Department)
John Easthope MSS
Malet Family MSS

DURHAM, UNIVERSITY OF (Department of Palaeography and Diplomatic)
3rd Earl Grey MSS
4th Earl Grey MSS
   (Pamphlet Collection also consulted)

The HUNTINGTON LIBRARY, SAN MARINO, CALIFORNIA
Huntington Library MSS (CB 129–361
                        H.M. 23367
                        Forster Collection
                        STG Box 118 and 129)

IMPERIAL COLLEGE OF SCIENCE AND TECHNOLOGY
Playfair MSS

INDIA OFFICE LIBRARY AND RECORDS
India Office Records (F/2/10 Board of Control Letter Book 1829–33, Mountstuart Elphinstone Collection, MSS Eur. F. 88)

KEELE, UNIVERSITY OF
Sneyd MSS

LAMBETH PALACE LIBRARY, LONDON
Benson MSS
Blomfield Letter Book
Selborne MSS
Tait MSS

LORD'S DAY OBSERVANCE SOCIETY, OFFICE OF (London)
Minutes of the Lord's Day Observance Society
Minutes of Working Men's Lord's Day Rest Association

NATIONAL REGISTER OF ARCHIVES, LONDON
Palmerston (Broadlands) MSS (GC/SH/)
Shaftesbury (Broadlands) MSS (SHA/PC, SHA/PD, SHA/EST, SHA/FH, SHA/MIS)
Wellington MSS

THE NEW YORK PUBLIC LIBRARY
Astor, Lennox and Tilden Foundations, Henry W. and Albert A. Berg Collection

NOTTINGHAM, UNIVERSITY OF
Portland MSS

THE PUBLIC RECORD OFFICE, LONDON
Cairns MSS (P.R.O. 30/51/8)
Ellenborough MSS (P.R.O. 30/12/12)
Russell MSS (P.R.O. 30/22)
Chancery Records P.R.O. C/16/217 L 134, P.R.O. C/16/242 W 176
Home Office Papers. H.O. 44–51
Ministry of Health Papers M.H. 5/2, 5/4, 50/1–24, 51/236

ST GILES'S HOUSE, SHAFTESBURY ESTATES, DORSET
Shaftesbury MSS

TEXAS, UNIVERSITY OF at AUSTIN (Humanities Research Centre)
Anthony Ashley Cooper/Shaftesbury Collection
John Ruskin MSS

UNIVERSITY COLLEGE LONDON (The Library)
Brougham MSS
Chadwick MSS

WINCHESTER, HAMPSHIRE RECORD OFFICE
Shaftesbury (Broadlands) MSS (27M60)

WORCESTER, THE RECORD OFFICE
Cobham Archives
(Note: these have now been withdrawn from the Record Office).

PRINTED SOURCES

(1) PARLIAMENTARY PAPERS
P.P. 1833   XX   (Factories, Employment of Children)
P.P. 1843   XIII   (Children's Employment, Trades and Manufactures)
P.P. 1847   XXXIII (Report of Commissioners in Lunacy to the Lord Chancellor)
P.P. 1859   III   (Lunatics and Lunatic Asylums)
P.P. 1868–9 XIII   (Agriculture, Children's etc Employment)
P.P. 1877   XIII   (Lunacy Law)
P.P. 1884–5 XXX   (Housing of the Working Classes)

(2) OTHER PARLIAMENTARY PUBLICATIONS
The Dorset Poll Book, October, 1831
Hansard, *Parliamentary Debates*, New Series and 3rd Series
Journal of the House of Commons

(3) NEWSPAPERS, PERIODICALS AND MAGAZINES, WORKS OF REFERENCE

(i) Newspapers
The Bath and Cheltenham Gazette
The Daily News

The Dorset County Chronicle and Somersetshire Gazette
Jackson's Oxford Journal
The League
The Leeds Intelligencer
The Manchester Courier and Lancashire General Advertiser
The Manchester Examiner and Times
The Manchester Guardian
The Morning Post
The Record
The Ten Hours Advocate
The Times

(ii) Periodicals and Magazines
The Annual Register
The Charity Record and Philanthropic News
The Journal of Mental Science
The Nineteenth Century
The Quarterly Review
The Ragged School Union Magazine
The Saturday Review

(iii) Works of Reference
Burke's *Genealogical and Heraldic History of the Peerage, Baronetage and Knightage*

(4) ARTICLES IN LEARNED REVIEWS ETC
Allen, P. R., 'F. D. Maurice and J. M. Ludlow: A Reassessment of the Leaders of Christian Socialism' (*Victorian Studies*, XI, No 4, 461).
Gash, N., 'Ashley and the Conservative Party in 1842' (*The English Historical Review*, LIII, 679).
Greaves, R. W., 'The Jerusalem Bishopric, 1841' (*The English Historical Review*, LXIV, 330).

Harrison, B., 'Philanthropy and the Victorians' (*Victorian Studies*, IX, No 4, 353).
Ozer, M. N., 'The British Vivisection Controversy' (*The Bulletin of the History of Medicine*, XL, 158).
Spring, D., 'Aristocracy, Social Structure, and Religion in the Early Victorian Period' (*Victorian Studies*, VI, No 3, 263).
Ward, J. T., 'A Lost Opportunity in Education: 1843' (*Researches and Studies*, No 20, Oct., 1959).
Ward, J. T. and Treble, J. H., 'Religion and Education in 1843. Reaction to the "Factory Education Bill"' (*The Journal of Ecclesiastical History*, XX, 79).

(5) THESES

Bentley, A., 'The Transformation of the Evangelical Party in the Church of England in the late Nineteenth Century' (Ph.D., Durham, 1971).
Ellis, G. M., 'The Evangelicals and the Sunday Question, 1830–1860. Organised Sabbatarianism as an Aspect of the Evangelical Movement' (Ph.D., Harvard, 1952).
Hardman, B. E., 'The Evangelical Party in the Church of England, 1855–1865' (Ph.D., Cambridge, 1963).
Orchard, S. C., 'English Evangelical Eschatology, 1790–1850' (Ph.D., Cambridge, 1968).

(6) SEPARATE WORKS (Select List)

Airlie, Mabel, Countess of, *Lady Palmerston and Her Times* (1922).
Arnstein, W. L., *The Bradlaugh Case* (Oxford, 1965).
Ashley, E., *The Life and Correspondence of Henry John Temple, Viscount Palmerston* (2 vols, 1879).
Aspinall, A. (ed.), *The Correspondence of Charles Arbuthnot* (Camden, 3rd ser., LXV, 1941).
Aspinall, A., *Politics and the Press, 1780–1850* (1949).
Aspinall, A. (ed.), *Three Early Nineteenth Century Diaries* (1952).
Bamford, F. and Wellington, Duke of (eds.), *The Journal of Mrs Arbuthnot, 1820–1832* (2 vols, 1950).
Barnardo, Mrs and Marchant, J., *Memoirs of the late Dr Barnardo* (1907).
Basset, A. Tilney (ed.), *Gladstone to His Wife* (1936).
Battiscombe, G., *Shaftesbury. A Biography of the Seventh Earl 1801–1885* (1974).
Bearce, G. D., *British Attitudes towards India, 1784–1858* (Oxford, 1961).
Benson, A. C., and Esher, Viscount, *The Letters of Queen Victoria, 1837–1861* (3 vols, 1907).
Bentley, J., *Ritualism and Politics in Victorian Britain. The Attempt to Legislate for Belief* (Oxford, 1978).
Best, G. F. A., *Shaftesbury* (1964).

Best, G. F. A., *Temporal Pillars: Queen Anne's Bounty, The Ecclesiastical Commissioners and the Church of England* (Cambridge, 1964).
Bickersteth, E., *A Practical Guide to the Prophecies* (4th ed., 1835).
Binfield, C., *George Williams and the Y.M.C.A. A Study in Victorian social attitudes* (1973).
Blake, R., *The Conservative Party from Peel to Churchill* (1970).
Boyson, R., *The Ashworth Cotton Enterprise. The Rise and Fall of a Family Firm, 1818–1880* (Oxford, 1970).
Bradley, I., *The Call to Seriousness. The Evangelical Impact on the Victorians* (1976).
Bready, J. Wesley, *Lord Shaftesbury and Social-Industrial Progress* (1926).
Bridges, J., *Memoir of Sir Andrew Agnew of Lochnaw, Bart.* (Edinburgh, 1849).
Brock, M., *The Great Reform Act* (1973).
Brose, O. J., *Frederick Denison Maurice* (Ohio, 1971).
Bunsen, F., *Memoir of Baron Bunsen* (2 vols, 1886).
Carnall, G., *Robert Southey and His Age. The Development of a Conservative Mind* (Oxford, 1960).
Chadwick, O., *The Victorian Church* (2 vols, 1966, 1970).
Checkland, O., *Philanthropy in Victorian Scotland: Social Welfare and the Voluntary Principle* (Edinburgh, 1980).
Cowling, M., *1867: Disraeli, Gladstone and Revolution* (1967).
Crowther, M. A., *Church Embattled: Religious Controversy in Mid-Victorian England* (1970).
Curry, K. (ed.), *New Letters of Robert Southey* (Columbia U.P., 2 vols, 1965).
Douglas, Sir George and Ramsay, Sir George Dalhousie (eds.), *The Panmure Papers* (2 vols, 1908).
Driver, C., *Tory Radical. The Life of Richard Oastler* (New York, 1946).
Edsall, N. C., *The Anti-Poor Law Movement, 1834–1844* (Manchester, 1971).
Esher, Viscount, *The Girlhood of Queen Victoria. A Selection of Her Majesty's Diaries between the years 1832 and 1840* (2 vols, 1912).
Finer, S. E., *The Life and Times of Sir Edwin Chadwick* (1952).
Fitzmaurice, Lord Edmond, *The Life of Lord Granville, 1815–1891* (2 vols, 1905).
Gash, N., *Aristocracy and People. Britain 1815–1865* (1979).
Gash, N., *Sir Robert Peel. The Life of Sir Robert Peel after 1830* (1972).
Gauldie, E., *Cruel Habitations. A History of Working-Class Housing, 1780–1918* (1974).
Gill, J. C., *The Ten Hours Parson* (1959).
Gill, J. C., *Parson Bull of Byerley* (1963).
Haley, K. H. D., *The First Earl of Shaftesbury* (Oxford, 1968).
Hammond, J. L. and B., *Lord Shaftesbury* (fourth ed. 1936, reprinted 1969).

Hare, A. J. C., *The Story of Two Noble Lives. Being Memorials of Charlotte, Countess of Canning and Louisa, Marshioness of Waterford* (3 vols, 1893).
Harrison, J. F. C., *The Second Coming. Popular Millenarianism, 1780–1850* (1979).
Harrison, R., *Before the Socialists. Studies in Labour and Politics, 1861 to 1881* (1965).
Hennell, M., *John Venn and the Clapham Sect* (1958).
Hewitt, M., *Wives and Mothers in Victorian Industry* (1958).
Hodder, E., *The Life and Work of the Seventh Earl of Shaftesbury, K.G.* (3 vols, 1887).
Hodder, E., *The Seventh Earl of Shaftesbury K.G. as Social Reformer* (1897).
Hollis, P. (ed.), *Pressure from Without in Early Victorian England* (1974).
Hutchins, B. L. and Harrison, A., *A History of Factory Legislation* (1903).
Ilchester, The Earl of (ed.), *The Journal of the Hon. Henry Edward Fox 1818–1830* (1923).
Ilchester, The Earl of (ed.), *Elizabeth, Lady Holland to her Son, 1821–1845* (1946).
Jones, K., *Mental Health and Social Policy, 1845–1959* (1960).
Kent, J., *Holding the Fort. Studies in Victorian Revivalism* (1978).
Kerr, B., *Bound to the Soil. A Social History of Dorset, 1750–1918* (1969).
Kirby, R. G. and Musson, A. E., *The Voice of the People. John Doherty, 1798–1854. Trade Unionist, radical and factory reformer* (Manchester, 1975).
Kitson Clark, G., *Peel and the Conservative Party* (2nd ed., 1964).
Lever, T., *The Letters of Lady Palmerston* (1957).
Leveson-Gower, The Hon. F. (ed.), *Letters of Harriet, Countess Granville, 1810–1845* (2nd ed., 1894).
Lewis, Lady Theresa (ed.), *Extracts of the Journal and Correspondence of Miss Berry from the year 1783–1852* (3 vols, 1865).
Lewis, R. A., *Edwin Chadwick and the Public Health Movement, 1832–1854* (1952).
Liddon, H. P., *The Life of Edward Bouverie Pusey* (4 vols, 1894).
MacDonagh, O., *Early Victorian Government, 1830–1870* (1977).
Marsh, P. T., *The Victorian Church in Decline. Archbishop Tait and the Church of England, 1868–1882* (1969).
Maxwell, The Rt. Hon. Sir Herbert (ed.), *The Creevey Papers. A Selection from the Correspondence and Diaries of the late Thomas Creevey, M.P., 1768–1838* (2 vols, 1904).
Meacham, S., *Lord Bishop. The Life of Samuel Wilberforce, 1805–1873* (Cambridge, Mass., 1970).
Mowat, C. L., *The Charity Organisation Society, 1869–1913* (1961).
Mozley, A. (ed.), *Letters and Correspondence of John Henry Newman* (2 vols, 1891).
Newman, J. H., *Apologia Pro Vita Sua* (1864).
Norman, E. R., *Anti-Catholicism in Victorian England* (1968).
Oldfield, S. H., *Some Records of the Later Life of Harriet, Countess Granville* (1901).

Olivier, W. H., *Prophets and Millenialists: the Uses of Biblical Prophecy in England from the 1790s to the 1840s* (Oxford, 1979).

Orton, D., *Made of Gold. A biography of Angela Burdett Coutts* (1980).

Owen, D., *English Philanthropy, 1660-1960* (Cambridge, Mass., 1965).

Parry-Jones, W. Ll., *The Trade in Lunacy. A Study of Private Madhouses in England in the Eighteenth and Nineteenth Centuries* (1972).

Philbin, J. Holladay, *Parliamentary Representation 1832. England and Wales* (New Haven, 1965).

Prest, J., *Lord John Russell* (1972).

Quennell, P. (ed.), *The Private Letters of Princess Lieven to Prince Metternich, 1820-1826* (1937).

Ransford, O., *David Livingstone. The Dark Interior* (1978).

Robbins, K., *John Bright* (1979).

Roberts, D., *Paternalism in Early Victorian England* (1979).

Robson, R. (ed.), *Ideas and Institutions of Victorian Britain* (1967).

Rosselli, J., *Lord William Bentinck. The Making of a Liberal Imperialist, 1774-1839* (1974).

Royle, E., *Victorian Infidels* (Manchester, 1974).

Russell, G. W. E., *Collections and Recollections* (1898, new ed. 1903).

Smith, C. Woodham, *Florence Nightingale, 1820-1910* (1956).

Smith, F. B., *The Making of the Second Reform Bill* (Cambridge, 1966).

Smith, P., *Disraelian Conservatism and Social Reform* (1967).

Southgate, D., *The Most English Minister. The Policies and Politics of Palmerston* (1966).

Speeches of the Earl of Shaftesbury, K.G. Upon Subjects Having Relation Chiefly to the Claims and Interests of the Labouring Class (1868, reprinted by Irish University Press, Shannon, Ireland, 1971).

Stedman Jones, G., *Outcast London. A Study in the Relationship between Classes in Victorian Society* (Oxford, 1971).

Stewart, R., *The Foundation of the Conservative Party, 1830-1867* (1978).

Storr, Anthony, *Human Aggression* (1968).

Strachey, L. and Fulford, R. (eds.), *The Greville Memoirs, 1814-60* (7 vols, 1938).

Sudley, Lord (ed.), *The Lieven-Palmerston Correspondence, 1832-1856* (1943).

Swartz, H. M., and Swartz, M. (eds.), *Disraeli's Reminiscences* (1975).

Symondson, A. (ed.), *The Victorian Crisis of Faith* (1970).

Thomas, M. W., *The Early Factory Legislation* (Leigh-on-Sea, 1948).

Thompson, F. M. L., *English Landed Society in the Nineteenth Century* (1963).

Tibawi, A. L., *British Interests in Palestine, 1800-1901. A Study of Religious and Educational Enterprise* (Oxford, 1961).

Tuke, D. H., *Chapters in the History of the Insane in the British Isles* (1882).

BIBLIOGRAPHY 619

Vincent, J. R. (ed.), *Disraeli, Derby and the Conservative Party. The Political Journals of Lord Stanley, 1849–1869* (1978).
Wagner, G., *Barnardo* (1979).
Ward, J. T., *The Factory Movement, 1830–1855* (1962).
Ward, J. T. (ed.), *The Factory System* (Newton Abbot, 2 vols, 1970).
Webster, Sir C., *The Foreign Policy of Palmerston, 1830–1841. Britain, the Liberal Movement and the Eastern Question* (2 vols, 1951).
Wellington, The Seventh Duke of (ed.), *Wellington and his Friends: Letters of the First Duke* (1965).
Whibley, C., *Lord John Manners and His Friends* (2 vols, 1925).
Wymer, N., *Father of Nobody's Children* (1954).
Wyndham, The Hon. Mrs Hugh (ed.), *Correspondence of Sarah Spencer, Lady Lyttelton, 1787–1870* (1912).
Ziegler, P., *Melbourne* (1976).

Index

Abbotsford, 17
Abercromby, James, 100
Aberdeen Coalition (1852-5), 337, 349, 364, 366, 439
Aberdeen, 4th Earl, 155, 156, 159, 209, 337, 338, 441, 442
Aberdeen, 7th Earl, 577
Aberystwyth, 32
Abyssinia, 159
Achnacarry, 264
Acrobatics, employment of children in, 479, 587
Additional Curates Society, 117
Admiralty, Board of, 97, 98, 100, 105
Afghanistan, 173, 174, 207, 561, 562, 571
Agnew, Sir Andrew, 76, 110
Agricultural gangs, 408, 478-9
Agriculture, employment of women and children in, 198, 499
Ainsworth, Peter, 185
Albert, Prince, 140, 141, 146, 148, 149, 158, 185, 251, 264, 272, 273, 309, 342
Alexander, Bishop Michael S., 154, 155, 156, 157, 159, 160, 162, 169 n. 53, 307
Alford, Dean Henry, 382
Alleged Lunatics' Friend Society, 351
Alnwick Castle, 128
Althorp, Viscount (later 3rd Earl Spencer), 60, 77, 78, 80, 81, 83, 85, 97
America, 48, 343, 344, 345, 460
American Civil War, 423, 432, 454, 458-9, 544
Anson, George, 146
Anti-Corn Law League, 142, 176, 177, 180, 195, 198, 201, 213, 225, 241, 300

Anti-Poor Law Movement, 125, 126, 134 n. 92
Apsley House, 61
Arbuthnot, Charles, 40, 45, 46, 53 n. 20
Arbuthnot, Harriet, 30, 32, 33, 40, 45, 53 n. 20, 55 n. 94, 61, 62, 63, 68
Arethusa, 545, 585
Argyll, Duchess of, 564
Arrow, 432, 445, 446, 447
Ashley, Lord: see Shaftesbury, Anthony Ashley Cooper, 7th Earl*
Ashley, Anthony (eldest son, later 8th Earl of Shaftesbury), 93, 94, 95, 130, 157, 158, 197, 224, 257, 346, 502, 565, 578; Shaftesbury's anxieties over, 253-4, 323, 324, 335, 425-6, 427, 428, 441, 500-1, 506-7, 605-6; joins navy, 323; elected for Hull (1857), 426, for Cricklade (1859), 436 n. 152, 501; marriage of (1857), 426
Ashley, Anthony (grandson, later 9th Earl of Shaftesbury), 500, 501
Ashley, Cecil (sixth son), 323, 425, 504, 505, 507, 565
Ashley, Constance (third daughter), 253, 323, 336, 425, 578; ill health of, 425, 504, 505, 506, 543; death of (1871), 505-6
Ashley, Edith (Hilda: fourth daughter), 268 n. 83, 501, 507
Ashley, Evelyn (fourth son), 130, 157, 319, 336, 364, 378, 425, 426, 429, 447, 448, 507, 578, 583; elected for Poole (1874), 564, 569 n. 161, for Isle of

622 THE SEVENTH EARL OF SHAFTESBURY, 1801–1885

Wight (1880), 569 n. 161; marriage of (1866), 502
Ashley, Fanny (daughter-in-law, wife of Lionel q.v.), 502, 564
Ashley, Francis (second son), 94, 130, 157, 158, 197, 336, 506, 507; death of (1849), 319, 323–4, 424
Ashley, Harriet (daughter-in-law, wife of Anthony), 426, 427, 500, 501, 502, 506, 565, 578
Ashley, Lionel (fifth son), 130, 336, 425, 507, 509, 564; marriage of (1868), 502
Ashley, Margaret (Poppy, granddaughter), 501, 507, 565
Ashley, Mary (second daughter), 196, 323, 506; ill health of, 424, 425, 427, 504; death of (1861), 424
Ashley, Maurice (third son), 130, 157, 506; ill health of, 254, 323, 335; death of (1855), 424
Ashley, Sybella (Sissy, daughter-in-law, wife of Evelyn), 502, 578
Ashley, Victoria (first daughter), 130, 323, 336, 425, 500, 501, 503, 506, 507, 594; marriage of (1873), 506
Ashley, Wilfred (grandson), 507
Ashley Cooper, Caroline (sister), 13, 16, 20, 25 n. 74, 91, 502; marriage of (1831), 20; death of (1869), 474, 503
Ashley Cooper, Charlotte (sister), 13, 14, 128, 275, 577; marriage of (1824), 20, 21, 25 n. 74
Ashley Cooper, Francis (brother), 13, 21, 23 n. 10; death of (1825), 20, 25 n. 71
Ashley Cooper, Harriet (sister), 13, 16, 20, 25 n. 74, 42; marriage of (1830), 20, 25 n. 74; death of (1868), 503
Ashley Cooper, Henry (brother), 13, 20, 23 n. 10, 29, 87 n. 35, 106 n. 3; death of (1858), 424
Ashley Cooper, John (brother), 13, 23 n. 10; death of (1867), 503
Ashley Cooper, Lionel (brother), 13, 20, 23 n. 10, 106 n. 3
Ashley Cooper, William (brother), 13, 15, 16, 23 n. 10, 27, 30, 33, 42, 54 n. 57; death of (1877), 564
Ashton-under-Lyme, 119, 144, 267 n. 47
Ashworth, Henry, 217
Ashworth, Messrs, 213, 234 n. 35
Athanasian Creed, 525

Athenian, 346
Austin, Alfred, 198, 200
Australia, 275; Southern, 274
Austria, 21, 444, 454, 455, 456, 462, 493, 494
Austro-Prussian War (1866), 493
Avesani, G. F., 457, 458
Azeglio, Emanuele d', 455, 456
Azeglio, Massimo d', 456

Babbage, Charles, 32, 53 n. 49
Balaclava, battle of, 441, 442
Balliol College, Oxford, 516
Ballot, 362; Act (1872), 476
Bankes, George, 200, 239, 296, 305 n. 142
Bankes, Henry, 60, 61, 63, 87 n. 31
Bankes, William, 61, 68, 71
Barclay, Bishop Joseph, 583
Baring, Bishop Charles, 380, 382, 400
Barmouth, 33
Barnardo, Thomas, 544, 545, 557
Bath, 260, 261, 262, 264
Bathurst, Earl, 31
Bathurst, Lady Georgina, 61, 87 n. 29
Battiscombe, Mrs Georgina, 255, 256, 603, 604
Baxter, David, 376
Beaconsfield, Earl, see: Disraeli, Benjamin
Beales, Edward, 460
Beaufort, Duchess of, 283, 324
Beaumont, Lord, 350
Bedchamber Incident (1839), 137–8, 139, 140
Bengal, 39, 449
Benson, Archbishop Edward W., 583, 584
Bentinck, Lord William, 38, 39, 40, 41, 54 n. 73
Berlin, 271; Treaty of (1878), 559
Bethlem Hospital, 415
Biblical Criticism, 364, 365, 377–80, 381, 386, 387, 394, 395, 398, 400, 494, 515, 516, 517, 526, 527, 562, 606–7; translation, 395, 517
Bickersteth, Revd Edward, 104, 115, 116, 155, 164, 246, 320
Bickersteth, Bishop Robert, 380, 381, 403 n. 53, 527
Binney, Revd Thomas, 563
Bismarck, Prince von, 494
Blandford, 200, 239
Blandford, Lord, 27

INDEX 623

Blenheim, 14
Blomfield, Bishop Charles, 303 n. 57
Bologna, 94, 95
Bolton, 144, 213, 257, 260, 267 n. 47
Bombay, 38, 39, 453, 572
Bonham, F. R., 141, 165, 166, 167, 177, 178, 179, 181, 195, 217, 218, 226, 244, 257, 263
Bonney, Revd T. G., 555, 562
Booth, William, 397, 582
Bournemouth, 581
Bowring, Sir John, 445
Bradford, 72, 76, 81, 121, 147, 233, 267 n. 47, 420, 484
Bradlaugh, Charles, 574
Brasenose College, Oxford, 162, 167
Brewer, John, 164
Brewster, George, 549
Brickfields, children employed in, 477-8
Bridport, 517
Bright, John, 210, 212, 221, 248, 273, 362, 363, 469, 574
Brighton, 33, 539
Bristol, 118
British Association for Advancement of Science, 517
British and Foreign Bible Schools Society, 118, 386, 387
British and Foreign Bible Society, 307, 308, 340, 343, 449, 529-30, 531, 556, 593
British Medical Association, 547
Broadlands, 131, 149, 225, 226
Broadmoor, 417
Brocket Hall, 422
Brodrick, Revd William, 381, 383
Brougham, Henry P. (later Lord Brougham and Vaux), 31, 63, 76, 237 n. 122, 260
Browne, Bishop Edward, 385, 403-4 n. 85
Buccleuch, Duke of, 185, 203 n. 61
Buckingham, Duke of, 482
Buckland, Professor William, 165, 382
Buddle, John, 184, 186
Bulgarian atrocities, 556, 566
Bull, Revd G., 72, 73, 74, 120, 121
Bunsen, Baron Christian von, 114, 115, 155, 156, 157, 160, 161, 162, 424
Burdett Coutts, Baroness, 545
Burial Laws, 581
Burnet, Robert, 429, 430, 437 n. 182

Burns, George, 546, 564, 610 n. 26
Burns, John, 506, 546, 564
Butler, George, 17
Butler, Henry, 17

Cairns, Earl, 535, 536, 538, 575, 581
Calcraft, John, 60, 86 n. 15
Calcutta, 450-2; Bishop and Bishopric of, 38, 41
Calico Printworks Act (1845), 227-8, 232, 233, 407
Cambridge, 549; Duchess of, 141; University of, 380, 403 n. 85, 505, 516
Cambridgeshire, 64
Camden Society, 518
Canada, 545
Cannes, 504
Canning, Earl, 449, 450
Canning, George, 28, 29, 33; Mrs, 28, 29
Canning, Lady Charlotte, 450-3
Canterbury, Archbishop of: see Benson, Edward W.; Howley, William; Longley, Charles; Sumner, John; Tait, Archibald C.; Dean and Deanery of, 382, 515
Canton, 445
Cardwell, Edward, 261
Carlisle, 128; Bishop and Bishopric of, 380, 389; Dean and Deanery of, 380, 381
Carlisle, George Howard, 6th Earl, 23 n. 11
Carlisle, George Howard, 7th Earl (until 1848, Morpeth, Lord), 13, 15, 16, 17, 18, 21, 23 n. 11, n. 12, 73, 74, 276, 277, 278, 285, 286, 287, 288, 289, 291, 303 n. 40, n. 44, n. 51, 373
Carlisle, Lady Georgiana (until 1825, Morpeth, Lady Georgiana, mother of the above), 13, 17, 18, 19, 20, 21, 22, 23 n. 12, 27, 46, 48, 52 n. 1
Carlsbad, 197
Carlton Club, 60, 177, 272, 302 n. 10
Carnarvon, Earl, 547
Carpenter, Dr Lant, 118
Castle Howard, 13, 15, 19, 128
Castle Wemyss, 506, 556, 564, 565
Catholic Association, 57
Catholic Emancipation (1829), 28, 29, 57, 263, 319
Cavendish, Lady, 42

Cavendish, Lord Frederick, 576
Cavour, Count, 342, 457
Cawnpore, 447
Census (Church, 1851), 364
Chadwick, Edwin, 80, 83, 250, 251, 252, 277, 278, 279, 280, 281, 282, 284, 285, 286, 288, 289, 290, 291, 292, 326, 332, 334, 336, 347, 349, 352, 353, 354, 356, 357, 358, 359, 360, 361, 480
Chamberlain, Joseph, 574
Chambers, Robert, 396
Charity Organisation Society, 544, 551
Chartism, 125–6, 176, 188, 195, 271–2, 273, 325
Chatsworth, 128, 129
Chelsea, 393
Cheltenham, 310
Cheshire, 178
Chester, 384
Chichester, 167
Chichester, 483, 545, 585
Children's Employment Commission (1840), 125, 127, 182, 189–90, 227, 407; (1861), 407, 408, 477, 478
Chillingworth Castle, 128
Chimney Sweeps, regulation of: Acts (1834) 124; (1840) 124, 350, 408; (1855) 350–1; (1863) 408, 410; (1864) 408–9, 410; (1875) 549; Bills (1851) 350; (1853 and 1854) 350–1; (1855) 351
China, 174, 175, 343, 432, 445, 446, 447, 460
Chiswick, Manor House, School at, 13, 16, 17
Christ Church, Oxford, 12, 13, 70
Christian Blind Relief Society, 531
Christian Remembrancer, 365
Christian Socialism, 321, 326, 603
Christian Vernacular Education Society, 453
Church Association, 519, 524, 526, 527, 528, 531, 533, 537, 538
Church of England, 111, 116–17, 118, 119, 128, 153, 154, 159, 162, 166, 167, 191, 192, 193, 252, 286, 313, 318, 343, 364, 376, 387, 397, 398, 471, 487, 488, 513, 521, 523, 529, 532, 533, 557, 559; Broad Church Party in, 377, 381, 382, 399, 400, 401, 515, 525, 557; Evangelical Party in, 109–19, 153–68, 307–21, 339–44, 364–5, 373–401, 515–39, 554–6, 580–4, 606–7, 608; High Church Party in, 117, 156, 157, 160, 161, 162, 163, 164, 165, 166–7, 307, 316–9, 340, 341, 364–5, 376, 378, 398, 399, 400, 401, 515, 518, 524, 525, 528, 538, 583, 607
Church of England Metropolitan Training Institution, 310
Church Missionary Society, 104, 154, 159, 160, 161, 527
Church Pastoral Aid Society, 111, 112, 116, 117, 151 n. 45, 153, 154, 160, 192, 262, 310, 311, 312, 387, 398, 530, 531, 556, 563
Church of Scotland, 128, 129, 557
Clancarty, Lord, 350–1
Clapham Sect, 49
Clarendon, Earl, 439, 440, 441, 444, 448, 449, 454, 455, 464 n. 85
Clarkson, Thomas, 84
Clay, Sir William, 354
Clerical Education Aid Fund, 310
Clerical and Lay Union, 532
Climbing Boys' Society, 350
Cobbe, Frances Power, 547, 564, 567 n. 30, 573, 577, 585, 586, 587, 601
Cobbett, J. M., 296, 297
Cobden, Richard, 211, 227, 273, 362, 363
Cockermouth, 89 n. 102
Colenso, Bishop John, 377, 387
Cologne, Archbishop of, 116
Colonial Church Society, 154
Colonial Office, 272, 274
Confessional, controversy over, 341, 527, 532–6, 538
Connolly, Dr John, 473
Conservative Party, see Tory Party
Constantinople, 443, 583
Convocation, reform of, 523; revival of, 340–2
Corn Laws, 62–3, 142, 213, 214, 227, 233, 239, 240, 241, 242, 246, 247, 248, 257, 263, 276, 325, 345, 377
Corry, Montague, 469
Corry, Thomas L., 25 n. 74
Costermongers, 483, 543, 585
Cotterell, Elizabeth, 123
Cowper, Earl (father-in-law), 43, 55 n. 112, 94, 128
Cowper, Lady Emily (Minny, wife), 43, 44, 45, 46, 47, 48; marriage of (1830), 49; see also Shaftesbury, Lady Emily

Cowper, Lady Emily (mother-in-law), 43, 44, 45, 46, 47, 48, 51, 52, 55 n. 112, 91, 92, 94, 104; marriage of to Palmerston, Lord (1839), 130, 131; see also Palmerston, Lady
Cowper, Fanny (sister-in-law), 143, 464 n. 85
Cowper (-Temple), William (brother-in-law), 378–9, 381, 489, 504, 528, 555, 559
Crabbe, George, 129
Crabtree, Mark, 144, 146, 147, 149, 180, 210
Creevey, Thomas, 44
Cricklade, 436 n. 152, 501
Crimea, Sanitary Commission to, 442, 443, 444
Crimean War, 335, 361, 366, 427, 432, 439, 440, 441, 442, 443, 444, 461
Criminal Law Amendment Bill (1883–4), 587
Crockford's Club, 33, 51
Crofts, Mr, 200
Cross, Richard A., 548, 549, 550, 551, 557, 558, 573, 587, 589
Crystal Palace, 339, 392
Cumberland, Duke of, 67
Cyprus, 559, 582

Daily News, 281, 458
Dardenelles, The, 335
Darveston, 200
Darwin, Charles, 396
Davis, Revd George, 511 n. 196
Dawes, Dean Richard, 381
Deccan, 38
Defoe, Daniel, 376
de Grey, Earl, 217
Delane, John, 456, 464 n. 85
Delhi, 447, 448
Denison, Archdeacon G., 516
Denison, John E., 27, 52 n. 4
Denmark, 462
Derby, 155, 546
Derby, Earl (until 1851, Stanley, Lord), 214, 242, 272, 337, 338, 340, 341, 352, 355, 356, 363, 364, 388, 392, 421, 449, 456, 468, 469, 470, 477, 482
Derbyshire, 17
Devon, Earl, 185, 186, 187
Devonshire, Duke of, 23 n. 12

Dillon, John, 575
Dillwyn, L. L., 552, 554
Disraeli, Benjamin, 168, 337, 358, 388, 405 n. 163, 421, 456, 467, 469, 473, 477, 481, 482, 534, 538, 557, 560, 561, 562, 571, 576, 583; Shaftesbury's comments on, 470, 472, 537
Dissenters, and burial grounds, 284, 286, 288; and burial laws, 581; and education (1843), 191–3, 194, 204 n. 115, (1870) 487–9; and missionary effort, 387–8, 389–90, 398; and ragged schools, 252, 326; and Sunday labour, 314, 339; Shaftesbury on, 192–3, 252, 531, 532, 557, 581, 607
Dissenters' Chapel Act (1844), 166
Dodd, William, 212–3, 234 n. 33, 234 n. 35
Doherty, John, 85, 120, 124
Donegal, 426
Dorchester, 12, 27, 30, 58, 59, 60, 62, 87 n. 35, 332, 333, 367 n. 16
Dorchester Agricultural Protection Society, 244
Dorset, 12, 33, 34, 60, 61, 62, 63, 64, 65, 67, 68, 69, 70, 75, 86 n. 15, 89 n. 102, 91, 93, 99, 106 n. 3, 137, 142, 198, 199, 200, 211, 239, 240, 244, 245, 246, 249, 499, 500, 511 n. 196
Dorset County Chronicle, 61, 63, 68, 200, 240
Dover, 216
Driver, C. H., quoted, 300
Dryden, John, 11
Dublin, 576; Archbishop of, 383
Dudley, Earl, 30
Dunbrody, 506
Duncan, Viscount, 262, 263
Duncannon, John George, Viscount, 391
Duncannon, John William, Viscount, 60
Duncombe, Thomas, 219, 231
Dundee, 264
Dunraven, Earl, 580
Dupetit-Thouars, Admiral, 208
Durham, 203 n. 78, 382; Archdeacon of, 384; Bishopric of, 382; Cathedral, 128; County, 549; Dean of, 381
'Durham Letter', The, 316–17

Early Closing Movement, 393, 394
East India Company, 38, 39, 53 n. 22, 75, 446

Easthope, Sir John, 192, 208, 211, 240, 244, 245
Ecce Homo, 377, 387, 394, 453, 526, 527
Ecclesiastical Commission, 149, 153, 165, 168 n. 3
Ecclesiastical Courts, 521–3, 536, 537
Ecclesiastical Titles Act (1851), 318; Bill (1851), 318, 320
Edinburgh, 322, 420
'Edinburgh Letter', The, 242
Edouard, Revd A. G., 389, 391
Education (1839) 118–19; (1843) 191–3; (1870) 487–90
Egypt, 113
Ellenborough, Lord (created Earl 1844), 40, 41, 54 n. 88, 62, 63, 173, 174, 176, 207, 209, 449, 450
Ellesmere, Earl, 45, 258, 259
Elphinstone, Mount Stuart, 38
Ely, Bishopric of, 385
Emigration, 273–6, 346, 369 n. 98
Ems, 334, 336, 349, 356, 357, 359
English Church Union, 518
Epsom, 273
Eros Monument, 599
Essays and Reviews, 377, 386, 395, 400, 515, 516
Estates, Shaftesbury, 198, 327, 331–4, 338, 366 n. 4, 427–32, 497–8, 499, 512 n. 207, 565
Eton College, 20, 224–5
Evangelical Alliance, 531
Evangelical Union, 532
Evangelicalism, characteristics of, 49–50; see also Church of England, Evangelical Party in, and relevant items under Shaftesbury, 7th Earl
Exeter, Bishopric of, 516, 524; Cathedral, 527
Exeter Hall, 109, 168, 209, 211, 313, 339, 344, 389, 390, 392, 533, 546, 577, 580, 605

Factory: Acts (1831) 72, 88 n. 94; (1833) 83–4, 85, 120, 121, 122, 123, 124, 126, 133 n. 66, 188, 221; (1844) 221–2, 223, 293, 299; (1845) 228, 232–3; (1847) 259, 269 n. 125, 292, 293, 294; (1850) 300, 345; (1864) 407–8; (1867) 477; (1874) 550, 557; (1878) 550; see also 433 n. 5; Indian Factory Act (1881), 572, 594 n. 9

Bills (1832) 72, 88 n. 96; (1833: Ashley's) 77, 79, 80, 81, 82, 83, 99; (1833: Government's) 83; (1836) 120–1; (1839) 122; (1841) 123–4, 176, 178, 181, 191; (1843) 191–4; (1844) 210–21, 234 n. 25; (1845) 227–8; (1846) 248, 256; (1847) 257–9; (1850) 296–300; (1883) 587
Question (1815–33) 72–85; (1834–41) 119–24, 144–5, 146–7, 149; (1841–2) 176–82, 188–9; (1843) 188–94, 210; (1844) 210–21, 224; (1845) 227–8, 233; (1846) 248–9; (1847) 256–66; (1847–50) 292–301; (1861–4) 407–8; (1866–7) 477–8; (1874) 550, 557; (1878) 550; (1883) 587; Indian Factory Question (1875, 1877, 1879, 1881) 572
Royal Commissions (1833) 78–85; (1875–6) 550
Select Committees (1831) 72–3, 76, 77, 79, 84, 85; (1840–1) 123–4
Farnham, 289, 290
Farquharson, J. J., 62, 244
Farr, Dr William, 482
Field Lane Ragged School, 251, 520, 545
Fielden, John, 217, 249, 256, 260, 293, 294
Fielden, Samuel, 294–6
Fielden Society, 295
Fishbourne, Admiral, 582
Florence, 94, 342
Flower and Water Cress Girls Mission, 543, 585
Floyer, John, 244, 245
Folkestone, 593
Forster, John, 563; Mrs, 563
Forster, W. E., 487–90, 577
Fox, Henry Edward (later 4th Baron Holland), 15, 22, 23, 24 n. 26, 600
France, 20, 27, 32, 57, 58, 94, 208–9, 271, 439, 440, 444, 455–7, 493, 494
Franco-Prussian War (1870), 493, 494
Frederick William IV, King, 114, 155, 156, 158, 161, 162
Frere, Sir Bartle, 565

Gainsborough, Lady, 505
Garbett, James, 162, 163, 164, 167, 171 n. 114
Garibaldi, Guiseppe, 457, 458, 460, 465 n. 114
Garter, Order of the, 338, 374, 375

INDEX   627

Gash, Professor N., 247, 327
Gateshead, 358
Gavazzi, Signor, 461
Gavin, Dr Hector, 442, 443
General Elections (1826) 27; (1830) 57, 58; (1831) 59, 60, 86 n. 15; (1832) 71, 72; (1835) 99, 100, 137; (1837) 137; (1841) 137, 142, 143, 147, 239; (1847) 262; (1852) 337, 341; (1857) 421, 426; (1865) 422; (1868) 472, 473; (1874) 534, 559; (1880) 574
General Land Drainage and Improvement Company, 430, 431, 495
Gent, Joseph, 564
George IV, 28, 51, 55 n. 94, 57
Germany, 141, 161, 254, 386, 495, 556
Gibbon, Edward, 95
Gibson, Thomas Milner, 212
Giffard, S. L., 79, 81, 89 n. 140, 116, 123, 198
Gilbert, Bishop, 167
Gladstone, W. E., 189, 318, 341, 364, 384, 385, 399, 467, 468, 470, 472, 473, 476, 486, 489, 515, 516, 517, 523, 527, 528, 534, 537, 538, 559, 574, 575, 585, 599, 602, 604; Shaftesbury's comments on, 162, 261, 576
Glasgow, 111, 129, 249, 264, 275, 322, 492–3, 531, 549, 557, 608
Glasgow Herald, 557
Glasgow Working Men's Sabbath Protection Society, 531
Gloucester and Bristol, Bishop and Bishopric of, 379, 380
Gobat, Bishop Samuel, 159, 160, 162, 307, 308, 386, 394, 583
Goderich, Viscount, 29
Golightly, Revd C. P., 165
Goode, Revd William, 403 n. 78
Gordon, John, 350
Gordon, Robert, 34, 35, 36, 37
Gorham Case (1850), 316, 328 n. 54, 341
Goulburn, Henry, 145, 164
Graham, Sir James, 40, 195–6, 199, 212, 244, 250, 364; and factory reform (1841–2) 176–8, 180–1, 188–9; (1843) 190–4; (1845–6) 227–8; (1846) 248; and mines reform (1842) 184, 185, 187; and consideration of offers of office in Ireland to Ashley, 217–18, 226; and lunacy reform (1844) 230; (1845) 230,

231; Shaftesbury's comments on, 194, 231
Granville, 1st Earl, 28
Granville, 2nd Earl, 446, 447, 451, 571
Granville, Lady Harriet, 28, 44, 46, 48
Great Exhibition (1851), 308, 327 n. 6
Greenock, 289
Greg, Samuel, 217
Greville, Charles C. F., 47, 59, 64, 68, 107 n. 46, 168, 170 n. 69, 235 n. 53, 451, 452, 464 n. 78
Grey, 2nd Earl, 63
Grey, 3rd Earl, 274
Grey, Sir George, 257, 283, 285, 286, 287, 288, 289, 291, 294, 296, 299, 313, 353, 354
Grosvenor, Lord, 199, 392
Grosvenor Square, London (No. 24), 19, 336, 344, 393, 458, 599
Gull, Dr W., 504, 580
Gurney, Russell, 537
Guthrie, Dr, 420
Gwydyr House, 278, 282

Hague, The, 323
Haldane, Alexander, 320, 365, 422, 424, 428, 519, 521, 522, 527, 529, 530, 561, 562, 563, 579
Halifax, 267 n. 47
Hall, Sir Benjamin, 393
Hammonds, J. L. and B., 255, 446, 601, 602, 603
Hampden, Bishop R. D., 328 n. 60
Hanwell, 413
Hardinge, Lord, 209
Hardwicke, Earl, 350
Hargreaves, Mr, 452, 453
Harrow, 14, 16, 324, 336
Harrowby, Earl, 300, 359, 375
Hatherton, Lord, 165
Havannah, 323
Hay, Captain, 347
Hayter, William, 282
Health, Board of; of Towns Association: see Public Health
Heber, Bishop Reginald, 38
Hereford, Dean of, 381
Hertford, 104
Hickman, Revd J., 309
Highbury, 310
Hill, Octavia, 551

Hill, Revd Robert, 376
Hindley, Charles, 595 n. 45, 599, 604, 606
Holland, George, 564
Holland House, 24 n. 28
Holland, Lady Elizabeth, 15, 19, 21, 24 n. 28, 29, 30, 48, 53 n. 32, 61
Holland, Lady Mary, 19
Holmes, William, 61, 62
Hong Kong, 445
Horne, Revd Thomas, 16
Horner, Leonard, 133-4 n. 67, 235 n. 39, 293
Housing, 249-51, 348, 409, 479-80, 551, 587, 588-90
Howard, Blanche, 18, 19
Howard, George, see Carlisle, George Howard, 7th Earl
Howard, Harriet, 19
Howard, Mrs Henry, 351
Howarth, Mary, 123
Howley, Archbishop William, 115, 118, 155, 156, 159, 161, 164, 312
Huddersfield, 72, 144, 147, 267 n. 47
Hull, 426, 430, 501
Hume, Joseph, 100, 101
Huskisson, William, 86n. 15; Mrs, 47, 48
Hyde Park, 339, 392, 467, 469
Hyderabad, 207

India, 37, 40, 41, 173, 448, 449, 451, 452, 453, 461, 560, 571, 572; Board of Control, 30, 32, 38, 41, 46, 47, 53 n. 22, 58, 59, 97, 209, 272
Indian Mutiny, 432, 447-54
Indigent Blind Visiting Society, 129, 153
Industrial schools, 409
Infernal, H.M.S., 157
Inkerman, battle of, 441
International Arbitration and Peace Association, 584
Ireland, 30, 57, 116, 154, 166, 168, 217, 218, 226, 242, 243, 246, 247, 309, 474, 506, 574, 576, 577
Ireland, Church of, 97, 473-5
Irish Society of London, 154, 309
Italy, 20, 21, 94, 95, 96, 102, 115, 116, 271, 342, 454, 455, 456, 457, 458, 493

Jackson, Thomas, 273
Jacobson, Bishop William, 384, 385
Jaffa, 156

Japan, 343, 378
Jenkinson, Lady Selina, 42, 43, 48
Jeremie, Dean James, 385
Jerusalem, 112, 113, 114, 307, 448
Jerusalem, Bishop and Bishopric of, 114-15, 117, 131, 154-9, 160-4, 167, 168 n. 13, 169 n. 48, 307, 308, 318, 386, 440, 583, 584
Jeune, Bishop Francis, 385
Jews, disabilities of, 264-5, 582-3; plans for conversion and repatriation of, 112-16, 154-9, 308, 440, 441, 444-5, 460, 559, 560, 601
Jocelyn, Lord, 143, 213, 214
Jones, Inigo, 16
Jowett, Benjamin, 246
Jowett, Benjamin (son of above), 117, 133 n. 46, 516, 527
Juvenile crime, 349, 586-7

Kabul, 173
Kay Shuttleworth, James P., 188, 204 n. 90
Keble, John, 162
Kenworthy, William, 217
Keswick, 94
King's College, London, 33, 155
Kingsley, Charles, 321
Kinnaird, Lord, 128

Labouchere, Henry, 101
Labourers' Friend Society, 250
Lamb family, 43
Lamb, Sir Frederick, 47, 55 n. 112
Lamb, William, 55 n. 112
Lambeth Palace, 157
Lambton, Hedworth, 187
Lambton, Lord, 184
Lancashire, 72, 77, 79, 119, 120, 123, 178, 215, 217, 224, 233, 248, 256, 257, 258, 262, 272, 294, 298, 345, 469, 544
Lancaster, 78; Duchy of, 286, 374, 468
Langton, J. H., 27
Lausanne, 335, 424
Law, H. S., 123
Leeds, 88 n. 97, 128, 143, 144, 267 n. 47, 278
Leveson Gower, Francis, see Ellesmere, Earl
Leveson Gower, Harriet, see Granville, Lady Harriet

Lewer, Edward, 431-2; Frederick, 431, 432, 495, 498
Leykham, Antoinette von, 21, 23, 41, 42, 55 n. 101
Leykham, Baron von, 25 n. 79
Liberal Party, 467, 468, 470, 472, 473, 574
Lieven, Princess, 48, 55 n. 101
Lincoln, Deanery of, 385
Lincoln, Lord, 276
Little Bolton, 77
Liverpool, 64, 155, 189, 278, 410, 443, 549
Liverpool, 2nd Earl, 28
Liverpool, 3rd Earl, 42, 47
Livingstone, David, biography of, 601
Loch, John, 39
Lodging Houses, 322, 347, 483-4; Acts (1851) 347-8, 589; (1853) 348; Bills (1851) 347, 409; (1853) 348; (1857) 409
London, 13, 34, 36, 64, 69, 70, 71, 72, 75, 79, 84, 92, 120, 129, 158, 197, 228, 229, 249, 251, 252, 257, 264, 265, 273, 276, 277, 278, 279, 280, 282, 284, 289, 296, 313, 314, 322, 336, 345, 356, 362, 391, 409, 418, 429, 461, 480, 481, 482, 483, 484, 490, 493, 503, 508, 531, 537, 545, 549, 551, 556, 566, 577, 578, 582, 585, 588; Bishop of, 157, 159, 161, 283, 381, 382, 389, 390, 526; Burial Grounds of (see also Public Health), 280, 281, 284, 288, 292, 303 n. 57, 304 n. 80, 352-4, 355, 356, 357; Treaty of (1852), 462; Water, supply of (see also Public Health), 284-5, 288, 289, 290, 292, 304 n. 103, 354, 354-5, 356, 481, 482
London City Mission, 111, 112, 251, 252, 531, 581
London Reformatory, 419
London Society for Conversion of Jews, 113, 114, 154, 155, 158, 159, 160, 162, 307, 308, 311, 382, 386, 387, 434 n. 49, 524, 531, 556, 583
London Society for Improvement of Condition of Factory Children, 77
London Society for Prevention of Cruelty to Children, 586
Londonderry, Lord, 186, 203 n. 78
Longley, Archbishop Charles, 382, 395, 398, 400, 503, 506, 520
Lonsdale, Earl, 87 n. 31
Lord's Day Observance Society, 109, 110, 111, 313, 314, 339, 394, 402 n. 5

Lord's Day Working Men's Society, 531
Lords, House of: Shaftesbury's dislike of, 337, 338, 418-19, 471; his desire to strengthen role of, 362-3, 472; his views on role of after 1867, 472-6, 575-6
Lothian, Lord, 128
Louis Napoleon, 356
Louis Philippe, 271
Lowe, Robert, 467 468, 469; see also Sherbrooke, Lord
Lowther, Lord, 87 n. 31
Lucknow, 447
Lunacy: Acts (1711) 34; (1774) 34, 36; (1808) 35; (1815) 35; (1819) 35; (1828) 36-7, 54 n. 67, n. 68; (1832) 54 n. 68; (1842) 229; (1845) 231-2, 237 nn. 132 and 133, 352, 414; (1853) 352, 413; (1862) 416-7, 590
  Bills (1828) 36; (1842) 181; (1845) 230-1; (1852) 352; (1885) 592
  Commission (Metropolitan, 1828-45) 36-7, 228-30; (post 1845) 230-2, 253, 351, 411, 412, 413, 414, 415, 416, 417, 420, 553, 555
  Question (to 1828) 34-5; (1828-44) 228-31; (1845) 231-2; (1850s) 351-2; (1860s) 410-17, 433 n. 26, 434 nn. 34 and 49; (1870s) 551-4, 558; (1880s) 590-3
  Select Committee on (1807) 35; (1859) 411, 591; (1877) 552-4, 562, 591
Luther Commemoration (1883), 580
Lyell, Sir Charles, 396
Lyme, 273
Lyster, Henry, 20, 128
Lyttelton, Lady, 93
Lyttelton, Lord, 357

McCaul, Revd Alexander, 154, 155, 160, 162, 246, 282, 382, 383, 386
Macaulay, Thomas B., 88 n. 97
Madiai, Francesco and Rosa, 342
Madras, 39
Magdalen College, Oxford, 165
Magee, Bishop William, 537
Mahon, Lord, 502
Maitland, Revd Brownlow, 555, 562
Malmesbury, Lord, 456
Malta, 20; Protestant College at, 160, 309, 428, 498
Manchester, 71, 85, 122, 134 n. 67, 142,

144, 188, 212, 217, 233, 249, 257, 259, 267 n. 47, 278, 293, 295, 297, 350, 393, 469, 489, 585
Manchester Guardian, 294
Manners, Lord John, 296, 298, 305 n. 142
Manners Sutton, Charles, 100
Manning, Cardinal, 535
Manor House School, Chiswick, 13, 16, 17
Marlborough, Duke of, 27, 60
Maurice, F. D., 321
Mawdsley, Thomas, 295, 296, 297
Mayhew, Henry, 340
Mayne, Sir Richard, 391
Maynooth College, 166, 167, 320, 373, 529
Mazzinglia, Mr, 342
Mearns, Andrew, 588
Mehemet Ali, Pasha, 113, 114
Melbourne, 346
Melbourne, 1st Viscount, 55 n. 112
Melbourne, 2nd Viscount, 15, 43, 47, 59, 97, 106 n. 21, 110, 111, 118, 137–8, 139, 140, 141, 319
Mentone, 504, 505
Merchant Shipping, 546
Metropolitan Drapers' Association, 393
Metternich, Prince, 41, 55 n. 101, 197, 271
Middlesex, county of, 35
Midlothian Campaign, 574
Milan, 94, 95; Cathedral, 96
Mildmay Conferences, 528
Millis, Maria, 14, 15, 51
Milltown, Lord, 590, 592
Milman, H. H., 365
Mines: Acts (1842) 188, 189, 407; (1872) 479
Bills (1842) 182–8, 189, 203 n. 78; (1872) 479
Question 125, 182–8, 189, 190, 479
Molesworth, Sir William, 357, 359
Montgomery, Revd Robert, 129
Moody and Sankey, 554, 555, 556, 562
Moore, George, 563–4
Moore, Revd Robert, 33
More, Hannah, 103
Morley, Samuel, 397, 399, 429, 574
Morning Chronicle, 208, 211
Morning Post, 179, 180, 241, 242, 608
Morpeth, George Howard, Lord: see Carlisle
Morpeth, Lady Georgiana: see Carlisle

Mount Stuart Elphinstone, Lord, 38

Nanking, Treaty of (1842), 174, 445
Napier, William, 290, 441
Napoleon III, 343, 440, 455, 456, 457, 461, 495
Natal, Bishop of, 377
National Education League, 487
National Education Union, 487, 488, 489
National Gallery, 334
National Lord's Day Rest Association, 394
National Society, 118, 119, 531, 545
National Sunday League, 392, 393, 394, 401
Natural History Museum, 587
Neeld, Joseph, 25 n. 74
Neology, 364, 365, 377–8, 381, 386, 387, 394, 395, 398, 400, 494, 515, 516, 517, 526, 527, 562, 606
Netherby, 129
Newark, 72
Newbattle Abbey, 128
Newby, 128
Newcastle, 358, 359
Newman, John H., 161, 162, 165, 170 nn. 74 and 76, 316
Nice, 94, 95, 335, 456, 457, 504, 521
Nicholl, Burnet and Newman, Messrs, 429
Nicolayson, Revd John, 113, 114
Nightingale, Florence, 442, 443–4, 600
Norfolk Street, London, 99
North London Sunday Rest Association, 392
Northampton, 574
Northumberland, 203 n. 78
Norwich, 547; Bishopric of, 380
Nuisances Removal Act (1848), 279, 280, 358

Oastler, Richard, 72, 74, 76, 83, 89 n. 117, 120, 121, 124, 126, 133 n. 66, 134 n. 92, 143, 144, 151 n. 36, 210, 295, 300, 483
O'Connell, Daniel, 57
O'Connor, Feargus, 195
Oldham, 249, 267 n. 47
Opium question, 174–5, 445, 446, 447, 461, 584
Origin of Species, 396
Orsman, W. J., 483, 543

INDEX

Osborne, 372
Osborne, Revd Sydney G., 200, 210, 499, 500
Oudh, 449, 450
Owen, Richard, 396
Oxford, 260; Bishop and Bishopric of, 161, 165, 258; University of, 13, 15, 17, 18, 19, 23, 102, 162, 167, 193, 254, 261, 338, 365, 380, 381, 384, 385, 503, 516, 527, 602
Oxford Movement, 117, 160, 161, 162, 163, 164, 165, 166, 307, 538; see also Church of England, High Church Party in

Palestine, 112, 114, 115, 159, 439, 559, 583
Palmer, Roundell, 163, 167; see also Selborne, Earl
Palmer, William, 165
Palmerston, 3rd Viscount, 112, 132 n. 18, 244, 421, 442, 445, 457, 462, 463 n. 34, 468; likely relationship to Minny, 43, 44; marriage of to Lady Cowper (1839), 43, 55 n. 112, 130, 131; offers Ashley office (1830), 58–9; and Near East Crisis (1839–41), 113–5, 155; at Home Office in Aberdeen Coalition (1852–5), 349, 357–8, 359–60; becomes Prime Minister (1855), 366, 442, (1859) 383; offers Shaftesbury office (1855), 373–5, 402 n. 19; awards Shaftesbury Garter (1861), 375–6, 402 n. 27; Shaftesbury's influence over appointments of, 376; Shaftesbury's influence over ecclesiastical policy of, 376–85, 394, 400, 403 n. 49, 432, 446, 447; and Sunday question (1856), 393; warns Shaftesbury of Waters (1861), 428–9, 430, 431; generosity to Shaftesbury's family, 429; death of (1865), 399, 422, 423, 467, 515
Palmerston, Lady, 131, 319, 374, 402 n. 19, 503–4; see also Cowper, Lady Emily
Panmure, Lord, 404 n. 115, 442, 443, 448, 463 n. 34
Panshanger, 92, 99, 128
'Papal Aggression' (1851), 316–9, 339, 341, 518, 527, 529
Paris, 28, 44, 94, 96, 322, 356, 444, 495, 556
Parliamentary reform (1820s) 57; (1830–2) 57, 58–9, 60, 64, 70–1; (1851) 363; (1859) 421; (1866–7) 467–70; (1884) 576
Parnell, C. J., 575
Paternalism, Tory, characteristics of, 74–6; see also relevant items under Shaftesbury, 7th Earl
Patten, Wilson, 77, 78
Payne, Joseph, 503
Payne-Smith, Dean Robert, 384, 515, 517, 524
Peach, W. N., 89 n. 102
Peel, Sir Robert, 29, 30, 31, 32, 41, 58, 59, 63, 97, 104, 105, 111, 118, 133 n. 36, 137, 138, 140, 144, 166, 167, 241, 251, 256, 261, 263, 300, 325, 326, 602; offers Ashley office (1834–5), 97–8, 106 n. 29; in office (1834–5), 99–102; opposes Ashley over Ten Hours day (1838), 122–3; offers Ashley Household office (1839), 139–40; (1841), 145–50; offers Ashley place on Ecclesiastical Commission (1841), 149; and plans for building new Churches (1843), 153, 312; and creation of Jerusalem Bishopric (1841), 115, 155, 156, 157; and Oxford Movement (1840s), 164, 165; and Afghan Crisis (1841–3), 173–4, 176; and Opium Trade (1842–3), 174–5, 176; and social issues (1840s), 176, 195–6; and factory reform (1841–2), 176–82, 188–9; and mines reform (1842), 182, 187, 203 nn. 61 and 78; and factory reform (1843), 192–4; and annexation of scinde (1843), 207–10; and Tahiti (1843), 208–10; and factory reform (1844), 213–5, 220, 221, 235 n. 39, 248; and consideration of offers of office in Ireland to Ashley, 217–18, 226; and Corn Law repeal (1845–6), 242–4, 246–8; resignation of (1846), 243; and Ashley's resignation from Commons (1846), 245–6, 266–7 n. 31; death of (1851), 319; Shaftesbury's comments on, 142, 143, 175, 195–6, 222–3, 246–8, 319
Pelham, Bishop John T., 380, 381
Pembrokeshire, 64
Pentonville, 251
Persigny, Duc de, 456
Peterborough, Bishop and Bishopric of 385, 519

Phillips, Sir George, 84
Phillpott, Bishop Henry, 316, 328 n. 54, 341
Piedmont-Sardinia, 432, 454, 455, 456, 457, 460
Pisa, 94
Playfair, Lyon, 485
Plimsoll, Samuel, 546
Plymouth, 154, 341, 435 n. 88
Poland, 154
Polish Rebellion (1863), 432, 458, 459–60
Pomare, Queen, 208, 209
Ponsonby, W. F. S., 60, 63, 65, 66, 67, 68, 69, 70, 71, 86 n. 16, 87 nn. 29 and 40
Poor Law (1834), 125, 126, 188, 210, 211, 276, 321, 544; Medical Relief under, 302 n. 29
Portman, Lord, 69–70, 496
Portsmouth, 426
Pottinger, Sir Henry, 208
Powerscourt, Lord, 147, 148
Prague, 197
Prest, Archdeacon, 384
Preston, 267 n. 47
Principles of Geology, 396
Protestant Alliance, 386
Prussia, 114, 116, 117, 157, 159, 161, 462, 493–4
Public Health: Acts (1848) 276–7, 332; (1858 and 1859) 480; (1866) 480–1; (1871) 481; (1872) 482; (1875) 550–1
Bills (1845) 276; (1847) 276
Question, 250, 252, 256; (1848–51) 276–92; (1851–4) 352–61, 370 n. 145; (1850s–70s) 480, 481–2, 485, 550–1
Public Worship Regulation Act (1874), 535–9
Pure Literature Society, 584
Purton Estate, 333
Pusey, E. B., 133 n. 45, 162, 163, 164, 167, 170 n. 74, 171 n. 114, 365, 395, 396, 400, 506, 524, 528, 579, 607

Quarterly Review, 113, 116, 122, 126, 127, 252–3, 255, 347

Ragged Schools, 251, 252, 253, 255, 256, 262, 264, 273, 274, 275, 276, 322, 346–7, 417, 418, 419, 420, 422, 435 n. 87, 469, 485, 488, 490, 545, 557, 580, 585, 593
Ragged School Union, 251–2, 261, 338, 346, 349, 368 n. 95, 368–9 n. 96, 369 n. 98, 418, 422, 423, 486, 488, 489–90, 491, 503, 545, 562, 564, 577
Raglan, Lord, 441, 442, 463 n. 19
Ransford, Oliver, 600–1, 604
Ravensworth, 128
Rawlinson, Robert, 482
Read, T. G., 67, 69
Record, 167, 320, 395, 455, 474, 529, 561, 593, 605
Reeve, Canon, 564
Reform Acts, see Parliamentary reform
Religious Worship Act (1855), 388, 389; Bills (1855), 387–8
Renan, E., 377, 387
Ricasoli, Baron, 457
Rice, Thomas Spring, 78
Richmond, 331, 424
Richmond, Duke of, 185, 482
Ripon, 128; Bishop of, 380, 404 n. 15; Dean of, 403 n. 78
Ripon, Lord, 209
Ritualism, 515, 518–26, 532–5, 554, 559, 607
Rochester, Bishop of, 157
Roebuck, John A., 219, 262, 263
Roman Catholic Hierarchy, creation of (1850), 316
Rome, 94, 95, 116, 494
Romsey, 378
Rosebery, Earl, 557
Rossie, Priory, 128
Rothschild, Baron, 264–5
Rowton Castle, 20, 128
Royal Titles Act (1876), 560–1
Rugby School, 224, 253, 254
Ruskin, John, 586
Russell, G. W. E., 605
Russell, Lord John, 48, 71, 78, 97, 121, 127, 256, 264, 272, 273, 337, 340, 345, 351, 352, 355, 362, 363, 364, 399, 421; and Parliamentary reform (1831–2), 58, 59, 60, (1851–2), 363–4, 421; (1866) 467–8; and corn law repeal (1845), 242, 243, 246; and factory reform (1830s and 1840s), 121, 134 n. 67, 134 n. 73, 257, 258, 259, 294; and Ashley over Bath Election (1847), 262; and removal of Jewish Disabilities (1847), 265; and Ashley over public health, 280, 283, 287, 288, 361; and subdivision of parishes

(1848), 312; and Sunday Labour in Post Office (1848), 314, 421; and creation of Roman Catholic Hierarchy (1850-1), 316-8; and Ashley over ecclesiastical appointments, 317, 328 n. 60, 340, 525
Russia, 159, 439, 440, 444, 459, 460
Ryder v. Mills, case of (1850), 295

Sabbath School Union, 531
Sadler, Michael, 72, 73, 74, 75, 77, 79, 81, 88 nn. 96 and 97, 93
Salisbury, 430
Salisbury, Marquis of, 538, 588
Salvation Army, 397, 582, 607
San Marino, 94
San Remo, 94
Sandon, Viscount, 111, 235 n. 39
Sanitary reform, see Public Health
Sardinia, 343
Saturday Review, 400, 452
Saunders, Robert, 235 n. 39
Savoy, 456, 457
Scarlett, Sir James, 89 n. 102
Schleswig-Holstein, 462
Scinde, Ameers of, 207, 208, 209, 450
Sclater-Booth, George, 550
Scotland, 17, 18, 19, 79, 128, 264, 289, 322, 323, 329 n. 100, 397, 416, 427, 506, 556
Scott, Revd Thomas, 51
Scott, Sir Walter, 17, 18
Scripture Readers Society, 153, 310, 339
Scutari, 442, 443
Sebastopol, 441, 444
Second Coming, 50, 103, 111, 112, 115, 127, 160, 265, 308, 320, 343, 421, 490, 528-9, 571, 600, 606
Seeley, J. R., 377, 394, 515
Seeley, R. B., 145, 151 n. 45, 246, 267 n. 33, 314, 377
Selborne, Earl, 558, 592; see also Palmer, Roundell
Selwyn, William, 517
Seymer, Henry, 244, 245
Seymour, Lord, 287, 288, 289, 290, 291, 304 n. 110, 353, 354, 356, 357, 360, 361
Shaftesbury, 585
Shaftesbury, Anthony Ashley Cooper, 1st Earl, 11, 12

Shaftesbury, Anthony Ashley Cooper, 2nd Earl, 11, 23 n. 3
Shaftesbury, Anthony Ashley Cooper, 3rd Earl, 11, 12, 23 n. 4
Shaftesbury, Anthony Ashley Cooper, 4th Earl, 12, 23 n. 5
Shaftesbury, Anthony Ashley Cooper, 5th Earl, 12, 23 n. 5
Shaftesbury, Cropley Ashley Cooper, 6th Earl (father), 12, 23 n. 5, 25 n. 71, 28, 29, 64, 91, 106 n. 3, 226, 337, 428; career and characteristics of, 12-13; relations with family, 13, 14, 15, 16, 19, 20; relations with eldest son 13, 14, 15, 16, 19, 20, 21, 30, 91, 130, 198, 200, 201, 207, 225, 231; death of (1851), 324
Shaftesbury, Anthony Ashley Cooper, 7th Earl (until 1851, Ashley, Lord), mentioned in review of first Earl, 11, 12; childhood, schooling and relations with parents, 13-17, 20, 21; and Maria Millis, 14, 15; at Oxford (1819-22), 13, 17, 18; early correspondence with Lady Georgiana Morpeth, 13, 17-22, 27; social life as a young man, 18, 19, 28; undertakes 'Grand Tour' (1823), 20, 21; attachment to Antoinette, 21, 23, 41-2; moods of depression and elation (1820s), 22, 23, 31; enters Parliament for Woodstock (1826), 27, 28; refuses offer of office by Canning (1827), 28-9; accepts offer of office by Wellington at India Board of Control (1828), 29-30, 32; and lunacy reform (1828), 34, 36-7; work at India Board (1828-30), 37-41, 51; desire to marry and search for a wife, 41-3; courtship of and marriage to Lady Emily Cowper (1829-30), 43-9, 51; religious development of in relation to Evangelicalism (1820s), 49-52; and parliamentary reform (1830-2), 58-71, 85; returned for Dorchester (1830), 58; loses office at India Board (1830), 58; refuses offer of office by Palmerston (1830), 58-9; returned for Dorchester (1831), 59-60; candidature at Dorset and petition against return (1831-2), 60-71; returned for Dorset (1832), 71, 106 n. 3; depressed by political prospects (1832-3), 71-2; and factory reform (1833), 72-86; influence of

Paternalism and Evangelicalism on, 74–6, 85; relations with Lady Cooper, 91–2, 99, 104; happiness of marriage, 92–4, 104, 106 n. 21; on holiday in Italy (1833–4), 94–6; accepts offer of office by Peel at Admiralty (1834), 97–8, 106 n. 29; returned for Dorset (1835), 99–100; at Admiralty (1835), 100–2, 107 n. 46; closer ties with Evangelicalism (1834–5), 102–5; and Sunday observance (1830s), 105, 109–11; and missionary work (1830s), 111–12; efforts for repatriation and conversion of Jews (1830s), 112–16, 132 n. 18; and Jerusalem Bishopric (1830s), 114–16, 132 n. 30; clash with High Church party (1830s), 116–17, 119, 133 n. 36; upholds Anglican doctrinal orthodoxy (1830s), 117–18, 119; opposes Whig plans for education (1839), 118–19, 133 n. 54; continuing efforts over factory reform (1835–41), 119–24, 133–4 n. 67, 134 nn. 73 and 77; and chimney sweeps (1840), 124; efforts to extend protection to other employment (1840–1), 125; sources of paternalistic concern (late 1830s), 125–7; reputation as public speaker (1838) and doubts about own abilities, 127–8; tour of North of England and Scotland (1839), 128–30; temporary reconciliation with father (1839), 130; attitude towards marriage of Lady Cowper and Palmerston (1839), 130–1; political future in late 1830s, 137; and Queen Victoria, 138–9, 140; accepts Household office (1839), 139–40; and marriage of Victoria and Albert (1840), 140–1; returned for Dorset (1841), 142; supports Protection (1841), 142, 239; and Peel, 142–3; and factory reform (1841), 143–4; first tour of factory districts (1841), 143–4; declines Household office (1841), 145–50; accepts place on Ecclesiastical Commission (1841) and role there (1841–7), 149, 153, 168 n. 3; continuing association with Evangelical societies (1841–7), 153–4; and Jerusalem Bishopric (1841–7), 154–9, 160–2, 167, 169 n. 53, 170 n. 69; and Protestant College at Malta, 160; disputes with Oxford Movement, 160–5; and Peel over ecclesiastical matters, 165–6; place and activities within Evangelical party in Church of England (1841–7) assessed, 166–8; and foreign issues (1841–3), 173–6; and factory reform (1841–2), 176–82, 188; and mines reform (1842), 182–8, 203 nn. 61 and 78; tour of factory districts (1842), 188–9; speeches on social issues (1842–3), 189–90, 204 n. 94; and factory bill (1843), 192–4, 204 n. 115; dealings with Tory government over social issues (1841–3), 176, 180–1, 194–6; and schooling of Anthony, 197; paternalistic concern over conditions on father's Estates, 198–9; speech at Sturminster (1843), 199–200, 225, 239; effect of speech, 200–1; and factory reform (1843–4), 207, 210–23, 234, n. 25 235 n. 53; and foreign issues (1843), 207–10; and agricultural grievances (1844), 211; attack on by Bright (1844), 212–3; and Dodd, 212–13, 234 n. 33, 234–5 n. 35; dealings with Tory government (1844), 217–18, 222–4; family matters (1844–5), 224–6; rumours of office in Ireland, 217–18, 226; and Calico Printers (1845), 227–8; and lunacy reform (1841–5), 228–32, 237 n. 122; and factory reform (1845), 233; political standing in Dorset (1840s), 239; abandons Protectionism (1845–6), 239–48; resigns seat (1846), 245–8, 266 n. 30, 266–7 n. 31, 267 n. 33; resumption of factory reform (1845–6), 248–9; social and paternalistic efforts while out of Parliament (1846–7), 249–53; family worries, 253–4; journeys abroad and financial worries, 254, 268 n. 84; significance of period out of Parliament (1846–7), 255–6, 260, 268 n. 93; continuing interest in factory reform and in Factory Act (1847), 256–60; contemplates return to Parliament (1846–7), 260–1; returned for Bath (1847), 261–4; and Jewish disabilities (1847), 264–5; personal satisfaction with events (1845–7), 265–6; interest in 1848 Revolutions, 271; and Chartism, 271; maintains political independence, 272; and Albert over scheme for social improvement (1848), 272–3; and emigration of Ragged Scholars (1848–9), 273–6; and public health (1848–51), 276–92; and factory reform (1847–50), 293–301; and Evangelicalism (1846–51), 307; attitude to Bishop Gobat, 307–8; and Great Exhibition (1851), 308–9, 327 n. 6; and Malta College, 309; and Irish missions, 309; and Church of England Teacher Training schools, 310; and schemes for surplus episcopal funds, 311; and subdivision of parishes (1849), 311–12; and Sunday labour at Post Office (1847–50), 313–16; and 'Papal Aggression' (1850–1), 316–19; and Russell over ecclesiastical appointments, 317; his Evangelicalism in late 1840s assessed, 319–21; dislike of Christian Socialism, 321; reviews his career in 1850, 321–2; poor health and overwork, 322; financial problems, 322–3; family worries, 323; death of Francis (1849), 323–4; death of father (1851), 324; his career to 1851 assessed, 325–6; succeeds to title and work on Estates (1851–5), 331–3, 367 n. 29; financial problems, 333–4, 366 n. 4, 367 n. 17; worries over family and health, 334–6; enters Lords, 336–7; feels out of touch with political events, 337–8, 367–8 n. 57; refuses Garter from Aberdeen (1854), 339; and Sabbatarian issue over Crystal Palace (1852), 339–40; skirmishes with High Church party (1852), 340; and revival of Convocation (1852), 340–2; and Protestantism abroad, 342–3; and U.S. slavery, 343–5; visits Lancashire (1851), 345; and Ragged Schools (early 1850s), 346–7; and Lodging Houses (1851), 347–9; and housing, 349; and juvenile crime (1853), 349; and chimney sweeps (1853–5), 350–1; and lunacy legislation (1851–3), 351–2; and public health (1851–4), 352–61; anxiety over political and religious prospects of country (early 1850s), 362–6; offered office by Palmerston (1855), 373–4, 402 n. 19; accepts Garter from Palmerston (1861), 375–6, 402 n. 27; influence on Palmerston's appointments, 376; and biblical criticism, 377–8, 386–7; influence on Palmerstons' ecclesiastical appointments (1855–8, 1859–65), 378–85, 403 nn. 49, 53 and 78, 403–4 n. 85, 404 n. 89, 405–6 n. 163; and Religious Worship Act (1855), 387–9; and Theatre Services, 389–92; and Sabbatarianism, 392–4; his Evangelicalism (1855–65) assessed, 394–6; and scientific advance, 396–7; and Dissenters, 397–8; his doubts about future of Evangelicalism in Church of England, 398–400; the 'Shaftesbury Bishops' assessed, 400–1; efforts to extend protection to other employment (1860s), 407–8; and chimney sweeps, (1861, 3, 4) 408; and vagrancy, 409; and housing, 409; sources of paternalistic concern, 409–10; and health issues, 410; and lunacy (1859), 410–17; extra-parliamentary pursuits (1855–65), 417–18; and Ragged Schools, 418, 435 n. 88; pessimism and increasing isolation, 419–21; depression on death of Palmerston (1865), 422; and family deaths, 422–4; distress at Anthony's marriage (1857), 426–7; ill health and dislike of visits abroad, 427; efforts to improve Estates, 428; financial problems of, 428–9; and Waters (steward), 429–31, 437 nn. 182 and 183; and Lewer, 431–2; and Crimean War, 439–45, 463 nn. 19 and 34; and seizure of *Arrow* (1857), 445–7; and Indian Mutiny (1857), 447–54, 464 nn. 78 and 85; and Italian Unification, 454–8, 465 n. 114; and American Civil War, 458–9; and Polish Rebellion (1863), 459–60; views on foreign policy, 460–1; and second Reform Act (1867), 468–9, 471; dealings with and disapproval of Disraeli, 469–70; dealings with and disapproval of Gladstone, 470; views on role of House of Lords after 1867, 472–5; and disestablishment of Irish Church (1869), 474–5; and Ballot Act (1872), 476; pessimism at political prospects, 476–7; and children in brickyards (1871), 477–8; and agricultural workers (1867), 478–9; and children in acrobatic performances (1872–3), 479; and mines reform (1872), 479; and housing (1866, 1868), 480; and public health (1866–72), 480–2; extra-parliamentary pursuits (1866–72), 483–4; dislike of House of Lords, 484–5; and Education Act (1870), 486–90; fears for future of Ragged Schools, 490; growing isolation and feeling that paternalism no longer possible in widened electorate, 485, 491; self-assessment at age of 70, 492–3; presented with freedom of City of Glasgow (1871), 492–3; attitude to foreign issues (1866–70), 493–5; law suits with Lewer and Waters, 495–6; later dealings with Waters, 496–7; financial problems and demands, 497–8; and Estates, 498–500; family matters, 500–4; deaths of Minny and Constance (1872), 504–6; continuing opposition to biblical criticism, 515–17; opposition to new translation of Bible (1870s), 517; continuing support for scientific investigation, 516–17; opposition to Ritualism (1866–74), 518–19; and Vestments issue (1867–8), 519–21; and attempts to reform ecclesiastical courts (1869–72), 521–3; and attempts to reform Convocation (1872), 523; dealings with High Church party, 524–5; dealings with Archbishop Tait, 526; discontentment with Evangelicalism, 526–7; feeling of isolation in Church matters, 527–9; his views assessed, 529–30; still retains prominent place in Evangelical party, 530–2; and issue of Confession (1873), 532–3; and Public Worship Regulation bill (1874), 535–8, 542 n. 136; pessimism about future, 539; and Emily Loan Fund, 543–4; and Charity Organisation Society, 544; and Temperance, 544–5; dealings with Barnardo, 545; and Ragged Schools (1870s), 545; and *Arethusa* (1874), 545; and Merchant Seamen, 546; and vivisection issue (1876), 546–8; and chimney sweeps (1870s), 548–9; and factory reform (1870s), 549–50; and public health (1870s), 550–1; and housing (1870s), 551; and lunacy (1877), 551–4; and Moody and Sankey, 554; and continuing opposition to biblical criticism, 555; continuing support for scientific development, 555–6; and Turkish Atrocities (1876), 556; receives freedom of City of Edinburgh (1878), 556; isolation, public and personal (1870s), 556–8, 561–5; and foreign issues (1877–8), 559–60; opposes Royal Titles bill (1876), 560; reconciliation with Anthony and Harriet, 565; and Indian factories, 572; and habitual drunkards, 572–3; further interest in vivisection, 573–4; alarm at Liberal Ministry (1880s), 574–7; at eightieth birthday (1881), 577; receives freedom of City of London (1884), 577; financial, family and health worries, 578–9; continuing public activities (1880s), 580; and Sunday observance, 580–1; and missionary efforts, 581; co-operation with Dissenters, 581–2; dislike of Salvation Army, 582; continuing interest in Jewish question, 582–3; and Jerusalem Bishopric (1880s), 583–4; and Opium question, 584; and Ragged Schools, 585; and Training Ships, 585; and vivisection, 585–6; and protection of children, 586–7; and factory reform (1883), 587; and housing, 587–90; dislike of increasing State intervention, 590; and lunacy (1883–5), 590–3; final illness and death, 593–4; funeral, epitaph, assessment of personality and public life, 599–609

Shaftesbury, Lady Anne (mother), 13, 14, 16, 23 n. 9, 25 n. 71, 331; death of (1865), 424

Shaftesbury, Lady Emily (Minny, wife), 51, 59, 62, 70, 71, 91–6, 99, 104, 106 n. 3, 130, 131, 138, 157, 188, 196, 197, 198, 254, 264, 323, 324, 335, 338, 374, 378, 424, 426, 427, 429, 498, 501, 506, 543, 564, 605; death of (1872), 504–5; see also Cowper, Lady Emily

Shaftesbury Park Estate, 493

Sheerness, 323

Sherbrooke, Lord, 571, 574; see also Lowe, Robert

Sheridan, R. B., 199, 205 n. 157

Shoe Blacks Brigades, 346, 368 n. 95, 417

Short-Time Committees, 72, 73, 79, 84, 134 n. 67, 147, 178, 180, 181, 188, 189,

216, 219, 224, 248, 249, 256, 257, 260, 264, 294, 295, 296, 297, 298, 299
Siena, 94
Simon, Sir John, 480, 481, 482
Smith, Dr Thomas Southward, 277, 280, 282, 356, 359, 360, 424
Snow, Dr John, 303 n. 43
Social Science Congresses, 410, 420, 469, 609
Society for Bettering the Conditions of Female Operatives, 256
Society for Church Missions to the Roman Catholics of Ireland, 309
Society for Improving the Condition of the Labouring Classes, 250–1, 252, 253, 255, 273, 347, 417, 419, 551
Society for the Establishment of the Dalrymple Homes or Retreats for Inebriates, 573
Society for the Medical Education of Women, 483
Society for the Prevention of Cruelty to Animals, 547
Society for Promoting Christian Knowledge, 104, 555, 562
Somerset, Duke of, 287
Somerset, Lord George, 229
Somerset, Lord Granville, 98, 99
South, Sir James, 32, 53 n. 47, 503
Southampton, 528
Southey, Robert, 74, 75, 76, 84, 85, 94, 129, 376
Spurgeon, Charles, 397, 398, 532, 564, 576, 582
St Albans, Church of (Holborn), 519, 520, 525
St Davids, Bishop of, 259, 517
St Giles Estate and St Giles's House, 15, 16, 19, 130, 188, 197, 198, 207, 225, 324, 331, 332, 333, 334, 335, 427, 485, 498, 500, 503, 506, 564, 565, 575, 578, 594, 599, 600
St Leonards, Lord, 352
Stafford House, 344
Staffordshire, South, 185
Standard, 79, 116, 174
Stanhope, Edward, 499, 500
Stanley, A. P., 381, 382, 383, 384, 399, 579
Stanley, Lord, see Derby, Earl
Stanley, Lord, 590
Stephens, A. J., 521

Stephens, J. R., 295
Stowe, Mrs Harriet Beecher, 343, 344
Stratfield Saye, 29
Sturminster Agricultural Society, 199
Sturminster Newton, 199, 201, 239
Sturt, H. C., 244, 499
Sumner, Archbishop John, 283, 307, 312, 340, 390, 393, 400
Sunday Observance, 76, 105, 109–11, 313–16, 339–40, 368 n. 63, 373, 392, 401–2 n. 5, 580–1, 596 n. 79
Sutherland, Duchess of, 344, 503
Sutherland, Duke of, 185
Sutherland, John, 443
Sutteism, 40
Swansea, 552
Swindon, 430
Swine (Yorkshire), 333, 498
Switzerland, 20, 254
Sydenham, 339
Sydney, 323
Syria, 157, 440, 441, 560

Tahiti, 208, 209
Tain, 329 n. 100
Taiping Rebellion, 343
Tait, Archibald C., as Archbishop of Canterbury, 506, 508, 525, 526, 533–6, 539, 576; as Bishop of London, 381, 389, 390, 397, 398, 400, 521, 522, 526; as Dean of Carlisle, 381
Tamworth Manifesto, 100
Targitt, William, 431
Temperance, 485, 544, 607
Temple, Dr Frederick, 516, 524, 527
Ten Hours Movement, 72, 74, 79, 80, 81, 84, 85, 93, 119–21, 125, 128, 133 n. 46, 180, 210, 215, 217, 223, 248, 256, 293, 294, 300, 301, 326, 527
Thames, River, 284, 285, 483
Theatre Services, 388–92, 404 n. 115, 521, 527, 563, 581
Thiers, Louis Adolphe, 495
Thompson, Dr Henry, 579
Thornhill, Thomas, 151 n. 36
Thurlow, Lord, 580, 581
Times, The, 73, 123, 174, 179, 211, 216, 251, 297, 298, 344, 355, 420, 422, 423, 450–2, 456, 459, 517, 534, 547, 549, 592
Torrens, Robert, 587, 589
Torrington, Lord, 560

Tory Party: in 1820s, 28; and Catholic Emancipation (1829), 57; criticism of Ashley's work at India Board (1828–30), 40; and Parliamentary reform (1831–2), 57–8, 59, 70; and formation of Carlton Club (1831), 60; and Ashley's election at Dorset (1831), 62–4, 67–9; after 1832, 71; and paternalism, 74–5, 76; in office (1834–5), 96–102; leaves office (1835), 102, 105; in later 1830s, 137, 141; and Bedchamber crisis (1839), 137–8; in office (1841), 141; and Jerusalem Bishopric (1841), 155; and social issues (1840s), 176, 194–6, 203 n. 78, 325; split in 1846, 242, 272; possibility of Ashley being offered office by (1849), 272, (1851), 367–8 n. 57; 1852 Ministry, 337, 340, 356, 363–4; 1858–9 Ministry, 366, 421, 456; and parliamentary reform (1859), 421, (1867), 467–70; 1874–80 Ministry, 549–51, 557–62, 571–4
Townley, R. G., 64
Tractarianism, see Church of England, High Church Party in; also Oxford Movement
Trench, Archbishop (of Dublin), 383; as Dean of Westminster, 382
Trinity College (Dublin), 154; (Oxford), 162
Tristram, Dr, 583
Trollope, Anthony, 124; Frances, 124
Truck system, 198, 332
Truro, Lord, 573
Tunbridge Wells, 44, 279
Turkey, 113, 439–41, 444, 559
Turkish Atrocities, 556, 559
Turnbull (steward), 499, 578
Turner, James, 151 n. 48
Turner, Mrs, 410
Tuscany, Grand Duke of, 342
Tyler, Mrs, 345

Uniformity of Public Worship Bill, 520
United Evangelical Church of Prussia, 156
United Wesleyan Committee, 192
Universities, tests at, 475
Upper Brook Street, London, 99, 336

Vaccination, 357, 370 n. 145
Venice, 94, 95

Venn, 527
Vestments Bill (1867), 519, 524, 526, 541 n. 72
Victoria, Queen, 15, 93, 106 n. 21, 118, 137–8, 139, 140–2, 148, 149, 157, 182, 215, 251, 264, 272, 283, 293, 315, 318, 339, 342, 374, 380, 381, 383–5, 393, 399, 457, 516, 533, 560, 572
Victoria Institute, 517, 555
Victoria Street Society for Protection of Animals from Vivisection, 547, 548, 586
Vie de Jésus, 377, 387
Vienna, 21, 197, 271
Villiers, Bishop Henry, 380, 382, 389
Vivisection, 546–8, 562, 573–4, 585–6
Voltaire (quoted), 11

Waddington, Dean, 381
Wake, Lady, 381, 384
Waldegrave, Bishop S., 400
Waldensians, 342, 455
Wales, 118, 229, 232, 416
Wallich, Dr, 41
Walmsley, Sir Joshua, 401 n. 5
Ward, W. G., 164, 165
Washington (Co. Durham), 549
Waters, Robert S., 334, 428–32, 437 n. 182, 495, 496, 498, 499, 578
Weldon v. Winslow, case of, 590
Wellington, Duke of, 12, 29, 30–3, 51, 54 n. 57, 57, 58, 60, 61, 63, 65, 66, 69, 86 n. 15, 92, 102, 118, 113 n. 54, 185, 186, 263, 338
Wells, Cathedral of, 381, 383
Wesley, Charles, 599
West Dorset Agricultural Society, 199
West Riding, 79, 144, 147, 264
Westminster: Abbey, 390, 503, 594, 599; City of, 34, 165; Deanery of, 165, 382, 383
Wharncliffe, Lord, 184, 186, 187
Whibley, Charles, 602, 603
Whig party: and Canning Ministry (1827), 28; and parliamentary reform (1831–2), 58, 59, 64, 70, 325–6; in office after 1832, 72; dismissed by William IV (1834), 96; and Peel Ministry (1835), 105; growing weakness of in late 1830s, 137; plans for education (1839), 118–19, 192; and chimney sweeps (1840), 124; and factory reform (1840), 123–4;

defeat of (1841), 137, 142; and Jerusalem Bishopric, 155; and Corn Law repeal (1845-6), 242, 246; and Factory Act (1847), 257-9, 277; defeat of (1852), 337; and Aberdeen Coalition 337; and parliamentary reform (1852), 272, 363-4, 421; and Palmerston Ministry (1855), 373
Wight, Isle of, 197, 223
Wigram, Bishop Joseph, 400, 403 n. 78
Wilberforce, Bishop Samuel, 165, 258, 259, 320, 341, 388, 390, 394, 396, 400, 405 n. 143, 517, 524, 525, 563
Wilberforce, William, 123, 181, 197, 344
Wilkinson, Revd G. H., 565
William III, 376
William IV, 59, 70, 96, 97, 116, 137
Williams, George, 585
Williams, H. R., 577
Williams, Revd Isaac, 162-4, 167
Williams, Robert, 60
Williams, William, 483
Wimborne Minster, 449, 450
Wimborne St Giles, 12

Winchester, Bishop of, 116, 517, 525; College, 12
Windsor, 57, 94, 138, 141, 158, 264, 560
Wiseman, Cardinal Nicholas, 316, 318, 319
Woodstock, 27, 29, 30, 32, 58, 60
Worcester, Bishop of, 383
Working Men's Lord's Day Rest Association, 394
Wycliffe Commemoration (1884), 580

York, 410, 411, 536; Minster, 128
Yorkshire, 72, 177, 178, 233, 272, 298, 333, 430, 498
Young England Movement, 196, 205 n. 137, 326
Young Men's Christian Association, 393, 395, 531, 580, 581
Young Men's Society for Aiding Missions at Home and Abroad, 154
Young Men's Society for Religious Improvement, 531
Young, William, 112-5

---

* The family surname 'Ashley Cooper' was used by the 7th Earl and his brothers and sisters, but 'Ashley' was more commonly used by the next (but not the present) generation. This explains the discrepancy of usage in the index entries above (see Battiscombe, p. 351).